Indians In The Americas

The Untold Story

by William Marder

Edited by Paul Tice

Foreword by Joe S. Sando

The Book Tree
San Diego, CA

Inquires shoud be addressed to:
The Book Tree, PO Box 16476, San Diego, CA 92176
www.thebooktree.com

ISBN 1-58509-104-9

Published in the United States of America

LCCN #2003115428

Published by
The Book Tree
P O Box 16476
San Diego, CA 92176

We provide fascinating and educational products to help awaken the public to new ideas and
information that would not be available otherwise.
Call 1 (800) 700-8733 for our *FREE BOOK TREE CATALOG*.

Dedicated

To all my Family - To all Indians in the Americas

and the future generations

who will eventually recognize, appreciate,

and take pride in the human values represented in this book.

THE CONNECTED SPIRIT WITHIN by William Marder

As awesome as the ocean seems
It is a tiny manifestation of the world we live in
There are oceans in us all
And much more you see
Because a part of our past is inside you and me
We are connected to our
Mother Earth and supplied with a power
To create our own dreams
Each and every hour
As we align ourselves with our source of
Beauty, Love, and Grace
We discover the sameness on each and every face
We see it in the birds as they soar high over the land
We see it in the waves as they pound against the sand
We see it in the early morning dew that
Forms on the blades of grass
We see it in the beauty of a sunset as
Another day comes to pass. Then when a new day dawns
We discover all this has a connection
Just as we are joined to our brothers, sisters and family
We discover the awesome spiritual presence within, and begin
to realize
We are joined together with our environment
and All in this worldly connection

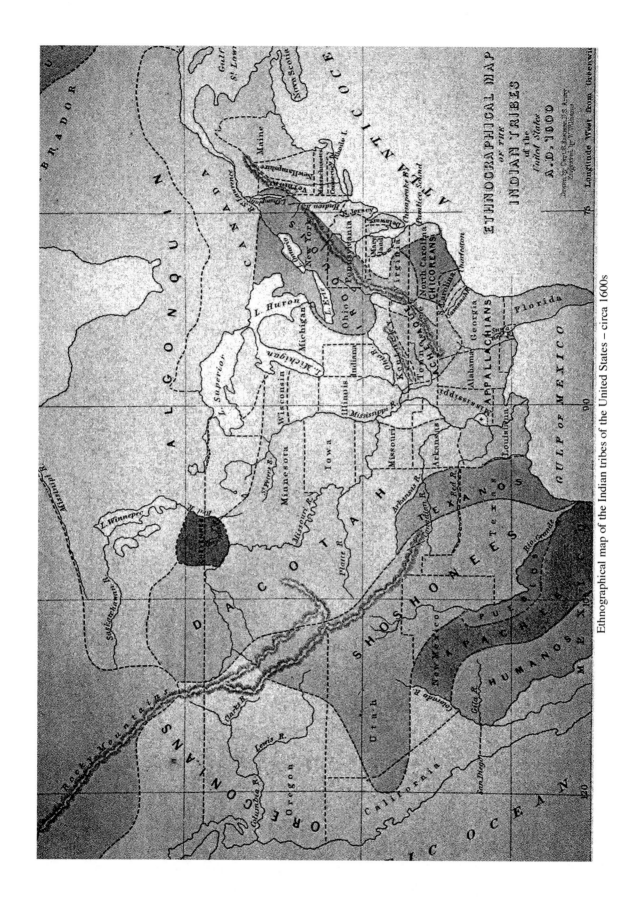

Ethnographical map of the Indian tribes of the United States – circa 1600s

Acknowledgements

I started working on this book over twenty years ago after completing the photographic book, *Anthony, the Man, the Company, the Cameras*. The large amount of research for the *Anthony* book led to an accumulation of photographs as a preparatory for this present book.

Studying Indian history relating to photography and viewing the early noble images of the Indians by George Catlin, Charles Bird King, Edward Curtis, etc., at a time when humanity and nature were still harmonious, coupled with later photographs of their depressing conditions, brought up the question as to how and why there was such dramatic changes. After reading two historic books, *A Century of Dishonor* (1881) by Helen Hunt Jackson and the *The Indian Dispossessed* (1905) by Seth K. Humphrey, the extent of the Indian tragedy became apparent. Visiting many of the Indian tribes over the last twenty years gave me additional evidence of their mistreatment.

The main purpose of this book is to set the record straight with the latest documented evidence of DNA studies and archaeological discoveries. New Pre-Columbian evidence of early contacts continues to be reported with each passing year. The historical account of *Indians in the Americas* would not be complete without the details of broken treaties and promises. The Indians' fight for survival is not primarily an Indian problem. All oppressed minorities throughout the world face similar problems. By revealing the past, hopefully this book can help to build a future based on mutual respect and understanding. We can all learn a great deal from the Indians. Through their battle for independence and self-determination, we can improve our treatment and respect towards other indigenous peoples throughout the world.

Every effort was made to be as accurate as possible, calling on a variety of different sources to document my writing. I was astonished in my research to find an embarrassing assortment of misinformation in our textbooks and history books pertaining to the Indians in the Americas. This has managed to instill ignorance and unfounded hatred towards an entire culture. I have traced the Indians in the Americas from their encounters and influence from outside forces, beyond their control, to their genocide and forced removal, to their present day struggles for self-determination.

Information and books accumulated after visiting Indian tribes and museums through the years added to the sources of much of my information. My widespread bibliography and extensive notes to the text list most of these sources. Of the many places visited, I especially want to thank the archives and information from: The Apache Cultural Center Museum, Ft. Apache, AZ; Canadian Museum of Civilization, Hull, Quebec, Canada; Cherokee National Museum and Archives, Tahlequah, OK; Choctaw National Museum, Tuskahoma, OK; Crazy Horse Indian Museum of North America, Black Hills, S. D; Montana Historical Society, Helena, MT; Museum of Anthropology of Vancouver, Canada; National Museum of the American Indian, New York City; Museum of the Plains Indians, Browning, MT; Nez Percé National Historical Park and Museum, ID; Pequot Museum and Research Center, Mashantucket, CT; Pueblo Cultural Center, Albuquerque, NM; Secwepemc Native Heritage Park and Museum, Kamloops, BC, Canada; Sioux Indian Museum, Rapid City, SD; Tamastslikt Cultural Institute, Pendleton, OR; Yakama Nation Museum and Library, Toppenish, WA, etc.

Invaluable information and research facilities from the following libraries were; Boston Massachusetts Public Library; Broward County Library, Ft. Lauderdale, FL; University of Massachusetts Library, Amherst, MA; Library of Congress, Washington, D.C.; National Anthropological Archives, Washington, D.C., and Widener Library of Harvard University, MA.

Special thanks to my publisher Paul Tice who took over the tremendous task of following through with detailed editing and persevering with all the back and forth interchanges. I also wish to thank for their assistance with this book: Larry Barasch, John and Lucia Beall, Robert Chadell, Vincent Chasse, Jack Forbes, Paula Fleming, Neil and Ursula Freer, Ingrid Goldstein, Stetson Kennedy, Vernon Murray, Scott Olsen, Carol and Nathan Rutstein, Joe Sando, D. Ray & Mike Smith, Dodi Sodos, Barbara and Fred Troiano, White Buffalo Society, Inc., and especially to my dear wife Estelle for all her help, patience and support.

FOREWORD

Indian culture is facing its stiffest challenge at present, due to the influence of liberal government, television and replacement of indigenous language with English. Native religion as well as sacred ceremonies and dances are in danger of destruction in the modern world. Native language is essential to the preservation of native religion and culture.

The Pueblo Indians of the American Southwest have, in particular, struggled to survive, retain their aboriginal land base and preserve their culture. They have struggled against three domineering governments—Spain, Mexico and now the United States. The 1980 United States Census reported that the Pueblo Indians of New Mexico were the last of many tribes to retain a greater portion of their original language and native religion.

There have been many books written over the years promising to tell the true story of the Indians in the Americas. Many have been filled with misinformation or derogatory views of the Indian. Finally, here is a book by William Marder that anyone can believe in. It is well researched and tells the true story of Indian accomplishments, challenges and struggles. This book represents years of study and is filled with over 1000 photographs and illustrations. It also contains a complete bibliography with periodicals, along with 780 richly documented, extensive notes to the text to aid the reader in further study.

Joe S. Sando

Pueblo Indian Author, Educator, and Historian

Joe Sando, born at the Jemez Pueblo, was raised traditionally in the way of Pueblo children. Sando graduated from Eastern New Mexico College at Portales, New Mexico and Vanderbilt University in Nashville, Tennessee. He has lectured and written five books on Pueblo history and lore. On April 13, 2004 Sando received the Bravo Award for excellence in Literary Arts. Joe Sando was the Director of The Institute of Pueblo Indian Studies, founded by him in 1986.

CONTENTS

Map of Americas by Joducus Hondius, from *Mercator's Atlas* – circa 1600s

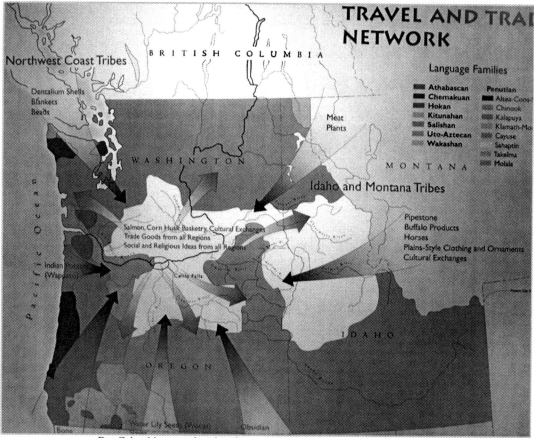

Pre-Columbian travel and trade network of the Indians in the Americas

INTRODUCTION

1494 Woodcut, Columbus Landing in Hispaniola

On October 12, 1492, Columbus landed on one of the Bahamian islands in the West Indies. Believing that he had landed in Asia and that he was on Indian soil, he referred to the island's inhabitants as "los Indos" (Indios). Other European explorers adopted this appellation, although it was a name that the indigenous peoples themselves had never heard before.[1] Throughout the years the first inhabitants in the Americas have been known by various names including "Aboriginal", "American Indians", "Amerinds", "Amerindians", "First Nations of Canada", "Indigenous peoples", and "Native Americans". To avoid confusion, "Indian" is the name used throughout this book when referring to the first inhabitants of North and South America and the Caribbean. Most of the Indian tribal names in use today are derivatives of names mistakenly and inaccurately given them by their Conquerors.[2]

The attribution to Columbus for the discovery of a land, which, by 1492, had already been inhabited for many thousands of years, has fostered the belief that the Europeans "owned" the continent, and produced a culture of intolerance towards all non-Europeans that was condoned by many in the scientific community. On the return of Columbus from his first voyage, as an incentive to the occupation of the New World, Pope Alexander VI issued a bull (edict) in May, 1493, dividing the government of the non-Christian world between Spain and Portugal and instructed them that "Barbarous nations be overthrown, discovered, and converted to the Catholic faith, to propagate the Christian religion."[3]

Chief Roanoke
Eastern Indian of Virginia

The Indian belief system was as complex and sophisticated as that of the Indians' European counterparts, although the two groups were far apart. The Indians neither imitated nor comprehended the Europeans' desire for material possessions, gold and land. The European political systems and spiritual beliefs lacked the spirit and wholeness that had supported the Indians' efforts to survive for generations. Spirituality was their way of life. In almost all of the Indian cultures, to accumulate, hold on to, or to have more than you need was humiliating. The teachings and beliefs of the Indians advocated that we are all close relatives of every living thing and creature on earth. We should care for all inhabitants for the benefit of all.

Bartolomé de Las Casas

Shortly after landing, Columbus and his men, in search of gold, began to enslave and brutalize an innocent people. There were devoted missionaries traveling with Columbus who, seeing the plight of the Indians, spoke out in their defense. Among the most popular of these missionaries was Friar Bartolomé de Las Casas, who often wrote of the spirituality of the Indians and appealed on their behalf to the Spanish government and the Pope, begging them to enact laws that would rescue the Indians from their sufferings. Las Casas, born in Seville, Spain in 1474, traveled in 1502 to Hispaniola. In 1510 he became the first Christian priest to be ordained in the New World. Bartolomé de Las Casas had in his possession an important injunction to the Indians from King Ferdinand of Spain and his daughter to be delivered to the new Governor in the Pacific area. It was called "The Requirement" because royal law required it to be read in Latin or Spanish, and to be witnessed by a notary before hostilities could be undertaken against the inhabitants.[4]

1598 engravings by Theodor de Bry, from
Narratives by Las Casas on
Spanish Atrocities in America

Referring to this letter in his book *History of the Indies*, Las Casas wrote, "The King gave instructions to Governor Pedrarias Davila regarding his conduct in the New World which included an injunction requiring the allegiance of the Indians to the King of Castile, the text of which was later used through the Indies..." The injunction was taken to an Indian village in Panama on June 14, 1514 to be read by the notary Fernández de Gonzalo Oviedo. Oviedo, on finding the village deserted, wrote, "My lords, it appears to me that these Indians will not listen to the theology of this Requirement, and that you have no one who can make them understand it; would your Honor be pleased to keep it until we have some one of these Indians in a cage, in order that he may learn at his leisure and my Lord Bishop may explain it to him."[5] There were Spaniards and missionaries that could not decide whether to laugh or cry at this injunction. The Requirement was read to any Indian who was available. If not, to "trees and empty huts when no Indians were to be found… into their beards on the edge of sleeping Indian settlements… Spanish notaries hurled its sonorous phrases after the Indians as they fled into the mountains…. Ship captains would sometimes have the document read from the deck as they approached the island."[6] The purpose of the Requirement was to absolve all Spaniards of any responsibility for the depravity and horror of their actions wherever they set foot in the New World. One of the many issued stated:

Columbus taking possession of Hispaniola by Theodor de Bry, 1594

> In the name of King Ferdinand and Juana, his daughter, Queen of Castile and Leon, etc., conquerors of barbarian nations, we notify you as best we can that our Lord God Eternal created Heaven and earth and a man and woman from whom we all descend for all times and all over the world. In the 5000 years since creation the multitude of these generations caused men to divide and establish kingdoms in various parts of the world, among whom God chose St. Peter as leader of mankind, regardless of their law, sect or belief. He seated St. Peter in Rome as the best place from which to rule the world but he allowed him to establish his seat in all parts of the world and rule all people, whether Christians, Moors, Jews, Gentiles or any other sect…. The late Pope gave these islands and mainland of the ocean and the contents hereof to the above-mentioned King and Queen, as is certified in writing and you may see the documents if you should so desire. Therefore, Their Highnesses are lords and masters of this land; they were acknowledged as such when this notice was posted, and were and are being served willingly and without resistance; Therefore, we request that you understand this text, deliberate on its contents within a reasonable time, and recognize the Church and its highest priest, the Pope, as rulers of the universe, and in their name the King and Queen of Spain as rulers of this land, allowing the religious fathers to preach our holy Faith to you…. Should you fail to comply, or delay maliciously in so doing, we assure you that with the help of God we shall use force against you, declaring war upon you from all sides and with all possible means, and we shall bind you to the yoke of the Church and of Their Highnesses; we shall enslave your persons, wives and sons, sell you or dispose of you as the King sees fit; we shall seize your possessions and harm you as much as we can as disobedient and resisting vassals. And we declare you guilty of resulting deaths and injuries, exempting Their Highnesses of such guilt as well as ourselves and the gentlemen who accompany us. We hereby request that legal signatures be affixed to this text and pray those present to bear witness for us, etc.[7]

Indians forced labor at Potosi, Peru silver mine, 1536, engraving

The Conquistadors' greed for gold and silver gave rise to some of the most cruel and inhuman treatment ever to be inflicted on an entire nation. Wherever the Spanish set foot in North and South America they butchered, raped, tortured and enslaved as many as twenty million Indians. Las Casas' eyewitness accounts of these massacres in *The Tears of the Indians* reveal the extent of the brutality they endured.[8]

Columbus reported in his diaries that the Indians of Hispaniola had told him that "there had come to Hispaniola people who have the tops of their spears made of a metal which they call quanin, of which he had sent samples to the Sovereigns to have them assayed, when it was found that of 32 parts, 18 were gold, six of silver and eight of copper." These samples were sent back to Spain on a mail boat, and the proportion was found to be identical to what was being forged in African Guinea. On his third voyage he journeyed to the Cape Verde Islands. Columbus wrote, "Canoes had been found which start from the coast of Guinea and navigate to the west with merchandise."[9] Las Casas also wrote of these same sightings. Indian myths and stories passed down orally relate of foreign visitors before the arrival of Columbus. We are now uncovering artifacts of skulls, pottery and sculptures that point to ancient foreign inhabitants in the Americas. Was it possible that there were a large number of landings in America before Columbus by other earlier civilizations? This would make the Indians inheritors of the achievements of a number of previous civilizations.

Series of Inca canals, fountains & walls Sacsahuaman, Peru

Long before Columbus, Indian technology was sufficiently advanced that they were able to build roads, irrigate their fields, construct houses using different materials, design elaborate buildings and cultivate a vast number of plants for food and medicine. From the late 15th century until the 17th century, public power in many European countries was concentrated in the hands of landowners. The majority of the population lived in slums, and was prey to epidemics of disease, the most gruesome and virulent of which was Bubonic Plague, also known as the Black Death. The population of slaves and peasants struggled in this feudal society under a supreme monarch who dispensed the law. The poor were ignored, and many of the cities were decimated by wars. The peasants had no rights, and the feudal system restricted their liberty and prevented the emergence of any kind of democracy.[10]

Inca straw suspension bridge over the Apurimac River, Peru

As they ventured into the New World and away from the turmoil of life in Europe, the European discoverers were astounded to find evidence of highly evolved civilizations. Vast ceremonial temples and cities of gold were built by the Inca, Maya, and Aztec people. The Indians inhabited vast areas of two continents from the Arctic to the tip of South America. They spoke more than 2500 different languages and thousands of dialects. Over 2000 large and smaller tribal bands were living throughout all of the Americas, with an estimated population of 75 to 112 million. As of 2004, 567 federally recognized tribes or nations live on 331 reservations. 55 million acres of Indian land is held in trust by the U.S. Canada presently has over 633 organized aboriginal tribal bands (now called First Nations), and about 198 in British Columbia in addition to about 2364 reserves.[11]

Before the Europeans invaded the Americas, the Indians were organized into small clans, tribes, nations and then confederacies. The Six Nation Iroquois Confederacy was in existence long before the Europeans arrived. The confederacy, a political union of North American Indian nations, covered a vast territory in the eastern part of the United States and into Canada. Benjamin Franklin had been familiar with the social and political organization of the Six Nation Confederacy and used this as a model for the formation of independent states into the United States of America.[12]

Mural by Diego Rivera illustrating ethnobotanical medicines from pre-Columbian to modern times

The Mayan, Aztec, and Inca civilizations, were sophisticated empires with large cities and religious centers, while other tribes roamed the Americas, fishing and hunting or settled in small agricultural villages. The Indians were astronomers, engineers, mathematicians, farmers, musicians, fishermen, hunters, and craftsmen. They utilized herbal medicines, mined minerals, and practiced surgery to heal their sick. The Mayans, by observing the universe over the years, used three different accurate calendar systems (and some variations within the systems). The three systems are known as the tzolkin (the sacred calendar), the haab (the civil calendar) and the long count system. In the field of mathematics, the Maya probably were the first to use the concept of zero.[13] The Inca population consisted of approximately 10 million, the largest and most complete nation in the Americas. They engineered, built and maintained an extraordinary road system over 2000 miles long through the Andes with intricate suspension bridges, and built extensive irrigation canal systems.[14] The Inca, Aztec, and Mayan civilizations developed a unique form of hieroglyphic writing, and built immense pyramids and cities. The Indians of the Americas cultivated over 150 different varieties of plants, fruits, herbs and vegetables unknown to the Europeans. The Indians have contributed an enormous amount to the advancement of our society. They domesticated over 40 varieties of plants, including corn, and it was they who first cultivated over 130 of the foods that are consumed throughout today's world. They excelled in the use of herbal medicines and understood the properties and use of drugs like quinine, cocoa, curare and many others. About ninety percent of pharmaceuticals worldwide are derived from American plants. Much of these are found in the Amazon and high in the Andes Mountains, where they were first found and utilized by the Indians. They discovered rubber and its use before anyone else, and they even practiced a form of surgery (trepanation).[15]

The Indians followed a communal lifestyle, with each person remaining loyal to his or her own tribe. The land and individual or communal possessions were considered to be gifts from their creator, and were regarded with great reverence. The many tribes, although different in dress, language and customs, whether hunters or agriculturists, all shared this same philosophy regarding the land and its use. Their chiefs, the servants of the tribes, were elected for their outstanding abilities as warriors and hunters rather than for their wealth or power. They were allowed to assume this leadership only after passing many tests over a period of years, which

The Historian, by E. Gause, 1900s

proved their superior skills and gradually increased their status over time.[16] The Indian elders passed down stories of their origins to the children through oral tales, animated mythologies, vision quests, seasonal celebrations, harvest festivals, daily prayer, dances, drums and chants. In many tribes elaborate costumes were used to act out their myths and legends. Tribes in different areas of the Americas told similar stories of their origins that included a great flood. Artist George Catlin, who visited over 48 Indian tribes, was told that most of

Obsidian knives and copper tool

the tribes connected their origin with a "Big Canoe" that settled on a summit of a hill or mountain, apparently after a large flood, as in Noah's Ark. They also celebrated a religious ceremony called "Settling of the waters." The Indians have always held the dove sacred, and their stories of a dove bringing a branch from a willow tree to the Indians echoes that of the dove returning to Noah's ark in the Book of Genesis.[17]

Pre-Columbian trading market, Cartenga, Columbia
Engraving by Theodor de Bry

A large trade network existed between the various tribes that extended throughout the Americas and allowed them to exchange or barter minerals, animal skins, agricultural products and other goods from one area to the other. Copper mined in the Northern Michigan area was traded over large distances to find its way as manufactured products in the Mississippi Mound and Mayan civilizations of Central America. In the ruins of Pueblo Bonito, in the vast ceremonial center of Chaco Canyon in Northwestern New Mexico, dating from about 850 to 1150 A.D., evidence of an extensive Pre-Columbian trade network was discovered in the form of copper bells, marine

shells, parrots and macaws—all of which were carried from the south to the upper Americas. The Indians extracted a valuable blue stone, turquoise, from mines around Cerrilos, Mexico. They fashioned some of it into jewelry and probably traded it for additional goods. Mica mined in Minnesota has been found in ornamental objects in the temple mounds of Ohio. Flint and obsidian for making arrowheads was manufactured in the midwestern areas of the United States and traded to the east. In a reverse direction, multicolored slate found its way to the Mississippi River from the east. This trade was by foot or water. Hernándo Cortés did not introduce horses into Central America until late in the 16th century.[18]

1755 Map of Colonial Indian Frontier, by John Mitchell

When the explorers from Spain, France, England and other European countries entered the Americas, they disregarded these well-established communities of indigenous tribes. The Europeans were initially regarded with reverence as gods or supernatural beings. The early European settlers were welcomed as honored guests, presented with gifts, and saved from starvation. As the early invaders plundered the Americas they were cautioned by the priests to treat the Indians as a spiritual people. This plea was totally ignored by the conquistadors in their thirst for gold.[19] The European invaders arrived in America with a completely different view of life and laws developed to serve the European population. Gradually, the new settlers began to believe that they had a "Manifest Destiny"—a notion that translated into the assumption of their right to take the lands of Indians, believing it was God's will that the United States control the continent.[20]

Alliances were forged between various European countries and some Indian tribes, allowing the Europeans to divide and conquer the Indians both economically and culturally. It was impossible for the Indians to win in this scenario because of the strong tradition of tribal loyalty, which effectively prevented the formation of any major confederation of tribes, which could have driven the Europeans off the continent. As a consequence, the various Indian tribes became dependent on the mercy and generosity of conquerors that, in fact, displayed neither of these qualities. In an attempt to control the tribes, the U.S. government established a reservation policy in 1786, which further demoralized and marginalized the Indian people.[21]

Reception given by the Indians to the Spanish arriving in the Caribbean.
1500's engraving by Theodor de Bry

By 1890 there were 162 reservations, most of which were located west of the Mississippi River. The Indians were confined to these designated parcels of land, stripped of their equality, their self-esteem, and their traditional hunting grounds. A new United States policy was developed, following a communication to the House of Representatives from Secretary of War, John C. Calhoun, on December 5, 1818. The aim of the policy was to dissolve the Indians' status as a nation, to end the practice of moving the Indians to reservations and force them instead to assimilate into white society. Individual Indian families were to be allocated plots of land to enable them to become independent farmers. This, of course, was intended to sever their connections to their tribes. The outcome was the removal of the Indians' land, which was then sold to white settlers.[22]

John Collier, Commissioner, Bureau of Indian Affairs

The Europeans undertook a systematic destruction of the Indians' lives, their land, language, science, art, religion and traditions and set about replacing the Indian culture with their own. White Wolf of the Crow Tribe predicted, "Our entire way of life will change. The coming of the white man will make this change... but it will never die, because it is of the Spirit. It is a Truth, and Truth cannot die."[23]

The Indians in the Americas are attempting to hold on to their spiritual convictions passed down orally and in sacred ceremonies from generation to generation. Their own religious priests and shamans instructed the tribes in ceremonies that bonded them to their ancestral past. This has allowed them to survive all adversities. The European onslaught and our modern world has brought photography and worldwide publicity. This has impacted the Indians' spiritual privacy, causing a backlash by many tribes that now restrict photography by outsiders, so as to protect and maintain their religious heritage.

John Collier, former Commissioner of Indian Affairs, reflected on the value of the spiritual lives of the Indians in his 1947 book, *Indians of America*. "They had what the world has lost. They have it now. What the world has lost, the world must have again, lest it die. Not many years are left to have or have not, to recapture the lost ingredient.... What, in our human world, is this power to live? It is the ancient, lost reverence and passion for human personality, joined with the ancient, lost reverence and passion for the earth and its web of life. This indivisible reverence and passion is what the Indians almost universally had, and representative groups of them have it still. They had and still have this power for living, which our modern world has lost."[24]

Spanish burn villages in the Caribbean, 1500s
Engraving by Theodor de Bry

Christopher Columbus praised these Indians as spiritual people as he wrote of converting them, and then of his own lust for their gold. On his first voyage when he encountered the Indians of Cuba, Columbus recorded in his journal on November 11, 1492, " I see and know that these people have no religion whatever, nor are they idolaters, but rather, they are very meek and know no evil, they do not kill or capture others and are without weapons."[25]

The Spanish Conquistadors devastated the Indians, dispossessing them of almost all their land by intimidation, bribery, threats, misrepresentation, fraud, and force. The Spaniards burned the Indians' books, brutally crushed any opposition, spread European diseases, and enslaved the native populations. The English viewed them as converts and the French as a source of trade.[26] Zealous Christian missionaries considered it their duty to elevate the standards of the Indians with forced conversion. By 1650, the Indian population was reduced through disease and war to no more than five million.[27]

The Europeans, in their search for riches, showed a complete lack of understanding Indian values, a fact emphasized by Sioux author, Luther Standing Bear:

Spanish let loose dogs on the Tainos
1500s, Engraving by Theodor de Bry

The white man does not understand America. He is too far removed from its formative processes. The roots of the tree of his life have not yet grasped the rock and the soil. The white man is still troubled by primitive fears; he still has in his consciousness the perils of this frontier continent, some of its vastness not yet having yielded to his questing footsteps and inquiring eyes. He shudders still with the memory of the loss of his forefathers upon its scorching deserts and forbidding mountaintops. The man from Europe is still a foreigner and alien. And he still hates the man who questioned his path across the continent. But in the Indian the spirit of the land is still vested; it will be until other men are able to define and meet its rhythm. Men must be born to belong. Their bodies must be formed of the dust of their forefathers bones.[28]

By the 18th century, some people in Europe who were aware of the scandalous mistreatment of the Indians began to speak against it. Despite a huge outcry and debates that concluded that the discovery of America might have been a mistake, the genocide against the Indians continued.[29] In 1840, an article in the London Saturday Journal asked, "Are the Indians capable of civilization?" It continued, "The Redman cannot exist with the white man, (and) it is useless to alter his wild condition, for attempts at civilization only serve to degrade instead of elevating his character. Therefore the Indians must be driven beyond the pale of civilization." It continued, claiming that "Indians clogged the lands inhabited by the white settlers... and, it becomes necessary for the security and prosperity of the whites to push the Indians further west.... The Journal added that whiskey was used deliberately to "sink them lower still."[30]

The Indians had a spiritual relationships with the trees, stars, plants and all animals. They understood the importance of this spiritual relationship as it related to their own survival. For the Western Indians living in the wide-open plains, the buffalo was an important part of their lives. They used its meat, its leather, its hair and its bones for food, clothing and for ceremonial purposes. A Blackfeet tribal legend relates the close relationship of the buffalo to the Indian through a mythical intermarriage, death and rebirth. Most of the Western Indian tribes believed that the buffalo skull kept evil spirits away.[31]

Offering the Buffalo Skull, Mandan, by Edward Curtis

Buffalo hide yard with 40,000 hides at Dodge City, Kansas, 1876

Slaughter from train

In the early 1800s buffalo ranged from the eastern U.S. to the Rocky Mountains in numbers estimated as high as 30 to 60 million. By the 1840s the arrival of vast waves of white settlers signaled the end of the buffalo as conflicts arose with the Indians about land use. About a million buffalo remained west of the Mississippi. Among the earliest settlers were trappers and traders, people who made their living selling meat and hides. By the 1870s they were shipping hundreds of thousands of buffalo hides eastward each year. More than 1.5 million were packed aboard trains and wagons in the winter of 1872-3 alone. In the 1880s the white man put an end to the buffalo when they were slaughtered for sport. Governor and Congressman, James Throckmorton of Texas stated in the 1800s, "It would be a great step forward in the civilization of the Indians and the preservation of peace on the border if there was not a buffalo in existence." Organized groups of tourists shot at the buffalo from trains with repeating rifles, decimating the herds. By the late 1890s only about 1200 buffalo were left. It was the end of an era of reverence for the buffalo, and the end of the Western Indians' traditional way of life. Without food and clothes for survival, the Western tribes began to depend on the federal government for their survival.[32] Black Elk, a holy man of the Oglala Sioux, witnessed this wanton destruction:

THE LAST of the BUFFALO Comprising a history of the Buffalo herd at the Flathead reservation and an account of the last great Buffalo roundup.

History of Buffalo Herd, 1909, Flathead Reservation

...I can remember when the bison were so many that they could not be counted, but more and more Wasichus (white men) came to kill them until there were only heaps of bones scattered where they used to be. The Wasichus did not kill them to eat; they killed them for the metal that makes them die. I have heard that fireboats came down the Missouri River loaded with dried bison tongues. You can see that men who did this were crazy. Sometimes they did not even take the tongues; they just killed and killed because they liked to do that; when we hunted bison, we killed what we needed. And when there was nothing left but heaps of bones, the Wasichus came and gathered up even the bones and sold them.[33]

Black Elk
Oglala, Sioux

During the late 1800s anthropologists and archaeologists feared that the Indians were a vanishing race. The Indian then became an object of study and fascination for anthropologists and scientists, as well as for novelists, poets and missionaries. In 1879 the United States government created the Bureau of Ethnology under John Wesley Powell to bring together all past survey information and to continue the study of the American Indian languages, myths and legends, technology, and religious beliefs.

The chapters in this book travel along the same path as the Indians. We will traverse through their possible origins, foreign contacts and invasions, to their displacement, suffering and dependency. The final chapters will provide an insight into what can be gained from the study of their proud culture, oral traditions, beliefs, ceremonial traditions, accomplishments and their present fight for self-determining their future and possible outcome in their relation to all indigenous people of other countries facing the same predicament today.

CHAPTER 1 INDIAN ORIGINS: PRE-COLUMBIAN

The body of knowledge regarding the Indians' origins is a mélange of fact and fiction contained in old manuscripts, myths, ancient geographical maps, and petroglyphs, some of which date back to 2250 B.C. The accumulated information is a record of the diffusion of ancient civilizations into the many Indian tribes that inhabited the Americas long before the arrival of Columbus.

Stele of bearded man
Chichen Itza, Mexico

Despite the proliferation of documented archaeological and scientific findings and the technology that now enables DNA (deoxyribose nucleic acid) analysis, there are still many unanswered questions. Were the Indians descendents of the ten lost tribes of Israel? Is information on their origins mentioned in the Bible? Did Minoans, Egyptians, Phoenicians (descendants of the Canaanites), Carthaginians, Africans, Hindu, Welsh, Scottish, Celtic and Norse seafarers, as well as Greco-Roman traders and Chinese and Japanese voyagers travel to America to interact with the Indians?[34]

Clay bearded man
Mexico City
circa 900 A.D.

Bearded man w/earplugs
Cerreo de las Mesas,
Mexico, circa 800 A.D.

Did the people we know as the Indians know how to make ships capable of transporting them across the Pacific or Atlantic Oceans as early as 100 B.C.? Did the Indians arrive primarily across the Bering Strait from Asia in one or several migrations? Did they inhabit the Americas from ancient times evolving from an earlier species of man in the Americas or are they the lost inhabitants of a sunken Atlantis or a lost continent in the Pacific called Mu (Lemuria)? The corn plant, an important grain for survival and culture of the Indian, was thought to have originated in America, or was it brought over from a far off land? Mummification and cranial surgery has long been thought to be a sole practice of the Egyptians. There is evidence of a similar embalming and a trepanation (cranial surgery) procedure used by the first inhabitants of the Americas as well as in Africa and Europe.[35]

Inca trepanation

The Spanish reintroduced the horse into America and some of today's breeds are descended from animals brought by Juan Ponce de Leon and Hernando de Soto. There is evidence, however, that there were horses in the Americas long before the arrival of Columbus. In 1933, archaeologist Junius Bird discovered in "Fell's Cave" (Patagonia, Chile) in Tierra del Fuego, South America, remains of fire pits, stone spear points and bones of a prehistoric relative of the common horse known to inhabit South America.[36]

The pyramids built by the Aztecs and Mayans in America resemble those in Europe, China, and Southeast Asia. They have long fascinated the archaeological community. Pyramids exist today in Egypt, India, Algeria, Canary Islands, Hawaii, Poland, Tahiti, China, and Mexico. Megalithic dolmen-type structures, which were

Uruk ziggurat, Anna precinct
Mesopotamia, circa 2000 B.C.

Teotihuacan Pyramid, Mexico
circa 1-250 A.D.

used for astronomical observations and burials, appear in England, Ireland, Scotland, Denmark, Malta, and West New Guinea as well as in North and South America. There are similarities in appearance of these structures on both continents that reveal a worldly connection.

The Cherokee Indians tell of a white people who landed in America in the 12th century. The Mayans and Aztecs speak of the return of their white god from the East. Daniel Boone related that a tribe of "blue-eyed Indians" he met was related to the Welch. Discoveries of three ruined forts of pre-Columbian origin in the southeastern part of the United States and a site in Tennessee with its walls, single gateway and

Megaliths: Tiahuanaco, Bolivia
circa 5000 B.C.

Malta megaliths, circa 5000 B.C.

moat, resembled ancient remains in Wales. Parts of the Mandan tribal language appeared to resemble the Welsh language. George Catlin was a firm believer that the Mandan tribe was related to the ancient Hebrews. In 1840 the *London Journal* quoted Catlin as saying, "A stout believer in the Jewish origin of the North American Indian would at once trace a connection between this "big canoe" and the ark of the Israelites, which occupied the centre of their camp when in the wilderness." James Adair, in his 1775 *History of the American Indians,* claimed that some American Indian chants among the Choctaw and the Chickasaw tribes utilized Hebrew words such as Jehovah in their Green Corn ceremonies. In the 19th century, Edward King published manuscripts relating to the Mexican *Aztec Codex.* He was convinced that parts of the Aztec pictorial writing illustrated biblical events.[37]

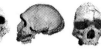

Australopithecus Africanus

With the development of advanced techniques for carbon dating, computer technology simulation, DNA analysis, linguistic studies, geophysical unearthing and other means, our leading scientists and archaeologists are in the process of making important new discoveries and getting closer to answers to determine the origins and time periods of the establishment of the first peoples to arrive on the American continent. We have been conditioned to believe that our ancient ancestors evolved in Africa 100,000 years ago and came to the Americas as big game hunters only about 12,000 years ago over the Bering Strait, before the last ice age, by way of Asia. Folsom artifacts first excavated in 1926 and Clovis, in the early 1930's, have left an indelible impression on the archaeological and scientific community, and in our society, that the origins of man in the Americas are dated to about 12,000 years or less. This firm stance taken by conservative archaeologists have quieted the numerous new discoveries. Prejudices towards any findings predating Clovis-Folsom in the Americas have castigated many archaeologists and scientists into losing their employment or keeping quiet. A 1989 report stated that at least five South American archaeologists admitted they held back on new data on pre Clovis-Folsom dates "out of fear that their funds would be cut off by American colleagues who endorse the short-chronology school of thought."[38] New archaeological data and discoveries estimate that the age of mankind started much earlier than was previously imagined.[39]

Left, *Homo Erectus* to right, *Homo Sapien*

The most recent scientific theory is that our universe was formed about 4.5 billion years ago under a continual bombardment of meteors. This massive upheaval brought about great changes in the environment. "For billions of years simple creatures like plankton, bacteria and algae ruled the earth." These single-celled microscopic organisms, along with photosynthesis, eventually oxygenated our earth making it possible for fish, insects, reptiles and humans to evolve.[40]

The continents were once linked together as part of one supercontinent called Pangaea (from Greek, meaning literally, "all of Earth"). From the study of geology and plate tectonic movements it has been determined that radical changes took place approximately 100 million years ago, causing the single supercontinent to start breaking up into separate land masses.[41] The African continent shifted until it collided with southern Eurasia, and the continent of South America drifted westward over what is now the Atlantic Ocean, finally colliding with what we now call North America. In recent times our continent has felt the stress of the past with periodic floods and earthquakes. Indians have passed down stories of these catastrophic events orally for thousands of years.[42]

1996 news reports

DNA evidence has determined that Africa may have been the cradle of civilization. Fossils found in Africa point to a number of different types of human ancestors.[43] The discovery of a skull on July 19, 2001, shook up the scientific community. The skull, which was nicknamed Toumai, had chimp-like features from the rear and human features in the front. Paleoanthropologists Milford Wolpoff, Martin Pickford and Dr. Brigette Senut of the Natural History Museum in Paris, France, claimed the skull was instead from a female gorilla and suggested that another species, *Orrorin tugenensis,* found in Kenya, was the earliest human. The discoveries pushed the origins of our human family tree back to about 6 million years B.C. There have been more fossils of human ancestry found in Africa than anywhere else on earth. One link to this chain was the *Australopithecus Africanus,* found in Southern Africa and identified by a South African anatomist, Raymond Dart, in 1924. The *Australopithecus Africanus* had ape-like features, walked upright, used tools, and had a larger brain capacity than the other apes of that same period. *Australopithecine,* sometime between 2 and 3 million years ago, evolved into a new species of human, *Homo erectus.*

1.7 million year-old skull Dmanisi, Georgia

Chopper tools

In 2001 a 1.75 million-year-old skull was found outside of Africa in Dmanisi, Georgia on a hilltop overlooking the ancient Silk Road. The finding points to our human ancestors leaving Africa with primitive tools at a much earlier date than had been previously estimated. This skull, found with stone chopper and scraper tools, had a small brain and chimp-like features. At present, a controversy exists in the scientific community as to whether we should dismiss the idea of a separate species and simply claim that everything after *Australopithecus Africanus* are *Homo sapiens*. Genetic evidence now supports a theory that present-day humans co-evolved at least 6 million years ago from a combination of different species of ape like-humans who inhabited the earth.[44]

Mastodon Indian hunters

Homo erectus had about half the brain size of modern man. Fossils of *Homo erectus* with different brain sizes and at various stages of evolution have been found throughout Europe, Asia, and Southeastern Asia. *Homo erectus* was theorized to have evolved into our present-day *Homo sapiens*. Recent evidence finds that our present day ancestors, *Homo sapiens*, appeared at least 150,000 years ago in Africa. Discoveries of *Homo erectus* fossils found in Java were dated to have lived as recently as 27,000 to 53,000 years ago. This evidence has persuaded anthropologists that *Homo erectus* did not disappear 200,000 years ago, as previously thought. They suggest *Homo erectus* lived during the same time period of *Homo sapiens*, in both Africa and Europe.[45]

Java was once connected to Asia by a land bridge. As the sea level rose, Java became an island, trapping these primitive humans. Advanced *Homo sapiens*, who were capable of building primitive boats, arrived in Java about 40,000 years ago and mixed with their primitive *Homo erectus* ancestors. Milford Wolpoff of the University of Michigan, a proponent of the multi-regional evolution theory, stressed that the Java fossils represent *Homo sapiens* from a population so advanced that some of its members migrated to colonize Australia. The skeletal remains found in Java, Wolpoff said, are "incontrovertibly ancestral to living (indigenous) Australians", a resemblance that "shows a continuity in the region as we expected to happen."[46]

In 1998, stone tools and fossilized bones of stegodons (elephants) and other animals were found on Flores, an island in the Lesser Sunda island chain, east of Java. Fission-track dating (see below) put the finds at about 800,000 to 900,000 years ago. It has been suggested that these tools belonged to *Homo erectus*, who would have had to travel by some type of raft to reach the island of Flores from Southeast Asia. It is likely that *Homo erectus* coexisted with *Homo sapiens*, interbred, and then migrated throughout the world. This would account for the differences in appearance and variations of the world's population. New discoveries and new, more accurate scientific ways for determining time periods mean that we are constantly recalculating the date of the appearance of the earliest humans in the Americas and the world. The history of the first inhabitants in America has been variously estimated to start 3000, 10,000 and possibly 50,000 years ago. New archaeological data estimates this may have occurred earlier.[47]

The current method of assessing the time period is determined by radiometric age dating. This is determined by studying the way radioactive elements decay. All living matter, whether plants or animal life, gives off radioactive chemical particles at a measured rate of release. This can be studied to determine a specific time period. Stone implements, animals, and fire pit sites can be tested to determine a date when humans may have occupied the site. Carbon 14 is one technique used for dating organic substances such as wood, bone or shells, but it is accurate only to about 50,000 years. A more precise method for determining a date is a newer fission-track method. A date is determined by tracking fragments of crystals from uranium-238 given off after it undergoes spontaneous fission. The density of the tracks per unit on its mineral surface is related to the uranium concentration. This technique can be used for age dating. The science of dendrochronology or tree-ring dating can also be used to reconstruct a time period from volcanic activity and other archaeological findings. Plants and animal fossils have enabled archaeologists to assess the approximate date of our last Pleistocene time age in North America to 1.6 million to the end of the Ice Age, 10,000 years ago.[48]

Mastodon trapped in ice

A number of Pliocene species of early humans also lived in Africa. During this epoch more than one species of early humans flourished at once and sometimes coexisted in the same geographical area.[49] The *Encyclopedia Britannica* also calls this the Paleolithic period, stating, "At sites dating from the Lower Paleolithic Period about 2,500,000 to 200,000 years ago, simple pebble tools have been found in association with the remains of what may have been the earliest human ancestors...." Due to the recent start and end of this Pleistocene epoch, a great deal is known about its geologic, climactic, and evolutionary history. During this epoch the polar ice sheets expanded and contracted and for this reason the Pleistocene epoch is commonly known as the Ice Age. Modern humans evolved and spread throughout the world during the Pleistocene era. During interglacial periods of the Pleistocene epoch the climate was warm and damp, allowing vegetation to flourish. Humans living in or traveling through Arctic areas found a simple source of food such as berries for sustenance. During the present ice age, glaciers have advanced and retreated over 20 times, often blanketing North America with ice. Our climate today is actually a warm interval between these many periods of glaciations. The most recent period of advancing glaciers, which many people think of as the "Ice Age", was at its height approximately 20,000 years ago. It began its advance about 70,000 to 150,000 years ago with a

Mountain glacier, southeast Alaska

severe cooling of world temperatures accompanied by a major advance of huge ice sheets in the northern latitudes. In North America this ice covering is called the Wisconsin glacier. Northward, it locked in the waters that formed the Bering Strait.

The glaciers began at two points in North America. One began its formation at the North Pole and spread down the eastern half of Canada as far south as Kentucky. The other glacier spread south from Alaska, following the mountain range in America's west that created Glacier, Yellowstone, Grand Teton, and the Rocky Mountains. There is evidence of paths made by humans as they advanced southward into America between the two ice glaciers, probably during warm periods. As one ice age ended and the earth warmed, humans and animals were able to migrate southward through the ice. During the last ice age a great deal of water was trapped in the ice caps and glaciers, lowering the sea level about 155 feet to expose a wide land area in the Bering Strait (Beringia) and allowing humans an easy access to cross from Siberia to Alaska. This land area of 900 miles wide was above the water from about 25,000 B.C. to 11,000 B.C.[50]

In his book, *The Ice Age History of Alaskan National Parks*, published in 1995, Scott Elias describes the geology, climate, ancient plants and animals from a study of core samples of pollen, plant fragments and insect remains collected by him and his colleagues. It led them to conclude that, "Beringia (Bering Strait) was not a treeless tundra, as has been thought, but was covered with birch, heath, and shrub willow. The plants and insects indicate that summers 25,000 years ago were warmer than today." Humans went southward, following the game and vegetation. About 11,000 years ago the glacial ice from the last ice age began melting, covering the Bering Strait with water and making it more difficult to cross over from Asia to America.[51]

Translated *Wallam Olum* (Red Score)

The "Bering Strait theory", estimating the Indians' arrival on the North American continent 3000 years ago, was accepted as historical fact after the discovery in 1833 of a chronicle of the Delaware (Lenape Lenni) Indians that seemed to document, among other things, their migration from Asia to Alaska. The chronicle was called the *Wallam Olum,* or *Red Score*. (*Red Score* was a pictographic history, later found to have probably been a hoax, perpetrated by naturalist Constantine Samuel Rafinesque, who claimed to have deciphered the original tablets, which, he said, had been lost).[52] In 1830, six years before Rafinesque published the *Wallam Olum,* Joseph Smith, founder of the Mormon Church, announced that he had "found a set of golden tablets buried in upstate New York written in the language of the Egyptians."[53] Smith attempted to substantiate his claim that the Delaware (Lenape) and the Mound Builders were descendants of the ancient Jews. Rafinesque challenged Smith's findings by publishing an article called *The American Nations and Tribes are not Jews,* in which Rafinesque assailed *The Book of Mormon,* calling Joseph Smith's tablets a hoax. Instead, Rafinesque may have perpetuated his own hoax, claiming the Indians were not the lost tribes of Israel but were Central Asian tribes that crossed into America over the Bering Strait. These false findings contributed to a belief that the Indians were newcomers from Asia and therefore had no rights to the land that was taken from them.[54]

Folsom arrowhead

In the 1950s, questions about the Rafinesque findings were raised when radio carbon dating revealed evidence that the Delaware had inhabited the northeast coast of the United States for at least twelve thousand years. Rafinesque's original manuscript of the *Walum Olum* was "replete with crossed-out Lenape words that had been replaced with others that better matched his English 'translation'. In other words, Rafinesque had been translating from English to Lenape, rather than the other way around; his manuscript was the rough draft of a forgery."[55]

This hoax may have fooled leading historians, ethnologists, and linguists for more than a century and is still claimed as a fact in many history and school textbooks, as well as fostering other books demeaning to the Indian.[56] A similar possible hoax arose in 1979 in a novel, *Hanto Yo*, by Ruth Beebe Hill. Hill claimed to have deciphered the Dakota language before any missionaries had recorded it. She said she translated the language from an early English dictionary and wrote a fifteen hundred-page book in the Dakota language. The Sioux Lakota tribal community disputed this as untrue.[57]

Projectile point, southern Chile circa 10,000 years

There was a time when the scientific archaeological community never imagined the possibility of finding a mastodon in the Eastern region of the United States, or that humans could have traveled to America over 15,000 years ago. There have been a number of archaeological discoveries that now reveal earlier and earlier dates of arrival of the first humans in the Americas. In 2003, Russian scientists uncovered a site on the Yana River in Siberia not far from the Bering Strait. Butchered bones of mammoths, bison, bear, etc., along with stone tools and ivory weapons, were all carbon dated to 30,000 years. Evidence at the site "makes it plausible that the first peopling of the Americas occurred prior to the last glacial maximum."

In the early 1950s, Thomas E. Lee of the National Museum of Canada uncovered man-made implements dating back about 65,000 years in glacial deposits at Sheguiandah, on Manitoulin Island in northern Lake Huron, Ontario, Canada. Geologist John Sanford of Wayne State University proposed that the oldest of these tools were at least 65,000 years old and might be as much as 125,000. The finding in 1951 outraged the scientific community to where Thomas Lee was harassed from his Civil Service position into unemployment. His funds were cut off and Lee was unable to publish his findings. "All the evidence was misrepresented by several prominent authors... the tons of artifacts vanished into storage bins of the National Museum of Canada; for refusing to fire the discoverer, the Director of the National Museum, who had proposed having a monograph on the site published, was himself fired and driven into exile."[58] Beginning in 1977, University of Kentucky archaeologist Tom Dillehay and his research team discovered at Monte Verde in Chile more than 700 stone tools, a child's footprint, fire pits, remnants of hide-covered huts and other artifacts. Peat from a stream had covered the area and preserved it. By 1978 Dillehay believed the site pushed human habitation of the New World back by 1300 years, to about 12,500 years ago. After further research in 1991, Dillehay radiocarbon-dated the Monte Verde site and, based on some tools, dated the site to about 30,000 B.C.[59] We have to remember that before about 16,000 B.C. the carbon dating of artifacts could have been underestimated by about 8000 years. An archaeological artifact presently dated 20,000 B.C. could in fact be dated to 28,000 B.C. Carbon dating is based on a false assumption that the percentage of carbon has been constant over the years, but it is known that carbon was more prevalent from 20,000 to 45,000 B.C. and varies from year to year.

Prehistoric butchered bone cut marks with straight cut end by humans

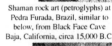

Shaman rock art (petroglyphs) at Pedra Furada, Brazil, similar to below, from Black Face Cave Baja, California, circa 15,000 B.C.

The discovery in a New Mexico cave in 1989 by archaeologist Richard MacNeish (of the Andover Foundation for Archaeological Research) of numerous stone artifacts, hearths, butchered animal bones and a clay fragment dating back at least 35,000 years could provide proof that the Americas were inhabited long before the generally accepted date of 12,000 years ago. These findings were in the Organ Mountains near Alamogordo, New Mexico in the Pendejo, Orogrande cave. MacNeish unearthed a roasting pit and found a bone spear point lodged in a horse's hoof at the site. The findings were estimated, with the help of radiocarbon dating, to be between 36,000 and 50,000 years old.[60] In 1991 *Science Frontiers* commented on MacNeish's findings, "It is certain that these discoveries will be disputed—and rightfully so. Even if they stand, it takes a generation to erase a false paradigm from the roster of science."[61] Archaeologist Niede Guidon of the Institute of Advanced Social Science in Paris reported on the Pedra Furada site in northeast Brazil in 1986. He reported finding ash-filled hearths and flaked stones estimated by the carbon-14 method to be at least 35,000 years old. The Pedra Furada site contained 400 prehistory sites including 340 stone walls filled with ancient paintings. Only two have been excavated suggesting this date. New remains are being found at the rate of 40 per year. American archaeologists reject these claims but French and South American archaeologists, after studying the findings, concluded the site clearly establishes a human presence to this date. Pedro Furada, in addition, has rock art dating to this period, making it the oldest art in the Americas. Conservative archaeologists questioned if the flaked tools were of human origin, stirring up a controversy.[62]

Cut bones and a stone tool were found at Toca da Esperanca (Grotto of Hope), in Central Brazil dating to 300,000 years ago by uranium-thorium testing at the Weak Radiation Laboratory in France.[63] In Arizona, in southwestern United States, there is a fire pit site that dates back 150,000 years. In another site in Southern California, archaeologists have used the fission-tracking method on pottery finds and discovered that they are at least 200,000 years old. For those adhering to standard views on North American prehistory, such ages were unacceptable.[64]

Flaked tools

The Calico site in Southern California dates back 200,000 years. This was confirmed by L.S.B. Leakey (discoverer of our early ancestor, *Homo habilis* in Kenya, Africa) who, with Ruth Simpson, Calico's chief archaeologist, unearthed an ancient pebble tool. Numerous tools show use-wear patterns through microscopic examination. Uranium thorium testing gives dating of 200,000 +/- 20,000 years. Due to this extremely early date, a controversy and debate developed over whether the artifacts were made naturally or by the hand of man. Many experts in the scientific community are now convinced of the authenticity of the site.[65]

At Valsequillo, Puebla, a site in Mexico, human artifacts were dated at 250,000 years by potassium-argon dating of igneous rocks and the similar dating of a camel pelvis. At the lowest layer of rock, fission-tracking assessed the site to be approximately 250,000 years old. The bones and stone tools were made by using flakes of filing to work the edges to make them sharp. Both the upper and lower layers of this site contained spearheads and over 100 partial skeletons of mastodon, mammoth, and smaller animals such as camel, horse, and antelope were uncovered at this site, along with evidence of human beings having hunted and eaten these animals. A spear point was found imbedded in the jaw of a mammoth.[66] Archaeologist Dr. Cynthia Irwin Williams (in charge of the project), geologist Virginia Steen-McIntyre and local paleontologist Juan Armenta Camacho, were all criticized for their dates and findings. Jose Luis Lorenzo of the Instituto Nacional de Antropologia e Historia had also investigated the site. It was reported that due to a disagreement and professional jealousy between him and Dr. Irwin-Williams, the Mexican government closed the site from any further investigations.[67]

Bearded Teracottta head Veracruz, circa 800 A.D. Roman features

A site on the Nottaway River of Virginia called Cactus Hill yielded preclovis radiocarbon dates of about 15,000 to 17,000 years old. Excavated by Joseph and Lynn McAvoy was a grouping of stone tools with a heavy percentage of blades and pentangular projectile points. This discovery makes Cactus Hill and the Meadowcroft Rock Shelter site in Pennsylvania (dating to about 18,000 years) the two earliest known sites for human occupation in eastern North America. Dennis Stanford of the Smithsonian believes the tools found at the Cactus Hill site are remarkably similar to older tools recently found in use by the Solutrean people of Spain and France. He suggests that these early Solutrean's might have sailed across the Atlantic to the Americas about 18,000 years ago with skin-covered boats, following the edge of the ice covered Atlantic to the eastern Americas.

Thor Heyerdahl, by studying the Pacific currents, realized travel was possible from the South Pacific to South America. Heyerdahl has also provided evidence that the Incas and the inhabitants of the Pacific islands and Southeastern Asia shared similar genetic blood groupings as well as styles of workmanship.[68] Heyerdahl did extensive research into both the cranial shapes and the texture of the hair of mummies found in Peru. He discovered a similar embalming technique as those used by the ancient Egyptians, as well as among other cultures. Similar mummification procedures of prominent individuals were also found "throughout the far-flung islands of Polynesia, from Easter Island in the east to Hawaii in the north, to New Zealand in the southwest... royal mummy bundles recently brought from a cave in Hawaii to the Bishop Museum in Honolulu correspond in striking detail with the sophisticated mummy bundles of the pre-Inca Tiahuanaco Culture."[69]

Bearded, Phoenician style Gulf Coast, circa 500 A.D. Museum of Anthropology Mexico

In 2003 a 5000-year-old Egyptian mummy was found lying in a fetal position with linen wrappings around the body, partially mummified. Although the ancient Egyptians were reputed to have had the best techniques for embalming mummies, they were not the first. A very sophisticated fishing tribe called the Chinchoros, who lived on the north coast of what is now Chile, was embalming their dead as early as 5000 B.C. Some of the early ancient Peruvian mummies were found with brown, soft, wavy hair lying in a fetal position wrapped with cloth. European anthropologists, after uncovering many of these Peruvian mummies and examining their cranial shapes, texture and color of their

Chinese mummy European features

hair, found that "they displayed physical traits thought to be alien to the aboriginal inhabitants of America."[70] In the late 1980's, perfectly preserved 3000-year-old mummies were discovered in a remote Chinese desert. They had long, reddish-blond hair, European features and appeared different than the ancestors of modern-day Chinese people. "Archaeologists now think they may have been the citizens of an ancient civilization that existed at the crossroads between China and Europe."[71] An anthropologist, T. D. Stewart, noticed in 1943 that when the wraps were removed from 2000-year-old coastal (Paracas) Peru mummies, that they were taller in statue and the skull shape was narrower than the present inhabitants. Dr. M. Trotter, a hair expert, examined the hair from the Paracas mummies in 1943. On reexamining the hair in 1951, Dr. Trotter, with a collaborator formerly with the Federal Bureau of Investigation in hair analysis, found that "The hair of the Paracas mummies, which I examined in 1943, may have changed colour and texture slightly. However, the amount of change in either colour or texture from any evidence we have, would not deny that the original color was a reddish brown and the original texture was fine." The Mayans of Yucatan, Mexico and tribes in the Umatilla area of Oregon, as well as societies in Africa, Egypt, Europe, and Southeast Asia practiced the custom of flattening and elongating their childs' heads.[72]

Nazca mummies, South Coast, Peru
straight brown hair

There are definite and distinct differences in size and facial features between the inhabitants of the Americas. Differences are also apparent in their culture and languages. It is plausible that the early inhabitants arrived in America at different stages and came from many different places. This would account for the many diverse tribes and cultures, whose bones and artifacts have been discovered in America. Native skulls found in ancient burial sites show Mongoloid or Asian features along with European and African features.[73] Early explorers, settlers and missionaries reported numerous encounters with black Indians as well as blonde Indians with white skin.[74]

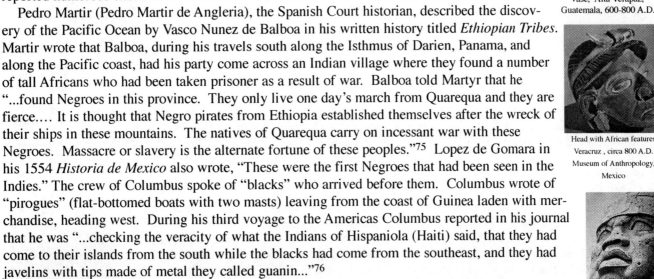
Chama polychrome ceramic vase, Alta Verapaz, Guatemala, 600-800 A.D.

Pedro Martir (Pedro Martir de Angleria), the Spanish Court historian, described the discovery of the Pacific Ocean by Vasco Nunez de Balboa in his written history titled *Ethiopian Tribes*. Martir wrote that Balboa, during his travels south along the Isthmus of Darien, Panama, and along the Pacific coast, had his party come across an Indian village where they found a number of tall Africans who had been taken prisoner as a result of war. Balboa told Martyr that he "...found Negroes in this province. They only live one day's march from Quarequa and they are fierce.... It is thought that Negro pirates from Ethiopia established themselves after the wreck of their ships in these mountains. The natives of Quarequa carry on incessant war with these Negroes. Massacre or slavery is the alternate fortune of these peoples."[75] Lopez de Gomara in his 1554 *Historia de Mexico* also wrote, "These were the first Negroes that had been seen in the Indies." The crew of Columbus spoke of "blacks" who arrived before them. Columbus wrote of "pirogues" (flat-bottomed boats with two masts) leaving from the coast of Guinea laden with merchandise, heading west. During his third voyage to the Americas Columbus reported in his journal that he was "...checking the veracity of what the Indians of Hispaniola (Haiti) said, that they had come to their islands from the south while the blacks had come from the southeast, and they had javelins with tips made of metal they called guanin..."[76]

Head with African features
Veracruz , circa 800 A.D.
Museum of Anthropology, Mexico

Four gigantic heads six to nine feet in height weighing about forty tons each, carved from round basalt block with Negroid features have been found at Tres Zapotes near La Venta on the Gulf of Mexico from the Olmec civilization, circa 1500 B.C. They were each placed in front of four large plazas in front of colorful temple platforms. In 1940, an expedition by the *National Geographic Society* and the *Smithsonian Institution,* led by Matthew Stirling, found on the western border of the state of Tabasco, Mexico, five mammoth heads, eight feet high, each weighing about 20 tons. A photograph in the New York Post of March 26, 1940, shows Negro features and a close resemblance to the colossal head of Hueyapan, Veracruz. A total of about 20 of these gigantic heads have been uncovered so far.[77] In 1972 Dr. Andrzej Wiercinski, craniologist and head of the anthropology department at Warsaw University, after an analysis of the skeletons at various Olmec sites, wrote "Skeletal remains from these sites make it clear that African or black people made up a considerable segment of the Olmec population." Dr. Wiercinski maintains that 13.5 percent of the skeletons from Tlatilco were of Africans and 4.5 percent of the skeletons from Cerro

Olmec culture
circa 800 B.C.

African Kingdoms
circa 1000 B.C.-1600

de las Mesas, Vera Cruz were of Africans. He added, "There is no one type of African on the African continent. These blacks have various facial characteristics and hair types." Olmec writing has been identified as possibly having North African origins.[78]

Clay kinky-hair heads, woman and man
La Venta Museum, circa 500 B.C.
Villahermosa, Tabasco, Mexico

A number of black figures in clay and stone have been unearthed in Costa Rica, Western Guatemala and the La Venta area.[79] A painted polychrome vase dating to 800 A.D. was found in Chama, Guatemala. A section of the vase was decorated with the illustration of a central figure with what appears to be a Mayan merchant trader painted black with a spear, a jaguar and other items draped over his shoulder. The black figure is shown dominating over a white figure kneeling at his feet.[80] A man painted black carrying a spear is pictured in both the *Dresden* and *Madrid Codices*. Both books survived after Franciscan Diego de Landa ordered the burning of almost all of the Mayan books.[81] The image of a black child with kinky hair was inscribed on a ceramic sculpture dating to approximately 250 A.D.[82]

A pottery fragment found in Tabasco, Mexico was decorated with what appeared to be a dead black man with closed eyes. This was unearthed on the Pacific coast of Guatemala and dated at 260 to 600 A.D. Numerous Negroid skeletons and skulls have been found in North and South America, together with skeletons having European facial appearances, buried along with native pottery. In his book, *They Came before Columbus*, Ivan Van Sertima establishes a parallel between the African and Indian civilizations of this time period. Sertima found a connection between the rise of the Olmec civilization in Mexico and the "...first pyramids, mummies, trepanned skulls, stele and hieroglyphs..." At this time in Africa, negro-Nubians gained power in Egypt to become the first black Pharaohs. Phoenician and Egyptian fleets sailing through the Mediterranean were under payment and orders of the black Nubian rulers of Egypt. Phoenician artifacts were unearthed with the remains of a European who had been buried in West Virginia. In Tennessee, archaeologists unearthed pigmy (pygmy) and European remains in the same early pre-Columbian burial mound.[83]

Earplugs Olmec   Earplugs Mayan

Earplugs Africa   Earplugs Mexico

Earplug
Moche culture, Peru

A priest of the Dominican order, Gregoria Garcia (1554-1637), spent nine years in Peru in the 1500s. In his *Origins of the Indians of the New World*, published in 1607, Garcia wrote that "The Indio's come from many nations of the Old World. Some are probably descended from Carthaginians, some are descendants of the Ten Lost Tribes of Israel; others came from Atlantis, Greece, Phoenicia and China."[84] Garcia also mentioned an island off Cartagena, Columbia, as the first point of encounter between blacks and the Spanish explorers in the New World. Garcia wrote, "Here were slaves of the chief, Negroes, which were the first ones our people saw in the Indies."[85] Both Darien (Panama) and Colombia lie within the end currents, which moved swiftly and forcefully from Africa to America. This can well account for early purposeful and unplanned landings of Africans. The Conquistadors found other blacks dispersed in small tribes and villages throughout the New World. There were colonies of blacks in Northern Brazil called the Charruas (Chares), and in western Columbia's Choco Region. There were other blacks found at Saint Vincent on the Gulf of Mexico (in present-day Venezuela), where black Caribs clustered around the mouth of the Orinoco River. The last of the pre-Columbian potters, the Mixtecs, have left behind clay sculptures of African faces that include the flared nostrils, the bone formation of the cheeks and the darkened grain of the skin. Some include the Gambian earrings, which can be definitely tied to villages in early Ghana and later Mali. Alvise da Cadamosto, a Portuguese explorer, saw similar earrings on warrior boatmen in Africa.[86] Numerous African skeletons were also discovered in Mexico. Carlo Marquez claimed the skeletons had prominent cheekbones.[87]

Olmec head
La Venta, Mexico
circa 800 B.C.

Missionary Francisco Tomás Garcés with Juan Bautista de Anza explored Arizona, California, and the areas surrounding the Gila and Colorado rivers from 1768 to 1776. He visited the Hopi and Zuni tribes. Garcés claimed he found a race of black men living side by side with the Zuni Indians of New Mexico. It was his contention that the blacks had inhabited there first. La Perouse (1741-1788), a French explorer, found blacks in today's California. He called them Ethiopians.[88]

Armond de Quatrefages, an anthropologist at the Museum of National History in Paris, in his book *The Human Species*, wrote that black inhabitants were found in small numbers and isolated areas in America. Some examples were the Jamassi (Yamassee) of Florida, the Charruas of Brazil (Uruguay), the black Caribs of Saint Vincent on the Gulf of Mexico and the black Zuni of present-day Arizona and Mexico. In Columbus' *Journal of the Third Voyage* he said he wanted to find out about the black people the Indians had told him about. Indians were found farming yams and taro, an African food, while the Portuguese explorers in Africa saw natives cultivating maize, an Indian product.[89] The Pima Indian tribe, Arizona members of the Uto-Aztecan family of languages from the Southwestern area of the United States, now living in Southern Arizona, have been identified as speaking a Semitic language. Analysis of the language of the Pima Indians revealed that it may be derived from Phoenician Iberian Punic colonists who settled in America from the Basque area of Spain between 800 and 600 B.C.[90] Inscriptions in the Zuni language on Mimbres pottery as well as certain mystic symbols have been discovered to bear a close resemblance to the North African group of languages used in the ancient kingdom of Libya. The Zuni language is an enigma because it is unrelated to any Indian tribal language in North America. The Haida Indians of the Northwest and the Kutenai (Kootenay) of the Rocky Mountains in the United States and Canada both speak a language that have no close relatives. The languages contain words that are impossible to achieve in today's modern languages.[91]

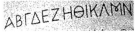

The tribal diversity of the Indians is revealed from the approximate 1100 different tribal languages spoken in the Americas before the arrival of Columbus.[92] The Stanford University linguist Joseph Greenberg identified three distinct periods of migration from Asia to America based on his analysis of the Indian language.[93] In 1985, linguist Richard A. Rogers plotted and compared the densities and exclusiveness of the various Indian languages in North America. He researched in two areas: those once covered during the last ice age and those never touched by the last ice age. In a study involving more than 213 native languages, Rogers found there were a smaller proportion of languages in the areas covered by the last ice age. Rogers concluded that the areas south of the continental ice sheets had been occupied for a far longer time, producing greater linguistic differentiation. The northern parts of North America contain only three language groups, from which he concluded that the Athabaskan-speaking inhabitants in the Northwest, the Algonquin (Algonkin) speakers in the central and eastern parts of North America, and the Eskimo-Aleutian speakers in the Arctic and part of the Pacific coast, occupied the area prior to the last Wisconsin ice age. Rogers further pointed out that the wide distribution of languages on the Pacific coast of North America suggested that there was a great migration to this area before the last ice age. Evidence of the evolution of the three language groups into many different languages suggests that there might have been three, four, or possibly more migrations to the Americas. In the first migration from about 30,000 years ago, the language groups were classified as Amerinds. The Na Dene was part of the second migration about 10,000 years ago. The third migration from 7,000 to 5,000 years ago contained Eskimo-Aleuts. Studies now determine, along with the three language groups, that migrations dating from 10,000 or 50,000 years ago or longer contained other groups that made their way to the Americas.[94] This substantiates other scientific studies suggesting that the Pacific coast of North America might have been settled first, then spread out from the coastlines into Central America around the Gulf of Mexico and into the inland regions of South America.[95]

Another way to discern the date of our ancient ancestors' arrival in the Americas is through mtDNA (deoxyribose nucleic acid) analysis. Extracting total genomic DNA such as a tooth, blood or hair does this. Mitochondrial DNA (mtDNA) is labeled into several types and groups called haplotypes. There are variations in the genetic code of mitochondria that fit into clusters. These clusters can trace a person's lineage back into time. The DNA blueprints in mitochondria, the energy factories of cells, are passed from mother to child. Although changes in it occur only by random mutation, they have taken place often enough over the past 500,000 years to serve as markers for scientists who are then able to construct extended "family trees" and trace patterns of migration. For example, in east Africa, where modern humans first appeared around 200,000 years ago, the mtDNA of the Turkana people has 44 mutations. But as humans left Africa and fanned out in successively smaller groups across Asia and the Pacific, that genetic diversity was gradually reduced.[96]

In 1981 Dr. Douglas Wallace headed a Stanford research team which found that ethnic groups could be identified and linked to their continent of origin by the mutation patterns in their mtDNA. He has looked back more than 100,000 years to the first humans in Africa. Dr. Wallace reported instances of prehistoric migrations that emerged from the study of DNA. He found prehistoric, courageous mariners who moved not out of Siberia as

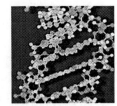

Haida Chief Wiah
of Masset, 1860

DNA double helix, 1952 X-ray photo by Rosalind Franklin, discovery credited to Nobel prize-winners Dr. Francis Crick and Dr. James Watson

anthropologists have long assumed, but out of Southeast Asia, then crossed the Pacific and came to the Americas at least 6000 to 12,000 years ago. Dr. Wallace said, "They either came across the Pacific to Central and South America or they went up the east coast of Asia and across the northern Pacific to Alaska and Canada." If this picture is accurate, it makes many Indians distant cousins of the Polynesians. Dr. Wallace and his Emory colleagues, in a 1992 report on mtDNA analysis, claimed the ancestors of the Amerinds, who comprise most Indians, entered the Americas in a single migratory wave at least 20,000 to 40,000 years ago.[97]

DNA outside cells

On the basis of DNA analysis of the different blood groups, geneticists have theorized that every full-blooded Indian tested carries at least one mtDNA (of four different haplogroups called A, B, C, and D). Three of these mtDNA groups (A, C, and D) are found primarily in Siberian Asians. The B haplogroup is found only in Southeast Asia, China, Japan, Melanesia and Polynesia. They are not found in Europeans or Africans. This finding claimed that all Indians are descended from four founding mothers who traveled to America and interbred with men from other groups that later became extinct. A band of these early settlers contained women with these four mtDNA characteristics. The A, C, and D groups were estimated to have appeared in America about 35,000 B.C. or possibly earlier. The B group began its migration to the Americas much later, at about 11,000 B.C., and possibly arrived partly by boat from different locations. The different tribes throughout the southern sections of North America inherited components of the four lineages. Only a single mtDNA lineage is found in the Na Dene speaking tribes of the Pacific Northwest, suggesting their arrival in America at a later date.[98] Christy Turner, a physical anthropologist who studies teeth, determined from detailed dental studies that the Indians of North and South America share the same dental pattern as those in Asia and are descended from an ancient Neolithic people who lived in Siberia over 200,000 years ago. Turner claimed they can be divided into three groups, thereby supporting evidence of different migrations.

A fifth mtDNA group called X was found in 1997 both in living Indians and in prehistoric remains. Haplogroup X is found in a minority of Indians who lack A, B, C, and D. The X mtDNA was not identified with any Asian origins but was found in Europe and the Middle East and in the Basque region of Spain. The X mtDNA was also found in Bulgaria, Finland, and Israel and in extreme southern Siberia. In the Americas the X group has so far been found in small numbers among the northern Indian tribes of the Na-Dene speaking Navajo, Yakama (Yakima), Nuu-Chah-Nulth, the Sioux, in larger numbers among the Ojibway (Ojibwe, Chippewa), Iroquois and Oneida tribes, and in ancient remains in Illinois near Ohio and near the Great Lakes. The geneticists are certain this X type is very ancient and not a result of intermarriages. The X mtDNA findings trace back to a population in Siberia that carries one of the mtDNA variants. It is possible that the Siberian people contained a Caucasoid link to an ancient racial stock that predated the present Siberian population and could possibly have arrived in America in limited numbers between 12,000 B.C. and about 30,000 B.C., via a Eurasian migration (of which no trace remains in Asia).[99]

South American
Amazon tribe

Geneticist Andrew Merriwether of the University of Michigan has questioned the four-mtDNA variant theory. Merriwether's analysis has concluded that the four-mtDNA variants can be subdivided into nine additional mtDNA types that are found in humans of Mongolian and Indian ancestry on both sides of the Bering Strait.[100] Merriwether's data indicated that the Indians came to the Americas from Mongolia in an exodus that lasted thousands of years, "...with lots of people in a sort of continuous migration over a long period of time."[101]

The dialects of many of the Indians in the northwestern parts of the United States—that is, those closest to Asia—are similar in some ways to some Asian languages. The Eastern tribes are widely diversified and their language is completely different from that of tribes in the northwest. The native people of South America and the inhabitants of Tierra del Fuego are of varying features, yet they coexist despite cultural differences and traditions, a fact that was observed in 1520 by Ferdinand Magellan.[102] The indigenous people in South America are so varied in appearance, stature, color, blood type and languages that if they were scattered throughout the world they would be taken as belonging to many different types of human ancestry. Christopher Columbus, on arriving in the West Indies in 1492, was astounded to find the Antilles inhabited by thousands of Indians from innumerable tribes, all speaking different dialects.

South American
Brazil tribe

The different traits and features of the Caribbean tribes of South America have long been a source of fascination for archaeologists and anthropologists. Their skin color is yellow but they are tall, and their facial characteristics are unlike the Asian features. They have distinctive oval faces with high, broad foreheads, large eyes, high

16

cheekbones, thin lips and well-developed facial hair. Their eyes are hazel gray or bluish. Author A. Hyatt Verrill spent many years among the Indians of Central and South America on behalf of the *Museum of the American Indian*, studying the Caribbean tribes. Verrill stated, "I believe that the Carobs (Caribs) are of southern European origin, perhaps the descendants of Phoenician voyagers, perhaps survivors of Atlantis, or possibly the result of an admixture of Indians and shipwrecked European navigators. Many of the men are decidedly Semitic in appearance, and many of the women would be indistinguishable from Europeans in a photograph."[103] The early Caribs lived in well-built houses in small villages. They were excellent hunters, fishermen, and farmers, and were well known for their distinctive multi-toned Carob pottery and exquisite basketry.[104] In February, 1975 the *Washington Post* reported that a Smithsonian Institution team of archaeologists had reported the discovery of two black male skeletons in a grave in the U.S. Virgin Islands. One had on a pre-Columbian Indian wristband. The Caribs had abandoned the grave centuries ago. Soil from the earth around the grave of the black skeletons was dated to circa 1250 A.D., and closer examination of the skeletons' jaws revealed dental mutilation practice with characteristics similar to those practiced in Africa.[105]

Human and animal sacrifice was practiced throughout the world. A document was found in 400 B.C. containing *The Carthaginian Law of Sacrifices*. It stated "...for a calf, whose horns are wanting, in case of one not castrated, or in case of a ram as a whole burnt-offering, the priests shall have 5 shekels of silver for each...."[106] Sacrifice was used for many reasons, but mostly to appease the gods or to guarantee a successful harvest. For example, "Global child sacrifice was practiced by the Irish Celts, the Gaul's, the Scandinavians, the Egyptians, the Phoenicians, the Moabites, the Ammonites and, in certain periods, the Israelites. Archaeologists have dug up thousands of bones of sacrificed children, often with inscriptions identifying the victims as first-born sons of noble families, reaching in time all the way back to Jericho in 7,000 B.C."[107] The Phoenician and Carthaginian civilizations, although advanced educationally and culturally, utilized ritual sacrifice of young children to their gods. Archaeological relics, such as the altars on high mountains in which children were sacrificed, and stone markers, which marked the burial place of the remains, have been found, along with stone carvings on markers depicting the children who were sacrificed. Clay jars were used to hold the charred remains. Entire burial grounds full of these slaughtered children have been uncovered.[108]

Aztec *Florentine Codex*

The Mesoamerican societies of the Aztecs, Mayans and Olmec, used young children as sacrifices to their gods at times. Friar Diego de Landa wrote that "In order to carry out these sacrifices they would purchase the children of slaves, or else those of people who out of devotion delivered their children, who were greatly regaled until the day of the feast."[109] Sylvanus Morley of the *Carnegie Institute*, Washington, D. C., wrote extensively on the ancient Maya. "Human sacrifice was performed in several ways; the most common manner and the most ancient... was by removing the heart. The intended victim, after being stripped, painted blue (the sacrificial color), and having a special peaked headdress set on his head, was led to the place of sacrifice, sometimes the temple courtyard, sometimes on the summit of the pyramid supporting the temple.... Women and children were as frequently sacrificed as men."[110] The *Florentine Codex* and the wall murals dating to about 300 A.D. in the Maya city of Bonampak, in southeastern Mexico, depict colorful, hand-painted scenes of human sacrifice and bloodletting. Sacrificial scenes are clearly depicted in Mayan sculpture, pottery, and murals.[111] In ancient Indian burial mounds in Florida, archaeologists have found ceremonial objects with evidence of child sacrifices. The Aztec life and death, earth-serpent goddess was known as Coatlicue. She was often depicted in Aztec sculptures with a skull head, cat paws, snake-serpent skirt, and a snake crown. In Aztec mysticism the male god Ometecuhtli had a dual, feminine wife named Ometecuhatl. The dual aspects were good and evil, light and darkness, and creator-destructor. Similar dual attributes can be found in the ancient mythologies of India as well as in other societies. Kali, as the India mother goddess, has been described as a blood drinker and companion of the demons, as both a destroyer and creator, interchangeable with the process of life and death.[112] In Mexico, the belief that the sun needed human nourishment prompted human sacrifice on a massive scale, and it has been estimated that as many as 20,000 victims perished in the Aztec and Nahua calendrical maize ritual in the 14th century A.D.[113]

Gruesome scenes resembling the Mayan murals and dated to that same era were found on the walls of the Assyrians, some of which are in the British Museum in London. They

Coatlicue, Aztec   Kali, India

depict scenes of horrible savagery and torture. Men were sometimes skinned alive or impaled on poles to slowly die outside the gates of a city. Renowned archaeologist Sir Austen Henry Layard rediscovered and unearthed the ancient Mesopotamia Assyrian cities, and graphically described the scenes in his book, *Discoveries In the Ruins of Neneveh and Babylon.* Regarding these wall murals Layard described the following: "Captives... were stretched naked at full length on the ground, and whilst their limbs were held apart by pegs and cords they were being flayed alive. Beneath them were other unfortunate victims undergoing abominable punishments. The brains of one were apparently being beaten out with an iron mace, whilst an officer held him by the beard. A torturer was wrenching the tongue out of the mouth of a second wretch who had been pinioned to the ground. The bleeding heads of the slain were tied round the necks of the living that seemed reserved for still more barbarous tortures."[114]

In the jungles of the Amazon in South America, a few primitive tribes were cannibals—a practice that, from primitive times, had enabled them to survive. The surrounding neighboring tribes lived in fear of these cannibalistic tribes. Amerigo Vespucci, after returning from his first voyage to Brazil, wrote a letter in 1502 describing the Guaranis, a primitive, cannibalistic tribe. Vespucci lived, ate and slept with the Guaranis for twenty-seven days. Accepted by the tribe, he described how they lived and shared all their possessions with each other. Vespucci found the people he encountered were "...completely nude, men as well as women, without covering their shame. They have bodies well proportioned; white in color, with black hair, and little or no beard.... They have no laws or faith, and live according to nature. They do not recognize the immortality of the soul, they have among them no private property, because everything is common; they have no boundaries of kingdoms and provinces, and no king!... Their cabins are truly wonderful...they slept in nets (hammocks) woven of cotton, exposed to the air without any covering... The meat which they eat commonly is human flesh, as shall be told.... They are warlike people... the enemy dead they cut up and eat. Those whom they capture they take home as slaves, and if women, they sleep with them; if a man, they marry him to one of their girls.... We found much human flesh in their houses placed in the smoke; and we purchased of them ten creatures male and female, who had been marked for the sacrifice...."[115]

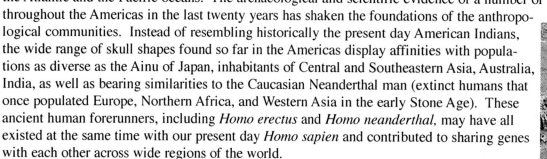

Primitive South American tribe

Hammock, pre-Columbus
Credited to the Taino's

Summarizing this chapter, the idea that the American Indians originally came from northeast Asia only 3000 to 6000 years ago across the Bering land bridge (Beringia) has now become outmoded due to recent findings. Both archaeological and genetic research, along with linguistic studies assembled over the last two decades, now support the idea of not one, but multiple migrations for the first Indians voyaging to the Americas across the Atlantic and the Pacific oceans. The archaeological and scientific evidence of a number of skulls unearthed throughout the Americas in the last twenty years has shaken the foundations of the anthropological communities. Instead of resembling historically the present day American Indians, the wide range of skull shapes found so far in the Americas display affinities with populations as diverse as the Ainu of Japan, inhabitants of Central and Southeastern Asia, Australia, India, as well as bearing similarities to the Caucasian Neanderthal man (extinct humans that once populated Europe, Northern Africa, and Western Asia in the early Stone Age). These ancient human forerunners, including *Homo erectus* and *Homo neanderthal,* may have all existed at the same time with our present day *Homo sapien* and contributed to sharing genes with each other across wide regions of the world.

South American tribal village homes

Most American Indian tribes strongly contest the early 3000 to 6000 year arrival theories on the grounds it is contrary to their oral traditions which relate that their ancestors have always been in the Americas. A number of tribes believe that their ancestors emerged from beneath the earth into the present world through a hole in the earth's surface. Either way, a large number of cultures, languages and social traits were brought to the Americas following a remarkable series of journeys over many thousands of years, long before the arrival of Columbus. Voyagers from far off lands overcoming numerous obstacles traveled the perilous seas in primitive vessels to bring their diverse and intermingled cultures to the shores of the Americas.

CHAPTER 2 CROSS-OCEAN VOYAGES TO THE AMERICAS

The existence of lands across the oceans was recorded as early as 2250 B.C. and in the ancient writings of China, Egypt, Greece and the Roman Empire. How did these ancient civilizations cross the oceans to the Americas at this time? If it was done, can we find evidence of these travels in sagas and archaeological findings?[116]

Clay tablet map with Babylon at center, showing oceans on a flat world

During this early period the sea level was much lower, leaving vast areas of land exposed. Civilizations inhabiting the coastal lands improved the size and construction of rafts and balsa ships. They added sails and rudders, enabling them to take advantage of the prevailing winds that propelled them far out into the oceans. Early Egyptians, Babylonians and Chinese developed maps based on compass readings, mathematical calculations and celestial observations. Thousands of years before Columbus early maps of the Chinese, Arabic, Greek, Roman and later, medieval maps, depicted lands across the oceans—what we now know as North and South America. The Piri Reis map of 1513, showing undiscovered land, was possibly recopied from maps made well before 4000 B.C.[117]

Egyptian dugout canoe circa 5000 B.C.

Scholars have theorized that the history of raft building in Southeast Asia is so ancient that they are the true precursors of the East Asian junk. The design of the East Asian junk is an evolutionary copy of the raft's distinctive curves and blunt ends. A tiny drawing of what looked like a raft was one of the earliest Chinese designs for a ship. We can trace the raft's appearance in the Southeast Asian Sea back to at least 60,000 to 70,000 years. Primitive hunters who utilized both fire and stone-cutting tools to hollow out wooden logs constructed the forerunner of the earlier ships. Some seaworthy ships from 5000 B.C. or earlier were constructed from reeds and had sails made from woven flax. Others were large dugout canoes with sails made from a bark fiber. These vessels were built with tools of stone, bone and coral. The canoes were dug out from tree trunks with crude axes or made from planks sewn together with cordage of coconut fiber twisted into strands and braided for strength. Cracks and seams were sealed with coconut fibers and sap from breadfruit or other trees. An outrigger was attached to a single hull for greater stability on the ocean, or else two hulls were lashed together with crossbeams and possibly a deck added between the hulls to create double canoes that enhanced the capability to travel long distances. During this early period expert seafarers depended solely on their observation of the ocean, sky, and traditional knowledge of the patterns of nature for clues to the direction and location of land. The canoes were paddled when there was no wind and sailed when there was. Incredibly, these ancient ships were seaworthy enough to make voyages of over 2000 miles along the longest sea roads of the South Pacific, between Hawaii and Tahiti. Although these double-hulled canoes had a smaller carrying capacity than the broad-beamed ships of the European explorers, the Polynesian canoes were faster. One of Captain James Cook's crew estimated a Tongan canoe could sail "three miles to our two." These travelers with their double-hulled sailing ships were able to carry a hundred people with their belongings, pigs, chickens, plants, and food for long voyages. As Cook explored the South Pacific in 1772-1775, he remarked that his ship, Endeavor, was no match for the speed and larger length of the native ships. He called the natives and their ships "Vikings of the sunrise."[118]

"How They Build Boats in America" Engraving by Theodor de Bry 1500s

Migration eastward from Southeast Asia could not be done without crossing substantial stretches of open sea. The Western Islands on the Sunda Shelf (Sumatra, Java, Bali, and Borneo) were joined to each other and to the Asian mainland by land bridges during the glacial periods when the sea was at a low level. Oral legends of the south Sea islanders and the Maori traditions claim their land once had close contact with Australia (of a great land mass connecting the islands of Papua New Guinea, with Australia). This runs contrary to the present scientific theories. The oral traditions speak of sunken lands, submerged ruins and megalithic structures off eastern Australia and in the Torres Strait. The Maoris recall a large land mass they called Waing-roa, beyond Cape Reinga, that was submerged in a volcanic eruption along with a large population and cultural center. In the mid 1970s divers uncovered a large number of carved stone heads and found remains of temples, as well as submerged, crumbling remains of a pyramid-type construction. The Australian aborigines' oral legends tell of pale-faced people visiting their land from across the sea, erecting sacred stones and other monuments and worshipping the stars. Mayan jade items as well as similar ancient

Hawaiian balsa double canoe

19

Inca items and stone heads similar to those on Easter Island have been dug up in Papua, New Guinea, Cape York and other areas in the Australia and New Guinea region. "A number of overseas archaeologists, anthropologists and ethnologists who have undertaken extensive field research over the years have come to the general agreement: Based upon present day New Guineans' ancient relics, customs and beliefs, and their knowledge of agriculture, which they practiced over a wide area for thousands of years before the coming of the Europeans, a super-civilization of highly advanced Megalith-building people may have once existed in New Guinea and left its mark upon the Melanesians. Other mysterious ruins that have raised much speculation exist near Alice Springs, Northern Territory. They con-

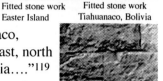

Fitted stone work   Fitted stone work
Easter Island   Tiahuanaco, Bolivia

sist of terraces up to 40 feet tall. The terraced walls are constructed of large stone blocks closely fitted together in a way not unlike the mysterious stonewalls of Tiahuanaco, Bolivia. Similar stone walls form the ruins which lie submerged off the Queensland coast, north of Brisbane. In the late 70's, similar stone ruins were reported found in Western Australia...."[119]

Phoenician fitted
stone work construction

In 1998 a joint Dutch-Indonesian team made a controversial claim that humans were contemporaries of stegodons. These extinct primitive elephant-like animals lived as long as 15 million years ago until the end of the last ice age. They were found at a site called Mata Menge on the Indonesian Island of Flores. In 1991, 1994 and 1997 archaeological expeditions to the island found flaked stone tools along with animal bones of stegodon, crocodile and giant rat. The bones were dated to about 800,000 years ago. This suggests that Paleolithic humans might have made ancient sea voyages with crude boats about 800,000 years ago.[120]

Anthropologists in Brazil have found numerous pre-Columbian skulls with negroid features. In 1975 after carbon dating the skull of a woman with African features (whom they named Lucia), it was possible to ascertain that it belonged to a woman who lived 11,500 years ago. This could revolutionize theories relating to the continent's early inhabitants. Scientists believe that Lucia's ancestors were from the same line of descent as Australia's aboriginal peoples, who crossed the northernmost Pacific Ocean by boat 15,000 years ago or earlier, next to glaciers that were forming at that time. In July, 1996, remains of an individual over nine thousand years old, known as the Kennewick Man, were found on the shores of the Columbia River in Washington State. Scientists believe that this person may be of Ainu extraction and, thru DNA studies related to the early Joman, distinct from the Japanese by having some caucasian features.[121]

Australian   Brazilian fossil
Aborigine   Lucia
                    Artist's rendition

A number of other ancient looking humans have been found in America dating about 13,000 years. On October 9, 1933, a grave containing the remains of a man and artifacts (originating from an unknown area) were found on the border between Minnesota and North Dakota, known as the Brown's Valley man. It was estimated to be 11,000 years older than the last Ice Age. In 1940, a well-preserved 9400 year-old man was found in a Nevada cave. The upper part of his body was mummified with a head of red hair. Known as the Spirit Cave man, he had been found on his left side with knees flexed upward in a fetal position, as with bodies found in the ancient pre-dynastic Egyptian burial sites. In the Mexico City National Museum of Anthropology lies a 13,000 year-old elongated skull of a woman known as Peñon Woman III, estimated to have died at the age of 27. Silvia Gonzalez, a geologist, sent the skull to Oxford University for carbon dating and surmised that she "was part of a fair-skinned population that resided in the Americas during the last Ice Age." In 1965 the 9700-year-old body of Gordon Creek woman was found in Colorado. The body and artifacts were sprinkled with red ochre. Clovis burials in Montana also contained red ochre. C. Vance Haynes, a prominent Paleo-Indian geochronologist, compared Clovis to Czech and Ukrainian burials and noted the similarity in the burials of two children at Lake Baikal with a Clovis burial in Montana. Both contained similar tools, points, and red ochre. In 1997, anthropologist Anne Pyburn discovered two Mayan tombs in Belize. The bones were red with the dust of cinnabar. The bodies of Olmec and Mayan royalty were often liberally coated with red cinnabar after death. The Kurgans, a seminomadic culture of Eastern Europe, used red ochre about 5000 B.C. in their mound burials as did the Adena mound culture about 500 B.C. The use of red ochre dates back about 800,000 to 900,000 years as a possible worldwide ancient ritual symbol, used as a body decoration to impart the essence of life. Skeletal remains have been found covered in red ochre in the Americas and among the ancient Africans, Asians, Australians, Egyptians, Europeans, Sumerians, etc. Archaeologists along the east coast, from Maine to Labrador, found burial sites with red ochre color in the contents of the graves. The coastal Beothucks were called "Red Paint Indians" due to the use of red ochre for decoration and burials. This is fairly common and existed in the ancient seafaring cultures in the Atlantic and early

Scandinavian coastal communities. In northwestern Australia, archaeologists have found thousands of circles engraved by people some 75,000 years ago. Buried at the bases of the circular monoliths are red ochre and stone artifacts dating 60,000 to 176,000 years old. From 1968, human skeletal remains buried in red ochre have been found at Lake Mungo in New South Wales, Australia, radiocarbon dated to about 40,000 years. Then we have Wilhelm Schouten van Hoorn's voyage, pioneering the way around Cape Horn. He landed at Rio Deseado on December 8, 1616, to stock up with food and water. The Dutch saw some strange things, including a burial ground, where they uncovered skeletons up to twelve feet in length, the skulls of which could be worn like helmets. In Terra del Fuego they found the inhabitants well proportioned and a similar height to Europeans. They had long black hair and sharp teeth, and painted themselves red and white all over.[122]

Dr. Theodore Schurr, a University of Pennsylvania molecular anthropologist, wrote an abstract entitled *Mitochondrial DNA and the Peopling of the New World*. Published in May, 2000, it claimed that genetic data shows humans may have been in America as early as 25,000 to 35,000 B.C. Schurr also claimed many of these early arrivals closely resembled the Joman people of Japan and their closet descendents, the Ainu, from Hokkaido, Japan.[123]

Most scientists, archaeologists and anthropologists now recognize there is no distinct race. All humans are 98 plus percent related. We may have certain different characteristics in color, nose, hair, skin, skull, etc., that will give us different traits through our DNA, but in essence we are related to each other in one way or another. Many Indian tribes from North America have a language association that reaches into South America. Over thousands of years we find that these linguistically related languages spread into different areas, along with some genetic traits that were absorbed through intermarriage.

Genetic variations of humans

Jack Forbes, an anthropologist, wrote in 1967:

> The physical characteristics of Native American peoples were at one time thought to link them with so-called mongoloid peoples of Asia, but the problem is now generally seen to be much more complex.... For one thing, the Indian peoples did not comprise a physically uniform population. Although the variations in physical type found in the Americas are not as great as those found in Eurasia or Africa, they nonetheless are great enough to suggest that perhaps several different ancestral groups mixed.... This writer would suggest that Native Americans... comprise a population standing somewhat between the extreme Caucasoid and Mongoloid types and may represent either the end-product of the mixture of several Mongoloid Caucasoid type groups or the survival of the type from which Mongoloid and Caucasoid are both derived.[124]

Thor Heyerdahl, through the voyages of the Kon-Tiki and the RA expeditions, discovered that it is possible to cross the Pacific Ocean following the existing natural currents. Heyerdahl discovered that boats he had constructed from balsa, reed or papyrus, using a design similar to that used by boat builders in 2000 B.C., were watertight and could be used for long ocean voyages. Heyerdahl used a balsa raft, built to ancient Inca specifications, and the accurate description given by Juan de Sáamanos, to build the first Kon-Tiki and found that it was possible for ancient travelers to voyage from South America to Polynesia and Australia.[125]

Early ships traveling across the Pacific Ocean from Asia to the Americas would have been diverted towards British Columbia by the swift Japanese currents—the strongest in the Pacific. Drawings of boats by ancient aboriginal artists on rock petroglyphs support this theory. They are shown as having a very high prow. Such an innovation would have been unnecessary in calm inland waters, but absolutely essential for an ocean journey. It was possible that early crude ships leaving from Kyushu, southern Japan, were diverted to the shores of Ecuador in South America. Due to the powerful western current flowing in a northerly direction from Asia, it was extremely difficult for Asian vessels to reach the Polynesian Islands. Instead they would first pass Japan and then move south of the Aleutian Islands, pushed on by prevailing western winds north of Hawaii until they reached the west coast of North America. They would have landed in Canada and then probably followed the coastline to migrate south to California and South America.[126]

Evidence also points to ancient voyages around 5000 B.C. or earlier from Southeast Asia to Indonesia and eventually to the east and west, where the explorers would have found themselves in the Pacific Islands. There also is a 1988 genetic study that point to pre-Columbian migrations from America to the South Pacific islands. Genetic tests of blood samples have shown that, in most instances, Indians from America and not from Asia settled these South Pacific Islands. Several of the same species of plants exist in

Prevailing Pacific currents

21

both South America and the Pacific, from Polynesia to New Zealand. They are all useful plants that explorers might take on a long voyage to a new land. The plant list includes the yam (Ipomoca batatas), the bottle gourd (Lagenaria), coco palm (Cocos nucifera), cotton (Gossypium), and the totora reed (Scirpus riparius), which was used to construct the reed ship. This reed grows extensively on the shores of Lake Titicaca near Tiahuanaco and in the Crater Lakes of Easter Island. Other useful plants found in both regions include the tomato, sweet potato, tobacco, papaya, and the wild pineapple. Those discovered in America have been found to pre-date those grown in Polynesia, suggesting a western migration from South America. The seeds could not have survived the long ocean drift nor being carried by birds on a migratory flight, so there is strong evidence that humans transported them.[127] The great numbers of American crop plants that pre-date European exploration in Polynesia are positive evidence of overseas voyages from and to South America and to the South Pacific or beyond. Oral legends of both the Incas and Easter Island link a connection between the two.[128]

These reed and balsa ships were extremely seaworthy and able to carry a heavy load of passengers and cargo weighing up to 40 tons. The early Spanish ships in America carried the same comparable tonnage. Due to their unusual design and construction, these ships were able to withstand the heavy ocean waves. Unlike ships constructed by the Europeans that were made buoyant by a watertight, air-filled hole so big and high that it could not be swamped by waves, the ancient Incas' ships could never be filled by water. Due to the open construction of the balsa wood, there was no place to retain the invading seas. The ocean water simply washed through. The raft-type vessels were made of light balsa wood, "or of bundles of reeds or canes lashed together in a boat fashion, or by making pontoons of inflated sealskins carrying a sort of deck."[129] A deck of "slender canes was raised so that crew and cargo remain dry while the main logs were awash and covered the underbelly of balsa logs. The logs as well as the canes were lashed securely together with henequen rope." The rafts carried masts and yards of very fine wood and cotton sails in the same shape and manner as the ships that first arrived in America from Spain.[130] On his many voyages with these balsa and reed boats, Thor Heyerdahl noted that they were "...exceedingly seaworthy craft, perfectly adapted for carrying heavy cargoes in the open and unsheltered ocean. Of all the valuable qualities none surprised and impressed us more

Balsa raft of the Pacific,
off Ecuador

than their outstanding safety and seaworthiness in all weather conditions." In addition, the ancient Incas equipped their ships with an unusual inventive navigational system they called "guara." This simulated our own rudder system. It was more advantageous with their own balsa and reed ships, allowing the boats to be steered and maneuvered by thrusting a number of these guaras in between the balsa logs and down into the water. The guara could be adjusted to sail in the desired direction into the wind, at any angle, to duplicate the same movements as a regular sailing boat with a keel.[131]

The early Spanish explorers record the many voyages the Inca made with these balsa and reed raft-type ships out into the ocean, to the Easter Islands and back. A Spanish missionary, Father Jose de Acosta, who spent 14 years in Peru, recorded in his *Natural and Moral History of the Indies* that, "The Inca Indians at Ica, and those of Arica (Chile), 750 miles to the south, told the Spaniards that in ancient times they used to sail into the south seas where they visited some islands very far away toward the west."[132]

Balsa boat,
Egyptian model   Inca balsa boat

Before the Spanish landed in Peru a report was sent by Juan de Sáamanos to the Spanish Emperor Charles V (Carlos) of a large raft sighting and capture by Francisco Pizarro and his pilot Bartolomo Ruiz in 1526, as they sailed south off northern Ecuador. They reported seeing a large raft of "almost equal size" of their own ship going in the opposite direction. The large raft was captured by the Spaniards and was found to have a crew of twenty Indian men. They noted it was a merchant vessel "...heavily laden with cargo… estimated… about thirty-six tons as compared with the forty tons of their own caravel." The descriptions match similar historic records of simply constructed large rafts. Many thousands of years ago ancient travelers, utilizing primitive rafts along with the lower sea levels, could possibly have traveled from island to island to cross the Pacific.[133]

There were a number of other sightings and captures of balsa rafts by the Spaniards. Pizarro, as he invaded the Northern coasts of the Inca Empire and approached Santa Clara Island, overtook five sailing balsa rafts in the open gulf of Guayaquil. As he crossed the gulf to the Peruvian port of Tumbe, Pizarro "...saw a whole flotilla of balsa rafts standing towards them, carrying armed Inca troops."[134] Las Casas had stated that he knew the aborigines in Peru possessed balsa rafts in which they navigated with sails and paddles, and that this fact was also known in pre-conquest times to the oldest son of Comogre, a great chief in Panama, who spoke to Balboa of a rich coastal empire to the south, where people navigated the Pacific Ocean with ships a little smaller than those of the Spaniards, propelled by sails and paddles."[135] Other accounts were by Fernández de Gonzalo Oviedo in 1535 and Andagoya in 1541. Zorate, who was the Royal Treasurer in Peru in 1543, also described the rafts, stating they were made of "long and light logs... five, seven or eleven tied together with cross beams; the navigation with sails and paddles; the ability of the large ones to carry up to fifty men and three horses."[136]

Ocean-going balsa raft

Thor Heyerdahl, in his *Early Man and the Ocean,* mentioned two main ports below Tiahuanaco as favorable starting points for traveling to the Pacific islands as described in Captain de Cadres' recorded interrogation of a wise old Indian named Chepo, said to be 115-120 years old. After two months journey, somewhat south of westward, they would first reach an uninhabited island called Coatu, in which there were three mountains and many birds. Keeping this island to their left, they would then reach the inhabited island of Quen, that had a chief named Quenteque. To reach Easter Island, one would follow the course given, and would first encounter the barren bird-island of Salay Gomez, which has three peaks. Keeping that on your left and passing north of it, Easter Island is not far beyond.

Spanish Historian Pedro de Gamboa Sarmiento, noted for glorifying the Spanish conquistadors, referred to the Inca voyages in his *History of the Incas.* Sarmiento obtained the information from forty-two of the best educated native historians in Peru during seven years, from 1559 to 1565. Heyerdahl, in his 1951 book *American Indians in the Pacific,* relates, "We learn from Sarmiento that when Tupac Inca traveled on the Pacific coast of northern Peru and Ecuador he 'conquered the Huancavelicas although they were very warlike, fighting on land and at sea in balsa (ocean-going rafts), from Tumbez to Huanapi, Huamo, Manta, Turuca and Quisin.'" Heyerdahl later gives an account by Sarmiento of a horse trophy brought back by the Incas before the Spanish came to America. "These trophies were preserved in the fortress of Cuzco until the Spaniards came. An Inca now living had charge of this skin and jaw-bone of a horse. He gave this account, and the rest who were present corroborated it. His name is Urco Huaraca. I am particular about this because to those who know anything of the Indies it will appear a strange thing and difficult to believe."[137] Father Cabello de Balboa, who came to Peru in 1566, provided additional evidence of the Incas visiting islands across the Pacific before the appearance of the Spanish. He questioned surviving Inca historians. He was told by them that two or three generations before the arrival of Pizarro, the Inca King Tupac Yupanqui "...had embarked a whole army upon a vast number of rafts and sailed away from the coast. On the return of the flotilla to Peru, the Inca and his captains claimed to have visited two inhabited islands far out in the ocean."[138] Garcilasso de la Vega, of Inca descent, claimed the Incas sailed their rafts "fifteen to twenty-four miles and more if necessary."[139]

Phoenician ship
circa 700 B.C., length 100 feet

By 1000 B.C. new construction methods using wooden planks and metal tools changed the appearance of the reed and bark ships. In addition, by studying the stars and the solar system the Aztecs, Arabs, Celts, Chinese, Egyptians, Greeks, Hindus and the Phoenicians developed navigational methods, as well as maps and charts of far-off lands. Ancient wall paintings, rock inscriptions, pottery and coins of this period show the variety of large sailing vessels able to travel across the oceans.

Information about the sizes and other details about these ships are found in written documentation and archaeological findings from sunken vessels. In an Ancient Egyptian tomb in Cheops, a 143 foot dismantled ship was found in 1200 pieces dating from about 2000 B.C. An inscription in a pyramid built in 1900 B.C. depicts a ship 180 feet in length and 60 feet wide that sank in the Red Sea. In the tomb of Queen Hatshepsut, dating to 1500 B.C., a relief illustrates a 200 foot long barge carrying two 100-foot obelisks to Aswan. In this same tomb is an illustration of a fleet of ships returning from far off lands. In the Old Testament it is noted that in 900 B.C., King Solomon employed Hiram of Tyre, in Phoenicia, to build large ships that would enable him to trade in Ophir, Somalia, or India.[140]

Egypt ship towing reed ship
Bani Hasan Tomb sketch
circa 2000 B.C.

Egypt ship, circa 2000 B.C.
celebration stamp

From 500 B.C. to 1 A.D. the Minoans, Etruscans, Phoenicians, Celts, Libyans, Greeks and Romans left records of their ships on pottery decorations and inscriptions. A 600 B.C. relief shows a full-hulled trading ship from Spain with an approximate length of 110 feet. The Greek historian, Herodotus, gives a detailed description of a Phoenician fleet hired in 500 B.C. by Pharaoh Necho. About 450 B.C. the Carthaginians fully integrated and superseded the Phoenicians. From their seaports along the

Mediterranean, their large ships traveled to Africa, India and Britain, and were reported to have crossed the ocean waters to America.[141] Greek history records how the Carthaginian captains Himilco and Hanno sailed along the Atlantic coast of Africa. Hanno describes an apparent colonizing expedition of sixty ships and thirty thousand men and women to a far off land that may have been America. A reference to the sun god Bel, inscribed with Ogam Celtic lettering, and a Phoenician monogram, were found in Vermont on a stone lintel over an entrance chamber and inside the entrance.[142]

Phoenician ship, 700 B.C.

Phoenician merchant boat loading cedarwood for export, 700 B.C.

The Romans were recorded to have built as many as a hundred giant 1200-ton ships to transport grain from its far-flung colonies. In 240 B.C. Athenaeus, a Greek writer, described an enormous 240-foot ship that carried 2000 tons of merchandise. Athenaeus went on to describe the largest galley ship ever built. Commissioned by Ptolemy IV of Egypt in 260 B.C., it was 420 feet long. Most of these ships were four times larger than the ships Columbus sailed to America. In his book, *The Gallic Wars*, Julius Caesar described naval battles in the Atlantic off France in 56 B.C. and wrote of his victory against an armada of 200 Celtic ships from France and England.[143]

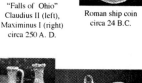
Roman Coins found at "Falls of Ohio" Claudius II (left), Maximinus I (right) circa 250 A.D.

Roman ship coin circa 24 B.C.

Caesar described these ancient enemy ships as being so large that his own ships, even with their high towers, were unable to reach their decks. The Celtic ships were reported to be over 180 feet in length, and made of oak with one-foot beams and iron nails as big as a thumb. A sunken Celtic ship was found off Marseilles with oak beams two feet thick. Such ships would certainly have been able to cross the ocean to America at least 1500 years before Columbus. A wreck of a Roman freighter has been found off the coast of Brazil. Artifacts of Roman coins, amphora, and statues have been discovered in North and South America, giving possible evidence that these ancient civilizations did travel to America.[144]

Roman marble of Venus, found in Gulf of Mexico

Roman amphora jugs found off Brazil

Roman lamps found in Alabama

Stone carvings at Angkor, a relief carving at Borobudar, Java, petroglyphs in Peru, temple paintings in India, and other early engravings illustrate the junks, outriggers, and galleys from Southeast Asia utilized as sailing vessels, many with triangular masts and outriggers. Fifth-century B.C. manuscripts of the Puranas and Jatakas of India relate tales of nearly 6000 round trip voyages from India to Malaysia and Indonesia.[145] A first-century Hindu manuscript, the *Periplus*, mentions two-mast sailing ships with dual rudders. Second-century murals and Chinese chronicles describe seven Hindu sailing ships 160 feet long, carrying 2000 tons of merchandise.[146] Chinese junks were well adapted for ocean voyages by the addition, in 200 B.C., of a rounded hull, a deep keel and a retractable stern rudder. Chinese expeditions to America took a coastal route south of Siberia and the Aleutian Islands and down the Northwest coast of America. Historical sightings by Coronado and other Spanish explorers in the mid 1500s of exotic ships with "pelican-shaped bows" in the Gulf of California confirmed the visits to America by the Chinese.[147] By 100 B.C. the population of the Asian continent numbered approximately ten million. Its coastal inhabitants were excellent travelers and traders who, by 140 B.C., were reported to have ocean-traveling junks that sailed to Madras, India, with gold and silk.[148] Inscriptions on turtle bone illustrated the transport of large armies. About the 5th century B.C., large numbers of ocean traveling ships as large as 100 feet long were built in Hong Kong shipyards.[149] As early as 400 B.C., China led the world in navigation, exploring the neighboring seas and venturing into the Pacific. By 100 A.D. they knew how to use the sternpost rudder to keep ships on course. By 300 A.D. they were able to calculate sailing speeds and estimate the length of their voyages as they extended their travels throughout the world. In 300 A.D. the kingdom of Wu was reported to have a navy of about 5000 ships with several decks for 3000 passengers. American archaeologist Robert Moriarty of the University of San Diego found stone anchors, of the kind that had been used in China for thousands of years, off the California coast dating to 1000 B.C. Additional stone anchors weighing about 450 pounds have been found off California.[150]

Ship carving on stone coffin, Sidon, Phoenicia, ca 200 A.D.

Java (Borobudur) ship stone carving with outrigger, circa 800 A.D.

Chinese Junk by Theodor de Bry, 1500s

Chinese merchant ship 60 ft., circa 1300 A.D.

Stone anchor San Francisco, Calif.

24

CHAPTER 3 LOST CULTURES OF THE AMERICAS

Copper alloy ring

Smithy (furnace)

Viking ship fitting

Viking artifacts at
L'Anse aux Meadows,
courtesy of Canadian
National Park Service

A site at L'Anse aux Meadows in Newfoundland, Canada, shows evidence of the Vikings having settled there on or around the year 1000 A.D., five hundred years before Columbus. They traveled from Norway to Iceland, from there to Greenland, and onward to Newfoundland. The settlement consisted of dwellings made of sod over wood frames, and each dwelling had five or six rooms placed around a central hall. Two large outdoor cooking pits, a smithy (furnace) for heating iron, iron nails, copper, and wood ship fittings that matched similar fittings used on ships in Norway, were found on the site. Other artifacts were found such as a copper alloy ring-headed pin of Norse origin, that would have been used to fasten outer garments of a woman or a man. A stone oil lamp and a type of soapstone spindle whorl used for spinning wool were also found. Viking sagas tell the story of their travels to Vinland with accounts by the survivors of their findings and encounters. Two in particular—*The Greenlander's Saga* and *Eric the Red's Saga*—give an account of what happened when they arrived, but it was only when the Viking artifacts were uncovered in Newfoundland that scientists identified that the sagas were accounts of voyages to the shores of Nova Scotia and probably New England.

Two of the Viking Sagas relate the story of the Viking journeys to the Americas. Sagas were central to the Norse oral tradition of transferring history and myths from generation to generation. The sagas describe the voyage to America when they left the southern part of Greenland and sailed in a northerly direction till they hit a large island. "They then went up and looked about in fine weather. Then they sailed through the Sound which lay between that island and the cape which projects northward." This direction implies they sailed north to Baffin Island, and then they took the Northwest Passage "west" to Alaska. They then sailed westward around the cape of Alaska to Helluland, a barren land with arctic foxes and massive herds of reindeer. From there they sailed southeast to Markland on the 58 parallel. An island lay to the south. This would have been in the vicinity of the Queen Charlotte Islands, Nova Scotia. Nova Scotia appears to be where the Vikings first landed. The sagas relate that they found "...immense number of elder ducks, ears of wheat and grapes that grew wild in the region." The land was described as a place so mild, no snow covered the ground during the winter and it was a 3-day voyage from Greenland. The second saga describes the voyage in 985 A.D. of Bjami Herjolfsson, a Norse settler in Greenland whose ship was blown off course. He had sighted a continent west of Greenland but did not go ashore. About 15 years later Leif Ericson, son of Eric the Red, explored the continent, making a number of voyages from Greenland to America during the next ten years. An extensive account of the Vikings' voyages were documented in 1892 by Sir Daniel Wilson, President of the University of Toronto in his book, *The Lost Atlantis and other Ethnographic Studies*. Wilson, in "The Vineland of the Northmen", relates accounts in detail of the

Vikings' sagas that were once disputed and now accepted. There is also a written record in the *Icelandic Annals* (records) of a post-saga voyage to Vinland. It relates that the Pope in Rome had designated Eric Gnupsson to be Bishop of Greenland in 1112. The Bishop set out for Vinland about 1121 but never returned. The *Icelandic Annals* record that the Vikings were sailing back and forth to North America from Greenland to fetch lumber and furs up until the mid 1300s.[151]

Controversial Vinland Map

A map from about 1440, with the name Vinland inscribed on the upper left corner, was published by Yale University in 1965. The map depicted Vinland as a separate continent located to the west of Ireland. A caption on the map, which was originally believed to have been lost, mentions "...the second journey to Vinland by Henricus." This was about 120 years after Leif Ericson's voyage to Vineland. Within the scientific community a dispute exists as to the authenticity of the Vinland map. Carbon-dating techniques used to analyze the parchment on which the map is drawn revealed a date of about 1434 A.D. The American Chemical Society tested the ink and confirmed that in their view the writing is a forgery. The map writes of two voyages to Greenland and a return to Vinland in the year one thousand seventeen. This appears to coincide with the route taken by the Vikings and with Leif Ericson's descriptions.

Viking artifacts were found at various other sites in North America. In 1961 a Norse penny, dating from circa 1065 to 1080 A.D., was found near the mouth of Penobscot Bay in Maine. Numerous rune

Norse penny,
found in Maine

stones have been found in many locations across the Northeast coast of the United States, from Newfoundland into Martha's Vineyard, Massachusetts, and as far west as Minnesota and Oklahoma. An ancient Viking two-sided iron battle-axe was found in Washington, Ohio. In a house built in the 1300s, a wooden figurine wearing carved "clothing" in a European style and a cross carved on its chest was discovered on the South coast of Baffin Island. The sagas tell of contacts and battles with the Indians who desperately desired the Vikings' iron axes. The Indian Algonquin language near the east coast is scattered with Gaelic and Norse words, which would suggest that there might have been intermarriage between the Indians and the invaders.[152]

Viking 2-sided iron axe found in Washington, Ohio

Giovanni de Verrazano sailed up the New England coast in 1524 on a voyage of exploration for King Francis I of France. On his first stop in Newport, Rhode Island he wrote, "We spent many days with the natives who were friendly and generous, beautiful and civilized. They excel us in size, and are of a bronze tawny color, some inclining more to whiteness and others of tawny color. Their faces are sharply cut, and there were among them two kings of so goodly stature and shape as is possible to declare, the eldest being forty years of age. Upon his naked body he wore an animal skin, and his hair was tied up behind with various knots. About his neck he wore a large chain garnished with stones of different colors. The women are very handsome and fair. Some wear very rich skins of the lynx. Their hair is adorned with ornaments and hangs down before on both sides of their breasts. We saw many of the men wearing breast-plates wrought of copper." Verrazano described their villages as being small, surrounded by cultivated fields of corn, peas, squash and pumpkins. Their homes were made of saplings covered with reed mats. It was only in Newport, Rhode Island, that Verrazano found these fair-skinned Indians whose resemblance to the Vikings was unmistakable. It is probable that he may have been describing the Beothuks, early inhabitants of Newfoundland, who the Vikings called Skraelings. The Beothuks, also called "Red Indians" from their custom of spreading red ochre over their bodies, were a distinct, light-skinned tribe with different ancestors and a different language (Beothukan) than the neighboring Algonquin tribes. By the 1700s they were massacred to extinction.

Indian Women Planting Maize, by de Bry

In Newport, Verrazano also reported his discovery of a "tall stone Norman Villa." This was a man-made tower similar to those built by the Vikings in Normandy and Norway in about 1300 A.D. He described it as "...round with eight pillars supporting eight arches." It had two floors with a lookout tower that faced the sea. In 1946, two Norwegian archaeologists discovered runic inscriptions deeply cut into the stones inside the tower in Newport. In 1971 similar runic markings were found on five carved stones buried along the banks of the Spirit Pond, west of the Kennebec River in Maine. Verrazano, leaving Newport, Rhode Island, traveled north to Maine where he found and described a different type of Indians, calling them "dark and less civilized."[153]

Newport Tower w/ Runic markings

Professor Roy Drier, on an expedition for the Michigan University of Mining and Technology in the 1950s, claimed to have found 5000 ancient copper pit mines around the northern shores of Lake Superior in Michigan. Drier estimated the mines he discovered were in operation from at least 2000 B.C. Mining engineers and metallurgists have estimated that over 500,000 tons of copper was taken from these mines on Michigan's Isle Royale, the Keweenaw Peninsula and Canada. The "Old Copper Culture", named for the copper tools found at the various sites, indicate that mining for copper in America started at least by 5000 B.C., preceding the Bronze Age. The oldest radiocarbon date known so far on a finely made native copper tool is about 6700 years. This tool was found at South Fowl Lake, Minnesota. The copper mines were in use until about 200 A.D. The large number of pits indicates that the copper could have been mined by Indians and possibly by different civilizations over a period of five thousand years. The copper was mined and made malleable by the use of fire and water to the copper ore and then through the use of stone hammers and manpower, annealed and hammered into copper articles. Copper tools, knives, barbed harpoon heads for spearing fish, awls, needles, earpieces, ornaments and axes have been found all along the water routes from the upper Great Lakes to the New England coast and to the South in Alabama and Georgia, indicating a mutual trade exchange existed for copper products. The Menominee Indians at one time resided on 9.5 million acres of this land from the Mississippi to Michigan. A federally recognized tribe, they now reside on a small reservation in Wisconsin.[154]

Norse copper pendant found at 12th-Century site Hudson Bay, Canada

Copper mine, Lake Superior, Michigan

26

Due to the proximity and numerous copper items found in many of the mound culture burial sites, it is most likely that the copper mines were an important part of the Adena and Mississippian cultures, or so-called mystery Mound Builders. Mound societies and the wealthy would adorn themselves with copper earpieces, breast plates, breech clouts and other forms of decoration. The Spiro Mound in Oklahoma contained about 25 solid copper axes with parts of their wooden handles, along with 266 copper plates depicting human figures. At the Moundsville site in Alabama, burial mounds were found with copper fishhooks, ear spools and copper pendants. At the Etowah mounds in Georgia were found 70 copper axes, hair ornaments and plates all made out of copper. In the Pee Dee mound culture of Southern North Carolina, the bodies of several infants and small children were tightly wrapped and placed in large pottery burial urns and then buried. A few of the Pee Dee burials were richly adorned with a variety of exotic artifacts made from copper imported from the Great Lakes area, and shells from the coast. Copper artifacts placed in the burial mounds were copper-covered wooden ear spools, rattles, pendants, sheets of copper, and a copper ax.[155]

Copper designs from the Hopewell mounds, circa 500 B.C.

Sometime around 6000 B.C., while Neolithic farming began in the near and far East, it also began in North America. There are indications at several sites in North America of established settlements, and evidence of agricultural societies in operation as early as 7000 B.C. The Koster site in Illinois and the Annis shell mound in Kentucky show that agricultural practices took place in the heart of North America during these times. There are indications that some of these sites are older still. Archaeological findings in the year 2000 indicate some forms of agriculture as early as 10,000 B.C. Today, over 50% of the world's domesticated produce comes from plants domesticated by the Indians.

Researchers have suggested that mound building occurred simultaneously with agricultural development and the stationary lifestyle associated with it. Agricultural development may have been a part of the lives of later mound builders but almost no evidence has been found to suggest that the people of the Adena culture pursued a lifestyle other than that of hunters and gatherers. It is likely that having to return to the same locales of abundant food year after year resulted in the degree of permanence required to construct their mounds. The Hopewell culture rose as the Adena seemed to fade. The former spread southward as far as Florida. Rather than forming a cohesive national identity, the organization of these groups was an informal network of trading relationships. Trade goods were exchanged; architectural ideas, religious concepts and other socio-political concepts were shared or borrowed. There is evidence that some of the groups in the Hopewell culture were adept at formal agriculture. This culture lasted about 700 years, to be followed by the much more advanced Mississippian culture.

Viking ship, 900 A.D.

An enormous number of ancient, crude tools, which would have been used for mining the copper, were found in the pits. The oldest copper tool was found at South Fowl Lake, Minnesota, and it was carbon-dated to about 4500 B.C. Items made from copper have been found on other native sites or with native artifacts throughout the Upper Great Lakes, as well as in the burial sites of the mound dwellers throughout the Ohio Valley. Some of the copper objects found in the burial mounds had complex geometrical designs and motifs that may have had meanings related to rituals. The same motifs appear in rock art inscriptions found in Canada, near Peterborough, Ontario. Some of the several hundred petroglyphs in the region are estimated to go back to 1500 B.C. The late Dr. Howard Barraclough (Barry) Fell, an Emeritus Professor at Harvard, deciphered one petroglyph with an ancient ship and a solar disk on top. Fell, with David Kelley, an epigrapher and amateur archaeologist, recognized that the script and picture carvings resembled an ancient Germanic language used by the Scandinavian's during the Bronze Age of about 2500 B.C. Rock petroglyphs that closely resemble those found in Peterborough have also been found in Norway and Sweden. Inscriptions on a white limestone rock, forty by seventy feet northeast of Toronto, Canada, relate of a Norseman King from Ringerike, Norway, named "Woden-lithi", who sailed on a "trading mission to America some 3500 years ago... for ingot-copper of excellent quality."[156]

Viking ship, stone carving Peterborough, Canada

Ancient iron or copper-smelting furnaces that may be related to these mine sites have been found in Ross County, Ohio. Of the number of furnace pits found, at least 130 were in Ohio with a few in Virginia, Georgia, and

Kentucky, and as far west as Arizona and New Mexico. In his 1951 book, *The Rediscovery of Lost America*, Arlington Mallery, an amateur archaeologist, noted that these furnaces bear a resemblance to ancient Old World pit smelters. This ties in with the discovery at L'Anse aux Meadows of a furnace used by the Norse to smelt iron. Mallery claimed that the evidence pointed to the "Norse of Greenland" as the builders and users of the iron furnaces, which are scattered over the United States.

British Bronze Age mound   Monks Mound, Cahokia
Stonehenge vicinity   100 feet in height

In the mid 1840's Ephraim George Squier and Edwin Hamilton Davies, amateur archaeologists, explored the ancient antiquities of Ohio. In 1848 they finished a manuscript of *Ancient Monuments of the Mississippi Valley*, which was to be published by the Smithsonian Institution. On completing the manuscript they discovered reports from British archaeologists that convinced them that the mounds of the Mississippi Valley were identical to those found in the British Isles and Scandinavia. In addition, their research on the art of plating metals found that the numerous copper ornaments discovered in the mounds "...are absolutely plated, not simply overlaid with silver... and if it is admitted that these are genuine remains of the Mound Builders, it must at the same time be admitted that they possessed the difficult art of plating one metal upon another." In a letter to Squier dated February 16, 1848, Joseph Henry, the secretary of the Smithsonian, insisted that Squier "adhere to the manuscript as it was submitted and remove everything he had added later on." At this time in American history no one could have imagined that either the so-called "Savage Indians" who were fighting for survival, or their ancient ancestors, could have had the capability to build the geometric-designed mounds or be the ones that manufactured copper items or of possibly plating intricate objects. Until their destruction, the Natchez Indians appear to be the direct descendants of the Mound Builders.[157]

One of the lasting effects of the last glacial period on the Great Lakes Region was the scouring of the rock that holds the copper deposits. This glacial scouring action exposed veins of native copper as well as shearing off copper pieces of varying sizes and transporting them miles, or even hundreds of miles, to the south. This transported copper, found mostly in glacial gravel deposits, is known as "float copper." It was deposited as the glaciers melted and receded northward. This float copper is found in sizes from that of less than a pea to many tons in weight. Float copper was readily available to the indigenous population during the Archaic Period. Experimentation would have demonstrated that this copper was malleable and could be fashioned into useful shapes. It is only a small step from finding the float copper to finding the exposed copper veins.

The first indigenous peoples who actually mined and utilized the copper have been labeled "Old Copper Complex" or "Old Copper Culture" by archaeologists. There is disagreement among the archaeological community as to the time period to ascribe to the Old Copper Complex. Dates range from over 5000 years B.C. to 700 years A.D. The copper artifacts from the Old Copper Complex differ from those of later manufacture.

In the mid 1840s, when the first modern copper mines were opened in the Keweenaw Peninsula, miners began to find traces of earlier mining efforts. Throughout the Keweenaw Peninsula and Isle Royale, pits and trenches dug into the rock were discovered, some as deep as 20 feet and others only a few feet deep. These pits and trenches showed evidence of copper having been removed from surrounding rock, and in some cases, copper was found partially worked out of the rock but still in place. In these pits and trenches were found a tremendous quantity of stone hammers, as well as additional copper artifacts of knives, spear points, awls, etc.

Copper chopper   Copper bracelet

In May of 1945 two fishermen found some artifacts projecting from the eroding bank of the Mississippi River at an old steamboat landing-site known as Osceola Landing, in Grant County, Wisconsin. Following this initial discovery, numerous copper artifacts were removed from the site by local collectors and were subsequently identified as Old Copper Complex artifacts. Old Copper Complex artifacts consist of fishhooks and harpoon points, conical spear points, awls, rat-tail spear points, knives, and spear points—many with holes for handles. Of great importance was the discovery by archaeologists of skeletal remains in association with copper and chipped stone artifacts. It is estimated that there were approximately 500 burials at the Osceola site. The major contribution of the Osceola site was the demonstration of a cultural complex that included Old Copper Complex artifacts. The Osceola site tied Old Copper Complex artifacts in with a distinctive chipped stone industry and burial complex.

Copper
fish hooks

It was not until June of 1952 that another Old Copper Complex site was discovered. This occurred on the western edge of Oconto, in Oconto County, Wisconsin, near the Oconto River. Thirteen year-old Donald Baldwin was playing in an abandoned gravel pit when he found human skeletal remains.

Initial investigation by the Oconto County Historical Society revealed burials accompanied by copper artifacts. Staff from the Wisconsin Historical Society and Milwaukee Public Museum examined the site more closely. It was found that a major portion of the original burial site had been removed by commercial gravel operations in the 1920s, but 45 burials were identified as remaining. Associated with these burials were Old Copper Complex artifacts in the form of awls, clasps, a spear point, fishtail spear point, fishhook, coiled copper beads, etc. Awls were found to be the most frequently occurring artifact, just as they had been at the Osceola site.

In 1953, a late Old Copper Complex site (approximately 2500 B.C.) was discovered in Algoma Township, Winnebago County, Wisconsin, on the south shore of Lake Butte des Mortes, on the farm of Matt Reigh. The Reigh site, like the Oconto site, was uncovered in part by commercial gravel operations. Burials of 43 individuals were uncovered along with copper artifacts identified as Old Copper Complex. As with the Oconto site, an unknown number of burials were destroyed by the gravel operation prior to the archaeological investigation being undertaken. These three sites, with their skeletal remains, distinctive chipped-stone and Old Copper Complex copper artifacts, support the unbroken continuity of indigenous peoples in the Upper Great Lakes.

Copper-plated bird
Peoria, Illinois mound

Old Copper Complex artifacts have been found at sites in the Canadian Provinces of Alberta, Manitoba, Ontario, and Quebec. The Morrison Island-6 site, located on an island in the Ottawa River, was found to contain 18 burials and 276 copper artifacts, with new and used copper scraps, indicating copper implement and weapon manufacture on the site. A carbon-14 date places this site at 2500 B.C. The Caribou Lake site contained a cremation pit with skeleton fragments and tooth enamel remains, along with copper artifacts. Carbon-14 dating placed this site at 1700 B.C. While Old Copper Complex artifacts have been found from Alberta in the west, to Quebec in the east in Canada, and as far west as North Dakota, as far east as New York and as far south as Kentucky in the United States, the center of the Old Copper Complex is generally agreed to be in Wisconsin.

Where did all this mined copper go? Some scholars believe that Phoenicians, Berbers, Bronze Age Europeans or Vikings may have mined the vast majority of copper in a huge international copper trade centering in the Lake Superior Region. There is a number of findings of script and artifacts to lend some support to this theory. There is also compelling evidence, from mound builders burial sites, to demonstrate that it was also possible the indigenous mound builders mined the copper and fashioned it into implements, weapons and ornaments.[158]

Evidence from nearby rock art points to a Scandinavian presence around 2500 B.C., and numerous artifacts found on the trails to the copper mines indicate that the Phoenicians may have possibly worked in them. In Egypt and other areas of Europe copper was a desirable item. Some of the Egyptian copper items are made with copper of the same quality as was used by the mound builders. Unsubstantiated theories persist that the Phoenicians mined the copper along the Susquehanna and Delaware River Valley. They then followed the earlier cultures to mine copper of a superior grade in the Lake Superior region. In 1974 a student found a 40 pound, 9 x 12 inch sandstone slab named the Knapp Stone along the west branch of the Lackawaxen near Pleasant Mount, Pennsylvania. It contained a sketch of the mountains with the sun and trees and Iberic script markings, circa 200 B.C. The script read, "On the appointed day, the sun sets in the notch opposite the house of worship." Nearby in the mountains are the ruins of what might have been an ancient, "corbelled, slab roof chamber." It was surmised that travelers used the stone to mark the position of the sun each day. In *The Search for Lost America,* author Salvatore Trento connected many of his findings relating to the Celtic-Phoenicians to their search for minerals, especially copper. It explained why mine artifacts of Celtic-Phoenician origin were found near old mine roads extending all over the Delaware River Valley from New York to Pennsylvania, to Pahaquarry township in New Jersey, to four miles away from Lake Superior, Michigan.

Iberic/ Script markings
found in Vermont

A French Jesuit missionary in the sixteenth century reported in northern Michigan that there were thousands of worked copper mines of which the Indians had no knowledge. All of these places had a substantial amount of copper. It was estimated by metallurgical engineers that an ancient civilization mined more than a billion tons of copper out of these mines. Carbon-14 tests of organic matter found in the mines date back to about 1000 B.C. In the Bronze Age, copper and tin were important ingredients in the making of bronze weapons, tools and jewelry in European and Egyptian civilizations.[159]

Ancient civilizations flourished from in the valley of the Indus River and its tributaries in the northwestern portion of the Indian subcontinent, to what is now present-day Pakistan.

At its height, its geographical reach exceeded that of Egypt or Mesopotamia and archaeologists have unearthed over 30 sites containing lost cities and villages that flourished from about 5000 B.C. to 1500 B.C. The sites extend from the Eastern Mediterranean to as far as India. Forests and lush green vegetation once surrounded settlements where the land is now arid and barren. The ancient city of Mohenjo Daro was discovered 300 miles north of today's Karachi, in Pakistan. Another site at

Pyramid complex, Teotihucan, Mexico, circa 1200 A.D.

Mesopotamian ziggurat complex Nippur, Sumer. circa 2500 B.C.

Harappa, near the Ravi River, was part of the pre-Harappan period that lasted from approximately 2700 B.C. to 2300 B.C. The sites contained sophisticated cities with large and complex hill citadels, housing palaces, granaries and baths. The arts flourished there, and many objects of copper, bronze and pottery, including a large collection of terra-cotta toys, have been uncovered. The Harappan culture of Northern India lived along the coastal areas from about 3000 B.C. to 1500 B.C. They were trading partners with the Sumerian civilization in the Indus Valley. It is likely that they had boats and trading ability to travel from island to island, finally arriving in America. Female statuettes found in the Harappan settlements of Northern India as well as along the western coast of South America and in Central Mexico showed topless women with huge upswept hair and headdresses clad in pantaloons and wearing ornate hip belts, large decorative earrings and other jewelry.[160] The cities in the Indus Valley were equipped with irrigation and sanitation networks, including sophisticated toilets similar to those found in the Aztec capitol city of Tenochtitlan . The houses were built along the four cardinal directions made of kiln-baked bricks. The four directions were similar to those used by the Mayan, Aztec, Chinese, Sumerians, and Pacific Coast tribes. Their religion appeared to be in some ways similar to the Indians. They had human deities of a mother goddess and worshipped the bull and water deities. The Harrappan culture used symbols of the swastika in a possible religious context. This same reverse swastika symbol is found in artifacts in Egypt and in the Indian mound culture, as well as appearing in Zuni and Hopi blanket and basket designs.[161] Chief Joseph of the Nez Percé, after his surrender, gave a pendant to General Miles and this object eventually found its way

Hopewell mound

to West Point. A few years ago it was examined and turned out to be a Mesopotamian tablet, recording the sale of livestock. How this tablet got into Chief Joseph's family and became his possession is a matter of assumption. Our understanding of the prehistory of America is not as complete as we may imagine.

Indus Valley goblet swastika design   Zuni baskets swastika design   Egyptian swastika design

The pre-Inca Moche (Mochica), a coastal dynasty that existed about 275 B.C., used building methods similar to those in use in the Indus Valley. Gigantic stone blocks were used for building above and below-ground reservoirs, along with carefully designed irrigation canals. In Mesopotamia (today's Iraq), the city of Uruk existed as one of many cities that were part of the Sumerian civilization. Uruk contained canals, reservoirs, bath houses, irrigation dikes and pyramids with stairways and temples on top, comparable to the Aztec and Mayan temples. Gold, decorative artifacts and small, white or purple/black beads that resembled those treasured by the Indians were unearthed in these excavations. The Indians called them trade beads (wampum) and they were valuable to them as currency as well as for belts of friendship with European colonists. Wampum first appeared in use with the Indians at approximately 2500 B.C.[162]

Great Baths, Mohenjo-Daro Indus River , West Pakistan c.1500 B. C.

Great Inca Baths Machu Picchu, Peru circa 1400 A. D.

After the conquest of Mesopotamia in 1760 B.C. by King Hammurabi, a water code was written that described similar techniques as those used by the Incas for taking care of their irrigation system. King Hammurabi wrote, "Each man must keep his part of the dike in repair." Catalhöyük, unearthed in south central Turkey circa 6000 B.C., contained homes built of sun-baked bricks and reed bundles covered over with dried mud. The construction and interior of the buildings resembled the Pueblo villages of today, along with movable ladders to reach the rooftops.[163] In the

American Indian trade beads (wampum)

Indus Valley beads

30

Mexican state of Veracruz, archaeologist Jaime Cortez Hernandez discovered a major ceremonial center that had been inhabited from 400 to 800 A.D., with stepped pyramids resembling those in Mesopotamia. In the site called Cuajilote he found two rows of stepped pyramid mounds flanked by an avenue a mile and a half wide, containing a temple at one end, a ball court at the other end, and a steam bathhouse for community bathing. The bathhouse and temple mounds were constructed of solid mud bricks with flat tops on the roofs. Stairways will remind one of a three-tiered stairway to the 70 foot-high Ziggurat of Ur step pyramid, similar to El Tajin on the Gulf Coast of Mexico.

North African pueblo

Taos pueblo, New Mexico

Dating to about 3000 B.C., the city of Uruk was a religious center in Mesopotamia (now southern Iraq), belonging to the Sumerian civilization that existed from about 3500 B.C. to 1800 B.C. The Indus Valley civilizations were advanced in pottery making, and were noted for their red earthen designs related to the Indian Anasazi pottery. The Harappan culture along the Indus River, now in west Pakistan, ended about 1500 B.C.—possibly due to climactic earthquakes and floods, or being overrun by war-like Aryans. [164]

Mud ziggurat, Mesopotamia circa 3500 B.C.

El Tajin, Yucatan, Mexico pyramid, circa 300-1200 A.D.

Step Ziggurat of Ur Mesopotamia circa 2100 B.C.

Clay cylinder script found at Ur, British Museum

We can speculate with some incidental information that the Harappan, Indus and Mesopotamia civilizations did not totally disappear and instead many may have escaped east to India, China, the Pacific Islands and then to America. In the ruins of Mohenjo Daro, bodies were scattered about in homes and alleyways, many with sword marks in their skulls as they tried to escape the invaders. The number of slaughtered was small compared to the city's total population. Most notable, however, are the steatite (clay seals), exquisitely engraved with animal figures and numerous writings of a pictographic script. Pictographic or hieroglyphic writing in the Americas among the Aztec, Olmec, Mayan, and Peruvian societies can be traced in some cases to a similar root and style to the pictographic writing found in the Southeastern peninsula of Asia as well as in Africa, China, Egypt, Mesopotamia and back to its birthplace in Sumeria. Based on about 20 wooden tablets located in museums throughout the world, we know the Easter Island script is dated to around 2000 to 3000 B.C. The tablets have remained an enigma with suggestions they are relics from the lost continent of Mu, but they either date to a later period or are related to the script of the Indus and Mesopotamia Civilizations of about 2500 B.C. The glyph script is almost identical to the Indus script except one is with and the other without outlines. [165] China, India and the Pacific Islands contain artifacts and structures that have similar characteristics in America that possibly may be connected to the Indus Valley culture and America. The Maya Temple complex in Tikal, Guatemala, resembles a similar temple complex in Madurai, India, both with pyramidal vertical towers. A Mohenjo Daro seal is pictured with a reed raft resembling a Moche Pot with Quetzalcoatl on it. The Moche culture existed from about 200 B.C. to 600 A.D., was located on the coast of Peru and preceded the Inca culture. They built sun-baked brick pyramids, decorated ceramic pottery and worked with copper and gold metals. Moche metalwork was more ornate and technologically advanced than that of earlier civilizations. Body ornaments of gold, silver, copper and alloys were frequently inlaid with turquoise and lapis lazuli. Geometric patterns and mythological motifs, especially the feline deity, were used. Other Moche pottery shows Quetzalcoatl painted black on a raft, as if on a voyage to America. The same Quetzalcoatl with a black face can be found on many of the Aztec codex writing. [166] In the Pacific Islands, stone faces and phallic statutes have been uncovered that are very similar to those found on the Marquesas Islands and in San Agustin, Columbia. [167] The mathematical concept of zero has also been credited to India as far back as 3000 B.C. and introduced to the Mayan civilization possibly at a later date. In the Chavin culture of Peru, which existed about 1200 B.C. to 200 B.C., a stone cat was found in 1919. The mouth was the

Egyptian hieroglyphics, Egyptian Museum, Cairo circa 2000 B.C.

Sumerian/Mesopotamian pictographic writing on clay tablet circa 3000 B.C.

Olmec

Mayan Codex writing on bark paper

Mayan glyphs on stone, ca 1000 B.C.

Southeast Asian Naxi Dongba script (Tibet Burma area) used by shamans in ceremonies

Olmec script circa 1000 B.C.

Rongorongo (Easter Island script)

Mesopotamian/Sumerian cuneiform script

Indus Valley script, circa 2000 B.C.

Sabaean bronze inscription, South Arabia, circa 100 B.C.

Adobe frieze wall design and bird decorations, Chan Chan, Peru

most prominent feature and the body was covered with geometrical designs. In the Chinese Shang dynasty from 1523 B.C. to 1027 B.C. we find bronze figures with similar open mouth faces and geometrical designs. Other artifacts found in Chavin of "a dragon with an elongated body… an anthropomorphized felinoloid monster, a humanized bird monster… humanized felines…" all bear a resemblance to Shang Dynasty figures of tigers, cats, dragons, birds, etc., of about the same time frame.[168]

Earthen mound, Indus Valley, circa 2500 B.C.

Mississippi earthen mounds circa 2500 B.C.

The ancient Peruvian city of Chan Chan, 305 miles north of Lima near the Pacific, covered about 25 square miles and was inhabited by more than 30,000 people from 1000 to 1470 A.D. Chan Chan contained pyramids, underground aqueducts, and walls decorated with intricate frieze murals. The city was built of solid earthen mud brick, the same material utilized in the building of the religious center or ziggurat of Ur, as well as other ancient cities throughout Southeast Asia.[169]

Around 3000 B.C., as the ancient Egyptians were building their first step pyramids, Indians in the lower Mississippi valley built a community surrounded by earthen mound pyramids. These mounds were varied in shape, size and number and consisted of flat-topped pyramids, cones, ovals, and circular shaped stones. Some were little more than barely-discernible undulations on the landscape. The most recent sites discovered in America were at Watson Brake and Hedge Path, near modern-day Monroe, Louisiana. This site, the earliest known site of flat-type mounds in America, consists of eleven mounds from three to twenty five feet tall, connected by ridges to form an oval, eight-hundred fifty-three feet across. The Watson Brake site in the flood plane of the Quachita River has been dated to about 3400 B.C., a date confirmed with the help of radiocarbon tests of organic acids and sand grains from the Watson Brake mound sites, undertaken at the University of Texas in Austin and the University of Washington. This predates the first Egyptian step pyramids and ziggurats in Mesopotamia by 1000 years. There were no human remains found in these mounds, but ninety-five percent of the items collected, pieces of cracked rock almost certainly from cooking pots, indicated the use of the site by humans.[170]

Mound site, Poverty Point

Eleven mounds, Watson Brake, circa 3500 B.C.

In 1500 B.C., Indians constructed a more advanced site in northeastern Louisiana called Poverty Point, particularly notable for its size and elaborate earthworks. It had a large number of concentric, semi-circular mounds bordered by large conical mounds that had, in their center, a great bird-shaped mound. Non-native stones found on the site originated from as far away as Wisconsin, Tennessee and Georgia, indicating that Poverty Point was a major trade center.

Natchez mound Grand Village, Tennessee

Silbury Hill mound Wiltshire, England

None of the mounds at Watson Brake or Poverty Point were considered burial mounds. The Poverty Point culture flourished for more than 1000 years. By 600 B.C. it had virtually disappeared—when people began to live in smaller, scattered communities (but continued to build mounds). It appears that the mound culture continued to exist along the path of the Mississippi River in the Natchez society.

A resurgence of mound building across much of the areas east and west of the Mississippi took place between approximately 300 A.D. to 1300 A.D. During this period an unknown group of people constructed between 10,000 and 30,000 earthen mounds. Mississippian mound culture flourished at places like Etowah in northern Georgia, Moundville in Alabama, and Spiro, Oklahoma. Along the Mississippi some villages usually had from one to twenty flat-topped mounds. They were

Dolmen stamp, Portugal

rectangular, flat-topped earthen platforms upon which were erected temples or residences for the elite. Along the Mississippi, platform mounds ranged in height from eight to almost 60 feet in height and were from 60 to as much as 770 feet in width at the base. By 500 A.D. quantities of pottery were produced for the first time. In the Northwestern Florida area, in excavations of the Weeden Island culture (circa 200 A.D.), burial mounds were found containing goods from other areas of America. This indicates that trade exchanges had taken place with other cultures. Mounds and stone circles in all sizes and shapes have been found throughout the World such as India, New Guinea and in many countries of Europe, including Germany, Russia, France and England. The mound-building period occurred after 3500 B.C. From the Mississippi Valley to the Yucatan, China and Egypt, these mounds and pyramids

Dolmen, Columbia, South America

Dolmen, Salem, Mass.

show similar alignments for astronomical use. In North America we call them mounds instead of pyramids, although they bear a close resemblance to many of the early earthen pyramids in the world.[171]

World step pyramids

Candi Sukuh, Indonesia

Canary Islands

In America these dolmens, pyramid mounds, and stone circles extended from Canada to as far south as Argentina. In a broader context, when we take into account the similarities in construction and their placement in relation to the sun and moon, we find they were used for forecasting seasonal changes and for religious purposes. From the astronomical viewpoint, many of these man-made constructions are oriented towards the solstice-points on the horizon (points of sunrise and sunset at summer and winter solstice), as well as to

El Chiapas, Yucatan, Mexico   Step pyramid, Tahiti

points of the rising and setting moon at the largest distance of the moon from the ecliptic (called major and minor moonrises and settings). An orientation towards certain fixed stars also appears possible. There were, however, apparent local reasons that accounted for differences in the orientation of these monuments. In 1891 J. W. Powell of the Bureau of American Ethnology wrote of the mound-building cultures, "For more than a century the ghosts of a vanished nation have ambuscaded in the vast solitudes of the continent, and the forest-covered mounds have been usually regarded as the mysterious sepulchers of its kings and nobles. It was an alluring conjecture that a powerful people... once occupied the valley."[172]

Stone circles at Wassu, Gambia, circa 750 A.D.

According to Barry Fell of the Epigraphic Society, the language on a stele in a burial mound in Ohio called the Davenport tablet was of the same languages used in the Mississippi Valley area about 700 B.C. and in ancient Egyptian texts from about 800 B.C. to 1400 B.C. Fell has stated that the Atakapas, and to a lesser extent those of the Tohome and Chitimacha tribes, inhabitants of the Louisiana area, have affinities with Nile Valley languages. Words in their language are similar to those used in Egyptian trading communities 2000 years ago.[173]

Megaliths, Carnac, France circa 5000 B.C.

In addition to earthen work mound and ziggurat pyramids there are many man-made earthen constructions around the entire world that go under different classifications. They are called cairns, dolmens, henges, mastabas, megalithic stonework, stone and earth chamber tombs, etc. These strikingly related constructions have been found in the Americas as well as in Africa, China, Cambodia, the Canary Islands, Easter Islands, Egypt, France, Germany, Greece, Tahiti, Korea, Japan, Poland, Scotland, Spain, Sudan, Tibet, Turkey, and many other places in the world. There must have been diffusion of information through human contact throughout the world to explain the similarities in all these dolmens, megaliths, rock circles, stone chamber tombs and earthen mounds, as well as the pyramids. Throughout the world there may have been a gradual development from the early mounds, ziggurats and smaller step pyramids to the advanced, higher, and elaborate pyramids. Archaeologists found most of these man-made complex geometric constructions were for ritual ceremonies and astronomical purposes. The similarity of mystic symbols carved on many of the monuments and prehistoric rock petroglyphs also shows an underlying unity of beliefs.

Megalithic circle, Patagonia area of Argentina, circa 3000 B.C.

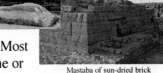
Megalith ceremonial burial chamber Sardinia, circa 4500 B.C.

Before the construction of the great pyramids in Egypt, mound-type chamber tombs called mastabas were used. These were low, rectangular structures that owe their name to the modern Arab word for "bench." During the first dynasties at around 3100 B.C., the Egyptians began to build mastabas from sun-dried mud brick. Most have long since crumbled to dust. Old Kingdom mastaba tombs were flat-topped stone or mud brick superstructures that marked the tombs of wealthy individuals and their families.

Mastaba of sun-dried brick Saqqara, Egypt, circa 3000 B.C.

These early mastabas consisted of a rectangular-shaped chapel above ground with a burial chamber below ground. The step pyramid began as a normal mastaba burial mound, but was subsequently enlarged by adding on to it, one mastaba on top of another. The surface was originally encased in smooth white limestone that must have caught the sunlight and reflected its rays. The Saqqara step pyramid, estimated to have been built about 2500 B.C., is considered to be one of Egypt's earliest pyramids. An ancient stone circle of megaliths surrounded by ancient mounds is located nearby. Similar megaliths and mounds can be found from the Saqqara area all the way to Sudan and Algeria. The Egyptian complex at Saqqara is not circular like Stonehenge. It is spread over an area of 1.8 miles by about three-quarters of a mile. It includes 10 large slabs about nine feet high, 30 rock-

Single standing stone (menhir), portion of a stone calendar Saqqara, Egypt

lined ovals, nine burial sites for cows (each under a pile of 40 to 50 rocks weighing up to 200 or 300 pounds each) and a "calendar circle" of stones. Many of these features line up in five radiating lines, including one running due east-west. It was described thus by the researchers on site: "The calendar circle is a 12-foot-wide arrangement of slabs about 18 inches long, most of them lying down. Two pair of upright stones stand directly across the circle from each other, defining a view that would have displayed sunrise at the summer solstice." The circle also contains two

Djoser step pyramid, Saqqara, Egypt, 2630 B.C.

other pairs of standing stones that defined a north-south view. Charcoal from hearths around the circle and wood from one of the burials date the sites to about 5000 B.C. Numerous similar stone circles and megalithic stones have been found throughout the world. Among them is Stonehenge, noted for a circular earthen work built under the present site, and the ancient Miami circle of stones uncovered in Miami, Florida.

Nebuchadnezzar step pyramid, Babylon, circa 600 B.C.

Ziggurat of Ur, model Mesopotamia, circa 2100 B.C. British Museum

Across the Great Court of the step pyramid complex of Djoser stands another step pyramid, built for a king of the third dynasty in about 2800 B.C. by the architect Imhotep. It was also a step pyramid with a series of six levels of stone that decreased in size as the steps ascended to about 200 feet in height. The burial chamber was situated below ground. Contrary to popular belief, the earliest Egyptian pyramids were not of stone but were, in fact, ziggurats made of sun-dried, mud-brick whose tops were platforms used as temples. As they decayed, new pyramids were built on top. The design was very similar to the flattop pyramids in Central and South America.

Ruins of top of ziggurat made of sun-dried brick Borsippa, near Babylon

Nimrud ziggurat construction

Sun-dried mud brick was also used in the first South American pyramid complexes in Caral and Tucume, Peru. These early pyramid sites date to approximately 2500 B.C., coinciding with the ziggurats in Mesopotamia and the Egyptians first step pyramid at Saqqara. The ziggurats were built of sun-dried mud brick, with facades made from glazed brick. Austrian archaeologists determined that King Nebuchadnezzar built a pyramid in Iraq some 2500 years ago that was of the same design as a Mesopotamian ziggurat. The 231 foot-high temple tower consisted of

Ziggurat at Choga Zenbil, Mesopotamia, circa 2500 B.C.

Mound complex Tucume, Peru, circa 2500 B.C.

seven terraces constructed of millions of mud bricks. There are approximately 25 ziggurats still scattered throughout Mesopotamia today. The base of the ziggurat was either square or rectangular. All walls were sloping, and all horizontal lines were slightly convex in order to make them less rigid when seen by the human eye. It is believed that the sloping walls were covered with trees and shrubs. Ascent to the top was achieved by a triple stairway or by a spiral ramp. However, for half of the existing ziggurats there are no visible means of ascent. The stairs of the ziggurats and Mesoamerican pyramids were built to human scale for climbing. Throughout the world, ziggurats, pyramids and mounds were normally not erected alone, but were a part of an entire complex. The Mayans followed the design typical of all Mesoamerican complexes. They built their ceremonial centers containing tall, flat-topped pyramidal temples, single story palaces, and the ever-present ball court around a broad central plaza. Distinctive architectural features of Mayan pyramids included corbel archways, towering roofs and elaborate decoration with stucco reliefs. The flat-topped pyramid complexes were utilized as religious and political centers and as residences for their leaders.

The Saqqara step pyramid, like the ziggurats, were the central part of an intricate complex of buildings and courts surrounded by a massive limestone wall enclosure. The Egyptian, Mesoamerican, Mexican and South American pyramids were utilized for the burial of important individuals and their possessions. Inside these large structures were small burial rooms. There were narrow corridors that led to these chambers. The pyramid complex of Huaca Rajada in Peru, which contains the tomb of the Lord of Sipan, is the richest intact burial chamber found in the Americas. This Moche warrior priest was found surrounded by gold, silver and copper ornaments; several family members and a llama accompanied him in death. Found near his burial tomb were two sun-dried mud brick adobe pyramids. Four additional tombs have been found in Sipan's Huaca Rajada, near the coastal city of Chiclayo. The Huaca is a mausoleum built by the Moche culture that ruled the northern coast of Peru from the

Egyptian burial items circa 1300 B.C.

Tell el-Dab'a warrior burial, Egypt circa 1500 B.C.

Royal tomb offerings, Mayan, circa 500 B.C.

Pyramid tomb Lambayeque, Lord of Sipan circa 200 A.D.

time of Christ to 700 A.D., centuries prior to the Incas. In Mesoamerica the burial chambers often contained treasures such as jade. Ornate wall carvings inside the pyramids show detailed calendars that can still be used to predict eclipses and other astral events. The massive temples on top of the pyramids served as astronomical observatories designed to track the movements of the night sky. The windows and doors are perfectly aligned to channel the light of the sun at different times of the year or to highlight a sparkling planet. The Mayans were also expert geologists. Each of their great cities is situated next to a cenote, or natural well, that provided drinking water and irrigated the crops. The Inca civilization continued the astronomical calculations of the seasons for planting and harvesting their crops. It was deemed so important that an astrologer was in charge of these predictions.

"Andean astrologer, who studies the sun, the moon, and all other heavenly bodies in order to know when to plant the fields"
Guamán Poma , circa 1600 A.D.

The pyramids of Comalcalco, built about 600 to 900 A.D., are unusual because they are made of clay bricks instead of being encased with stone or cement. The Mayans could not find stones in the region, so they made mortar from clay mixed with sand and ground oyster shells. They used the lime obtained from the shells to cover walls, floors and to manufacture plaster sculptures. It is believed that

Comalcalco inscribed bricks

Comalcalco pyramid Yucatan, Mexico

Comalcalco was one of the first pyramid complexes built with bricks. It is unusual among Mayan sites because its 375 structures, including a large stepped pyramid, were constructed using millions of fired bricks. Many of the bricks, when separated from their mortar, display various symbols as well as their makers' fingerprints. Neil Steede, who worked for 11 years as an archaeologist for the Mexican government and subsequently examined other sites throughout Mesoamerica and South America, collected a sample of these bricks (4612 bricks weighing 21 tons) and photographed the inscriptions that decorated some 1500 of them. He discovered what he interpreted as "masons' signs." Steede deemed the bricks to be virtually identical to those found on Roman, Minoan, and ancient Greek sites.

Architects who built the pyramid of the sun at Teotihuacan, Mexico, about 100 A.D. must have been acquainted with the specifications and design of the Cheops (Khufu) pyramid at Gizeh. Both pyramids in Egypt and Mexico

Pyramid of the Sun, Teotihuacan, Mexico circa 1-250 A.D.

Cheops pyramid, Egypt circa 2500 B.C.

occupy an identical area at the base of 44,000 square meters. The only difference is that Mexico's pyramid of the sun is only half as high. The pyramids of Central and South America have only flat tops used for religious purposes. The tops of the Mexican pyramids were rectangular platforms that at one time were covered with mica. Both the Egyptian and Mexican pyramids have the same geographical alignment. The Cheops pyramid lies in the exact center of all the land area of the world, dividing the earth's land mass into approximately equal quarters. It is possible that the Egyptian pyramid served as a model. At the Copan pyramid in Honduras a base line of nine degrees north of west, set up with a sundial, indicates the sunset at the solstices and equinoxes. At the Mayan site at Uaxactum in Guatemala, three temples along with two steles give the exact orientations of the sun's position during solstices and equinoxes. At the great pyramid of Xochicalco, the sun, when shining down a vertical shaft, casts an exact round shadow twice a year at its peak. At the pyramid of the sun at Teotihuacan, Mexico, stone markers line up with the pyramid to indicate the rising and setting sun at the solstices and equinoxes. All of the pyramids are built with accurate proportions and dimensions that clearly demonstrate an ancient knowledge and complex understanding of the geometric principles of trigonometry, as well as an under-

Pyramid mounds site Caral, Peru, circa 2600 B.C.
Photos, Field Museum, Chicago, IL

standing of astronomy and geography. The builders were able to forecast the precise length of a year. They knew the speed of the earth's rotation, the length of its orbit and, in fact, displayed a complete knowledge of the cosmos. The pyramids resembled modern astronomical laboratories for the study of the planets and stars. Near the top were shafts used for observation slits from which to view the sky during the time of the equinoxes in spring and autumn. All of these feats, including the construction, were achieved with knowledge of an arcane, prehistoric science that nevertheless seems to have been universally understood.

Pyramids were built in the Americas during or before the same time-period as the Egyptian pyramids. The site at Caral has shattered the myth that civilization got a late start in the New World. Dr. Ruth Shady Solis, a Peruvian archaeologist, is the lead investigator of Caral and has worked on this project for years. In the year 2000, Jonathan Haas from the Field Museum in Chicago and Winifred Creamer at Northern Illinois University did radiocarbon tests on the remains of woven reed bags that were probably used for carrying stones from a nearby quarry. They estimated the age of the reeds and the six immense pyramids at about 4600 years old, which situates them in about the same time period as the building of the great Egyptian pyramids. Nearly 5000 years ago, around the time that the Sumerians developed writing and during the time the Egyptians built the Great Pyramid at Giza, people here in Caral, Peru, were building a city. They probably knew nothing about writing or the knowledge of ceramics. They did know how to plan and build huge public works, and they evolved a specialized and stratified society which functioned with a sophisticated and diversified economy. Caral is located in Peru, 14 miles west of the coast and about 120 miles north of Lima in the Supe valley, on a sand-dune terrace. Dr. Soils believes that Caral was a thriving urban trading center about 5000 years ago, at the time of or before the Egyptian pyramids. The 150-acre complex consisted of a series of plazas and pyramids, with the largest pyramid covering land the size of four football fields, with a height of 60 feet, and a 30-foot wide staircase to reach its pinnacle. The ancient Peruvians also developed at Caral what may have been one of the first cities in the Americas. It had hundreds of upper, middle and lower-status dwellings and irrigated fields. Two partially excavated pyramids reveal adjacent, circular sunken plazas—a combination of square and round that would come to characterize later structures throughout Peru. They contained staircases and circular walls built of colored plaster and squared brickwork. The presence of plazas suggests that the early society had evolved a need for large ceremonial gathering places. Archaeologists unearthed 32 flutes made of condor and pelican bones in an amphitheater, suggesting a knowledge of music and, perhaps, public ceremonies. It is possible that Caral developed a division of labor with people specializing in different

Moche pyramids
Túcume, Peru
circa 3000 B.C.

trades. A civilization evolves because it controls or conquers something important. Mesopotamians prospered when they learned to irrigate and cultivate the desert. The residents of Caral diverted water from the Supe River to irrigate fields, where they grew staples such as squash and beans. Learning how to grow and process cotton also changed their society; with it they made fishing nets and traded the fish they caught with the communities on the Pacific coast 12 miles away. Archaeologists have unearthed thousands of fish bones, including those from anchovies and sardines, along with items not native to Caral such as the seeds of the cocoa plant and necklaces made from snail shells. Dr. Winifred Creamer, an archaeologist and professor at Northern Illinois University, believes that Caral could be the birthplace of civilization in the Americas.[174]

In South America the Moche complex at Tucume appears to contain the largest pyramid center in Peru. There were originally 26 major pyramids and some smaller structures at the time. They were built around 1100 A.D. and have eroded over time. The pyramids of Tucume were known for their huge size— the largest pyramid was estimated to contain more than 130 million sun-dried bricks. It measures about 1500 feet long, 400 feet wide and 500 feet high. In 1987, when the archaeologist Walter Alva visited Tucume with Thor Heyerdahl, the latter remarked, "Crossing the wood of carob trees far away from the culture, I thought that was just one of my dreams. I had never seen before in my entire life such a thing... the hugest complex of monumental structures made of sun-dried bricks in the new world. I could appreciate 26 huge pyramids and many other smaller ones altogether in a sacred site of 500 acres. I literally felt that I was from another planet, there was nothing like these strange and colossal ruins in our own familiar earth."[175]

Pyramid remains, Akapana

In the Andes, close to the southern shore of Lake Titicaca at an altitude of 12,500 feet near La Paz, Bolivia, lies Tiahuanaco, a major ceremonial center. These ancient people built the nearby Akapana pyramid of crude stones. The Akapana, a step pyramid (found in Egypt as well as Mesoamerica), is aligned perfectly with the four cardinal directions. It originally had a covering of smooth andesite stone, but 90% of that has disappeared. The pyramid used to be a multi-stepped, T-shaped pyramid encased in stone (and filled with dirt). Most of the stones were removed and used to build the modern city of La Paz. Centuries of rain and weathering made its shape almost unrecognizable. The top of the pyramid was apparently once covered in small green stones. Hundreds of tiny green stones lie scattered in the dirt of the pyramid. Its interior is honeycombed with shafts in a complicated grid pattern, which incorporate a system of blocks used to direct water from a tank on top, going through a series of levels, and finally ending up in a stone canal surrounding the pyramid. Near the Akapana pyramid is a path that leads to Kalasasaya, a semi-subterranean temple. Professor Posnansky, an authority on Tiahuanaco, measured the alignments and the tilt of the earth's axis compared to the present and determined that the temple was built in approximately 15,000 B.C.

Chinese pyramid

Cahokia mound
near St. Louis, 100 ft.

Metal clamp in
Tiahuanaco stone

There are pyramids made from cut stone in Ecuador, close to the equator. In the jungles of Brazil are 12 pyramids that have been viewed via satellite and through infrared lenses. They are positioned side by side, in 2 rows of 6. In Japan, underwater pyramids have been found. Near Hiroshima, at Hiba, pyramids can also be found at Mt. Ashitake. In China there are over 100 pyramids made of mud and dirt that have become hard as rock. Many of these pyramids were built at least 2000 years ago. A number of pyramids dating to the Mayan era of about 210 B.C. were built as burial mounds for the Chinese emperors. The white pyramid of Tibet is in the Qin Ling Shan mountains near the city of Xian. The Chinese pyramids are remarkably similar in construction to the mound pyramids found throughout the Americas. In the Canary Islands, Easter Islands and at Tiahuanaco, Bolivia, the pyramids were built with precisely cut stone blocks that fit so perfectly together they did not need cement. Some of these stone blocks were connected with metal clamps. There are many ancient pyramids in Greece, some of which could pre-date those found in Egypt. One pyramid at Hellicon dates to about 2720 B.C. In Begrawiya, Sudan, about 50 black pyramids were connected to the Meroite civilization and date between 592 B.C. to 400 A.D. The Meroites worshipped the same gods as the Egyptians. Unconfirmed reports state that ancient pyramids were discovered in the remote Southern mountain areas of Russia in Kashkadaryin and the Samarkand regions. They were reported to be similar to the ones at Giza, Egypt, though in contrast to them, the Uzbek pyramids have a flat surface, as those in Mesoamerica.[176]

Meroite step mounds
Begrawiya, Sudan

Ceramic pottery was found containing the "Re" (Ra) glyph, Egypt's symbol for the sun god, in the sun pyramid at Teotihuacan, Mexico. Placed as a scroll and an eye motif inside a circle, this signified "the eye of the sun." Some inhabitants of Teotihuacan identified their sun god as "Re." Thor Heyerdahl discovered that the name "Ra" was known as the name of the sun on all the hundreds of islands of Polynesia. It was also in the name of an ancient Peruvian culture hero called Kon-Tici Viracocha, referring to the Inca legend of their high priest and sun-king. Polynesian oral legends relate that a man named Tiki led their fair-skinned, red-haired people to South America. In 1527 Pizarro, the Spanish conquistador in Peru, found the Inca people tall, with fair complexions and beards. The light-skinned Incas claimed to be descendents of Viracocha who supposedly created the large stone stepped pyramids and statues found near Tiahuanaco in Bolivia. The name Viracocha has turned up in numerous Inca legends and poems as well as stone sculptures and pottery. A Chimu effigy jar shows Viracocha as a bearded man. The Incas recall ancient cities in the Andes, built by light-skinned, blue-eyed warriors who were called Chachapoyans, and whose ancestors still live in the jungles of Peru. Francisco Pizarro, the 16th-century Spanish conqueror, remarked that the Inca head, Atahuallpa, and his family, were "whiter than the people of Spain" and "corn blonde." When Pizarro asked the Inca Indians who the white-skinned redheaded Indians were, they replied that they were the descendents of the "virachoias," a divine race of white men with beards, who had lived there before the Incas became rulers. They were wise, peaceful instructors who had come from the north a long time ago and had taught the Incas' primitive forefathers architecture and agriculture as well as manners and customs."[177]

Viracocha
Tiahuanaco,
Bolivia

Quetzalcoatl

The Toltec, Maya and Inca all have oral legends relating to a teacher they called Viracocha, who came across the ocean from the east with other men to instruct the people in the arts and agriculture, and then leaving with a promise to return again from the east. The Aztec name for this god from the east was Quetzalcoatl in Nahuatl, or Kukulcan in Mayan— both names with the same meaning. Quetzal is the name of the paradise bird and coatl is the word for serpent. In Mexico, Cortés confirmed that Montezuma assumed that Cortés was the return of a white European god from the past. Quetzalcoatl's appearance was of a middle-aged man with long red hair, a grizzled beard and holding a shield. Portraits of light skinned, bearded men have been portrayed on stone and ceramic sculptures and have been sighted by early explorers in Brazil and the Amazon. In the Aztec *Nahuatl Codex*, the illustration shows bearded men, possibly Quetzalcoatl's men, attacking a village with rafts. The Mixtec writing system from Oaxaca, Mexico, repeats the oral legends of Quetzalcoatl by illustrating what appear to be bearded warriors in their codex.[178]

Aztec Quetzalcoatl,
plumed serpent
Musee de l'Homme, France

In the *Mexican Codex*, written in the native Nahuatl tongue, it recalled several attempts of those from a land across the eastern sea to civilize the savages and barbarians of Central America. All failed until Quetzalcoatl made his appearance. According to the *Popol Vuh*, the Bible of the Mayan Quiches of western Guatemala, it was from the east, "...where red and white men lived in joy: their aspect gentle and sweet, their language pleasant, and their minds very intelligent." Friar Juan Torquemada, the Franciscan missionary, collected traditions of Quetzalcoatl in Mexico in the 1600s. Torquemada, in the book *Monarquia Indiana*, wrote that the Toltecs and their leader Quetzalcoatl came from a land not submerged, like the Atlantis legend states, but from where the ruling class became so unstable, due to occasional catastrophes, that they looked elsewhere to settle their people. "Quetzalcoatl, it is held for certain, was a man of upright character, elegant carriage and was white and blonde (blanco), with a ruddy face (rubio) and bearded. His beard was long. He was of benevolent disposition and learned, and a great personage. His hair was long and black...." In the same book Torquemada says, "Quetzalcoatl had blonde hair, and wore a black robe sewn with little crosses of red color." The native historian Fernando de Alva Ixtlilxochitl, in his two-volume, *Relaciones and Historia de Chichemecas*, provides a detailed account of the important part played by his great-grandfather Don Fernando in the conquest of Mexico and the path of the Tultecs (Toltecs) to their destruction. Ixlilxochitl writes, "...and the Tultecs ...came to these parts, having first passed over great lands and seas, living in caves and passing through great hardships, until getting to this land."[179]

Outside: Peruvian Pottery of white skinned captives
Inside:From wall Painting in Temple of Warriors, Chichen Itza, East coast, Mexico, of white captives

The Seri Indians in the Gulf of California have a legend that men landed on their Island in a longboat and were worshipped as Gods. The men had blue eyes and white or yellow hair and at least one of the women had red hair. In the same area, a Mexican tribe tells of blue-eyed, yellow-haired people who sailed up the Mayo River from the Gulf of California. The Mayo tribe intermarried with these foreigners and each generation had produced individuals with blonde hair and blue eyes. These foreigners were probably the Toltec. Spanish historian Francisco Saverio Clavigero gave a similar description of Quetzalcoatl as Juan Torquemada, with some additions. In his 1781 *History of Mexico*, Clavigero claimed Quetzalcoatl was a high priest of Tula in the capital of the Tulteca, and described his appearance as "white in complexion, tall and corpulent, broad in forehead, with large eyes, long black hair, thick beard, a man of austere and exemplary life, clothed in long garments, gentle and prudent. He was expert in the art of melting metals and polishing precious stones, which he taught the Tultecans."[180]

Much like pottery portraying black-skinned traders with spears and jaguar skins, the wall mural paintings at the temple of warriors in Chichen Itza in the Yucatan show white-skinned captives bound and led away by dark-skinned warriors. A northern Peruvian pottery scene also shows white-skinned captives being led away with ropes by dark-skinned, armed warriors.[181] The Spanish considered statues of Viracocha as a heathen deity because the figures wore the same Mediterranean-style robes and sandals as their own statues of the Apostles. These statues were destroyed wherever the Spanish found them. Unearthed painted ceramic statues portray this Semitic-looking man, Viracocha, as a culture god hero.[182]

Many ancient cities in Southeastern Asia, as well as in Egypt, contained wall paintings and pyramid-type ceremonial centers that bore similarities to the later Inca, Maya and Aztec religious centers.[183] The Egyptian, Maya and Inca civilizations observed similar burial customs. Similar mummification and embalming procedures were practiced in Egypt, in the southern and southwestern United States, the Aleutian Islands and Peru. In each case the bodies were wrapped with a covering that served as a shroud. Natural and artificial means were utilized for the preservation of the human body such as drying by air or fire, or filling the body cavities with plant or other materials. Artificial methods of embalming with chemical substances such as resins, oils, herbs and other organic materials were also employed.[184]

Both the Maya and the Egyptians built burial chambers at the base of their pyramids. One unusual custom observed by both cultures was the destruction of certain personal items before the body was placed in the burial tomb. The Maya would deliberately slit the gown and slippers of a dead woman before burial. During the early Egyptian dynasties, burial customs required

Osiris and Isis statues

that vases were to be broken before being placed in the store-chambers under the Kings' burial pyramid.[185] Two Egyptian amulets of Horus, the Egyptian sun god, were recently discovered in a native burial ground of the Ojibway (Chippewa) Indian tribe.[186] In 1940, historian Mariano Cuevas published illustrations and reports of two Egyptian figurines called shawabtis, in her book, *Historia de la Nacion Mexicana*. The figurines were reportedly found buried in 1914 about three feet below the surface on the property of Reverend Senior Velloso, archbishop of El Salvador, near the Pacific port of Acajutla, El Salvador. One of the figurines is of a Pharaoh's sarcophagus (mummy case or coffin) wearing the crown of Osiris, god of the dead. The other figure is similar to the mother goddess, Isis. An inscription on the male statue appears to be the cartouche of Pharaoh Osorkon of the 22nd dynasty, dating to 1000 B.C. Both figurines are decorated with Egyptian motifs and hieroglyphs. What makes the find perplexing was their disappearance in a burglary, setting off a controversy as to whether these are original or forgeries.[187]

On April 5, 1909, there appeared a lengthy front page story in the newspaper *Phoenix Gazette,* headlined, "Explorations in the Grand Canyon: Mysteries of Immense Rich Cavern Being Brought to Light." It reported: "The latest news of the progress of the explorations or what is now regarded by scientists as not only the oldest archaeological discovery in the United States, but one of the most valuable in the world, which was mentioned some time ago in the Gazette, was brought to the city yesterday by G. E. Kinkaid, the explorer who found the great underground citadel of the Grand Canyon during a trip from Green River, Wyoming, down the Colorado, in a wooden boat, to Yuma, several months ago.... According to the story related to the Gazette by Mr. Kinkaid, the archaeologists of the Smithsonian Institution, which is financing the expeditions, have made discoveries which almost conclusively prove that the race which inhabited this mysterious cavern, hewn in solid rock by human hands, was of oriental origin, possibly from Egypt, tracing back to King Rameses II. If their theories are borne out by the translation of the tablets engraved with hieroglyphics, the mystery of the prehistoric peoples of North America, their ancient arts, whom they were and whence they came will be solved. Egypt and the Nile, and Arizona and the Colorado will be linked by a historical chain running back to ages, which staggers the wildest fancy of the fictionist."

In 1996 David Hatcher Childress of the World Explorers Club called the Smithsonian Institution and reported their denial of any findings. The Smithsonian claimed to have absolutely no knowledge of the discovery or its discoverers. Childress then wrote a paper called "Archaeological cover-ups", delving further into this incident. Childress wrote that, "Historian and linguist Carl Hart, editor of World Explorer, then obtained a hiker's map of the Grand Canyon from a bookstore in Chicago. Poring over the map, we were amazed to see that much of the area on the north side of the canyon

Egyptian petroglyph Australia

has Egyptian names. The area around Ninety-four Mile Creek and Trinity Creek had areas (rock formations, apparently) with names like Tower of Set, Tower of Ra, Horus Temple, Osiris Temple, and Isis Temple. In the Haunted Canyon area were such names as the Cheops Pyramid, the Buddha Cloister, Buddha Temple, Manu Temple and Shiva Temple. Was there any relationship between these places and the alleged Egyptian discoveries in the Grand Canyon? We called a state archaeologist at the Grand Canyon, and were told that the early explorers had just liked Egyptian and Hindu names, but if that was true why was this area off limits to hikers or other visitors, because of dangerous caves?"[188]

Ancient Egyptian hieroglyphs have been found in the early 1900s in New South Wales, Australia. The mysterious carvings were located on a rock cliff in the National Park Forest in Hunter Valley, north of Sydney. There are more than 250 separate carvings of familiar Egyptian gods and symbols, including a life-sized engraving of the god Anubis. The hieroglyphs tell the story of explorers who were shipwrecked in a strange and hostile land, and the death of their royal leader, "Lord Djeseb." Scholars have estimated the date of the voyage at between 1000 B.C. and 2748 B.C.[189]

The stone buildings constructed by the Maya and Inca in South America show a similarity to the buildings built by the Phoenicians in the Mediterranean region. The Maya originated in the Yucatan around 2600 B.C. and were noted for the highly decorated

Inca construction, Ollantaytambo, Peru

ceremonial temple-pyramids, palaces and observatories—all built without metal tools. Mayan stonework has survived in the remote jungles of Mesoamerica at Palenque, Tikal, Tulum, Chichen Itza, Copan and Uxmal. It had similar architectural designs, stepped terraces, corbelled arches, and simulated air-conditioning ducts, such as those found at the Castillo at Chavin de Huantar in Peru. In the pyramids found in Crete and Easter Island and in those which were built in Egypt's third-dynasty—in fact, all the stonework built during this same time period is similar in construction to that found in Peru. The style of Inca stonework underwent a radical change during the

1400s. The Inca stones were rounded rather than squared at the edges. The stonework of the Old World was squared off and fitted together in the same style used today.

The Inca stonework was so unusual that one will never see an Inca stone wall with a square corner, straight line, or flat plain unless it had been constructed this way by accident. Every single stone in the wall fits in only one place, which means that a wall must be erected one stone at a time, with each stone very carefully fitted into its own particular location. The quarries of the Incas were simply large boulder fields where loose rock had fallen from mountain faces and each were chosen for its quality and rough shape, then dragged down to the building site for finishing. At the site of Sillustani, near the shores of Lake Titicaca in Peru, stonecutters used the same method of quarrying the stones as the Egyptians. Very little information exists regarding the methods used by the Incas to move these huge boulders. Similarly, engineers can only theorize as to how the Egyptians managed to move their stones, some of which weighed close to ten tons. One theory suggests the use of pulleys, but at that time there was no written language except the Inca quipu, containing knotted strings on which records were kept. Information that might be helpful to understand how the stones were moved remains hidden. We can read the numerical values of the quipu knot; we cannot interpret what those numerical values signify.[190]

Artifacts which apparently originate from North Africa have been unearthed in Cuenca, Ecuador, in southern California and in sites in the American Midwest previously inhabited by mound builders. Stone tablets inscribed with Libyan text have been discovered in Cuenca, Ecuador and in Oklahoma, and stone sculptures resembling North Africans were found in the Hopewell mound site. All date from approximately 300 to 1000 B.C. Facial features of the large stone heads from the Olmec civilization in Mexico dating from about 1500 B.C. bear a strong resemblance to the people of North Africa. The distinct helmet crown worn on their heads is similar to the crowns worn by West African chiefs in Ghana. A Nicaraguan throne was described by Fernández de Gonzalo Oviedo (1478-1557), a Spanish historian, in his *Journal of the Second Voyage,* as "a small stool with four feet, made of fine, smooth wood." This description is a close match to that of an Ashanti throne-stool from West Africa. The civilizations of Africa developed very sophisticated vessels that included reed boats (with and without sails), rafts made from logs lashed together, wide double dugouts, double-canoes, lateen-rigged dhows, jointed boats, and rope-sewn plank vessels with straw cabins and cooking facilities. These vessels were used throughout the Nile and Niger rivers. The ships could travel distances of up to 2600 miles carrying cargoes as diverse as food, people, elephants and building materials. In addition, the shortest distance between Africa and North America is a mere 1500 miles.[191]

Popol Vuh, one of the few important Mayan books not destroyed by the Spaniards, mentions "blacks" that came to America from "the land of the sunrise." Mayan colored murals at Bonampak and Chichen Itza in Mexico show black and light-skinned warriors together.[192]

Phoenician alphabet

Phoenician script found in Parahyba, Brazil

Ogham writing found in Oklahoma
Barry Fell, *Saga America*

There is a large body of evidence indicating that the Phoenicians traveled to America. Ancient Egyptian records show that in the 6th century B.C., Pharaoh Necho commissioned the Phoenicians to sail around Africa to the New World. The Phoenicians were noted for their seafaring skill and adventures, and for their ships, which were larger than those used by Columbus. Their route would have taken them to the eastern part of Central America, an idea corroborated by the similarity between the pictorial hieroglyphic style of writing and pyramid-type structures found in Egypt, and in sites inhabited by the Olmec and Maya civilizations in Central America. Neil Stead, an archaeologist, found a form of Ogham (Ogam) carved on to the surfaces of the Olmec figures. Ogham is a writing system that originated in the British Isles and has been found at various cave sites and on stones in the United States. A translation of the script on the Olmec heads has yet to be determined. However, the implication is that there was either contact with the indigenous peoples of areas of the United States where this same writing system is found, or that there was some kind of contact with a culture, or cultures, who used Ogham in the ancient world.

Many of the ancient Greeks who studied science, astronomy and philosophy described lands visited by the Phoenicians. During the 3rd century B.C., Erasthothenes, the first man known to have calculated the world's circumference, wrote in the *Oecumene* (Known World) of three continents surrounded by "Oceanus", and of a place, "Terra Incognita", that was

European head, found in Calixtlahuacan, west of Mexico City circa 200 A.D.
National Museum of Anthropology, Mexico City
Photo by Romeo H. Hristov

beyond unknown lands. In 360 B.C. Aristotle spoke of a land that was fertile, well wooded and had navigable rivers. He also reported that the Carthaginians were attempting to build a colony in this "secret land" but later abandoned their efforts. In the 5th century B.C. Herodotus and Avienus speculated that the Phoenicians were quite capable of crossing the Atlantic, in view of their earlier spectacular voyage which had taken three years to complete on a route from the Red Sea, through the Straits of Gibraltar, around the African continent and back to Egypt. Herodotus wrote of the superior trading methods of the Phoenicians and Plato, in his *Dialogues*, wrote of an ancient civilization beyond the western horizon which he called a "great continent, Atlantis." In 378 B.C.

Bronze inscription, Bylbos Imitation of Egyptian hieroglyphics and Phoenician alphabet, circa 1800 B. C.

Strabo, the Roman geographer, wrote, "For wherever it has been possible for men to reach the limits of the earth, sea has been found and this sea we call 'Oceanus'." He stressed that, "The ancients will be shown to have made longer journeys, both by land and sea." The most revealing description of a land discovered across the oceans comes from Didorus Siculus, a Greek geographer living in Rome. In 56 B.C., Siculus finished his voluminous forty books, *Historical Library (Bibliothek),* a thirty-year opus in which he described a place the Phoenicians had traveled to in the 12th century B.C., located beyond the Pillars of Hercules (Straits of Gibraltar): "For there lies out in the deep off Libya an island of considerable size, and situated as it is in the ocean it is distant from Libya a voyage of a number of days to the west. Its land is fruitful, much of it being mountainous and not a little being a level plane of surpassing beauty. Through it flow navigable rivers which are used for irrigation, and the island contains many parks planted with trees of every variety and gardens in great multitudes which are traversed by streams of sweet water.... In ancient times this island remained undiscovered because of its distance from the inhabited world, but it was discovered at a later period for the following reason. The Phoenicians, who from ancient times made voyages continually for purposes of trade, planted many colonies throughout Libya and not a few as well in the western parts of Europe. And since their ventures turned out according to their expectations, they amassed great wealth and essayed to voyage beyond the Pillars of Heracles (Hercules) into the sea, which men call the ocean.... The Phoenicians, then awhile exploring the coast outside the Pillars... were driven by strong winds a great distance out into the ocean. And after being storm-tossed for many days they were carried ashore on the island we mentioned above, and when they had observed its felicity and nature they caused it to be known to all men. Consequently, the Tyrrhenians, at the time when they were masters of the sea, purposed to dispatch a colony to it; but the Carthaginians prevented their doing so, partly out of concern lest many inhabitants of Carthage should move there because of the excellence of the island, and partly in order to have ready in it a place in which to seek refuge against an incalculable turn of fortune, in case some total disaster should strike Carthage. For it was their thought that, since they were masters of the sea, they would thus be able to move, households and all, to an island which was unknown to their conquerors."[193]

The Atlantic currents do, in fact, run straight at South America from that region, so it would have been possible for a lost ship to travel there, and make the return voyage. Oceanic currents have, in more recent times, pulled vessels north, then back east across the ocean. A small African fishing boat lost in a storm ended up on the coast of Brazil; and, in 1488 (four years prior to the more famous voyage of Columbus), Jean Cousin of Dieppe France was sailing down the west coast of Africa and his ship was caught in a storm and blown across to Brazil.

Carthaginian gold coin w/map

Mark McMenamin, a Mount Holyoke geologist, found a Carthaginian gold coin minted in the Punic/Phoenician city of Carthage in North Africa, dated between 350 and 320 B.C. McMenamin, working in 1996 with computer-enhanced images of the gold coin, believes the designs represent a map of the ancient world. The detail of the gold coin shows what he believes is a map of the central and western Mediterranean area surrounded by Europe, Britain, Africa, and (at right) the Americas—Central and South America. Parts of this map matched a similar, later world map compiled in the 2nd century A.D. by the Greek geographer, Ptolemy. If this is true, the coin not only depicts the oldest known maps in existence, but would also indicate that Carthaginian explorers had sailed to the New World.[194]

The Phoenician trade center of Tartesus (Tarshish, Spain) is mentioned in the Bible as a "source of valuable commodities." Archaeologist Robert Marx discovered a map dated 1367 at Madrid's National Library. On the map is a notation that claimed the location of King Solomon's mines as a land called "Bracir", which Marx believes to be Brazil. Artifacts and inscriptions indicate that the Phoenicians traveled to Brazil and other parts of South America.[195] The Phoenicians were noted for

Phoenician era vase found Binghamton, N. Y. circa 1000 B.C.

41

developing the alphabet, for the invention of glass, for a purple dye called Tyrian purple, and for superb stonework. They developed industries, particularly for the manufacture of textiles and dyes, metal working—for the manufacturing of bronze tools using copper as an alloy, glassmaking, and stone masonry of buildings, including the placing of huge fitted stones in walls.

Further compelling evidence to indicate the presence of the Phoenicians in the Americas comes from the fact that they traveled with dogs—two of their favorite breeds being similar to Peruvian dogs of today. Peruvians and Mayans utilized the same methods as the Phoenicians to produce a red dye for their textiles.[196] Hugh Fox, Professor at Michigan State University and author of *Gods of the Cataclysm,* researched the Phoenician connection to the Americas and concluded, "I had an artist draw pictures of Phoenician funerary masks that were close doubles of their counterparts among the Olmecs in Mexico, and side by side presented drawings of the Egyptian-Phoenician god, Bes, from both western Mexico ("Yopi" territory) and Egypt. There was no question in my mind that the "Yopis" were a Phoenician colony in Mexico and that probably the Olmecs themselves were derived from Phoenician settlers—with a strong infusion of black African influences."[197] Fox also established a relationship between the figures on Chimu-Moche pottery with the mythological gods of the Phoenicians. Bes, a dwarf god with a headdress, appears in the Mayan as well as in the Egyptian, African, Phoenician and Roman societies. The smaller or deformed individuals were respected in these societies as having special qualities given to them by the gods.[198]

Phoenician ships, circa 1000 B.C.

If the Phoenicians, the inventors of the alphabet, did, in fact, discover America, it is not improbable that the lost and controversial Paraiba Stone should be the only written evidence of their passage on these shores. A large number of dolmens, megalithic upright standing stones with inscriptions of old Phoenician writing, have been found in all areas of North America. Salvatore Michael Trento made an exhaustive study of these dolmens and megalithic stones and concluded that they were indeed built and inscribed by Old World traders. Trento, with a band of professional anthropologists and geologists and more than two hundred volunteers, formed the Middletown Archaeological Research Center (MARC) and spent many years recording, measuring and photographing these old-world ruins in hills, valleys, and riverbeds in seven states. Trento's accumulated evidence and findings provide an amazing record of Celtic-Iberian and Phoenician artifacts left in America from approximately 1000 B.C. to about 1000 A.D., at a time when the Phoenicians were at their peak as a naval power, with a major port in Spain and a role as a leading trade nation that exported goods all over the Mediterranean region. Copper played an important role in these early civilizations. The Egyptians needed large amounts of copper-headed chisels and other copper tools for their temple pyramids, while the Greeks used enormous amounts of copper in their elaborate buildings and roads.[199]

Stone dolmen
Brittany, France
circa 1500 B.C.

Stone dolmen
N. Salem, New Hampshire
circa 3000 B.C.

Interior, Malta stone
burial chamber,
circa 3000 B.C.

Stonehenge, England
circa 1800 B.C.

America's dolmens, stone circles, megalithic standing stones and pyramids parallel the same type of construction that was used throughout the world, apparently for observing astronomical meridians and the position of the sun and moon at the solstice and equinox days. Some seven thousand years ago in Brittany, people moved stones weighing up to 180 tons and placed them strategically in the landscape. The most famous megalithic site is Stonehenge, on Salisbury Plain in southern England. Stonehenge, with its precise construction is not, however, a typical example of structures built at the same time as those in Brittany, but was, in fact, built much later. According to the latest studies, the current monument stands on the site of an earlier simpler Stonehenge, constructed in approximately 2200 B.C. A mathematical knowledge of the Pythagorean theorem would have been required to build these monuments. It was not until 2000 years later that Pythagoras said, "the square of the hypotenuse of a right angle is equal to the sum of the square of the other two sides." In August 1998, in Miami, Florida, excavations exposed an archaeological treasure consisting of a circle of holes chiseled into the limestone

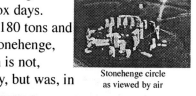

Stonehenge circle
as viewed by air

Miami circle of stones
Miami, Florida
circa 2000 B.C.

First model of
Stonehenge, England
circle of stones, circa 3000 B.C.

bedrock. Pottery shards, stone axe heads and other artifacts were also found in this circle, whose function is still unknown. It may have been a structure of some importance, such as a house for the tribal chief. It is a unique site—nothing like it having been found previously in the region. Although the overall site is approximately 2000 years old, the date of the earliest portion of the complex is not known. The Miami circle, tentatively attributed to the Mayans, resembles similar circular layouts uncovered throughout the Americas and worldwide.

Circle of 13 stones Calanais, Britain

Stone circle, Caral, Peru circa 3000 B.C.

The Miami circle is described in a report as follows: "The circle is depicted by at least 20 irregular cut basins which vary in size from one to three feet. Peculiar to the circle are numerous postholes, and a carving in the rock similar to an eye, that appear on the circle's east-west axis suggesting an alignment to the equinox, however, any astronomical alignments remain to be fully documented. Also particular to the site are several offerings, including two basaltic stone axes not manufactured in Florida, and a five-foot shark deliberately buried in the circle.... Probably also dating to this time are the four Station Stones (two of which survive) and, on the northeast side, an earthwork which runs from the break in the bank-and-ditch."[200]

We can surmise that Stonehenge, the Miami and Caral circles and the other sites worldwide were aligned with astronomical meridians and the position of the sun and moon at the solstice and equinox days. This alignment must have also reflected a feeling of alignment with the cosmos that served to tie far-flung communities together to the central group. This was almost certainly the purpose of the alignments at Chaco and other Anasazi cities. The ruins at Poverty Point, Louisiana and other mound cities east and west of the Mississippi share similar alignment points with some Mayan cities of Central America, leading to a possible conclusion that cultures were in contact with one another.

"Sun Dagger" spiral sun calendar. Winter solstice, rays of sunlight fall between the two huge stone slabs. Summer solstice, single band of light bisects the center of the spiral. During spring and fall equinoxes, an additional light falls on the smaller petroglyph, to the left of the larger one. Fajada Butte, Chaco Canyon. Discovered by Anna Sofaer in 1977.

Solstices and Equinoxes Fajada Butte, Chaco Canyon, by "Light Years Ago Tim O'Brien"

The positioning of all stone constructions suggests a higher degree of advancement than was previously credited to these ancient civilizations. Their dependence on agriculture meant that it was extremely important to follow the planting and harvesting seasons, as well as to know the shortest and longest days of the year. The placements of the stones were based on sophisticated astro-mathematical computations that we cannot understand even today. Many monuments are oriented towards the solstice-points on the horizon (points of sunrise and sunset at summer and winter solstice), as well as to points of the rising and setting of the moon at the largest distance of the moon from the ecliptic (called major and minor moonrises and settings). There also is an orientation towards certain fixed stars. It appears as though there were varying degrees for the orientation of the monuments according to which celestial bodies the community worshipped. Many megaliths and dolmens acted as observatories and were constructed in such a way that the rising sun will, on the day of the winter solstice or the spring or autumn equinoxes, send its first rays into the depths of the chamber or fall on markers of stone surrounding the dolmens. Many ancient civilizations in the Old World and in the so-called New World were sun-worshippers. The adobe walls and canyons surrounding many of these ancient civilizations in the Americas were engineered to line up astronomically with our sun, moon and stars. Symbols of spirals and waves are sometimes found on ancient carvings at the sites of the stone monument, apparently utilizing the sun in conjunction with the spiral or waves for lining up the solstice at different seasons to act as an astronomical calendar.

Spiral sun petroglyph Arizona

Spiral sun petroglyph

The Pueblo and Navajo Indians of the Southwestern United States share a close relationship. The two cultures are found in the Four Corners area, a very sacred place for both groups. The Pueblo and Navajo societies are products of this Southwestern desert environment. For this reason, there are many similarities between the two cultures, despite their vastly different histories. Among the many Pueblo tribes are the Hopi and the Zuni. The term Pueblo refers to a group of Indians who descended from cliff-dwelling people long ago, known as the ancient Anasazi. Archaeologists have determined that the Pueblo inhabitants have resided in the Southwestern United States area for more than 4000 years.

Spiral, Ometepe Island, Nicaragua. Photo J. Martin

Each Pueblo village consists of a tight organizational structure headed by a priesthood that controls the social, political and religious aspects of daily life. It is generally agreed that all Pueblo tribes descended from a common ancestor. This notion is reinforced by the fact that all Pueblo tribes have shared agricultural and irrigational techniques throughout their histories that have been almost identical, with maize being the primary staple crop for all these groups. The primary function of the priesthood in Pueblo society was to perform ceremonies to control the weather and the movements of the sun, to promote fertility in all living things, and to exorcise and to cure. They were also believed to maintain harmony between the people and the environment. Most of Pueblo astronomy can be linked directly to the sun. Extensive observations of the sun led to the development of an advanced sun-based religion among the Pueblo cultures. Solar alignments were made to indicate proper times for ceremonies and other important events. In particular, the solstices were regarded as special occasions and many of the calendrical markers were designed to indicate precisely when a solstice would occur.

Astronomical alignments
Pueblo Bonito kiva

At Hovenweep Castle, an ancient Anasazi ruin, a chosen room acted as a solar observatory. Several holes cut into the walls align with the rays of the sun at particular times. These times match the summer and winter solstices, and the spring and fall equinoxes. Many ancient ruins in the Americas have uncovered similar findings.

The southwestern Chaco Canyon area has been identified as a vast astronomical and cosmological ceremonial complex comparable and probably related to the astronomically and geometrically prearranged constructions of Mesoamerica. From about 900 A.D. to 1130 A.D. fourteen major buildings, after extensive planning and engineering, were constructed of sandstone and wood to form a complex celestial pattern. Eleven of the fourteen major buildings are associated with one of the four solar or lunar azimuths on the sensible horizon.

Supernova explosion, sun, moon and
star petroglyphs.
Penasco Blanco, Chaco Canyon

Three buildings (Pueblo Bonito, Pueblo Alto, and Tsin Kletzin) are associated with the cardinal directions (meridian and equinox). One building, Casa Rinconada, was built in an almost perfect circle. It was built on a hill, isolated from other structures on the south side of the canyon, across from Pueblo Bonito. The four main supporting posts in the ancient kiva were located in the corners, indicating their four cardinal directions: north (white), west (black), east (red) and south (yellow).[201] Pueblo Bonita, four stories high, contained over 700 rooms with 36 kivas. The major axes of symmetry and the location of the holes found in the ruins allowed light to enter different areas on these special dates, coinciding with the summer solstice and the equinoxes. The sun shines through the windows and illuminates wall niches according to the solar and lunar cycles, making the structure into an enormous solar calendar. Archaeological discoveries of large numbers of shattered pots, the absence of burials and household refuse, and 30-foot wide roads leading north, reveal that Chaco Canyon was not developed as a livable complex, but instead for seasonal, ceremonial visitations by great numbers of residents from the outlying communities.[202]

The alignments of many of these ancient observatories were based on the use of a circle of stones as at Stonehenge, Miami and other sites throughout the world. Big Horn Medicine Wheel, located on a ridge on Medicine Mountain in northern Wyoming, used a circular arrangement of stones measuring 80 feet across, with 28 rows of stones radiating from a central mound to an encircling stone rim. Placed around the outside edge of the wheel are five smaller stone circles. The medicine wheel contains 28 "spokes", possibly to represent the number of days in a lunar month. The Big Horn Medicine Wheel is not unique to the area. There are at least 28 other stone structure observatory cairns or altars of stone circles, some with spokes that are located only on the front range high plains area of the Rocky Mountains. None are as high as the one on Medicine Mountain, but all are on their highest point, with a full observational horizon. The Indians would go to these sacred mountains to offer prayers and to seek spiritual harmony with the powerful spirits there. The center mound, once occupied by a large buffalo skull, was a place to make prayer offerings. The area was used for those going on a vision quest. They would offer prayers and thanks to their mother earth that afforded them past and future sustenance.[203]

Big horn medicine
wheel

We now know from hieroglyphic writings that the ancient Egyptians were well advanced in astronomy and mathematics. The source of the ancient Egyptians' advanced knowledge has been a great mystery. Construction of their pyramids required knowledge and use of the square, the triangle, the circle and a five-sided pentagram. Little is known of the ancient religions or of the early inhabitants of Britain, Scotland and France. The Druids and the Beaker People were two that remain somewhat mysterious. The Druids were the priests, teachers and judges among the ancient Celts. The Beaker culture lived during the Bronze Age, from about 2500 to 1000 B.C. We can only surmise that the

Serpent mound, Ohio

ancient Celt or Beaker cultures, or another ancient culture, built the giant earthworks of a great serpent in Carnac, located in Brittany, France, and similar ones throughout Britain. The name Carnac is derived from *Cairn-hac*, which denotes "Serpent's Hill." A similar serpent mound can be found in Brush Creek, Ohio, called the "Great Serpent Mound", estimated to have been built about 1000 A.D. This serpent has an open mouth with the shape of an egg by its head. Studies indicate that parts of the Serpent Mound are aligned with both the summer solstice sunset and, less clearly, the winter solstice sunrise. A pile of burned stones once located inside the oval head area was several feet northwest of its center, possibly to make a more precise alignment with the point of the "V" in the serpent "neck" and the summer solstice sunset. In Kansas, Kentucky, West Virginia, Ontario, Canada, and Oban, Scotland, similar serpent mounds have been found.[204]

Snake, Mayan

The symbol of the snake is found in many ancient societies throughout the world from Egypt, Greece, India and to the Americas. The Aztecs, Maya, Toltecs and Incas of South America used the serpent in their buildings, statues, and vases to illustrate a serpent deity. The Egyptian sun god of the Pharaoh, with a serpent apron and headdress, compares almost perfectly to the Mixtec sun god with a serpent apron and headdress. The Mohave Indians of southern California have a legend of a giant rattlesnake god. In the Spiro mounds of eastern Oklahoma, snakes were painted on ceramic plates by the Mimbres culture. These plates, inscribed with images of snakes, show people in a ceremony, handling and dancing with the snake. In some Indian cultures a snake priest performs a ritual with the participants of the snake clan. One of their beliefs is of a "Snake Maiden" who gives birth to the "Corn Maidens". A similar belief was associated with the Mother Goddess in Crete. The Mother Goddess (right) is pictured with a snake in each hand. The various snake rituals and corn maidens were related to the aspects of a Mother Earth Goddess, bestowing fertility and life.

Snake goddess, Crete   Snake, Adena mound, Ohio

Mayan stone serpent

Serpent plate, Mississippi mound

Serpent sculpture Tiahuanaco, Mexico

In the Aztec civilization the snake deity was called Coaticue (She of the Serpent Snake). The Aztec calendar depicts the birth of a new sun as an elaborate fire serpent. The feathered serpent is found carved in stone throughout Mexico City and nearby at the temple pyramid of Quetzalcoatl, in the Citadel of Teotihuacan. The Pueblo villages hold ceremonies relating to a similar feathered serpent. The Hopi ceremony, held each summer, includes a snake dance and the handling of the snake. Shamans dress in unusual costumes and perform elaborate snake rituals. A flute ceremony is derived directly from the ancient mythology of the Hopi. Holding deadly rattlesnakes in their arms and mouth, the Hopi dancers pray to their gods for life-giving rain. At the Mayan ruins at Copan, Honduras, two carved heads of priests, each holding a snake in his mouth, bear a strong resemblance to the Hopi snake ceremony performed today, 2000 miles away.

Zuni Snake, Hopi wall painting

The snake dance was also performed at one time by other Pueblo tribes. The Acoma, Cochiti, Laguna, Zia, and Zuni of New Mexico, as well as the Yokut tribe of California, hold a snake ceremony similar to the Hopis. Both the Cherokee and Iroquois tribes also perform snake dances. The Algonquin believed that crossing a bridge in the shape of an enormous serpent would lead to the road of the afterlife. All those who were strong and true in their past life would cross this bridge. The others would fall into the waters below and turn into snakes.

In Dahomey, West Africa, their deity Dan (Da) is depicted as a snake with the tail in its mouth. In Egyptian mythology the rearing serpent is associated with the " Eye of Ra", or god's all seeing eye. In Hindu mythology, "nagas" are serpentine creatures with human faces and a serpent's tail. In American Indian mythology, serpents function as mediators between gods and humans associated with the sun. At the temple of Kukulcan (meaning feathered-serpent), an illusion is created with shadows, at each Vernal Equinox, of a serpent twisting down the steps of the pyramid. In Greek mythology Apollo struggles with a monster snake that he finally defeats. Japanese mythology tells of a hero, Susanoo, who battles a two-headed serpent. The Norse god Thor fought a constant battle with a serpent that was

Petroglyph, Inscription rock, Arizona

"The Monkey" with spiral tail, Nazca Lines, Peru.

45

encircling the world. Pliny the historian relates a tale of the Druids' contact with a serpent's egg. "Hissing serpents throw this up in the air", referring to an energy center surrounding the serpent.[205]

Soboba swastika maze stone Riverside, Ca.

Maze stone petroglyph Hemet, California

There are numerous giant, geometrical earthworks in varying maze shapes of circles, ellipses, oblongs, octagons and triangles, scattered throughout North and South America. In the Nazca plains of Peru similar earth constructions shaped like birds and animals have been discovered. These works date from about 3000 years, and have been attributed to the ancestors of our present Indians. In Peru's ancient Nasca Valley the famed "Nazca Lines" can be seen from the air. The source of these drawings, which consist of geometric patterns of triangles, spirals, zigzags and intricate etchings of birds and animals in the sand, has remained a mystery.[206] Archaeologist Maria Reiche has identified the Nazca designs as a spiral labyrinth, and others as a pointer for their gods to subterranean water acquifers and rivers that have long dried up and collapsed into the sand.[207]

An enormous oval labyrinth stone covered with a complex petroglyph was found 90 miles south of Los Angeles, California. Known as the Hemet Maze Stone, it is covered with a light coating of desert varnish. Located in a valley, it was determined by geologists to have fallen from a mountaintop into the valley about 15,000 years ago. The petroglyph stone carving is esti-

Brazil dolmen

mated to be at least 3000 years old. Inscribed on the stone is a labyrinth maze pattern with a swastika design in the center and corner, surrounded by a geometric square line. At least 50 other similar maze stone petroglyphs have been found on mountaintops in Orange, Riverside, San Diego and the Palm Springs area of California. All designs are rectangular and vary in size from four inches to several feet in diameter. There is a faint indication of a mineral-based red coloring that was originally painted on the stone along with its unique maze design. The red coloring with its geometrical designs have been found in many pyramid type mounds in the Americas, China, and in the ruins of Mesopotamia. Many of these precise earthen works can only be seen in their entirety from the sky. The question remains—how did these people acquire the knowledge and design capabilities to illustrate these designs so they could be viewed from far in the sky?[208]

Celtic-Phoenician landmarks are in many areas of North and South America, Europe, Asia, Australia, Easter Island and in other parts of the world. Two of the more mystifying man-made monuments are located in South America. In the Brazilian southern state of Rio Grande do Sul, there is a megalithic site with dolmen structures very similar to those that exist in Europe. Giant single standing stones and stone circles can also be seen throughout the extreme north of

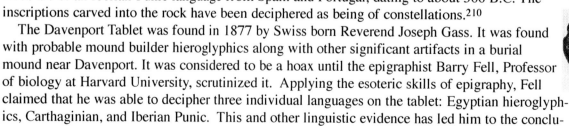

Dighton Rock, Mass.

Brazil. The Celtic dolmens are big stone structures sustained by two or more stones. The dolmens discovered in South Brazil are some of the biggest in the world. At least three of them have more than 100 square meters of area in the upper stone, sustained by three or four stones. The entire ancient Celtic tradition surrounds these dolmens, bringing it into a much broader context with the dolmens in other countries.[209]

Some of the inscriptions on the stones have been deciphered. Artifacts attributable to the Celtic-Phoenicians, or to a culture that used a similar language, are frequently discovered in the Americas. In the 18th century, the Dighton Rock was found on the banks of the Taunton River in Massachusetts, bearing a strange inscription which Ezra Stiles, then President of Yale College, claimed to be Phoenician. The authenticity of these and similar finds have been re-examined. In the past their origins were dubious enough to convince scientists that they were a hoax. Archaeologists had explained the markings as accidents of nature, from plows or scratches. Advanced knowledge of deciphering by a new breed of epigrapher (the study of ancient inscriptions) has provided a clearer picture. One attribution is that the letters on the Dighton Rock are of an Iberian-Punic language from Spain and Portugal, dating to about 500 B.C. The inscriptions carved into the rock have been deciphered as being of constellations.[210]

Davenport, Iowa stone tablet,

Grave Creek Mound, W.V.
Cincinnati Chronicle, 1939

The Davenport Tablet was found in 1877 by Swiss born Reverend Joseph Gass. It was found with probable mound builder hieroglyphics along with other significant artifacts in a burial mound near Davenport. It was considered to be a hoax until the epigraphist Barry Fell, Professor of biology at Harvard University, scrutinized it. Applying the esoteric skills of epigraphy, Fell claimed that he was able to decipher three individual languages on the tablet: Egyptian hieroglyphics, Carthaginian, and Iberian Punic. This and other linguistic evidence has led him to the conclu-

Grave Creek stone Smithsonian

sion that the Phoenicians colonized Massachusetts for a short while around 400 B.C. In 1641 Jesuit priests reported finding bronze figurines with Phoenician writing in Brazil. In addition, Phoenician artifacts and motifs featuring their Mother Goddess Tanith have been found throughout North and South America.[211]

The Grave Creek stone was discovered in 1838 during the excavation of the Grave Creek Mound in Moundsville, West Virginia, on the Ohio River about 10 miles south of Wheeling. The stone was a small inscribed sandstone disk, about 1 7/8" wide and 1 1/2"high. In 1838 the mound where it was found was reported to have been 69 feet high and 295 feet in diameter at the base, making it the largest of the Adena mounds. Today the mound, dated from between 250 B.C. to 150 B.C., is preserved in the Grave Creek Mound State Park. The Smithsonian Institution made four casts of the Grave Creek stone in 1868. In his 1976 book, *America B.C.*, Barry Fell translated the inscription and claimed the script to be Iberian, and the language Punic. Another example includes an ancient stone axe found in Pemberton, New Jersey, which showed up in a Currier and Ives engraving with an inscription attributed to the Tartessian in the Iberic language. It was published in the American Ethological Proceedings in 1861. Deciphered by Fell it read, "Stand firm, On Guard, Parry, Close in and strike." Near the same location in the Delaware River valley were found numerous inscribed stones, some polished. One stone appeared to be an Andalusian amulet. The text appeared to be of Iberic script, dating to about 200 B.C. to 100 A.D.[212]

Bat Creek Stone, Tennessee

In 1872, four pieces of a stone tablet inscribed with strange characters were found on a Brazilian plantation near the Paraiba River. It told the story of Phoenician merchants ("Canaanites of Sidon") and their ships being blown across the Atlantic in 536 B.C. The owner of the property sent a copy of the inscription to Dr. Ladislau Netto, who was Director of the National Museum in Rio de Janeiro. After studying the document carefully, Dr. Netto announced to a startled world that the inscription recorded the arrival of Phoenician mariners in Brazil, centuries before Christ. Unfortunately, an Indian rebellion broke out in the Paraiba region that same year. In the ensuing confusion, the plantation in question was never located and the stone itself was never recovered. A copy of the inscription was sent to the eminent French historian and philologist Ernest Renan who declared it a fake, and Netto was ridiculed by the academic establishment of his day. Renan based his conclusion on the fact that the text contained certain grammatical errors and incorrect expressions that forced him to question its authenticity.

A century later, a Brandeis University professor and distinguished scholar of ancient Near Eastern civilizations, Cyrus H. Gordon, studied the Paraiba inscription and arrived at the opposite conclusion. The inscription, he claims, contains grammatical forms and expressions that have only been recently deciphered, and were unknown to linguistic experts of the 19th century like Renan and Netto. Therefore, he contended, the document could not have been a fake. Gordon's translation reads, in part, "We are sons of Canaan from Sidon.... We sailed from Ezion-geber into the Red Sea and voyaged with ten ships. We were at sea together for two years around Africa but were separated by the hand of Baal and we were no longer with our companions. So we have come here, twelve men and three women... may the exalted gods and goddesses favor us."[213]

Los Lunas Stone, New Mexico

The Bat Creek Stone was discovered in 1889 in an undisturbed burial mound in eastern Tennessee by the Smithsonian's Mound Survey Project. *The Smithsonian* published a report by Cyrus Thomas about the stone. At this time the writing was considered to be letters from the Cherokee alphabet. In 1964 it was found that the published engraving of the stone was upside down. When reversed, it immediately became obvious to Henrietta Mertz and Cyrus Gordon, a noted semanticist, that the inscriptions were Hebrew, from the Middle East, dating to 135 A.D. In 1971, Cyrus Gordon identified the letters inscribed on the stone as Paleo-Hebrew, of approximately the first or second century A.D. The five letters to the left of the comma-shaped word divider read, from right to left, LYHWD ("for Judea"). In 1988, wood fragments found with the inscription were Carbon-14 dated to somewhere between 32 A.D. and 769 A.D. These dates are consistent with the apparent date of the letters. The Bat Creek stone is among countless artifacts in storage at the Department of Anthropology. Given the sheer volume of the material, all can not be displayed.[214]

There is a fascinating old site some few miles west of a little town called Los Lunas, located south of Albuquerque, New Mexico. The site has been known as "Mystery Mountain" by the locals for many years. At the foot of this mini Masada-like natural plateau there is an inscription written in Paleo-Hebrew. The inscription contains a slightly abridged version of the Decalogue, or Ten

Newark/Ohio Stone

Commandments. Anyone who is familiar with the Hebrew language and the well-established ancient Hebrew alphabet used prior to the Common Era, can easily read this inscription. In 1995 Cyrus Gordon proposed that the Los Lunas Decalogue is in fact a Samaritan mezuzah. The familiar Jewish mezuzah is a tiny scroll placed in a small container mounted by the entrance to a house. The ancient Samaritan mezuzah, on the other hand, was commonly a large stone slab placed by the gateway to a property or synagogue, and bearing an abridged version of the Decalogue. Prof. Frank Hibben, a local historian and archaeologist from the University of New Mexico, is convinced the inscription is ancient and thus authentic. He reports that he first saw the text in 1933. At the time, it was covered with lichen, making it hardly visible. A guide who had seen it as a boy back in the 1880s took him to the site. David Deal, an archaeologist, also claimed to have discovered an ancient Mediterranean zodiac carved on a rock near the Los Lunas stone.[215]

In November of 1860 David Wyrick of Newark, Ohio, found the Newark/Ohio Decalogue inscribed stone in a burial mound adjacent to the extensive, ancient Hopewellian earthworks. The stone is inscribed on all sides with a condensed version of the Ten Commandments in a peculiar form of post-exilic, square Hebrew letters. The robed and bearded figure on the front is identified, in letters fanning over his head, as Moses. The figure has a mild expression and fine features. He is wearing a turban and flowing robe, and is either holding a tablet or wearing a breastplate. The inscription is carved into a fine-grained black stone, identified by geologists Ken Bork and Dave Hawkins of Denison University as limestone. The inscribed stone was found inside a sandstone box, smooth on the outside and hollowed out within, to make an exact fit for the stone. The Decalogue stone measured 6-7/8" long, 2-7/8" wide, by 1-3/4" thick. Cyrus Gordon believed the Newark Decalogue stone to be a Samaritan mezuzah like the Los Lunas Decalogue. Several months earlier, in June of 1860, Wyrick had found an additional stone, also inscribed with Hebrew letters. Wyrick found this "Keystone" within what is now a developed section of Newark, Ohio, at the bottom of a pit adjacent to the extensive, ancient Hopewellian earthworks. This stone dated to circa 100 B.C. to 500 A.D. There have been questions as to whether Wyrick's fascination with the Hopewell culture and its relationship to the lost tribes of Israel affected his judgment regarding the origins of these stones.

Bar Kokhba coin found in Kentucky, circa 135 A.D. Gordon, *Before Columbus*

A third discovery, by credible citizens, of a stone bearing the same unique characters as the Decalogue stone strongly confirmed the authenticity and context of the Decalogue Stone, as well as Wyrick's reliability as an expert. When the Paraiba, Bat Creek, Newark Decalogue, Los Lunas and additional stone inscriptions are placed in the broader context of additional evidence, it becomes plausible that ancient peoples may have visited the Americas. Dr. Fell and Dr. Cyrus Gordon presented these views at meetings of the Epigraphic Society.[216]

Additional evidence of a Judean migration to America exists in the numerous Judean coins and Semitic objects found in the Americas. Alexander von Wuthenau discovered on the Pacific coast of Ecuador evidence of the presence of early Hebrews. A figurine of a lovely girl was found who wore a headdress with a remarkable Phoenician affinity. Other Ecuadorian heads show definite Semitic features. At Veracruz, a figure with Semitic features was found with a false beard, styled like an Egyptian beard, with a snake-like protrusion on the forehead.[217] Hebrew coins were found in different areas and at different times. The coins were found in Kentucky and Missouri in 1932, 1952, and 1967. They are all coins from Bar Kokhba's rebellion against Rome, dated from between 132 and 135 A.D. The date of 135 A.D. coincides with the date found on the Bat Creek stone, discovered in nearby Tennessee.[218]

Celtic sun god Stark County, Ohio

Celtic-Ogham Oklahoma

Contact between the ancient civilizations of the Mediterranean and the budding cultures of pre-Columbian America would explain why nicotine and cocaine had been detected on Egyptian mummies in Germany. Extensive tests in 1992 in Munich by Dr. Svetla Balabanova of the Institute of Forensic Medicine in Ulm (Germany) on the ancient Egyptian mummified remains of a 3000-year-old 21st dynasty mummy of Henut Taui had found both nicotine and cocaine in her hair shafts. Both tobacco and cocoa are Indian plants that were not grown anywhere else before Columbus arrived in the New World. It would also explain why a ball court in the Mayan city of Chichen Itza in the Yucatan has a running motif of

Celtic petroglyph Oklahoma

Iberic-Punic inscription Paraguay, Fell, *American B.C.*

Celtic Circles New Grange, Scotland

Celtic, Eye of Bel Mystery Hill, Mass. Fell, *America B.C.*

48

lotus blossoms, a flower unknown in the area, but sacred to the ancient Egyptians and a traditional design in Egyptian art.[219]

The name "Celts" was the designation given to those peoples who emerged from the same geographical location where the so-called "Lost Tribes of Israel" had disappeared from at an earlier stage of world history. These people migrated across Europe to settle in the British Isles and the coasts of France and Spain. They were a well-organized sea power at the time when Julius Caesar and his Roman legions invaded Britain in 55 B.C. The Celtic influence is found in megalithic stone structures with Ogham writing concentrated in Ireland, scattered across Scotland, the Isle of Man, South Wales, Devonshire, to the ancient Roman city of Calleva Attrebatum. Similar markings, dating to 500 B.C., have been found on standing stones in Spain and Portugal. It is from this area of the Iberian Peninsula that the Celts, who colonized Ireland, may have come. The discovery of similar

Chief Oconostota
by Frank Parson, 1732

carvings in the state of West Virginia to New England, along with many petroglyphs with Ogham writing found as far west as Oklahoma, have caused some speculation that the Celts may have come to the New World as early as 100 B.C. A number of archaeologists now agree that the dolmens were both entrances to burial chambers and were used as astronomical observation temples for sun worship—their openings usually pointed towards the east. Circles and other designs have been found on many of these stone structures that are similar to those on both sides of the European continent. Inscriptions with Celtic writing (Ogham) have been found on North American dolmens, along with Celtic stone altars to their sun god. One inscription reads, "Pay heed to Bel, his eye is the Sun."[220]

Chinese   Mayan
circa 500 A.D.   circa 800 A.D.

Accounts of the remains of early forts in America and the arrival of the Welsh under a Prince Madoc, have persisted in Native American oral legends. Former Governor Sevier of Tennessee recorded an account by Oconostota, Chief of the Cherokees, in a letter in 1810. The letter told of a Welsh Prince, Madoc, and his followers, fleeing from violence and bloodshed in Wales, escaping by ship and, using ancient Celtic maps and charts, crossing the Atlantic and landing on American soil at Mobile Bay in 1170 A.D. Moving inland, they built fortified settlements in Alabama, Georgia and Tennessee, giving rise to later claims of discovery of "Welsh Indians" between the mid 1500's and early 1800's. George Catlin believed that he had traced the descendants of these Welsh settlers among the Mandan Indians, many of who were blue-eyed and whose language contained elements of Welsh.[221]

Lake Titicaca,   Mayan
South America   Asian features
Asian features

There is documented evidence of Asian influence in Central and South America prior to the arrival of Columbus in 1492. Olmec and Chavin civilizations, as well as the Moche culture, that existed in America from approximately 1500 B.C. to 500 A.D., contain oriental similarities. Designs on pottery and sculpture bear too close a resemblance to each other for them to have been developed separately. The first Emperor of China, Sui-jon (3000 B.C.), invented the art of knot writing, called quipu by the Incas. The second Emperor, Shon-nung (2737-2705 B.C.), was represented as having a head of an ox and the body of a man, very similar to the Chavin. A six-foot Peruvian stone monolith, called the Stele Raimundi, was carved with the head of an ox and the body of a man. Many of these objects found in America are related to objects of the earlier Chinese Shang Dynasty of 1523 to 1027 B.C. Additional Chinese influences relating to gold metal work, pottery and weaving first appeared in South America about 3000 to 300 B.C.

Java   Mayan

Dragon detail   Chinese dragon
Chan Chan, Peru   carved box

These artifacts show similarities to the work from the Middle and late Chou Dynasties, probably originating from the coastal states of ancient China. Additional influences on the arts of Central America are of Hindu-Buddhist origins. Asiatic influences on the Mayan society began to show in the Mesoamerican culture about 500 B.C. During this same phase, the Mayan burial customs imitated those of China when they buried their "important individuals in stepped chambers using wooden planks, and the use of cinnabar and jade as primary burial offerings."[222] Throughout Asia and Mesoamerica, shrines were dedicated to serpents, and the cult of the serpent is seen in the most ancient civilized sites of Mesoamerica, including the Olmec civilization.[223]

Bark container
snake design

Both Asia and America seemed to share a fondness for mandalas, the drawn or carved circles of divine meditation that was favored by Hindus and Buddhists. The scroll shape and other Asian motifs

49

were universally used in the architecture of the Mayan and Asian cultures. The mandalas of Mesoamerica were of Teotihuacan origin with a close similarity and shape as those in Asia. The mandalas were also located in Mesoamerican architecture. In Asia they were prominent in their temples. The "pecked circles" of Mesoamerican mandalas are similar to the "pecked circles" in the Asian mandalas. Both designs show a cross within a circle, with arms pointing in the direction of solstices and equinoxes, making it probable that they were utilized as a type of astronomical calendar.[224]

Mayan Dresden Codex detail on bark paper

The making of paper from the inner bark of trees began about 3500 years ago in Asia. In China around 600 B.C., written records on wooden tablets and stone beater tools suggested that man had been writing on paper from as early as 1200 B.C. The complex process for converting the inner bark from tropical and subtropical trees to paper was invented in China and traveled to Southeast Asia, the South Pacific Islands and to the Mayans in the Yucatan. Bark was extensively used for boats, shelter, clothing and other uses by cultures as diverse as the Eskimos of Alaska, the Unyoro tribe of Uganda and the Japanese. Bark has assumed a mystical, religious importance in many parts of the world.

The Maya used a similar bark manufacturing paper process to that used in Southeast Asia. The Maya used it for their tunics, elaborately decorated hieroglyphic codex folded books, ceremonial clothing, banners, etc. The Toltecs improved on the manufacture of bark and passed along to the Aztecs the technique to produce scrolls 35 feet long. In the 1990s anthropologist Professor Paul Tolstoy of the University of Montreal did extensive research on the manufacturing of paper from bark and found similarities in about 92 of the 121 complex steps in both Mesoamerica and Southeast Asia. Tolstoy claimed the technique and tools for making bark paper appeared about 4500 years ago in Southeast Asia, and by trans-Pacific voyages the process was transferred to Mesoamerica 2500 years ago. Bark cloth was in widespread use throughout Papua, New Guinea, Polynesia and parts of Oceania when the explorers first landed. It was used for clothing and other everyday items and for ceremony. As early as 1888, a German archaeologist, Max Uhle, noticed a close similarity between certain stone artifacts of Mexico and others in Indonesia. He discovered shaped and grooved flat stones that were used in Southeast Asia as bark beaters in the manufacture of paper. These same stones were found in ancient Mexico. Uhle believed they were used for the same purpose in both Mexico and Indonesia.[225]

1774 map of North America inscribed as Fousang (Fusang) on the west coast of America

In 1774 a map was published dividing North America among "the European Powers." It was unusual that on the map was inscribed "Land which is supposed to be the Fousang (Fu-Sang) of the Chinese Geographers." Outlines of the coast and entries about Spanish and Russian discoveries date it prior to the voyages of captains Cook and Vancouver. It is also remarked that this is the "Coast seen by the Spanish in 1771 with inhabitants who go naked." A map from 1630 (Dutch) shows a Chinese junk in the area. "Fusang" shows up on other charts and maps, one from 1768 places it near the River of the West, of what might be Puget Sound.[226] It is identified on 15th- century Ming Dynasty world maps as an island on the far side of the Pacific Ocean, adjoining a continent that borders an ocean. These maps, dating to the 1300s, were based on earlier Han dynasty 100 B.C. maps. China was placed at the center

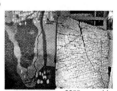
Chinese map of Africa   2200 year-old map, Chinese

of the world. Europe, India and Asia were depicted as one land mass surrounded by a ring of oceans with a concentric outline resembling North and South America. These ancient Chinese maps can be found in the collections of the British museum in London and in the French Ecole Des Langues Orientales Vivantes in Paris. An ancient Tibetan manuscript mentions a "green land" across the Eastern Sea. China has a long history of map making. In Russia, stone slabs with a relief map of the Ural Region was reported and found to be 2200 years old. "The map contains civil engineering works: a system of channels with a length of about 12,000 km, weirs and powerful dams. Not far from the channels, diamond-shaped grounds are shown. The map also contains numerous inscriptions. Originally, scientists thought it was an old Chinese language. Later it was discovered that the inscriptions were done in a hieroglyphic-syllabic language of unknown origin. A "Map of the Great Ming

Chinese compass 100 A.D.

Empire" dates back to 1389 and is arguably the oldest world map in existence. It accurately reflects the African continent and has been found to include suggestions of a Chinese voyage around Africa to the Americas about 100 years before Columbus, in the early 1400s. The use of stars for ocean travel is mentioned by the Chinese in 200 B.C. By 400 B.C. the Chinese were using a magnetic needle with a primitive compass.[227]

The first tale of a voyage to a strange land across the oceans, called Fusang, can be found in a book of Chinese mythology, *Shan Hai Jing* (*Classic of Mountains and Seas*), compiled by Emperor Yu of the Xia dynasty. It is both a geography and a shaman's book of myths and legends. The book mentioned a "Great Luminous Canyon", a possible reference to the Grand Canyon. The land was named Fusang, and was described as having hundreds of mountains, rivers and mineral resources, amazing creatures and plants, and many diverse and strange peoples. In 225 B.C. Emperor Shi Huang Ti spoke of a paradise across the Eastern Sea called the "Isle of Immortals". The geography of this era pictures the American continent encircling the world. Two names on the encircling continent confirm the name "Fusang Mountains" and "Land of Woman." Chinese poetry refers to this canyon as the birthplace of the sun.[228] Supposedly, Chinese Emperor Shi Huang-Ti ordered explorer Hsu Fu to search for islands in the Pacific, where palaces of gold and silver and pharmaceutical medicines were reported to exist. Hsu-Fu left in 219 B.C. with a large fleet of ships carrying many men and women. When they did not return it was presumed that they had found a rich and habitable land.[229]

Emperor
Shi Hwang-ti

A more documented record of a trip to the Americas by Buddhist monk Hui-Shen (Hoei-Shin) was mentioned by Liang Shu in his *History of the Liang Dynasty* (502 to 556 A.D.). Liang Shu claimed that in the Southern Dynasties period a monk named Hui-Shen crossed the ocean and discovered a land named Fusang. This was later compiled by Si'lian Yao and Wei Zheng in 629 A.D. as a *Biography of Eastern Nations*, during the reign of Emperor Taizong of the Tang Dynasty. Liang Qichao (1873-1929), a Chinese journalist and scholar, believed Fusang to be today's Mexico. This age was of intense commercial trade and economic activity for China. A French Chinese scholar, Joseph Deguignes, wrote a paper about Fusang in 1761. He had limited material, and his work set off much controversy. A German professor, Karl Frederick Neumann, published Hui-Shen's narrative in 1841, along with a commentary. An American, Charles Leland, translated Neumann's work in 1875. For some reason it has fallen out of favor in the last century's history and literature. Hui-Shen was among the first of the Buddhist missionaries to reach China from Afghanistan. Hui-Shen, with four other Buddhist missionaries, sailed off from China in 459 A.D. and returned in 499 A.D.

Javanese/Chinese style junk
circa 1500s, by de Bry

On his return journey, Hui-Shen arrived at Kinh-Chow, the capital of the Tsi Dynasty, situated on the Yangtze. Hui-Shen waited three years for an audience with Emperor to report on his activities. Unable to meet the Emperor due to a civil war, Hui-Shen met with Emperor Wu Ti of the new Liang Dynasty in 502 A.D., and told him an incredible tale of a 7000-mile journey to the land of Fusang. He claimed they had stopped off in Japan. Once leaving Japan they would have been in the grip of the Kuro Shiwo, the so-called Japan Current. This sets to the northeastward at such a rate that there was no returning. To the Japanese it was known as the Black Current, or the "Current of Death." Detailed descriptions of Fusang were given in the *History of the Liang Dynasty*, including marriage customs, crime and slavery. Much of this appears to relate to ancient Mexican society and the Amazon (women). The Fusang tree was a sacred tree that provided food, bark cloth, and a type of writing paper. The land of Fusang was noted as located 20,000 Li (7000 miles) east of Siberia, which would put it in the vicinity of the west coast of Mexico.[230]

The reported discovery of ancient Chinese artifacts in Victoria, B.C. and in Mexico seems to support the story of Fusang. Hui-Shen's party appears to have traveled down the California coast to Mexico. Archaeologist James R. Moriarty has unearthed possible Chinese stone anchors encrusted with manganese, which shows they had been lying on the seabed for 2000 or 3000 years. The Fusang plant that gave the country its name was apparently the century plant, a cactus-like agave, American (maguey, Mexican) plant commonly used for food and clothing found in the American southwest, Central America, and in the areas of Mexico. Religious symbols and scrollwork from South America to the Northwest coast have Buddhist and Taoist motifs resembling similar designs on southwest petroglyphs, Mayan hieroglyphs and Peruvian textiles. Chinese artifacts dating to 1200 B.C. have also been found in the Fraser Valley of British Columbia.[231]

Mound pyramid, Xian,
China

Parts of the *Maya Dresden Codex* relating to lunar and solar cycles and eclipses match closely those of the Han Chinese astronomical calculations.[232] At a Neolithic site at Bampo near Xian, China, artifacts were unearthed from a matriarchal clan society that existed 6000 to 7000 years ago. More than 10,000 tools and utensils, earthenware, and over 200 tombs and skeletons were found here. This discovery in China, in 1954, reveals similarities to ancient Indian burial methods,

Aerial view, part of over 70
Chinese pyramids

pottery designs, and implements of daily use.[233] There are about 100 Chinese mound pyramids, many near Xian, dating from at least 2000 B.C. to 21 B.C., that resemble the mound pyramids throughout the world and in the Americas.[234] In 1996 archaeologists in Russia announced the discovery of step pyramids dating to the 4th century B.C. in the Sentelek Valley of the Charysh district. Their design was similar to those in Latin America. In February, 1997, in the remote Altai territory of Siberia, funeral pyramids were found. Throughout Russia there are a large number of dolmen structures dating from about 2000 B.C. that resemble similar dolmens found throughout Europe and in the Americas.[235]

Signs of Japanese influence in South America have been discovered and dated to approximately 3000 B.C. Coastal currents from Japan show that it is possible to sail from Japan and be carried by the ocean currents southward to land in Peru or Ecuador. In the Japanese Ainu culture, similarities can be found among the Yakama and Kutenai Indians. Both cultures used the tule (Scirpus, Bulrush) for making place mats for serving food, coverings for their dwellings, as well as, at times, for wrapping their dead.[236] In 1960, pottery, fishing hooks, refuse, and stone figures were unearthed along the coast in Ecuador at a site known as Valdivia, near La Venta. These pots closely resembled pots of the Jomon people of Japan, who are noted for their fishing abilities. Decorations on the ceramic pots found in Ecuador and in the Jomon culture of Japan are identical in design and technique, with chevron and meander motifs engraved or stippled into the pots. These Neolithic designs found in Japan, denoting supernatural power, were utilized in the Neolithic areas of Southeastern Europe on ceramics dating to 5000 B.C., as well as in Mexico's Olmec culture 3000 years ago. In ancient Mesoamerica and Japan (Joman culture), serpents are pictured on the ceramics or on the walls of the temples. In the Jomon culture, the vessels themselves were made in the form of serpents with serpent-like clay belts surrounding the ceramic as a form of protection.[237]

Jomon snake pottery

Possible evidence that early travelers visited America from Egypt to Mesopotamia to India and across the Pacific exists in related architectural artifacts and plants. India, Pakistan and the Mayan calendars and zodiacs have similar names for their days. In his 1974 book entitled *Ancient Egyptians and Chinese in America*, R. A. Jairazbhoy found 21 such parallels between the myths and religious practices of ancient Egypt and those of Mexico.[238] Astronomy provides another connection within the Mayan calendar, which incorporates a 365-day solar calendar as found in Egypt, and a 260-day lunar calendar like that of Mesopotamia. Both are linked by means of a scale that spans 52 solar years or 73 lunar years. The Mayan calendar is a better system for measuring time than any Eurasian calendar because the Mayans eliminated the need to keep the moon and sun in step, a brilliant idea for this time. They used mathematics to understand and explain their history.[239]

Elephant vessel detail
Aztec Mexico

Elephant pipe, found in
Davenport mounds
in S.D. Peet, 1892
Moundbuilders

Elephants are featured in Mayan sculptures, although the mammoth supposedly was extinct during the time of the Mayan civilization. One of the oldest artistic works found dates to 30,000 B.C., done on an elephant bone. Found in Puebla, Mexico, it illustrates an elephant as well as other extinct animals. In March, 1952, Mexican pre historians Maldonado Koerdell and Luis Aveleyra found at Ixtapan a complete skeleton of an elephant with stone artifacts, including two spearheads between the ribs of the elephant and nearby, the remnants of "Tepexpan man." The radiocarbon date was determined to be at about 10,000 B.C.[240] Indian myths and legends tell about an animal similar to the mammoth. In Indian life we find tales about monsters and heroes that effectively describe an animal very similar to a modern day elephant, but bigger and with more hair. There were oral tales from the Inuit traditions of Alaska, to tales from the Naskapi Indians of the Labrador Islands, to the tribes in the southeast areas of North America, all similar in their descriptions of this giant animal.[241] Elephants were common in India and played an important role as the elephant god, Ganesa, in the Hindu religion. Artifacts featuring elephants in a seated position, posed as though praying, have been uncovered as stone pipes in mounds in North America, on temples in the Yucatan, Mexico and in Copan, Honduras. These elephants bear a strong resemblance to the Hindu elephants carved on the temples in India and Southeast Asia. In the ancient sacred Hindu text of *Ramayana*, the elephant and deeds of King Rama of Ayodhya are featured in the Hindu creation myth.[242] Architectural stone carvings in Hindu temples of India and the extensive Mayan temple ruins of Chichen Itza in the northeastern Yucatan state of Mexico have similar stone carvings. These structures were built with perfection; utilizing copper clamps to join the gigantic stone blocks, and tools such as the plumb bob, bronze crowbars, and chisels. The blocks were individually cut and beveled to exact dimensions and positioned without mortar.[243]

Stone box corn cobs (maize)
Mexico, circa 1300 A. D.

Corn woman, Mexico

52

Maize and other varieties of corn are thought to have their origins in America. The oldest example of the existence of an ancestor of maize is in Mexico, where fossilized pollen has been unearthed. By plant synthesis, botanist Paul Manglesdorf estimated the pollen to be about 80,000 years old. These samples were taken from geological core samples drilled 200 feet below Mexico City. Scientific evidence and Mayan oral legends point to about 2500 B.C. for maize (corn) to have been introduced in the Tehuacan valley in Mexico.[244] Representations of maize appear on sculptured statues from India dating from the twelfth century A.D. Indologist and Ethno-Botanist Shakti M. Gupta of Delhi University confirms the presence of maize and at least five other New World plants in pre-Columbian temple sculptures in India.[245] The oldest sculptures of maize appear at Sanchi, India, dating to the 2nd century B.C. These numerous statues, especially in northern India, show Hindu deities holding maize cobs partially wrapped in the husk. Hindu religious text called maize one of the twelve original plants bestowed by the gods. It is known as "the Fruit of Rama." Maize was indicated as playing an essential role in rituals celebrating the birth of Buddha.[246]

Maize statue, India

The evidence of maize in both Asia and Africa before 1492 is sufficient to set aside the claim that maize was transported from North America to Europe after the arrival of Columbus. In Scotland, maize and aloe cacti have been discovered, carved in the 1400s in the Rosslyn Chapel, built before the birth of Columbus. In the Middle East (Tigris-Euphrates Valley), on a bas-relief on the wall of the Assyrian Palace of Nations of Clah (Nimrod), a figure representing a god is seen standing in front of some corn-like plants. A man with a small bag or basket in his left hand holds an ear of corn in his right hand. In the Cairo museum in Egypt are two golden urns—on one side of each urn are carved grains of corn. The other side has flower blossoms in bas-relief. In the National Museum in Beirut, Lebanon, are several ears of corn made of iron found in the ruins of Baalbek.[247] Maize designs have been unearthed in pre-colonial ceramics in South Africa. Fragments of pottery with maize imprints dated to the 12th century have been excavated in Nigeria.[248] The question of the origin of maize and whether it traveled from America to India, Scotland, or Africa, is under debate by the scientific community.[249]

Dr. Eduard Seler, an important scholar of middle American research, studied the enormous Aztec calendar and its four "ages". He said, relating to them, that he "...observed with undisguised amazement, the powers represented in these four correspond to the very elements hypothesized by the Greek philosopher Empedocles as the 'roots,' ritsonata, of all things. The four distinct prehistoric and pre-cosmic ages of the Mexicans, each oriented toward a different direction of the heavens, are astonishingly related to the four elements: earth, wind, fire, and water, known to classical antiquity and which even now determine the way in which the civilized people of East Asia look upon nature." The Indians of North America, the Hebrews and the Hindus use the same numbers and symbols in many of their rituals and ceremonies. The Creek Indians used seven ears of corn from fields of their seven different clans in their sacred ceremonial dance. The Hebrews believed in seven archangels; and their Menorah holds seven candlesticks. The upper levels of Hindu temples are constructed with seven pillars. The ancient Dravidians of southern India used a creator symbol of a serpent with a seven-petaled, flowerlike headpiece. The seven lotus centers of Kundalini used in yoga were the primary power centers of the body.[250] The number seven is a sacred number in Indian, Hindu and ancient Hebrew teachings. Indian legends tell of their origins from the seven stars arriving on Earth as seven tribes. The origin is the Pleiades, part of a larger constellation called Taurus. The Indians used the Pleiades as an astronomical point to mark the change of seasons. Pleiades appears about the time of the last frost, giving information that would have been important for successful crop cultivation. The Seneca Indians celebrated their midwinter ceremony when the Pleiades passed directly over their villages at approximately 42 degrees latitude in early February, signifying the beginning of the planting season.[251]

Skidi Pawnee star chart
Field Museum, Chicago

The serpent itself is a symbol for rebirth and regeneration, as well as healing related and utilized in ancient and modern civilizations throughout the world. The Hopis in their snake dance utilize the snake as a messenger to their creator to deliver their prayers. A winged staff today symbolizes modern medicine with two serpents coiled around the staff. The snake or serpent in Minoan, Egyptian, Greek and other early societies is often portrayed and associated as the female Mother Goddess, who assumes a serpent form as a symbol of female wisdom and council.[252]

Indians have always considered the earth as the mother, while the fruits of the earth, such as "mother corn", are also referred to as female. In the Indus Valley and other

Aztec Serpent
Quetzalcoatl

Serpent, India

sites throughout Western Europe and Asia, numerous quantities of steatite seals and female figurines, many represented in a pregnant condition, have been unearthed. Limestone sculpture images resemble female deities, similar to the Indian symbolic deities of an all-powerful Mother Earth.[253] The twin Hindu goddess Shiva, both a destroyer and healer, is often shown as a twin partner of the male god Bhairava, each one half female and the other half male, encircled with a serpent. This symbolized Mother Earth and the bonding of the female with the male.[254]

Aztec calendar face
Tenochtitlan, Mexico

The Aztec calendar showed this male/female figure, and indicated that the human race may have evolved from the Pleiades. Pleiades in the Aztec calendar signifies the final year of their 52-year cycle, called calendar round, and was celebrated with a ceremony. The Muslim religion in its holy book, the *Koran*, relates that the angel Gabriel came from the constellation Pleiades. After a lapse of about 1500 years and the decay of Mohenjo-Daro and other great cities of the Indus civilization, Hinduism began to evolve. The Indians and Hindus both utilized similar symbolic deities as intermediaries to their creator. Trees, snakes, mother earth, as well as the sacred white buffalo and the Hindu bull of Shiva are held in respect by the Indians, Hindus, Mesopotamians, ancient Egyptians and the Minoan civilization. Plato's writings on Atlantis related that bulls were allowed to roam free. Hindus hold the cow sacred, and Hinduism's major deity, Lord Shiva, rides on Nandi, a sacred white bull. The Indians use the white bull in their sun dance, starting with the "White Buffalo Calf Woman's" appearance from the East.[255]

Aztec calendar round

Plato has written of the existence of Atlantis and told stories of this long lost civilization. Evidence of man-made ruins of a walled city off the island of Crete and in Bimini in the Caribbean have led to speculation that Atlantis, once a large continent, suffered a tremendous catastrophic earthquake and sank under the ocean. A finding of stone construction and possible underwater pyramids in the waters off Cuba has increased the possibility of a large continent disappearing in a great catastrophe. In their book, *Echoes of Plato's Island*, by Anton and Simon Mifsud, Chris Agius Sultana and Charles Savona Ventura, a strong case is made that the Maltese and Pelagian Islands were part of a larger land mass and are remnants of Atlantis. They found an ancient text written about 620 B.C. by historian Eumalus of Cyrene in his *History of Libya*, that confirms the existence of Plato's Atlantis between Sicily and Libya. Underwater sites off Malta have been discovered that show submerged temples, megaliths and pottery.

Underwater step pyramid
off Okinawa, Japan

Colonel James Churchward, who spent over 50 years studying ancient Nahuatl stone tablets from Mexico and India, concluded that Atlantis was once the home of Indians who were later forced to abandon their Atlantean cities and escape to America. In the Pacific Ocean a legendary continent called Mu was said to have existed off Okinawa. Mu is reputed to have sunk and disappeared under the sea about 12,000 years ago as a result of an earthquake. Professor W. Masaaki Kimura of the National University of Ryukyu, Okinawa, has discovered geological evidence that Mu existed.[256] Fifteen inscribed stone tablets with images and glyphs were excavated from the mouth of the river Hija and off islands underwater near Okinawa. Illustrations on the tablets resemble depictions of the ancient stepped pyramid structures that exist in present day Egypt, Iraq, Mexico and Peru. This is discussed in detail and illustrated with photographs in Dr. Schoch's book *Voices of the Rocks*. Dr. Schloch wrote, "For many decades, indeed for centuries and even millennia, various researchers and writers have searched for the truth behind Plato's lost continent of Atlantis (usually, but not always, considered to have been located in either the Mediterranean Sea or in the Atlantic Ocean), or for the presumed sister continent of Atlantis in the Indian or Pacific Ocean, referred to variously as Mu or Lemuria." Plato's chronology, when interpreted literally, shows that Atlantis was destroyed cataclysmically around 9500-9600 B.C., and the supposed civilization of Mu is thought to have been even older. In the 1990s, Professor W. Massaki Kimura found ruins and remains of what appeared to be pyramid stone structures off the coasts of Okinawa and the islands of the Ryukyu Island chain, Japan. Kimura considered this to be tangible evidence of a lost, highly sophisticated, and very ancient civilization. Could this be Mu or Lemuria? The best-publicized and most spectacular of these structures is one located off the southern coast of Yonaguni Island. It is a small Japanese island located east of Taiwan and west of Ishigaki and the Iriomote Islands in the East China Sea. The man-made structure off the coast of Yonaguni has been hailed as "the world's oldest building", taking the form of a "stone ziggurat" dating back to 8000 B.C. The pyramid-type structure has the superficial appearance of a platform-like or partial step-pyramid-like

Petroglyph step pyramid
Japan

54

structure. It has been compared to various pyramid and temple structures in the Americas, such as the ancient "Temple of the Sun" near Trujillo in northern Peru.[257] Petroglyphs in Japan have been found on rocks near the top of mountains inscribed "Sa-Ra-Mu" (translated as "Sacred Sun Earth"). On the small neighboring island of Tokunoshima, among the ruins of Tomori in the town of Amagi, rock petroglyphs can be seen that illustrate an ancient seagoing ship that resembles early Celtic and Phoenician ships from 1200 to 2500 B.C.[258]

Massive stone construction
Sacsahuaman, Peru

In Peru and Bolivia, high in the Andes, lie two sites that still mystify archaeologists as to their date and their importance in their relationship to past civilizations in other parts of the world. We can only speculate that these two sites were part of a past civilization that encompassed the entire world, to eventually disappear mysteriously. A massive, ancient stone structure can be found in Sacsahuaman (Sacsayhuaman), Peru, near Cuzco, the capital city of the Inca Empire. It has puzzled archaeologists because the stones in this construction weigh over 300 tons, predating the polygonal-shaped Inca stones of 3 tons. Instead of cutting the stone in regular shapes, as in the Inca style, the ancient ancestors of the Incas used very irregular shapes and some stones have about 32 different angles. With all these angles, the stones fit so perfectly on every side that a knife blade cannot be inserted in the joints. All the stones are slightly convex, giving them a slight bulging appearance. All this was beveled at the edges and built without mortar. The walls are sixty feet high and so heavy they are able to resist the earthquakes that are common in the Andes region. Garcilaso de la Vega, a Spanish historian, raised by the Incas in the shadow of these walls, wrote of Sacsahuaman, "...this fortress surpasses the constructions known as the seven wonders of the world. For in the case of a long broad wall like that of Babylon, or the colossus of Rhodes, or the pyramids of Egypt... an immense body of workers... overcame all difficulties by employing human effort over a long period.... But it is indeed beyond the power of imagination to understand how these Indians, unacquainted with devices, engines, and implements, could have cut, dressed, raised, and lowered great rocks, more like lumps of hills than building stones, and set them so exactly in their places."[259]

The builders of these massive walls and the method used to erect, shape and position these giant stones is still a mystery. The old ruins of the city of Luxus, in Morocco on the Atlantic shore of North Africa, supposedly built by the Carthaginians, has at least three levels of construction representing totally different cultures. The Romans built the last on top, and beneath were Carthaginian structures. Below these was a style of buildings from an unknown civilization. Like the pre-Inca masonry in Peru, this bottom style incorporates massive polygonal stones as those used in Sacsahuaman, Peru. Thor Heyerdahl noticed this similarity and questioned why these similar masonry styles were on opposite sides of the Atlantic Ocean. Besides these massive ancient ruins, ruins of megaliths also exist on the island of Malta, where they taper off into the Mediterranean. Underwater ruins have also been discovered off the Maldives Islands in the Indian Ocean. Underwater ruins in the Atlantic Ocean can also be seen off the Bahamas. This entire area has been long believed to have been part of the lost continent of Atlantis. In Carnac, France, stone ruins stretch from the land out into the Atlantic Ocean. The extensive underwater ruins of large stone blocks off Okinawa, Japan, are located in the Pacific Ocean, giving credence to the existence of another lost continent called Mu. All of these underwater ruins would have been built before the last Ice Age ended, with the rising of sea levels about 10,000 to 12,000 years ago.[260]

The ancient ruined city of Tiahuanaco (Tiahuanacu), parts of which were built about 10,000 to 15,000 B.C., lies 12,500 feet above sea level in the Bolivian Andes, 15 miles from Lake Titicaca. This date would account for the findings of carvings of elephants and other animals that have been extinct for at least 12,000 years in South America. Evidence surrounding this ancient city suggests that when it was built it was at ground level, just above the sea. Tiahuanaco, besides being high up in the Andes, was an unusual feat of construction. It is near an ancient shoreline that apparently was once a harbor. Enormous stone blocks weighing between 100 and 150 tons are scattered all over the site. Numerous earthquakes took place here, and much of the site was covered in solidified mud. It has now been partially restored and geologists have determined that some of the blocks were brought from quarries 200 miles away. Arturo Posnansky, a German engineer who spent his life researching the ruins, wrote four large volumes, *Tiahuanacu, The Cradle of American Man,* on its archaeological construction and astronomical features. A ceremonial center with pyramids, temples, stone idols, and a 10-ton, 10-foot high "Gateway of the Sun" entrance, also called Tiwahaku, dominates the site. The upper portion of the gate is carved with beautiful and intricate designs, with various symbols of birds, elephants, extinct toxodon, and a human figure in the

Extinct Toxodon

Tiwahaku, "Gate of the Sun"

55

center, thought to represent the Sun god, Viracocha or Quetzalcoatl. Large stone images up to 7 feet tall were uncovered at the site. One was a bearded statue with large round eyes, a straight narrow nose and an oval mouth. Rays of lightning are carved on the forehead, and animals are carved around the head. His arms are crossed over an ankle-length tunic, decorated with pumas around the hem. Serpents are on each side of the gate. The temple area of Kalasasaya is a square, sunken pit with heads protruding from stone walls.

Stone statues Stone statues
Easter Island Tiahuanaco

Each head is different, and according to various writers, these stone heads depict all of the known (and some unknown) races of man on the Earth. Some believe that Tiahuanaco was a great religious center and place of pilgrimage, to which people journeyed from the four corners of the Earth. There are numerous similarities in Tiahuanaco and discoveries found in Easter Island as well as in the Pacific Islands. In 1955, Thor Heyerdahl uncovered at Rano Raraku in the oldest part of the statue quarries, a "...missing link between the oldest types of stone statues in Tiahuanaco and those on the nearest inhabitable island in the Pacific. They also discovered additional columns and stone heads without bodies that conformed closely with characteristic statues from Tiahuanaco. The sun gate leading into Tiahuanaco, facing in an east-west direction, is similar to a monolithic gateway that is standing in Tongatabu, Polynesia. There are megalithic stonework and pyramids throughout the Pacific that resemble those in Tiahuanaco and other areas of South America."[261]

Kalasasaya Temple
Tiahuanaco, Bolivia

Easter Island, known to the islanders as Rapa Nui, is in the Pacific, 2000 miles west of the South American coast. It contains a mausoleum of giant stone statues, skillfully erected on tall cliffs on a colossal platform made up of megalithic stones. One figure is about thirty feet high. There are more than 550 of these large stone images of men, mostly without feet. The jaws are big and the chins jut out. Four stone causeways from the platform of giant statues of men lead to an open plaza with a domed temple containing more giant statues of men, and one of a giant woman. There are also sculptured carvings of three masted ships and extinct, four-footed birds. In addition to the statues, the islanders possess the *Rongorongo* script, the only written language in Oceania. It is an ancient pictorial language that has now been deciphered. The island is also home to many petroglyph rock carvings. The mystery remains as to how these mammoth statues that are twenty feet thick at the base and fifteen feet high, and which weigh many tons, were moved. Today, over 500 of these statues lie on the ground as though a major calamity pushed them on their sides. Thor Heyerdahl proposed that the people who built the statues were of Peruvian descent, due to a similarity between Easter Island and the unusually fitted stonework of the Incas. Archaeological evidence indicates the discovery of the island by Polynesians in about 400 A.D. The stones and statues tell a story of an earlier age, and of the similarity between the Andes and Easter Island. Easter Islanders grow the potato and the totora reed, both of Andean origin. In the old legends, Easter Island and Cuzco, Peru, were both called "The Navel of the World." The legends also recall a similar Sun god, called Viracocha.[262]

Easter Island stone statues

Geologically, both Easter Island and Peru lie on an underwater ridge connected to the coast of Peru at the Nazca Plain. At one time, in the distant past, this underwater ridge would have provided a partial land bridge between Easter Island and South America. These two locations are at the opposite edges of the Nazca plate. The new science of plate tectonics has found a shift under the South American plate. As it pushes under the South American plate, lifting its edge, the shift is usually smooth and steady. At other times, however, there are violent earthquakes. In the distant past it is probable that the Nazca plate slipped suddenly under the South America plate, drastically lowering one and raising the other. Evidence supplied by respected scientists and geologists support the theory that the axis of the earth shifted about 10,000 B.C., causing a great catastrophe. Lake Titicaca, on the border of Peru and Bolivia, is now more than two miles above sea level. The ancient city of Tiahuanaco is currently 12 miles away from, and 100 feet higher, than the lake. The area around Lake Titicaca is littered with millions upon millions of fossilized seashells. The city has ruined docks, which implies that sometime in the history of civilization, this area was subject to a major upheaval that may have happened about 12,000 years ago. Stone roads and extensive ruins of temples built of huge blocks were found under the waters of Lake Titicaca in the 1980s by two cinematographers. If this major upheaval did occur, involving an entire mountain chain being created or thrust up 15,000 feet, it would have easily effected the rest of the world and could explain the disappearance of other civilizations under water, as well as the vast number of flood legends and catastrophes that exist in almost every culture on earth.[263]

Evidence of explorers who traveled to America from West Africa have been passed along in oral traditions and recorded by Arab historians. A tribal chief from Ghana sailed across the Atlantic in the 9th century B.C. Tales recorded in the 14th century by the Arab historian Ibn Amir Hajib in his *Arabian History of Africa,* refer to expeditions by the sultans of the West African Kingdom dispatching a trading flotilla of four hundred ships to the far side of the ocean.264

Phoenix., February 1828

Ancient Cherokee oral records told of the visit a long time ago, long before the coming of the white man, of black people from Africa landing on the shores of Turtle Island. Unable to conquer the inhabitants, they left after finding the Indians spiritually self-sufficient.265

Records of early events were produced in the form of pictorial writing using hieroglyphic characters. A number of these inscriptions have been found in North America. The Micmac tribe from the northeastern section of the United States, for example, used a pictorial hieroglyphic script similar to the ancient Egyptian symbols. This was in use before the Rosetta Stone was deciphered in 1823. Several thousand of the Indian hieroglyphic characters were found to be similar to the characters used in Egyptian hieroglyphics. The Algonquin tribes in the northeast also used a similar style of writing, inscribing Egyptian-style hieroglyphic script symbols vertically on the bark of trees. The Egyptians also used vertical writing. The Algonquin tribes and a number of southwestern plains tribes use a form of pictorial writing that reads horizontal, and from right to left. This remains in use today.266 This writing

Indian pictograph signatures

was non-phonetic and, in place of an alphabet, syllabary was utilized—with hundreds of pictorial signs that could convey a story. For example, a picture of a temple on fire would mean conquest; a wrapped mummy figure was a symbol for death. The Indians of Columbia and Peru used a very similar hieroglyphic writing system called *Parejhara.* Catholic texts and prayers contain pictures of this writing. Supposedly invented by the early missionaries, the native Indians recall this complex hieroglyphic system, in use by their ancestors before the Spanish invaded their lands. They also claimed they had other writing systems such as the quipu for keeping a financial count, and tile writing called "Tocapu", based on geometric abstract patterns. The Andes Indians also were found to have woven these same writing designs into textiles still in use today. A bean writing system may have been invented by the Moche culture before the Inca. Dot and line signs on a special bean legume (Spanish, pallares), have been found in burial offerings and on painted vases. The Panama tribes also use a similar hieroglyphic script emphasizing body language and gestures as in the Parejhara script.267

"Inca Chief accountant and treasurer, charge of the knotted strings, or khipu." Guamán Poma

The cotton first cultivated in Egypt about 375 B.C. has been found to be genetically similar in chromosomes to the cotton found in Peruvian textiles discovered in graves dating from 2500 B.C. The original Peruvian cotton appears to have been crossed with an Asiatic strand to produce much stronger cotton. It was also found that these same cottonseeds had again changed their makeup about seven thousand years ago, to be transported back to Eurasia.268 Cotton was first discovered in North America in the Tehuacan Valley in central Mexico, dating from 7000 to 5000 B.C. In the Indus Valley, the earliest cotton discovered was dated to around 2500 B.C. There are three basic kinds of cotton: Old World cotton, which has thirteen large chromosomes, and American cultivated, as well as Hawaiian wild cotton, both of which have 26 chromosomes—13 large and 13 small. This

Madrid Codex writing

indicates that the American and Hawaiian cotton resulted from mixtures from the Old World cotton. In addition, the 26 chromosome wild cottons have been found along the Pacific islands. It appears that in ancient times cotton was carried back and forth throughout the Pacific, leaving a genetic trail. In 1466, hybrid cotton superior to the African and Egyptian cotton was found in Guinea, West Africa. African traders before Columbus most likely took this hybrid cotton to West Africa from America.269

Information regarding the travels of cotton is gleaned from the DNA evidence of the people having the same genes as those from the Pacific Islands of Samoa, Tahiti, Easter Island and the rest of Polynesia as well as to the inhabitants of South America.270 Douglas C. Wallace, an Emory University genetic scientist, traced some of these migrating populations and determined that they started out from the Mongolian region of China. The same mutated gene shows up in four of these spread-out Indian populations: the Mayans of Central America, the Pima and Hopi of the Southwest, and the Ticunas tribe in Brazil, South America. This gene also appears in the indigenous inhabitants of Southeast Asia, and the islands of Melanesia and Polynesia in the South Pacific.271

In the ancient cities of Eurasia, craftsmen were part of a guild that was very similar to the Indian clan system. This striking similarity in the clan identification was that each craft was given a name of some animal such as the "snake" or "donkey" group. Artifacts, stone construction, pyramid shape temples, hieroglyphic inscriptions on stone, and burial customs from these lost Eurasian cities were similar to the temple and mound constructions of the Mayan and pre-Inca civilizations. The ancient southeastern Asian civilizations of Egypt, Sumeria, Mohenjo Daro, and others were at their prominence about 2000 B.C. Due to changing weather patterns and wars, the cities began to be abandoned about 500 B.C. and were left to eventually become part of the desert.[272]

Mayan complex at Tikal
Yucatan, Mexico

The great North American civilizations began in South America at Caral, Peru, and Tiahuanaco, Bolivia, about 3500 B.C. or earlier. Other great cities consisted of the temple complex of Chavin de Huantar in Peru, the Mayan city of Tikal, the ancient ceremonial center of Teotihuacan in Mexico, La Venta in Mexico (constructed by the Olmecs), Chichen Itza in Mexico, and Chan Chan in Peru. Numerous cities such as Machu Picchu were part of the great Inca Empire that stretched 3000 miles from modern Columbia to central Chile. They were built about 1000 to 50 A.D. The vast, impressive Mayan city of Tikal in Guatemala was built with plazas and immense temples of limestone masonry. The city reached its prime by 750 A.D., with a population of at least ten thousand inhabitants.[273]

The Adena mound culture in North America, 1000 B.C. to 200 A.D., had their burial mounds constructed into shapes of turtles, rabbits, serpents, etc. The Adena people were noted for burying objects with their chiefs, as the Egyptians did with their dead. Beautifully crafted ceremonial objects in stone, wood, copper, pottery, stone pipes, bone masks with bird designs, along with ornaments made from mica, pearl and copper, were buried with their leaders. The Hopewell mound culture in the Ohio Valley, West Virginia and Kentucky areas existed from about 500 B.C. to 700 A.D. Elaborate ceremonial centers were built with octagonal and square earthen enclosures. The architectural constructions were usually steep cones built over burial pits containing intricate log tombs that were beautifully furnished. The elite built their homes, staged religious events, and laid their ancestors to rest all around one great center. There appears to be a connection between the Hopewell mound culture and the Maya and Aztec civilizations, as evidenced by discoveries of carefully and well-crafted materials made of copper and bone, along with masks, elaborate feathers and headdresses. Ceremonial objects reveal a temple mound religion of powerful priests and evidence of human sacrifices. The Natchez (Mississippi) culture existed from about 800 to 1500 A.D. The paramount chief of the Natchez was called the Great Sun, and he lived in the Grand Village. Elaborate funeral ceremonies for the Natchez elite were conducted on the mound plaza. These rituals included the sacrifice of relatives and servants of the deceased. Natchez pottery vessels, as well as European trade goods obtained from the French, were buried with the dead. The Hopewell, Natchez, and Adena societies built some of their mounds in the forms of snakes or fanciful beasts. The great serpent mound in Adams County, Ohio is about a quarter of a mile long, and in the shape of a serpent about to swallow an egg. The Adena and other mound builders buried their dead in a similar fash-

Mound complex, Tennessee
Cahokia Mound complex, Illinois

ion to the Egyptians. The Adena bodies had deliberately flattened skulls, which imitated the Maya custom of flattening the head at birth. Intricately engraved, polished stone tablets from the Adena society have been unearthed, and the mounds of the Hopewell, Natchez, Adena, and Cahokia societies show a remarkable similarity to burial mounds (Cairns) found in England, Scotland, Ireland and parts of continental Europe. In both Egypt and America, the burial mounds were found to contain personal possessions alongside the human remains. Their dogs and stone statues accompanied the Adena, Hopewell, and Natchez dead, along with jars overflowing with pearls and other treasured possessions. In the Natchez society, when their king died all his wives and slaves willingly accompanied him to their death.[274]

Cat-God, ancient funerary vessel, northern Peru.
Scientific American, 1954

In the Cahokia site, near Collinsville, Illinois, there are more than 128 large mounds and evidence of wood posts in circles, "woodhenges", built to form an astronomical calendar for a civilization that flourished and was inhabited from at least 900 to 1100 A.D. The city itself covered six square miles with houses arranged in rows around open plazas. The main agricultural fields were outside the city. In these mounds, human remains as well as personal hammered copper ornaments were found. One artifact was a five-inch long serpent made from a thin sheet of copper.[275] The cat, as a female supernatural deity, has been found in ancient Egypt, carved on a rock face in Wichita, Kansas, engraved on Carthaginian coins dating to the third century B.C. and found along the Arkansas River, both up and downstream from Wichita. A wooden figure of a cat dating to 500 A.D. was also uncovered in Key Marco, Florida.[276]

Key Marco, Florida, Cat of carved wood
Egyptian Cat, Female goddess of Ra the Sun god

CHAPTER 4 MISSIONARIES IN THE AMERICAS

Columbus' 2nd voyage, by de Bry

Before he left Spain on his first voyage to the New World, Columbus was under the assumption that he was traveling to India. He had given the Spanish sovereigns information "concerning the lands of India ruled by a prince called the Grand Can." According to Columbus, the ancestors of the Grand Can "often sent to Rome for learned men who might instruct him in our Holy Faith, and how the Holy Father had never complied, so that many believing in idolatry were lost to the doctrines of perdition (the state of everlasting punishment in Hell)...." Columbus took it upon himself to find and convert these people. In a blatant statement he set down his purpose. "Your highnesses, as Catholic Christians and defenders against the doctrines of 'Mohamet' and all other idolatries, resolve to send me, Christopher Columbus, to these parts of India and to this prince and to his people to learn their disposition and the proper means of converting them to the Christian Faith.... Thus, after expelling the Jews from your domain in the same month of January, Your Highnesses ordered that I should go with a sufficient fleet to this part of India, and for that purpose most graciously elevated me to the title of Don, High Admiral of the Sea and perpetual Viceroy and Governor of all islands and continents that I should discover and gain both now and hereafter in the Ocean Sea, and that my son should succeed me and so on from generation to generation, forever."[277]

It is unknown whether Franciscan monks accompanied Columbus during his first voyage across the Atlantic in 1492. But after the discovery of the Americas, during his second expedition to the West Indies in 1493, two Franciscan missionaries accompanied Columbus from Belgium: Jean de la Deule and Jean de Tisin. Many Franciscans followed them to present-day Latin America and to the West Indies. Most of the missionaries who accompanied the first settlers to America wrote continuously about saving the souls of the "heathen and pagan savages." There were only a few missionaries who bravely championed the cause of the Indians. Among the few who risked their lives and reputations were Friars Bartolomé de Las Casas, Bernardino de Minaya and Bernardino de Sahagun. All three men petitioned the Pope on behalf of the suffering Indians. A missionary, Friar Motolina, made claims similar to those of Las Casas, saying that, "...countless natives were killed in labor at the mines", and furthermore, a Spanish Royal Official, Alonso de Zunta, said that in the Popayánn province, "...the bones of the dead Indians were so thick along the roads that no-one could lose the way."[278]

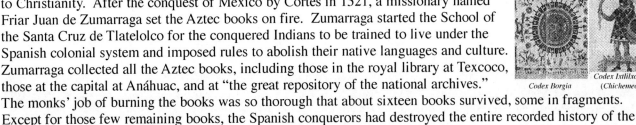

Codex Nahuatl, Mixtec

Codex Madrid   *Codex Aztec*

Codex Borgia   *Codex Ixtlilxochitl (Chichemeca)*

Book burning was undertaken with a fanatical zeal by the missionaries in their attempt to destroy the remaining traces of the Indians' culture and convert the populace to Christianity. After the conquest of Mexico by Cortés in 1521, a missionary named Friar Juan de Zumarraga set the Aztec books on fire. Zumarraga started the School of the Santa Cruz de Tlatelolco for the conquered Indians to be trained to live under the Spanish colonial system and imposed rules to abolish their native languages and culture. Zumarraga collected all the Aztec books, including those in the royal library at Texcoco, those at the capital at Anáhuac, and at "the great repository of the national archives." The monks' job of burning the books was so thorough that about sixteen books survived, some in fragments. Except for those few remaining books, the Spanish conquerors had destroyed the entire recorded history of the Maya and Aztec civilizations.[279]

The Mayan civilization underwent a similar purge at the hands of the missionaries. In 1562, a Franciscan missionary, Diego de Landa, in his zeal to eradicate heathen practices, ordered the mass burning of many of the Mayan manuscripts and books. This happened in the town of Maní, 40 miles from Merida in Yucatan, Mexico. A few manuscripts remained, scattered throughout other areas of the Maya nation. In later years Landa regretted his decision, writing, "We found a large number of books... they contained nothing in which there were not to be seen as superstition and lies of the devil, so we burned them all, which they regretted to an amazing degree and which caused them (Mayans) much affliction." Realizing the Mayan culture was doomed under Spanish rule, Landa wrote for posterity, "It may be that this country holds a secret that up to the present has not been revealed, or which the natives of today cannot tell." Landa, believing the Maya culture was destroyed, recorded in detail the Mayan religious practices, language, social life, chronology and laws. Landa noted his burning of the books destroyed many secrets of the Maya civilization.[280]

Bishop Diego de Landa

In spite of his regrets, Bishop Landa, as a Provincial head in Merida, conducted an inquisition in 1562, having determined that the powers granted to him by the Pope's Papal Bull laws of 1452 and 1493 allowed him the authorization.[281] Landa established his own court in the monastery in Mani and, with the aid of Spanish officials, brought the Indian leaders in to separately face charges. He had with him his official notary, Francisco De Orozco, and commissioned one Spaniard as a prosecutor and another Spaniard to defend the Indians. For three months Landa proceeded with mass arrests and torture of Indians that he seized in the outlying areas. The Indians who repented were sentenced to forcibly stand with idols in their hands and ropes around their necks. Wearing the high conical hat of shame, they had to endure a mass and sermon and then suffer their final punishment of being tied to whipping posts and given a prescribed number of lashes.

The Inquisitor of the Holy Office of this kingdom and his chief assistant, by Guamán Poma, 1600

A Spanish eyewitness, Sebastian Vasquez, observing Landa's inhuman methods of eliminating idolatry in 1562 in the city of Merida, Yucatan, wrote on March 25, 1565, "When the Indians confessed to having so few idols (one, two or three) the friars proceeded to string up many of the Indians, having tied their wrists together with cord, and thus hoisted them from the ground, telling them they must confess all the idols they had, and where they were. The Indians continued saying they had no more... and so the friars ordered great stones attached to their feet, and so they were left to hang for a space, and if they still did not admit to a greater quantity of idols they were flogged as they hung there, and had burning wax splashed on their bodies...."[282]

Three months later, when the inquisition had ended, an official inquiry established that more than 4500 Indians were tortured, 158 had died from the effects of the inquisition, and at least 13 people committed suicide to escape the torture, "...while 18 others, who had disappeared, were thought to have killed themselves. Many more had been left crippled, their shoulder muscles irreparably torn, their hands paralyzed 'like hooks'." Landa had been ordered back to Spain, arriving in October, 1564, to face questions by the Council of the Indies due to his misuse of authority in torturing, flogging, and in other brutalities against the Indians.[283] In May, 1565, in the city of Merida, Yucatan, the Council of the Indies exonerated Landa of the charges against him.[284] After the death of Francisco de Toral,

Spanish Hanging, 1500s, by de Bry

Bishop of the Yucatan, Landa was named the new Bishop, arriving in Campeche, Yucatan, in October, 1573, with thirty handpicked friars. The Indians in the Yucatan immediately lodged complaints to Landa regarding excessive punishments by his predecessors. Landa was forced to abide by new rules imposed by the Pope in Rome. In a regulation written in September, 1570, the Holy Office of the Inquisition granted the Indians freedom from flogging or imprisonment, "...because of their simplicity and lack of capacity, and because many of them have not been well instructed in the faith." The Maya resisted vehemently the attempt by the Spanish to convert them to Christianity. In 1613 Dominican Friar Antonio de Remesal was sent to Guatemala to win over the Mayans. In 1619 he recorded his experiences in a book.[285]

Unlike the Mayans, the Inca nation was without a written language and had no books to be burned. When the Spanish conquistador, Francisco Pizarro, captured the Inca capital of Cuzco in 1533, he proceeded to devastate the countryside and kill all the Inca rulers. The Spaniards put Tupac Amaru, the last Inca king and his family, to death in 1572, ending the Inca civilization. Fortunately, Spanish chroniclers and Inca survivors recorded some of the Incas' past history. Their history was passed down as an oral language. Accounts for recording decimal numbers and a form of writing were kept on knot strings called quipus. These knotted strings, as well as the Inca's musical instruments, believed to be from the devil, were destroyed.[286]

12th Inca ruler, Tupac Cuci Hualpa Huascar in chains 1525-1532 by Guamán Poma

The Pueblo Indians of the American southwest were not spared the cruelty of the missionaries. At Tumacacori, Arizona, the friars drilled the Indians in the rudiments of hygiene and "proper dress", and required them to greet one another with "Hail Mary!"—responding, "Conceived in grace!" Attendance was required at every mass, and the friars kept diligent records of all who went to confession. But they would not allow them to participate in Holy Communion, arguing that they were children who could never grow up. In spite of Friar Geronimo de Mendieta's warning against harsh treatment, the notion of the Indians as childlike was sometimes used to justify brutal punishment, generally by inexperienced friars who grew increasingly frustrated by the unwillingness of Indians to follow their directions. In New Mexico, friars punished the Pueblo Indians in several ways for maintaining their pagan traditions; they whipped, imprisoned and hung them, or forced them to do hard labor. Those who committed sexual infractions were whipped and placed in stocks, or underwent a particularly sadistic punishment by some friars who would punish particularly stubborn men by grabbing the testicles and twisting them until they collapsed. Pedro Acomilla of Taos accused a priest in 1638 of having "twisted his penis so much that it broke in half, leaving him without what is called the head of the member." In 1655, Father Salvador de Guerra whipped a Hopi he found worshipping idols until "he was bathed in blood." Later that day he whipped him a second time, inside the church, after which he poured burning turpentine over his head. Father Guerra told his superiors this was the only way to eradicate idolatry.[287]

The injustice and dehumanization endured by the Indians had its foundation in the medieval wars fought by the Crusaders against the Moslems. This was a war fought in the name of Christianity to keep the Moslems from the gates of Europe. In 1453 the Byzantine Empire fell and the Ottoman Empire occupied Constantinople. This gave the Muslim Turks the power to invade Portugal and Spain. The Christian church issued two doctrines, bringing about immense changes in the treatment and relationship between the Christian and non-Christian countries. These proclamations reverberated throughout the world and were used as an excuse to subjugate and disenfranchise the Indians. In 1452 Pope Nicholas V issued the first law,

Pope Alexander VI
(Borgia) 1492-1503

called *The Bull Romanus Pontifex*. "This law gave King Alfonso of Portugal the power to "invade, search out, capture, vanquish and subdue all Saracens and pagans whatsoever, and all other enemies of Christ wheresoever placed." Pope Nicholas further directed that all the land and possessions of these heathens be taken away and that these peoples be "reduced to perpetual slavery." This first doctrine gave future authorization to legitimize the conquest, removal of, and enslavement of the Indians.

In 1493 two more papal bulls were issued by Pope Alexander VI, including the devastating *Inter Cetra Papal Bull*, stating that "barbarous nations be overthrown and brought to the faith itself." In 1494 the "Treaty of Tordesillas" was initiated by the Pope between the monarchs of Spain and Portugal to divide the New World.[288] The primary objective of the church was to first convert the Indians by peaceful methods and if that failed, by force. This was enforced even after a new pope, Giuliano della Rovere, known as Julius II, became the church head in 1512. Pope Julius II declared at the Fifth Lateran Council that the Indians were the true descendents of Adam and Eve and hence human beings. The pope gave an account as to why the Indians were not mentioned in the Bible. This was due to the Indians having been expelled from the Old World because of the sins of the ancestors of the Babylonians.

A new Pope, Clement VII, asserted on May 8, 1529, his domination over all heathens. The Pope announced his Papal Bull (*Intra Arcana*) to the king (emperor) of Spain, Charles V.

Alexander VI, *Book of Privileges*

Pope Clement VII stated, "We trust that, as long as you are on earth, you will compel and with all zeal cause the barbarian nations to come to the knowledge of God, the maker and founder of all things, not only by edicts and admonitions, but also by force and arms, if needful, in order that their souls may partake of the heavenly kingdom."[289] During the years of 1529 to 1537 the Spanish conquistadors, Pizarro and others, in their search for gold throughout Central and South America, subjected the Indians to inhuman cruelties and slavery.

With the 1534 election of a new head of the Roman Catholic church, Pope Paul III, the church made another attempt to change and rectify the past Papal bull laws, by again recognizing the Indians as human beings so as to attempt a change in their conditions. On June 9, 1537, Pope Paul III announced the Papal bull law, *Sublimis Deus* ("Sublime God"), acknowledging that the Indians are "truly men", and interceded to abolish Indian slavery in any form in the New World by Spain.

Dominican Friar Bartolomé de Las Casas wrote often of the spirituality of the Indians, and appealed on their behalf to the Pope to enact laws to rescue the Indians from their sufferings.[290] In 1524, at age fifty, Las Casas sent thirty well-defined propositions to a council to bring about a fundamental change in the treatment of the natives. Las Casas proposed a *New Law for the Indies*, under Spanish rule. The Spanish King, Charles V, signed two royal decrees on November 20, 1542, and June 4, 1543, endorsing the propositions. The decrees stated, "The Pope derives from Christ authority and power extend-

Pope Paul III

ing over all men, believers or infidels, in matters pertaining to salvation and eternal life... that the Pope is under the solemn obligation to propagate the gospel, and to offer it to all infidels who will not oppose it.... The Pope is obliged to send capable ministers for this work.... The Pope may distribute infidel provinces among Christian princes for this work.... In this distribution should be had in view the instruction, conversion, and interests of the infidels themselves, not the increase of honors, titles, riches and territories of the princes."[291] Las Casas, in his *History of the Indies*, wrote that the principle for establishing the faith in the New World should be the same as that followed when Christ introduced his religion into the entire world. The devil could not have done more mischief than the Spaniards when they subjected the natives to cruelty, "treating them like beasts, and persecuting those especially who applied to the monks for instruction."[292]

The terms "encomienda" (allotment of Land) and "repartimiento" (assessment), were interchangeably used in reference to the process of forcing the Indians to work. In Peru the word *mita* (repartimiento or forced labor) was used to in reference to the work in silver mines. The encomienda system was first used over the conquered Moors of Spain. The Spanish adhered to an old tradition that non-believers taken in could be enslaved. Spain established a set of rules called "Requirement" to identify and register the captives, make payment to Spain, outline the duties for the new slaves, and to ensure that Indians were not taken into slavery against their will. This document, read to the Indians in Spanish, informed them that they were now part of Spain and needed to conform to Spanish rule and accept the Catholic faith. It decreed that if the Indians obstructed Spanish entry into their lands, then the Spaniards were justified in enslaving them. The Requirement gave the conquistadors control over the native populations by requiring the natives to give up their lands as tributes to deserving subjects of the Spanish crown. In addition, the grantee also became owner of any Indians living on the land.

"The Christian trustee (encomendero), granted the use of Indians and land by the Spanish crown." Guamán Poma

The concept of tributes was not new to the natives of South America. The Incas employed the tribute system as a tax to their subjects on agricultural or other goods that went to the Inca hierarchy. Recognizing this, the Spanish decided that the tributes given to the encomendero should only require the natives to offer goods that they were already producing, such as maize, salt, honey, hunted game, cotton clothes, beans and peppers. The Spanish added to this the tributes of human labor to work in the plantations and mines. Until the mid 1500s the encomendero could fix the tributes at whatever amount they desired, which led to shocking abuses of the Indians who were forced to labor in the mines—which were brutally dangerous and often deadly places to work. The native Caribbean population was drastically reduced from 4 million to less than 22,000 due to this kind of exploitation.

The encomienda system was one of the most damaging institutions implemented in the New World by the Spanish colonists. The original intent of the encomienda system was to enable Spain to indoctrinate the Indians in the Catholic faith. Under the Law of Burgos, any encomendero with 50 or more Indians had to educate one boy in reading, writing and religious doctrine, so that he could teach the other Indians these things. The encomendero seized this opportunity to exploit and utilize the Indians to their own ends, forcing the Indians to pay the encomendero a repartimiento (assessment) in return for protection and religious instruction.

The missionaries were under the assumption that the Indians were pagan savages, incapable of living Christian lives without proper direction. The primary task of the encomienda became to look after the welfare of the natives, as well as to educate and teach them about their God. The colonists decided that if the natives were left to their own devices, they would run away and not cooperate with the Spaniards in matters of commerce, which would hurt their trade goals. The encomenderos were responsible for the Indians who were supposedly not granted to the Spaniard for life, but only for two to three years at a time. During their time in service they were to be educated and protected by the encomendero. The Indians were to be paid for their labor and supplied with the necessities to live. Instead, the Indians were forced into a system of exchange that forced them to sell their goods at fixed prices and to buy unnecessary Spanish goods set at much higher prices.

Spain also encouraged the Indians to intermarry with the Spaniards, believing that this would have the effect of changing the Indians' behavior and converting them to Christianity. The rights of the Indians were disregarded due to the importance of their labor to the economy. New Spanish arrivals to the New World realized that it was easier to set up lands and use the encomienda system for Indian labor than for them do to the work. This superior attitude became a permanent part of their society, which still endures today. The system set a precedent for the degradation of the Indian population in the Americas. The encomienda system was never quite extinguished; it merely evolved and took on new forms, like that of American slavery.[293]

In the year 1542, when the number of chattel slaves still ran into the hundreds of thousands, Las Casas wrote the articles (numbers 25 and 27) for the *New Law of the Indies*, titled *Laws of Burgos*, abolishing chattel slavery.

Las Casas fought to bring laws into effect so as, "to prevent the absolute extermination of the natives." The New Laws did, however, give the Spanish the right to explore Indian lands and to live and trade on them without opposition from the Indians, but only as long as the Spanish colonists did not harm the Indians in any way. The Laws also abolished slavery in any form, and placed high monetary penalties on anyone breaking this law. They also forbade use of Indian labor in the mines. The *New Laws of the Indies* stated that, "The Spaniards have no more regard to their salvation than if their souls and bodies died together, and were incapable of eternal rewards or punishments." Christians were given the right to preach, but again, the church held no formal power over the Indians, so they could not force them to convert or take action against them for not believing or abiding by Christian beliefs. A new form of local government was created by the New Laws called audiencias, and it was decided by them that the large encomiendas must be reduced in size and that the creation of new ones should be forbidden. The laws made quite a stir in the Spanish colonies, and caused chaos with the Spanish colonists who had become used to having the Indians at their mercy. The encomenderos were particularly disturbed by the fact that the New Laws forbade Indian slaves, including their use in the mines.[294]

"The administrator of the royal mines punishes the native lords with great cruelty. " by Guamán Poma

The council decided to support the encomienda system as an institution of Spain, with modifications to several common practices, in order to alleviate some of the hardships placed on the Indians. Due to problems that the New Laws were causing in the colonies, the Council of the Indies, which was the body charged with implementing the Laws, recognized that if the legislature wasn't amended, then there would be a state of total anarchy in their colonies in America. The council decided on a fixed, low tribute that eliminated the aspect of the Indians being used for personal services and dictated that punishment for any mistreatment of the Indians by an encomendero would result in deportation back to Spain. The new rules and the decrees signed by the monarchs and the Pope were, however, impossible to enforce. King Charles V of Spain refused to acknowledge Pope Paul's bull, *Sublimis Deus*, and ordered that all copies that arrived in America should be confiscated. Dominican Bernardino de Minaya was imprisoned by his Dominican order for overstepping his authority and voicing his opinion against the *Sublimis Deus*. The Spanish landowners in the New World, as well as being constantly changed by succeeding Spanish kings, also continually circumvented these decrees.[295]

Juan Gines de Sepulveda, a Spanish Cordoban theologian and royal historian, crusaded in favor of the Pope's doctrines during the mid 1500s. He argued, "Heathens and heathenism invited and justified conquest by any method, however ruthless; that the rights of the Papacy and of the Christian monarchs would be periled by allowing any regards of sentiment or humanity to stand in the way of their assertion; and that even the sacred duty of conversion was to be deferred till war and tyranny had obtained the absolute mastery over the natives."[296] In 1551 Sepulveda and Las Casas squared off in a public debate that would decide the future fate on Spain's treatment towards the Indians. Sepulveda had written a book titled, *On the Just Causes of War*. In this book Sepulveda attacked Las Casas' former "laws and constitutions" drawn up in Valladolid, Spain in 1542, by a council of clergy under the influence of Las Casas and sanctioned by the King of Spain.[297] Sepulveda defended his position for armed expeditions against the Indians as justified, according to the rules of the Kings of Spain. He argued that, first of all, the Indians were "barbaric." Next, they were not skilled in the use of written language and the art of government. In addition they were, "completely ignorant, unreasoning, and totally incapable of learning anything but the mechanical arts; that they are sunk in vice, are cruel, and are of such character that, as nature teaches, they are to be governed by the will of others."[298] Sepulveda believed that those in control of the Indians were wiser and superior in both their virtue and learning, and therefore had the right to control those under them.

The administrator of the royal mines punishes the native lords with great cruelty. by Guamán Poma

Sepulveda quoted from Aristotle's philosophy and teachings that, "the fool ought to be slave to the wise."[299] Sepulveda's second argument was that, even though the Indians were unwilling, they must accept Spanish leadership so they could be punished for all the sins and crimes they had committed in the past. This especially alluded to the Indians' idolatry and customs of human sacrifice. Sepulveda contended that all heathens and pagans who did not observe the law given to them by Jesus Christ should be severely punished by the Christian people.

The third argument by Sepulveda was that the Indians should be punished for the injuries and misery they had inflicted upon the innocent with their practice of human sacrifice. The only way to avoid this evil, he claimed, was to subjugate and enslave these barbarians. His fourth argument was that unless the Indians were brought under control it would be impossible to advance and spread the Christian religion. Subjugation of the Indians was necessary to protect the missionaries so "they would not be massacred by either (pagan) rulers or priests."[300]

Sepulveda argued that the Roman Emperor Constantine used his power to close the pagan temples and to forbid the worship of idols under penalty of death, enabling him to bring Christianity to the Roman Empire. Sepulveda further asserted that the Roman pope, Alexander VI, in a decree to the College of Cardinals, declared any armed expedition against the Indians to be just, and gave permission to the Spanish kings to conquer the Indians and add them to the Spanish empire. For this reason Sepulveda declared "that wars undertaken by God's command are just, no one will deny that a war is just that God's vicar, after a mature deliberation and in the exercise of his Pontifical authority, declares to be justified."[301]

Pope Clement VII 1530 crowning as the Holy Emperor, by Hogenbred

Las Casas spoke for five days in 1552, reading his entire manuscript, *In Defense of the Indians*, chapter by chapter. Las Casas proceeded to demolish Sepulveda's book as being a polished, painstaking, persuasive document filled with tricky kinds of arguments to deceive the "thieves, these enemies of the human race, so that they will never come to their senses nor, admitting their crimes, flee to the mercy of God...." If Sepulveda's campaigns against the Indians were lawful, the very name Christian "will be hateful and detestable to all the peoples of the world to whom the word will come of the inhuman crimes that the Spaniards inflict on that unhappy race, so that neither in our lifetime nor in the future will they accept our faith under any condition...."[302]

Las Casas took on this debate and defense of the Indian to wipe these stains from the name of Christianity, allow the spread of the faith to continue and, as Christian doctrine dictates, to defend his sheep from the wolves. Las Casas summed up his preliminary arguments against Sepulveda, pointing out that his defense will contain two main topics. He would first show that Sepulveda and his followers were wrong, in distorting all their arguments against the Indians. Second, this distortion created a greater harm to the Indian souls. "For the Creator of every being has not so despised these people of the New World that he willed them to lack reason and made them like brute animals so that they should be called barbarians, savages, wild men, and brutes, as they (Sepulveda, et.al) think or imagine. On the contrary, they, the Indians, are of such gentleness and decency that they are, more than the other nations of the entire world, supremely fitted and prepared to abandon the worship of idols and to accept, province by province and people by people, the word of God and the preaching of the truth."[303]

Regarding the description of the Indians as barbarians, Las Casas noted that in ancient times the Greeks called the Romans barbarians and vice versa. Las Casas cited the barbarian as one who cared nothing for life in a society, living like a brute animal, eager to fight, and inclined to every kind of savagery. Las Casas stated that the Creator made all men in his image and if mankind were to be considered barbaric, it would follow that God's design had for the most part been ineffective, saying, "There is no room for distinction between Greek and Jew, between the circumcised and the uncircumcised, or between barbarian and Scythian, slave and free man."[304] He also remarked that long before the Spaniards had entered the

From Codex Ixtlilxochitl

New World, the Indians had a great civilization with excellent laws, their own religion and their own customs. "They cultivated friendship and, bound together in common fellowship, lived in popular cities in which they wisely administered the affairs of both peace and war justly and equitably, truly governed by laws that at very many points surpass ours...."[305]

Las Casas cited the book, *History of His Times*, by Paola Giovio, in which the Bishop of Nocera praised the aptitude and capacity of the Indians for educating themselves in the Liberal Arts. Las Casas related how at one time, Caesar Augustus, after he had conquered the world, turned his army against the Spanish people, whom he called barbaric and wild. Las Casas argued that in ancient times Spain itself was a barbaric nation under Roman domination. He reasoned that the Roman Empire, according to Sepulveda's argument, could have enslaved and decimated the Spanish people the same way Sepulveda was now condoning the extinction of the Indians. Las Casas concluded his argument on barbarians by saying, "The Indian race is not that barbaric, nor are they dull-witted or stupid, but they are easy to teach and very talented in learning all the liberal arts, and very ready to accept, honor, and observe the Christian religion and correct their sins... once priests have introduced them to the sacred mysteries and taught them the word of God. They are endowed with excellent conduct... and had political states that were well founded on beneficial laws. Furthermore, they are so skilled in every mechanical art that with every right they should be set ahead of all the nations of the known world on this score, so very beautiful in their skill and artistry are the things this people produces in the grace of its architecture, its painting and its needlework. But Sepulveda despises these mechanical arts..." Las Casas argued that, "Every nation, no matter how barbaric, has the right to defend itself against a more civilized one that wants to conquer it and take away its freedom."[306]

Last rites from *A Brief Telling of the Destruction of the Indians*, 1552

Las Casas replied to Sepulveda's argument that war against the Indians was justified because of their idolatry and human sacrifice. Las Casas argued that anyone outside the Christian religion, "no matter whether they be Jews, Mohammedans, or idolaters, they are in no way subject to the church nor to her members, that is, Christian rulers." Las Casas cited Saint Paul to make his point against using war to effect conversion. "This is my commandment: Love one another as I have loved you... love does no evil... pagans, therefore, must be treated gently and with all charity. Nor should any trace of evil be visible in our actions." Making the point that the Pope's words had been used out of context, Las Casas stated, "The bull of the Roman Pontiff, Paul III, expressly forbids these detestable wars that are waged against the Indians under the pretext of religion. He commands that they be led by the faith, not by the terror of war, but by the word of God and by holy living." Las Casas ended his debate by exhorting that, "The Indians are our brothers, and Christ has given his life for them. Why, then, do we persecute them with such inhuman savagery when they do not deserve such treatment? The past, because it cannot be undone, must be attributed to our weakness, provided that what has been taken unjustly is restored... finally, let all savagery, and apparatus of war, which are better suited to Moslems than Christians, be done away with.... The Indians will embrace the teaching of the gospel as I well know, for they are not stupid or barbarous but have a native sincerity and are simple, moderate, and meek, and finally, such that I do not know whether there is any people readier to receive the gospel."[307] After listening to the arguments of Sepulveda and Las Casas, the commission consulted and debated both points of view. It was determined that the Spanish conquests in the New World were evil, unlawful and unjust. The outcome amounted to no more than a ban on future similar ruthless expeditions against the Indians. Yet the commission voted that the existing conditions of slavery and wars in South America were to continue until the Indians surrendered.[308]

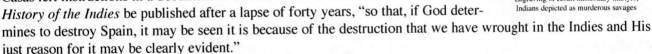

Although Las Casas failed to convert the king of Spain, he managed to attack his conscience. On July 13, 1573, King Philip II of Spain declared the Spanish settlers should only use as much force against the Indians as was necessary, and banned the word conquest. It was replaced with the term "pacification."[309] Las Casas left instructions in a document to be read after his death that his entire *History of the Indies* be published after a lapse of forty years, "so that, if God determines to destroy Spain, it may be seen it is because of the destruction that we have wrought in the Indies and His just reason for it may be clearly evident."

Engraving of Jesuit missionary martyrs; Indians depicted as murderous savages

A younger missionary, Dominican friar Bernardino de Sahagun, sided with the views of Las Casas and became a staunch advocate for the Aztecs. Sahagun spent his lifetime writing the history and customs of their culture. He had to first learn their language, Nahuatl. He learned of the spiritual aspects of the Aztecs, and their world known as the fifth sun. Sahagun compiled, during 1547 to 1569, a twelve volume work called *A General History of the Things of New Spain*. Sahagun wrote about the Aztecs and the history of their rise to power in the valley of Mexico, as well as their sophisticated religious customs and philosophies. He wrote that the Aztecs prophesied of the coming of the first white men and the catastrophic end of their world. He was lambasted as pro-Indian and as a potential subversive. His superiors in the church considered his work so controversial that the publication was buried in the Catholic archives until the nineteenth century.[310]

Before the arrival of the Spanish missionaries, the tribes in California were self sufficient, with an abundance of food growing near the shoreline and plenty of seafood and game animals at their disposal.[311] At Carmel, California, missionary Junipero Serra described this festive, happy scene of several different villages enjoying a

Sunday: "And so they passed Sunday camping on Carmel Beach, divided into countless groups, each with its fire, roasting and eating what they had caught.[312] The Indians followed their own traditions with lots of feasts, ceremonial music and dancing. "Generosity was a way of life."[313]

Father Junipero Serra arrived in California in 1769 with a contingent of soldiers under orders from the Spanish vice regent to pacify and convert the Indians to his god and way of life. Father Junipero Serra, founder and first president of the California missions, developed a fanatical desire for saving souls in imitation of Saint Francis of Assisi, founder of the Franciscan order. Serra was driven by his own private torments and his peculiar search for glory and martyrdom. He constantly carried with him a heavy chain, with which he would repeatedly flagellate himself before assemblies of awestruck Indians. His fellow missionary wrote, "He beat himself so unmercifully, that all the audience shuddered and wept."[314] Serra would stand upon the pulpit with the image of the crucified Christ in one hand, he would then take a heavy stone in the other and would strike himself again and again on the chest with such ferocity that the Indians thought he would fall dead before their very eyes. On other occasions, he would take a burning candle with four wicks, open the bosom of his habit and would then hold it against his naked chest.

Father Junipero Serra

His plan was to set up his version of an ideal Christian community for the Indians. His purpose was to bring the Indians into the missions for an apprenticeship, where under the guidance of the Franciscan fathers they would be taught to pray, eat with silverware, wear clothes, and become farmers, weavers, cattle ranchers and provide other by-products for Spanish society. In this ideal society the Indians would live according to the Catholic Church, with marriages and baptisms conducted and controlled only by the church.

Father Martín de Ayala flagellates himself in the presence of Diego Beltrán de Caysedo. by Guamán Poma

The Indians entered these missions for at least ten years of forced apprenticeship. As soon as they accepted baptism, their freedom ended. Physical punishment such as whipping, placing in stocks, and attaching shackles and chains were used as pressure tactics to force the Indians to follow the doctrines of the church. They were forced to listen to all the masses and sermons that were held in Latin. The young, unmarried Indian women were locked up in prison-like buildings to learn spinning and weaving and similar occupations. They were led out of these dungeon residences only two or three times a day in order to attend church and allow themselves a breath of fresh air.[315] This kept them away from the Indian men but did not keep the Spanish soldiers away, who used the women as prostitutes and paid them with food.[316] There were over a thousand Indians in each mission, with a detachment of soldiers on hand to preserve order and prevent anyone from trying to escape. The Indians were forced to learn blacksmithing, tile making and brick building, as well as other trades

Mother Maria Agreda preaches to Indians in the southwest, 1631 woodcut

needed for building and laying the thousands of adobe bricks for the mission buildings. The missions, according to one visitor, began to resemble slave plantations. "We declare with pain that the resemblance (to slave colonies in Santo Domingo) is so exact, that we saw both the men and the women loaded with irons, while others had a log of wood on their legs; and even the noise of the lash might have assailed our ears as that mode of punishment is equally admitted, although it is employed with little severity.... The day is divided into seven hours of work and two of prayer, but four or five on Sundays and feast days, which are wholly devoted to rest and religious worship. Corporal punishments are inflicted on any of the Indians of both sexes who neglect their pious exercise, and many faults, which in Europe are wholly left to divine justice, are here punished with irons or the log. In short, to complete the parallel with the religious communities, from the moment a neophyte is baptized, he seems to have taken an eternal vow. If he runs away and returns to his relations among the independent villages, he is summoned three times, and should he still refuse to come back, they apply to the authority of the governor, who sends a party of soldiers to tear him from the bosom of his family, and deliver him to the missions, where he is condemned to a certain number of lashes."[317]

Paiute baptism in Utah, 1850s

These living conditions and devastating epidemics contributed to a huge rise in the death rate among the Indians. The monks blamed themselves for all the unfortunate incidents, claiming that God was punishing the monks for their sins. Following Serra's example, the monks whipped themselves—and whipped the Indians even harder, having conceived a poisonous hatred towards the Indians because of their resistance to conversion. This period of missionary zeal in California lasted for over sixty years, until 1834. The damage that the Spanish mis-

66

sionaries inflicted upon the Indians of the area was irrevocable, affecting those who survived it for the rest of their lives. Evidence of the extent to which the population was decimated was discovered in the large burial pits beside the mission buildings.[318]

The Missionary, by
Frederic Remington, 1890s

In 1834 Governor Jose Figueroa of California, a mestizo of Aztec descent, was given the task, against his wishes, of turning each of the missions into an Indian village (Pueblo). Instead, the missions were plundered of their livestock and powerful Mexican families in California took tools, supplies and the best lands. Whatever Indians were left from the missions were forced to work as house servants or agricultural laborers without any pay except for food and possibly shelter. The fortunate Indians that survived and did not give in to alcohol and disease converted and intermarried into the Hispanic culture.[319]

In 1850 Adam Johnston, the first Indian agent in California, reported the story of an old man at the Mission Delores, who said, "I am very sad; my people were once around me like the sands of the shore—many, many. They have gone to the mountains—I do not complain; the antelope falls with the arrow. I had a son—I loved him. When the pale-faces came he went away; I know not where he is. I am a Christian Indian; I am all that is left of my people. I am all alone."[320]

Henry Benjamin Whipple (1822-1901), an Episcopal Bishop of Minnesota, attempted missionary work that he believed to be in the best interest of the Sioux, as he fostered the removal of the Sioux Indians from their homeland in the Black Hills in order to make room for white settlers. Whipple's purpose was to reduce the amount of land the Indians used for hunting purposes so they would be forced to abandon hunting in favor of farming the land. Whipple envisioned that these new, white settlers would be role models as neighbors of the now peaceful Indians.[321]

Bishop Henry
Whipple

In 1784 Benjamin Franklin, in an article titled *Remarks Concerning the Savages of North America*, had said, "Savages we call them, because their manners differ from ours, which we think of perfection of civility; they think the same of theirs."[322] Franklin described the civility of the missionaries in an example of a Swedish minister's sermon to an assembly of chiefs of the Susquehanna Indians. The minister proceeded with a sermon on the historical facts upon which the Christian religion was founded. The minister described Adam and Eve, the evil of eating the first apple from the Garden of Eden, the coming of Christ to repair the mischief, his miracles and suffering, etc. When he had finished, an Indian orator stood up to thank him. "What you have told us", says he, "is all very good. It is indeed bad to eat apples. It is better to make them all into cider." The Indians thanked the minister for being so kind as to come "so far and tell us these things you have heard from your mothers. In return I will tell you some of those we have heard from ours." The Indian then told the story of how in ancient times their ancestors subsisted on only the flesh of animals. During one hunt, two young hunters had killed a deer. As they were about to broil it over a fire to satisfy their hunger, they beheld a beautiful young woman that had descended from the clouds. They presented this spiritual woman with the best part of the deer. She was pleased with the taste of it and told them that their kindness would be rewarded. The young woman told them to return to the same place "after thirteen moons, and you shall find something that will be of great benefit in nourishing you and your children to the latest generations." They did so, and, to their surprise, found plants they had never seen before; but which, from that ancient time, have been constantly cultivated among them, to their great advantage. Where her right hand had touched the ground, they found maize; where her left hand had touched it, they found kidney beans; and where her backside had sat on it, they found tobacco. The good missionary, disgusted with this idle tale, said, "what I delivered to you was sacred truths; but what you tell me is mere fable, fiction and falsehood." The Indian, offended, replied, "My brother, it seems your friends have not done you justice in your education; they have not well instructed you in the rules of common civility. You saw that we, who understand and practice those rules, believed all your stories; why do you refuse to believe ours?"[323]

Red Jacket with
George Washington Medal

Red Jacket addresses Iroquois, 1752

In 1805 a missionary, Reverend Cram, refused to shake Seneca Chief Red Jacket's hand, saying, "There is no fellowship between the religion of God and the devil." Red Jacket replied, "Brother, our seats were once large and yours were very small; you have now become a great people and we have scarcely the place to spread our blankets and you have got our country, but are not satisfied; you want to force your religion upon us.... We understand that your religion is written in a book; if it was intended for us as well as you, why has not the Great Spirit given it to us and not only to you?... We only

67

know what you tell us about it; how shall we know when to believe, being so often deceived by the white people? Brother, you say there is only but one way to worship and serve the great spirit; if there is but one religion, why do you white people differ about it? Why do you not all agree as you all read the same book?" Red Jacket was named from the red coat given to him by the British as support in the wars against the colonies. A great orator, he said, "Our forefathers crossed the Great Water and landed on this island (Turtle Island). Their numbers were small. We took pity on them, and they sat down among us. We gave them corn and meat. They gave us poison in return."[324]

By the mid 1800s the European missionaries were destined to carry their brand of civilization into areas then occupied as what they called "wild inhabitants" of the prairies and forests. Others reasoned that no Christian could believe that God had created Indians and Negroes merely to be persecuted and exterminated by the white man. It follows that a wrong course has been pursued in the intercourse between the two. The white man refused to admit for a moment that his colored brother could ever be his equal. He drove him away instead of pressing him to his bosom. In the 1840s, a small minority recognized the racial problem and appealed to deaf ears for tolerance. "Remove this crying evil. Let the whites banish their disgraceful antipathy to the colored races; place them in society, and under the protection of the law as equals, not dependents and they will, in a real civilization, forget blood revenge and cease to be savages."

This "noble savage" has been held up by poets and orators as the very perfect ideal of man in what is strangely called his natural state. The year 1868 brought a futile attempt by a woman writer, Lydia Maria Child, to plead for the plight of the Indians. In *An Appeal for the Indians*, she wrote:

> We Americans came upon the stage when the world had advanced so far in civilization that our record ought to be much cleaner than it is. The plain truth is, our relations with the red and black members of the human family have been one almost unvaried history of violence and fraud. Our ancestors, whether Catholics or Puritans, were accustomed to regard heathen tribes as Philistines, whom "the Lord's people" were commissioned to exterminate root and branch, or to hold them as bondsmen and bondswomen.[325]

Kateri Tekakwitha, Indian convert to Christianity

The early settlers of this country, with the exception of a few like William Penn, treated the Indian tribes as inferior beings. Benevolent individuals tried, from time to time, to ameliorate this state of things; but their efforts availed little because the spirit of pride and violence pervaded all the laws, all the customs, and all the churches. Father La Jeune, a French missionary during the mid 1600s, labored with the Indians in Canada and found them equal if not greater in abilities than the Europeans. Despite the fact that he degrades them by calling them savages, Father La Jeune writes, "In point of intellect, the American red-man could be placed in a high rank. I can well compare them to some of our own (French) villagers who are left without instruction. I have scarcely seen any person who has come from France to this country who does not acknowledge that the savages have more intellect or capacity than most of our peasantry."[326] The English utilized a similar method as the Spanish and other conquerors to degrade, demoralize, and colonize, and to make a non-person out of the Indians. It started with the employment of simple words and phrases, such as "pagan society", and "heathen", then progressed to

Algonquin couple, drawn by a member of Samuel de Champlain's expedition in 1613 with use of the term "savages"

words in our history books such as "Indian menace", "Indian peril", "Savage barrier", etc. It was also used against the Irish and other groups who didn't share the same religious beliefs as the English.[327] It is worth noting that the English at one time lived in separate tribal kingdoms, hunting wild animals, raising herds of cattle and wearing clothing of animal skins. The inhabitants lived in small wicker huts covered with straw.[328] The very name Britain derives from an ancient word, "signifying part-colored; because the inhabitants painted their bodies with various pigments", similar to the Indians they first met in America.[329] In 1496 King Henry VII of England followed his own proclamation with a commission to John Cabot. This was issued to, "...conquer, occupy and possess the lands of 'heathens and infidels'."[330]

Depiction of Indians as savages

The technique intended to degrade and slowly disembody the Indian from a human being into a savage, barbarian, heathen, and pagan, relates back to the treatment to which Europeans subjected their own people under the feudal system.[331] In 1645, Roger Williams, an early advocate for religious tolerance and Indian land rights, denounced the distinctions being made between the English and Indians, Protestantism and Catholicism, and the use of the word heathen.[332]   The Greeks, who used this word for anyone they considered inferior or uncivilized, invented the word barbarian. Strangely, each succeeding civilization considered its own society superior and their neighbors as barbaric. With the Protestant Reformation, Protestant Germans used these same words against the Turkish governments' forcing its Muslim religion upon their conquests in Eastern Europe. The words barbaric, heathen and pagan were considered proper words to be used against any culture that was different. It included not only their religion but also an entire people.[333]

A Class for Mohawk Children
Published in London, 1786

In 1646, the apostle Elliot began to labor as a Christian missionary among the Indians in towns around Boston. Touchingly, the Indians asked him, "The English have been among us twenty-six years. If they thought the knowledge of their god so important, why did they not teach it to us sooner? If they had done so, we might have known much of god by this time, and many sins might have been prevented."[334]   By the late 1600s the English traders, followed by missionaries, were all across the east coast of America. The Cherokees' was a typical example of a tribes' contact with European society. The traders intermarried with the Cherokees and the missionaries followed to convert the Indians with the federal government's approval. Missionaries were supplied by the government with the necessary tools and given livestock to start the Cherokees off on their new, more civilized culture. The churches most steadfast about converting the Cherokees to Christianity were the Presbyterian, Baptist, Methodist and the Society of United Brethren of Moravians. The Moravians were German immigrants who established the first mission in Cherokee territory. There were two separate bands of Cherokees that were fierce rivals: one for the missions and one tribe opposing.[335]

Walter Posey, a sympathetic Presbyterian minister among the Cherokees, related a prophecy that the tribe was given. They were told that a white hairy man would appear. He would have gifts that they were not to touch. These were the burning drink, the black book and the cross (religion). With the Bible in one hand and a bottle of alcohol in the other, many missionaries approached the Nations. As Posey noted, "Distilling and selling was a respectable home industry conducted by laymen and sometimes by clergy."[336]

The first school to convert Indians to Christianity was established in 1568 by the Spanish Jesuit missionaries in Havana, Cuba.[337]   As there were very little original natives left on the island, the Indians from Florida were sent to Cuba for schooling. In the 1700s Reverend Eleazer Wheelock, with the backing of the English colony, conceived of the idea of a boarding school to remove the Indian children from the influence of their parents, language and culture. The purpose of the mission

Peter Jones, Ojibway
converted missionary
1845

schools, besides conversion to Christianity, was to train Indian teachers and preachers to go back to their communities and give the Indians skills that fit into a white society. The girls were taught sewing and other housekeeping chores, while the boys received instruction in farming, blacksmithing, etc. Samsom Occom, a Mohegan Indian, attended the Reverend Eleazer Wheelock's school and converted to Christianity, graduating as a Presbyterian minister and teacher to his people.

Hopi school children (Arizona), European clothed

Occom wrote a short autobiography of his life, recalling his past. "I was born a heathen and brought up in heathenism, till I was between 16 & 17 years of age, at a place called Mohegan, in New London, Connecticut, in New England. My parents 'livd' a wandering life, for did all the Indians at Mohegan, they chiefly depended upon hunting, fishing and fowling for their living and had no connection with the English, excepting to traffic with them in their small trifles; and they strictly maintained and followed their heathenish ways, customs and religion, though there was some preaching among them…."[338]

In 1800, the Brainerd Mission in Tennessee, under Abraham Steiner, became the first Moravian Indian mission established to serve as an example to all the Cherokees, "of the European approach to land use, one that stressed plow cultivation and the raising of livestock." The mission also taught the Cherokees how to build and maintain gristmills and dams. The federal government aided in the program of "agrarian reform" by sending missionaries and providing them with supplies. Congress supplied the funds to the Cherokees for livestock, farming implements and other supplies. In 1819 President James Monroe praised the work of the missionaries and on March 3, 1819, ratified a "Civilization Bill", an "Act making provision for the civilization of the Indian tribes adjoining the frontier settlements." This act was to give Federal funds to the missionaries to enable them to increase their schooling of Indian children in order to adapt them into white society.[339]   That same year President Monroe, accompanied by General and Mrs. Edmund P. Gaines, came to inspect a school he had approved two years earlier.

Monroe not only found much to praise, but recommended the construction of "a good two story house, with brick or stone chimneys, glass windows, etc.... at the public expense, for use as a girls' school."[340]

Indian Mission school

In 1787 after the Revolutionary War, missionary societies appeared such as "The Society of the United Brethren for Propagating the Gospel among the Heathen." In 1802 the American Board of Commissioners of Foreign Missions was formed. In 1817 the United Foreign Missionary Society proclaimed a similar goal. With the end of the War of 1812, a spirit of nationalism emerged in the U.S. with a new determination to send out missionaries to all the Indian tribes and to establish schools to convert the Indians and enforce the doctrine of "Manifest Destiny." Additional organizations joined the previous missionary societies, all intent on converting the Indians to their religion. The Baptists, in 1814, changed their constitution to have their organization use "the energies of the whole denomination in one sacred effort for sending the glad tidings of Salvation to the heathen, and to nations destitute of pure Gospel light."[341] This new phase of conversion propagandized the lie that the Indian was and would always remain a savage unless he became "a carbon copy of a good white man."[342] According to the missionaries, the Indian would never be accepted on equal terms unless they became fully Christianized and accepted the white man's way of life. A Methodist missionary wrote, "In the school and in the field as well as in the kitchen, our aim was to teach the Indians to live like white people." Another well known Sioux missionary, Stephen Riggs, wrote in 1846, "As tribes and nations, the Indians must perish and live only as men."[343]

Navajo Chief Black Horse shakes hands with missionary, circa 1890

The missionaries also acted as agents for the U.S. government. In 1817 the federal government signed the Treaty of Turkey Town, offering land in Arkansas to the Cherokees for their land in the east. The land was not theirs to give, as the Osage tribe mostly occupied it. In 1818, Tollunteeskee (Ata lunti ski), principal chief of the Arkansas Cherokee, requested from the American Board of Foreign Missions (ABFM) a mission for his nation in the west. They established the Dwight Mission in the spring of 1821 with Cephas Washburn and his assistant, Reverend Alfred Finney. The two immediately helped instigate a war between the Osage and Cherokees. Besides missionary work, Washburn relayed government instructions and arranged treaty parties. Once the Cherokees were removed to the Oklahoma territory his missionary work ended.[344] In the 1840s many missionaries opposed the Cherokees' removal to Oklahoma. They had succeeded in converting many Cherokees into the white man's culture. Ministers accompanied the Cherokees and endured the agony of their journey. As they were gathering to face this awful journey, a religious revival swept through the camps. The records of this journey (called the "Trail of Tears") show that along the way the churches were allowed to minister to the Cherokees to express their faith.[345]

Reverend Henry H. Spaulding

By 1887, with the backing of the federal government, the missionaries were in every area in the United States, attempting to indoctrinate the Indians to their faith and change their way of life. In 1887 the head of the Indian education program issued this statement. "Education cuts the cord that binds Indians to a Pagan life, places the Bible in their hands, substitutes the true God for the false one, Christianity in place of idolatry... cleanliness in place of filth, industry in place of idleness."[346]

The Nez Percé true name, Nimiipuu, means "real people." They orally recorded many events of the coming of the white man. When Lewis and Clark came to their land in 1805, sick and desperate for food, Chief Twisted Hair welcomed them as friends, fed them and guided them westward. In the 1830's, the Reverend Henry H. Spaulding came to the area to preach the gospel to the Nez Percé. The impact on the Nez Percé by the white man and the missionaries ended in their downfall. The Nez Percé, in their oral history called "Advent of the Missionaries", tell of, "Injums sitting on rocks all around. Injums sitting on ground inside rock circle. Lots Injums! Preacherman Spaulding stand about here. Maybe on platform and talk. Spaulding call to Injums. 'Look up. See Jesus. See Jesus up there!' One hand pointing Injums to Jesus: other hand stealing Injums land! That religion not good for Injum... I remember very well when the Spauldings came to Clearwater. The missionaries brought with them the Good Book, which told our people how to live and what to believe, that they might reach the land of a better life after death. A book that told all this to the Nez Percé. Changing their lives to a better way of living; a better spirit life. But the missionaries had something behind him, which came with him to the Nez Percés. Behind him was the whiskey bottle along with his Good Book. We know what the bottle has done. It would have been better had the Good Book and the whiskey bottle been kept from the Nez Percé."[347]

Old Chief Joseph's graveside

70

CHAPTERS 5 SLAVERY, MIXED-BLOODS, AND THEIR EFFECTS ON THE INDIAN

Trading in slaves was popular on the North American continent long before the white man and the fur trader became involved. The abduction of women for concubines is no doubt the oldest form of human bondage. The Indians themselves had always been traders of slaves. The majority of slaves were abducted in war and taken back to the victor's lands to become workers or used as barter with neighboring tribes. History records slave trading involving the Maya, Inca and Aztec, as well as among the North American tribes. The Blackfeet raided the Assiniboin; the Assiniboin raided the Cree, and so on. Slave trading among eastern tribes, such as the Huron and the Ottawa, was also common.

The Iroquois were known middlemen in the slave traffic between the eastern and western Indians, bringing back as many as three or four hundred slaves from Ohio. When Ohio was "the West", the Pawnee were known to have frequently sold Apache women and children to the French on the Missouri and Platte rivers. Possibly from this business, the French continued to call all Indian slaves "Panis" (Pawnee). It was a "Panis" woman who saved Alexander Henry the Elder from a massacre at Michilimackinac. The slave trade reached far and wide. The Illinois had slaves from the east coast and Florida, and the Great Lakes tribes owned Eskimo slaves. A Jesuit priest, Father Gulon, claimed while in China he had seen a slave woman he recognized as a Huron he had met while in Canada.

Africans and Indians interacting as Europeans observe, 18th century French engraving

According to Clark Wissler, a historian on Indians, none surpassed the Indians of the Pacific coast. He estimates that one third of the Indian population between British Columbia and Alaska were slaves of the lowest condition. According to Wissler, "To show how wealthy he was, the Tlingit owner of slaves would club some of them to death in public; in other words, he was rich enough to destroy property." Contrary to most other tribes, those of the northwest did not condone sexual relations with slaves.[348]

The Portuguese and the Spanish introduced slavery over a century before the English brought the first Africans to Virginia in 1619. After arriving in the Americas, Europeans turned first to Indians as a source of forced labor. They introduced African slaves to the region only after calculating the difficulty of coercing large numbers of Indians into their labor systems. The first black slaves were sent to America in 1508 to the island of Hispaniola. The black slave trade would not end until 1888 in Brazil. It is estimated that ten million black slaves were shipped to America during this period. Africans who fled from slavery frequently mixed with Indians to avoid being captured. Indians who escaped from slavery could evade the colonists through their knowledge of the surrounding areas, and some of them returned to help free enslaved Africans. In America it was not until 1620 that Indian slavery was completely replaced with African slavery. Along the Brazil-Paraguay border, Indian slavery endured until the 1750s.[349]

The European slave traders joined a well-established slave trade that had begun in the eighth century with West Africans selling slaves to Mediterranean traders. The small but continuous traffic in slaves, led by the Portuguese, exploded in the fifteenth century when the Portuguese applied slavery to the cultivation of sugar cane, first in their Atlantic island colonies and then in Latin America. The Spanish quickly followed, to be succeeded in the seventeenth century by the Dutch and in the eighteenth century by the English.

Spanish work slaves in the sugar plantations in Hispaniola
Engraving by Theodor de Bry

In 1404, Spanish explorers discovered the Canary Islands. They began to colonize the islands and enslave its people. Spain attempted to end this forced slavery in its colonies as early as 1435. With the assistance of the Catholic Church and the Popes, a plan was put into action fifty-seven years before Columbus landed in America. In 1435 Pope Eugene IV wrote to Bishop Ferdinand of Lanzarote in his Papal Bull, *Sicut Dudum*, "They have deprived the natives of their property or turned it to their own use, and have subjected some of the inhabitants of said islands to perpetual slavery, sold them to other persons and committed other various illicit and evil deeds against them.... We order and command all and each of the faithful of each sex that, within the space of fifteen days of the publication of these letters in the place where they live, that they restore to their earlier liberty all and each person of either sex who were once residents of said Canary Islands... who have been made subject to slavery. These people are to be totally and perpetually free and are to be let go without the exaction or reception of any money." The faithful who did not obey would be excommunicated.[350]

"They threw into those holes all the Indians they could capture of every age and kind.... Pregnant and confined women, children, old men left stuck on the stakes, until the pits were filled.... The rest they killed with lances and daggers and threw them to the war dogs who tore them up and devoured them."
by Las Casas
Engraving by Theodor de Bry, 1595

When the Spaniards arrived in the New World it did not take long before they were abducting Indian women—at first as their mistresses, and later, to work the mines and plantations. Expeditions of discovery were often nothing more than quests for more slaves. It was not long until there existed a fully-fledged trade in Indian slaves. Columbus, a slave trader himself, sent four ships loaded with Indian slaves to Spain in 1492. Upon his return to Spain, after his second trip to America, Columbus offered the Spanish Monarchs a group of Indian slaves, contravening his Queen's explicit prohibition of enslavement. Queen Isabella, showing great displeasure, ordered their freedom and their return to Hispaniola. Queen Isabella reprimanded Columbus, saying, "Who gave you the authority to make slaves of my subjects?"[351]

Eric Williams, in his *History of the Caribbean*, writes that seventeen Christian blacks were first brought to the Caribbean, and most of them worked in the mines. Due to the decline in the Indian population, Ferdinand, King of Spain, commented that he "...needed a hundred more so that 'all of these be getting gold for me.'" Many officials, religious and individuals, requested the importation of black slaves, even those from Africa. In 1518, Licenciado Zuazo expressed his concern in a letter about the decline of the Indian population: "...that of a million one hundred and thirty thousand at the beginning, there were then remaining eleven thousand and that in three or four more years there would be none." Another official, Gil Gonzalez Davila, blamed the Indian decline on the colonists for not taking suitable care of them. He blamed them "...first because of being delicate people... [who] suffered from a change of place and secondly, because the vecinos, being uncertain how long these Indians would be at their disposal, did not look after them properly." The Dominicans, along with others, realized that the Indians could not survive the labor and harsh conditions. Zuazo stated that his experience with Africans had taught him that they could work harder.[352]

Las Casas had initially requested that black slaves be used to replace the Indians, and was blamed as having promoted the black slave trade in order to rescue the Indians. Gustavo Gutierrez, in his book, *Las Casas: In Search of the Poor Jesus Christ*, depicted Las Casas as belonging to an age that accepted slavery. In 1516, Las Casas, in his *Memorial de Remedios*, asked the king "...to maintain in the mines of the communities that he, Bartolomé, is proposing 'some twenty blacks or other slaves'...meaning those slaves in Spain who were Christian." In 1531, however, he requested a license from the king to import four hundred blacks from Africa to serve in Chiapas, where he served as bishop from 1544 to 1547.[353] Las Casas had a change of heart shortly thereafter, in 1543. On a return trip from Spain, Las Casas stayed in Lisbon. The injustices of African slavery confronted Las

Slaves mining gold for the Spanish, by de Bry, 1595

Casas; he began to change his mind and regret his previous requests. Gutierrez writes that "...Bartolomé regrets what he had written years before, 'oblivious' he says, 'of the injustice with which the Portuguese take them and make them slaves.'" He began to rewrite his *Historia de Las Indias* to include the slave trade. In it, he wrote, "After he found out, he would not have proposed it for all the world because blacks were enslaved unjustly, tyrannically, right from the start, exactly as the Indians had been."

Las Casas, to whom Emperor Charles V gave the title "Protector of the Indians", was thought by many to be a man ahead of his time. He was also part of an unjust prevailing system, which at that time was accepted socially and justified philosophically and theologically. In short, he was a product of his times.

In 1538, Pope Paul III forbade all Indian enslavement. Years later, with the recommendation of Friar Bartolomé de las Casas, Charles V enacted "Leyes Nueves" (New Laws), with a formal title of *Laws of Burgos*, that recognized the Indians as human beings, entitled to the protection of the Crown with the rights and duties of all others protected. This, at least on paper, did away with legal slavery. Those intending to profit from slavery, however, ignored the laws.[354]

The trappers and traders made use of a long-standing business, which no doubt they had heard of as a money-making scheme as far away as France. The Indians themselves had been accustomed to trading in slaves, so it was more than likely accepted by them as a way of life. The French *coureurs des bois* were the first of the traders to partake in the slave trade in America. In 1788, John Askin, a respected businessman whose job it was to forward supplies and liquor from Fort Michilimackinac, the great depot of the North West Company, to posts in the Interior, wrote to Monsieur Beausoleille in Grand Portage that he was sending a "bark" (canoe) with goods, an officer and several soldiers to pass the summer with him at the Portage. A postscript to his letter read, " I need two pretty slave girls from 9 to 16 years old, have the goodness to ask the gentlemen (at the Portage) to procure two for me." Mention of the slave trade in journals of explorers, trappers, and traders is not common, however, it does exist. The *coureurs des bois*—fur trappers and traders who spent months or years at a time in the woods, trapping animals for their pelts—were scattered over the eastern and midwestern parts of Canada

Kutenai Indian Maiden

and much of what is now the United States. Because they were on good terms with the natives and were widely distributed, they had easy access to the slave market, which already existed. Some slaves procured by the "coureurs des bois" were sold to interior posts to be used however they might be needed, for mistresses of the officers and frontiersmen, and also for domestic purposes. The Mackinac baptism records mention many references to Indian slaves: "Marie, born a slave of Sieur Chevalier", "Marianne, about 20 years old, now the lawful wife of Jean Baptiste, formerly a slave." The slave pool was continuously added to by French troops who took captives while fighting on the Indian frontier. In 1745 the Royal Council sanctioned Indian slavery. Before that, by a royal edict in 1709, Canada also sanctioned slavery among natives. Even the French missionaries owned slaves, usually obtained as gifts from slave traders for the purpose of saving their "heathen souls." The French came to the Americas for wealth and power, but their methods were different. They did not seek to conquer the regions they explored and claimed. The French, unlike the Spaniards, were mild in their treatment of slaves. They considered their women slaves as goods for trade. With the influx of white women, the buying and selling of women for sex became less common.

There was less sexual involvement between the English colonists and their Indian slaves. Neither the Cavaliers nor the Puritans were completely insensitive to the charms of Indian girls. The New England soldiers even selected the healthiest and most beautiful women from the slave pool for themselves, before sending the rest to Europe. The capture,

"The Trapper's Bride" by Alfred Jacob Miller, 1850

open purchase and trade in Indian women did not appear to be as important to the English as it had been with the Spaniards and French.

In 1798, David Thompson wrote on his journey home that his baggage consisted of, "furs of wolves and foxes, with meal and corn; and two Sioux women which the Mandans had taken prisoners and sold to the men, who, when they arrived at the trading house, would sell them to some other Canadians." In spite of Thompson's reputation for having a strong moral sense, he appeared to have a blind spot where the selling and buying of slave women was concerned. Contrary to Edwin Thompson Denig's statement that "no system of concubinage was tolerated" at the Hudson Bay Company posts, evidence proves otherwise.

Pierre Raddison, in 1668–69, founded the Hudson Bay Company as a result of the exploration in the region. It was given an English charter in 1670, which conferred on them a trading monopoly as well as virtual sovereign rights in the region specified, as that drained by rivers flowing into Hudson Bay. This company initially started in Eastern Canada and the United States. In early operations of the Hudson Bay, the business of trading Indian women was important enough to draw attention of tribes from the distant western plains. The Blackfeet sold slaves they had taken in raids to the Cree and Assiniboin, who in turn sold

"The Penobscot (Indian) Belle." Engraved 1849 by F. Halpin from a daguerreotype

them to the Hudson Bay Company. At York they were traded along with beaver pelts and buffalo robes to the factories of "the Honorable Company."

Samuel Hearne, who was known to have taken many Indian women in trade for himself while often complaining of the price he had to pay, lectured his men piously on the impropriety, not to mention the dangers, of

Englishmen having intercourse with the daughters of the country. According to Hearne, Governor Moses Norton maintained a harem of native girls—"five of the finest he could select." While the Hudson Bay people tried to keep the stories of slave trade quiet, the North West Company did not, and left little in doubt that their slave trade was active. Archibald Norman McLeod, the Northwestern autocrat, routinely mentions in his following transaction, "I gave the Chef de Canard's widow to the amount of 28 plus, and took the slave woman, whom next fall I shall sell for a good price to one of the men." At Rainy Lake, Hugh Raries wrote of an Indian hunter with an unusual name—the Devil. He wrote, "...the Devil set off. I gave him a keg of rum, and a few goods, with 45 plus that he owed me for his daughter. Jourdain arrived from the Long Sault with 2300 plus. On his arrival I gave him the Devil's daughter for 500 lb. Grand Portage currency."

Indian woman
by Karl Moon, 1919

In the Department of Athabasca, Canada, the most remote, loneliest and richest of the North West Company preserves, the traffic in slave girls was carried on openly. James McKenzie, at Fort Chipeway, seized the wife of one of his Indians in payment for a debt. He comments in his fort journal, "Two advantages may be reaped from this affair; the first is that it will assist to discharge the debts of a man unable to do it by any other means... the second in that it may be the means of thickling (sic) some lecherous miser to part with some of his hoard. I therefore kept the woman to be disposed of in the season when the Peace River bucks look out for women in the month of May...." When the Indians, whose women McKenzie stole, tired of his actions and rebelled, McKenzie told them, "We would do as we thought proper, for it was not their business to prescribe rules for us." He often threatened to chop off the heads of those who rebelled.

According to Philip Turner, the Northwesterners and Canadians on the Bay were very much disliked by the Indians because of their thievery of Indian women. Turner records that the Northwesterners received, "from five hundred to two thousand livres", and if the father or husband of any of them resist, the only satisfaction they get is a beating." As the Northwesterners' trade pushed further west toward the Rockies they, as had the Spaniards before them, soon found in the wild Plains Indians a new source of women for the slave trade. There existed an active slave trade among the Cree, Assiniboin, Crow, Mandan, Blackfeet, Apache and Navajo, and the Northwesterners were prepared to purchase them. The highly respected John (the Priest) McDonnell notes all too casually, "Tranquille bought a slave women—i.e., taken in war—for two horses and 20 pluez of goods." Alexander Henry the Younger reports that, "The Crows had a handsome slave girl, about 12 years of age, who was offered to us for a gun, 100 balls, and enough powder to fire them; but those rascally Big Bellies would not allow us to purchase her, saying they wanted her for themselves."

In reference to the Blackfeet and the slave trade, there is mention of some of the Indian men having many wives who were offered to the whites. It was possible that these "wives" were actually slaves, not wives at all, and only seen in that light by Europeans who were not aware of the extent of the slave trade. New Mexico's early slave trade at Taos, in 1761, involving Comanche, Apache, and Navajo women, became a very profitable business. Any surplus slaves were taken to Chihuahua for trade with the trading caravans that journeyed there each spring.

In 1820 in America's southwestern region, the commodities most wanted by the Spanish traders were horses and young women. Taos, where the trade was most popular, drew Indian trappers and free traders from all over the southwest to trade furs, hides and slaves. James P. Beckwourth, who lived with the Crow, participated in their tribe's slave hunts. Beckwourth relates a story of a raid for Blackfeet women after surrounding them. "We marched them to an open piece of ground, made them form a line, and proceeded to make a selection. The aged and ill favored, and the numerous matrons we withdrew from the body, telling them to return to the village and depart without clamor. They went away in sullenness, with their eyes flashing fire. The remainder, to the number of fifty-nine, very attractive looking young women, we carried along with us...." According to Beckwourth, a Crow could not marry a female captive. He, however, "took a pretty young woman prisoner, but was obliged to give her to one of the braves...." When a warrior takes a woman prisoner, she is considered his sister, and he can never marry her. If she marries, her husband is brother-in-law to her captor. An occasional turn-about occurred when the Indians would raid a white traders' encampment and carry off his Indian wives to sell to other mountain men. Bending Reed, the wife of trapper La Bonté, was carried off by Blackfeet and later offered for sale at a trading post.

Crow Indians, 1890s

The missions of California and other locations in the southwest held an abundance of Indian girls, making it an easy target for slave hunters. In the years between 1700 and 1750 there were believed to be as many as 800 Apache women and children who were held as slaves in New Mexico. However, since they had been baptized as Catholics, the term esclavas (slaves) was avoided except in ecclesiastical records. As the fur trade progressed from beaver to buffalo, slaves of the Plains Indians were traded less and less, as the women's skills became more valuable to the Indians, particularly in dressing buffalo hides for white traders.

The Taos and Santa Fe slave markets evolved into a lucrative business of theft and selling of Indians. Whites and Indians alike, along with the Mexican traders, continued to expand the selling of male and female slaves into a profitable business. In 1850, the first Indian agent in New Mexico reported that, "The value of captives depends on age, sex, beauty, and usefulness. Good females... are valued from fifty to a hundred and fifty dollars each. Males, as they may be useful, one half less, never more." [355]

"True history and description of... America, whose inhabitants are savage, naked, very godless and cruel man-eaters." Dutch, by Hans Staden, 1596

Throughout the history of contact between the Indian and their European invaders, the Indian was constantly referred to as an inferior product of humanity, needing to be improved by any means available. This view of white American superiority to the Indian and opinions on how to end the Indian problem, were voiced in the 1700s by William Byrd of Virginia who stated, "If whites could stomach marrying Indians, desirable pragmatic results would emerge. Through intermarriage with whites, the Indians' dark complexion and paganism would be supplanted as well as their friendship and their land secured by the white race."[356] On December 21, 1801, Thomas Jefferson expressed a similar opinion to the Indians, advising them to give up their hunting and warfare for cultivation of the earth and added, "You will mix with us by marriage, your blood will run in our veins, and will spread over this great island."[357] Not content with destroying the pure, full-blooded Indian, an attempt was then made to destroy and degrade any hybrid or mixed offspring of the Indian. In America after hundreds of years, we have been conditioned to the stereotyping of many individuals of different skin color. Individuals with different skin color from Asia, the Caribbean, Europe, or America have been, consciously or unconsciously, incorrectly racially classified. Prejudicial stereotyping throughout America has forced many Indians and others of mixed-blood ancestry to renounce their ethnic heritage.

Derogatory music song sheet, 1904

Since the first landing in America by the Spanish, and subsequently by explorers from other European countries, and with the importation of African slaves, new names were devised to indicate the dilution of the Indian bloodlines through intermarriage. Presently they are classified as: Métis (derived from the old French word meaning "mixed"), a person who is the product of a French/Indian marriage. A mestizo (derived from the Spanish), is the name for a product of a Spanish/Indian union. The highly derogatory term "half-breed" was used to describe the offspring of a marriage between a white European and an Indian.[358] Names, some derogatory, were devised for other groups such as: Creole, half-bloods, half-bred, mixed-breed, mulatto, molattoe, mulat (Dutch), mustee, mongrel, moreno, negro, pardo, cholo, colored, coon, black, ladino, octoroon, quadroon, etc. All were used to define skin color resulting from the different intermarriages.[359]

A number of Indians were sent to Portugal and Spain as slaves during the 1500s. These Indian slaves were primarily from South America and the Caribbean. Columbus initiated this slave trade and was the major supplier of these slaves before 1500, sending between 3000 and 6000 slaves to Seville. Columbus wrote to King Ferdinand and Queen Isabella, "It is possible in the name of the Holy Trinity, we can send all the slaves it is possible to sell... of whom, if the information is correct, they tell me that one can sell 4000...."[360]

"The royal administrator and his low-status dinner guests: the mestizo, the mulatto, and the tributary Indian." by Guamán Poma, 1600

On a Sunday just before Christmas in 1511, Dominican Friar Antonio de Montesinos assembled the Spanish colonists on Hispaniola for mass in a thatched church. He shocked his congregation by being one of the first missionaries to make a stand in defense of human rights for the Indians and his position against slavery, declaring, "I have come up on this pulpit, I who am a voice of Christ crying in the wilderness of this island... this voice saying that you are in mortal sin, that you live and die in it, for the cruelty and tyranny you use in dealing with these innocent people. Tell me, by what right or justice do you keep these Indians in such cruel and horrible servitude? On what authority have you waged a detestable war against these people, who dwelt quietly and peacefully on their own land?"[361] In the congregation was one Bartolomé de Las Casas, the future heroic advocate and champion of human rights for the Indian.

The father of Las Casas, returning from service on Columbus' second voyage, had reportedly given an Indian slave to his son, then a student at the University of Salamanca. The younger Las Casas went to America as a conquistador to make his fortune in 1502. He acquired slaves who worked for him in the mines, enabling him to build a large estate. As a reward for his part in the bloody war in Cuba, he was given an encomienda (a Spanish royal grant of land), along with Indian slaves. He received his holy orders about 1512. It was not until 1514 that Las Casas, while preparing a sermon on his estate in Cuba, realized the injustices that were being done to the Indians. In his fortieth year he vowed to devote his life to defend and rectify the wrongs against the Indians. In a sermon on August 15, 1514, Las Casas publicly announced he was returning all his Indian slaves to the governor.[362]

Women committing suicide because of Spanish atrocities
Engraving by Theodor de Bry, circa 1600

Due to labor shortages, the American colonists under British rule used Indians and then Africans as slaves. The English form of slavery, called indenture (forceful bondage), was similar to the Spanish encomienda system. In the early 1600s the term of bondage in this system lasted seven years.[363] During the 1630s this form of indenture began to change, making it legal in some areas, where a labor shortage existed, to hold Africans or Indians for more than seven years, even for life. In Barbados, a British island in the Caribbean, it was announced, "...that Negroes and Indians should serve for life, unless a contract was made to the contrary."[364]

In 1636 an Indian from Massachusetts became the first Indian to be legally enslaved and sentenced to work until his death. Queen Elizabeth had expelled, in 1596 and again in 1601, all dark-skinned people from Britain, including 'negars and blackamoores', and had them returned to America. Many who were the product of mixed marriages were gathered up and resold as slaves to the Caribbean, possibly Bermuda.[365]

The British colony in America sent a large number of rebellious Indians from the northeast mainland to the West Indies, to an unknown homeland and fate. In 1637, Pilgrims in New England under British rule annihilated most of the Pequot tribe in Connecticut. A number were sold as slaves for cash to the West Indies. Others were sold as indentured servants or attached to the remaining Indian tribes that assisted the British.[366] After King Philip's war (1675-76) and a battle with the British colonist forces, Metacom (King Philip) was beheaded. His widow and son were sold into slavery in the West Indies for 30 shillings apiece.[367]

African slaves rapidly replaced Indian slaves by the mid 1600s. The rules of slavery changed in 1670. In Virginia they allowed the Indians to leave their bondage after being enslaved for 12 years. The Africans were forced to remain as slaves for life. During the period when the Indians and Africans were part of the slave system, there was much intermarriage. In most Indian tribes the African was adopted into the tribe, welcomed with his children as new members and offered full protection against the Europeans, who considered the Africans to be inferior. Although a New York law banned Indian bondage in 1679, a law was passed in 1682 that forbade negro or Indian slaves from leaving their master's "homes without permission."[368]

In 1680, the assembly voted that it was against the law for negro or Indian slaves to meet anywhere together in groups of four or more, "or (to be) armed with guns, swords, clubs, staves or any other kind of weapon."[369] A 1690 Connecticut law forbade "red or black people from walking beyond the city limits without a pass."[370] In 1751, South Carolina passed a law stating that, "The carrying of Negroes among the Indians has all along been thought detrimental, as an intimacy ought to be avoided."[371] Connecticut, Massachusetts and Rhode Island passed laws imposing a nine o'clock curfew on Africans and American Indians. These laws were enacted to prevent the Indians and Africans from meeting and planning insurrections.[372]

Kentucky runaway slave poster, 1853

In 1708, the United States census records for South Carolina documented 1400 Indian slaves compared to half that number of African slaves. By the mid 1700s, Africans had replaced the Indians as the main source of slaves. In South Carolina, the white plantation owners mobilized the free Indians to maintain a force against the growing population of African slaves. A prominent South Carolina physician set forth these racist views in 1763, when he wrote, "The blacks in this climate are necessary, but very dangerous domestics, their number so much exceeding Whites, a natural dislike and apathy that subsists between them and our Indian neighbors, is a very lucky circumstance, and for this reason: In our quarrels with the Indians... it can never be our interest to extirpate them, or to force them from their lands; their ground would be soon taken up by runaway Negroes from our settlements, whose numbers would daily increase, and quickly become more formidable enemies than Indians can ever be, as they speak our language, and would never be at a loss for intelligence."[373]

Indians working the silver mines in Peru

Indians were often hired as mercenaries by the Europeans to hunt, catch and return runaway slaves. These runaway slaves set up their own communities, known as maroon settlements. Former African and Indian slaves and their offspring situated the maroon settlements throughout North and South America where slavery was enforced.[374] During the 1800s, when Spain abandoned slavery, many of these slaves sought refuge in Spanish-controlled territory. The maroon settlements joined forces with a number of runaway Indians in Florida under Spanish control to help defeat the United States government in a series of three Seminole wars.[375]

From 1549, decrees were enforced on both the mestizos (Spanish-Indian) and mulattos (African-White) to establish a distinct separation between both classes of half-bloods. By the mid 1500s, rebellions against Spain by African and Indian slaves had spread throughout the Spanish colonies. Alarmed and fearful of this combined force of African and Indian slaves, Viceroy Martin Enriquez wrote to the king of Spain. "Your majesty... the time is coming when these (African) people will have become masters of the Indians, in as much as they were born among them and their maidens, and are men who dare to die as well as any Spaniard in the world.... I do not know who will be in a position to resist them."[376] This forced the Spanish to temporarily halt the importation of slaves from Africa. In 1615, King Philip III of Spain received a letter from Mexico urging him that, "Division of the races is an indispensable element..." for controlling his subjects.[377] In this instance it referred to those who were half Spanish and half Indian. The mestizos were usually of a lighter complexion than the mulatto, which supposedly gave the mestizo a closer affinity to his Spanish heritage. The mixing of the races was so common in Mexico during the 1600s that it was getting impossible to tell from the skin color who was free or who was a slave.

"La Mulata," Yucatan, Mesoamerica 800 A.D.

The increased importation of male slaves from Africa and the decimation of the Indian male from disease and other forms of extermination resulted in an imbalance between the sexes. From the early 1500s, approximately 60 percent of the blacks shipped from Africa to the Spanish colonies in America were male. In 1524, King Charles V of Spain had formed the Council of Indies to administer its colonies in the western hemisphere. It was decreed that one-third of the slave ships were to contain females. Twenty-five years later, he decreed that the child of an Indian woman and a black African slave was considered to be a free person, whereas the child of a Spaniard and a black African slave woman was still a slave. Many of the Indian men were killed laboring in the silver mines and the pearl fisheries, leaving a larger number of females at home. The African male slave filled in the gap by marrying the Indian women. A dividend of this mixed marriage in the Spanish colonies was the freedom of the children of these marriages. The Spanish conquerors lived in constant fear, as King Philip complained that black Indians committed crimes dressed as Indians and were able to "hide out with their mother's relatives and cannot be found."[378]

Holding instruments for slaves

In Mexico, where racial mixing was common, the use of the term mestizo has evolved over hundreds of years to refer to anyone who is not a true, traditional Indian or of white Spanish ancestry. Mestizo lost its biological racial connotation to become a social designation.[379] During the 1800s, the Spanish colonial government "sold 'certificates of whiteness' to Indians who had mastered Spanish language and culture sufficiently to make enough money to buy such a certificate."[380] The past stigma attached to the name mestizo has been accepted in modern American, Portuguese, and Spanish terms as "a person of mixed European and Indian ancestry."[381]

Branded slave with instruments of torture. Carte de Visite photo circa, 1863

A form of reverse stereotyping has taken place in our present era. The mestizos, now a majority, were previously discriminated and disenfranchised by their European conquerors. Now they discriminate against the minority full-blooded Indian. The term mestizo implied that the mestizo speaks Spanish and that the Indian (Indio) does not, and is therefore considered inferior. In Peru, the word cholo expresses the same meaning as mestizo and defines an individual whose parents and grandparents are of mestizo heritage, containing a mixture of predominately Indian and white ancestry. In Mexico and Peru, upper-class individuals of mixed ancestry are called criolle or cruzado instead of mestizo.[382]

77

The mulatto designated a marriage between a black and a white. The Spanish were prejudiced towards the darker children of mixed marriages and "...had come to favor the lighter American mestizos (mixed-bloods) over darker, part-African peoples."[383] In the *Heritage Illustrated Dictionary* of 1979, a mestizo is "A person born of mixed European and Indian ancestry, of a mixed race."[384] This evolved into a separate racial class and caste system. In Latin countries, mestizos were descendants of the Spanish, Portuguese, and Indians."[385] The mestizo was often referred to as someone who speaks Spanish but does not live on the Indian reservation. The mestizos ancestry includes non-whites.[386]

Slavery book, circa 1840

Although slavery was technically banned in the Spanish possessions, a way was devised to overcome this restriction by subjecting the Indians to forced labor and debt peonage (encomienda).[387] Males and females between the age of twelve to twenty were sentenced to years of forced labor in Spanish mines and missions. After the repossession of the Acoma Pueblo in January, 1599, male Indian slaves over the age of twenty-five had one foot amputated by a Spanish sword before starting their servitude, so they would be unable to escape.[388] In the southeast, in South Carolina and Georgia, soldiers, settlers, and allied Indians raided the Spanish missions for slaves.

Slavery was at its peak in America during the mid 1800s. In Cuba and the West Indies under Spanish domination the word "creole" was used to name those slaves now born in captivity in America. *The London Saturday Journal*, in their issue of March 28, 1840, described a visit to these islands. "As the experience of years had taught me to believe that the Spaniards are a kind and warm-hearted race... I was not a little surprised to find, as a result of personal inquiry and minute observation, that in this last particular I had been most miserably deceived, and that in no quarter, unless perhaps in the Brazils, which I have not visited, is the state of slavery so desperately wretched as it is at the moment on the sugar plantations of the Queen of the Indies, the far-famed island of Cuba." In an issue of *The London Saturday Journal* published in May, 1840, a more moderate tone was pleaded towards slavery and the harsh treatment of Negroes and Indians. "While we cannot doubt that the white men are destined to carry civilization into the countries at present occupied by the wild inhabitants of the prairie or forest, yet no reasoning Christian can believe that God created Indians and Negroes merely to be exterminated by the white men... remove this crying evil. Let the whites banish their disgraceful antipathy to the colored races; place them in society, and under the protection of the law as equals, not dependents, and they will, in real civilization, forget blood revenge, and cease to be savages."[389]

The Spaniards had extended the Indian slave trade bondage in their territory in the western region of North America by carrying out raids on Indian tribal areas. The Navajo, Apache, Yuma, Ute, Pima, Papago, etc., were forced into slavery.[390] This form of slave bondage by the Spanish was legally terminated by 1835, when the Mexican Republic declared all Indians free and independent. The Mexican war ended in 1848 with California becoming a part of the United States. Voting rights of the Indians, which had existed under the Mexican regime, was suspended. The Indians and their descendants were deliberately disfranchised by the new state constitution. From 1850 until 1868, Los Angeles maintained an Indian slave market on Monday mornings. Indians convicted of offenses, most commonly drunkenness, could be acquired by a white or Mexican rancher, who were entitled to keep the Indian for twice the length of his normal prison sentence. Indian slavery still continued in the United States after Abraham Lincoln's Emancipation Proclamation in 1863. African and Cherokee slavery ended in an 1866 treaty with the Cherokee Nation. It was not until the United States Congress outlawed the enslavement of Navajos by Americans and Mexicans (through a joint resolution on July 27, 1868), that there began to be an end to the enslavement of Indians. In 1872, California enacted laws to abolish slavery. [391]

Ute Indians, 1873, by
J. W. Powell and A. H. Thompson

The Indian could not legally challenge his enslavement. The Supreme Court in 1884 ruled that the fourteenth amendment to the United States Constitution freed the African slaves but did not grant citizenship or constitutional rights to the Indians, even to those who had left the reservation and entered white man's society. The Dawes Act, or Land Allotment Act in 1887, conferred citizenship only to those Indians who accepted allotted land, or who had left the reservations to become residents of any state or territory. The slavery practices towards non-citizen Indians continued until 1924 when the United States, under President

Pima Indian family, 1890s

78

Calvin Coolidge, finally gave the Indians full citizenship, without the protection of their individual civil rights as in our "Bill of Rights."[392]

Chief American Horse
receiving citizenship papers, 1917

The mixed marriages between black African slaves and American women resulted in a new caste classification called mulattos. The various dictionaries of the time gave different translations of the word mulatto. *Chambers Cyclopedia* of 1727 to 1741 stated, "Mulatto, a name given, in the Indies, to those who are begotten by a negro man on an Indian woman; or an Indian man on a negro woman." Other dictionaries designated mulatto as a black-white mixture or half-black mixture with half of something else. Mulatto was often used to describe an individual whose ancestry was unknown.

There were legal ramifications to designating an individual as a mulatto, a negro, an Indian or any of the other names that implied mixed or Indian parentage. In 1705, Virginia prohibited any negro, mulatto or Indian from holding public office. The act stated, "For clearing all manner of doubts which hereafter may happen to arise upon the construction of this act, or any other act, who shall be accounted a mulatto: Be it (etc.), that the child of an Indian, and the child, grandchild, or great grandchild, a negro shall be deemed, accounted, held, and taken to be a mulatto." In 1785 the law was modified to state all persons with one-fourth or more negro blood is a mulatto. In 1866 the law was changed again to state, "Every person having one-fourth or more negro blood shall be deemed a colored person, and every person not a colored person having one-fourth or more Indian blood shall be deemed an Indian."[393] Other states had similar laws that affected the status and legal rights of the mixed-blood. Indiana's laws stated that "No negro, mulatto or Indian could be a witness in cases involving a white person."[394] In 1850, California passed a statute that stated, "Persons having one-eighth or more of negro blood shall be deemed mulattos, and persons having one-half Indian blood, shall be deemed Indians... no black or mulatto person, or Indian, shall give evidence in a case involving a white person."[395]

Guatemalan of Mayan
& Spanish descent

Mestizo Parade, Beliz Guatemala
(Maya Yucatec) 2002

The hypocrisy inherent in the missionaries' attempts to Christianize the Indians is revealed in a letter from Dr. Elias Boudinot on the question of the enslavement of the Delaware Indians. "We had therefore sent them (Delaware Indians) two ministers of the Gospel, who would teach them these great things.... On their arrival, the chiefs of the natives were called together, who answered them, that they would take into consideration.... They spent fourteen days in council, and then dismissed them very courteously, with an answer to us. This answer made great acknowledgement for the favor we had done them. They rejoiced exceedingly at our happiness in being thus favored by the Great Spirit... to remember our Red Brethren in the wilderness. But they could not help recollecting that we had a people among us, who, because they differed from us in color, we had made slaves of, and made them suffer great hardships, and lead miserable lives. Now they could not see any reason, if a people's being black entitled us thus to deal with them, why a red color should not equally justify the same treatment. They therefore determined to wait and see whether all the black people amongst us were made happy and joyful, before they put confidence in our promise; for they thought a people who had suffered so much and so long, by our means, should be entitled to our first attention; that therefore they had sent back the two missionaries, with many thanks—promising that when they saw the black people amongst us restored to freedom and happiness, they would gladly receive our missionaries"[396]

Sinaloa Mestizo
Mexican American Folklore
2002

In 1829, in a ruling on a case from South Carolina, the Supreme Court stated that the words negro, mulatto, etc., as used in statutes for the purpose of designating a class, were to be interpreted "by their common acceptation which in the case of mulatto meant offspring of a black and a white." They further stated that there was no legal definition of the term mulatto and it would be up to a jury to decide on a final definition. There was, however, no mistaking the stigma attached to the word mulatto. "It is certainly true that every admixture of African blood with the European, or white, is not to be referred to the degraded class." The South Carolina court cases had to decide whether an Indian who was free of black African blood was to be considered a free Indian. It was noted in 1846 that the class of mulattos had a constant tendency to assimilate to the white, "and the desire for elevation presents frequent cases of embarrassment and difficulty..."[397] The ramifications of the South Carolina court decision for the black population were that the only way to escape being stereotyped as a mulatto or colored person was to prove "free Indian descent, unmixed with African blood."[398]

Many states noted the term "colored person" in their census records. Free persons of color were considered to be Indian to differentiate from colored blacks that were still considered slaves. In the 1870 United States census, the designation mulatto was changed to "include quadroons, octoroons, and all persons having any respectable trace of African blood."[399] In the 1880 and 1890 census, a black person was defined as one who had three-fourths or more of black blood. The census of 1930 included Indians of mixed ancestry as black, which increased the size of the black population. The word "mulatto" was not recognized as a legal term.

In the French areas of America, the designation Métis applied to anyone born of a marriage between a white French-Canadian and an American Indian. The predicament of the French Canadian Métis of later years was no different from that of the Spanish mestizos. Those who lived in isolation near white settlements were living in poor conditions. As a result of their mixed marriages, they were shunned and erroneously stereotyped as inferior by the upper class French Canadians and English due to the impurity of their blood. As the white Europeans expanded westward in the 1800s and boundary lines changed, they encountered thriving, settled Métis communities in Michigan, Illinois, Missouri, Wisconsin, Louisiana and parts of Canada.

The French Canadian men married their Indian wives according to Indian tradition, deviating from established church beliefs. They remained in the Indian villages and accepted the Indian culture, much to the dismay of their critics, who objected to their common-law marriages. The Métis, noted for their fierce independence, started out as established fur traders. They developed their own language, Michif, a mixture of Cree-French Creole, and wore garments featuring a bright red sash and elaborate beaded patterns on their clothes.[400] They were left on their own to trade with the Indians, far away from the colonial government. The Métis mostly inhabited Saskatchewan in the Northwest Territories of Canada in the 1860s. They had been forced to leave Ontario and Manitoba to escape prejudice from the mostly white Protestant settlers who settled the land when it was purchased from the North West Company and the Hudson Bay Company. The buffalo was vanishing as well as the fur trade. The mostly French-speaking Métis came into cultural conflicts with the new English-speaking white settlers.

After brewing for a number of years, the prejudice against the Métis led to the Red River rebellion of 1869 and subsequently to the formation of a provisional government under Métis leader Louis Riel, at Fort Garry, Manitoba. When soldiers arrived from eastern Canada to end the rebellion, Riel escaped to the United States. In 1870, Riel's Métis followers fled the province of Manitoba and went to Saskatchewan. In Saskatchewan, the Métis set up their own temporary government and elected Gabriel Dumont as their President. As the railroad pushed westward in the 1870s and 1880s, new immigrants were given the land under newly enacted land acts. This outraged the Métis, who had lived on the land for years as squatters. In 1884, with their petitions and complaints having been ignored by the provisional government in Ottawa, they asked Louis Riel to return to Saskatchewan from Montana to help them. Riel discovered catastrophic conditions awaiting him; the conservative government had withdrawn their help to both the Métis and the Indians, and they were now left to survive without the food rations and farming assistance that had been promised under their treaties with the Canadian government.

On March 8, 1884, a ten-point bill of rights was proclaimed for the Northwest Territories, recognizing the rights of the Indians, white settlers, and the Métis. When the Ottawa government did not respond, a provisional government was set up on March 19th by the Métis. They attacked Fort Carlton in the Battle of Duck Lake, with a victory for the Métis and the start of the Riel rebellion. Within a month over eight thousand troops, five hundred Northwest Mounted Police, and white volunteers arrived in Saskatchewan. The 150 Métis had no chance against this kind of manpower and, in 1884, the rebellion ended. Louis Riel was hanged on November 16, 1885, and Indian chiefs Poundmaker and Big Bear were charged with treason and sentenced to three years in jail. The cost to the Canadian government to end the rebellion was $5,000,000. The Métis lands were given to white settlers while the Métis were forced to flee to Spring River, fifty miles northwest of Prince Albert, to begin another round of poverty, hardship, and discrimination.[401]

It was not until 1982 that the Canadian constitution finally allowed "existing" aboriginal rights for the "Métis, Amerindians, and Inuit", of Canada, without defining the term "existing."[402] In 1994 the Métis were given the right for self-government.[403] Both the United States government and the Canadian government enacted treaties

THE

SLAVERY CODE

OF THE

DISTRICT OF COLUMBIA,

TOGETHER

WITH NOTES AND JUDICIAL DECISIONS EXPLANATORY OF THE SAME.

Slavery code of 1890s

Louis Riel, Métis

and laws against mixed-bloods. In the 1830s, special privileges were given to people of mixed parentage in an attempt to turn full-blooded Indians against half-bloods. Full-blooded Indians were forced to leave their traditional homelands to settle on reservations, while mixed-bloods were allowed to remain. The mixed-bloods did not, however, have any rights to live on the reservations, but were given sums of money in compensation.[404] In the U.S. treaty with the Poncas in 1858, all full-bloods were forced to relocate to a small reservation in Oklahoma, while "their half-breed relatives" were not. An 1865 treaty with the Blackfeet Nation of Indians clearly stated the United States government's position toward half-breeds. "The half-breeds of the tribes, parties to the treaty, and those persons citizens of the United States who have intermarried with Indian women of said tribes, and continue to maintain domestic relations with them, shall not be compelled to remove to said reservation but shall be allowed to remain undisturbed upon the lands herein ceded and relinquished to the United States."[405]

Mandan Indians, Catlin, 1850s

In the United States government 1887 General Allotment Act, full-blooded Indians were legally classified as "incompetents", and were restricted to living on small pieces of land without the opportunity for ownership until twenty five years had passed. In the same 1887 act, mixed-bloods were allotted larger parcels of land in better areas with immediate, full control of their land.[406] In the 1910 United Sates census only 56.5 percent (150,053 out of 265,683) of Indians in the United States were reported as full-bloods. A small portion, 8.4 percent (22,207), claimed they were Indian but did not report any blood mixture. In 1930, 46.3 percent (153,933 out of 332,397) were full bloods with 42.4 percent (141,101) declaring themselves as mixed-bloods. A jump in the 1930 census of Indians, without mentioning blood mixtures, increased from 8.4 percent in 1910 to 11.2 percent. In 1940, census instructions defined an Indian as black unless his Indian ancestry "very definitely predominates and he is universally accepted in the community as an Indian."[407]

United States census rules of 1980 disallowed an individual to be categorized in more than one racial classification. Boxes could only be checked for white, black, or Indian. A box checked as both Indian and black would be counted as black; there was no box for mixed-status citizens. Those with part-Indian ancestry had to be careful to check the box next to "Indian" only if they wished to be considered as an Indian.[408] This categorizing of an Indian by the amount of blood in his veins has been used by the United States government to rid themselves of their problems with the Indians. It was hoped that defining the percentage of Indian blood necessary to be called an Indian would result in the eventual disappearance of the Indians. The government's original treaties with the Indians contained no mention of this notion, and the present United States standard of setting the blood amount at one-quarter will eventually, through intermarriage, result in the Indians being defined out of existence.

In October, 1988, the NCAI (National Congress of American Indians) rejected this Federal policy of blood quantum. Charles Dawes, Second Chief of the Ottawa Indian tribe of Oklahoma, stated, "What could not be completed over a three-hundred year span may now be completed in our life-span by administrative law.... We must fight any attempt to limit any program by blood quantum.... We must dedicate our efforts to insuring that... Native American people will be clearly identified without reference to blood quantum... and that our sovereign Indian Nations will be recognized as promised."[409]

Mary Richards
Lipan, Apache
by Frank Rinehart, 1898

The general acceptance of the Indian of his half-blood relative proved, in time, to be detrimental to his own survival. At times, their half-blood relatives exploited the Indians, although the main damage was from the attitudes and customs the half-bloods acquired from their white parents, from their association with white society, or from their formal education in white missionary schools. Conflicts often arose on issues due to different viewpoints between full-blooded and mixed-blooded Indians. This was especially true early in the 1850s, when issues of tribal removal were under discussion. The government and missionaries attempted to use the educated half-blood as a link between the races that would facilitate the conversion of the full-blood Indian. The half-blood was viewed simply as a useful agent of the white race rather than a legitimate member of it. Due to his ability to communicate with both races, the half-blood was often used as an interpreter. The male half-blood experienced more difficulty in being accepted in white society than did the female. The half-blood found a greater acceptance among the Indians than whites because the Indians' culture was more tolerant, and this receptivity intensified the animosity towards the half-bloods from the whites.

Many white women who were captured and married to Indians were unable to return to white society because their half-blood children were not accepted. Due to the unavailability of women, the female half-blood was more readily acceptable and easier to marry into the male-dominated white society. The white father looked forward to seeing his mixed-blood daughter marry above her station in life, rather than below it. The woman was seen as a passive member of society and therefore, was less of a perceived threat than a half-blooded man. To the white female, the half-blood was erroneously classified as a semi-barbarian or of a class lower than her own.

This racial caste system remained ingrained into the minds of many white Americans through such novels as James Fenimore Cooper's *The Last of the Mohicans* (1826), Walt Whitman's *The Half Breed* (1846), Helen Hunt Jackson's *Ramona* (1884) and Edward Willett's and Bill Beeler's *Bonanza* (1892). In his book, *The Fur Hunters of the Far West*, published in 1855, Alexander Ross commented on the mixed-blood Indian, "Half-breeds, or as they are more generally styled, brulés, from the peculiar color of their skin, being of a swarthy hue, as if sunburned, as they grow up resemble, almost in every respect, the pure Indian. With this difference that they are more designing, more daring, and more dissolute... they are by far the fittest persons for the Indian countries, the best calculated by nature for going among Indians.... They are vigorous, brave; and while they possess the shrewdness and sagacity of the whites, they inherit the agility and expert-ness of the savage."[410]

Indian mother and child
European depiction by
John White

A year later, in his novel, *The Red River Settlement*, Ross wrote, "While enjoying a sort of licentious freedom, they are generous, warm hearted, and brave, and left to themselves, quiet and orderly. They are, unhappily, as unsteady as the wind in all their habits, fickle in their dispositions, credulous in their faith, and clannish in their affections. In a word, of all people, they are the easiest led astray and made dupes of by designing men."[411] In his 1849 book, *The Oregon Trail*, Francis Parkman refers to the mixed-bloods as "a race of rather extraordinary composition, being, according to the common saying, half Indian, half white man, and half devil."[412]

"The Indian Beauty," 1857
Currier & Ives depiction

Over the years there has been a constant deviation in the United States government policy towards the Indians in an attempt to destroy their culture and assimilate them into white society. In 1914 Frank G. Speck, a noted anthropologist from the University of Pennsylvania, addressed this issue, advocating a 20th-century approach to what was, in effect, a 19th-century problem. Speck's speech was published in the *Society of American Indian (SAI) Quarterly Journal*. Speck had observed the effects of the gradual erosion of tribal culture, language, and heritage on the Indians and realized that racial bias existed in America. He forecast what would happen to the Indian culture through mixed marriages. His main desire was to save the Indian race from disappearing altogether. The Indian, said Speck, "could serve himself and his country best by standing upon his own institutions, with, of course, modifications which are unavoidable nowadays, as the exponent of outdoor life, the ideal of the Boy Scouts movement... clean, natural pursuits, rather than becoming a sweat-shop, factory or office slave in our already crowded industrial sphere.... Moreover, the shame of it is that when thoroughly de-cultured, the Indians often lose their pride enough to mingle and marry with their social infe-riors among certain classes of Negroes and Whites. Now, how can we, in truth and honesty with ourselves and our friends, the Indians, ask them to lower themselves socially to the level of our heterogeneous dark skinned masses?... The ethnologist never takes a stand against native cultures in which he sees so much good, by contact, that he objects to educating the Indian down to the level of the average community white man."

The persistent attitude of white superiority, all a matter of perception, over a period of hundreds of years towards those of a darker skin color, conditioned the half-blood to accept a lower position in life and assisted in developing a caste and racial system based on skin color throughout North and South America. Indians have absorbed Spanish, French, English, African, and other nations' blood to mix with their own. Due to this blood mixture and generations of discrimination it has pressured many Indians, light skinned blacks and others to pass as white to increase their job prospects and escape racial discrimination. Unfortunately, it has also caused many Indians to relinquish their own culture and spiritual heritage. Surviving in our modern society has not been spiritually rewarding. Today, after years of genocide and approxi-mately thirty generations of complex intermixing, a large number of the Indians in the Americas are beginning to develop an awareness of their great culture and traditions. Many Indians are returning to their tribes to practice their traditional beliefs.[413]

"Payta Kootha—a Shawnee
Warrior," 1836, litho
McKenney & Hall

CHAPTER 6 GENOCIDE AGAINST THE INDIAN

THE LONDON SA

THE NORTH AMERICAN INDIANS.

NO. I.—ARE THE INDIANS CAPABLE OF CIVILISATION?

is received almost as an axiom by far too many of those who
the blessings of civilisation, that the red man cannot exist
the white man—that it is useless to seek to alter his wild
ition, for attempts at civilisation only serve to degrade
of elevating his character. Therefore it is argued the

The London Saturday Journal, May 2, 1840

We cannot deny that, from the first day European colonists settled on the shores of North and South America, an unceasing effort was made to mold the Indian in order to accommodate the Europeans' lust for gold, land, or other material benefits. The Indians were forced to accept these changes or be annihilated. Genocide against the Indians took place whenever the European nations laid claim to a new region, despite the fact that the Indians greeted the Europeans warmly and offered them help and hospitality. Throughout the entire history of North and South America there have been reports that capture the tragedies of the conquest of the Indians.[414] In 1840, an article in the *London Saturday Journal* asked, "Are the Indians capable of civilization?" It continued, "The Redman cannot exist with the white man, [and] it is useless to alter his wild condition, for attempts at civilization only serve to degrade instead of elevating his character. Therefore the Indians must be driven beyond the pale of civilization.... Indians clogged the lands inhabited by the white settlers... and it becomes necessary for the security and prosperity of the whites to push the Indians further west...." The journal added that whiskey was used deliberately to "sink them lower still."[415]

The history of this genocide began with the Spanish, who first landed on the shores of America. The Tainos were the first Indians encountered by Columbus when he landed in the West Indies on October 12, 1492. The Tainos were a tribe related to the Arawak who lived in the Amazon, in the northern part of South America, and also throughout much of the West Indies. Columbus was welcomed as god from heaven. Writing in his journal, Columbus used every adjective imaginable to praise the Tainos. He described them as friendly, kind, lovable, giving, shy, free, generous, timid and innocent. On November 4, 1492 in Cuba, Columbus noted, "These people are very meek and shy; naked, as I have said, without any weapons or government." On November 5, 1492, Columbus wrote, "All that these people have they will give you for a ridiculous price, they gave one great basket of cotton for the end of a leather strap. These people are very free from evil and war."[416]

On arriving on December 21, 1492, at the harbor Acul Bay (The Sea of St. Thomas), Columbus remarked, "They brought us all that they had in this world, knowing what I wanted, and they did it so generously and willingly that it was wonderful."[417] On December 22, 1492, he wrote, "The chief of this country, who lives near here, sent a canoe full of people.... He begged me to go with the ships to his country and said he would give me anything he had.... These people are so generous; they give whatever is asked of them, willingly, and it seems you are doing them a favor to request something from them."[418]

Burning Indians on Hispaniola, by de Bry

On December 24, 1492, Columbus wrote in his journal, "Your highnesses may believe that in all the world there cannot be a better or more gentle people. Your highnesses must be greatly pleased because you will soon make them Christians and will teach them the good customs of your kingdoms, for there cannot be a better people or country."[419] The Tainos greeted Columbus with gifts, and a good will offering of dry leaves (tobacco). They played with the Spanish steel swords, cutting their hands on the unfamiliar objects. Columbus was astounded to discover that these people did not possess any private property and, "that the people are so amiable and friendly that even their King took pride in calling me his brother...."[420]

As soon as he set foot in the Bahamas, Columbus considered taking back natives as servants or slaves. Exploiting and subverting the Indians became advantageous for the Europeans. Columbus gave a day-by-day written account of the capture of these friendly Indians. When he went ashore on October 12, 1492, in the Bahamas, Columbus wrote, "I believe the people from the mainland come here to take them as slaves. They ought to make good and skilled servants, for they repeat very quickly whatever we say to them. I think they can easily be made Christians. If it pleases our Lord, I will take six of them to your highnesses when I depart, in order that they may learn our language...."[421]

On October 14, 1492, Columbus wrote of the Indians, "Soon I, saw two or three of them, and the people came to the beach, shouting and praising God. Some brought us water, others things to eat.... By the signs they made they were asking if we came from Heaven... others shouted in loud voices to everyone on the beach, saying 'Come see the men from Heaven; bring them food and drink.' Many men and women came, each one with some thing. They threw themselves on the sand and raised their hands to the sky, shouting for us to come ashore, while giving thanks to God...."[422]

Spanish pillage village in Cusco, Peru, by de Bry

As Columbus wrote in his diary of these friendly greetings, he also noted his true intentions of taking the entire tribe back to Spain as captives. Writing in his journal on October 14, 1492, Columbus noted of the men he took captive, "Your highnesses will see for yourselves when I bring to you the seven that I have taken. After they learn our language I shall return them, unless your highnesses order the entire population be taken to Castile, or held captive here. With 50 men you could subject everyone and make them do what you wish."[423]

Columbus had written agreements with his royal sponsors for him to find and bring back "merchandise" and "goods". Columbus was never given the authorization to do missionary work. He was authorized only to bring back material wealth in any form.[424] It was primarily gold that Columbus sought as soon as he landed in the New World, as evidenced by the numerous references to it in his journal. On his first day in the Bahamas, on October 13, 1492, Columbus wrote, " I have been very attentive and have tried to find if there is gold anywhere."[425] In his journal of October 15, 1492, "I anchored at sunset near the cape in order to find out if there was any gold there...." On October 16, 1492, Columbus wrote, "They said there is a lot of gold there..." On December 6, 1492, Columbus landed in the north part of Haiti at Mole St. Nicholas. On December 24, 1492, Columbus established the first settlement in the New World with the sailors and with help from the Tainos, who salvaged a great part of the Santa Maria that had run aground on a reef. Columbus built a small fort and called this first settlement in the New World, "La Navidad" (The Nativity).

Columbus noted, with some apparent frustration, in his journal of December 6, 1492, that he was getting weary of not finding any gold. " I hope to God that I can have some good trade in gold before I return to Spain."[426] The day before he departed Hispaniola for Spain, on January 4, 1493, he wrote, "I wish to depart because nothing is gained by staying here. Too many disagreements have taken place; I have also learned the bulk of the gold is in the vicinity of Your Highnesses, Villa de la Navidad." [427]

Christopher Columbus arrived back in Palos, Spain, on March 15, 1493. With him were several kidnapped Tainos. Following the departure of Christopher Columbus, his brothers who now ruled La Navidad began to enslave and brutalize the Tainos. The Spaniards raped the women and sacked the island looking for gold and food. They were reported "stealing the Taino's property and wives and inflicting so many injuries upon them that the Indians resolved to revenge themselves on any that they found alone or in small groups."[428]

Spanish punish the Indians in Hispaniola
by hangings on ship, by de Bry

As soon as the Tainos put up resistance, the Spaniards assembled over two hundred soldiers armed with powerful crossbows, lances, and swords, with vicious dogs at their heels and horses to give them speed; they moved on the Tainos and completely massacred them. Las Casas reported, "For one Christian whom the Indians killed, the Christians would kill a hundred Indians." In addition, Las Casas said the Spaniards "made bets as to who would slit a man in two, or cut off his head at one blow; or they opened up his bowels. They tore the babies from their mother's breast by their feet, and dashed their heads against the rocks... they spitted the bodies of other babies, together with their mothers before them on their swords."[429]

As a further torture to the Tainos and a blot on their religious vows, they would hang the leaders in groups of thirteen from a gallows set up in the village. The rope around the Tainos where they hung was "... just high enough for their feet to nearly touch the ground and by thirteens, in honor and reverence for our redeemer and the twelve Apostles, they put wood underneath and, with fire, they burned the Indians alive."[430] For all these atrocities inflicted by the Spanish Conquistadors, Las Casas placed the blame on the Kingdom of Spain. He called this "cruelty never before seen, nor heard of nor read of."[431]

The peaceful Tainos resisted the Spanish to the best of their ability. The Spanish, under Columbus and his brothers Bartolomé and Diego, resorted to enslaving the Indians to prevent any further rebellion. They proceeded to round up 1500 Tainos to ship to Spain as slaves. King Ferdinand and Queen Isabella I of Spain became the first monarchs to traffic in Indian slaves.[432] Five hundred bodies were all the four ships could hold. The rest of the captives were divided among the Spaniards remaining in Hispaniola, and those they could not take were released to flee for their lives, with some women being forced to abandon their children. Two hundred of the

Tainos died aboard ship before they reached Spain.[433] Landing at Seville, Spain, the rest of the slaves were sold as "naked as they were born."[434] Andrés Bernáldez, a Spanish chronicler, noted that the voyage of Columbus and the slaves he returned with was "not very profitable since almost all died, for the country did not agree with them."[435] Many of the Tainos rebelled and fled to the hills and other islands. A leading Taino chief, Cacique Guacanagaric (Guatiguaná), a former friend of Columbus, attempted to unite the 250,000 remaining Tainos.[436]

King Ferdinand and Queen Isabella
of Spain, 1522
Bas relief, Royal Chapel, Grenada

In March, 1495, Guacanagaric and his Taino warriors attacked the Spaniards, but were overwhelmed and slaughtered.[437] Those captured were burned, tortured and mutilated, and thrown into pits to be eaten alive by the Spaniards' savage dogs.[438] In 1498, another cargo of six hundred Caribbean Indians was sent to Spain to be sold as slaves.[439] The Tainos who were taken prisoner were forced to work as laborers in the plantations and mines. Many of them were sent to serve a year as slaves in the silver mines of Bolivia. In 1508, a census taken by the Spanish found that in Hispaniola (Dominican Republic and Haiti), only 60,000 Indians were left. In 1514, the Spanish census listed over seventeen chartered Spanish towns, yet out of the approximately three million native Tainos who lived in the Caribbean before the arrival of the Spanish, this census reported that there were approximately 20,000 left. In 1548 Fernández de Gonzalo Oviedo, historian of the Indies, doubted their were even 500 native Indians of the islands left.[440]

According to Las Casas, by 1542 about 200 Tainos were left in Hispaniola.[441] This means that over 99 percent of them were annihilated in just over 20 years.[442] The small number of Taino survivors is consistent with the reports of atrocities of those who died as slaves, through torture, from epidemics of new diseases or as a result of their rebellion against their oppressors. This figure, in any case, places the despicable actions of the Spanish against the Tainos in the category of genocide.[443] In his will, read after his death in 1566, Las Casas revealed that he had been haunted by the injustices of his countrymen and country, saying, "I believe that because of these impious, criminal and ignominious acts, perpetrated unjustly, tyrannously, and barbarously upon them, God will visit His wrath and His ire upon Spain for her share, great or small, in the bloodstained riches, obtained by theft and usurpation, accompanied by such slaughter and annihilation of these people—unless she does much penance."[444]

Most of the European colonists who arrived after Columbus treated the Indians with disrespect and arrogance, displaying their superior weapons of war upon each encounter with the friendly Indians. They had no concept that the natives' temperament was an entirely different temperament from that of their conquerors. They were extremely hospitable because they were brought up to give rather than take. Their nature was to cooperate rather than compete. Their god was revealed through nature, rather than on Sundays in church. Sir Francis Drake found these same qualities in the Indians living on the California coast. The early Spanish chroniclers encountered these spiritual qualities in the Indians and in civilizations they found throughout South America.

Spanish massacre of Tainos
by Theodor de Bry, 1600

Additional acts of genocide were carried out against the Indians in the Americas. Over 30,000 Indians were used as slaves in the early mines and plantations in the Caribbean. In the United States, many of the Indians were sold as slaves to other settlers in distant parts of the country so they would be unable to escape due to the hostile environment. In parts of California, Spanish missionaries enslaved the entire Chumash tribe of Indians. They would amputate one foot of Indian men over 25 years of age to prevent them from escaping, and raped many of the Indian women. The entire tribe, with the exception of those individuals who intermarried or developed immunity to the white man's diseases, was eventually wiped out. The Spaniards used the genocide and enslavement of more than 10,000 Indians to finance the conquest of the new lands in North America. The Europeans, who arrived after Columbus, found a vast amount of gold and material wealth. In the process, the Europeans decimated the existing Indians and almost wiped out their way of life.

Before Cortés arrived in Mexico the Aztec civilization had reached its peak and was compared to the other great world civilizations. In the late 1920s in *A Cultural History of the Modern Age*, the Aztec civilization was given a glowing report, described as follows, "The culture of Mexico is to be imagined as... in the same stage as the Empire in Rome, characterized by a life of huge cities, of refined comforts, of autocratic forms of government and expansionist imperialism, of massiveness in architecture and extravagance in ornament, of ethical fatalism and barbarized religion. The capital, Tenochtitlan, built on platforms in a wondrous lake, displayed huge temples and obelisks, extensive arsenals, hospitals, barracks, zoological and botanical gardens, barber shops, vapour baths, fountains, tapestries and paintings of gorgeous feather-mosaic, costly goldsmith's work and finely tooled plates of tortoise-shell, splendid woolen cloaks and leather gear, ceilings of fragrant carved wood, hot-plates, scent-sprayers, and hot water systems. In the weekly markets, attended by hundreds of thousands, wares of every conceivable kind were exposed for sale. A wonderfully organized postal service of fast couriers, ply-ing on the network of well-built highways and ramps which traversed the land,

Pyramids of the Sun and Moon at Teotihuacan, Mexico City, circa 1- 250 A.D., restored rendering by Iganacio Marquina

carried every item of news with amazing speed and precision. Police and fiscal arrangements worked with the greatest accuracy and reliability. The kitchens of the wealthy were fragrant with the most select food and drinks, game fish, waffles, preserves, delicate soups, spiced dishes; and withal a number of things unknown to the Old World, turkey, [and] "chocllatl"—the favorite dish of the Mexicans.... The streets were so clean, a Spanish text tells us, that in passing along them one soiled one's feet no more than one's hands. The population was honest as it was clean; all houses were left open.... Writing was by means of very elaborate picture writing, and there were also lightning painters who could fix all occurrences with amazing rapidity in almost all speaking designs. The mathematical sense of the Aztecs must have been highly developed, for their arithmetical system was built up on the difficult principal of raising to a power, the basic number being 20, the next 20^2 number or 8000, and so on; further, the Maya are supposed to have invented, independently of the Indians, the idea of zero, a fertile and com-plicated notion which only made its way into Europe slowly, via the Arabs."[445]

The Spanish, under Cortés, systematically went about to completely destroy this great civilization. The Governor of Cuba, Diego Velasquez, was motivated to acquire the riches of the Aztecs after hearing of a wealthy Mexican empire in reports brought back by explorers, Francisco Hernandez de Cordoba and Juan de Grijalva. Cortés narrowly managed to undertake the expedition and on April 21, 1519, he arrived in Mexico with only about 500 men, 16 horses and several pieces of artillery. Cortés landed near Villa Rica de Veracruz and immedi-ately gained control of the city. Soon the Spaniards started to march inland and fought against the Tabascans (Tlaxcalans)—who surrendered and became Cortés' most faithful allies. By October, 1519, this combined force reached the Aztec village of Cholula, where they slaughtered over 3000 of its citizens. Montezuma II (Moctezuma), Aztec ruler of Tenochtitlan, was troubled as to how to handle Cortés after realizing that the appear-ance of Cortés exactly matched the expected time and prophetic description of their returning Aztec bearded god, Quetzacoatl.[446] Montezuma sent emissaries with gifts of gold and precious jewels in an attempt to turn Cortés back. It was reported that when the emissaries asked why they desired so much gold Cortés replied, "I and my companions suffer from a disease of the heart that can be cured only with gold."[447] Cortés arrived and entered the gates of Tenochtitlan (now Mexico City) on November 8, 1519, and was welcomed by Montezuma as a guest in his palace. Shortly thereafter, Cortés seized Montezuma and held him as a hostage, hoping to gain wealth from a large ransom and to forestall an Aztec attack. News then came that Spanish troops, sent by Governor Velázquez, had arrived at the coast to place Cortés under arrest for insubordination. During April, 1520, Cortés left Tenochtitlan to fight and defeat this army. While he was gone, Cortés' deputy, Pedro de Alvarado, who was suspicious of what he viewed as an alarmingly frenetic religious celebration, closed the pas-sages and gates to where the Aztec's Feast of Huitzilopochtli was being held. The Spanish ran among the dancers and massacred 600 Aztecs and seized all the gold in the city. When Cortés returned to the city they were attacked by thousands of Aztec warriors. Cortés brought out Montezuma to talk to his people, but they stoned him. Montezuma later died of the wounds. Fighting quickly broke out in full force and the sheer numbers of the Aztec army overwhelmed Cortés and his army, which numbered only 1250 Spaniards and 8000 Mexican warriors. Cortés retreated, but later returned with an additional army of Indians that were at odds with the Aztecs. The Aztecs fought valiantly under leadership of the last Aztec emperor, Cuauhtemoc. Ravaged by diseases introduced by the Spaniards, deprived of fresh water and food supplies, they withstood an 80-day siege, surrendering on August 13, 1521.

When the war ended, the city was totally destroyed. The survivors fled from the city and the killings continued. As the Aztecs left their homes, Spanish soldiers stationed along the roads searched for gold. The bravest and strongest warriors were separated and branded

Cortés meets and seizes Montezuma
Aztec *Florentine Codex*

with hot irons either on their cheeks or the lips. Cortés rounded up the lords that were alive. They were bound and taken to Coyoacan and their feet were burnt. Reluctant Indian laborers were used to destroy the Aztec homes and any remaining vestiges of their society. The Spanish succeeded in destroying any remaining opposition, confiscating their land and forcing the remaining Aztecs to serve in the encomiendo system to work the mines, more or less as slaves. The priests began their conversion, tearing down the Aztec temples to be replaced by churches. Cortés' greed for more and more gold destroyed the great city of Tenochtitlan and killed more that 240,000 Aztecs. Cortés was rewarded with Governorship, a Captain-General rank, and Chief Justice of the province of New Spain for the next four years.[448]

Aztec *Codex Mendoza* tribute scroll to Cortés

The Spaniards, for their part, were shocked that the Mayans and Aztecs were cruel and practiced human sacrifice. The Spaniards themselves were ruthless in their own brutal destruction of large numbers of the Indians. The Aztecs and Mayas lived in an agricultural society. Their crops, and therefore their lives, were at the mercy of the elements. They prayed and sacrificed individuals to a number of gods; a war god to defeat their enemies; rain, wind, and fire gods, etc. The mediator between the Aztecs and their supreme god and creator was called Quetzacoatl. The Mayan supreme founder was called Kukulcan. Both Kukulcan (Kukulkan) and Quetzacoatl were the same deity, worshipped by both societies and represented as a feathered serpent in their architecture. In Aztec and Mayan oral history, "It is believed among the Indians that with the Itzas who occupied Chichen Itza there reigned a great lord, named Kukulcan, and that the principal building, which is called Kukulcan, shows this to be true. They say he arrived from the west... after his return he was regarded in Mexico as one of their gods and called Quetzalcoatl; and they considered him a god in Yucatan on account of his being a just statesman...."[449]

Mayan Jaguar headpiece
Mt. Alban, Yucatan, circa 600 A.D.

The downfall of the Aztec empire followed with the downfall of the Mayan culture. By 1542 the Spanish established a foothold in the town of Merida and Campeche in the Yucatan. They proceeded to decimate the Mayans with smallpox and war. By 1549 the Mayan population had been reduced from about 800,000 inhabitants of the Yucatan "...to about 250,000 people when the fighting stopped."[450] The Mayan priests were burned at the stake and the survivors were forced into the encomiendo slavery system to work for the Spanish settlers. In place of gold (that was never found), Franciscan missionaries poured into the Yucatan to build missions and initiate the conversion of the Mayan Indians.[451] An extract from a Mayan chronicle gives a glimpse of their disaster: "It was then the first teaching of Christianity began that shall be universal over our land.... Then began the execution by hanging and the fire at the end of our hands. Then also came ropes and cords into the world. Then the children of the younger brothers passed under the hardship of legal summons and tribute... then the seven sacraments of the Word of God were established. Let us receive our guests heatedly; our elder brothers come!"[452] The entire advanced Mayan and Aztec civilizations were destroyed. These civilizations possessed a regular government, laws, and literature. "What an immense treasure", remarked the historian Niebuhur, "for the history of civilization has been lost forever on orders of the first Christian Bishop in Mexico to burn all the native literature." Smallpox and other diseases wiped out about half of the Indians in Central America. Regenerating their numbers, the Mayans rebelled in 1847 in the Yucatan's "War of the Castes." They held out against superior weapons in sporadic fighting until they settled for an uneasy peace in 1901.[453]

Life and Death, after a Stele at Tres Zapotes, Veracruz, Mexico

The Spanish were not finished in their quest for gold and silver. In South America they were about to find the Inca civilization. The entire Inca civilization was systematically and brutally destroyed over and over again from about 1527, when Francisco Pizarro invaded their land, to the 1820s, when Peru was liberated from Spain and received independence. In 1526, when Pizarro first seized a large balsa raft, he realized what lay in this land along the coast of South America. "They were carrying many pieces of silver and gold for adorning the body... crowns, belts and bracelets, armor for the legs and breastplates... mirrors decorated with silver, and cups and other drinking vessels. They carried many wood and cotton mantles, shirts... they had small weights to weigh gold, resembling Roman workmanship."[454] The gold and silver did not have any monetary

Painting, 1847 Mayan "War of the Castes"

value for the Incas. It was purely aesthetic, related to the worship of their sun gods. For the Spanish it was for the monetary possession. Francisco Pizarro read the *Requirement*, similar to the one delivered to Governor Davila in Darien, Panama. A section of the letter read to an Inca representative in 1527 stated, "I, Francisco Pizarro, servant of the high and mighty kings of Castile and Leon, conquerors of barbarian peoples, and being their messenger, herby notify and inform you... to recognize the church as your Mistress and as a governess of the World and Universe, and the High Priest called the Pope, in Her name, and His Majesty (king of Spain) in Her place, as Ruler and the Lord King.... And if you do not do this... with the help of God I shall come mightily against you, and I shall make war on you everywhere and in every way I can... and I shall seize your women and children, and I shall make them slaves, to sell and dispose of as His Majesty commands... and I insist that the deaths and destruction that result from this will be your fault."[455]

Mayan smallpox

After a massacre of about 10,000 Incas, their king, Atahuallpa, offered them roomfuls of gold and silver in return for his freedom. The Incas asked the Spanish, "Do you eat this gold? The Spanish replied, "Yes we eat this gold."[456] The Pre-Columbian goldsmiths of the Americas fashioned elaborate objects of gold, birds, fish, frogs, turtles, alligators, shells, lizards, armadillos, monkeys, deer, jaguars, mosquitoes, and flowers. Headdresses had golden feathers to which real birds' plumage was attached. The goldsmith knew sophisticated metalworking using the technologies of alloys, filigree, granulation, lost-wax casting and gold plating. Pre-Columbian gold and Mesopotamian gold working techniques evolved during the same time period. The Metropolitan Museum of Art timeline dates it at 1500 B.C. when gold was first hammered into a thin foil and placed into the hands and mouth of a youth upon burial at Waywaka, Peru, in the south-central Andes. Found there also was a gold worker's tool kit, along with small pieces of gold foil. In 1998 excavations at the site of Mina Perdida pyramid, south of Lima, Peru, found small hammered foil pieces of copper and gold with radiocarbon dates of at least 1300 B.C. Director Richard Burger and geologist Robert B. Gordon of Yale University's Peabody Museum of Natural History reported their discovery in the *Journal of Science*. The real skill of these early craftsmen began among the Chavin around 1200 B.C. The Chavin made gold ornaments by hammering fine sheets of metal and decorated them by embossing. The technique of casting gold was developed by the Nazca people in the deserts of southern Peru before 500 A.D. In the Chimu culture, which flourished from 1000 A.D. to 1470 at their capital, Chan Chan, thousands of gold artists and craftsmen worked on gold items. The goldsmiths were accomplished sheet-metal workers, hammering and annealing, then soldering a hundred pieces or more into a complex ornament that swayed and shimmered. A magnificent gold burial mask of the Chimu Empire was superbly created. Between A.D. 1150 and 1450, goldsmiths in the Chimu Empire learned how to do filigree by rolling gold under tension into fine wires. Plating was done with an alloy of 30 per cent gold and 70 per cent copper. After being poured onto an ornament, this alloy was treated with acids extracted from plant juices producing a copper oxide which could be cleaned off, leaving the surface covered with a thin film of pure gold. When the Incas conquered them in 1470, many of their goldsmiths were moved to Cuzco, the Inca capital in the central Andes. When Francisco Pizarro conquered Peru, the Inca emperor, Atahuallpa, was ransomed for gold after Pizarro had been given about five tons (150,000 troy oz.) of gold.[457]

"The Inka asks what the Spaniard eats. The Spaniard replies: 'Gold.'" by Guamán Poma, 1600

The Spanish had all the gold objects melted down and sent to Spain, abruptly ending 3000 years of gold working in Peru. Instead of keeping their bargain, Pizarro had Atahuallpa strangled in July of 1533, and then had his corpse burned. The Incas resisted with rebellions over the years. Terror, massacres and the beheading of their leaders met each rebellion. In 1572 they beheaded Inca king Tupa Amaru. Another brutal execution was of Tupa Amaru II, his wife Micaela, and their family on May 18, 1781. All were executed in the same square as Tupa Amura. A Spanish eyewitness wrote, "They cut off his hands and feet. They did the same with (Micaela), and from the others they took the heads, to send to different towns. The torsos of the Indian and his wife were taken to Piqchu where a bonfire had been lit. They were thrown in and burned to ashes, and these were then cast into the air and into a stream that runs nearby. Thus ended Jose Gabriel Tupa Amaru II and Micaela, whose pride and arrogance were such that they named themselves monarchs of Peru."[458] The population was reduced to less than half as the result of Spanish brutality and disease. This, coupled with the seizure

Inca gold headdress

Inca's working with gold
Engraving by de Bry, 1600s

88

of all Inca wealth, let their civilization sink into dire poverty. An article in the mid 1900s wrote of the past Inca Civilization, "The whole land was covered with miracles of engineering. Countless canals, aqueducts, and terrace works brought it to the extreme of fertility, and the utmost care was spent cultivating it, vertically no less than horizontally. Even above the clouds there were orchards. High roads, which overcame every obstacle, threaded the whole district, now making use of hewn steps and of leveled ravines, now passing through long tunnels and now over long ingenious bridges. Peru taught the whole of Europe the principle of manuring—the introduction of guano has revolutionized our agriculture. Incomparable was its textile art.... They were masters of carving... and it is probably no exaggeration to say that our own continent has never produced a form of government of like wisdom, justice and benevolence. In their splendid irrigation system, in their religion, which honored the sun as the highest god and the moon as his sister-wife, and in their mummy cult they remind us even more startlingly of the Egyptians than do the Aztecs."[459]

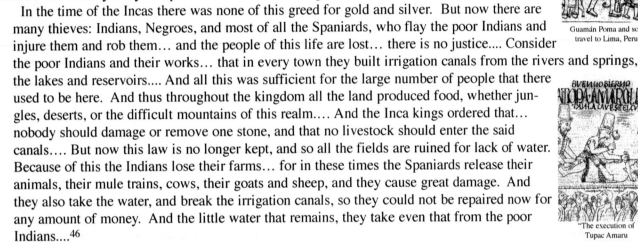

Francisco Pizarro

Inca King Atahuallpa
strangled by Spanish,
Engraving by de Bry, 1600

Guamán Poma and son
travel to Lima, Peru

"The execution of
Tupac Amaru

Felipe Guamán Poma de Ayala (Guamán Poma), in an enormous work of 800 pages of text with 400 illustrations, recorded the Spanish genocide in South America. Completed about 1615, Guamán Poma's book recounted his people's prehistoric origins, and openly and fearlessly attacked the cruel tyranny of Spanish rule. In his writings of the Incas he wrote:

In the time of the Incas there was none of this greed for gold and silver. But now there are many thieves: Indians, Negroes, and most of all the Spaniards, who flay the poor Indians and injure them and rob them... and the people of this life are lost... there is no justice.... Consider the poor Indians and their works... that in every town they built irrigation canals from the rivers and springs, the lakes and reservoirs.... And all this was sufficient for the large number of people that there used to be here. And thus throughout the kingdom all the land produced food, whether jungles, deserts, or the difficult mountains of this realm.... And the Inca kings ordered that... nobody should damage or remove one stone, and that no livestock should enter the said canals.... But now this law is no longer kept, and so all the fields are ruined for lack of water. Because of this the Indians lose their farms... for in these times the Spaniards release their animals, their mule trains, cows, their goats and sheep, and they cause great damage. And they also take the water, and break the irrigation canals, so they could not be repaired now for any amount of money. And the little water that remains, they take even that from the poor Indians....[46]

The Indian tribes in the southwestern parts of the now United States did not fare any better under Spanish colonial rule. The Spanish established a mission and encomiendo system with forced taxes to abolish the Pueblo culture and force them to learn what the priests brought them in religion, and a new way of life. With increased suppression, forced labor, religious persecution, rape and then starvation, it forced the Indians into resistance and then rebellion. This affected all the Rio Grande Pueblos, as well as the Hopis, Zunis, Apaches, Navajos, Yaquis, Yumans, Tarahumaras and a number of other southwestern tribes that were in contact with the Spanish. Each rebellion resulting in a death of a catholic priest brought in the soldiers and more reprisals against the Pueblo Indians. The Indians were hanged and slaughtered letting loose another round of retribution to all the Indians in the area. The Yaquis, a fierce independent tribe, fought back along with the Pueblos of the Rio Grande.

In 1680 the Pueblo tribes, under the leadership of a medicine man from the Taos Pueblo "El Pope", united and drove the Spaniards out. Many Pueblo lives had already been lost as a result of the Spanish occupation, as well as from war and diseases. According to an Indian prisoner taken captive by the Spanish, " the prime movers of the rebellion, and what he had heard were two Indians of San Juan, one named El Pope and the other El Taqu, and another from Taos named El Saca, and another from San Ildefonso named Francisco.... He knows that these were the principals, and the causes they gave were the alleged ill treatment and injuries received from the present secretary, Francisco Xavier, and the maestro de campo, Alonso Garcia, and from the sargentos mayors..."[461] Despite their success, the Spanish returned in 1692. By the end of 1696, the Spanish General de Vargas, "was able to secure the submission of all the Pueblos. They were now reduced in numbers because of the flight of many of their people to other areas, as well as by those killed in action...." Those who remained submitted to de Vargas and became allies of the Spanish." [462]

A deathbed confession addressed to King Philip II of Spain by Garcilaso de la Vega, a defender of the Incas and their culture, stated the attributes of the Incas. Vega wrote of the destruction of an entire civilization by the Spanish Conquistadors. "We found these lands in such a state that there was not even a robber or a vicious or idle man, or adulterous immoral woman: all such conduct was forbidden... everything from the most important to the least was ordered and harmonized with great wisdom. The Incas were feared, obeyed, respected and venerated by their subjects, who considered them to be most capable lords.... I desire His Majesty to understand why I have set down this account, it is to unburden my conscience and confess my guilt, for we have transformed the Indians who had such wisdom and committed so few crimes, excesses, or extravaganzas... this kingdom has fallen into such disorder... it has passed from one extreme to another. There was no evil: now there is almost no good."[463]

Pueblo Man

In 1607, colonists from England started the first permanent settlement at Jamestown, Virginia. The native tribes befriended Captain John Smith and, if not for the hospitality and food supplied by the Indians during the winter months, the new settlers might have starved. Peace between the Indians and the colonists reigned for fifteen years. Thanks to the generosity of Powhatan, the principal chief, John Smith stated they were given "corn and bread." With the increase of more colonists there was a desire for additional land. The best land to farm was the Indians' land that had been already cleared and cultivated. The only way to secure this land was through force. The British had to expel the Indians from their lands. Powhatan stated years later, "I am an old man and must soon die, and the succession must descend in order to my brothers, and then to my two sisters and their daughters. I wish their experience was equal to mine, and that your love to us might not be less than ours to you. Why should you take by force from us that which you can obtain by love? Why should you destroy us, who have provided you with food? What can you gain by war? You see us unarmed and willing to supply your wants, if you will come in a friendly manner, and not with swords and guns...."

Powhatan and council
by de Bry, 1600s

Powhatan went on that he wanted peace, friendship, and to "laugh and be merry with the English." Powhatan ended this message to Captain Smith stating that he did not want to leave his homeland to be hunted in the woods. He cautioned Captain Smith that, "This might soon be your fate too, through your rashness and unadvisedness. I therefore exhort you to peaceable councils." Captain John Smith supposedly was spared—saved from death by Powhatan's daughter, Pocahontas. Her age at the time was ten or eleven, much too early for a romantic affair.

The English were fascinated by the Indians and wrote detailed descriptions in the early 1700s that accurately described them:

> The Indians are of the middling and largest stature of the English: They are straight and well proportioned, having the cleanest and most exact limbs in the world: They are so perfect in their outward frame, that I never heard of one single Indian that was either dwarfish, crooked, bandy-leg'd, or otherwise misshapen. But if they have any such practice among them, as the Romans had, of exposing such children till they died, as were weak and misshapen at their birth, they are very shy of confessing it, and I could never yet learn that they had. Their colour, when they are grown up, is a chestnut brown and tawny but much clearer in their infancy. Their skin comes afterwards to harden and grow blacker, by greasing and sunning themselves. They have generally coal black hair, and very black eyes, which are most commonly grac'd with that sort of squint which many of the Jews are observ'd to have. Their women are generally beautiful, possessing shape and features agreeable enough, and wanting no charm, but that of education and a fair complexion.

Virginia Indian
by John White, 1585

> The men wear their hair cut after several fanciful fashions, sometimes greas'd, and sometimes painted. The great men, or better sort, preserve a long lock behind for distinction. They pull their beards up by the roots with mussel shells, and both men and women do the same by the other parts of their body for cleanliness sake. The women wear the hair of the head very long, either hanging at their backs, or brought before in a single lock, bound up with a fillet of peak, or beads; sometimes also they wear it neatly tyed up in a knot behind. It is commonly greased and shining black, but never painted. The people of condition of both sexes wear a sort of coronet on their heads, from 4 to 6 inches broad, open at the top, and composed of peak, or beads, or else of both interwoven together, and work'd into figures, made by a nice mixture of the colours. Sometimes they wear a wreath of died furs; as likewise bracelets on their necks and arms. The common people go bare-headed, only sticking large shining feathers about their heads, as their fancies lead them.

Their cloaths are a large mantle, carelessly wrapped about their bodies, and sometimes girt close in the middle with a girdle. The upper part of this mantle is drawn close upon the shoulders, and the other hangs below their knees. When that's thrown off, they have only for modesty sake a piece of cloth, or a small skin, tyed round their waste, which reaches down to the middle of the thigh. The common sort tye only a string round their middle, and pass a piece of cloth or skin round between their thighs, which they turn at each end over the string. Their shoes, when they wear any, are made of an entire piece of Buck-Skin; except when they sow a piece to the bottom, to thicken the sole. They are fasten'd on with running strings, the skin being drawn together like a purse on the top of the foot, and tyed round the anckle. The Indian name of this kind of shoe is moccasin.

Noble Matron of Secota, Virginia Indian

The upper part of his hair is cut short, to make a ridge which stands up like the comb of a cock, the rest is either shorn off, or knotted behind his ear. On his head are stuck three feathers of the wild turkey, pheasant, hawk, or such like. At his ear is hung a fine shell with pearl drops. At his breast is a tablet or fine shell, smooth as polish'd marble, which sometimes also hath etched on it a star, halfmoon, or other figure, according to the maker's fancy. Upon his neck and wrists hang strings of beads, peak and roenoke. His apron is made of a deer skin, gashed round the edges, which hang like tassels or fringe; at the upper end of the fringe is an edging of peak, to make it finer. His quiver is of a thin bark; but sometimes they make it of the skin of a fox or young wolf, with the head hanging to it, which has a wild sort of terror in it; and to make it yet more warlike, they tye it on with the tail of a panther, buffalo, or such like, letting the end hang down between their legs. The prickt lines on his shoulders, breast and legs represent the figures painted thereon. In his left hand he holds a bow, and in his right an arrow. The mark upon his shoulder-blade is a distinction used by the Indians in traveling, to show the Nation they are of—and perhaps is the same with that which Baron Lahontan calls—the arms and heraldry of the Indians. Thus, the several letter'd marks are used by several other Nations about Virginia, when they make a journey to their friends and allies.

Abdih-Hiddish "A Minatarre Chief" Tattooed by Karl Bodmer, 1832-1834

I don't find that the Indians have any other distinction in their dress, or the fashion of their hair, than only what a greater degree of riches enables them to make; except it be their religious persons, who are known by the particular cut of the hair, and the unusual figure of their garments; as our clergy are distinguish'd by their canonical habit. The habit of the Indian priest is a cloak made in the form of a woman's petticoat; but instead of tying it about their middle, they fasten the gatherings about their neck, and tye it upon the right shoulder, always keeping one arm out to use upon occasion. This cloak hangs even at the bottom, but reaches no lower than the middle of the thigh; but what is most particular in it is, that it is constantly made of a skin drest soft, with the pelt of fur on the outside, and revers'd; insomuch, that when the cloak has been a little worn, the hair falls down in flakes and looks very shagged, and frightful. The conjurer shaves all his hair off, except the crest on the crown; upon his ear he wears the skin of some dark-colour'd bird; he, as well as the priest, is commonly grim'd with soot or the like; to have his modesty he hangs an otter-skin at his girdle, fastning the tail between his legs; upon his thigh hangs his pocket, which is fasten'd by tucking it under his girdle, the bottom of this is likewise fring'd with tassils for ornament sake. In the middle between them is the huskanawpen.

The dress of the women is little different from that of the men, except in the tying of their hair. The women of distinction wear deep necklaces, pendants and bracelets, made of small cylinders of the conque shell, which they call peak. They likewise keep their skin clean, and shining with oil, while the men are commonly bedaub'd all over with paint. They are remarkable for having small round breasts, and so firm, that they are hardly ever observ'd to hang down, even in old women. They commonly go naked as far as the navel downward, and upward to the middle of the thigh, by which means they have the advantage of discovering their fine limbs, and compleat shape.[464]

Florida Indian Chief (King) and Maidens, by de Bry

These same Englishmen, who so vividly, aptly described their first encounters with the Indians, were also responsible for wiping out entire tribes of them down the east coast of the United States. In 1614, when a small group of 104 English explorers landed in the vicinity of Massachusetts Bay, they returned home with Indian slaves and left behind a smallpox epidemic. The Puritans who followed them on the "Mayflower" landed on December

11, 1620, and found that most of the New England natives had been decimated by small-pox. The Puritans built their colony, "Plymouth Plantation", near the ruins of a former Indian village of the Pawtucket Nation and were warmly welcomed by Squanto, a Wampanoag Indian. His first greeting to them was in broken English, "Welcome Englishman!", because he had spent years as a slave in England. Squanto befriended the early colonists, acting as an interpreter, and explained to them how to use the wild corn that was growing in the abandoned fields, to fish, and to survive utilizing the food,

Indians sick from diseases, 1600s, by de Bry

herbs, and fruits of the land. Squanto and Chief Massasoit also arranged a peace treaty between the Puritans and the Wampanoag Indians who surrounded their colony. Due to his effort the Puritans prospered, and there was peace for about fifteen years. Squanto was also credited with bringing about the first Thanksgiving. At the end of their first year, the Puritans gave a great feast made from their first harvest to honor Squanto and their Wampanoag friends. This was the first "Thanksgiving" celebration.

As word of the Puritans' success reached England, more Puritans arrived by the boatload. These new arrivals had no concept of what the Indians considered land ownership. The Puritans who came considered the land "public domain"—there for the taking. The Indians had not cultivated or farmed the land in the European style, and there were no fences or other boundary markings to denote owner-ship. The original Puritan settlers that Squanto helped were excommunicated and expelled from the Church. The new British immigrants were joined by British settlers, who began to seize the land, enslave the Native Indian populations and finance their expansion by selling Indian slaves. During

Chief Massasoit of
Wampanoag
1580?-1661

these early years, Massachusetts allowed owners to brand Indian slaves on the cheek or forehead to prevent their escape. This marked the beginning of a disastrous genocide against the Indians along the entire east coast. Puritan voices arose against the Indians, calling them subhuman creatures and wild beasts standing in the path of civilization. Cotton Mather, a Puritan preacher, wrote "...that probably the devil decoyed those miserable savages hither, in hopes that the gospel of the Lord Jesus Christ would never come here to destroy or disturb his absolute empire over them." William Bradford also viewed the Indians in New England as wild beasts, writ-ing in 1620, "The vast and unpeopled countries of America, which are fruitful and fit for habitation, being devoid of all civil inhabitants, where there are only savage and brutish men, which range up and downe (down), little otherwise than the wild beasts of the same."[465]

In 1636, the Massachusetts colony, with a force of about 200 colonists, commanded by Captain John Mason and Captain John Underhill, went to war against the Pequot Indians who had killed two slave traders. They enlisted the aid of several hundred Mohegan's, enemies of the Pequots. Almost the entire Pequot tribe was burned alive and massacred, village by village, while asleep. Women and children were cut to pieces while trying to hide under their beds. The colonists, with a force of drawn weapons, encircled their fort, and those who attempted to flee the flames were brutally shot down. The massacre was described as a "fearful sight to see them thus frying the fire, and the

Battle with the Pequots
and English in which
700 "savages" had their
heads cut off
Book title, 1638

streams of blood quenching the same, and terrible was the stink... victory seemed a sweet sacrifice and they gave the praise thereof to God... and to give them so speedy a victory over so proud, insulting, and blas-phemous an enemy.... It is supposed that no less than five or six hundred Pequot souls were brought down to hell that day." The colonists thought they were justified in their acts against the Pequots. Their success was sufficient evidence "that they had the divine approval for the destruction of the bloody heathen."

After this massacre the remaining Pequots were hunted down and more than one hundred were captured. The men were put to death and the rest were distributed as slaves to important colonists or sold into slavery in the West Indies, the Azores, Algiers, England and Spain. Even the friendly Wampanoag chief did not escape. He was beheaded and his head was placed on a pole in Plymouth, Massachusetts, where it remained for 24 years.[466]

In 1641, the Dutch government in Manhattan began their first scalp bounty against the Indians. The Puritans followed with bounties on Indians for slaves. The Dutch and the Puritans joined forces to exterminate all Indians from New England. The term "heads roll", was a literal translation of the atrocities against the Indians in the east. Each white victory resulted in a "Thanksgiving celebration" against what they named "heathen savages." The heads of Indians were hacked off and kicked through the streets of Manhattan like soccer balls. All these atrocities heightened the hatred

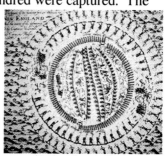

Attack on Pequots, Mystic,
Connecticut, May 26, 1637
From European engraving, 1638

between the colonists and the Indians, resulting in more conflicts with increased distrust, hatred, and revenge on both sides. The Indians believed that the colonists' main purpose was to take their land and destroy them as a people, while the whites regarded the Indian as a pagan savage. The cruelty inflicted upon the Indians was not forgotten, and Indian parents passed down painful memories and the desire for revenge to their children. In the same way, injuries that were sustained by the white people at the hands of the Indians inflamed the passions of their friends and relatives, which perpetuated the punishment and conflict from generation to generation.[467]

Pequot Warrior

There were some settlers living as friends with the Indians, but these were just a token few. One of these men, William Penn (1644-1718), along with his Quaker friends, lived in friendship with the Delaware and tribes of the Six Nations for over 100 years without one serious disturbance, due to their renunciation of war. In 1681 William Penn received a grant from the king of England to settle in America. An open letter dated August 18, 1681, was sent by Penn to be delivered to the local tribes by his Representative, William Markham. Penn relayed the power of God and to "all things, therein...." and that all must account for their actions to God. We are all "taught to love and help one another...." Penn voiced his desire for peace and friendship and that he wished to live together with the Indians as brothers and friends. He noted, "The unkindness and injustice that hath been too much exercised toward you by people of these parts... to make great advantages of you, rather than to be examples of goodness and patience unto you... sometimes to the shedding of blood, which has made the great God angry."[468]

In 1682 William Penn purchased the land in Pennsylvania from the Delaware (Lenape), Susquehanna and other Indians tribes. About 1684, at a treaty of peace, a wampum belt was presented to Penn coupled with a pledge of friendship made by the settlers to that, "The utmost good faith shall be observed toward the Indians; their land and property shall never be taken from them without their consent; and in their property, rights, and liberty they shall never be invaded or disturbed, unless in just and lawful wars authorized by Congress." To solve any disputes, twelve persons were selected, six English and six Indians.[469] The Abbé Raynal, a prominent Frenchman and author of the *Histoire des Deux Indes*, in 1770, voiced his approval of Penn's action and felt that Penn acted justly with the Indians with his love and friendship; it was "some kind of compensation for the disgust, melancholy, and horror..." wrought upon the Indians by the European settlers. Raynal wrote that the evil calamities the Europeans reigned on the natives of America was because "the insatiable thirst of gold has given birth to the most infamous and the most atrocious of all traffics, that of slaves."[470]

1829 Book

Wm. Penn Treaty, from Currier & Ives litho

William Penn's treaty with Indians from a painting by Benjamin West

In 1792 Red Jacket, the Seneca Chief, visited Philadelphia for the one-hundredth anniversary of the agreement between William Penn and their tribes. Red Jacket noted the deep friendship that existed for William Penn, and the peace between his tribes during this period. Voicing his fear of the future, Red Jacket said, "As you love peace, so do we also; and we wish that it could be extended to the most distant parts of this country."[471]

On September 8, 1760, the Governor of French Canada surrendered to General Lord Jeffrey Amherst. The Indians who had sided with the French found themselves no longer welcomed by the English. There was one last battle in the east by the Indians to prevent these new colonists from entering their land. Pontiac, an Ottawa Chief, enlisted the Miamis, Ottawas, Chippewas (Ojibways), Wyandots, Pottawatomies, Delawares, Shawnees and other tribes to drive the colonists away. In 1763 each tribe attacked a specific garrison or post in its locality. This was the last desperate attack to drive the English into the Atlantic Ocean. On February 10, 1763, at the Treaty of Paris, the war between France and England ended and France renounced all possessions east of the Mississippi. Pontiac agreed to peace terms on October 3, 1763. Spain had also ceded Florida to England and by this time the increasingly large numbers of colonists had began to press across to the west and south to settle on Indian lands.

By the time the United States gained independence in 1776, the Indian tribes in the Northeast had been greatly reduced in numbers by diseases brought by the European settlers. Smallpox was deliberately given to the Indians. General Amherst "had been determined to eradicate the Indian vermin—if necessary, by the further use of small-pox-infected blankets...." Amherst, in 1763, in his war against Pontiac's rebellion

George Washington presents medal to Red Jacket. Painting by Hal Sherman, 1792

against the British, "...urged every method be used against them, including that notorious directive about distributing smallpox-infected blankets in their encampments; he also advocated the use of drugs." In another letter on July 13, 1763, Colonel Henry Bouquet suggests "the use of dogs to hunt the Indians, the so-called "Spaniard's Method", which Amherst approves in principle, but says he cannot implement because there are not enough dogs.[472]

Africans, who were resistant to many of these diseases, were brought in as slaves instead. Boston had been a major slave-trading center for the Northeast Indians. Charleston, South Carolina, became the major market and port of entry and exit for slaves to the South. In 1670 the port of Charleston became the main exit for shipping southern slaves of Indian descent (particularly the Cherokee, Creek and Choctaw Indians), to the Caribbean plantations.

Smallpox, from Mayan codex

General Amherst 1717-1797

Pontiac, Ottawa 1720-1769

One of 3 letters, July 13, 1763, between General Amherst and Colonel Henry Bouquet on the use of smallpox

The Indian slaves were also forced to work as sailors and soldiers in almost every European nation. In 1778 during the United States war of Independence, George Washington impressed all Indian, Mulatto and African slaves into battalions to fight the British, offering these Indians freedom if the United States won the war. Abraham Lincoln abolished slavery for African Americans in 1865 and gave them citizenship, while Indians were still being enslaved. In a joint resolution on July 27, 1868, the United States Congress and Mexico outlawed the enslavement of the Navajos in both countries. Even after this, Indians were taken advantage of and cheated out of their lands.[473]

In 1884 the Supreme Court, in Elk versus Wilkins, ruled that the fourteenth amendment to the United States Constitution freed the African slaves, but did not grant the same citizenship or constitutional rights to the Indians. This right was not even granted to the Indian who had left the reservation to assimilate into white society. It was not until June 2, 1924 that the Indian Citizenship Act authorized the Secretary of the Interior to issue certificates of citizenship to Indians to give them the right to vote. Unfortunately, in some states, court action was required and it took about 25 years before the Indian Citizenship Act became a reality for all Indians.[474]

General Sullivan 1740-1795

In 1779 the United States government, under direct orders from George Washington, sent General John Sullivan to wipe out the Six Nation Iroquois Confederacy as punishment to them for siding with the British during the Revolutionary War. Washington instructed Sullivan, saying, "The expedition you are appointed to command is to be directed against the hostile tribes of the Six Nations of Indians.... The immediate objects are the total destruction and devastation of their settlements… that the country may not be merely overrun, but destroyed.... We may then listen to propositions for peace, and endeavor to draw further advantages from their fears."[475] Sullivan immediately attacked the Senecas and Cayugas. Framed houses and the

Iroquois village

gardens and fields full of produce in several towns and villages were completely burned and destroyed. The Indians fled before Sullivan's advance, and the Seneca capitol of Kanandalgus was destroyed as well as the entire valley of the Genessee area.

One of the worst atrocities was the slaughter of the Delaware Indians and converts from the Mohawk tribe that accepted the Moravian religion. Their religious principles forbade them to take up arms and, although they were neutral, their villages were completely destroyed in massacres at Pavonia (1643), Paxtung (1763), Gnadenhutten (1782) and Moraviantown (1813). In one village, the Indians were deceived into gathering together into one house and were butchered in cold blood. In the village were 62 grown adults, one third of whom were women (many nursing mothers), and the remainder were 34 children. Other highly civilized settlements were burned to the ground. Washington gave estates that had belonged to the Indians to the soldiers who had decimated their land.[476]

The Seminole Indians, originally part of the Creek (Muscogee, Muskogee) tribe, split apart from the Creeks and moved out of Alabama, Georgia and into Florida in the 1700's. They became known as Seminoles because the name means runaways. During the early 1800s, the fugitive slaves' only escape was into the Spanish territory of Florida. In 1825 the Creek Indians from Georgia were evicted from their ancestral homes. They tried to take shelter in Florida, then under Spanish control. This did not prevent the Georgia militia and vigilantes from invading Florida to seize the Indians and sell them into slavery. The Creek Indians paid a large sum to stop these attacks on their people. The Georgia slaveholders had demanded and had been given one hundred and forty thousand dollars by the Creeks as a payment for those children who would have been born to their slave masters. It forced the Creeks to make alliances with other fragmented Florida tribes, spawning the formation of the Seminole nation of tribes. [477]

Chief Hendrick
Mohawk, 1680-1755

Andrew Jackson had left his mark in Florida in 1818 in a punitive expedition against the Florida Seminoles and to take Florida by force from Spain. The Seminoles opposed the United States when they came to take the Seminole's land after the United States acquired Florida in 1819 from Spain. In the 1823 Treaty of Moultrie Creek, the Seminoles ceded most of their land in Florida to move to a reservation in central Florida. A problem arose with the African slaves in the custody of the Seminoles. The Africans had integrated into the Seminole culture as equals and they were now being forced to go back to the white southerners. The Treaty of Paynes Landing in 1832 forced the seven attending chiefs to sign an agreement calling for the Seminoles to be removed to Oklahoma. In 1834, at a treaty discussion, Osceola was reported to have said, "This is the only treaty I will ever make with the whites", as he stabbed the treaty paper with a knife. With their refusal, the United States government attempted to destroy the Seminole Indians in Florida. Another Seminole war soon broke out when Georgia slaveholders forcibly carried off the wives and children of Florida Indians who had intermarried with the fugitive slaves, lasting seven years and costing the United States over twenty million dollars. On April 30, 1836, General Winfield Scott, commander of the troops in Florida reported that, "The whole force of the enemy, including Negroes, does not exceed 1200 fighting men. It is probably something less." Colonel Zachary Taylor received approval from Congress to use bloodhounds to chase the Seminoles in Florida. It took a third Seminole war to remove approximately 250 additional Seminoles.

Osceola, a Seminole leader
From painting by
Charles Bird King, 1820s

The Seminole wars lasted over forty years, until 1858. Sam Jones (Arpeika), a Seminole spiritual leader and medicine man, helped warriors prepare for battle and participated in the wars as well. In research by balladeer Okefenokee Joe, it states, "Over 15,000 soldiers died, but Sam Jones was never captured or subdued, and the Indians never surrendered. They disappeared into the swamps to live." In 1911 the U.S. government created three reservations in South Florida. In 1935 a peace treaty was signed with the remaining Seminoles in Florida and the United States.[478]

The same course was pursued against Indian tribes living in Colorado. In 1833, soldiers killed one hundred ten Indians in Colorado. All the women above age 20 were massacred in cold blood, and the children were sold or given away as servants. In 1840, the *London Saturday Journal* reported, "The warfare is too bloody to last; the Christians are killing every Indian."[479]

During his travels to unmapped Indian lands from 1830 to 1839, George Catlin, at age of thirty-three, visited a number of the tribes and as a painter and pictorial historian. He summed up the genocide against them by saying, "The Indians of North America, as I have before said, are copper-coloured with long black hair, black eyes, tall, straight, and [have] elastic forms—are less than two millions in number—were originally the undisputed owners of the soil, and got their title to their lands from the Great Spirit who created them on it; were once a happy and flourishing people, enjoying all the comforts and luxuries of life which they knew of, and consequently cared for; were sixteen millions in numbers, and sent that number of daily prayers to the Almighty, and thanks for the goodness and protection. Their country was entered by white men, but a few hundred years since; and thirty millions of these are now scuffling for the goods and luxuries of life, over the bones and ashes of twelve millions of red men; six millions of whom have fallen victims to the small-pox, and the remainder to the sword, the bayonet, and whiskey; all of which means of their death and destruction have been introduced and visited upon them by acquisitive white men; and by white men, also, whose forefathers were welcomed and embraced in the land where the poor Indian met and fed them with 'ears of green corn and with pemican.' Of the two millions remaining alive at this time, about 1,400,000 are already the miserable living victims and dupes of white man's cupidity, degraded, discouraged and lost in the bewildering maze that is produced by the use of whiskey and its concomitant vices; and the remaining number are yet unroused and unenticed from their wildhaunts or their primitive modes, by the dread or love of white man and his allurements."[480]

Portrait of George
Catlin

CHAPTER 7 INDIAN DISPOSSESSED AND FORCED REMOVAL

The speculation and exploitation for Indian lands relate back to grants to individuals or groups willing to settle in the New World in exchange for land that did not rightfully belong to them. Realizing the Indians could not understand how you can own the land, every type of deception and trickery was utilized to take it. Speculation to own Indian lands go back before the

George Washington signs U. S. Trade and Intercourse Act of 1790, prohibiting sale of Indian land

Revolutionary War when George Washington, Benjamin Franklin and groups of leading citizens attempted to buy or successfully purchased Indian land. Although a proclamation by King George III in 1763 prohibited individuals from taking Indian lands, Washington wrote a letter to a William Crawford in 1767, stating, "I can never look upon the Proclamation in any other light.... By this time it be easy for you to discover that my plan is to secure a good deal of land...." Benjamin Franklin, on his trip to London in 1766, represented a group of associates who attempted to purchase 1,200,000 acres of land in Illinois, north to Wisconsin.

Greenville treaty, by H. Candler Christy | General Anthony Wayne

The mass expelling of the Indians westward began in 1789, when the United States War Department was created, in part to handle Indian matters. Between 1789 and 1871, the President was empowered by the Senate to make treaties with Indian Tribes in the U.S. These treaties recognized the Indians as supreme sovereign nations. Article II, Section 2, clause 2 (better known as the Supremacy Clause) of the U.S. Constitution gives priority to treaties should there be a conflict between a treaty and either a constitutional provision or state law. However, this statute did not alter or abrogate the terms of treaties that had already been made.

Greenville treaty Indian signatures, 1795 | Fort Stanwix 1768 treaty, with League of Iroquois signatures conceding land in the territory west of the Appalachian Mountains

Before 1871 about 800 treaties were negotiated, with the Senate ratifying less than 400. The Indians were under the assumption that approximately all 800 treaties were in effect with their signatures. They did not know the treaties had to be ratified by Congress. In all these signed treaties the Indian nations complied, and did not break their word on any. The President's authority to make treaties with Indians was terminated by the Act of March 3, 1871. After this date the treaties were called "agreements." The Supreme Court ruled that these agreements are the same as treaties and, under United States law, remain in effect today.[481]

The Delaware (Lenape) people signed the first Indian treaty with the newly formed United States government on September 17, 1778. Numerous betrayals and massacres, and liquor, eventually forced them to give up their lands. Most moved westward, first to Ohio, then to Indiana, Missouri, Kansas, and finally to the Indian Territory in Anadarko, Oklahoma. Other small bands fled to Ontario, Canada. On October 15, 1783, a Committee on Indian Affairs drew up a report for the Continental Congress on how to deal with the Indians regarding trade, territorial claims, etc. The Six Nations, on October 22, 1784, relinquished their land in the Ohio Valley in return for "goods to be delivered to the said Six Nations for their use and comfort...." During the 1790s, Chief Little Turtle led the Miami Confederacy to defeat the U.S. in two major battles. After a defeat by General Anthony Wayne, and weary of war, the Greenville Treaty of 1795 was negotiated with Little Turtle to take more Indian land for the white settlers in the northwest. With bribes and pressure, several more treaties followed, taking most of the northwest land from the Indians. Dragging Canoe, who lived from the early 1730's until 1792, was perhaps the first American Indian to organize and lead a serious resistance effort against white settlement on Indian lands. For the last 17 years of his life he fought and killed settlers who were encroaching on Cherokee hunting grounds in what is now east and middle Tennessee. Dragging Canoe strongly resisted the sale of Cherokee lands to whites and spoke at treaty negotiations, vehemently objecting to the continued sale of Cherokee land. He planted the seed of resistance to white settlement of Indian land that lasted over 100 years, and even beyond. Tecumseh and the Prophet, both students of Dragging Canoe, continued the Indian resistance into the 1800's. The Treaty of Hopewell, signed on November 28, 1785, with the Cherokee Indian nation, encompassed all their territory south of Ohio and east of the Mississippi. This treaty supposedly guaranteed the land only to the Cherokee nation. It stipulated that any citizen of the United States or any non-Indian who had settled, or intended to settle on the Cherokee land, must leave within six

Delaware Chief

Dragging Canoe, by Mike Smith

Chief Cumnacatogue, Cherokee, circa 1790s

months of the treaty's ratification or, "such person shall forfeit protection of the United States, and the Indians may punish him or not as they please." The treaty also guaranteed to the Cherokee nation "that the hatchet shall be buried forever", and that peace and friendship will be "re-established between the said states on the one part, and all the Cherokees on the other, and shall be universal." The treaty was signed and ratified on November 28, 1785. On July 2, 1791, another treaty was signed with the Cherokees, creating new boundaries.

Creek Indians surrender to Andrew Jackson after Battle of Horseshoe Bend, 1814

Between 1791 and 1819 the United States forced or bribed the Cherokee into making twenty-five treaties, which confiscated their land. Before the end of the 1830's, the U.S. government had taken all of the Cherokee's land east of the Mississippi River, consisting of over 50,000 square miles.

The Choctaws, Cherokees, Chickasaws and the Creek Indians all signed treaties which promised that "the hatchet shall be buried forever", and established defined land boundaries and terms advantageous to the U.S. government. Several boundary-changing amendments were made to each of these treaties, which gradually pushed the Indians further and further west. All the treaties were used basically as an implement for taking Indian land peacefully thru deception, instead of by force.[482]

By 1802 the five great southern tribes, the Choctaw, Creek, Chickasaw, Seminole and Cherokee had responded to Thomas Jefferson's earlier advice to integrate their cultures into white society.[483] The Cherokee nation had been a distinct community with boundaries recognized by the United States government, and had completely assimilated into white society. The Cherokees lived on forty thousand square miles of rich agricultural land in Tennessee. According to an 1825 census taken by the Cherokees, they had 33 grist mills, 13 sawmills, 1 powder mill, 69 blacksmith shops, 2 tan yards, 762 looms, 172 wagons, 2923 plows, 7683 horses, thousands of sheep and black cattle, eight cotton weaving machines, eighteen schools, public roads, a written constitution and their own newspaper, *The Cherokee Phoenix*, published in English and Cherokee. Sequoia (George Guess) had developed a syllabary (character pictures that represented words), making it possible to write in the Cherokee language.[484] In addition, many of the Cherokees had adopted the Christian religion, and had changed their political and justice system to that of the United States.

Thomas Jefferson letter January 18, 1803

Courtesy, Thomas Jefferson Foundation, Inc.

With the Louisiana Purchase of 1803, more Indian lands secured from the French were added west of the Mississippi. The Indians began to grow restless, fearful that the United States government would take their land. Thomas Jefferson was familiar with this unrest and on January 18, 1803, penned a confidential letter to Congress: "The Indian tribes residing within the limits of the U.S. have for a considerable time been growing more and more uneasy at the constant diminution of the territory they occupy... it excites dangerous jealousies and perturbations in their minds to make any overture for the purchase of the smallest portions of their land.... In order peaceably to counteract this policy of theirs, and to provide an extension of territory which the rapid increase of our numbers will call for, two measures are deemed expedient. First, to encourage them to abandon hunting, to apply to the raising of stock, to agriculture and domestic manufacture, and thereby prove to themselves that less land and labor will maintain them in this, better than in their former mode of living.... Secondly, to multiply trading houses among them and place within their reach those things which will contribute more to their domestic comfort than the profession of extensive, but uncultivated wilds; experience and reflection will develop to them the wisdom of exchanging what they can spare and we want, for what we can spare and they want...." Jefferson went on to recommend the expenditure of monies for the Lewis and Clark expedition to eventually open new territory to white settlers.

Chief Pushmataha Choctaw

After the War of 1812 there was pressure in Congress to displace all the Indians from their lands in the east. There were also constant demands from the United States government to the Indian commissioners to renegotiate treaties. The mood in the east was to remove the eastern Indians from the path of the white man. Two Presidents of the United States who played a principal role in enacting laws for this removal were President James Monroe (author of "The Principles of 1823", or The Monroe Doctrine) and Andrew Jackson. Their way of thinking regarding the Indian removal is best expressed in two letters. General Jackson wrote to President Monroe on March 14, 1817, concerning the Indians: "Their existence and happiness now depend upon a change in their habits and customs...." James Monroe, in a reply to Jackson on October 5, 1817, writes, "The

Choctaw "Treaty of Dancing Rabbit Creek", 1830

hunter or savage state requires a greater extent of territory to sustain it than is compatible with the progress and just claims of civilized life, and must yield to it. Nothing is more certain than if the Indian tribes do not abandon that state, and become civilized, that they will decline and become extinct. The hunter state, tho' maintain'd by warlike spirits, presents but a feeble resistance to the more dense, compact, and powerful population of civilized man."[485]

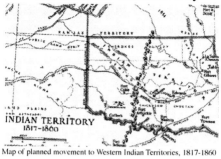

Map of planned movement to Western Indian Territories, 1817-1860

In 1819 Congress passed the first law that enabled the appropriation of $10,000 for the purpose of "civilizing" the Indians. In 1824, with the creation of a Bureau of Indian Affairs within the war department, Congress became actively involved. President James Monroe, in a special message to Congress on March 30, 1824, started the first steps for removal of the Indians west by arguing it would benefit the Indians. In December, 1824, President Monroe told Congress that it was too slow a process to change deplorable conditions necessary for their survival if they remained in their ancestral homeland. The only solution, Monroe suggested, was for the Indians to be induced to go out west, "from the lands they now occupied to land west of the Mississippi River." James Monroe, at the end of his term in office on January 24, 1825, addressed a special message to Congress for a bill that would satisfy both the Cherokees and Georgians, that would "shield them from impending ruin, but promote their welfare and happiness."[486] Quickly following, on February 1, 1825, was a bill drafted by Senator Thomas Hart Benton to acquire land from the Indians in the west, and to be used as an incentive to remove the Indians from the east. As President Monroe left office in 1825, he restated, "Experience has clearly demonstrated that, in their present state, it is impossible to incorporate them (Indians) in such masses, in any form whatever, into our system...." The Secretary of War, Calhoun, promised that ninety-seven thousand Indians would be moved from North Carolina, Georgia, Alabama, Tennessee, Ohio, Indiana, Illinois, Missouri, New York and the territories of Arkansas and Michigan. Before their forced removal, the five Indian nations occupied over seventy-seven million acres of land. Georgia had pressed for this ruling from President Monroe, urging that the Cherokee nation should be forced to move without delay, and their territory given to Georgia. This could not be arranged legally unless a way could be arranged to persuade the Cherokees and other eastern tribes to surrender their original treaty rights.

Peter Pitchlynn (Snapping Turtle), Choctaw political leader, 1806-1881, Catlin

Chief Ledagie, Creek

The Choctaws were the first to be removed west to Oklahoma. The 1786 Treaty of Hopewell with the Choctaw Nation made the United States' intentions clear. This treaty was the first attempt by the U.S. to establish control over the Choctaw. The treaty required the return of escaped slaves, the turning over of any Choctaws whom had been convicted of crimes by the U.S., and the return of any property which had been captured during the Revolutionary War. Additional treaties followed, taking more land. In the War of 1812, the Choctaws fought alongside Andrew Jackson in the battle of New Orleans. This did not prevent their removal. The 1820 treaty with the Six Nations forced the Choctaws to exchange 4,150,000 acres of the prime cotton-growing delta region of the Choctaw Nation for lands of questionable quality west of the Mississippi River, in the (then) new "Indian Territory."

The Treaty of Dancing Rabbit Creek was signed on September 7, 1830, and ratified by the Senate on February 24, 1831. The Treaty of Dancing Rabbit Creek abrogated all previous agreements and called for the removal of all Choctaws from their remaining ancestral lands to reservations in what was to eventually become Oklahoma. Due to a split over leadership of the Choctaw nation, leading Choctaw chiefs were bribed with the best lands to initial this treaty. Under the terms of the new treaty, all of the lands remaining under the control of the Choctaw Nation—10,421,139 acres—were to be exchanged for the same land in Indian Territory. The Choctaw Nation would receive title in fee simply to an area west of Arkansas Territory, lying between the Arkansas and Canadian rivers on the north, and the Red River on the south. The great majority of the Choctaws were bitterly opposed to the sale of tribal lands and their removal to the west. Small parties of Choctaws made their departure west as early as November of 1830. These first parties pressed ahead to the Saline River in Arkansas, where they stopped for five weeks to build a ferry for those who were to follow. After extreme suffering

Map of Creek Tribes Prior to 1776

from hunger and exposure to severe winter weather during much of the 550 mile journey, the surviving ninety-two Choctaws arrived in an emaciated condition at the Kiamichi River in February of 1831. Here they settled into the shelter of the abandoned and partially burned old Fort Towson, to barely survive on a scant supply of corn. During the following several years other groups from the Choctaw Nation went west. One group of 4000 Choctaws were scarcely in boats on the Mississippi River when a severe winter storm overtook them. This was the beginning of one of the worst blizzards ever experienced, leaving 2500 Choctaws huddled in the open near the Arkansas Post, some bare-footed, many without blankets, to suffer the fury of the storm. The next group of about 8000 were exposed to and contracted cholera in the waterfronts along the river while awaiting their turn to board the boats, resulting in a heavy loss of life. It is estimated that 17,500 Choctaws immigrated to Indian Territory, leaving 1200 who remained in Mississippi.

ME-NA-WA
Creek Warrior

The United States guaranteed the Creek (Muscogee) Nation a large territory covering most of Georgia and Alabama in the Treaty of New York in 1790. Many treaties followed in the years to come. On April 24, 1802, Georgia moved to oust the "Five Civilized Tribes" (Five Nations) of Cherokees, Chickasaws, Choctaws, Muskogee (Creeks) and Seminoles from their land by arranging the "Georgia Compact" to cede her land in the west to the United States government in return for a promise that the government would take title to the Cherokees land "as early as the same can be peaceably obtained on reasonable terms."[487]

The Muscogee and the Alabama were the largest of the Creek family of tribes. Most of them lived north of the other Creek tribes. They are called the Upper Creeks. The lower Creek tribes were either Yuchi or Hitchiti tribes. The Creek Indians were part of a 19 tribal group that once resided in much of what is now Alabama and Georgia. Today, many of the 20,000 Creek Indians live in Oklahoma. In the 1802 Georgia Compact, the State of Georgia sold all the Creek land to the United States, in which the State of Georgia was paid $1,230,000. The Georgia Indian Removal Bill of January 27, 1825, called for the removal of all Indian tribes within the State of Georgia. After the first Creek War in 1813-1814 that ended in the Battle of Horseshoe Bend, the Creeks were forced to sign a treaty that made them give up their land. In the 1830's, they were forced to move to the Indian Territory in what is now Oklahoma. Most of the Creeks refused to leave, resulting in the Creek War of 1836 to 1837. Upon their defeat, fourteen-thousand Creeks, about twenty-five-hundred in chains, were led by General Winfield Scott on a forced march to Oklahoma, without their belongings. The Creeks received very little payment for their lands and were forced to live in poverty for many years on poor land.[488]

The Cherokee territory in the east was fertile cotton-growing cotton land, and the Industrial Revolution in England had caused a sudden growth in demand for the raw material to be woven into cloth. In 1830, gold was discovered in Georgia and settlers rushed on to Cherokee land to stake mining claims. Political trickery was then used to divest the Cherokees of their land. Andrew Jackson led the removal of the Cherokees from their land before and after he became President in 1829. Jackson made it known that his sympathy was with the southern whites. He refused to honor any of the treaties between the United States and these tribes. The Cherokees protested against the attempt to remove them from Georgia. Under the administration of James Monroe, in January, 1823, the Cherokees issued a proclamation asserting their original treaty rights. They also claimed that these original rights preceded the sovereignty claimed by Georgia.[489]

Major Ridge, Cherokee
1771-1839

In 1829, President Jackson informed the Indians in Alabama and Georgia that they could not exist as an independent nation within those states and that their only alternative was to emigrate west of the Mississippi. Jackson also refused to stop the harassment of these tribes by groups of vigilantes and squatters who had moved onto the Indian land. On May 28, 1830, Jackson set the stage for the removal of all the eastern tribes from their homeland through an act of Congress, passing The Indian Removal Act—an act to provide for an exchange of lands with Indians residing within any of the states or territories, and for their removal west of the Mississippi."[490] On March 30, 1834, Congress, under the presidency of Andrew Jackson, passed additional laws that impacted the relationship between the United States government and the Indians for many years. The Indian Trade and Intercourse Act gave the government the power to rename and resettle the Indians. In 1834 Congress banned all alcohol sales on Indian land. The Indian Reorganization Act transformed the bureau; the head of the Indian bureau was now called the Commissioner of Indian Affairs, an efficient arm of the United States government, for determining the fate of the Indians. It also allowed the government to give annuities to tribal chiefs instead of, as was previously the case, to individuals. The government's intention was to force the

Indians to give up hunting for food to become farmers. The purpose of the acts of Congress was to remove and isolate the Indians into another territory until they were converted to the white man's way of life. The Indians were to be purposely removed to an area so unfit for farming that it was called by early American explorers Stephen H. Long and Zebulon Pike, "The Great American Desert."[491]

In two speeches, one by President Andrew Jackson and one by Speckled Snake, a Cherokee, the views of the United States and the Indian Tribes were stated regarding removal. Jackson, in his second annual message to Congress in 1830, justified the removal of the Indians to the west with this speech:

Se-Quo-Yah, Cherokee inventor of the Cherokee alphabet

It gives me pleasure to announce to Congress that the benevolent policy of the government, steadily pursued for nearly thirty years, in relation to the removal of the Indians beyond the white settlements is approaching to a happy consummation. Two important tribes have accepted the provision made for their removal... and it is believed that their example will induce the remaining tribes also to seek the same obvious advantages. The consequences of a speedy removal will be important to the United States, to individual States, and to the Indians themselves.... It puts an end to all possible danger of collision between the authorities of the General and State governments on account of the Indians. It will place a dense and civilized population in large parts of country now occupied by a few savage hunters. By opening the whole territory between Tennessee on the north and Louisiana on the south to the settlement of the whites it will incalculably strengthen the southwestern frontier and render the adjacent States strong enough to repel future invasions without remote aid. It will relieve the whole State of Mississippi and the western part of Alabama of Indian occupancy, and enable those States to advance rapidly in population, wealth and power. It will separate the Indians from immediate contact with settlements of whites; free them from the power of the States; enable them to pursue happiness in their own way and under their own rude institutions; will retard the progress of decay, which is lessening their numbers, and perhaps cause them gradually... to cast off their savage habits and become an interesting, civilized, and Christian community.... Toward the aborigines of the country no one can indulge a more friendly feeling than myself, or would go further in attempting to reclaim them from their wandering habits and make them a happy, prosperous people.... Humanity has often wept over the fate of the aborigines of this country.... To follow to the tomb the last of his race and to tread on the graves of extinct nations excite melancholy reflections. But true philanthropy reconciles the mind to these vicissitudes as it does to the extinction of one generation to make room for another. In the monuments and fortresses of an unknown people, spread over the extensive regions of the West, we behold the memorials of a once powerful race, which was exterminated or has disappeared to make room for the existing savage tribes.... What good man would prefer a country covered with forests and ranged by a few thousand savages to our extensive Republic, studded with cities, towns, and prosperous farms... and filled with all the blessings of liberty, civilization, and religion? Doubtless it will be painful to leave the graves of their fathers; but what do they do more than our ancestors did or than our children are now doing? To better their condition in an unknown land our forefathers left all that was dear in earthly objects.... Can it be cruel in this Government when, by events which it can not control, the Indian is made discontented in his ancient home, to purchase his lands, to give him a new and extensive territory, to pay the expense of his removal, and support him a year in his new abode? How many thousands of our own people would gladly embrace the opportunity of removing to the West on such conditions![492]

In response to President Jackson's removal act, Speckled Snake of the Cherokees made this speech:

Brothers! We have heard the talk of your great father, it is very kind. He says he loves his red children. Brothers! When the white man came to these shores, the Muskogee gave him land, and kindled him a fire to make him comfortable; and when the palefaces of the south made war on him, their young men drew the tomahawk, and protected his head from the scalping knife. But when the white man had warmed himself before the Indians' fire, and filled himself with the Indians' hominy, he became very large; he stopped not for the mountain tops... his hands grasped the eastern and the western sea. Then he became our great father. He loved his red children; but said, 'You must move a little farther, lest I should, by accident, tread on you....' I have heard a great many talks from our great father and they began and ended the same... 'Get a little farther....' He also said, 'It shall be yours forever.' Now he says, 'The land you live on is not yours; go beyond the Mississippi; there is game. There you may remain while the grass grows or the water runs.' Brothers! Will not our great father come there also? He loves his red children, and his tongue is not forked.[493]

Trail of Tears
Rendering by Robert Lindneux in 1942,
courtesy of the Granger Collection, New York

These speeches were in 1830, and the removal remained unresolved for 5 more years. After fierce debate in Congress and a Supreme Court ruling by Chief Justice John Marshall in 1832, it was granted that the Cherokees and all other Indian tribes "had always been considered as distinct, independent, political communities, retaining their natural rights...." This ruling gave all the Indian tribes sovereign immunity from state laws on their own reservations. President Andrew Jackson responded angrily to this decision. "John Marshall has rendered his decision; now let him enforce it."[494] Led by John Ross, who was part Cherokee, the Indians resisted intimidation and bribery, refusing to sign an illegal treaty that was being forced on them.

John Ross, Cherokee
1790-1866

Instead, the United States government arranged a treaty with a small opposition group. The following December, 1835, the "treaty party" of the progressive slave-owning Cherokees signed the Treaty of New Echota, relinquishing all lands east of the Mississippi and agreeing to migrate to the Cherokee lands beyond the Mississippi. Although the Cherokees killed the signatories—Major Ridge, his son and Elias Boudinot—for treason, the signatories impacted the entire Cherokee nation, causing the eventual removal of most of them. At this time, only about 2000 of this faction (a small part of the Cherokees) signed the Treaty of New Echota and moved peacefully from 1835 to 1838 to Oklahoma.[495]

Osceola knifes the Seminole Treaty, sketch

The Georgia Militia destroyed their crops, burned their homes and initially rounded up the Cherokees opposing the move. The federal troops stepped in and herded the Cherokees into concentration camps. In one of the saddest episodes of America—men, women and children were taken from their land, herded into makeshift forts with minimal facilities and food, then forced to march a thousand miles (some made part of the trip by boat in equally horrible conditions). Chief John Ross made an urgent appeal to General Scott, requesting that the general let his Cherokee people lead the tribe west. General Scott agreed. Ross organized the Cherokee into smaller groups and let them move separately through the wilderness so they could forage for food. The parties under Ross left in early fall and arrived in Oklahoma during the brutal winter of 1838-39, with a loss of much life among his people. About 4000 Cherokee died and were buried in shallow graves as a result of the removal. The route they crossed and the journey itself became known as "The Trail of Tears" or, in Cherokee, "The Trail Where They Cried" (*"Nunna daul Tsuny"*). All the tribes forcibly moved were subjected to their own "Trail of Tears".[496]

Tecumseh

Death of Tecumseh, 1768-1813, from engraving

In 1832, some of the Seminole leaders signed a treaty and promised to relocate. The Seminole tribe split because of this decision. After certain Indians agreed to move, the other part of the tribe fought to keep their lands. They fled into the Florida swamps. This became the Second Seminole War of 1835. Osceola led the Seminoles until General Thomas Jessup betrayed him. Osceola was seized and imprisoned by Jessup during peace talks under a flag of truce. Osceola died in 1838 while still in prison. After the war many Seminoles moved west, except for a determined group that remained hidden in the Florida swamps.[497]

During this period, countless Indians voiced their disapproval of the selling of their native lands. Kanekuk, a Kickapoo prophet, expressed a different view when he said, "Some of our chiefs make the claim that the land belongs to us. It is not what the Great Spirit told me. He told me that the lands belong to Him, that no people owns the land; that I was not to forget to tell this to the white people when I met them in council." Similarly, Tecumseh, a Shawnee chief, said, "No tribe has the right to sell, even to each other, much less to strangers... sell a country! Why not sell the air, the great sea, as well as the earth? Didn't the Great Spirit make them all for the use of his children?"

Chief Seattle
1786-1866

Tecumseh, witnessing the decimation of the eastern tribes, said, "Where today is the Pequot? Where are the Narragansetts, the Mohawks, the Pokanoet (Pokanoket), and many other once powerful tribes of our people? They have vanished before the avarice and the oppression of the White Man, as snow before a summer sun." Chief Black Hawk (1767-1837), from the Upper Mississippi Valley Sauk tribe, echoed Tecumseh's sentiments in his autobiography in 1833. "My reason teaches us that land cannot be sold. The Great Spirit gave it to his children to live upon and cultivate as far as necessary for their subsistence, and so long as they occupy and cultivate it they have the right to the soil, but if

Chief Washakie of
the Shoshone

War against the Shoshone, engraving

101

they voluntarily leave it then any other people have a right to settle on it. Nothing can be sold, except things that can be carried away."

In 1854 Chief Seattle (Suquamish and Duwamish), in his reported speech to the Governor of the state of Washington said, "To us the ashes of our ancestors are sacred and their resting place is hallowed ground. You wander far from the graves of your ancestors and seemingly without regret. Your religion was written upon tables of stone by the iron finger of your god so that you could not forget. The Red Man could never comprehend nor remember it. Our religion is the traditions of our ancestors—the dreams of our old men, given them in solemn hours of night by the Great Spirit; and the visions of our sachems; and it is written in the hearts of our people. Your dead cease to love you and the land of their nativity as soon they pass the portals of the tomb and wander way beyond the stars. They are soon forgotten and never return. Our dead never forget the beautiful world that gave them being.... Let him be just and deal kindly with my people, for the dead are not powerless. Dead, did I say? There is no death, only a change of worlds."498

In 1868 Chief Washakie of the Shoshones and his tribe moved voluntarily to their present reservation, east of the Wind River Mountains. Ten years later, Chief Washakie bitterly criticized the government for its failure to provide the Shoshones with promised supplies of tools for cultivating the land, seeds for planting, implements for harvesting, and animals for breeding as promised in the treaty. Chief Washakie, at a council in 1878 that was called by the Governor of Wyoming, stated:

"Captain Smith takes the King of Pamaunkee prisoner, 1608," by de Bry

> The white man who possesses this whole vast country from sea to sea, who roams over it at pleasure and lives where he likes, cannot know the cramp we feel in this little spot, with the undying remembrance of the fact, which you know as well as we, that every foot of what you proudly call America, not very long ago belonged to the Red Man. The Great Spirit gave it to us, there was room enough for all his tribes; all were happy in their freedom. The white man had, in ways we know not of, learned some things we had not learned, among them how to make superior tools and terrible weapons, better for war than bows and arrows, and there seemed no end to the hoards of men that followed them from other lands beyond the sea. And so, at last, our fathers were steadily driven out, or killed. We, their sons, but sorry remnants of tribes once mighty, are cornered in little spots of the earth, all ours by right—cornered like guilty prisoners, and watched by men with guns who are more than anxious to kill us off.499

There were innumerable additional episodes of Indian removal, each accompanied by arguments and rationalizations for their removal. It was said that the Indians had no right to block the white man's progress, that the Indians were an encumbrance and did not make use of their land, that they were subhuman and savages and incapable of assimilating into white society. There were even those who reasoned that this was the only way to preserve their "noble savage" civilization. Numerous voices arose from Europe and the United States in a campaign to demean and ridicule the Indian, in a plan to manipulate the public and Congress, so as to confiscate their land and convert them to the ways of the white man.

It began with Captain John Smith in the mid 1600s after he wrote how the generosity of the Indians saved his Jamestown, Virginia settlement from starvation. Smith later called on the enslavement of this, "viperous brood."500 Henry Knox, Secretary of War under George Washington, stated in 1793, "If our modes of population and war destroy the tribes, the disinterested part of mankind and posterity will be apt to classify the effects of our conduct and that of the Spaniards in Mexico and Peru together...." That same year Knox wrote, "a future historian may mark the causes of this destruction of the human race in sable colors."501

In 1809 Thomas Jefferson had told a delegation of Indians, "I consider my red children as forming one family with the Whites." By 1824 Jefferson underwent a dramatic change in his opinion, remarking on the increase of the non-Indian population and the fact that, "Barbarism has, in the meantime, been receding before the steady step of amelioration; and will in time, I trust, disappear from the earth."502 James Madison, in his inaugural address of 1809, stated it was his responsibility "...to carry on the benevolent plans which have been so meritoriously applied to the conversion of our aboriginal neighbors from the degradation and wretchedness of savage life to a participation of the improvements of which the human mind and manners are susceptible in a civilized state."

French depiction of Indians in book on a " dialogue between Baron de Lahontan and an American Savage," 1700s.

In 1817, James Madison, at the end of his Presidency, wrote that the right to Indian lands "was suggested by the principle of which has limited the claim of the U.S. to a right of preemption. It seemed also that [there exists] an unqualified right of a civilized people to land used by people in the hunter-state, on the principle that the earth was intended for those who would make it most conducive to the sustenance & increase of the human race...."[503]

A younger Chief Joseph, Nez Percé

Senator Thomas Hart Benton, a vocal opponent of Indian rights since the 1820s, claimed that whites should take over the land of the Indians because the whites used the land: "according to the intentions of the creator." Benton further said: "I know of no human event, past or present, which promises a greater and more beneficent change upon earth than the arrival of the Caucasian race.... The Mongolian, or Yellow race is there, four hundred millions in number, spreading almost to Europe: a race once the foremost of the human family in the arts of civilization, but torpid and stationary for thousands of years. It is a race far above the Ethiopian or Black—above the Malay, or Brown. If we must admit five races—and above the American Indian, or Red—it is a race far above all these, but still, far below the White and, like all the rest, must receive an impression from the superior race whenever they come into contact...."

Nez Percé camp at Wallowa, Oregon survey engraving, 1872

Benton considered the Indian to be a lost race. He further stated, "The Red Race has disappeared from the Atlantic coast: the tribes that resisted civilization met extinction. This is a cause of lamentation with many. For my part, I cannot murmur at what seems to be the effect of device Law... civilization, or extinction, has been the fate of all people who have found themselves in the track of the advancing Whites, and civilization, always the preference of the Whites, has been pressed as an object, while extinction has followed as a consequence of its resistance." The same derogatory comments about the Indian was maintained by Clay and endorsed by John Quincy Adams and Andrew Jackson, forming a consistent thread in the ideology of American expansion. It was still maintained at the end of the nineteenth century.[504] Martin van Buren, the eighth President of the United States, stated in his first year as president in 1837 that, "No state can achieve proper culture, civilization and progress... as long as Indians are permitted to remain."

President William Henry Harrison, a former ally of the Indians, had acknowledged the Indian's land as "...one of the fairest portions of the globe to remain in a state of nature, the haunt of a few wretched savages, when it seems destined by the creator to give support to a large population and to be the seat of civilization." William Tecumseh Sherman, a Union General in the Civil War and commander of the Union forces in the West, called the Indians, "bloodthirsty devils" and coined the phrase "the only good Indian is a dead Indian."[505] Major General Benjamin Lincoln, after an unsuccessful mission to negotiate with the Indians, noted at Lake Erie, Pennsylvania on July 14, 1793, "...if the savages cannot be civilized and quit their present pursuits, they will, in consequence of their stubborness, dwindle and moulder away from causes perhaps imperceptible to us, until the whole race shall become extinct..."[506]

Gold was discovered in the center of the Nez Percé reservation in 1860, in the area of the junction three states: Washington, Oregon and Idaho. In May, 1877, instead of accepting an ultimatum from General Howard to abandon their homes and move to a reservation, the Nez Percé instead fought a running battle toward sanctuary in Canada. After 3 months of outsmarting and outfighting their pursuers, they were captured within about 30 miles from Canada at Bear Paw Battlefield in Montana, and were exiled to the Lapwai Indian reservations in Idaho. Their leader, Chief Joseph of the Nez Percé, made an eloquent speech in Washington, D.C. in 1879. "If the White man wants to live in peace with the Indian he can live in peace.... Treat all men alike. Give them all the same law. Give them all an even chance to live and grow. All men were made by the same Great Spirit Chief. They are all brothers, the earth is the mother of all people, and all people should have equal rights upon it...."[507]

Bright Eyes (Susette La Flesche)   Reporter Thomas Tibbles

Chief Standing Bear, Ponca

Governments came and went and in 1877, when the peaceful Ponca tribe, who had lived in Nebraska for over one hundred years, were removed from their land, a chain of tragic events developed. During their removal and 500-mile journey to their new location, one third of the Ponca people died. Former Indian agent and newspaper reporter T. H. Tibbles, who had fallen in love with and married a Ponca Indian woman called Bright Eyes, toured the east coast. Tibbles proclaimed the plight of the Ponca tribe. This was the first time an Indian tribe received national attention. The Poncas had acted as a buffer between the warring factions of Sioux to the north and the white settlements to the south. In a treaty with the United States government in 1858, they ceded much of their territory to make gains in other areas, such as achieving peace and building schools for their children.

Ponca Indians, Standing Bear seated 3rd from left

Without consulting members of the Ponca tribe, the United States government gave the Ponca land to the Brule Sioux in 1865. The Brule Sioux refused to settle on the Ponca land. However, on August 15, 1876, the United States government "provided for the removal of Poncas to Indian territory whenever they consent." The United States government then proceeded to coerce the Poncas to move to a strange land without money, interpreter or guide. The Poncas said they would die before they abandoned their homeland, and on March 3, 1877, the United States government passed a law to remove the Poncas "without their consent", to an Oklahoma reservation far from their ancestral homes and sacred burial grounds. Their frantic protests were ignored and soldiers were sent to enforce their removal. Head Chief White Eagle was forced to comply.

The Poncas set out on the journey to their new land in the summer of 1877. More than one hundred and eighty-five members of the tribe lost their lives because of the excessive heat and various other weather disasters. Their Chief, Standing Bear, lost his son and his married daughter. Chief Standing Bear set out on foot during a blizzard in 1879 to bury his son in the Ponca burial grounds, not wanting to bury him in alien territory. The Poncas returned to eastern Nebraska where their friends, the Omaha tribe, gave them asylum. Learning of this, the Secretary of the Interior sent General Crook to have Chief Standing Bear arrested and taken back to Oklahoma, but there was a public outcry that caused the case to be tried in the Federal District Court in Omaha.

The trial was dramatic, with an emotional Chief Standing Bear telling his story and succeeding in moving the judge, General Crook, and the white audience to tears. Chief Standing Bear pleaded, "I see you all here today. What have I done? I am brought here, but what have I done? I don't know. It seems as though I haven't a place in the world, no place to go, and no home to go to." The lawyers for Chief Standing Bear applied for his release on a writ of habeas corpus. The United States government claimed that because Chief Standing Bear was an Indian, he was not entitled to protection of a writ of habeas corpus on the grounds that an Indian was "not a person." The attorney for Chief Standing Bear contended that he was protected in the same manner as "every human being, "and that any other interpretation of this law was in violation of the funda-

Chief Standing Bear and family, years after trial

mental principles of the Constitution. Judge Dundy finally made his ruling with these words, "During the fifteen years in which I have been engaged in administering the laws of my country, I have never been called upon to hear or decide a case that appealed so strongly to my sympathy as the one now under consideration. On the one side we have a few of the remnants of a once numerous and powerful, but now weak, insignificant, unlettered, and generally despised race. On the other, we have the representative of one of the most powerful, most enlightened, and most Christianized nation of modern times.... It may seem beyond belief that, in the one hundred third year of the declaration, 'all men are created equal,' it was necessary for a federal judge to determine at great length that every human being is a person, and as such entitled to a hearing in the courts." Judge Dundy even invoked the dictionary for a definition, saying, "Webster describes a 'person' as 'a living soul; a self-conscious being; a moral agent; especially a living human being; a man, woman, or child; an individual of the human race.' This is comprehensive enough, it would seem, to include even an Indian." Judge Dundy went on to praise the Poncas for their fine attributes and to commend Chief Standing Bear's protection of his dead son's body and his wish to bury him on his native land. He stated that Chief Standing Bear's "love of home and native land may be heathen in origin, but it seems to me that they are not unlike Christian in principle...." He concluded, "An Indian is a person within the meaning of the laws of the United States, and has therefore the right to sue out of a writ of habeas corpus in a Federal Court or before a federal judge in all cases where he may be confined, or in custody under color of authority of the United States, or where he is restrained of liberty in violation of the Constitution of the United States." The Judge stated that General George Crook was in violation of these laws and "that no rightful authority exists to remove the Indians by force." In addition, the Indians, as well as the more fortunate white race "have the inalienable right to life, liberty, and the pursuit of happiness so long as they obey the laws and do not trespass on forbidden ground." He released the Indians from custody. There was a public outcry after the judges' ruling.

Governor John DeLong of Massachusetts subsequently appointed a committee in Boston to investigate the bureaucratic mistakes made with the Poncas. The committee members launched a scathing attack on the entire United States government and its relationship with the Ponca Indians. The commission accused the United States

Chief Red Fox
Sioux, 1900

government of robbing the Ponca Indians of their homes and not making any attempt to rectify their errors. The committee claimed the government "blunderingly" had given the Ponca lands to the Sioux. On December 18,1880, a new President, Rutherford B. Hayes, appointed a government commission to attempt to right the wrongs done to the Ponca tribe. Four weeks later, on January 25, 1881, the special commission reported to President Hayes on the wrongs done to the Poncas. They recommended an allocation of one hundred sixty acres of land be made to

Captain Jack watches Federal troops, Modoc War

each man, woman and child of the Ponca tribe. This land was to be selected by them on their old reservation in Nebraska, or on land that they were actually occupying. There were also additional sums given for the construction of Ponca dwellings and schoolhouses on their old reservation in Nebraska, or in Oklahoma.

On March 3, 1881, an act of Congress carried out the recommendation of the commission. That same year, on August 20, 1881, the United States government entered into an agreement with the Sioux that declared that the Sioux "do hereby cede and relinquish to the United States so much of that portion of the present Sioux reservation as was formerly occupied by the Ponca tribe of Indians." This was already indicated in the treaty concluded between the United States government and the Ponca tribe on March 10, 1865. This concluded the long bureaucratic calamity that arose from the notion that Indians were "non-persons."[508]

Countless other Indian tribes were annihilated or forcibly removed to reservations. In 1859, the United States government rounded up the people who remained from numerous tribes—the Walla Walla, the Cayuse, the Umatillas, the Modocs, the Klamath, Paiutes, etc. They forced many of them to agree to a treaty and then removed them all to reservations in Northeastern Oregon.[509] The United States Army and loose bands of vigilantes during the 1860s to the 1890s, in their Western Wars with the Indians, were responsible for numerous massacres, many against innocent civilians. In 1854 over 150 Sioux were killed at Blue River in Nebraska; 500 Shoshones at Bear River, Idaho in 1863; 250 Cheyennes and Arapahos at Sand Creek, Colorado, 1864; 100 Cheyennes at Camp Robinson, Nebraska, 1878; and in 1890 at least 300 Sioux at Wounded Knee, South Dakota, among countless other massacres. The 1894 United States Census gave only an approximate number of those Indians slaughtered in fights with the Europeans. They estimated at least 8500 Indians in only individual dealings with the whites, rather than battles. In the over 40 Indian wars with the federal government, it cost the lives "...of about 30,000 Indians.... The actual number of killed and wounded Indians must have been much greater than the number given, as they conceal, where possible, their actual loss in battle. Fifty percent additional would be a safe number to add to the numbers given."[510]

Big Foot / Medicine Man

Wounded Knee massacre and burial December 29, 1890

Alexis de Tocqueville was a French political figure and historian. After visiting America in 1831 he criticized the United States government's policy of Indian removal. The Frenchman described how the Americans take the Indians "by the hand and transport them to a grave far from the lands of their fathers." He observed sarcastically that it was all accomplished "with singular felicity, tranquility, legally, philanthropically, without shedding blood.... It is impossible to destroy man with more respect for the laws of humanity." He predicted that the Indians would remain undisturbed after their forced removal beyond the Mississippi only until the white land seekers decided to take this land for themselves. He then indicated each Indian would then face the assaults of "the most grasping nation on the globe", who would drive the Indians from one "final" location to another until "their only refuge is the grave."[511] After over a century of displacement from their ancient homelands, and subjugation to all of modern society's enticements, many of the Indians resisted assimilation and continue to maintain their old traditions until this day.

Throughout American history the media, history books, Western dime magazines, and our movie films have presented a distorted image of the Indian to the world. Washington Irving, the famous American author, was aware of not only their displacement but also the demeaning of the Indians by other writers and their attempts to change the way readers view or interpret the Indians. In 1820 Irving, in his *Traits of Indian Character*, wrote of their displacement, "It has been the lot of the unfortunate aborigines of America, in the early periods of colonization, to be doubly wronged by the white men. They have been dispossessed of their hereditary possessions by mercenary and frequently wanton warfare, and bigoted and interested writers have traduced their characters. The colonists often treated them like beasts of the forest, and the author has endeavored to justify him in his outrages. The former found it easier to discriminate. The appellations of savage and pagan

Navajo "Long Walk" to Bosque Redondo, N.M., after 8000 surrender to Kit Carson in 1864

were deemed sufficient to sanction the hostilities of both; and thus the poor wanderers of the forest were persecuted and defamed, not because they were guilty, but because they were ignorant." Irving concludes his sketch of the Indian with these compassionate and gloomy words, "We are driven back", said an old warrior, "until we can retreat no far- ther—our hatchets are broken, our bows are snapped, our fires are nearly extinguished; a little longer and the white man will cease to persecute us, for we shall cease to exist!"[512]

Cheyennes and Black Kettle, seated center, September, 1864 at Fort Weld, Colorado at peace meeting before Sand Creek Massacre

The western dime novels began to appear in stores during the 1860s and they attracted an enormous amount of interest from the non-Indian public. Sales reached almost 400,000 copies a year and, as the white American population increased and expanded west into the lands of the Plains Indian tribes, interest in the books grew in North America. Indians played a prominent role in 45 percent of the 321 stories in print by the late 1800's. By 1910 circulation of these dime novels had increased to ten million a month. Such language as, "Crack! Crack! Three more redskins bit the dust!" left no doubt as to how the American public was meant to see the Indians. They were depicted as pagan, evil, treacherous savages who, without mercy, went around scalping white men, burning their homes and torturing their people. Their cul- ture was cast in shadows. When the movie industry was in its infancy, Hollywood lost no time in capitalizing on the fad with western movies showing conflicts between cowboys and Indians. In fact, if the movie industry had not jumped in, it is likely that the Indians would have disappeared in the minds of the American people. Some of the early Indian movies were Hiawatha in 1909, Deerslayer in 1911, and The Last of the Mohicans in 1920. In 1924, movie director John Ford introduced the film Iron Horse. This created an enduring image of the Indians in the minds of the white public. The movie depicted Indians as drunkards and bumbling fools. In 1930 a movie about the life of William F. Cody (Buffalo Bill) was released, depicting Cody as the hero and the Indian as the enemy. Cody's Wild West Shows always depicted the Indians attacking whites and killing them. This, of course, created an image of the Indian as being savage and ruthless, when in reality it was the opposite. Most Indian tribes had, by this time, been herded into reservations. As a last resort, to save themselves from starvation, many tribes attacked in defense against superior weapons and soldiers.

On December 15, 1915, Buffalo Bill himself remarked to Boy Scout Chief, Earnest Thompson Seton, at a din- ner in Washington, D.C., that, "I never lead an expedition against the Indians, but I was ashamed of myself, ashamed of my government, and ashamed of my flag; for they were always in the right and we were always in the wrong. They never broke a treaty, and we never kept one."[513] Inaccuracies were rampant in the movie depictions of the Indians. They showed the Indian chiefs wearing shawls, and invented scenarios of Indians avenging the deaths of their companions. They would be shown dragging a body behind a horse or using inhuman forms of torture and violence, despite the fact that it was customary for most American Indian tribes to bury their dead as speedily as possible, in order to return it to Mother Earth. The movie directors also featured the Indians as war- like and provocative. Naturally, they left out the broken treaties and attempts to coerce the Indian off his land. The older Indians, realizing that these films had the potential to influence a new generation against them, attempt- ed to shield their children from these Hollywood inaccuracies by telling them stories of their ances- tors' great courage, bravery, and their many attempts to make peace.

At a memorial presentation for the Mayor of Chicago, at a Grand Council Fire of Indians held on December 1, 1927, the Indians attempted to change many of these untruths:

You tell all white men 'America First.' We believe in that. We are the only ones, truly, that are 100 percent. We therefore ask you while you are teaching our school children about America First, teach them the truth about the First Americans. We do not know if school histories are pro British, but we do know they are unjust to the life of our people—the American Indian.

Sitting Bull & Buffalo Bill Cody, Wild West Show, 1885

They call all white victories battles, and all Indian victories massacres. The battle with Custer has been taught to schoolchildren as a fearful massacre on our part. We ask that this, as well as other incidents, be told fair- ly.... What is civilization? Its marks are a noble religion and philosophy, original arts, stirring music, rich story and legend. We had these.... We sang songs that carried in their melodies all the sounds of nature—the running waters, the sighing of winds, and the call of the animals. Teach those to your children that they may come to love nature as we love it.... We had our statesmen.... We played games—games that brought good health and sound bodies. Why not put these in your schools? We told stories. Why not teach school children more of the wholesome proverbs and legends of our people? Tell them how we loved all that was beautiful.

That we killed game only for food, not for fun. Indians think white men who kill for fun are murderers. Tell your children of the friendly acts of Indians to the white people who first settled here. Tell them of our leaders and heroes and their deeds.... Put in your history books the Indians' part in the World War. Tell how the Indian fought for a country of which he was not a citizen, for a flag to which he had no claim, and for a people that have treated him unjustly. We ask this, Chief, to keep sacred the memory of our people.[514]

A scene on the frontiers as practiced by the "humane" British and their "worthy allies," 1812

The Europeans, fully knowledgeable of scalping, developed the mass scalping and torture of prisoners to a science. As early as 440 B.C. ancient Scythians (Russians) practiced it. Herodotus, the Greek Historian wrote, "The Scythian soldier scrapes the scalp clean of flesh and, softening it by rubbing between the hands, uses it thenceforth as a napkin. The Scyth is proud of these scalps and hangs them from his bridle rein; the greater the number of such napkins that a man can show, the more highly is he esteemed among them. Many make themselves cloaks by sewing a quantity of these scalps together."[515] In the 11th century, the Earl of Wessex scalped his enemies. This activity was later brought to the new world, not so much as an official method of warfare, but as a bounty to ease the anger of the frontiersmen. The Europeans had taught the Indians first-hand the horror of viewing the mutilated remains of their families and friends after an attack by white settlers. By inflicting the same mutilation on their enemies they had hoped to stem the onslaught of these white settlers that were invading their land. To some Indians, if the attacks could not stop the whites, at least it would send the message that they were prepared to be as unscrupulous as the Europeans.

The Dutch government, and soon after, the English, created the scalp bounty as a means to pacify the settlers. They paid a fee for each scalp that was delivered to the locally appointed magistrate. "When the English and the Dutch came to the new world they brought the custom with them. Scalping was introduced by the Governor of New Netherlands to facilitate collecting bounties on Indians. Once the Indians had assisted them in surviving the first few winters, the Dutch, hand in hand with the British, carried out a systematic program of genocide on all the Eastern tribes."[516] The Europeans taught the Indians how to scalp in volume and without reason. England approved the practice of scalping in America by offering rewards to those Indians who could prove they killed their enemy. The New England Puritans, in 1673, were the first to offer bounties for Indian heads and then for their scalps. By 1724 the officials in the colony of Massachusetts were offering forty pounds sterling for scalps of Indian women and children.[517] The British began authorizing payments of eight dollars for an Indian scalp. On June 12, 1775, the British published a scalp bounty poster in Massachusetts. The poster offered rewards for the scalps of Indians allied to the French.[518] Eventually rewards for scalps were paid on enemies that were not Indians. The French and British offered premiums for Indian scalps in addition to paying for a white enemy's scalp. As the Indian wars extended to the western plains, rewards for Indian scalps from the United States government sometimes brought in as much as two hundred to four hundred dollars for each scalp.[519]

In 1791 William Bartram traveled through the southeastern section of the United States. Bartram observed the Indians and wrote of the accounts of other white traders who resided among them. Bartram wrote, "I cannot find upon the strictest inquiry that their bloody contests at this day are marked with deeper stains of inhumanity or savage cruelty than what may be observed amongst the most civilized nations: they do indeed scalp their slain enemy, but they do not kill the females or children of either sex: the most ancient traders, both in the Lower and Upper Creeks, assured me they never saw an instance of either burning or tormenting their male captives; though it is said they used to do it formerly. I saw in every town in the nation of Seminoles that I had visited, more or less male captives, some extremely aged, who were free and in as good circumstances as their masters; and all slaves have their freedom when they marry, which is permitted and encouraged, when they and their offspring are every way upon an equality with their conquerors."[520]

Ahyouwaighs, Mohawk Chief of Six Nations

During the War of 1812 Tecumseh, from the Shawnee tribe, allied with the British in 1813 and was astounded when he discovered that white American prisoners of the opposite side were being tortured and murdered. Tecumseh halted the torture and killing and in a rage told his British commander, Colonel Henry Proctor, "Go and put on petticoats, I conquer to save, and you to murder."[521] Lieutenant Governor Cadwallader Colden of New York related in his book, *History of the Five Indian Nations*, that the Indians, fighting with the French, would not stand for the cruelty of their French allies toward their Mohawk Indian enemies. As the French and Indian allies attacked Mohawk Indian villages during the winter of 1693, Calder stated, "The French designed to have them all put to the sword, but their own Indians would not suffer it, and gave them Quarter."[522]

The western border of the colonies was being populated with settlers that were comprised of outlaws and runaways. With them they brought disease and alcohol. The frontier was a breeding ground for conflict with the Indian population. Initially the frontiersmen turned on the Indians in an attempt to move them off the land. When the Indians retaliated, the settlers turned to the government for help. The settlers demanded retribution for the Indian reprisals. The Spaniards did not hesitate to use a bounty for scalps of every Apache man, woman and child in the Mexican state of Sonora during the mid 1700s. The Spaniards had also condoned the giving of alcohol to the Indians so that they would become addicted and dependent on the Spanish for a supply. Bernardo de Galvez, Viceroy of Mexico in 1786, urged the local authorities to give gifts of food and alcohol to make the Indians dependent on the Spanish authorities. He wrote, "The supplying of drink to the Indians will be a means of gaining their goodwill, discovering their secrets, calming them so they will think less of conceiving and executing hostilities... which will oblige them to recognize their dependence upon us more directly." Galvez also advised giving the Apaches defective arms, so they would have to ask the Spanish for parts.[523] Alcohol played a significant part in dominating the Indians. All the Europeans used it as a means to influence and subdue the Indians. Benjamin Franklin had once stated that rum might be the agent of Providence, "to extirpate these savages in order to make room for the cultivators of the earth." In 1786 Franklin, in a letter written to a French friend, said, "Almost every war between the Indians and the whites has been occasioned by some injustice of the latter towards the former."[524]

The horrendous methods of torture of prisoners was practically unknown by the Indians until it was initially introduced by the Spaniards into America. The Indians used torture as a part of their ceremonial rituals. "Among many tribes the torture of a prisoner was more of an honor than a punishment, and a captive killed without being tortured would have felt that he was being insulted and slighted by not being permitted to exhibit his bravery and fortitude before his enemies."[525] Any part of the warrior's body, his ribs, thigh bone, or teeth was considered a trophy. Some tribes would consider the touching of an enemy in battle as a coup or trophy, more important than taking a part of his body. The French and Indian War (1754-1760) is filled with incidents of scalping by French, English and Indian warriors. Newspapers, diaries, journals and other sources all document these occurrences. Scalping predated these wars, with historical records and archaeology indicating the practice originated among certain Indian tribes. The scalp (part of, or the whole head) was considered as a coup or trophy of a battle between warriors, not as an excuse for brutality against innocent women and children. As a part of their spiritual beliefs, the Indian warriors in battle would cut off the trigger finger, heads or eyes of their enemy so as not to be seen or harmed by their opponents in their next life.[526]

Despite the indiscriminate annihilation by the Europeans throughout America, despite the ravages of disease and alcohol, regardless of the intermarriage between the Whites and Indians, despite the influence the Europeans wielded on every aspect of Indian life, and even despite all efforts to Christianize the Indians, many of the tribes have persevered and increased in numbers. Many are attempting to restore their ancestral customs, language and arts. There are still primitive tribes living in parts of Central and South America which have never been in contact with a white man and have happily retained their ancestral way of life. Religion is the core of the Indians existence, day by day. They believe that all things in nature have a soul, and that mankind must live in harmony with nature. Their religious belief is so strong that it is impossible to separate religion from everyday life.

Their ancient sacred ceremonies, dances and music have been censored and forbidden. Their children were forcibly removed from their families to attend schools where they were not allowed to speak their language. In South America we have the same story. The Spanish have mixed freely with those they have conquered. Most of the wealthy and prominent in South and Central America have Indian blood. There are still innumerable tribes in Central and South America living in primitive conditions and working for wealthy landowners under a feudal system. Many of these countries have a majority of Indians in the population. In spite of this the Indian is miserably fed, housed and paid very little for his labor. In Peru, Quechua speaking natives, remnants of the Incas, live in extremely poor conditions. In Mexico, the remnants of the Mayans and Aztecs live in degraded conditions and are subservient to their government. In other parts of South America such as Chile, the Mapuches Indians have managed to unite and have succeeded in accomplishing recognition.[527]

CHAPTER 8   RELIGION OF THE INDIAN

"At The Shrine"
Photo by Edward Curtis
"Scattered about the Navaho reservation are many cairn shrines. The Navaho, when alone or in parties, on approaching one of these gathers a few twigs of pinon or cedar, places them on the shrine, scatters a pinch of sacred meal upon it, and makes supplication for that which he may habitually need or which the moment demands."
The North America Indians

The religion the Europeans encountered in America was unfamiliar and mysterious to them. The Indians had a kind of spirituality that the Europeans and missionaries could not fathom. The missionaries believed, of course, that the force of life was concentrated on one God—their sole Creator—whereas by contrast, the Indians believed that the source of their life force was a power that penetrated the entire world. The Indians prayed to their spiritual creator and his intermediaries every day. Most Indian tribes revered the animal spirits because they represented the animals' ability to survive and the Indians' dependence on them for their food and clothing. Many clans adopted the animal names of those they believed were their magical ancestor creators that enabled them to survive.

Religion formed a large part of the Indians' daily lives, and their beliefs and traditions appear to have worldwide counterparts that may have been brought here by the Indians' ancient ancestors. The Indians were not accustomed to a rapid pace of life. They were trained at a young age to use silence and meditation as a reservoir for spiritual strength. From childhood they were taught self-control by sitting still, observing and listening to sounds and smells. One who constantly talked and did not listen was considered rude and insincere. Silence was considered the foundation of the individual's personality. It was impolite to discuss matters without first greeting and getting to know your visitor. Silence and moderation were signs of courtesy, patience was a virtue, and any important matter would be discussed at length and voted on by the tribal elders before an answer was given.

Their supreme force was considered untouchable because it belonged to a supernatural world. The Melanesian people of the South Pacific utilize the word *mana* to refer to an invisible force that pervaded the cosmos, believed in by a widespread primitive faith. The Algonquin tribes singled out one supreme being—the Great Spirit (Kitshi Manitou)—as their true god, or simply their creator (Manitou). This concept of one Supreme Being preceded the Christian worship of a single God. Their supreme being was the protector of the caribou, and directly after the completion of a hunt, sacrifices were made to Manitou.[528] A number of the Plains Indian tribes called their Great Spirit "Wakan Tanka." In the ideology of the Dakota, Plains and Winnebago Indians, the word "Wakan" signifies sacred, mysterious, or wondrous. It could also mean "coming from a supernatural power."

Chief Smohalla

The Indians used a shaman (medicine man) as their intermediary between themselves and the Supreme Being, primarily in times of sickness. The belief in shamans was extensive in the northwestern tribes and spread into a number of other tribes. Shamans played an important role in the history of ancient man, as found in mystical cave paintings in Europe and later among the ancient tribes of northeast Asia. The shaman was believed to have supernatural powers and these were used to solve almost any problem. There were shamans who had magic against war or snakes, and those who were able to make it rain. Some were visionaries who predicted the future or who provided magical solutions to solve tribal problems.[529]

In the 1880's in Washington state, Chief Smohalla, shaman priest of the Wanapan tribe, explained the Indians' religious belief system, their origins and bonds to the earth as follows:

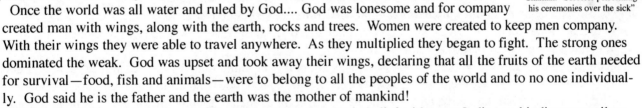

Shaman: "Sorcerer performing his ceremonies over the sick"

Once the world was all water and ruled by God.... God was lonesome and for company created man with wings, along with the earth, rocks and trees. Women were created to keep men company. With their wings they were able to travel anywhere. As they multiplied they began to fight. The strong ones dominated the weak. God was upset and took away their wings, declaring that all the fruits of the earth needed for survival—food, fish and animals—were to belong to all the peoples of the world and to no one individually. God said he is the father and the earth was the mother of mankind!

The concept of the earth as the mother of all creation is a basic belief with most Indian and indigenous tribes throughout the world. Smohalla told his people to obey this ideology; he called it the Washani (dancer's) creed. He claimed God's anger would be vented on those who cut up the lands and cheated the people. Smohalla said:

You ask me to plow the ground! Shall I take a knife and tear my mother's bosom? Then when I die she will not take me to her bosom to rest. You ask me to dig for stone! Shall I dig under her skin for bones? Then when I die, I cannot enter her body to be born again. You ask me to cut grass and make hay and sell it, and be rich like a white man! But how dare I cut my mother's hair? It is a bad law, and my people cannot obey it. I want my people to stay with me here. All the dead men will come to life again. Their spirits will come to their bodies again. We must wait here in the homes of our father and be ready to meet them in the bosom of our mother.[530]

Charles Alexander Eastman, an Ohiyesa, Santee Sioux author, explains this great mystery in the first pages of his book, *The Soul of the Indian*, as:

Charles Eastman
1858-1939

> The original attitude of the Indian toward the Eternal, the "Great Mystery" that surrounds and embraces us, was as simple as it was exalted. To him it was the supreme conception, bringing with it the fullest measure of joy and satisfaction possible in this life.... The worship of the Great Mystery was silent, solitary, and free from all seeking. It was silent because all speech is of necessity feeble and imperfect.... It was solitary, because they believed that He is nearer to us in solitude, and there were no priests authorized to come between man and his Maker. None might exhort or confess or in any way meddle with the religious experience of another. Among us, all men were created sons of God and stood erect, as conscious of their divinity. Our faith might not be formulated in creeds nor forced upon any who were unwilling to receive it. Hence there was no preaching, proselytizing, nor persecution; neither were there any scoffers or atheists....[531]

According to Ruth L. Bunzel in a 1932 ethnology report, the Zuni Pueblo society was rooted in a belief that all life was based on the individual's spiritual soul that was connected with his head, heart and breath. The head contained the individual's knowledge and intelligence. The heart was the foundation of the individual's feeling and reflection. With their breath the Indians communicated or inhaled the ceremonial blessings from the creator. The Zuni believed that their dreams were a supernatural creation and, when interpreted, could foretell the future. Certain rituals could cure bad dreams. Bunzel said:

> To the Zuni the whole world appears animate. Not only are night and day, wind, clouds and trees possessed of personality, but also even articles of human manufacture, such as houses, pots and clothing, are alive and sentient. All matter has its inseparable spiritual essence. For the most part this spiritual aspect of things is vague and impersonal.... Of this animate universe man is an integral part. The beings about him are neither friendly nor hostile. Insofar as all are harmonious parts of the whole, the surrounding forces sustain and preserve humanity in the status quo.... There is no Satan in Zuni ideology, and no Christ.

In other words, the battle against good and evil or religion against religion had no place in the Zuni ideology.[532]

The idea of the spiritual was with the Indians at all times. The notion of attending church, of having one day each week set aside for worship, or of a holy book, was completely foreign to them. Their spiritual lives were inextricably tied in with nature and the blessings and calamities that it brought them. The word "sacred" did not apply to the same things for the Indians as for the Europeans. Medicine or power was sacred, as was the number four, because it as stood for the four quarters of the earth. It represented the power from the Great Spirit that came from these four corners into all the things that existed. The Europeans, who observed the rituals and ceremonies related to the unfamiliar belief system, saw the Indians as carefree, innocent savages. The Indian considered themselves as caretakers of the environment. All the animals, air, water and vegetation coexisted in a fragile harmony and needed to be maintained so as to

"A Medicine Man Curing A Patient" (engraving)
1870s, by Capt. Eastman, U.S.A.

ensure the continuation of all living matter on this planet. This, they believed, was the sacred circle of life in which humans are equal to that of all other creatures.

According to the Sioux holy man Black Elk (Hehaka Sapa), everything done by an Indian is done in a circular fashion, because the power of the universe always acts according to circles and all things tend to be round:

> All power came from the sacred circle of the nation; as long as the circle remained whole, the people flourished. The blossoming tree was the living centre of the circle and the circle of four quarters nourished it. The east gave peace and light, the south gave warmth, from the west came rain, and the north, with its cold and powerful wind, gave strength and endurance. This knowledge came from the external world (the transcending world, the universe) and with it, our religion. Everything done by the power of the universe is made in the form of a circle. The sky is circular and I have heard that the earth is round as a ball and the stars too are round. The wind whirls, at the height of its power. The birds build their nests in a circular way, for they have

the same religion as us.... Our tipis (tents) were circular like the nests of the birds, and were always laid in a circle—the circle of the nation, a nest made of many nests, where the Great Spirit willed us to brood our children.[533]

Tipi (Tepee), 1920s

Four is the sacred number and this circle is divided into four quarters. The four directions, north, south, east and west are significant, as are the four sacred colors, red, yellow, white and black, representing the colors of the human races and the parts of the world from which they come. There are four seasons: spring, summer, fall and winter. Indians, in their sacred ceremonial rituals, address these times and movements with their ritual pipe. When they have covered the entire circle they speak the words, "all my relations", thus acknowledging the relationship between all beings in the universe and their common vision of peace.[534] The American Indians' concept of the sacred circle represents physical and spiritual unity. This circle of life is interpreted according to particular individual beliefs of each Indian nation, but is broadly symbolic of an encompassing creation.... While non-Indians quite willingly admit to the complexity of the circle of 'things' around them, what has been left behind by the scientific, post-Renaissance, non-Indian world, is the universal sacredness—the living mystery—of creation's circle.[535]

"Chippewa Lodge" engraving by Capt. Eastman

The Indian had a close relationship with his family, community, tribe, and all the creatures of the earth, and a well-ordered, balanced society. They also believed that the human being possessed the only great intelligence. The foundation of all their songs and all their ceremonies celebrated the differences between the Indians and the other creatures in the world. At the same time, they believed that all creatures, including human beings, were related and owed their existence in this world to the same creator, the Great Spirit who oversaw everything in the universe. They believed all of us on earth were connected in some way with each other and to their creator.

Inuit (Eskimo) igloos, engraving

The Judea-Christian view is based primarily on commandments that set down rules and laws that all good Christians have to follow in order to enter heaven. The Indian religion focused on their own self-esteem and the right of all creatures to exist harmoniously. This is seen in the Indian idea of the medicine wheel, sacred hoop, or circle, that represent the dynamic, moving, harmonious, unified world in perfect balance. The Indians were unable to comprehend the religious beliefs that the missionaries attempted to impose on them. The notion of salvation was a particularly mysterious concept to the Indians, as the idea of Jesus appearing after his death was contradictory to their beliefs.

Indian thatched lodging, 1898, by Rinhardt

The Judea-Christian faith taught that God is entirely separate and distant from man. The Indians believed that their Great Spirit existed in every part of their life and allowed them more freedom as they worshipped the earth, wind, sun and stars. In some ways the Indians' religious beliefs echoed those of the white man. The Indians pondered the creation and origins of our earth, the sea, the stars, animal and plant life, and the presence of man. The Great Spirit inhabited the caves, forests, mountains, canyons, animals, rocks, water, sun, etc. and the Indians' religion evolved in a process of adaptation to the natural surroundings.

Tlingit interior, 1887
Togiak, Alaska, 1877

White America misunderstood the Indian's worship of nature, calling it idolatry. In 1851 an article in the *United States Democratic Review* falsely questioned and attempted to degrade "The Race of American Indians", and their religious beliefs.

As a race, there never was one more impracticable; more bent on a name-less principle of tribality; more averse to combinations for their general good; more deaf to the voice of instruction; more determined to pursue all the elements of their own destruction. They are still, as a body, nomadic in their manners and customs. They appear, on this continent, to have trampled on monumental ruins, some of which had their origin before their arrival, or without their participation as builders, though these are apparently ruins of the same generic race of men, but of a prior era. They have, in the north, no temples for worship, and live in the

Inside and outside Navajo Hogan, 1920s

wild belief of the ancient theory of a diurgus, or Soul of the Universe, which inhabits and animates everything. They recognize their Great Spirit in rocks, trees, cataracts, and clouds; in thunder and lightning; in the strongest tempests and the softest zephyrs; and this subtle and transcendental spirit is believed to conceal himself in titular deities from human gaze, as birds and quadrupeds; and, in short, he is supposed to exist under every possible form in the world, animate and inanimate. The influence of the civilization of the Zen Maize on the semi-civilization and history of the Indian race of this continent has been very striking. It is impossible to resist this conclusion in searching into the causes of their dispersion over the continent. We are everywhere met with the fact that those tribes who cultivated corn and lived in mild and temperate latitudes reached a state of society which was denied to the mere hunters. The Indian race that named the Mississippi Valley at the era of the first planting of the American colonies were but corn grow-

Grinding corn, from the Aztec *Florentine Codex*

ers to a limited extent. It was only by the labor of females, while the men were completely hunters and periodical nomads. They spent their summers at their corn fields, and their winters in the wild forests, doing just what their forefathers had done; and the thought of their ancestors having had the skill or industry to raise mounds, or throw up defenses on the apex of hills or at sharp defiles, never occurred to them till questioned on the subject by the whites.[536]

The Indians' worship of objects, associated with their everyday life, was primarily symbolic. It was the supernatural power of the spirit within the object that they worshipped as an intermediary between themselves and their creator. The Indians have given more attention to nature than any other existing culture or religion, thus providing an example that is relevant today. Defiling the earth is abhorrent to their society. For the Indian, the universe was controlled by a mighty being who lived in the great beyond. Edward Goodbird summed up the white man's misrepresentation of the Indians' worship of their many sacred objects as, "White men think it strange that we Indians honored these sacred bundles; but I have heard in Europe men once honored relics, the skull, or a bone, or a bit of hair of some saint, or a nail from Jesus' cross; that they did not pray to the relic, but thought that the spirit of the Saint was near, or that he was more willing to hear their prayers when knelt before the relic. In much the same way, we Indians honored our sacred bundles. They contained sacred objects, or relics, that had belonged each to some god—his scalp, or skull, the pipe he smoked, or his robe. We did not pray to the object, but to the god or spirit to whom it had belonged, and we thought these sacred objects had wonderful power, just as white men once thought they could be cured of sickness by touching the bone of some saint."[537]

The Indian utilized a number of methods to reach the Great Spirit; by daily prayers, fasting, vision quests, medicines, through a shaman as an intermediary, with ceremonial dances and even with self-mutilation. This contact with their creator through intermediaries was necessary for them to maintain constant balance and harmony between their spiritual world and man. J. R. Walker, a physician who lived for many years among the Oglala Sioux, of the Dakota family of tribes, explains this intermediary trans-

Virginia Indians preparing meal with corn
from John White painting, engraving by Theodor de Bry

formation to the Great Spirit as, "When Wakan Tanka (Great Spirit), wishes one of mankind to do something he makes his wish known either in a vision or through a shaman.... Wakan Tanka is like sixteen different persons; but each person is kan. Therefore, they are all only the same one...."[538]

The Indians' tipis (tepees) faced east, to welcome the morning sun; they prayed to the sun as an intermediary to the Great Spirit. They believed that the souls of their dead entered into another world beyond this world. They believed in one God as did the Christians, a God who controlled the entire universe. He was their Great Spirit, called by a different name in the languages of the different tribes: Orenda, Wakan Tanka, Watauinaiwa, Manito, Tirawa, Awonawilona, Ometeotl, Olelbis, Yahgan, Agriskoue, Maona, etc. The Wintun tribe of California call their supreme being Olelbis, to whom they prayed at sunrise. In northern California the Pomo tribe worships a hybrid God called Dasan. Their God came out of the ocean, turned into a man and built the world through the power of his words. Then he created the first humans. The Algonquin family of tribes, who were the first to welcome the Dutch, English and French to North America, called their Great Spirit Manitou. Every Algonquin man of importance was expected to have a supernatural guardian spirit. In their legends thunder and lightning became lesser gods, and from these stories came the great bird known as the Thunderbird. A number of Indian tribes passed down many other similar mysterious legends concerning their own gods.

The Pawnee tribe of Indians called their Great Spirit Tirawa. Tirawa ruled the lesser Gods. The Pawnees were once neighbors of the Algonquin Iroquois tribe, and spoke the same Caddoan language. The Pawnees developed a complex belief that strongly emphasized the importance of figures as being subordinates to Tirawa. They were astronomers who utilized the stars and the sky to determine the planting time for their primary crop, corn. They worshipped corn as one of the lesser gods of their one supreme creator, Tirawa. The Pawnees also gave prayers to the earth as the source of all life, including the corn. They believed that the arrival of the new corn each year symbolized the birth of human life. They believed their Great Spirit Tirawa was omnipotent, and reigned

Florida Timucuan Indians worshipping statue set up by French
Depiction by French artist Jacques Le Moyne, 1596

supreme throughout the world. Tirawa alone could bring good or bad, success or failure. All prayers were made to Tirawa. According to George Grinnell, "When the pipe is lighted, the first whiffs are blown to the Deity. When food is eaten, a small portion is placed on the ground (or in the fire) as a sacrifice to Him."[539]

The Pawnee observed a ritual called "Hako", which encompassed more than 20 smaller ceremonial rites, and was a direct link to reaching Tirawa. It was performed only in the spring, summer and fall, never in the winter. It addressed the belief of there being a holy place in the Universe where they could send their prayers. The Pawnee believed that performing this "Hako" ritual would guarantee that their prayers would be received and answered by Tirawa. The Pawnee "Hako" ritual bears a striking similarity to a religious ritual practiced in 600 B.C. This was held in the city of Eleusis, in a mountainous region called Attica, near Athens. This ritual was called the "Eleusinian Mystery", and was practiced to celebrate life, death and immortality. It was centered on the growing season. The ancient Greeks used corn as a measure of their life cycle. They believed, as did the Pawnees, that the winter season was considered a bad omen, and that participation in the ritual (in other seasons) guaranteed them life after death.[540]

The Creek tribe believed in a supreme creator who was related to the sun, and who lived in the sky on a solid spherical covering. The sun was worshipped as his messenger—an agent of life to all the plants on earth. The creator's intermediary on earth was the spirit that lived in their sacred fires. Their entire spiritual life was controlled by their religious beliefs.

In the Pacific Northwest the creator of the Nootka tribes was called Quawteaht. Their creator lived in the heavens, and the Nootkan believed that he had power over their fish. In Tierra del Fuego in South America, the Indians, far removed and out of contact with the North American tribes, had an invisible and lonely creator who ruled the world and was known as Watauniewa. The Indians prayed to him but did not offer sacrifice because he was considered to be the owner of everything—thus to sacrifice his own belongings to him would not have made sense and would have been wrong. Other tribes in different areas such as the Winnebagos, related to the Siouan family, prayed to four different earth gods.

Kwakiutl, Koskimo house post
by Curtis, 1915

The Mayan civilization was based on agriculture. They firmly believed in life after death and made prayers and sacrifices to four leading earth gods. Out of these four, one, Huitz-Hok or "Mountain Valley", ruled supreme. The four earth gods represented the four world directions of east, north, west and south, and their four leading colors were yellow, red, white and black. Mayan life and religion revolved around these gods just as it revolved around the crop cycles.[541]

The Inca people were religious in their every expression. Their religious temples were covered with shining sheets of gold as the priests prayed to Mother Sun and made sacrifices of young boys and girls. Beyond the worship of their lesser gods and their great temple gods stood their overall creator, Viracocha. Viracocha had appeared in a dream to the Inca ruler called Pachacuti Inca Tupac Yupanqui, when the Chanca were besieging the Inca forces. Upon victory, Pachacuti raised a temple to honor Viracocha

"Shaman consulting a Sorcerer"
Florida Indians depiction, by de Bry

in Cuzco. He was represented by a gold figure, the size of a small child. Inti, the sun god, was one of the Incas' ranking deities, considered to be the divine ancestor of the Inca. Apu Illapu, the rain giver, was an agricultural deity to whom the common man addressed his prayers for rain. Temples to Apu Illapu were usually on high structures; in times of severe drought, pilgrimages were made to the temples and prayers were often accompanied by human sacrifices. The people believed that Illapu's shadow was in the Milky Way, from where he drew the water when he poured down rain. Mama-Kilya, wife of the sun god, was the Moon Mother and the regulator of women's menstrual cycles. The rising and setting of the moon was used to calculate monthly cycles, and to set the time periods for Inca festivals. Silver was considered to be tears of the moon. The stars had minor functions. The constellation of Lyra, which was believed to have the appearance of a llama, was prayed to for protection. The constellation Scorpio was believed to have the shape of a cat; the Pleiades were called "little mothers", and festivals were celebrated on their reappearance in the sky.

Algonquin shaman

Earth was called Paca-Mama, or "Earth Mother." The sea was called Mama Qoca, or the Sea Mother. Their creator was worshiped with this prayer: "To Viracocha, power of all that exists, be it male or female, Saint, Lord, Creator of newborn light. Why art Thou? Where art Thou? Is it not possible for me to see Thee? In the world above or the world below or wheresoever in the world thy mighty throne is to be found? In the heavenly ocean or the seas of the earth, where is Thy habitation? O Pachacamac, Creator of man, Lord, thy servants desire that their feeble eyes may behold Thee...."[542]

Charles Alexander Eastman, an (Ohiyesa) Santee Sioux, was well aware of the changes in the Indian due to their exposure to modern society. Eastman recollected from his early years. "As a child, I understood how to give; I have forgotten that grace since I became civilized. I lived the natural life. Whereas I now live the artificial. Any pretty pebble was valuable to me then, every growing tree an object of reverence. Now I worship with the white man before a painted landscape whose value is estimated in dollars! Thus the Indian is reconstructed, as the natural rocks are ground to powder and made into artificial blocks that may be built into the walls of modern society.... We of the twentieth century know better! We know that all religious aspiration, all sincere worship, can have but one source and one goal. We know that god of the lettered and unlettered, of the Greek and the barbarian, is after all the same god."[543]

Indian oral story-telling, by Edward Curtis

Many other Indians voiced their views on life and their Great Spirit. Chief Luther Standing Bear (Oglala Sioux) stated, "The man who sat on the ground in his tipi (tepee) meditating on life and its meaning, accepting the kinship of all creatures and acknowledging unity with the universe of things, was infusing into his being the true essence of civilization. And when native man left off this form of development, his humanization was retarded in growth."

Chief Joseph of the Nez Percé declared, "The earth is part of my body, and I never gave up the earth." Sitting Bull, the Great Indian Chief and shaman (medicine man) of the Teton Sioux said, "All the Indians pray to god for life, and try to find out a good road, and do nothing wrong in this life. This is what we want, and to pray to god. But you did not believe us. You should say nothing against our religion, for we say nothing against yours. You pray to god. So do all of us Indians, as well as the whites. We both pray to only one god, who made us all."

Red Jacket (Sagoyewatha), an Eastern Seneca Chief of the Six Nations, said, "Brother, you say there is but one way to worship and serve the Great Spirit. If there is but one religion, why do you white people differ so much about it? Why not all agree, as you can all read the book? Brother, we do not understand these things. We are told that your religion was given to your forefathers, and has been handed down from father to son. We also have a religion, which was given to our forefathers and has been handed down to us, their children. We worship in that way. It teaches us to be thankful for all favors we receive, to love each other and be united. We never quarrel about religion because it is a matter which concerns each man and the Great Spirit. Brother, we do not wish to destroy your religion or take it from you; we only wish to enjoy our own."

Red Jacket, Forest Lawn Cemetery, Buffalo, N. Y.

Crowfoot, of the Midwest Blackfeet tribe, said, "What is life? It is the flash of the firefly in the night. It is the breath of the buffalo in the wintertime. It is the little shadow which runs across the grass and loses itself in the sunset." Charles Alexander Eastman, an educated physician and author, wrote in 1911, "In the life of the Indian there was only one inevitable duty—the duty of prayer—the daily recognition of the unseen and eternal. His daily devotions were more necessary to him than daily food... each soul must meet the morning sun, the new sweet earth and the great silence alone! He sees no need for setting apart one day in seven as a holy day, since to him all days are god's."

"Magic Pile Erected by the Assiniboin Indians"
Karl Bodmer, 1832-1834

Bishop Henry Whipple was the first Episcopal Bishop of Minnesota. Described as a friend to the Indians, he also did them a disservice by believing the answer to their problems would be solved by Christianizing and educating them into white society. He wrote, "The North American Indian is the noblest type of heathen man on earth. He recognizes a Great Spirit; he believes in immortality; he has a quick intellect; he is a clear thinker; he is brave and fearless; and until betrayed, he is true to his plighted faith. He has a passionate love for his children, and counts it a joy to die for his people. Our most terrible wars have been with the noblest types of the Indians and men who had been the white mans' friends. Nicolet said the Sioux were the finest type of wild men he had ever seen."[544] In an 1860 letter to President James Buchanan, Whipple called on the government to embrace a paternalistic scheme to uplift the Ojibway (Chippewa), Sioux and Winnebagos. In a series of eight proposals he stated, "The only hope for the Indian is civilization and Christianization. They understand this, and I believe would welcome any plan which will save them from destruction. The curse of the Indian country is the firewater, which flows through its borders. Although every treaty pledges to them protection against its sale and use, and the government desires to fulfill this pledge, thus far all efforts have proved ineffectual.... First, whether in future, treaties cannot be made so that the government shall occupy a paternal character, treating the Indians as their wards.... Seventh, whether some plan cannot be devised to create in the Indians an interest in securing themselves homes where they can live by the cultivation of the soil.... Eighth, whether practical Christian teachers cannot be secured to teach the Indians the peaceful pursuits of agriculture and the arts of civilization."[545]

Tom Newcomb, who lived with the Sioux under Crazy Horse during the early 1870s, stated, "I tell you I never saw more kindness or real Christianity anywhere. The poor, the sick, the aged, the widows and the orphans were always looked after first. Whenever we moved camp, someone took care that the widows' lodges were moved first and set up first. After every hunt, a good-sized chunk of meat was dropped at each door where it was most needed. I was treated like a brother; and I tell you I have never seen any community of church people that was as truly Christian as that band of Indians."[546] Another missionary, the Jesuit Father Lafitau, widely recognized for his work among the Indians, described the medicine lodge of the Sioux as a "true church of god, and we have no right to stamp it out."[547]

Two white authors, one in 1834 and one in 1927, quite adequately laid down the basic concept of the Indian religion. Washington Irving, after a visit to the Nez Percé and the Flatheads, prior to their contact with the Europeans, wrote in *The Adventures of Captain Bonneville,* "Simply to call these people religious would convey but a faint idea of the deep hue of piety and devotion which pervades their whole conduct. Their honesty is immaculate, and their purity of purpose and their observance of the rights of their religion are most uniform and remarkable. They are certainly more like a nation of Saints than a hoard of savages."[548] In 1927 John James, in *My Experience with Indians,* wrote, "I claim for the North American Indian the purest religion, and the loftiest conceptions of the Great Creator, of any non-Christian religion that has ever been known to this world.... The North American Indian has no priests, no idols, no sacrifices, but went direct to the Great Spirit and worshipped Him who was invisible, and seeing Him by Faith, adored Him who seeketh such to worship him in spirit and in truth, who is a Spirit and planted a similar spirit in His creatures, that there might be a communion between the two."[549]

"Idols of the Mandan Indians"
by Karl Bodmer, 1832-1834

115

CHAPTER 9 INDIANS ON DEATH AND THE SOVL

"Offering of the Mandan Indians"
by Karl Bodmer, 1832-1834

The Indians believed in an afterlife and understood the concept of a soul, and they manifested their beliefs through their customs and respect for the dead. Most tribes regarded death as a happy experience rather than a tragedy. The individual bravery and devotion to tribal existence insured a lasting place for their spirit in their other life. The Indians were daring in combat, and had no fear of death.

Although there was as wide a variety of gods as tribes, to rule the fields, the ocean and the weather, there were certain beliefs that were common to all tribes, irrespective of the name and personality of their creator. One was the nature of the afterlife and the journey of the soul. All Indians believed that, while their bodies would decompose and nourish the earth, their spirits would return in visions. For most tribes the afterlife was situated across a distant river, somewhere in the heavens, in a volcano, or in an underworld. The Indian's devotion to the souls of the dead earned them the admiration of a few of the early missionaries and priests. Father Joseph Francois Lafitau, a French missionary, speaking of his work among the Algonquin tribes during the early 1700s, wrote, "It could be said that all their work, all their sweating and all their trade comes back almost solely to doing honor to the dead. They have nothing precious enough for this. And so they sacrificed their beaver robes, maize, axes and wampum in such quantity that it could be believed they attach no importance to them, although they constitute all the wealth of the country. They can be seen almost naked in the winter cold, while they have, in their chests, good fur or woolen robes destined for the funeral duties. On these occasions, each person makes it a point of honor or religion to appear liberal to the point of magnificence or prodigality."[550]

Tlingit religious ritual

Many Indian tribes shared their beliefs that animals also possessed a soul, although an animal soul was considered less important than those of the Indians themselves. The Indians nevertheless considered the animals to have a spiritual power that had to be taken into account upon the death of the animal, and different animals were believed to have certain mysterious and unusual qualities. The bear was especially admired and believed to possess human intelligence. The Indian believed a power was transformed back to the individual Indian hunter after the bear's death. Animals that managed to elude the hunter were considered to have special powers. When an animal had been killed, the Indians followed special ritualistic procedures for its disposal in order to show respect for its soul. The creator had permitted the taking of its life and it was forbidden to kill more animals than necessary.

The northwest coast tribes universally believed in the immortality of the salmon, on which they were dependent for their food. They believed the salmon were supernatural creatures that inhabited a great house beneath the sea, and rose out of it each year to make their run upstream for the benefit of the Indians. The Pacific salmon was the only fish that changed color and appearance during its run upstream in fresh water, and then in the salt waters of the Pacific, giving it apparently magical properties. The Indians performed ceremonies of renewal that included rituals around the birth and death of the salmon, as well other important seasonal crops such as huckleberry and root feast ceremonies. It was important for the salmon bones to go back to the sea after the fish had been consumed, otherwise, "On resurrection the salmon-person might lack an arm or leg, or some part, and he may become angry and refuse to run again in the stream in which they had been so unappreciatively treated."[551]

Salmon effigy

Burying or burning the personal possessions of the deceased in or near the grave was a universal custom among ancient civilizations. Many, like the Egyptians, believed that the soul would need sustenance in the afterlife. For this reason it was important for the deceased to have the weapons, clothing, ornaments and utensils that had been used in life. The *Codex Vaticanus A* bears so close a resemblance to the Egyptian *Pert-Em-Hru* that it has been called, "The Mexican Book of the Dead." In its pages the corpse is depicted as dressed for burial; the soul, like the Egyptian ba (human-headed bird), is shown escaping from the mouth. The deceased is ushered into the presence of Tezcatlipoca by a priest in an ocelot skin, just as the Egyptian was brought before Osiris, and stands naked with a

Moche (Mochica) burial items of
Lord of Sipan
Lambayeque, Peru, circa 500 B.C.

wooden yoke about his neck to receive judgment. He then has to undergo the tests which precede entrance to the abode of the dead. Most tribes universally practiced removal of the body through a hole in the wall of the home, so that the living could avoid following the same path as the dead. The Pueblos (Hopi), as well as other tribes, considered that the body became a mere husk after death—an empty case whose disposal was a ritual of comfort for the survivors. It was the comfort of the soul that was of primary importance, and food and clothing were placed in the grave for sustenance during the journey to the next world. During the first four days the spirit of the deceased was believed to stay close to home. Food and drink was left

Florida Indian burial of Chief Priest, by de Bry

for the spirit. Many Indian tribes, as well as the ancient Egyptians, broke pottery and left it in the grave to prevent the evil spirits from taking possession. Often a hole was made in the pottery, signifying that it was also dead, and it could accompany the dead soul to the next world.

The methods of disposal of the body varied among Indian tribes. Some practiced cremation, others buried their dead lying prone in the ground, or seated with knees drawn up close to the chin, while others placed their dead on platforms above the earth, or in trees. Some tribes placed the dead in burial mounds, complex tombs, or to be buried in their house. The northwestern tribes used decorated wooden boxes to bury their dead. It was believed that the soul would emerge from the body and go on to construct for itself a new and better body in the afterlife. The lyrics of a Pueblo death song illustrate the expectations of the Indians. "I care not where my body lies. My soul goes marching on." The Pueblo view was that the dead would go to the sun or return from whence he came—a place Pueblo people called "Sipapu." In this other world the dead will live as before, except everything would be reversed. Day will be night, and summer will be winter, etc. In the Pueblo perspective, the living, the dead and the unborn continue to be part of mankind's circle, without a beginning and without an end, "...which the Pueblos hope will last as long as the earth will bring forth corn and the sky, clouds, heavy with raindrops, and as long as the sun god will give warmth and life to this world."[552]

Blackfeet tree burial, 1900s

The Catholic Europeans were unable to tolerate the Indians' beliefs, which they found primitive and shocking. Their own god's demands were revealed to them through the works of Jesus Christ and in the Bible. A religion without a written history was beyond their understanding, as was one in which the notions of heaven and hell were absent. For the Indian, the notion of god-given reward or punishment for a devout life was likewise incomprehensible. In the 16th century, William Penn attempted to understand the soul and the religion of the Algonquin tribes, but was unable to see any sophistication or true meaning in the Indian burial rites. He spoke of the natives with love and admiration for their culture, without ever understanding that their traditions (ceremonies, sacrifices and hospitality) constituted the everyday practice of their religion. Penn wrote of their religion, death and of their belief in an afterlife, "If they die, they bury them with their apparel, be that men or women, and the nearest of kin fling something precious with them, as a token of love.... These poor people are under a dark night in things of religion; to be sure, the traditions of it they have only; yet they believe in a god and immortality, without the help of metaphysics; for, say they, there is a great King that made them, and that the souls of the good shall go thither, where they shall live again. Their worship consists of two parts—sacrifice and cantico; their sacrifice is their first fruits; the first and the fattest buck they kill goeth to the fire, where he is burnt, with the mournful ditty of him that performeth the ceremony.... The other part... round dances, sometimes words, sometimes shouts; two being in the middle, that begin, and by singing and drumming on a board, direct the chorus."[553]

Dakota and Plains Indians sky burial

The violent Aztec civilization had its own traditions and concerns about death and dying. These were passed down orally and appeared in their pictorial writings. After the conquest in the sixteenth century, Aztec scribes, in the Nahuatl language, under Spanish rule, made translations. The Aztecs pondered, "Is it true that one lives only on earth? Not forever on earth, only a short while here. Even jade will crack, even gold will break, even quetzal feathers will rend, not forever on earth: only a short while here." Another verse stated, "If in one day we leave, in one night descend to the mysterious regions, here we only come to meet, we are only passers-by on earth. Let us pass life in peace and pleasure; come, let us rejoice. But not those who live in wrath: the earth is very wide! That one could live forever, that one need not die." Another poetic poem reaffirmed the destiny of one's soul: "In heaven you live; The mountains you uphold, Anahuác is in your hand, Everywhere, always you are awaited, You are invoked, your fame are sought. In heaven you live: Anahuác is in your hand."[554]

"Digging the Grave", Kansa Indian burial

William H. Warren, son of an Ojibway mother and a white father, became a member of the House of Representatives in St. Paul, Minnesota. Warren was educated with the customs of his own tribe. He died in 1853 at 28 after completing a history of his Ojibway nation. He described their traditions and religious beliefs. The following aptly describes their burial customs and belief in an after life: "When an Ojibway dies, his body is placed in a grave, generally in a sitting position, facing the west. With the body are buried all the articles needed in life for a journey. If a man, his gun, blanket, kettle, fire steel flint and moccasins; if a woman, her moccasins, axe, portage, collar, blanket and kettle. The soul is supposed to start immediately after the death of the body on a deep beaten path, which leads westward; the first object he comes to in following the path is the great Oda-e-min. After camping out four nights and traveling each day through a prairie country, the soul arrives in the land of spirits, where he finds his relatives accumulated since mankind was first created; all are rejoicing, singing and dancing; they live in a beautiful country interspersed with clear lakes and streams, forests and prairies, and bounding in fruit and game to repletion—in a word, abounding in all that the red man most covets in this life, and which conduces most to his happiness. It is that kind of paradise which he, only by his manner of life on this earth, is fitted to enjoy." A common burial practice for many tribes was to place the body facing west.[555]

The Cherokee view of birth to death and rebirth was a process that went on for eternity. The Cherokee were taught to live each day as if it was their last day on earth. In ancient times a Cherokee died fearlessly, surrounded by family and friends. They believed in the harmony of life and the ability to communicate with each other without any harsh speech. They believed that they had seven lifetimes during which to transform themselves into perfect beings. They also believed in a higher level of consciousness, that certain rituals and ceremonies would enable them to choose the relationships and friends they would have in the next lifetime. They viewed the experience of dying much as they viewed the cycle of the changing seasons. "Old age is as wonderful as the beauty of autumn. When one has lived with care and mindfulness, death is another quality to be explored."[556] Cherokee oral legends tell of their origination in the cluster of stars known as Pleiades, or The Seven Sisters. Star woman fell to earth, precipitating the birth of the planets, animals and the twelve original tribes of the Cherokee nation. It was claimed that these star people came to earth in Elohi Mona, five islands in the Atlantic Ocean, later called Atlantis. Before they came from the stars, great waters existed on earth inhabited by one body that contained both the female and the man. The Cherokees believed that the children of the sun on earth greeted the seven sacred children of the stars, and the people from these two worlds intermarried. Their descendants are the Cherokee, Creek, Choctaw, Yuchi and other Indian nations of the southeastern part of the United States. Atlantis was eventually destroyed by the misuse of their sacred power and their enslavement of others. During the ten-thousand-year breaking up of Atlantis, its inhabitants migrated throughout South and Central America and five of the original twelve tribes were lost.[557]

"Mourning the Dead," engraving

According to Apache mythology, a spirit (soul) is released at the time of death, and is guided to the underworld by the ghosts of its dead ancestors. The underworld is divided in two sections—one is a beautiful, forested green place that is inhabited by the ghosts of pure and chaste people. The other is dismal and barren, and is inhabited by the ghosts of witches. Burial rites are held instantly after death occurs, so as to hasten the spirit's departure. The Apache believed that unless the funeral was quick and thoughts of the dead were forgotten, the ghosts might return from the underworld to create havoc. The members of the immediate family would begin a period of mourning by cutting their hair or wearing old clothes. The family and relatives of the dead would isolate themselves from the rest of the tribe in the belief that the ghosts might return to familiar grounds. The dead person was taken away from the tribal grounds and buried with his favorite possessions. The dead person was buried in the hole left after the removal of a small rock or stump of a tree.[558]

The Choctaw tribe, according to their mythology, originated in the western part of North America, possibly among the Sioux tribes. Two brothers, Chahta and Chikasa, led them from their ancestral home to seek better lands, finally arriving in south-central Mississippi. Under Chikasa the tribe split in two, with one being called Chickasaw and the other Choctaw. The tribes believed in an afterlife and one Great Spirit they called Hush-tahli, who related to and acted through the sun creator.[559] The Choctaws also acknowledged the existence of lesser spirits that appeared as a force "in the sigh of the wind, the flight of the birds, the howl of the lone wolf, and the midnight hoot of the owl."[560] As in many other tribes, the dead men and women were buried with their food and personal possessions. In their early history the living honored the dead by covering them with skins and placing them on a burial platform near their home. Their possessions were arrayed near to them and the surviving members collected at the foot of the platform to mourn. An elaborate ritual prepared the dead for the next world. When the body had decomposed, a special group called "bone pickers" ascended the scaffold to clean the bones of flesh. The skeleton was painted with vermilion and placed in a coffin in the village bone house. Once a year a common burial was performed during which time a "Choctaw Cry" ceremony was performed, the names of all who had died during the year were announced and then all the dead were buried in a common mound. When the "Cry" was concluded, it signaled the end of mourning for the deceased. With the coming of the white man and the end of their nomadic existence the custom changed, and the dead were buried in the yard with a small house built over the grave.[561]

"How the Aztecs Treat their Dead," by de Bry, 1600s

The Cheyenne, who inhabited the Great Plains, called the soul the "tasoon", which meant "shadow", or the vital substance and spiritual essence of the body. When the soul left the body for a certain time, they believe that death had come. Death, in simple terms, was a state of existence after the soul had separated from the body. Their creator, known as Heammawihio, had, in ancient times, departed the earth for the heavens. The sun represented Heammawihio. At tribal gatherings it was customary to make the first offering of the pipe to the creator. The Cheyenne believed that after death their soul traveled through the Milky Way, called in Cheyenne "ekutsihimmiyo", to eventually reach the home of Heammawihio. The Cheyenne reported similar after-death experiences to people in the present day. During a coma they saw the villages of their family who were dead, and they were sent back to earth by their spirits to recover from these vivid experiences. In Cheyenne tradition there was no hell, nor was there any punishment, judgment or damnation in the afterlife. When they left this world for the next they left free of fear of recrimination for any past wrongs, except in the case of suicide, which, they believed, prevented the soul from finding the promised tranquility of the afterlife. The Cheyenne believed it was important to dispose of the body immediately after death, to enable the soul to be able to the separate from the body and to prevent the soul from taking one of them on a journey with the deceased.

Virginia Indian shamans

The dead Cheyenne was dressed in his finest clothing by his relatives and close friends and the body was wrapped while it was extended with the arms at the sides. Robes were lashed around the body with great lengths of rope. This burial bundle containing the rolled-up dead body was then carried on a platform held by two poles to its burial site, and placed upon a scaffold or the branch of a tree. At times the favorite possessions of the deceased were left at the graveside. A man would be buried with his weapons, while a woman would go to the afterlife with her utensils. Everything else was given away to non-relatives who had come to the dead person's home to mourn. Mourners would cut their hair or gash their foreheads to make the blood run, and a husband or wife in mourning would isolate themselves from their relatives for a year.[562]

Amazonian tribes had a variety of beliefs. Some tribes believed the body split into two parts at the moment of death and the soul linked to their creator, while a spirit or ghost returned to earth.[563] Their shaman or medicine man or woman acted as a mediator between the two worlds, enabling intercession with the soul and the spirit on behalf of the tribe, often through dreams. One of their prayers to their dead was, "I have two loves: The Indians of the earth. The Indians of the skies. A rope, filament of the soul, mythical link, connects me to them. I have two shores: That of the river. That of the Milky Way. Down here I was your guide. Up there, I will be your lucky star."[564]

Yanomamo Amazon Indians,
Shaman curing ceremony

Many other tribes shared the belief of two souls. The Crow Plains Indian tribe believed one soul traveled to the next life and the other soul or ghostly spirit haunted the grave. The Mandan tribe believed in four souls. Two souls symbolized by the white sage and meadowlark merged to form one soul to travel to the next world. The third soul stayed in the dead persons' lodge and the fourth left the village to occasionally return to scare its people.

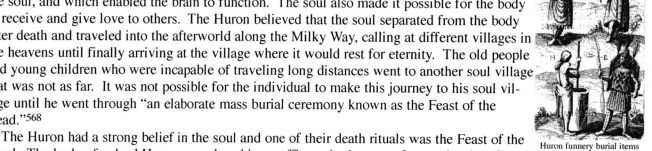

The Salish tribes of the Pacific Northwest believed in the oneness of life between man and the animal life surrounding him. They believed that man contained two souls, one of which departed into the sunset to the next world, where it remained forever. The soul that was left behind with the body remained on earth and was good or evil depending on the kind of life its owner had had while on earth.[565] The dead would be buried in various ways, depending on

Mandan Chief Mato-Tope by Karl Bodmer, 1832-1834

where they had lived. They might be placed in storage boxes, in a cave, suspended from a tree, placed on top of a memorial pole or set out in a canoe that was raised up on scaffoldings, or they would be cremated with only the charred bones and ashes brought home. Their personal possessions would either be buried or burned with the body, or left at the graveside. Some tribes would declare a ceremony of feasts and potlatches on the death of a chief. This included the period of mourning and rites to pick the chief's successor.[566]

A Nakoaktok Mawihl, by Curtis

With the conversion of many Indians to Christianity, the concept of a place similar to hell began to creep into their mythology. A Shawnee Catholic related the story to Father de Smet of how the Great Spirit resided on the top of a mountain in the midst of a beautiful island. It was to this place that the good Indians went, here among beautiful vegetation and all the food you could eat. Separating this land of beauty was a tree of supernatural length, with a delicious grape vine in the center that the spirit had to cross. If the Indian led a good life, he would pass in safety. If his life was bad when he approached the grape vine, "...he was sure to lose his footing and fall into the rushing waters beneath, by which he was borne onward to a cold and barren and desolate country, where he was doomed to wander forever in a state of misery and famine."[567]

The Huron believed in five components which radiated throughout the body and gave life to the soul, and which enabled the brain to function. The soul also made it possible for the body to receive and give love to others. The Huron believed that the soul separated from the body after death and traveled into the afterworld along the Milky Way, calling at different villages in the heavens until finally arriving at the village where it would rest for eternity. The old people and young children who were incapable of traveling long distances went to another soul village that was not as far. It was not possible for the individual to make this journey to his soul village until he went through "an elaborate mass burial ceremony known as the Feast of the Dead."[568]

Huron funnery burial items

The Huron had a strong belief in the soul and one of their death rituals was the Feast of the Dead. The body of a dead Huron was placed in a coffin or, in the case of a warrior, in a flexed position in a shallow grave. Infants were buried along a road between the villages so that their souls might enter women passing by and be born again. At intervals of eight, ten or twelve years, all the dead from each Huron village were removed from their temporary grave to a mass burial site. The bones were stripped of the remaining flesh, cleaned lovingly and placed in beaver skin bags by relatives of the deceased. The bones were dressed in fine robes and adorned with bracelets and strings of beads. They were then taken on a ceremonial journey to the place of burial. The bodies were hung from poles on a high scaffold surrounded by a platform. Bundles of bones were placed on the platform. Underneath this platform was a large pit about forty feet square and up to ten feet deep. Ceremonies and rituals were performed in which all Hurons participated. After the ceremony, "The bodies were placed in the pit along with beautiful fur robes, pottery, weapons, tools, ornaments, food and utensils.... At the end of the Feast of the Dead, the souls of the Hurons buried in this way departed from Huronia and went to the various soul villages in the sky. Such elaborate burial rituals and lavishing of wealth upon the dead is reminiscent of Hopewell death rites practiced more than one thousand years earlier in the Upper Great Lakes region. It is quite probable that Huron death rituals perpetuated a part of the religious tradition that once had been Hopewellian."[569]

Hopewell mound burials with 7 ft. tall individuals Engraving from Bureau of Ethnology report, 1890s

CHAPTER 10 INDIAN WOMEN, CHILDREN AND THEIR CLANS

The first European explorers to land in America were astonished at the beauty of the Indian women. Verrazano called them "comely to behold: very graceful and well formed: of a sweet and pleasant countenance... well mannered."[570] Another European wrote of their average height, attractiveness, and their pleasing proportions, finely cut long hair and black eyes.[571] The women in the southwestern Pueblo tribes cropped their hair in the front and used a headband to form a topknot. Their hair was usually parted in the middle, adorned with turquoise or pierced shells that were strung in chains that hung from their ears or neck.[572] One early journal described the Indian women in New England as "very comely, with good features, many petite Brownettoes and spider fingered lasses... among them", many with "slender limbs, cleanly straight, generally plump as a partridge and, saving now and then, one of a modest deportment with black eyes and very white teeth."[573]

"Chippewa Squaw & Child"
McKenney & Hall litho, 1855

Captain John Smith wrote, in 1624, of his observations of the Indian women he encountered in Virginia. The women were "generally tall and straight, of a comely proportion, and of a color brown when they are of any age, but are not born white.... The women's hair is cut in many fashions, agreeable to their years, but ever remaineth long." For dress the women were covered during the winter with animal skins. During the summer months, mantles of deerskins, turkey feathers, grass and the leaves of trees were intricately woven together to cover their nakedness. Smith noted that they were "very shamefaced to be seen bare." It was normal with most of the Indian tribes for a married couple to take their clothes off on retiring and sleep nude. It was the custom for women as well as the men to adorn their legs, hands, breasts and face with tattoos, and to paint their heads and shoulders with a blood root (puccoon), which they ground into a powder and mixed with oil. In each of their ears were three large holes where "they hang chains, bracelets, or copper."[574] Smith further wrote that, "Their women are careful not to be suspected of dishonesty without the leave of their husbands.... Each household knoweth their own lands, and gardens, and most live for their own labors."[575]

Body decorating with red dye was a common practice of Indians throughout North America, as was tattoo designs that could not be rubbed off. When they landed in South America on September 20, 1519, Caballero Antonio Pigafetta, a Spanish explorer who sailed with Magellan, described the men and women they found there as "...well built, not very black but rather brown, though they paint their bodies all over with red, also their faces. Naked except for a girdle made of large parrot feathers, they openly show their shame, for they cover only their posterior parts, which is a cause of much laughter and mockery. They have no hair on the whole of their bodies, or on their faces, because they pluck it out. Nearly all except the women and children have three holes in the lower lip from which hang three round stones about a finger in length...."[576] Women also had considerable credibility as petitioners for fairness. A well-known example is that of Pocahontas, who interceded with her father, Chief Powhatan, to spare the life of Captain John Smith after the tribal council had sentenced him to death. Chief Red Fox in his autobiography wrote, "We, long ago, learned that some women are wiser than some men. If the woman produced the chief, she must be as wise as the chief."[577]

Mo-Hon-Go, Osage
woman and child
McKenney & Hall, 1838

Friar Gaspar de Carvajal, who accompanied an expedition down the Amazon River in 1541-42, recalled a battle between the Spanish and a tribe of Amazon warrior women, when an arrow wounded him. Carvajal wrote, "These women are very white and tall and have long hair, braided and wound about their heads. They are very robust and go naked, their privy parts covered with bows and arrows. One drove an arrow a span deep into one brigantine, and this kept up until both vessels looked like porcupines." Another Spanish explorer, Antonio de Herrera, wrote of his voyage with Francisco de Orellana down the River of the Amazons, "...he learned that the land was controlled by women, who lived in the same way as Amazons, and were very rich, possessing much gold and silver. They plated their houses with gold. Their own houses were of stone, and their cities defended by walls..." In Brazil, an Xingu Indian myth recalls a female-dominated society that went to different villages to capture the men. They sang as they walked and "use bows and arrows and do not have a right breast, so they can pull back their bowstrings more easily." Other reports from missionaries and explorers tell of their warlike dispositions and how they fought astride certain strong and agile animals, such as cows. One missionary, Joao dos Santos, reported in the sixteenth century that a similarly ferocious tribe of women in Abyssinia, Ethiopia, also burned off their right breasts so they could have full use of their right arm. There was speculation that the African tribe might have its origins with the Queen of Sheba, and possibly have had a Phoenician connection that brought these same traits to the Amazon women of America.[578]

A Piegan woman

The mythology and oral legends that pertain to Indian women were passed down through generations with songs and stories. Women were glorified as dynamic and powerful arms of the creator, to be worshipped and respected. Her power came from her ability to give birth and as a teacher to her children. The Cochiti Pueblo tribe often referred to and even performed childbirth in a sacred or ritual way. To call someone "mother" was to show her the highest respect. In the Sioux Lakota tribal legends it was a woman who was endowed with strong healing power. She was called the White Buffalo Woman. It was she who had brought the sacred pipe to the Lakota so that they could perform their ceremonies and rituals. The White Buffalo Woman lived in a cave and held power over the four winds. Before any Lakota business or ceremony could be performed, the pipe was first offered to the four different wind directions.[579]

The tribes that cultivated their own food had ritual dances and ceremonies that celebrated the corn woman or corn mother. The ideal woman, symbolized as Mother Earth, was represented in different tribes by different universal names: the Hopi and Navajo Spider Woman, the Sioux tribes had their White Buffalo Woman, the Iroquois as Grandmother Turtle and Sky Woman, Laguna Pueblo as Thought Woman, Abenaki as First Woman. The Pueblo tribes had several who were named Yellow Woman, Coyote Woman, Grandmother Spider, Earth Woman, Corn and Sun Woman, etc.[580] In the Six-nation League of the Iroquois an oral myth states, "According to the legend, the corn plant sprang from the bosom of the mother of the Great Spirit, after her burial."[581] The Seneca tribe told their story of the creation of earth through their legendary Sky Woman, whom her jealous and fearful husband catapulted into space. A waterfowl then carried her to safety and placed her on the back of grandmother turtle, thereby stopping her tremendous fall. From the body of this grandmother the earth was formed. The shell of the turtle, being strong and hard, represented the toughness and firmness of women. A number of other Indian tribes tell similar creation legends.[582]

Through the women in these various creation legends, all tribes and nations were connected to one source that made brothers of all of mankind. The sun and fire were idolized as a gift from the creator, and to both the Cherokee and the Iroquois tribes, the sun and earth fires were female. The Spider Woman of the Pueblo tribe was considered the grandmother of the sun, responsible for populating the world.[583] According to the Navajo legend, there was only one sex and all lived beneath the earth. After they were separated, a great flood drove them upwards and Changing Woman was then created. When she reached womanhood, Changing Woman was impregnated by the sun's rays and by water from a waterfall, and subsequently gave birth to twin sons. Changing Woman is the symbolic nurturer and protector of the Navajo nation—the benign bestower of corn and other things that were vital to their survival. In Navajo mythology, man is secondary. "Next to Changing Woman in importance is her husband, the Sun."[584] Tribal ceremonies were performed relegating to women the power to deal with droughts or floods, and to increase the production of corn. In Indian mythology, as well as in their ideology, the mother had special status and was considered the central and most important part of the household. Her importance as a mother continued as long as she had a living child. Indian legends and myths credit women for planting the first wild seeds and producing the first crops. The woman in many tribal legends was portrayed as the giver of life. In many of the Pueblo tribes the community prayed for "female rain" to sustain life. In most tribes, agriculture was the responsibility of women who owned the farmland, the crops and the homes.[585]

White Fawn, Shoshone Bannock woman

The archaeological record shows that the most ancient religions centered on the worship of a goddess or goddesses. Some artifacts that remain of the Paleolithic culture, which goes back approximately 50,000 years, are small flint carvings of goddess figures. These symbols, developed in Paleolithic times, survived into the Neolithic period, particularly in "Old Europe" (the area of Yugoslavia, Hungary, Bulgaria and the islands of the Mediterranean). Their cities were without fortification or weapons. There are relics from a matriarchal society, from Minoan Crete, that date to about 23,000 B.C. This society flourished until about 1450 B.C. due to its isolation. It was eventually wiped out by a patrilineal, war-like society from the north.[586]

122

Most of the largest, important tribes throughout North America followed the matrilineal traditions. In the east these included the Iroquois, Mohegan, Delaware, along with other nations of southern New England and the Powhatan Confederacy in Virginia. In the south were the Creek, Choctaw, Chickasaw, Seminole, and the nations of the Caddoan linguistic family. In the midwest and southwest were the Pawnee, Hidatsa, Mandan, Oto, Missouri, Crow, Siouan nations, Navajo and Pueblo cultures, Hopi, Laguna, Acoma and Zuni. The women, especially in many of the agricultural tribes of North, South and Central America, were recognized for creating life and for the capacity to understand and teach the laws of life. The Cágabá tribe of Northern Colombia described the

"The Queen is carried to the King of Florida"
by Jacques le Moyne, engraving by de Bry, 1600s

woman as "...the most elementary expression of fertility and the most exalted deity of culture; she is the Mother, the creator. From her are born mankind, the good black earth, the edible plants, the animals, and all of nature. All these elements are 'Children of the Mother' and are subject to her law."[587] The Fox tribes in the Great Lakes of North America said, "The earth on which we live is a woman.... She provides us with all the food we eat and lets us live and dwell upon her."[588] The Delaware (Lenape) tribes of North America consider the earth as a goddess and pay homage to her at the annual Thanksgiving Day festival, thanking her for the blessings conferred on their people.[589]

In the primitive patriarchal tribes that were non-agricultural and nomadic it was important for the man to assume an outward appearance of power, primarily because of his larger role in using his physical strength to supply the vital necessities for survival. When in total command, the man used brute force and relied on the principle of the survival of the fittest. The woman, however, desired peace and stability, and showed compassion and concern for humanity. The men, without the teachings and patience of the women, were quick to opt for power and nationalistic pride.[590]

"Florida King Receives his Bride"
by Jacques le Moyne, engraving de Bry

The women were responsible for the building and upkeep of the house, and even made the household furniture. The men looked after the tasks of fitting the heavy beams of wood. In most of the Indian tribes, except for the Pueblo, the women did the weaving. The women would gather the plants for making the fiber, make the dyes, dye the fiber threads, and spin and weave the cloth. The women were required to have many talents and occupations that included homemaker, botanist, herbalist, potter, weaver, tanner, artist, craftsperson and shaman. The husband was responsible for catching fish and for trapping, hunting and butchering of the game. The men cut down large trees and cleared the areas for planting. They found the stone and flint from which they manufactured weapons and canoes. Both men and women broke up fields and harvested maple sugar. Sometimes men helped plant and harvest, as did the children. A man who helped his wife was more highly esteemed, particularly among the women, than one who did not.

Before the Europeans landed in America the women had very good health, and childbirth was apparently easier for native women than for European women. Children were considered an enormous asset in any tribe. With the help of midwives and medicine women, who used their expertise with herbs to increase or decrease fertility, it was possible to have a certain degree of family planning. Midwives also understood pre-natal care and were highly skilled in birthing techniques. Babies were nursed until they weaned themselves. They were carried close to the warmth of the body during waking hours, at first by the mother, later by grandparents, aunts, and older sisters. After a few months they went into a cradle-board and hung where they could watch the mother's activities. In the early years girls and boys played together, but soon the boys would become interested in their fathers' occupations and the girls would begin to imitate their mothers. Girls would build small play lodges, prepare food, and make clothes and baskets for their dolls. The children were educated in the family arena—simply by observing. Families slept in one room, and sex education was a natural process, rather than a secret or shameful thing. When an Indian girl reached puberty, her first menstruation, which represented her entry into womanhood, it was celebrated in a particular way. This was because most tribes regarded menstruation as a supernatural phenomenon. At this time the girl was usually required to avoid people and live apart, not to serve food or to touch medicines for fear of contamination. She secluded herself in a "little house", or moon lodge, and an elder woman would come and instruct her in the responsibilities of adulthood and womanhood. She would be told that this time of the month was natural, not an occasion for fear of either men or women, but that she was

Teaching the young

then the focus of such cosmic energies that she should not come near ceremonies or ceremonial objects so that she might not disturb their use with her personal power. After four days there would be a ceremony and celebration by the whole village, with feasting, singing, dancing and gift-giving. It was a merry festival, full of joking and often acting out of sexual desires and fantasies on the part of the older and more experienced tribe members, in a general atmosphere of tolerance and good humor. The shaman, who brought supernatural aid to the young woman, directed the ceremony and formally announced that she had reached womanhood and was marriageable. This was the most important time in a woman's life, next to birthing children, and a powerful and magical time for all the women of the tribe.[591]

Indian woman menstrual lodge, by Captain Eastman, engraving, 1870s

Children were the foundation of Indian society. The child was a sacred being given to the parents as a gift from the creator. The Lakota believed that the creator decided on the best home for this Wakan yeja (sacred being). "Unlike the European children who were born with the Christian burden of original sin, an Indian child came into the world carrying within it divine qualities. The spiritual qualities were meant to be nurtured so they can flourish."[592] In some tribes the birth usually required very little assistance. The birth would normally take place in a regular dwelling house. Older female relatives or friends would attend the mother. If traveling, the mother, on feeling labor pains, would leave to go into the woods with an older woman who served as a midwife. The mother had prepared herself for an easy birth by eating sparingly and exercising. After birth the newborn infant was washed in cold water or snow. A few hours later the mother would rejoin the group with the baby in her arms. The Indian woman seldom ran into difficulty during childbirth. The infant was "...ordinarily quickly and easily delivered, and many times so strong that a few hours after, they will go about their ordinary vocations."[593] A newborn infant was laid on its back, on a bed of soft material made up from the surrounding vegetation. Its bedding was made from milkweed fluff, duck feathers, cattail grass, sphagnum moss, or a soft cedar bark. These natural materials provided a soft and absorbent bed for the infant.[594]

Chippewa woman & baby in cradleboard by J. Otto Lewis

"Indian Woman procuring fuel" with child

The child's father would have made a smooth flat cradleboard, about two to three feet long and about a foot wide, onto which the infant was strapped from birth in order to be close to its mother. The cradleboard made it easy for the mother to carry the child while working or to keep the baby nearby, suspended by two ropes from the ceiling as a kind of hammock. It could also be converted to a crib by being placed on the ground on top of poles.[595] An infant would spend most of the first year of life in this cradleboard with his feet against a footboard and his head resting comfortably against soft vegetation. His "diaper" of moss or cedar bark was changed often. If it cried, a baby would be taken with his cradleboard outside, hung on a tree limb, and be left alone until his crying stopped. Babies were nursed on demand, rocked by its mother or grandmother, and soothed with lullabies. After a year of confinement in the cradleboard, a child would be allowed to crawl and walk at will.

Arthur Cercle and baby brother, Nez Percé, 1903

Cradle Song, 1900s

Cradleboards go back to ancient times. Human skulls, which were flattened at the back, have been found in ancient Anasazi ruins, an apparent indication of the use of cradleboards.[596] In the colder areas, in Canada, for example, the baby was carried in a warm parka and strapped in place by a belt slung around the mother's waist and under the baby's buttocks. Alternately, under extremely cold conditions, the baby was held directly against its mother's skin beneath the parka, to benefit from direct body heat.[597] The Mayas considered a particular shape of the head and squinting eyes to be signs of beauty. About five days after birth the infant was placed mouth downward on the cradle. One board was tied to the back of his head, another to the front. Both were lashed tightly together to cause the child's head to take a sugarloaf shape. Suspending a small object from the child's hair, so it dangled between the eyebrows, encouraged squinting.[598]

Ute woman and papoose

From the moment of birth the child was surrounded by its relatives and other important tribe members, all of whom played an important role in the future of the child. This is a formal acknowledgement that the child belongs not only to the family, but the clan and its tribe.

The newborn infant is loved, petted, fondled and held immediately after birth, by anyone old enough to do so. Older sisters as well as grandmothers helped care for the child. Infants and young children accompanied their parents wherever they went and adapted to the adults' eating and sleeping schedules. The Indians believed an infant provided a place of safety for an ancestor's soul. To beat or to speak harshly with the child might force the soul to leave, causing death to the child. Most tribes believed that punishing the child physically could affect the child's health and personality, and would eventually result in death.[599] The Indians did not believe in corporal punishment but tried to bring up their children as individuals whose rights and wishes were to be respected. Exclusion, making the child an outcast from games with his companions or helping their parents, would be a form of discipline. For the child this punishment was more severe than a beating and did not break their spirit. It was associated

Indian ceremony, relieving pain from birth

in his mind and could be quickly comprehended. Sarcasm or ridicule would be used as a punishment instead of a beating to teach the child. Bad Arm of the Sioux tribe indicated, "It is better to use ridicule early—to keep the young on the good road."[600] Chief Red Fox of the Sioux wrote in his autobiography of the deep love his people had for their children. "They never punished their children by beating or whipping them. Many white people slap their children, snatch them by their ears, and drag them by the arms, or beat them with straps or sticks.... Only recently American educators have recognized the harmful effects that come from manhandling children."[601]

Anthropologists, studying the upbringing of Zuni children, came to the conclusion that the use of ridicule was "quite possibly the most important single sanction in the upbringing of the Zuni child, and more than any other one factor, shapes overt behavior in later life."[602] The Zuni child, throughout life, was very sensitive to being ridiculed and laughed at from his tribe. It prevailed on him to act properly. "The calmness of adult Zunis and many other Indians can be related to fear rather than trust of their fellow tribesmen." This ridicule was seldom meted out to the child in public. Any criticism would remain among the immediate clan family.

Cradleboard by E.Curtis   Learning the Indain Traditions

Their elders taught Indian children the value of praise, reward and respect. An example of this is found in the Shawnee tribe. "Children were taught that good conduct would earn a reward and evil conduct would bring sorrow.... A few words of praise from a parent or an elder was regarded as the highest prize that could be given for good conduct. A child would strive with all his might to win such praise while he would be indifferent to bodily punishment. One punishment that was always a bitter one to an Indian child was to have some of his faults told to a visitor or friend."[603]

Poor Dog & family, Sioux by Rinhardt, 1890s

When born, the baby is given to the mother who is entrusted with the role of acquainting the child to all in nature, and helping him to develop into a spiritual being. The sisters, aunts, fathers, and all his brothers and uncles all bear the responsibility for caring and teaching the child. Instead of being reared by one or two parents in our western culture, considered primitive by Indian standards, the Indian child is reared by the mother, family and their entire tribe.

Charles A. Eastman, author of *The Soul of the Indian*, explained the Indians' philosophy of child-rearing and the high regard in which mothers were held. "Silence, love, reverence—this is the trinity of first lessons; and to these she later adds generosity, courage and chastity.... Men may slay one another, but they can never overcome the woman, for in the quietude of her lap lies the child!... This wild mother has not only the experience of her mother and grandmother, and the accepted rules of her people for a guide, but she humbly seeks to learn a lesson from ants, bees, spiders, beavers and badgers. She studies the family life of the birds, so exquisite in its emotional intensity and its patient devotion, until she seems to feel the universal mother-heart beating in her own breast. In due time the child takes of his own accord the attitude of prayer, and speaks reverently of the Powers. He thinks that he is a blood brother to all living creatures, and the storm wind is to him a messenger of the 'Great Mystery'. At the age of about 8 years, if he is a boy, she turns him over to his father for more spartan training. If a girl, she is from this time much under the guardianship of her grandmother, who is considered the most dignified protector for the maiden. Indeed, the distinctive work of both grandparents is that of acquainting the

"Keokuk Chief of the Sacs & Foxes", with child McKenney & Hall, 1838

Wasasku family by F. Rinhardt, 1890s

125

youth with the national traditions and beliefs.... The old are dedicated to the service of the young, as their teachers and advisers, and the young in turn regard them with love and reverence."[604] The boys would learn to hunt, haul firewood, watch the sheep and other animals or guard the horses. The girls would fetch water, learn to cook, make pottery, grind corn and help the mother with other tasks. A Hopi chief, Don Talayesva, described the young child's education. "Learning to work was like play. We children tagged around with our elders and copied what they did. We followed our fathers to the fields and helped plant and weed. The old men took us for walks and taught us the use of plants.... We joined the women in gathering rabbitweed for baskets, and went with them to dig clay for pots. We watched the fields to drive out the birds and rodents, helped pick peaches to dry in the sun.... All the old people said that it was a disgrace to be idle..."[605]

Cheyenne family, by Rinhardt, 1890s

Chippewa family, by Rinhardt, 1890s

Puberty ceremonies varied slightly according to their surroundings. In the Apache tribe the beginning of puberty for young women was celebrated in a four-day ceremony, symbolizing the young woman's passage into motherhood. The ceremony began at the onset of menstruation with the girl taking on the appearance of a mythological, white-painted woman who symbolized a woman budding with the fruitfulness of the earth. The complex ceremonial ritual began before sunrise. During the ceremony the young girl is sprinkled with yellow pollen, from a southwestern cattail rush plant (tule). This medicine, which the Apaches consider magical, is also used for healing the sick and wounded, and for crop growth. The ceremony is based on the importance of women in the survival process for living in the harsh desert land.[606]

A Cheyenne legend describes the fierce independence of Indian women in their tribe. Corn Woman left an abusive husband and when her brother ordered her to return to her husband she did, but told him, "Don't ever try to beat me again. If you do, I'll fight you with whatever is at hand. I don't care if you kill me. From that day on he was her slave."[607] In the Cheyenne way of life the women were the driving force possessed

Hopi girl   Apache girl
by E. Curtis   by E. Curtis

with discipline and wisdom. G. B. Grinnell, in his authoritative 1923 book *The Cheyenne Indians*, noted, "The women are the rulers of the camp. They act as a spur to the men if they are slow in performing their duties. They are far more conservative than the men, and often hold them back from hasty, ill-advised action. If the sentiment of the woman of the camp clearly points to a certain course as desirable, the men are quite sure to act as the women wish."[608] In

Apache, morning bath
by E. Curtis

the wars fought among the Iroquois, Cherokee, Susquehanna or Huron, the tribal penalty for killing a woman was twice that for the killing of a man, because it was believed that killing a woman implied the murder of any children she might have borne.[609] Most white women who had been taken captive in warfare and had assimilated into Indian tribes "refused to be ransomed; they would not return to the drudgery and subordination accorded women in Colonial society."[610]

Even though the leadership was generally passed on patrilineal, the daughters of a tribal chief could assume succession if their were no male heirs. There were many important Indian women tribal leaders. "Queene of Appamatuck" was one of the women chiefs who decided on the death of John Smith. Pocahontas overturned this decision. An important treaty to preserve peace between the Indian tribes and the British, in the 1677 "Treaty of Virginia", included the signatures of a number of Indian tribal chiefs along with Queens, Pomunckey, and Queen Wayonaoake. Although most of the European history books left out the designation of women as chiefs, there were a few writers that paid homage to these brave women calling them Queens or Empresses.[611] When the Europeans arrived in the Rhode Island area the chief of the Narragansett tribe was a woman called a "sunksquaw." In their defeat by the English in 1675, their last woman leader named Magnus was executed with 90 other members of the tribe. During 1673 George Fox, the founder of the Quaker religion, wrote that, "The old empress (of Accomack) sat in council." In 1705 a man named Robert Beverley noted two towns that were governed by queens named Pumgotenque and Nandeuye. Beverley wrote that these queens governed these nations. Women tribal leaders in southern New England were Quaiapen (Narragansetts), Weetamoo (Pocassets), Weunquesh (Eastern Niantics) and Ashawonks (Saconnets). They all assumed power as queens, sunksquaws or squaw-sachems. Queen Weetamoo was married to Wamsutta (Alexander), the eldest son of Wampanoag, Chief Massasoit. Wamsutta (Alexander), reigning chief

1677 Treaty signatures

Queen Wayonaoake

Queen Pomunckey

of the Wampanoag, died of poisoning by the British, who were displeased with his independent behavior. King Philip (Metacom), then became chief of the Wampanoag. Queen Weetamoo, as a war chief, allied herself with her brother-in-law against the British. In June, 1675, she led 300 warriors against the British, trying to repulse the settlers who were stealing their lands. It was the first large-scale organized Indian attempt to repel the European invaders. This engagement today is referred to as "King Philip's War." Queen Weetamoo drowned while trying to escape. The English cut off her head and put it on display in Taunton, Massachusetts. From a prewar estimate of 15,000, the remaining 4000 Wampanoag tribal members fled for safety to other tribes.[612]

Sarah Winnemucca of the Paiute tribe defies forced removal to Oregon, 1880s

Although the Saconnets were initially allied with the Wampanoag Confederacy, Queen Ashawonk of the Saconnet tribe was persuaded by the English to remain neutral in King Philip's War of 1675 to prevent her warriors from enslavement in the West Indies. Mamanuchqua, a woman, reigned as one of the five chiefs of the Esopus confederacy. In many tribes these women, or the women under them, had the power to decide the fate of their captives.

In most Indian tribes the social, religious and political life of the tribe was based on a clan structure. The clan system revolved around tribal family loyalties that revert back to prehistoric times. It is a complicated family and social structure that is made up of either matrilineal (descent from women), patrilineal (descent from men), phratry (a group of clans with descent from one ancestor), or moiety (two households, representing two halves of the tribe) systems, all developed to bind the individual together with their tribe. Most Indians of North America at the time of its discovery were organized in clans under a matrilineal clan system. There were other tribes organized according to a patrilineal clan society. The concept of clans and their relationship to the Indian culture was unique in that it reached, in many cases, into many parts of North and South America and was based on the mother's ancestry. The European clan system was based on paternal lineage. The origin of for the word "clan" is the Gaelic "clan", meaning "offspring." This term was used as early as 1000 A.D. to designate Scottish or Irish family groups. Many early Mediterranean societies consisted of many tribes and clans.[613] Most clans stressed mutual obligations and duties. Clan descent is traced in one line only, male or female. The Greek word "phratry" meant the kinship of a group, or descent from a single line of ancestors. The ancient Roman kinship group was basically similar to a patrilineal descent through the father instead of the mother. The name "gens" is also used to describe a clan group descended from the father. Several of these clans, when combined into a larger social group, are called a phratry. If a tribe includes two clans or phratries, each clan or phratry is called a moiety. Moieties are taken from a French word, "moitie"(half), representing two parts of the community. The distinction between phratries and moieties is not simply a matter of the number of groupings based on descent. Moieties were also for the purpose of producing a balanced opposition within the tribe. The frequent interaction between the groups resulted in economic equality and peaceful stability. Children inherited the clan moiety of their father. People from clans of the same moiety did not intermarry and had no inherited rights to each other's lands. When clans gathered for ceremonies, sports, or to settle disputes, allegiance to clans of the same moiety overrode all other loyalties. The moiety society can be found not only in tribes in America but also in Africa, Australia and India. European colonists did not understand the significance of these clan groups and different categories when they attempted to move all the Indian people to live in the same area.[614]

Assiniboin family, by Rinhardt, 1890s

Florida Seminole family, 1930s

There were a number of woodland tribes as well as the southern Siouan, Ho-chunk and Menominee that were divided into the dual divisions of earth and sky, each of which consisted of a number of clans. Thus, the clans named for those creatures that dwelt in the sky formed one division, and those named after land dwellers, water-inhabiting animals, or fish formed the second division. The Pueblo society contained moieties divided into squash or winter people, turquoise or summer people. Each half of this moiety shared the responsibilities of taking care of the village during six months of the year. The Tsimshian, Northwest Coast Indians, divided their moieties into killer whale and raven, and whale and eagle. Traditionally, the moieties may also have functioned as neighborhoods within villages. The moieties could also function in game rivalries, particularly in lacrosse, with one side competing against the other.[615]

Inuit family, 1920s

127

Lewis Henry Morgan, a pioneer ethnologist, published a detailed study of the League of the Iroquois matrilineal clan system in 1851, which revealed a close similarity to the Greek and Romans' patrilineal society. Indians and Greeks used the same term—phratry—to describe a league, brotherhood, or group of clans within their society. Kinship organizations were designated by animal names in Indian tribes, similar to the kinship animal names of the Greeks and Romans.[616]

Lewis Henry Morgan

The members of the clans relied on each other for help, protection, and especially for assistance in avenging injuries perpetrated by strangers. An individual looked to fellow clan members for his security and could rely upon receiving it; to wrong any person was to wrong the entire clan. From the bonds of blood uniting the clans sprang the obligation of blood revenge. If any person from outside the clan killed a member of the tribal clans, the obligation of blood revenge rested on the entire clans of the slain man. Mediation was, however, the first recourse taken by the fellow clan members of the perpetrator. They proposed methods of settlement to the council of the clans of the slain person. In the case of the one who was killed, the clan of the victim could appoint one or more avengers, whose duty it was to pursue and kill the slayer. The clans could adopt strangers and thereby admit them into the tribe. In the Seneca tribe, prisoners of war who were not killed were adopted into a clan as members entitled to tribal rights. An adoption took place on the proposal of any one member of the clan and the adoptee's were welcomed as brothers, sisters or children of those who had adopted them. The adoption was confirmed by ceremonial acceptance into the tribe. A clan that had been drastically reduced in numbers by war or sickness was often replenished through mass adoption from another clan, with its consent. Among the Iroquois, the ceremony of adoption into the clan was performed at a public council of the tribe and was considered a religious rite. The clans had a common burial place. Among the Iroquois of New York State, this has disappeared with the influx of white people, but it existed formerly. It exists still among other Indians, including the Tuscaroras, who are closely related to the

Joseph Brandt of
Iroquois Confederacy

Sister Molly Brandt
Canadian stamp

Iroquois. Although they are mostly Christians, each clan has a separate row in the cemetery. The mother is therefore buried in the same row as her children, but the fathers are buried separately. For the Iroquois the whole clan of the deceased attends the burial, prepares the grave, the funeral addresses, etc. All the members of an Iroquois clan were personally free, and bound to defend each other's freedom; they were equal in privileges and in personal rights, the sachem and chiefs claiming no superiority; and they were a brotherhood bound together by the ties of kin.[617]

Yakama woman

In some tribes the children of sisters would be considered siblings, while the children of a man's brother would be cousins to his children.[618] An important social principal of the clan was that it limited marriage choices. It was forbidden to marry anyone who carried the same family name or was from the same clan, no matter how distant a relative he or she may be. In general, all tribe members were considered related. A brother or sister would be considered part of the same family. To maintain the common tie, a widower could marry his dead wife's sister and a widow could marry her brother-in-law. A man could also marry the daughter of his wife's brother, or his wife's father's sister. In most tribes, for each person there were four clans of primary importance. First was the clan of the mother and maternal grandmother; second, was the father's clan, which included the paternal grandmother; third in importance was the clan that included the individual's maternal grandfather's clan; fourth, was the paternal grandfather's clan. This created a strong bond, not only between a husband and wife, but also among all the members of the family clan. It promoted a sense of community awareness and of responsibility to the clan, and removed the emphasis

Family from *Travels through parts of North America, 1776-1778* by Jonathan Carver, 1710-1778

from the individual. If the clan was in danger of dissolving thru wars or attrition, then to perpetuate the clan name the surviving members would join another clan or, if necessary, join a clan from another tribe and bring with it their old clan name into the new tribe. This method of survival in ancient times brought diverse tribes together to eventually integrate into one.[619]

Although most marriages were monogamous, polygamous relationships were allowed if they were expedient for the survival of the clan family. In the Indian culture this was not considered degrading to the women, and until the 1830's, when the practice was outlawed, some men had as many as five or six wives. It was reported in the 1860s in the Crow tribe that, "Some men have had five or six wives. If a man marries the oldest sister, he is entitled to all the others if he wishes them."[620] The men in the Choctaw tribe had multiple wives, and the practice was not outlawed until the 1830's. In some tribes the husband was entitled to marry his eldest wife's sisters as they grew up. If he did not marry them, however, they needed his consent to marry someone else. In a number of tribes a man was required to marry his brother's wife if she was widowed. In order to ease the workload of the women in his family, a man might also marry more than one wife, if he had the means.

Sioux mother and child, 1900s

Adultery was strictly forbidden and anyone caught in the act of adultery would have part of his or her nose, ears or scalp cut off. A traveler in the southeastern region of the United States wrote in 1791, "They are given to adultery and fornication, but I suppose in no greater excess than other nations of men. They punish the delinquents, male and female, equally alike, by taking off their ears. This is the punishment for adultery. Infamy and disgrace is supposed to be a sufficient punishment for fornication, in either sex."[621] Divorce for women in the Sioux tribe was easy; if she was unhappy with her husband she was allowed to throw all his possessions into the village circle to show the marriage was at an end. The tipi was hers and the man returned to his own mother's or sister's dwelling until he remarried. It was customary in most tribal clan communities to show deference to the father's clan, praising it while disparaging one's own clan.[622]

The Hopi Pueblo tribe taught their children that their mother's side must be favored because she bears the children. As the Hopi say, "The man is the slave. The clan is on the woman's side." In the Hopi and other Pueblo societies the man was in charge of carrying out the clan's religious beliefs and secret rituals, which were carried out in the clan's *kivas*, sacred chambers used for the Pueblo tribes' religious ceremonies. Clans performed a pivotal role in social and religious functions. Each clan claims its special sacred fetishes and ceremonies. Hopi society is divided into twelve phratries, or clan groups, containing many clans within each phratry.[623]

Chippewa woman, by Rinhardt, 1890s

Women had a strong voice in tribal affairs. Since the woman inherited the name, in most tribes, they decided the matter of adoption and the fate of captives. In many tribes women were healers, herbalists or shamans (medicine women). In many tribes, the high chief was a woman; these were called women sachems, royaneh (rowainers), sunksquaws, queens or rainbow women, according to the tribe to which they belonged.[624] Succession to chief was usually from the male on the mother's side. The children of the chief of the tribe were, thus, not able to succeed their father, but a chief would be succeeded by his brother or by the children of his sister. The word "sachem" is often translated as "chief." It was the sachem's duty to uphold the laws of the clan and the Confederacy. He acted as arbitrator of disputes between clan members. He attended tribal and Six Nations councils. To help him carry out day-to-day clan affairs, the clan mothers appointed a war chief. If the clan mothers were displeased with the sachem, it was the war chief's duty to tell him so. If the clan mothers became unhappy with the way the war chief carried out his duty, they could take away his title and give it to another male relative.[625] In the Iroquois Confederacy the council would consist of women sponsors who had the right to vote for each chief, and also the right to recall him or her. When a chief died or was ejected, the woman head of his clan would pick a new chief in consultation with the other women council members. This ensured that there would be unanimous approval before a new chief was named. When a new chief was installed, deer horns were placed on his head as a symbol of his office. If the new chief did not perform his tasks as expected, the woman sponsor of his clan would give him three warnings. At the end of the third warning she would remove his deer horns, and he would step down.[626]

Hayne Hudjihini
"The Eagle of Delight"
McKenney & Hall, 1850

In 1724 a missionary father called Joseph Francois Lafitau summed up the Indians' thoughts about women, specifically the women in the Iroquois confederacy, saying, "Nothing is more real however than the women's superiority. It is they who really maintained the tribe, the nobility of blood, the genealogical tree, and the order of generations and conservation of the families. In them resides all the real authority: the lands, fields and all their harvest belong to them; they are the souls of the councils, the arbiters of peace and war; they hold the taxes and the public treasure; the slaves are entrusted to them; they arrange the marriages; the children are under their authority; and the order of succession is founded on their blood. The men, on the contrary, are entirely isolated and limited to themselves. Their children are strangers to them."[627]

Pierre de Charlevoix, a French Jesuit priest, was astonished to find how important the role women played in the Huron culture he had encountered in 1761. "Among the Huron's, where this dignity is hereditary, the succession

129

is continued through the women, so that at the death of a chief, it is not his own, but his sister's son who succeeds him; or, in default of which, his nearest relation in the female line. When the whole branch happens to be extinct, the noblest matron of the tribe or in the nation chooses the person she approves of most, and declares him chief.... These chiefs generally have no great marks of outward respect paid them, and if they are never disobeyed, it is because they know how to set bounds to their authority. It is true that they request or propose, rather than command; and never exceed the boundaries of that small share of authority with which they are vested.... Nay more, each family has a right to choose a counselor of its own, and an assistant to the chief, who is to watch for their interest; and without whose consent the chief can undertake nothing.... Amongst the Huron nations, the women name the counselors, and often choose persons of their own sex.... The women have the chief authority amongst all the nations of the Huron language.... But if this be their lawful constitution, their practice is seldom agreeable to it. In fact, the men never tell the women anything they would have to be kept secret; and rarely any affair of consequence is communicated to them, though all is done in their name, and the chiefs are no more than their lieutenants...."[628]

Jicarilla Apache women on horseback , E. Curtis

As was the custom in most tribes, names for their clans were related to their source of food and spiritual importance. The southwestern tribes used animals: buffalo, snake, owl, wolf, elk, beaver, bear, etc. The central midwestern tribes such as the Shawnee utilized the names of wolf, raccoon, turtle, turkey, snake, hare, rabbit, buzzard, panther, deer, loon, bear and owl. In some tribes there would be a warrior clan that would be called upon in time of battle. The size of a tribe usually determined the number of clans. Large tribes could have hundreds of clans. As their numbers decreased, many of these clan names would disappear.

Sioux women on horseback, Pine Ridge, 1920s

In Aztec society, as well as in many tribes of the American northwest, it was the community of different clans that owned the land. These clans would farm the land that belonged to the entire community and each clan was given a share of the food produced. Each clan had a totem (badge, or coat of arms). This identified the entire clan. The Aztecs called their clan "calpulli." Each calpulli contained a number of houses, which were owned by individuals. Clan families lived here, but were not given the deed of ownership for the land. When an individual married, a piece of land was loaned to him so he could produce his share of food for the community. Women and men had equal rights to land and to ownership of a house. When someone left the clan, his or her plot of land reverted back to clan ownership. As the clan grew, more land would be annexed to give to new members of the community. Exact records of land owned by the clan were kept, with the member's name being recorded on "amatl" paper. The Aztec clan system existed for the benefit of the entire community, guaranteeing each member the right to share the land so they could feed and take care of their families. Marriage was permitted only between members of different clans. A clan council decided marriages, with the elder women acting as marriage brokers.[629]

Although the cultures of the Northwest Coast Indians were different in some ways from the tribes who lived in the east, the village communities were similar. The northwest Indians based their clan system on the totem. This allowed kinship ties between relations living in different villages. The totem pole, created by many of the northwest tribes, stood at the entrance of the head of the clan. It was carved with clan emblems and depictions of events, legends and myths that recalled family histories. The totem representing the clan was usually an item that could be seen or touched as a bird, animal or plant (or a group of animals or plants of the same species) that is particularly revered by members of the social group because of a mystical or ritual relationship that exists within that group. The totem embodied the spirit that represented the bond of unity within a tribe, or clan. The members of the clan believed that they were descended from a totem ancestor, or that they and the totem were "brothers." The totem could be regarded as a group symbol and as a protector of the

Kaw-Ciaa, Tlingit woman dressed for potlatch, 1906

members of the group. In most cases it was usually forbidden to kill or eat the totemic animal or plant. The symbol of the totem may be tattooed on the man or woman's body, engraved on weapons, pictured in masks and, by the Indians of the Pacific northwest, carved on totem poles. Each totem pole had its own history including the clan, victories in war, and other important events. The totem poles, usually made of red cedar, are not worshipped and have no religious meaning. Totem poles represented no special power; they are only carved and mounted to tell a story by the family that owned them. In

Dancers in potlatch regalia, Ft. Ruppert, 1914 photo by E. Curtis

some cultures men and women have different totems but, generally speaking, totemism is associated with clans or blood relatives. Marriage between members of the same totemic group is prohibited.[630]

Salish bride & groom potlatch arrival, 1919

The potlatch played an important part in the northwestern tribes clan society. The potlatch hospitality was provided for visiting clan members. The potlatch format varied among tribes, but its function was universally the same, a gathering called specifically for giving away extra personal items, electing a new chief, or the favorite daughter for marriage.[631] Among the northwest coastal tribes that included the Tlingit, Haida, Kwakiutl, Nootka and Chinook, the act of giving at a potlatch demonstrated the superiority of those of high rank. In Canada the government confiscated many totems and banned the potlatch from 1880 to 1951.[632]

Potlatch gifts for distribution, 1900s

One of the worst atrocities committed by the missionaries who tried to "civilize" the native tribes was the degrading and upheaval of the traditional power of the woman. Their western beliefs encouraged hundreds of tribes to accept the man as the master of their society. As early as 1530, the intentional disembodiment of the Indian woman began. European engravings of America depicted an Indian woman as a symbolic figure in an unfavorable light. It hinted of the change of status of the Indian woman from a leading figure in her culture to a servant in the new European society. A Florentine artist, Francesco Pellegrino, published a woodcut engraving in 1530. It illustrated the figure of a woman wearing a yoke and a ball and chain. A later copy identified the woman as a servant with the inscription, "The servant is happier in accordance with his patience."[633]

In 1575 an engraving pictured America as a nude woman holding a bow and arrow, accompanied by an animal. In 1588 Ludovico Buti painted frescos in the Uffizi palace in Italy showing figures representing America as Indian women, bare-breasted, accompanied with symbols of wealth, showing her wearing a feathered headdress with American animals. A sixteenth-century German lead plaque illustrates America as a bare-breasted women with a bow and arrow, surrounded by monkeys, a parrot, pearls, urns of precious metals and a sack of gold nugget's. Sixteenth-century engravings of America illustrated a bare-breasted woman on top of a giant armadillo watching a battle between the Europeans and Indians. The back-

Indian woman on armadillo, circa late 1500s

ground represented the Indians as savage cannibals, portraying a scene of the Indians cutting up and roasting human flesh. The inscription read, "America is far the strangest continent; here people live like lawless savages.... The inhabitants of this land take each others' lives.... Like mindless and innocent animals, they destroy each other, then roast the flesh as their usual fare." Other engravings in 1579, 1595, 1600 and 1603 depicted the Indian as a female cannibal or as an Amazonian woman, either carrying a trophy head or stepping over parts of the bodies or animals. One engraving illustrated the woman native turning away from the roasted human flesh on a spit, and pivoting towards a figure of Christ on a cross to ask forgiveness.[634]

"The American Amazon" from Joan Blaeu, Atlas Major, Amsterdam, 1662-63

During British colonial rule in America there was a movement to remove the traditional power of the Indian women. The British, coming from a patriarchal society, had no understanding of the social structure in the Indian tribes, and were unfamiliar with the notion of women having power. They sent Indian men to England in order to teach them about the workings of the male-dominated European judicial system. When the men returned to their tribes, their mission was to change the views of the other tribespeople towards their women. This was a major issue in the Cherokee nation. During the early 1800s men in the male-dominated Cherokee society now replaced the women chiefs. Under the leadership of Elias Boudinot, Major Ridge and John Ross, a committee of men drafted a constitution that disenfranchised women and African Americans. This constitution, written at the beginning of the 19th century, was modeled after the Constitution of the United States in order to appeal to the government from whom they wanted favors. The Cherokee women were now the underdogs. They no longer had a voice in the Cherokee nations' business, or in the struggle for the possession of the Cherokee land. The staff of the *Cherokee Phoenix* newspaper was now made up entirely of men.

In 1817, as soon as the new written Cherokee constitution was adopted, Nancy Ward, one of the last women leaders in the Cherokee council, turned in her cane of leadership and resigned her office. The Cherokees revered her as a war woman (Agi-ga-u-e) that rallied her people to defeat the Creeks in 1755. Before she reached the age of 20 she was chosen by the seven clans of the Cherokees to fill the office of Beloved Woman (Ghighau), similar to being knighted. She was admired as follows: "It was believed that the Great Spirit often used the voice of the Beloved Woman to speak to the Cherokees and consequently her words were always heard, if not always heeded. In the matter of what to do with prisoners she did have absolute authority, which she did not hesitate to use. Perhaps most important, the Beloved Woman was the head of the influential Woman's Council, made up of a representative from each clan, and she sat as a voting member of the Council of Chiefs." The value placed on women by the Cherokee Nation was not limited to Nancy Ward. Attakullakulla, a Cherokee leader in the 18th century, when asked by the British governor of the position of women in their tribe, replied, "It is customary among our tribe to admit women to our councils.... (Since) the white people, as well as the red, are born of women, is not that the custom among them also?"[635] Attakullakulla also said, "Women could be become warriors if they wished."[636]

Sacajawea 1788?-1812
Shoshone, women guide &
interpreter for Lewis and Clark

Well into the 20th century, Canadian Indian women were stripped of their power. From 1869 to 1894 the government of Canada, acting as a trustee of the Indian people, subjected the Indians to legislation. The 1869 "Act for the Better Protection of Indian People" caused an upheaval in the traditional matriarchal system of the Indians and replaced it with a patriarchal system. Section 12 (1) (b) of the 1869 Indian Act stated that an Indian woman married to a non-Indian man ceased to have any rights as an Indian and could no longer hold or inherit property on the reserve. She was also denied the right to be buried on her ancestral land with her relatives. Indian men, on the other hand, were free to marry anyone they chose, including non-Indian women. The non-Indian women were rewarded with status and received the same rights and privileges taken away from the Indian women—in effect, she was considered to have become an Indian through marriage. In 1880 a law was passed in Canada banning the potlatch, thus continuing the breakdown of the cultural heritage of all Indians.[637]

Nancy Ward,
Cherokee heroine
courtesy, Mike Smith

In the 1890's, Canada passed a law forcing the removal of Indian children from their homes to residential schools. The children were forbidden from speaking their native language on pain of punishment, which often involved beatings. It was not until June 12, 1985, that the last vestige of the old laws was removed, ending one hundred and sixteen years of legislated discrimination against women based on race, sex, and marital status. Amendments to the old law restored the rights of Canadian Indian women. Although guaranteeing some inalienable rights, the new law also subdivided the Indians into classifications.[638]

The United States enacted similar laws to Canada, restricting Indian women's rights and contributed to the breakup of the Indian culture by removing their children. In 1969 the "Indian Child Welfare Act" and the "Freedom of Indian Religion Act" was introduced. It did not become a law until nine years later, in 1978, when Congress passed it. This finally gave the Indians the right to teach their own cultural heritage and gave the Indian tribes exclusive jurisdiction over child custody proceedings involving an Indian child. This was to halt the "alarmingly high percentage of Indian families that were broken up by the removal, often unwarranted, of their children from them by non-tribal public and private agencies."[639]

Princess Angeline,
daughter of Chief Seattle

Encouraged and sustained by their strong heritage and their traditional roles as clan leaders, the Indian women are leading the struggle to revitalize their culture. In 1993, Yet Si Blue (Janet McCloud), of the Tulalip tribes, near the town of Marysville, Washington, forecast: "It is going to be the job of Native women to begin teaching other women what their roles are. Women have to turn life around because if they don't, all future life is threatened and endangered. I don't care what kind of women they are, they are going to have to worry more about the changes that are taking place on this Mother Earth that will affect all of us." How would our present society have evolved had we followed the basic concept of Article 44, Great Law of Peace of the Iroquois Confederacy? It stated, "The lineal descent of the people of the Five Nations shall run in the female line. Women shall be considered the progenitors of the nation. They shall own the land and the soil. Men and women shall follow the status of their mothers." The 21st Century has brought forth new women leaders actively involved as mothers and environmentalists to fight for the rights of all the Indians in the Americas. [640]

First woman's basketball team
Tulalip Indian school, 1912

CHAPTER 11 CEREMONIES, DANCE AND MUSIC OF THE INDIAN

Ceremonial dance, ritual and music have been important to man throughout history. Many of our modern day feasts, holidays, and dances have survived from ancient times, providing man with formal ways of expression, celebration and mourning. In some instances, many of our present ceremonial celebrations are carryovers from ancient celebrations that have changed and evolved to suit the times. With other observances we have forgotten the evolution, significance and origins of these ceremonies. To the Indians, the ceremony connects them to the sources of life.[641]

Hopi bean planting ceremony, 1890's

Ceremonies and dances are performed by the Indians in the Americas in honor of corn, rain, snakes, eagles, fire, sun, ghosts, buffaloes, healing, creation, baskets, hoops, beans and women. The origins of some of the present-day Indian corn ceremonies and European May Day celebrations have similarities to suggest they go back to the earliest formative stages of ceremonial religious rituals as a reference to Mother earth.[642] Figurines representing the female as a symbol of fertility to the earth or a Mother Goddess and dating back to about 20,000 B.C. have been unearthed in many parts of the world.[643] These Mother Goddess statues have been found throughout Europe and in the Americas at Tlaticlo, Mexico, in South America at Cuenca, Ecuador, and in sites formerly inhabited by the North American Mississippian mound builders in Georgia, to as far north as Illinois.[644] Some statues celebrating the corncob and the goddess of corn have been found in Mexico. "Many representations of fertility gods found in Mexico are goggle-eyed, just like their counterparts in Sumer (ancient Babylon)."[645] These female statues, found throughout the world, are clearly associated with fertility and the cultivation of the mother earth. In North and South America they are associated with numerous corn mother creation legends and ceremonies related to the American Indians. Corn, the main sustenance of Indian Pueblo life in the southwest, is also referred to as corn mother and mother earth. The Pueblo corn ceremonies practiced by all the Pueblo Indians relate this similarity in their ceremonies of dance, songs and poetry.

Phoenician female idol, circa 1000 B.C. Olmec corn god circa 500 B.C. European female idol, c. 1500 B.C.

The dance and music of the American Indian were inextricably bound with their religion and spirituality. The ceremonies, dances and music brought their people together and allowed them to maintain their traditions throughout peace and war. Their traditional music is as diverse as their individual tribes. When they danced the Indians used drums, rattles or bells on their clothes or in their hands. With these instruments and with their feet, they marked the beat. Early petroglyphs and archaeological findings, as well as the legends and Indian mythologies passed down orally through generations, give us an insight to the early ceremonies, dances, and musical instruments. Ceremonial dances were performed to the accompaniment of voices and musical instruments—drums, rattles, and sometimes flutes. A new piece of music is first presented in song. The singing style is characterized by melodies with ranges of between one and two octaves. At the top of their range, the singers' voices are extremely loud, forceful, and shrill. The lead singer begins the first part, "A", and is interrupted by the other singers with the same phrase, "A". Several musical phrases follow, each one pitched lower than the previous one until the ending is reached in the lower part of the singers' range. Just before it is completed, there is a brief break in the drumming to signal the end of the song. Dancers were aware of this and were able to know exactly when to stop at the end of each dance. The singers beat simultaneously on the drum in an even double (two) pattern, which coordinates the dancers' most common step of toe-heel (right foot) and toe-heel (left foot).[646]

The Indians believed that music was not a human creation but was given to them by their creator to serve various purposes. The community dances were held for the purpose of solidifying the tribe. Songs and dances were used for religious rituals, healing, accompanying work or games, storytelling and social events. Throughout North and South America the pitch, melody, songs, instruments and dances varied according to the culture and environment, but all Indians believed that the dances and songs had spiritual and supernatural sources. The traditional dances relate to seasonal or life-cycle events, and the ceremonies unfold according to ancient calendars and belief systems. Among most American Indian tribes, many songs are the personal property of

Virginia Secoton Indians pole feast dance
Depiction by John White, 1585

the singer or the group sponsoring a ritual or celebration. The music begins as a song. When it is accompanied, the instruments are mainly drums, rattles, and sometimes flutes. Singing is the traditional way of presenting a new piece, and the melody is taught to others by repeating it. The style of singing, the form of the song and the range of the voice all vary by group.

Many of the groups use vocals exclusively. There are numerous American Indian songs. The personal songs of the Arctic peoples of Alaska and northern Canada, for example, are often used on social occasions, such as the potlatch. Gifts are given to the guests to thank them for coming and to ask that the songs they have heard that day be remembered for next year. There are also songs for dancing, game songs, and songs given to children by their close relatives. A song given to a child belongs to that child his or her whole life.

Tlingit Indian potlatch music ceremony, 1900s

Sometimes the songs use vocals instead of full lyrics. Usually, the only accompaniment is drums. The natives of coastal Canada and the northwestern United States, including the Tlingit, Kwakiutl, Makah and Chinook, consider their songs to be private property that can be sold, inherited and loaned to another. Originally, there were curing songs sung by shamans. Hunting songs were sung just for entertainment, as well as lullabies and children's songs. The Indian instruments were noted for their intricate carvings and the use of a large amount of percussion instruments and whistles, flutes and horns.

There appear to be similarities between the music and ceremonial cultures of Indian tribes in Baja, California, and those of the native peoples living on the islands of Tierra del Fuego at the southernmost tip of South America, and in Papua, New Guinea and Australia. The Yumas, Guaícuris, Pericu and the Seri, that are now confined to an island in the Sea of Cortez, origi-nally peopled Baja, California—all of them belong to the primitive hunter cycle and, except for the Yumas, share similar physical proportions. According to Ruth Underhill, "The Yuman consider that all things were born of earth and sky, but they have no myth of emergence.... The chief ceremonies are those of death and war... the speeches are informal and the songs are clan songs.... The Yuman are, in many ways, equally different from the California seed-gathers to the west of them. They stand alone as a pocket of different culture and tradition left, by chance, in the corn country."[647]

Bella Coola animal mask ceremony
Photo by Carl Gunther, 1885

The songs of these southern California tribes, the Fuegians from Tierra del Fuego, as well as the Papua tribes from New Guinea and the songs of the central and western Australians tribes are all related. "Every verse begins with a downward glide through a whole tone (or less) and then remains on the lower tone thus reached until the next verse, where the level is again shifted one step downward. If the two-verse stanza is repeated, the result is a three-tone melody with a range of about a third. In other songs with every repetition of a single verse, the level is shifted one step downwards; the result is the same variant of the "stair-pattern", which the Papua of Torres Straits use in their ancient ceremonial songs. An expert might find it difficult to distinguish between a Corroboree of the Arunta and a song of some Plains Indian tribe, judging only from the musical notation."[648] "These facts lead to the hypothesis that the bearers of the same

Rabbit, monkey and jaguar musicians playing drums and dancing, Mayan codex, 1500s

primitive culture originally were neighbors—perhaps somewhere in central or northern Asia—then migrating from there, under pressure from more advanced tribes, until they gradually reached the southernmost regions of the continents and the islands outside of these: some to Tasmania, southeast Australia, the Andaman Islands, Ceylon through the Australians of the present time, Papua, etc.; others to Tierra del Fuego and California through Indian tribes which pressed after them over the Bering Strait."[649]

Many of the additional Indian tribes of Nevada, Utah, and parts of Colorado, Wyoming, Idaho, Oregon and California, that include the Utes, Shoshones and Paiutes, have a strong music and dance tradition. Songs and dances are included in every ceremony. Harvest festivals, birthing and naming ceremonies, mourning ceremonies (funerals), war dances, hunting and honoring dances all have their own distinct music. The Pueblo tribes of southwest Arizona, New Mexico, and parts of Utah and California, including the Hopi and Zuni, have a fairly complex and dramatic music structure. Their ceremonies often center on farming, including the green and blue corn dances. There was often an exchange of dance and song styles among the Pueblo tribes.

The tribes of the plains area, whose land stretched from Wyoming to Minnesota and North Dakota to Texas, have used song as a means of communication and expression among themselves. Songs were also used to ask other groups for help in hunting or for trade among the people, but they are also known for singing just as entertainment. Their song lyrics blend words with vocals. The Plains people are one of just a few groups of Native Americans who use the flute regularly. They primarily used a large bass drum played by a group of chanting singers. They are very well known for their powwow dances, guessing games, or hand-game songs.

Zia Pueblo dance festival, 1890s

The Great Lakes tribes of Minnesota, Wisconsin and Michigan, such as the Ojibway (Chippewa), Menominee and Ottawa, focus on group songs for their ceremonies. Most of their music is religious. The musical form of their songs is very specific. Songs can be received in a dream or in a "vision quest". Individual Great Lakes people make it a point to learn songs from other neighbors. Flutes, drums and rattles are common instruments, although the drum is the most important of these. Over the centuries these groups have absorbed European influences, including Christian hymns and fiddle playing, into their music.

The social songs of the northeast and Algonquin tribes stretching from the Mississippi Valley to New York and south to Virginia, including the Seneca, Mohawk, Huron and Delaware, are often humorous, with a wide vocal range. Their style of singing is more relaxed than some Indian tribes, and include more instrumental accompaniment and even solo flute playing. The music and the choreography of their social dances are both quite complicated.[650]

The music of the southeast Indians from North Carolina to Florida and west to Texas, including the Creek and the Choctaw, are also centered on ceremony and dance. The style of the Creek Stomp Dance songs is unusual because each song set is sung in a type of call-and-response style. The solo singer sings several different songs, with the melody becoming more complicated for each song. The singers and dancers who respond keep their responses the same, but may sing in three-part harmony by the end of the song sets, with frequent sweet and low tones. Young men from the Creek Indian tribes sing for personal enjoyment and not for ceremonial use, and they often played the flute. There were three types of Creek dances: social, ceremonial and animal dances. John Swanton, an anthropologist, remarked that the Creek social dances began at sunset when the moon was full. In 1790 William Bartram remarked on the Creeks and their enemies, "Some of their most favorite songs and dances, they have from their enemies, the Choctaws; for it seems these people are very eminent for poetry and music; every town amongst them strives to excel each other in composing new songs for dances; and by a custom amongst them, they must have at least one song, for exhibition, at every annual busk (entertainment)."[651] The

Choctaw women in pre-game festival, by Catlin, 1840s

Choctaw Social Dance songs originated with the Ballgame Festival, a sacred community event. Ballgame is an athletic event similar to lacrosse. The musical events surrounding the sport contain songs of healing, personal songs by the players, and dance music before and after the game. A soloist may sing songs and the music is varied and complex. The Seminole corn dance is a religious ceremony with a song leader, leading a line of dancers that include men and women holding hands. Time was kept by the sound of small turtle shell rattles worn on the knees by the women.

The most common instruments used in American Indian ceremonies are drums and rattles. Other percussion instruments include rasps, bells (usually attached to clothing), clap-sticks, flutes, whistles and stringed instruments for providing melodies. The Apache violin is a single-string instrument made from the stalk of the agave plant, and is unique to the Apache people. The Yaqui violin, on the other hand, is closely modeled upon European instruments played at missions during the 17th century. Folk guitars and harps, also copied from European models, may be found among some southwestern peoples.

Drums can range in size from large powwow drums (played by a number of people) to the palm-sized water drums found among some northeastern peoples. Some are constructed from wood with skinheads, or are simply hollowed logs from a tree with skinheads, while others require more sophisticated construction techniques. The word "drum" often refers to the group of players as well as the instrument. Rattles are made from many materials, but gourd or bone is used most frequently, usually covered with leather and bound with thongs. Gourd rattles are made from gourds that have been carefully dried, prepared and decorated according to the individual or to tribal preference. Bone rattles are most commonly made of a section of horn that is cut to a desired size. Gourd and bone rattles are filled with seeds or other objects. Turtle rattles are made from turtle shells, with objects such as turtle bones or cherry pits placed inside. This instrument honors the turtle for its role in the creation of "Turtle Island", a name for North America that is frequently used by Eastern Woodlands Indians. Other rattles may be made from such diverse materials as carved wood, cans and plastic bottles. Songs accompany the drums and rattles at both the dance and religious ceremonies.

Mayan codex, blowing trumpet, 1500s

Flutes date back at least 5000 years and may have evolved from whistles. They have been found in ancient Greece, and flutes made from condor and pelican bones were discovered in ancient South American Pyramids. This ancient instrument traveled into Mesoamerica and into the Anasazi culture of the southwest area of America.[652] Although once used exclusively in courtship or healing rituals, the American Indian flute is used in contemporary culture for a variety of purposes and is rapidly gaining popularity among non-Natives. Flutes are usually made from wood or cane. Examples of ceramic and metal flutes exist, but are not common. Whistles are considered by many archaeologists to be the forerunner of the American Indian flute. The whistle has always been a sacred object, used in specific rituals to call spirits. Even when used during hunting or battling with enemies, it was still used for calling the spirits. The whistle was made from a material that was special, if not sacred, to the area of the tribe—eagle bone in many cultures, cane in the southeast and cedar in the northwest coastal tribes.

Indian dances and songs are used for social purposes and in religious ceremonies. In each area of North and South America the Indians practice similar ceremonial rituals pertaining to their area. At times many of the ceremonies and dances were suspended or forced to go underground due to a misinterpretation by their conquerors. Without the continuation of their tribal cultural ceremonies, including dances and music and the involved participation of the entire tribe, the

Flute and drum, Darien, Panama

Indians would not have survived hundreds of years of European domination. Many ceremonies are based on ancient religious rites that involved sacrificial ceremonies. Humans were used for sacrificial purposes throughout the world to appease the gods in ancient times. Today some Indians still make animal sacrifices to their gods. In the Chilean Andes an elaborate sacrificial ceremony—"gnillatum"—is called by the chief of the Mapuche tribe and performed after severe hardships such as an earthquake, bad crops or lack of rain. Songs are sung while dancing in an elliptical circle, with young girls each riding a white and yellow or tan horse, paired with two men also on horseback. A hen is sacrificed to their supreme god, Chau. One of the prayers is, "Hear us, Chau! We are all united in this prayer. Hear us, Father in the far above and woman with him. Hear us! Give us blue skies so that we will have a good harvest."[653]

Ceremonial worship was very important to the Aztec, Maya, Inca and all the agrarian Indian tribes, as were the instruments used in the ceremonies: flutes, whistles, drums, and trumpets made from large conch shells. Gourd and wooden trumpets have been found, as well as drums decorated with gold and silver and set with precious stones. Dances performed by elaborately-dressed dancers were also an important part of the ceremonies. Among the Inca dances were the Ritual Dance (Taqui), with singing, accompanied by four large drums that were beaten by Incas of a high rank, and a Warriors Dance (Cachu), danced by men and women whose hands were joined, making a circle.[654] Ceremonies were performed for different reasons; some were to encourage bravery in war, others to produce endurance, courage and the ability to withstand pain. Many ceremonies and dances were for peaceful purposes pertaining to birth, life, death and nature. Others were to celebrate puberty, educate their children, honor the seasons and encourage abundant crops, rain, fishing, hunting, etc. The ceremonies and dances of the American Indian were both a religious ritual and a spiritual experience through which the American Indian could make contact with their various intermediary spirits. The dance, music and ritual procedure was what their individual spirit asked of them.

The Iroquois ceremonial dances, with participants of individual men or women or both, numbered throughout the year to at least 32, ranging from their Great Feather Dance to their False Face Dance. The main Iroquois festivals included the New Year Festival in winter, the Maple Festival in spring, the Corn Planting Festival, the Strawberry Festival, the Green Corn Festival, and the Harvest Festival of Thanksgiving. The festivals were held to give thanks to the good spirits for health, clothes, food and happiness. The Shawnee tribe performed at least 21 different dances by individual women, men or together in groups.[655]

"Chippewa Tomahawk Dance", Otto Lewis, 1820s

The Apache religious ceremonies are centered on the conviction that a supernatural power manifests itself in almost every facet of the Apache world and, through visionary experiences, they can commune with the power and develop a healthy and cooperative relationship with it. In shamanic ceremonies, the practitioner interacts with this particular power alone. But other rituals require a priest to officiate. Both shamanic and priestly rituals are patterned. Four is the sacred number; songs and prayers occurred in quartets. The ceremonial circuit moves clockwise, and rites last for four successive nights. The Apache perform life-cycle rites, including the rite for a child who takes his first steps and a girl's puberty rite.[656]

Olmec shaman with bag, sculpture of serpent, circa 800 B.C.

Before the arrival of the white man the Sioux were nomadic, horse-riding Plains Indians who lived in tepees and hunted buffalo. Their religious system was dominated by cosmology and the appeasement of supernatural beings to ensure successful buffalo hunts. The "Seven Sacred Rites" form the basis of Lakota religion. These seven rites include: The Sweat Lodge, the Vision Quest, Ghost Keeping, the Sun Dance, Making Relatives, the Puberty Ceremony, and Throwing the Ball. Six of the seven rites have endured in contemporary worship—the last, Throwing the Ball, is no longer performed. The Yuwipi, an ancient Sioux ceremony for healing, divining and for finding lost persons or objects, takes place in total darkness with a special altar to allow the medicine man to call on the spirits to appear and work with the people.[657]

Songs are used by the Navajo nation to keep individual members of the group in harmony with nature. The Navajo call their song and dance ceremonies "ways." They are somewhat like plays, which can last for several days and include sand painting and chanting. The Navajo use gourd rattles and water drums to accompany their singing. The Navajo origin myth explains their emergence onto the Earth from a series of underworlds. In the myth, the natural and supernatural intertwine. The Navajo believe in powerful Holy People, with whom the Navajo aim to live harmoniously. There were over 50 Navajo chants, or ways, not counting all the variations. Sand painting and fire ceremonies, songs, along with dances, chants, symbolism, prayers and herbs were used for healing. The Navajo ceremonies were for the purpose of maintaining and restoring a balance in their world or the individual. The main ceremony in Navajo life is that of the Blessingway Ceremony. In this ceremony the "benevolent holy

Petroglyph, shaman with serpent Utah, circa 1000 B.C.

people" are explained as those that are inherently good for mankind. Changing Woman and/or White Shell Woman and Earth Woman are brought into the story to show that order out of chaos exists within the Navajo culture and illustrates the basic good versus evil in man. The Blessingway ceremonial chant recounts the Navajo creation myth after their emergence. The evil side of this pendulum is First Man. He represents the first chief when evil was prevalent on the land. Throughout the ceremony, the culture of the Navajo way of life is explored. It is believed that the Navajo's sense of knowledge will overcome evil and that the forces of Changing Woman will ultimately win. Yeibhichai songs and dances for the nine day Nightway Curing Ceremony showcase some of the most electrifying forms of traditional music. In this ceremony, masked dancers impersonate gods with mystical powers to help cure someone who is sick. The men who sing these songs are grouped into organized teams based on where they live. It is up to each team to come up with new songs or sing old favorites through this nightlong singing and dancing. This night is the conclusion of the nine-night ritual. [658]

The Navajo Fire Dance ceremony is performed nine nights during November to cure sick people. The dance involves a number of individuals; some who have names such as the cactus dancers or the sun and moon dancers. Each one of these dancers has a certain appearance, which illustrates the symbol they are representing. The cactus dancers, for example, carry sticks that protrude out and are the points of the cactus. The sun and moon dancers carry shields that are painted with a mouth and eyes, so that each shield represents the face of either the moon or the sun. The dance is comprised mostly of individuals representing different aspects of the Navajo community. As the dance progresses, there are intervals at which new dancers come in and the old ones leave the circle. In certain parts of the dance, ill individuals are brought to the center and have direct interaction with the dancers, mostly by means of the dancers pointing their arrows at the ill individuals. At other times, the ill are taken back to the outskirts of the circle and wait until it is time for them to rejoin the center. At the end of the Fire Dance about forty-seven men, each carrying a bundle of cedar, light the wood until it is burned out. They then leave the dance floor as the audience gathers the charred remains for medicinal purposes. [659]

Medicine man (shaman) performs ceremony, by de Bry, 1500s

Religious practice and belief is similar in all of the Pueblos and is based on fertility, moisture, harmony in nature and between nature and man. Harmony is achieved through a cycle of ceremonies. With the arrival of Christianity in the so-called New World, both Christian and Indian ceremonies and rituals were celebrated and continue to be celebrated today. Almost all of the Pueblo tribes believe the same basic creation story. They believe that their ancestors emerged from a world beneath this one, through a hole in the roof of the underworld. The Pueblos ceremonial buildings, known as kivas, are circular structures with a hole dug in the middle and only a rooftop entrance, to remind them of the creation story.

Arikara medicine men in "Mother Night Men" ceremony

Some of the ceremonies were similar to those of other tribes and other ceremonies were unique to particular villages. Many of them included dances that celebrated the corn, woven baskets and the act of hunting. There were also animal dances celebrating animals sacred to the tribes: deer, turtle, buffalo, eagle, water serpent and the snake. Butterfly and Turtle Dances are symbolic of Mother Earth's annual renewal and regeneration processes and were usually performed in the spring. Deer and Antelope Dances take place in the fall, a traditional time for hunting and preparation for winter. Buffalo Dances are winter dances, celebrating the abundance of food and the continued survival of the tribe. The kivas were and still are used for different types of sacred religious events in the Pueblo culture. The ceremonies that take place in these buildings are considered to be very private. Only grown men or adolescent boys who are considered on the verge of manhood are allowed into the kivas.[660]

The Flute Ceremony in Pueblo society is performed to produce rain. The other reason for the ceremony is to "enact mankind's emergence to this present Fourth World."[661] At the beginning of a sixteen-day ceremony, elaborate flute altars are established in the clan homes. The ceremony in each village is led by the Grey and Blue Flute Societies. A religious priest and two flute-playing women lead the way, carrying small reed rings with thin rods. On the way to the main plaza corn meal is thrown on the ground to signify their many migrations.

Kachina rain dance ceremony Shanghopavi, Hopi Pueblo

The Pueblo Indians of the southwest made the Hoop Dance popular in the early 1900s. Dancers must touch only one hoop at a time with the hand, and the hoops must be picked up from the ground with the feet. The Hoop Dance was originally part of a healing ceremony, designed to restore balance and harmony in the world. It also represents man emerging from the underworld. Some of the early dancers believed that each time a dancer passed through a hoop while dancing, he added one year to his life. The colorful and energetic dancer maneuvers all of the hoops on his body while dancing, to create multiple designs. One Hoop Dance tells the story of a young eagle's overwhelming desire to fly. In recent years, a public form of the dance has been developed.

The Eagle Dance is important in the mythology of the Pueblo people as well as for the Plains tribes. The Eagle Dance is a remnant of a much more extensive ceremony to solicit rain for crop growth. Because of its ability to fly so high that it disappears from view, the eagle is seen as a messenger between the earth and the gods above by many Indian cultures. For this dance, young men or boys wear white caps with yellow beaks and bands of feathers running along each arm to imitate the eagles. They pivot and flap their arms to the beat of a drum to replicate the soaring, diving, perching or resting movements of the eagle. The dancers blow on whistles fashioned from bones taken from eagle wings. This simulates the cry of an eagle. As they dance and whistle, their prayers fly high into the air towards the creator.

The Turtle Dance ceremonies held in December in the Pueblos of Acoma Cochiti, San Ildefonso, San Juan, Santa Clara and Taos, are dedicated to the rain-making spirits and are a very important thanksgiving ritual for the clouds, rain, snow, lightning and thunder. The dance honors Mother Earth for providing plentiful crops and gives thanks for the many beauties of life. The water-loving turtle has a long life and represents time, longevity, persistence and strength. The singing tells about the gourd rattle, the turtle, and of evergreens, which symbolize strength and eternity. It tells of the creation of the kachinas that

Pueblo Eagle Dance, 1890s

make the clouds, lightning, thunder and rain. Woven into the singing is the story of corn, its pollination, growth and ripening process, and finally the harvest.

The Zuni Pueblo tribe holds an elaborate religious ceremony every December called "Shalako", that commemorates their tribal history, pays tribute to their dead and offers respect to their spirit world. The dancers wear costumes that resemble gargoyles, with long bird beaks and eagle feathers, all topped off with buffalo horns. Another ceremony is called "dancing the corn" and takes place during the winter. The Zuni take six perfect ears of corn, hold them up in a basket and sing to them.[662]

Ute Eagle Dance, 1920s

138

The Hopi perform an annual ceremonial cycle in thirteen villages that are spread over three mesas in northeastern Arizona. According to the Hopi, life and death, day and night, and summer and winter are all counterparts in a system of alternation and continuity. Death is not an end but rather a birth into a new world. For the Hopi, the spiritual world is reflected in the physical world. They believe that there is no clear division between human beings and spirits. For the Hopi, the spirits of the dead return to the material world as kachinas and acquire supernatural qualities. As these spirit-beings can come to the human world and even leave it again, they are able to contact living humans and affect their lives. The Hopi believe that spirits can even take possession of human beings during certain sacred times—for example, during the mask dance, when dancers who wear masks are considered the manifestation on earth of the beings represented by the masks. A kachina can

Pueblo ceremonial dance

take the form of things such as animals, plants, clouds, stars and abstract elements. They allow the rain to grow Hopi crops and help keep the world in balance. The kachinas' home is in the San Francisco Peaks, west of the Hopi mesas. They live there for half the year, but at the winter solstice or shortly thereafter, they go to the Hopi villages where they live until the summer solstice. While among the Hopi, they are the focus of several ceremonies, during which the kachina spirits pervade the souls of Hopi men who dance in elaborate regalia. The belief that the kachina becomes the man is fundamental to this Hopi ceremony. The right and obligation to wear the sacred masks, even one representing a woman, is inherited through a man's membership in a particular clan. Both Hopi boys and girls are present at an initiation when they are eight or nine years old, at which time they learn the secret of the masked figures. Often the most important rituals take place within the kiva, the sacred ceremonial structure of the Hopi. These rituals are hidden from public view, but in the major ceremonies the kachinas always make their appearance in public

Christmas Pueblo Dance, 1890s

dances or dramas. Sometimes carved images of the kachinas are given as gifts to Hopi children and women during ceremonies in February. The kachina dolls are known as "Tihu" in Hopi, and are carved by Hopi men from the roots of cottonwood trees. Considered as precious representations of these vital spirits, the kachinas dolls are cared for by the children and help them to learn to recognize the many different kachinas.[663] In the middle of these sacred ceremonies, usually during the spring or summer, a troupe of clowns will appear and swarm into the plaza from the rooftops, climb down ladders head-first, fall and stumble. They reverse life and turn everything upside down, even with such grave matters as the treatment of the dead. The clowns and tricksters behave shamefully so as to force us to contemplate on our true moral standards.

Hopi Trickster

The clowns are also known as anti-Kachinas because they act as sacred fools. They inspire the Hopi to protect their social and sacred values and at the same time to laugh at their inevitable human weakness.[664]

The Snake Ceremony, practiced by the Hopi Indians of northeastern Arizona, centers in the belief that rattlesnakes are spirit gods who bring rain and never harm anyone with a good heart. The snake dance developed and spread northward from Aztec and Mayan ceremonies celebrating the feathered serpent. The serpent is carved on the temple pyramids in Teotihuacan and at the Tenayuca pyramid in Mexico City. In the Maya city of Copan, Honduras, stone carvings show the heads of priests holding a snake in each mouth. The Hopi dancers of today, 2000 miles away, imitate the Mayan snake ceremony. A Hopi oral legend tells of an inquisitive adventurous Hopi youth named Tiyo who decided to investigate the path of the Colorado River. Unable to return up the swift river, he met Spider Woman, who showed him the passage to the underworld. After many encounters he entered the land of the snake people where he saw a snake kiva. It was there he met a young maiden who then turned into a rattlesnake. Spider Woman appeared and gave him a charm to catch the maiden rattler. The young man was then admitted into the snake clan and was taught all the secrets and prayers for the snake ceremony that would please the gods to make rain. Tiyo returned with the snake maiden to his people. They were overjoyed until she gave birth to baby rattlesnakes. When the snakes bit the Hopi children, the Hopi village banished the young snakes and their mother. A terrible drought then covered all the land, which became a desert. They approached Tiyo, who told them the underworld gods were angry that they drove the snake maiden and her children away. The only way to appease the gods was to bring them back. Tiyo taught his people the songs he learned to bring the snakes back. For four days the Hopis hunted the serpents in all four directions, using songs and flutes to round them up. The

Aztec serpent sculpture, circa 1200 A.D.

Mayan snake sculpture circa 800 B.C.

snakes were brought into the kiva and washed as the Hopi danced and offered prayers and songs. At the end of the ceremony the snakes were carried out into the desert. The next day the gods were pleased and sent down rain to save the Hopi crops. From that day, each year the Hopis hold their Snake Dance to bring rain.[665]

Hopi Walpi snake priest, by Curtis

The Snake Dance usually takes place in August and lasts nine days. During the first four days the Snake Society hunts rattlesnakes. During the next three days the Antelope Society erects an altar and performs sacred ceremonial rites. During the eighth day a large amount of green cottonwood boughs, with their leaves, are placed in a round recess in the main dance plaza. This is called a "kisi." A buckskin cloth is hung over the entrance that faces east. A deep hole is hollowed out in front of the "kisi" and covered over. This hole, called "Sipapu", signifies the entranceway to the underworld. Late in the afternoon of the eighth day the antelope priests, followed by the snake priests, leave the kiva and march into the plaza to perform part of the ceremony with dances and chants. On the afternoon of the ninth day, the dance takes place. As the dance begins, the snakes are brought to a priest in the center of the plaza, where the crowds gather to watch. When a male snake member passes the priest he is given a snake that he puts between his teeth. Another dancer comes with a stick covered with many eagle feathers. He waves the feathers that represent large birds, the snakes mortal enemies. They

Hopi Snake Ceremony, 1920s

brush the snake on the head with the feathers to deter them from biting. Members of the snake clan march around the kisi (snake house) and dance with big, live snakes in their hands and between their teeth. When the dance ends, the snakes are thrown into the center of the plaza, where there is a rain symbol made of cornmeal. The feathered sticks keep the snakes in a circle until it is time for them to be carried away and released. When released, the snakes go in all different directions, eventually disappearing underground, where it is believed they ask the water god to bring rain. In 1912 Edward Curtis, a photographer, was invited to a Hopi snake ceremony and described the experience:

Clad in a loincloth, I entered the kiva with the Chief Priest and followed his orders and directions in every detail. I slept beside him. I fasted through the nine days as prescribed by Hopi priests. I had no contact with members of my party and followed the rules of celibacy. The snake hunt began on the tenth day. We stripped and smeared our bodies with red paint, which is considered the pollen of snakes. At the same time the chief offered a prayer that the snakes would not harm us… then we climbed the ladder out of the kiva and proceeded single file down the trail to the land of the north wind. The Hopi understand that on this day no one may go into the valley northward from the village… a prayer is said and an offering of cornmeal is scattered in a spring at the foot of a cliff. Then each priest sets out to find snakes. Fortunately, I was the first to see a snake. We surrounded it and threw meal on it… then I quickly seized the snake by the neck…. Our sacks soon became heavy with the weight of snakes…. They searched for snakes for four days, from the four cardinal directions. The snakes are placed in the kiva with the priests. Sand from the desert is spread on the floor of the kiva to mark the trail of any snake that escaped the earthen jars in which they were contained. The snakes were treated like special guests. They were sung to, washed, fondled and readied for the ceremonial dance to invoke the gods to provide rain…. As

Apache Snake Ceremony

Snake Ceremony, 1900s

preparation for the dance, we smeared pink clay over our moccasins and other parts of our costume and corn smut mixed with "man medicine" (a concoction of root juices and what not) over our forearms, calves and the right side of our head. We whitened our chin and blackened the rest of our face. Around our waist we placed the customary brightly woven fringed belt and in the rear, we hung a fox skin, which moves in rhythm of the dance…. Two fraternities participated in the dance—the Snake and Antelope. After the snakes had been brought into the plaza, the Snake and Antelope stood facing each other. They each held a snake. From time to time they would wrap the snake around their neck or hold it between their lips…. I followed the dancers four times around the plaza, and tossed the snakes aside to be picked up the "catcher", then received another snake for the continuation of the dance.[666]

The Six Nations of the Iroquois inhabited central New York State and the Ohio Valley. Their federation was the most complex of any Indian group. Their creation myth begins in a similar way to that of the Indians of the southeast, with the Sky People who inhabit a world above the earth, and

Hopi snake priest

140

one pregnant woman descending to propagate the earth. Women owned the homes and held ceremonial precedence. In their ceremonies, the Iroquois rid themselves of woman-fear. Honors to food spirits were paid regularly throughout the season, interspersed by other rites and dances.[667]

Nicaragua dance, 1500s
Central America, by de Bry

Involved in all these religious ceremonial functions was the shaman or medicine man or woman. The shaman, known to have Asiatic origins, was very common in the northwest coastal tribes and throughout many tribes in North and South America and other parts of the world. In the northwest tribes, wood rattles, spirit drums and numerous charms used by the shamans in their healing rites have been found. The basis of shamanism is that illness is caused by the presence of a foreign body, which must be cured by the shaman, who sucks out the foreign object and destroys it. Shamanism can also be used for negative purposes, as well as for healing. In parts of South America the shamans are called "machis." An Araycanian Indian from the Andes recalls his visit to a machi. "A machi has the power to discover the real source of an illness.... He began to treat me. First, he pretended to stab me with a knife—he did not do so actually, of course—and then he sucked the point of sickness in my heart, the place in which I had severe pain, and out came a great deal of green-looking and vile smelling matter. The next day I began to feel better.... Some say the machi sucks them out, but others say he has them in his mouth and merely spits them out.... There are both men and women machis who treat by sucking, but not every machi does so. Some say certain machis have their fingertips split, and with them draw out the spirit of sickness."[668]

A shaman receives a calling to his vocation, unlike doctors in western cultures where becoming a doctor is at least partly the result of choice. Sometimes shamanistic abilities run in families, but when a person feels called to be a shaman, he or she must develop and maintain a special relationship with the spirit world and bring that special relationship with spirit to the person or situation in need. Many times, the shaman will receive revelations from nature or through a song, for example, concerning particular objects to be used in rituals. Each shaman has a personal spirit, usually an animal, but sometimes the spirit of

Sioux dog dance, 1851 sketch by Catlin

a lake or a water hole. Shamans doctor people for illness and injury. A shaman usually works with an interpreter who translates the mumbles, songs and other words of the shaman for the participants in the ritual. Both the shaman and interpreter are paid for their work. Curing invariably includes singing and chanting, and smoking a pipe. White paint or white clay is used by the shaman to decorate the attending family and friends and, usually, the patient. Failure to follow the shaman's instructions will result in failure of the cure, and sometimes illness or death to the shaman. There are some shamans who call upon various animals to assist in their work. The most powerful are believed to be able to control the weather. There are shamans who could find lost things, and if they had been stolen they could identify who had stolen them.[669]

The Corn Dance and festival are the most popular of all those celebrating the annual harvest, particularly among the Creek, Cherokee, Seminole, Yuchi and Iroquois, each of whom have their own activities and particular ways of welcoming the corn harvest. The festival typically lasts for three days and is performed during spring and summer by all the southwestern tribes to mark the planting and harvesting, and includes prayers for rain and a bountiful harvest. The dance is also an occasion for weddings and birth celebrations. In the present era, villagers usually attend a Catholic mass before the dance to blend their Christian beliefs with their traditional ceremonies. The festival takes place at different times between May and October, depending on when the corn ripens in different regions. Corn can only be eaten until proper thanks have been offered to the Great Spirit, the rain and the sun that brought forth a good harvest. Some tribes believe their origins began with the corn, made from the creator, so the Green Corn Festival is also a time of religious

Aztec ceremonial rope dance

renewal. Members of the tribe join at a religious gathering and stand with bowed heads bent to show reverence. The Great Feather Dance is performed at this time. In some tribes only men perform the dance and in others, women are allowed to participate.

Although it is not part of the ceremonial purpose of the Green Corn Dance, council meetings take place during the dance and festival. Babies and young men who have come of age are given their names at the Corn Festival. *Busk* is another part of the religious ceremony celebrated by Indian tribes. The word busk comes from the word *boskita* and means "to fast". The Creek New Year is marked with this part of the religious ceremony. At this time, members of the tribe clean out homes, throw out ashes and buy or make new clothes. Refuse and broken items from the tribe are put into one common heap and burned as an outward sign of the inward commitment to their religion. A feast of beef, cornbread, tortillas and soup, as well as beans and squash, marks the end of each day.

Pueblo Harvest Dance, 1920s

About 200 dancers perform the Hopi Green Corn Dance as a prayer for rain and successful growth of the corn crop. The leader of the dance carries a pole with yellow feathers to represent the sun. The men dance in moccasins while the women dance barefoot, which gives them closer contact with the earth. The dancers carry pine boughs as symbols of all living things. The male dancers wear blue headdresses to represent the sky; tufts of eagle down hang from the headdresses as "clouds." The headdress is a fundamental part of the process of praying for rain. Another type of Pueblo dance is the Blue Corn Dance. In this dance, the dancers act out the planting, growing and harvesting of corn.

The Black Drink Ceremony by the southeastern Indians (primarily the Creeks and Seminoles) was performed at the Green Corn Ceremony, before the Indians went hunting or to war. This was a cleansing ritual and another method of religious renewal. The drink itself was a strong emetic, which cleansed the digestive tract. It purified participants from minor sins and left them in a state of perfect innocence. It also gave them courage to be daring during war and strength to keep friendships. The Creeks called this drink ceremony "asi." The drink was brewed as a tea from the leaves of the shrub *Ilex vomitoria* and given by the shaman to the group, often sitting in a circle.

The vision quest is a very important part of American Indian spirituality. It is not a part of all Indian tribal traditions but has, nevertheless, become a very widespread practice. The practice is hundreds of years old, and is documented by Black Elk as having been a part of the Lakota culture in the early 1800's. Young warriors would seek visions on isolated mountains, where it was believed they would be closer to the Great Spirit. Being far from their villages and therefore from the possibility of seeking help from others forced the warrior to use his own wits and resources to combat danger from animals or weather.

The process is as follows. Immediately prior to reaching the chosen location, the seeker uses a sweat bath and then, using sage or pine needles, produces a smoke called smudging. He may then paint his body with white clay. He carries a buffalo robe, pipe, and moccasins, and wears a breechcloth. When he reaches the place where he is to meditate, he builds a bed of flat rocks and covers it with pine branches, sage or cedar—all of which are, in some way, sacred to the Indians. Traditionally, the vision quest was taken by a male youth who was preparing to enter manhood, but it could also be undertaken by anyone at any age needing guidance and a connection with the spirit world. When a young man approached the age of adulthood, he would prepare to take a vision quest to meditate upon the path he should take in life. The usual length for a vision quest was three days. At the end of the three days the elder who was in charge of this youth would come to get him and take him back to the group. His vision would be discussed and analyzed regarding its true meaning and application to the boy's life. During this time the youth would be totally alone, without food or water. He was expected to stay awake for the entire three days and to stay in the sacred area that he had prepared for himself. He would pray, sing and chant in order to produce a meditative state conducive for a visionary experience. Often the vision is of an animal or plant that would agree to be his guardian spirit for life, available to help him when the need arose. Sometimes the seeker would be taken to the spirit world in order to be given information. Black Elk, an Oglala Sioux, describes his vision quest: "Once, I went to pray at the top of the sacred mountain of my ancestors. As I climbed to the top I heard voic-

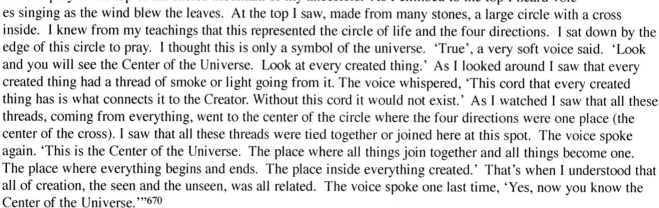
Kashka, Tlingit

es singing as the wind blew the leaves. At the top I saw, made from many stones, a large circle with a cross inside. I knew from my teachings that this represented the circle of life and the four directions. I sat down by the edge of this circle to pray. I thought this is only a symbol of the universe. 'True', a very soft voice said. 'Look and you will see the Center of the Universe. Look at every created thing.' As I looked around I saw that every created thing had a thread of smoke or light going from it. The voice whispered, 'This cord that every created thing has is what connects it to the Creator. Without this cord it would not exist.' As I watched I saw that all these threads, coming from everything, went to the center of the circle where the four directions were one place (the center of the cross). I saw that all these threads were tied together or joined here at this spot. The voice spoke again. 'This is the Center of the Universe. The place where all things join together and all things become one. The place where everything begins and ends. The place inside everything created.' That's when I understood that all of creation, the seen and the unseen, was all related. The voice spoke one last time, 'Yes, now you know the Center of the Universe.'"[670]

The American Indian tribal traditions are filled with many sacred objects and symbols. These sacred objects and their use varied in each of the tribes for protection and as a spiritual connection to their creator in a manner similar to the use of rosary beads in the Catholic religion. The earliest written accounts of purification ceremonies mention "ritual baths" in which the participants seek spiritual renewal in their lives. Archaeologists have found great baths in the Harappan civilization that indicate they were used for ritual bathing and spread

Ute Bear Dance ceremony, 1890s

westward to India to be used by the Hindu religion. Two thousand years ago the Romans enjoyed the use of natural spa water for healing and cleansing. A Jewish ritual bath ceremony called Mikvah is performed once a month for women, including right before a wedding. The baptisms performed by John the Baptist were a carry over from ancient pre-Christian religions. In Africa, Asia and Europe, as well as by the Indians in the Americas, purification rites are an important part of their religious and spiritual beliefs.[671]

Sweat Lodge

The Indian Purification Ceremony, also known as the Sweat Lodge Ceremony, is utilized by one or more individuals. Most North American and Central American Indian tribes have traditionally used the sweat lodge for purification, cleansing and healing of mind, body, emotions and spirit. The Indian word for purification is "oenikika", which means "breath of life." The sweat lodge is made of branches, often willow, but other kinds of wood may be used. Blankets or tarps are used as coverings to hold in heat produced by lava rocks which are heated, then taken into the lodge where water is poured on them to produce steam. A fire built in the center heats some sweat lodges. Black Elk wrote, "The sweat lodge utilizes all powers of the universe: earth, and things that grow from the earth; water; fire; and air."[672] The circular shape of the lodge is like a womb or a protective bubble. When the door of the lodge is closed there is absolute darkness, so that participants are aware of the presence of the Spirit. The ceremony is shrouded in secrecy, with the prayers and songs said and sung in the sweat lodge being known only to the participants. The sweat lodge ceremony is one of physical and spiritual purification practiced by American Indians to overcome illness and to prepare for other ceremonies. The water slowly releases the heat in the stones, which rises as steam and permeates the air to create a hot, humid atmosphere conducive to manifestation of the particular intent of the ceremony. Alex Saluskin of the Yakama Nation described his upbringing and tribal customs and how each child was assigned a mentor. Referring to the sweat lodge ceremony, Saluskin says, "I was told that the sweat house and the hot rocks which were prepared for the great sweat house were blessings handed down from the Great Spirit. This hot water cause by cold water on the hot rocks would cleanse you

Navajo sandpainting healing ceremony

Sandpainting, 1900s by E. Curtis

and purify your scent, so the wild animals wouldn't detect you. You would have the scent the same as the fir bough and reeds that grow in the mountains.... This kind uncle of mine and his wife took time to explain these things step by step. They didn't leave one thing untold and it was shown physically to me, then asked me if I could do it."[673]

The Winter Dance is a renewal ceremony performed by the Salish people on the Colville Reservation, north of Spokane, Washington. The Winter Dance is intended to produce heavy rains to water the root crops. The winter dance is performed for four days, from eight in the evening until nine the next morning. The first day of the winter dance is usually for family. By the fourth day there may be as many as 100 or 150 people in attendance. A shaman chooses the location of the ceremony. It is held in a single room; the windows are covered and there is a pole made of pine in the middle of the room that extends from the floor to the ceiling. This pole is referred to as "the old man", and is a symbol for the Indians' relationship with the spirits that created and gave meaning to this world. During the winter dance itself, spirits call out in songs. Those who can hear the songs will sing them. This exchange between the spirits and human beings is called *samish* in the Salish language, a word that implies that a special sound is being imparted to a person by the creative presence of

Kiowa Horn ceremonial dance, 1920s

the world. No one touches the pine pole except for the singers, who begin to sing very slowly, one at a time, in no set order. The singers enter a kind of altered state during this process and a translator is usually present to give the English interpretation, or if the words are already in English, to project the message loud and clear for everyone in the room to hear. These are personal statements about ethical and moral life, about community, about spirit presence, and about the origin of the song. As time passes, the pace of the singing becomes faster, and people get up to dance.

The traditional Inuit (Eskimo) culture is similar to those found in the regions of northern Russia and the northern Scandinavian countries. Life has been insecure with the challenges of the cold and the continual threat of starvation. Their religious belief is grounded in the belief that "anua" (souls) exist in all people and animals. Individuals, families and the tribe must follow a complex system of taboos to assure that animals will continue to make themselves available to the hunters. Many rituals and ceremonies are performed before and after hunting expeditions to assure hunting success. An underwater goddess, Sedna or Takanaluk, is in charge of the sea mammals. She is part human and part fish. She observes how closely the tribe obeys the taboos and releases her animals to the hunters accordingly. There is a corresponding array of deities who release land mammals—these are Keepers or Masters, one for each species. The angakut or shaman is the spiritual leader of each tribe. He is able to interpret the causes of sickness or lack of hunting success; he can determine the individual or family responsible and isolate the broken taboo. In a manner similar to shamans in other cultures, he enters a trance with the aid of drum beating and chanting. This allows his soul to leave his body and traverse great distances to determine the causes of sickness and other community problems.[674]

Tlingit dancers, 1912

The northwest coast Skokomish tribe performs the Salmon Spirit Ceremony in order to thank the earth for its supply of food. When the salmon start to appear, the people hold a ceremony where they sing songs and offer the first salmon caught that year back to the river. The Tlingit tribe and other northwest coastal tribes celebrated the Potlatch Ceremony. It was traditionally a festive gathering of tribal families to dedicate a new totem pole, and a time for gift giving. The potlatch lasted for several days and was hosted by one family who gathered and stored large amounts of prepared food. The guests began their journey in a dugout canoe, heading along the coastal waters towards their host village. They sang a song of peace when approaching the landing area on the beach. The host (who was sometimes a chief) and his family answered them with another song. The guests and their hosts danced on the beach for part of the day, an event that was followed by a formal presentation to the host by a master of ceremonies. Everyone continued the celebration with a feast of boiled or roasted meat, fish, soup and berry cakes. There were speeches by the host, storytelling, games and finally a gathering around a campfire. Less important guests slept beneath canoes turned upside down, while selected visitors were invited to sleep in the chief's house. The host or chief gave the visitors gifts each day. It often took the host family two or three years to accumulate enough gifts to be given away at a potlatch. A totem pole was often erected near the last few days of the potlatch to signify the special event, to make the host's ownership known, or sometimes as a monument to the dead. The totem pole carvings told of family histories and ancestral spirits, in human and animal form. The hosting family and visitors shouted and clapped as a drummer gave a roll on the drum while the pole was dragged and raised into its hole, and dancers trampled and stomped the ground at its base. Once the dance was over and the earth packed down, the host chief commanded the drums and clapping to stop. The host followed by explaining what the carved figures meant, beginning with those at the top of the pole. This ended the ceremonies and the guests started for home in their dugout canoes, loaded down with food and gifts. Other celebrations marked various parts of the year or particular occasions in the life of the tribe's people.[675]

The Buffalo Dance, a sacred ceremony of the Plains and Pueblo tribes, was an invocation to their creator for the continuation of the bounty provided by the buffalo—their primary source of food, tools and clothing. The hunter thanked the spirit of that animal and asked for good luck with the next year's hunting. The dancers would be dressed in buffalo skin headdresses with arm, wrist and knee bands of porcupine quills, and carried gourd rattles in one hand and pipes in the other. The dancers imitated the actions of the buffalo to the music and one of them used sticks to imitate a hunter using a bow and arrows. With mock weapons pointed at the buffalo, he fell to the ground and lay there as the dancers circled four times. The dancers "imitate the pawing of a buffalo bull in rage or defiance and... manifest a defiant bravery of the dancers equal to that of the buffalo bull." At the end of the fourth circle the buffalo dancer arose to show he would still be available for the next hunt.[676]

The Horse Dance is a religious dance performed by the Sioux in which four wild horses and four singers participated. Fools Crow, a spiritual leader of the Teton Sioux, gave a description of this sacred dance. "After the shaman blew a mixture of red-hot ashes with the smoke from the fire into the faces of the horses they began to calm down. The horses were then mounted bareback and, as they passed through the corral gates, the singers broke into song. As the drums were played and the riders

Mandan Buffalo Dance by Catlin, 1830s

prayed, the wild horses began to prance and then to dance. After each of the horses was halted at each of the four cardinal directions, they were taken back to the corral, wiped down with sage grass and let go."[677]

Deer Dance, Tesuque Pueblo, 1920s

The Deer Dance relates back to ancient Mayan roots depicting the struggle between humans and animals. Today it is a celebration of thanksgiving in which the hunter imitates the deer he has hunted during the year. The deer dance is usually performed in the winter and pays homage to the soul of the deer. The deer dancer wears a deer headdress, breechcloth around his waist, a belt of deer hoof rattles, and cocoon rattles around his legs and ankles. The sounds of the rattles are meant to recreate the sounds of the rustling leaves and of the wind. The headdress is a stuffed stag's head tied with a leather thong around the dancer's chin. The dancers may wear antlers and hold long sticks to represent the front legs of the deer. The dancer covers his forehead and part of his eyes with a white scarf. The solitary deer dancer carries gourd rattles and is accompanied by the sounds of wooden rasps and of a drum made of a gourd floating in a dish of water. The musicians sing about the beauty of nature and celebrate the lives of the animals whose flesh and skins have sustained the Indians throughout the long winter.

Pueblo Deer Dance, 2004

The Uweepe Ceremony is a little-known healing ritual performed by only a few medicine people in South Dakota. During this ceremony the leader will travel into a spiritual dimension where the wisdom of the past, present and future are available so as to diagnose and find a cure for the patient.

The Making of Relations Ceremony is to combat loneliness and to create a sense of community and continuity. Ben First Eagle, a Watatome and Choctaw Indian from the Black Hills of South Dakota, explains how and why the ceremony is performed. "This is a ritual that we have for making a new relation. To Native Americans, the worst thing that you can call a person is an orphan. It means that the person is disconnected, that they have no relations, that they have no bloodline. These things happened in the past. The mother and father would be killed or disease would take them. And they happen today. In this ceremony, another family or group takes in a young person who has been left alone. Or it can be a middle-aged person or someone older. Age doesn't matter. Anyone who loses his or her relatives can partake in this ritual. Another family will say, 'this one is pitiful. We need to help. So, let's make this one our aunt, our brother, our sister, nephew, niece, grandson, or granddaughter.' The Making of Relations Ceremony insures that no one is an orphan, no one is alone. In this ritual we use the pipe, we use blankets, and these days we use a chair.... Songs are sung. An eagle feather is tied in the person's hair, complete with a medicine wheel that could be made of rawhide and painted, or made of porcupine quills. That's done to symbolize their connection to the four directions, and to the hoop of life. Hair represents the person's life because it grows. It contains a person's wisdom, and a connection to the past."[678]

Indian powwow, 1898, by Rinhardt

The powwow was utilized in the early days to gather medicine men and spiritual leaders together for ceremonial dances for the spiritual benefits of the tribe. Since the time when the Indians were moved to reservations, the powwow became an inter-tribal social event held either indoors or outdoors, in a dance circle. The powwow begins with the grand entry, with dancers entering from the east entrance of the dance ring. The eagle staff and flag bearers enter first, followed by the male dancers in different groups: traditional dancers, grass dancers, and fancy dancers. The female dancers follow them: traditional dancers, jingle dress dancers, and fancy shawl dancers. All the dancers dance in a circle clockwise. Male traditional dancers come from all the tribes. They wear moccasins, leggings, breechclout, bells, armbands, headpieces made from porcupine quills and deer tail fur, and an eagle feather bustle on their backs. Eagles are not killed for their feathers and these feathers are not considered as a decoration, but rather they are thought of as sacred and are to be respected. The female traditional dancers wear dresses made from tanned and smoked hide. Rows of elk's teeth, shells or porcupine quills are strung on the upper and lower parts of the dress. They wear eagle feathers on their heads and carry an eagle wing fan. They dance with a weaving and slide-step motion, sometimes staying in one spot. Grass dancers dance in a freestyle form, moving swiftly, bobbing, weaving and stepping with a bounce. Their outfits are of colorful yarn fringes, ribbon and beaded streamers. Fancy dancers dance mainly for competition and the dance style is related to the dance of the Plains Indians of the late 1800s. Today's fancy dance was developed in the 1950s. The fancy dancer wears a colorful two-piece

White Buffalo Society Powwow, 2001

Powwow poster, 1983

145

bustle of dyed turkey or goose feathers worn on the back. The male dancer displays an array of colors as he twists, whirls and bounces energetically. The Fancy Shawl dancer dances a modern and free-style dance. The girls make up dance steps while moving clockwise around the dance circle. Their dance resembles a ballet, and is danced on the toes while spinning, causing their shawls to fly outward. The jingle dress dancer's outfit

Powwow shawl dance, New Mexico, 1999

is made from calico or velvet with several rows of attached tin cones. Can lids can also be used to make the jingles. The female dancers wear eagle feathers on their heads and often carry an eagle-wing fan. They dance with one hand on their hips while twisting and bouncing. Their dance shows how the path of life twists, curves and turns suddenly. In the 1920's, some powwows became inter-tribal and the practice of "contesting" began. Dance competitions were held, often lasting an entire weekend. World War II brought a revival to the powwow world as the Indians recognized the need to keep their culture intact, and as a means to interact with other tribes. Powwows have been growing, constantly changing and adapting to modern ways, while retaining their cultural roots.[679]

Fancy dancer, 2001, Ojibway, White Buffalo Society

The Sun Dance is the predominant tribal ceremony of Great Plains Indians, although numerous tribes practice it today as a prayer for life, world renewal and thanksgiving. The original significance was to honor the Sun and to give thanks to all forms of life. A similar ceremony held by the Crow tribe is called the Medicine Lodge Ritual. Both ceremonies have in common the fact that the participants make supplications to the creator and indulge in self-torture. The Mandan Okeepa Ceremony and Kiowa Warrior Dance were early predecessors to the Sun Dance. The ceremony was performed with drums, rattled percussion instruments and mythical and animal impersonators. Part of the ceremony featured a bull dance, during which the dancers wore masks from the skins of the buffalo. "On the

Comanche dancer 1990s

last day, the dancers were pierced as in the sun dance—skewers thrust through their chest muscles and tied to ropes—whereupon they were hoisted above the ground and hung suspended in the air until they tore loose. Some of them would also induce intense pain by piercing their backs and hanging the heads, skulls or hides of buffalo from them. Other men would dance and move around the village, dragging objects attached to their piercings."[680] The Sun Dance reflected the relationship with, and included symbolic representations of, various animal species—particularly the eagle and the buffalo. For many tribes of the Plains Indians, whose buffalo-hunting culture flowered during the 18th and 19th centuries, the Sun Dance was the major communal religious ceremony. Although details of the event differed among various groups, certain elements were common to most tribal traditions. The annual ceremony was held in late spring or early summer, when people from different bands gathered together again following the dispersal that customarily took place in winter. The Sun Dance was a ritual of sacrifice performed among the Arapaho, Arikara, Assiniboin, Blackfeet, Blood, Cheyenne, Plains Cree, Crow, Gros Ventre, Hidatsa, Kiowa, Mandans, Ojibway, Omaha, Ponca, Shoshone, Sioux and Ute. Generally, each Sun Dance has a sponsor, usually the main dancer, who bears the expenses of the ceremony. The dance was performed as a prayer for a relative or friend, or to determine the dancer's place in the universe. American Indians believe that unless the Sun Dance is per-

Sun Dance, by E. Curtis
Mandan Sun Dance Ceremony , by Catlin, 1838

formed each year, the earth will lose touch with the creative power of the universe, thereby losing its ability to regenerate. Before this ceremony the Indians would fast at least three or four days. The sponsor, usually a person who has lost a relative, sets up a circle of tipis. The entrance faces east, and some tribes celebrate the dawn in their Sun Dance ceremonies. Inside one of the tipis was an altar on which rested a decorated buffalo skull. A tree was cut and set up in the center of the space to be used for the dance. Ropes made of hair or leather thongs were fastened to the top of the pole. Men tie these ropes to sticks, which were stuck through the flesh of their chests or backs. The men danced, gazing at the sun, whistling through pipes and pulling back on the ropes until the sticks tore through the flesh. Dancers would blow on eagle-bone whistles, fixing their eyes on the fork on the center pole that is known as the Thunderbirds' or Eagles' nest, and members of the tribe would respond with cries of, "What formed us… make us fortunate… deliver us from diseases… furnish us with game… deliver us from great cold weather, deliver to us our enemies…."[681] The Sun Dance was outlawed in the latter part of the nineteenth century, partly because certain tribes indulged in self-torture as part of the ceremony. The white settlers found this gruesome and against their religious

War Dance of the Sauks and Foxes
McKenney & Hall, 1830s

upbringing. During the 1890s there was a fear by the federal government that the Sun Dance, with the Ghost Dance, would revive a rebellion against white authority. In the 1930s, after the religious ban on the Sun Dance was lifted, it was relearned and is now practiced by some tribes once again.[682]

"Chippewa Pipe Dance" by Otto Lewis, 1820s

The Pipe Ceremony is a sacred ritual for connecting physical and spiritual worlds. The prayer or ceremonial pipe consists of two parts, a bowl representing the Great Spirit and the stem representing the people. The two parts remain separate until used. This represents the joining of the Great Spirit and the people as one. The tobacco represents the prayers of the people. As the smoke travels upward, the prayers of those smoking the pipe were carried to the Great Spirit. The pipe, at times, was decorated with fringe, representing rain; an eagle feather symbolizing the creator; and buffalo hides to signify the earth. Tobacco is seen as a way to connect the worlds because the plant's roots go deep into the earth, and its smoke rises high into the heavens. There are different kinds of pipes and different uses for them. There are personal pipes and family pipes as well as pipes for large ceremonies. The particular stone used depends upon the tribe's location, and various symbols are added to attract certain spiritual energies. Also, the type of tobacco used depends on tribal custom. Despite these differences, there are certain important similarities. The ceremony invokes a relationship with the energies of the universe, and ultimately the creator, and the bond made between earthly and spiritual realms is not to be broken; it is unimaginable for an Indian to break his word after

Peace Pipe

smoking the pipe. In the past, the signing of treaties was always accompanied by pipe ceremonies because Indians believed that smoking the pipe would seal the arrangement. No one would be foolish enough to lie or go back on their word once the pipe was smoked because the pipe was the vehicle for carrying their word up to the creator and, in return, a blessing would descend from the creator to the individuals smoking it. The United States government did not abide in these understandings, and sent representatives to the Indians to use the pipe as a means of deception.

The Tobacco Ceremony was performed in the Crow tribe, acted out over a period several months during all phases of the planting, harvesting, curing and use of the tobacco, which was considered a healing medicine. The Tobacco Society performed the ceremony of initiation, planting and harvesting of the tobacco. The initiate into the society was given a medicine bag containing tobacco which, it was believed, would bring the wearer good luck and prosperity. The planting ceremony lasted an entire day and along the way, four stops were made. At each stop, four songs were sung and the women danced.[683]

The introduction of the Ghost Dance ceremony marked a turning point in American Indian tribal culture that led to the end of their freedom to conduct their ancient ceremonies. The Ghost Dance was created in the 1870s with the "Shohola" religion and practiced in Oregon. It was followed by the first Ghost Dance celebrated in Northern Paiute, by Tavibo, possibly the father of Wovoka. They prophesied that those participating in this circular dance would witness a return of their dead relatives, good health and prosperity. The dance gradually lost popularity until 1889 when Wovoka (Jack Wilson), a holy man of the Paiute tribe, received a vision of a new circular dance that would return the Indians lost lands, bring back the buffalo, revive deceased relatives and make the white people disappear. Initially it was manifested as a peaceful religious ceremony urging the participants, "You must not fight."[684] The Ghost Dance was to be a ceremony for the regeneration of the earth and, subsequently, the restoration of the earth's caretakers to their former life of bliss. Not surprisingly, the religion experienced its height of popularity during the late 19th century when devastation to the buffalo, the land, and Indian culture was at its peak. Between 1888 and 1890, various tribes sent emissaries to Wovoka, who claimed to be a visionary, and who was hailed as a messiah by many desperate Indian nations. Wovoka maintained that spirits had shown him certain movements and songs after he had died for a short period of time. Wovoka preached non-violence, and most tribes abandoned their warlike ways in preparation for future happiness. The dance quickly spread to various American Indian nations and as it spread, it took on additional meanings. It was believed that while performing the Ghost Dance one could visit relatives who had left their bodies. As so many Indians had lost friends and relatives, this aspect of the ceremony was particularly healing. The Sioux, Cheyenne and Arapaho expanded its meaning further, after being told in dreams that wearing certain designs on clothing would protect them in battle. These beliefs served to ward off fears of imminent danger from

Wovoka

Wovoka, Paiute medicine man (shaman) and Ghost Dance participants, 1890s

suspicious and sometimes hostile white onlookers, but proved futile in the end.[685] In 1933, Alexander Lesser, an American anthropologist, wrote of the significance of the Ghost Dance. "Indian ways were not gone, never to be recovered, Indian ways were coming back. Those who had lived before in the 'Golden Age' were still carrying on old ceremonies, old dances, old performances, and old games in the beyond. They were coming back; they were bringing the old ways and the buffalo, Dance, Dance, Dance. The white man would be destroyed by a great wind. The Indian would be left with the buffalo, with his ancestors, with his old friends and his old enemies. Cast aside the white man's ways like an old garment; put on the clothes of the Indian again. Get ready for the new day and the old times."[686]

Arapaho Ghost Dance Ceremony, photo by James Mooney, 1890s

The Ghost Dance unified Indian people, even tribes with a tradition of conflict. The solidarity of these groups frightened government officials, whose worst fears were realized years earlier when the Arapahoe, Cheyenne and Sioux came together to defeat Custer. Most ghost dancers did not embrace warlike behavior. Yet, the government reacted to this outburst of Indian behavior by gunning down ghost dancers at Wounded Knee during a peaceful ceremony. Even women and children were shot in the back as they were trying to escape. Many say this was in retaliation for the massacre at Little Big Horn, since the seventh cavalry was again involved. According to a historian of that time, James Mooney, during one investigation of the Ghost Dance, U.S. troops reported seeing approximately 125 people at the beginning of the dance, and twice that number at the end, with no one new coming into the circle. The end of the Ghost Dance resulted in the death of Chief Sitting Bull of the Sioux. Major James McLaughlin ordered his arrest and on December 15, 1890, when he refused to leave with them, he was shot by Bullhead, of the Indian police. Before his death, Sitting Bull, when he found out they were coming to arrest him, stated, "Why should the Indian police come against me? We are of the same blood, we are all Sioux, we are relatives.... Let the soldiers come and take me away and kill me, whenever they like. I am not afraid—I was born a warrior.... I did not start the Ghost Dance; Kicking Bear came here of his own accord. I told my people to go slow, but they were swept into this thing so strong, nothing could stop them. I have not joined the sacred dance since I was told to stop way back."[687] Two years after the Wounded Knee massacre in 1892, the United States government arrested the leaders of the Ghost Dance in Oklahoma and then banned all their religious ceremonies, along with the Ghost Dance and the Sun Dance. It was not until the 1934 Indian Reorganization Act that the ban on religious ceremonies was lifted, and 1978 when Congress passed the "American Indian Religious Freedom Act" that finally promised to protect and preserve American Indian religious liberties.[688]

Smudging plays a central role in traditional healing ceremonies because it is believed that once negative energies are cleared out, a sense of peace and relaxation take over, putting spiritual difficulties to rest. Smudging is a common practice among Native Americans for the cleansing of energy through the burning of sage, tobacco, cedar, dried herbs and sweet grass. The smudging itself is performed by mixing the sweet grass, sage and tobacco in a bowl, usually an abalone shell, burning the ingredients, and then blowing or fanning the smoke over a person. Often, an eagle feather fan is used, as American Indians believe that the prayers and thoughts contained in the smoke are carried to the creator on the wings of eagles, which fly the highest and are in direct communication with the creator. Smudging is often combined with other natural treatments, such as talking to a shaman, taking long walks, fasting, praying and engaging in purification ceremonies. Indian men used medicine shields or mandalas for spiritual as well as physical protection. The shields were circular and decorated with power symbols and objects of personal significance, as an important animal or insect such as a buffalo, an eagle, or an ant. The creature would come to the man in a vision or be given to him by someone else. The animal or insect would give the warrior further power and protection by allowing him to see where the enemy was. Sometimes parts of animals such as eagle feathers would be attached as well. Smaller shields, known as replica shields, were also made by the men and worn for spiritual protection from evil. Physical safety was aided by the size of the shield and the material used to make it, which was a hard rawhide from the hump of the buffalo. The rawhide was cured, making it dense, so that no arrow could penetrate it. Bullets from early flint rock rifles didn't always go through the rawhide, although later more powerful bullets did. In present times the medicine shield or mandalas are hung in the homes to give protection from danger and evil, and to ensure prosperity, good health and happiness for the entire family.

Smudging ceremony
Lame Wolf
White Mountain Apache

The Medicine Wheel, also called the "Spirit Hoop", is revered in American Indian culture as a symbol of power without limit or end. It is a common religious symbol for many tribes and is placed in front of every tipi, decorated in special symbols, colors and stones, to let people know about its inhabitants. It consisted of a circle of which horizontal and vertical lines went to its center, where an eagle feather was attached as a sign of the power of the Great Spirit. In actuality, it is a circle divided by a cross to create four directions—the north, east, south and west. Each person is represented somewhere within that circle, according to their birth date. The medicine wheel was a reflection of an individual's strengths and weaknesses, and it gave people guidelines to follow for personal growth. The medicine wheel was often marked with the four sacred colors—black, white, red and yellow, signifying the four seasons, four cardinal directions, and the races of humanity. Tribes used different colors to represent the four cardinal directions. In Cherokee legends the Medicine Wheel represented the red road (NS) that was the path of good. The opposite, black (EW), represented fear and trouble. The four cardinal directions for the Cherokees were, 1: the red (east), for the direction of the sun. 2: black (west), associated with the moon, represented the souls of the dead and death. 3: blue (north), represented cold, trouble and defeat. 4: white (south) was warmth, peace, and happiness. For the Mayans, yellow represented south, or the sun, as to where the dead went.

Prayer feather, sweet grass, ceremony rattle, medicine wheel, medicine bag. Courtesy, White Buffalo Society

The dream catcher is a device that is hung to catch dreams. The good dreams, knowing their way, go through the hole in the center and then fall off the feather to the dreamer lying below. These good dreams were believed to nourish the dreamer and to aid his or her spiritual growth. The bad dreams, not knowing the way, would get trapped in the webbing and vanish at the first light of day. A dream catcher hung over a burial site would guide the spirit of the departed on its journey to the next world.

Dream catcher

The prayer feather was a gift from the Great Spirit to the winged birds he favored and who were close to him. Bird feathers, obtained in the proper manner, are used by the American Indians to help guide the smoke from smudges of tobacco, sage and sweet grass in their ceremonial prayers to the Great Spirit.

The medicine bag established a close relationship between the wearer and his spiritual protectors, especially among the southwestern plains tribes. It contains an assortment of natural materials such as beads, stones, buffalo hide, deerskin and various other animal parts in a pouch made from the skin of the creature that is the wearer's guardian spirit. The items, representing the embodiment of the spirit of the animal, are worn around the neck in a bag. Its contents were for healing his body and mind and to give him courage and strength to protect him for the tasks ahead.

Sioux medicine bag

The talking feather (talking stick) was used in the stories passed down through generations to preserve their culture. To keep order and to allow each tribal member to speak, a talking feather or talking stick was passed along to those wishing to speak. The holder of the feather or stick was obligated to speak only the truth.

The coup stick was used by Indian warriors that believed it was more courageous to touch an enemy with a stick and humiliate him rather than to kill him. For this practice of humiliation, he used the coup stick—and the action was called "counting coup". A ceremonial coup stick was made of fur, leather, and wood, with brightly colored beads along with an animal or bird claw. The choker around the necks of the Indians was believed to protect the neck area from injury from a knife or arrow or later, from bullets. Animal furs and special beads made the choker a status symbol.

Peyote religious ceremony 1920s

The Native American Church (N.A.C.) was formed as an alternative to the Christian church to combine fundamentalist Christian elements with American Indian culture. The movement began among the Kiowa about 1890 and, led by John Wilson (Big Moon), soon spread to other tribes. The hymns developed in this style are in sharp contrast to traditional music. This style, known as "peyote", is simpler to sing. Peyote meetings can be held anywhere. Prayers and the use of instruments that include the water drum and a rattle accompany the services. The members came to be known as peyotists due to their ingesting a sacramental food, peyote, taken from the tops of a small hallucinogenic cactus plant. In 1918, peyotists from a number of tribes incorporated their movement as the Native American Church. The N.A.C. draws a lot of its teachings from the Christian religion using peyote as its sacrament. The church stresses high morality, which includes love towards one another, their family, self-reliance and absence of alcohol. In 1940 the church was declared illegal by the Navajo Tribal Council, which saw it as a threat to Navajo culture and to Christianized Navajos. The church flourished underground, however, until 1967 when the tribe reversed its decision. Federal legislation legalized the use of peyote in 1994 for sacramental use. The use of peyote is not required to attend the church. By 1996 the church had 250,000 members in the United States, Mexico and Canada.

CHAPTER 12 AMERICAN INDIAN ACCOMPLISHMENTS

A significant amount of Indian technology, inventions and methods of farming and production were adopted by the European settlers and played a large part in their survival in the New World. The Indians in the Americas were the original discoverers. Many of their inventions and beliefs endure today and continue to make meaningful contributions to our lives. One of the main contributions has been the appreciation that the Indians traditionally held for the environment. The *Encyclopedia of American Indian Contributions to the World: 15,000 Years of Inventions and Innovations* claims, "More than 450 inventions and innovations can be traced to indigenous peoples of the North, Middle and South America." Below is a brief summary of these vast accomplishments.[689]

"Transporting Water and Grass Seed"
Valley of San Joaquian, California, 1880s

Agricultural products: John Rolfe acquired tobacco seeds from Indians in the Caribbean. The seeds were brought to Jamestown around 1612. John Rolfe married Pocahontas who was Chief Powhatan's (Algonquin) daughter. American settlers adopted the agriculture and technological procedures used by the Indians to cultivate tobacco, cotton and other crops. Indians cultivated crops of tomatoes, hundreds of varieties of sweet and regular potatoes, squash, pumpkins, all varieties of beans, peanuts, pecans, hickory nuts, black walnuts, corn, sunflower seeds, cranberries, blueberries, strawberries, maple syrup, artichokes, all kinds of peppers, prickly pears, chocolate, vanilla, allspice, sassafras, avocados, maize, cacao bean, fruit of the breadnut tree, papaya, plums, pears, wild rice, etc. From the Indians in the Americas, chicle, chewing gum, was developed. In thousands of years of plant breeding, Indian farmers developed and passed down their knowledge of plant genetics. They were able to grow at least 3000 varieties of potatoes, 300 varieties of grasses, many varieties of corn and other agricultural food crops. In over 400 years since the European settlers landed in America, not a single plant has been found that was not already domesticated by the Indians. In 1775, on a visit to the Muscogee (Creek) tribes, one visitor wrote, "They make pancakes; they dry the tongues of their venison... they eat much roasted and broiled venison, a great deal of milk and eggs... also dried peaches and persimmons and other fruit and berries, as well as their particular boast, a prepared drink known as 'hickory milk'.... In a word, the greatest abundance available."[690] James Adair gave a full description of the natives agricultural capabilities in his 1775 *History of the American Indians*. "Every dwelling-house has a small field pretty close to it... there they plant a variety of large and small beans, peas, and the smaller sort of Indian corn, which usually ripens two months from the time it is planted.... The Indians begin to plant their out-fields when the wild fruit is ripe.... Corn was their chief produce, and main dependence.... In July, when the chestnuts and corn are green and fully grown, they half boil the former... the women pound it with a large mortar... then they knead both together, wrap them up in green corn blades of various sizes, about an inch-thick, and boil them well.... This sort of bread is very tasty.... They have another sort of boiled bread which is mixed with beans and potatoes.... The women also plant pompions, and different sorts of melons.... They commonly have pretty good crops, which is owing to the richness of soil.... They have a great deal of fruit, and they have such kinds as will bear it.... It is surprising to see the great variety of dishes they make out of wild flesh, corn, beans, fruits, herbs, and roots. They can diversify their courses as much as the English, or perhaps the French cooks: and in either of the ways they dress their food, it is grateful to a wholesome stomach.... Their old fields abound with more strawberries than I have seen in any part of the world."[691]

Corn, pumpkin, squash
1600s French engraving

Air gun: A simple tube or barrel about six feet long and an inch in diameter. Fired a slender arrow two feet long. At the foot of the arrow, down or floss of the thistle was attached, which allowed it to be airtight in the barrel. The force of blown air discharged the arrow. It was generally used for shooting birds.

Domestication, hunting and use of animals: The Indians hunted wild buffalo, bear, elk, deer and moose and used their meat, skins and bones for various purposes. The Indians domesticated turkeys, ducks, dogs, guinea pigs, and, in the Andes, birds. In Guatemala the macaw, quetzal bird, and others were raised for their feathers. The

"Sneaking up" disguised as buffalo
by George Catlin

Incas also raised herds of domesticated rhea's (an ostrich-like bird) for both food and feathers. Herds of deer were kept and raised for food. Various animals were raised to be used for sacrifices to their Gods. The Mayans raised bees for their honey.

Navajo dwellings,
Monument Valley, Arizona

Architecture: Magnificent Mayan pyramids up to 180 feet high. Stone buildings with beams placed along the walls or supported on pillars. Walls constructed from rubble and mortar and covered with mosaics made from small stones. Some of the architecture resembled Greek temples. The early wood longhouses of the northeast Indians relied on arch construction with arched ceilings resembling the interior of some European churches. The Pueblo Indians made their homes from mud bricks. Mud topped by roof timbers were stacked two and three stories high with wooden ladders connecting to the other levels.

Mayan Castillo, Chichen
Itza, Yucatan, Mexico
Inca
construction

The early Pueblo tribes built their villages into the surrounding mountain rock. The Plains Indians built semi-subterranean sod houses that were well insulated against the cold winters and hot summers. On the Pacific coast the European settlers copied the American Indian early style homes. The homes resembled rectangular cedar or redwood plank houses built above the ground with gables. The Incas arranged their major religious and political buildings around large plazas.

Art: Mayan sculptures were created using stone tools. Great carvings were done in 3/4 or full length with dimension and perspective and colored with natural dyes, usually red, black, blue and green. Codices, wall frescos and designs on ceramic ware were decorated with elaborate colors and elaborate designs.

Astronomy and the calendar: Long before the arrival of Columbus in the Americas, Indian astronomers used a sophisticated system of astronomy which could calculate celestial events such as solar eclipses. Mayan astronomers were so accurate at observing the movements of the stars and planets that by the fifth century B.C. they had calculated a year's length so accurately that it was only 19 minutes off. The development of the calendar was a supreme achievement by the Mayans, who had studied the lunar system and evolved a method of judging the best times for planting according to the cycles of the moon and the eclipses. The Mayans were able to predict eclipses and the rising and various positions of the stars. The Maya understood 17 different calendars based on the cosmos. Some of these calendars go back thousands of years and are so difficult that you would need an astronomer,

Tzolkin Calendar, Mexico
260 days, 52 day cycles

astrologer, geologist and a mathematician just to work out the calculations. They also made tables predicting eclipses and the orbit of the planet Venus. The calendars that are most important to beings of earth are the Haab, the Tun-Uc and the Tzolkin. The Tzolkin is the most important and the one with the most influence. The Tzolkin is a cycle of 260 days and the haab is a cycle of 365 days. The Tzolkin cycle and the Haab cycle were combined to produce a cycle of 18,980 days, known as the calendar round. 18,980 days is a little less than 52 solar years. The Aztec Calendar or Sun Stone was basically similar to that of the Mayan. The Inca calendar was based on the observation of the sun and the moon, and their relationship to the stars. Names of 12 lunar months are recorded, as well as their association with festivities related to their agricultural cycle.[692]

Bark canoe: The art of construction was common to most of the American Indians. Birch, as well as red-elm, butternut and hickory were used—although birch bark was the most suitable material because it retained its shape without warping, and was light enough that two men could easily carry it around water obstructions. The bark was stripped from the tree, shaped into the form of a canoe and stitched together with pieces of white ash or other elastic wood using bark thread or twine, and splints. The ribs were made of narrow strips of ash, set a foot apart along the bottom of the canoe, having been turned up at the sides under the

Bark dugout canoe

rim. Each end of the canoe was made the same, inclining towards each other until they formed a sharp vertical prow. Their size varied from twelve to forty feet, and canoes were designed to carry between two to thirty men. These canoes were used extensively during the fur trade and frequently carried about 1200 pounds of fur.

Cotton: Textiles made from cotton dating back to at least 2500 B.C. have been found preserved in the acidity of coastal Peru. It was quickly discovered by the Europeans that cotton grown by the Indians produced a far superior fabric to that produced in the Old World. The Indian cotton was so fine that it was often mistaken for Chinese silk. Cotton clothing quickly replaced garments made from wool and allowed the Indians to catch more fish because cotton made stronger fishing nets. Large plantations sprang up in the south in which the owners used Indian and later, African, slave labor. As the demand for American cotton spread throughout the world and the Industrial Revolution began to unfold in England, mass production became possible. Southern plantation owners moved through the Carolinas and Georgia and built new plantations as far west as Texas. In their path, they annihilated or scattered numerous eastern Indian nations: Choctaw, Chickasaw and Cherokee, as well as the Seminole and smaller tribes, taking their valuable cotton producing land. By 1850 the money earned from the sale of cotton accounted for half of the total annual export trade income of North America. The Indians also produced over 109 distinct hues of superior dye colors made from natural substances. Evidence of the durability and brilliance of these colors can still be seen in recently discovered 2000-year-old Peruvian textiles. The Europeans immediately adopted the technology of the Indian techniques for making these dyes, some of which were made from the Brazil wood tree, found in Brazil. Cochineal was an important dye found in Mexico from the bodies of females of the scaled insect called *dactylopius coccus*. It provided the distinct scarlet dye used for the uniforms of the British "Redcoats."

Arawak Indians gathering crops, engraving, Drake's voyage, 1500s

Chocolate, vanilla: Mayans called "Ek Chuah" the word for black, and also referred to the Mayan god of cocoa (chocolate). The cocoa bean was the universal currency for the Maya. The Indians discovered how to cure the cocoa fruit and separate the seeds from the beans. In addition, the beans had to be prepared for the making of chocolate by a delicate and complicated process. The same basic technology is still used today for the extraction of the seeds through drying, roasting and grinding the cocoa pods to make chocolate. An additional complicated process was developed by American Indians to extract vanilla from the vine *vanilla planifolia*. The Indians of Mesoamerica invented a four-step process to cure vanilla and convert it into a flavoring ingredient. Due to the Indians' elaborate processing techniques, vanilla-processing plants were not established in Europe until the 1700s.[693]

Cereals, hominy grits and tortillas: Many crops involved complicated processing procedures developed by the Indians. The making of a tortilla involved soaking corn in water to which was added additional ingredients. The mixture was then ground to yield masa and made into a tortilla. "Hominy" (Algonquin word) grits were made in a similar fashion from corn, by soaking it in water and wood ashes and then grinding it. In the late 19th century, a man called Kellogg developed a revolutionary breakfast food by flattening the corn into a flake and toasting it, rather than grinding it, to produce Kellogg's Corn Flakes. The amaranth cereals found in Mexico were very popular because of its 16 percent high protein count, compared with 7 percent for rice and 13 percent for wheat. This was a popular delicacy eaten by the Aztecs during their ceremonies. The Aztecs would form the amaranth cakes into the shapes of their gods. Sometimes the cakes were made with honey or at times with human blood. Amaranth is now widely grown as an important cereal in Nepal, India, China and Pakistan.

Cooperative labor and sharing of food: The Inca agricultural system was based on a cooperative sharing of all the agricultural products for the entire community. Each subject of the Inca Empire paid taxes by laboring on the myriad roads, crop terraces, irrigation canals, temples, or fortresses. In return, rulers paid their laborers in clothing and food. In addition, there were "feasts of charity" held for the specific purpose of sharing food. In 1714, a European observed the community spirit that prevailed in a Carolina tribe: "It often happens that a woman is destitute of her husband, and has a great many children to maintain; such a person they always help, and make the young men plant, reap and do everything that she is not capable of doing herself."[694] The American Indian culture pioneered a socialist system based on their spiritual principles. The Indians matrilineal (descent from the mother), non-materialistic, extended family society allowed Indians to absorb the new technologies and incorporate it with their ancient spiritual values. The Incas promoted this philosophy in South America. The Incas cared for the aged, sick and those unable to fend for themselves. There was resentment towards anyone who had too many possessions. If one accumulated too much, it was customary to have a feast to distribute the extra items to those less fortunate. The entire tribal laws were based on sharing and taking care of the unfortunate. Gold, land or possessions did not have monetary value to the American Indian. The tribal elders determined fairly how the land and resources were to be used. All material goods belonged to the entire tribe and not to the individual. No individual American Indian could own the land, animals or food. All persons were considered free and equal with the right to pursue individual happiness as long as it was not at the expense of one of their own.[695]

Professions of the Tarascan peoples, Mexico
Loom, a Bow and Arrow, Writing Instrument, Feathers, Etc.

Corn (maize): Corn was the chief agricultural product of the Indians, next to the potato. More maize is raised in North America for feeding cattle and hogs than any other food product.

Dancing and songs: The American Indians were fond of dancing and singing. Prayers were offered to the Great Spirit in the form of a dance before hunting or planting. One Mayan dance resembled a Russian folk dance performed in a circle with two dancers in the center. One dancer armed with reed lances hurled them at the other dancer who parried them with a shield as he squatted on his haunches.

Indian women gathering crops, 1500s
by Theodor de Bry

Storytelling: Storytelling was a precise art because of the nature of Indian languages. Some tribal languages had as many as twenty words to describe rain, snow, wind and other natural elements; languages had precise words to describe the various states of human emotion, the intensity of human physical efforts and the serenity of the land itself. If the stories began "Once upon a time...", they quickly gave the listener a completely accurate rendering of a specific experience, which Western languages could not possibly duplicate. In this context, everyone understood the philosophical overview, and ad hoc explanations were treated as facts that must be understood, but whose time for understanding had not yet come. In some of the larger Indian nations elders functioned pretty much as scientists do today. That is, no one person could remember all the information about the trivial past, the religious revelations and the complex knowledge of the physical world. Consequently, people specialized in certain kinds of knowledge. With drama, poetry and story telling, a rich native heritage is now an accepted part of our society.

Most of the American tribes had outstanding singers and speakers who would pass down the stories, chants, songs and folklore of their tribes from one generation to the next. An enormous number of these legends were ultimately written down and preserved in books for future generations. Many of the prophecies, tribal creation stories, chants and music have now been preserved. Religious ceremonials generally involved the recitation of the origin and migration stories, and most of the accumulated wisdom of the tribe was familiar to everyone. Special knowledge regarding other forms of life, if revealed in visions or dreams, was made available to the larger community on a "need-to-know" basis, since it was generally regarded as personal knowledge. Garcilaso de la Vega, in his book, *El Inca*, tells of composed comedies and drama that were performed by professional actors for the Incas. The actors used a superior style to give dramatic performances that told of the Inca history and greatness. The comedies were skits on Inca life that concerned family and household themes. The theatrical plays were accompanied by music played with the flute and drums. The Incas were widely known for their folktale story telling and poetry with measured syllables and word rhyming.[696]

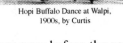
Hopi Buffalo Dance at Walpi,
1900s, by Curtis

Fishing: The Indians and Inuit tribe of the Pacific coast were advanced in their knowledge of catching fish with nets, hooks, harpoons and spears. The men caught the fish and the women gutted, scaled, cleaned and dried it, and placed it in the smoke houses where it was preserved through the winter. The Chickasaw Indians would fish in their canoes, making spears from cane—some of them between sixteen and twenty feet long. Throwing the spears twenty or thirty feet, they "seldom failed to pierce a fish through at every throw. This was doubtless an invention of great antiquity, and practiced by their fathers ages before the use of iron was known amongst them."[697] James Adair, in his 1930 *History of the American Indians*, wrote that the Indians devised other ingenious methods for catching fish:

In dry summer season, they gather horse chestnuts, and different source of roots.... They scatter this mixture over the surface of a middle-sized pond, and stir it with poles, till the water is sufficiently impregnated with the intoxicating bitters. The fish are soon inebriated, and make to the surface of the water, with their bellies uppermost. The fishers gather them in baskets and barbecue the largest, covering them carefully over at night to preserve them.... It seems the fish caught in thus manner are not poisoned, but only stupefied; for they prove very wholesome food to us... when they are speedily moved into good water, they revive in a few minutes.... Those Indians who are unacquainted with the use of barbed irons are very expert in striking fish out of their canoes, with long sharp pointed green canes.... In Savannah River I have often accompanied them in killing sturgeons with the green swamp harpoons, and which they did with much pleasure and ease.... They have a surprising method of fishing under the edges of rocks, that stand over deep places of a river. There, they pull off their red breeches or their long slip of stroud cloth and, wrapping it round their arm, so as to reach the lower part... they dive under the rock where the catfish lie to shelter themselves from the scorching beams of the sun, and to watch for prey: as soon as these fierce aquatic animals see that tempting bait, they immediately seize it with the greatest violence in order to swallow it... the diver...

Arawak Indians fishing, engraving, 1600s

accordingly opens his hand, seizes the voracious fish by his tender parts, hath a sharp struggle with it against the crevices of the rock, and at last brings it safe ashore.[698] The Indians also developed a technology to extract oil from fish, which was used in cooking and as fuel for oil lamps.

Flute: A flute found in a Caral, Peru, archaeological site was dated to about 5000 B.C. The flute was an instrument used universally in ancient civilizations. The Indian flute was mostly carved from wood, and was usually about eighteen inches in length and an inch in diameter. Six finger holes were placed at equal intervals apart, with the mouthpiece at the end. Its tone was mellow and relaxing.

Freeze drying: The Incas were the first to develop the technique for freeze-drying food. Potatoes developed for high altitudes would be left out in the cold evening, able to withstand the frost at 15,000 feet. In the morning the women would step on the potatoes until all the water disappeared. The Incas reduced the potato into a light flour. The potatoes could then be kept in storehouses for up to six years. When needed, they would be re-hydrated with water.

Cherokee ball playing, 1900s

Games and sports: Indians played a large number of games. Many were played during ritual ceremonies. Foot races were popular because they were an endurance test and gave different tribes an opportunity to congregate and compete. One of the oldest games was Indian stickball (Ball-Play) played in various ways, using a single or double stick. Ball courts were always found in the Mayan temples and in the Olmec civilization at La Venta, in the hot land of the Gulf Coast, where rubber grew. The game called "tlachtli" was the forerunner of basketball, and was played as a religious ritual in all regions of Mesoamerica to Arizona as early as 500 B.C. It was played in a rectangular court and the ball was made of hard rubber. The rubber used for the ball was derived from the palaquim tree. Unlike natural rubber, it was a natural latex material that hardened on contact with the air. The object of the game was for players to put the ball through a ring hung in the middle of the court without using hands or feet to touch the ball, only using their elbows, hips or legs. Often the losing team was sacrificed by decapitation. Another game, patolli, was similar to modern-day backgammon or parcheesi. Patolli was played on a marked board or bark, with beans for counters. The first person to travel around the board and safely return home won the game. This game was observed by the Five-Flower Goddess, but did not involve human sacrifice. Totoloque was a gambling game using pellets made of gold. The gold pellets were tossed some distance towards gold slabs. In five strokes or tries, the stakes of gold or jewels were won or lost by the players.[699]

The game of lacrosse, so named by the French in Canada because they believed that the stick resembled a bishop's staff or crozier, is still played by the Indians today, as well as in the rest of the world. Originally, the ball (the size of a golf ball), was made of scraped deerskin, moistened and stuffed with deer's hair and sewn tight. The sticks were about two feet long with the bottom being the size of the palm of the hand and netted with deerskin thongs. Goal posts were about 500 feet apart and the game was played in teams. In 1834 George Catlin painted "Ball Play of the Choctaws-Ball Up" and described a game as follows. "In every ball-play of these people, it is a rule of that no man shall wear moccasins on his feet, or any other dress than his breech-cloth around his waist, with a

Lacrosse sticks

beautiful bead belt, and a 'tail' made of horse hair or quills, and a 'mane' on the neck of horse hair dyed of various colors. The game had been arranged and 'made up' three or four months before the parties met to play it, and in the following manner. The two champions who lead the two parties, and had the alternate choosing of the players through the whole tribe, sent runners, with the ball sticks most fantastically ornamented with ribbons and red paint, to be touched by each one of the chosen players, who thereby agreed to be on the spot at the appointed time and ready for the play. The ground having been all prepared and preliminaries of the game all settled, and goods all 'staked' (wagered), night came on without the appearance of any players on the ground."[700] The game of lacrosse was a feature of large gatherings that included dances and other ceremonial events. At times, as many as

Choctaw Indians play lacrosse
by Catlin, 1838

600 players played for the ball during a game that gave an opportunity for a release of tension between the opposing teams. Another game was called "chunkey" (chungke), and involved a smooth 3-inch rounded stone rolled across the ground and players trying to stop it with an eight-foot long pole as it rolled across the ground. A javelin toss, called ga-na-ga-o, was played by the Iroquois by fifteen or thirty players who threw a five or six-foot long javelin stick made from maple or hickory at an eight-inch diameter circular hoop with an empty center. Variations of this hoop and pole game were played for sport. There were also button games that were thrown on a

154

blanket with points given as to how many colors were shown face up. There were many other games of chance using dice out of seeds, beans, stones, etc. Over 80 different tribes played a hand guessing game to music. One party held and hid two objects—one marked and one unmarked in each hand. The guesser has to identify which hand contained the marked object. These games were often played day and night, non-stop, with teams who stood or sat in rows behind the players to wait their turn. The Incas played a game with a spinning top, which they called "pisqoynyo."[701]

Indian bone game, 1900s

In an address to the Folklore Society in 1897, Stuart Culin observed a similarity between the games played by many different tribes throughout America:

The games of this class, comprising the platter or dice of the Atlantic coast, the plumstone game of the Sioux, and the game of tossed canes or staves in the southwest, I have found recorded as existing among some 61 tribes, comprised in 23 linguistic stocks, described or collected by some 75 observers, extending from the year 1634 down to the present, and represented by some 90 specimens of implements from 41 tribes, 18 stocks, and 39 collectors in the five principal American museums of ethnology: Washington, New York, Chicago, Cambridge and Philadelphia, and the hands of five individuals. The older accounts of the game among the Indians of Mexico are not included in this enumeration. Among all these tribes the principle of the game is invariably the same. Two-faced lots are tossed and numerical values attributed to the various combinations. The number of these lots varies from three to 13, four being the most common. Their form and material range from slips of cane, about a span in length, through wooden staves and blocks of various sizes, to fruit stones, disks of bone and even beans. The numerical counts attributed to their falls in general bear a relation to the number of heads or tails that come uppermost, but the count is often augmented by one or more of the lots, distinguished by marks from the others, turning in a specified manner. The methods of tossing are much diversified.

Indian Stick Game
courtesy Toppenish, Oregon Mural Society
Artist Mavis Wilson

The fruit stones and bone disks are usually thrown in a bowl or platter or in a small basket; the canes tossed or shot against a suspended blanket or skin, and the wooden staves struck on a stone, ends down, so that they rebound, hit sharply on a stone held beneath, or allowed to fall from some little height upon a blanket placed upon the ground.... A more popular game in Zuni is called *Ta-sho-li-we*, " wood canes", or "arrows", and is played with staves instead of canes. It would appear that the wooden staves are substitutes for canes, a fact which is abundantly confirmed by the wooden lots used by adjacent tribes.... My general conclusion as to the interrelation of American Indian games is extended, in the case of the particular game I have described, to the belief that its various forms are not only derived one from another, but that its place of origin may be definitely fixed in the country of the reed arrow and the *atlatl*, or throwing-stick; that is, in the three arid regions of the southwestern

Children's game, Aztec codex, circa 1200 A.D.

United States and northern or central Mexico. It is in ancient Mexico that I conceive we find evidences of its highest development. What indeed is that pictured diagram in the *Fejervary Codex* not without parallels in other manuscripts, but the counting circuit of the Four Quarters, set with colored grains on the north, west, south and east, and in the middle the god with three arrows and the *atlatl*, here, as in Zuni, is the presiding genius of the game.[702]

Maple sugar: The American Indians were manufacturing sugar from maple long before the arrival of the Europeans. Tribes of the Iroquois Confederacy had invaded Algonquin land and learned how to make sugar from the sap of the maple tree. Their ancient religious festivals included a maple dance. They developed ingenious implements to be used in the manufacture of maple sugar. One of these was the sap-tub, which was made from a strip of bark about three feet in length by two feet in width. The first European settlers followed the Indian example and used the maple sap to make syrup. French trappers were first introduced to this new delicacy of popcorn and crackerjacks during the 1600s when they were served popcorn over which was poured hot maple syrup. One of these visitors wrote back to France, praising this new food and advocating its introduction to France as "snow food", as he called it. Our modern day term for this is crackerjack.

Medicines: Over 2000 plants from North and South America are utilized to make valuable pharmaceutical medicines to treat a variety of illnesses, from diabetes, cancer, to the common cold. Seventy-five percent of these medicines were derived from plants known to the American Indians. Foxglove was used by the Indians to treat heart problems. Hemlock was one plant used to cure scurvy. With the inner bark, the Indians were able to heal sores and relieve the swelling. The Ojibway Indians pulverized hemlock and swallowed it to prevent diarrhea. The twigs were boiled as a tea by the Penobscot as a cure for the common cold.

Landing of Pilgrims as Indians make maple sugar, Currier & Ives litho, 1840s

Metallurgy: Gold and silver, copper and jade: The Old Copper Culture in the Great Lakes region of North America, developed at least 5000 years ago, is considered by many scientists to have been the oldest mines in use in the world. Long before man used iron, the Great Lakes Indians were making intricate objects out of copper. Pre-Columbian metal workers invented sophisticated techniques for working with other metals. Before Columbus, Indians living in what are now Ecuador and Guatemala learned how to work with platinum, a metal that has the extremely high melting point of 3218 degrees, by developing a technique called sintering. Europeans were unable to work platinum until the 19th century. Metal workers in other parts of the Americas knew how to solder, could make foil, and used rivets to fasten pieces of metal together. The Maya used copper and bronze, sometimes mixed with tin, to make jewelry and other objects. Gold was worked into various objects by many cultures in the Americas over a period of almost three thousand years, from 1500 B.C. to 1500 A.D. The Chavin, Nazca, Sican, Chimú and Inca cultures in Peru, the Canar in Ecuador, the Calima, Tolima, Muisca and Zenu in Colombia, the Cocle in Panama and the Diquis in Costa Rica, all produced gold treasures at different or overlapping dates. Even the Mixtec people in Mexico, although not always included with pre-Columbian artisans, made wonderful ornaments. Gold was a metal that produced great reverence, being referred to as "the sweat of the sun", while silver was "the tears of the moon." In Waywaka in the south-central Andes of Peru, a gold worker's tool kit was found, along with small pieces of gold foil, dating about 1500 B.C. The Moche of Peru, between 200 B.C. and A.D. 600 A.D., invented the process of electroplating, a chemical process for gilding copper and alloys made from silver, copper and gold. The Incas knew how to smelt and cast metals, enabling them to make many different types of instruments such as trumpets and bells out of materials such as brass. Mercury, a metal produced with the contact of cinnabar as a reducing agent, was discovered at a stele architectural site at Copan, Honduras. Significant quantities of copper ax heads and chisels and vast amounts of gold ornaments have also been found. In South America, gold was also utilized for decorating the temples and palaces of many South American structures. Inca goldsmiths lined the walls and edifices of the temples with flattened thin sheets of solid gold. Despite the fact that large nuggets have been found near several of the ancient sites, gold and silver were not valued for monetary purposes until the Europeans arrived in the new world. The gold was valued more for its aesthetic and religious purposes. The Spanish invaders enslaved the American Indians to work in the

Inca funerary mask, 1200 A. D.   Mayan, jade and gold sculpture, Guatemala, 800 B. C.

Inca burial with poured gold , de Bry, 1600s

gold and silver mines and later in tin and lead mines. Most of the gold and silver was melted down into bars or coins and shipped back to Spain. Ultimately, these massive amounts of gold changed the entire feudal system of Europe into a new world economy based on the amount of gold or silver a country acquired. What remains of Pre-Columbian gold, however, is well displayed in museums—most notably at the Museo del Oro in Bogota, Colombia; Museo del Oro at the Banco Central de Costa Rica in San Juan Nacional Museo in San Juan, Costa Rica; Nacional Museo del Banco Central del Ecuador in Quito; Museo de Oro del Peru in Lima; Brooklyn Museum in New York; American Museum of Natural History in New York; Dumbarton Oaks Research Library and Collection, Washington, D.C.; Metropolitan Museum of Art (Jan Mitchell collection), New York; and the British Museum in London. Jade ornaments were highly regarded in the Maya civilization. Examples of these were found at many of the ancient architectural sites. Working only with stone tools, the Maya developed unusual ways of working to make this intractable jade material into a finished product. They manufactured jade beads, earplugs and masks on flat plaques that were sculptured with their god-like figures.[703]

Moccasin: This amazing invention of the American Indians compared favorably with any footwear utilized by any country at that time. As a fashion item it surpassed any footwear and was far superior to the sandals worn by the Romans and Greeks. It was made of one piece of deerskin. In earlier times it was made out of elk. It was seamed up the heel and also in front, above the foot, leaving the bottom of the moccasin as one piece. One style of moccasin extended several inches above the ankle and was fastened with deer strings. The Indians learned how to tan deerskins using the brain of deer, which was mixed with moss and made into a cake substance. It was then hung over a fire to dry, and could then be preserved for years. The deerskin was soaked for a few hours in this boiled brain cake solution with added water and then wrung out and stretched until it becomes dry and pliable. Finally, it was smoked on all sides until all the pores closed, and the skin was thoroughly toughened and the color changed from white to brown.

"Costumes" of the Indians, drawn from originals by Capt. Eastman, 1880s

Names and sign language (Indian to European): European settlers in America did not have words for the many fish, plants, food and animals they found, so many Indian words were adopted into European languages. Words such as cigar, potato, tomato, and hammock come from the Maya, Taino and the Nahuatl languages. The Amazon gave us piranha, condor, and toucan. Quinine, mescal and peyote are also Indian names, as are poncho, moccasin and parka. Trees and plants with Indian names include hickory, pecan, mahogany, mesquite, yucca, maize, squash, avocado, papaya, tapioca and succotash. The toboggan was a Micmac Indian word for the canoe, dory and kayak were other names for watercraft. Many American cities, states and towns carry Indian names. Some of these are Dakota, Ohio, Nebraska, Kansas, Kentucky, Alabama, Iowa, Massachusetts, Wyoming and Minnesota. Indian sign language was devised by the Indians with gestures of the hands as a system of intertribal communication. Origins date to at least the early 1500s.

Pottery: The American Indians perfected this ancient art. Almost all of the Indians made pottery. The Iroquois made various kinds of black pottery vessels and clay pipes. Some were made with clay and pulverized quartz, which gave them a fine texture, polish and firmness, and the appearance of stone. This pottery was often formed in the shape of a human face, a wolf or other animal. In South America, the Incas and the Maya were both noted for their exquisite pottery. All pottery was made by hand in one of three ways: the simplest consisted in modeling or shaping the item from a lump of clay, with the fingers. Larger pots were built by coiling a flat ribbon of plastic clay, spiraling around the item until the desired size was reached. The clay was then smoothed off with a flat, spoon-shaped implement. Smaller pots were made in clay molds. The pottery was engraved or painted with images of men or women, birds, animals or plants.

Hopi clay potter, by Curtis, 1900s

Rubber: Rubber was extracted from the trees in a sap or latex form and used by the Indians in South America for making ponchos or raincoats. The Olmecs, in the Yucatan Peninsula, invented a way to treat raw latex in order to make usable items from rubber as early as 1700 B.C. The American Indians had vulcanized rubber by heating it and mixing it with sulfur to make it strong and pliable long before Charles Goodyear accidentally discovered this same process in a laboratory in 1839.

Mayan jaguar with ball

Surgery: Head surgery through trepanation was practiced thousands of years ago, beginning with the Indians of South America. Flint and obsidian blades were sharpened to make surgical instruments that were so thin that the incisions they made could not be duplicated until the advent of laser surgery. In addition to performing surgery, most American Indian tribes knew how to heal the wounds with the use of plant antiseptics or to apply botanical plants on the wound to promote healing. They made syringes out of bird bones and animal bladders to administer plant medicine. The *Encyclopedia of American Indian Contributions to the World* claimed that, "The operations they performed included plastic surgery, skin grafts, thoracentesis to remove fluid from the chest cavity, and arthrocentesis to remove fluid from the knee. American Indian healers routinely cleansed wounds with boiled water and used botanical antiseptics on them, a practice not routine in Western medicine until the early 1900s. Pre-Columbian Aztec healers, in urban areas, practiced in government-funded hospitals."[704]

Tar and asphalt: Discovered by the American Indians in both the northeast and on the western coasts. It was applied to their baskets and cloth containers to make them waterproof. It was also used for boat caulking by the Indians of southern California. They also made tar-coated tarps, used for protection from the rain.

Trails and modern roads: We have lost sight of the fact that many of our modern roads and the roads built by early European settlers were made on top of the well beaten and well-selected Indian trails. The Europeans exploring this vast continent often resorted to the American Indian forms of transportation, Indian trails, snowshoes and toboggans. The Incas built a road system that included suspension bridges for their runners. The early settlers with their horses, farm animals and wagons traversed the wilderness using Indian trails. In the early years they were the only routes available. An educated chief, Dr. Peter Wilson, who chanced to be present, delivered a speech at the May, 1847 meeting of the New York Historical Society. Dr. Wilson spoke about his people and culture and the removal of the Senecas and Cayugas from their land and into the western wilderness. Regarding the former Indian trails, he stated, "The Empire State as you love to call it... was once laced by our trails from Albany to Buffalo, trails that we had trod for centuries, trails worn so deep by the feet of Iroquois, that they became your roads of travel, as your possessions gradually eat into those of my people. Your roads still traversed those same lines of communication, which bound one part of the long house to the other. Have we, the first holders of this prosperous region, no longer a share in your history? Glad were your fathers to sit down upon the threshold of the long house. Had our forefathers spurned you from it, when the French were thundering at the opposite side to get a passage through and drive you into the sea, whatever might still have been a nation, and I, instead of pleading here for the privilege of living within your borders, I might have had a Country."

Mohawk King Hendrik
(Tiyeeneenhogarow) Wolf Clan
with wampum belt, 1700s

Wampum: Used as currency or for gifts among the northeastern Indian tribes. It was also used for ornamentation, as a tribute from a weaker tribe to a stronger one, to ransom captives, compensate for crimes, as prizes in victory games, as payment and incentives for peace or war, to accompany marriage proposals, bribes, burials, etc. Wampum was a collection of small, white or dark purple/black beads made from shells gathered along the east coast. The dark beads were more valuable than the white. To make the wampum, shells were ground and polished into small cylindrical tubes. They were then fashioned into various finished products and woven into belts, girdles, earrings, headpieces or necklaces. Belt-wampum beads were rectangular cutouts with drilled holes, rolled smooth on sandstone, that were woven into a shell-beaded fabric. They were also used to record agreements, with the purple color predominant if the agreement was considered important, serious or sad. The Hiawatha Belt made from wampum represented the first United Nations agreement, the first time in history anywhere on the globe where independent nations were able to join together under a unified government that allowed individual customs and governments of member nations. This belt memorialized the Haudenosaunee, League of the Pine Tree (center), or Great Peace, of the five original Iroquois Nations. It became six nations after they received the fleeing southern Tuscarora nation into the League. Wampum became a beautiful and sacred medium for remembering an agreement or treaty. The invaders considered it local currency, since the Indian people always seemed to be giving it to each other, and to white people.[705]

War club and tomahawk: The war club was a heavy weapon usually made out of ironwood, about two feet long, with a ball five inches in diameter, and worn on the belt for close combat. The tomahawk succeeded the war club, just as the rifle succeeded the bow as an instrument of war. The tomahawk used by the Indians was fashioned like an axe. Originally made of stone, and later steel, brass, or iron, it had a deep groove cut around the outside, whereby the handle was attached with a thong. This was worn in the girdle, or behind their back. With oval stones replacing the blade, this tomahawk could be turned into a war club.

Iroquois war club

War; Guerrilla warfare: The Indians taught the Colonists the practice of guerrilla warfare. Using hunting techniques such as traps, lures, decoys and calls, they were able to creep up and surprise the enemy. This was called "bush fighting" by General George Washington. These strategies helped defeat the British in the war for independence and the same strategies were used in future wars. Adept at camouflage techniques, the Indians were responsible for Roger's Rangers and the Green Mountain Men who, dressed in their green-colored buckskin, could conceal themselves in the forest. Robert Rogers educated both the British and the Americans in fighting wars against the Indians. During the second World War the Hopi, Navajo, as well as members from other Indian tribes served in the United States army as code-talkers. The entire invasion of Iwo Jima had six code-talkers working around the clock to send and receive more than 800 critical messages. Le Hockey, the communications officer of the fifth Marine division stated, "Without the Navajos the Marines would never have taken Iwo Jima." More than 10 percent of the American Indian population, or one-third of every able-bodied Indian from 18 to 50 years of age, volunteered for the war. In some tribes the percentage reached 70 percent. Several hundred women also served with the Women's Army Corps and the Army Nurse Corps. One of the Flag raisers at Iwo Jima, Ira Hamilton Hayes, was a Pima Indian.

Hopi code talker

CHAPTER 13 INDIAN CREATION, FLOOD AND PROPHESIES : MYTHS AND LEGENDS

Throughout the Americas many tribes shared numerous pre-Columbian myths and legends. Similar Indian tribal myths and legends were also part of the mythology in other cultures of the world. Evidence of a common myth can be found in the "Vengeful Heroes" tale. This myth, from the Amazon and Guiana, is "...widely known from the Mediterranean to Kazakhstan, Mongolia and Tuva...." The "Vengeful Heroes" myth was widely used to describe "deeds of the main deities or epic kings...."[706] Indian tribes shared similar creation, flood and prophesy legends with other worldwide civilizations. One foretold of the return of a white man from the east. The creation stories were not unique to Indian tribes. Similar references have been found in artifacts from ancient Egypt, Sumer (Sumeria), Babylon, Persia, India and Greek civilizations dating back to at least 6000 years, and possibly much earlier.

Legend of Kukulkan: after the flood he travels to Chichen Itza, Yucatan

The first eleven chapters of the Bible recount creation stories of the world that are very similar to ancient Mesopotamian myths. The stories of the great deluge and the creation of mankind are recorded in *Genesis*, the first book of the Bible. "Recent scientific investigations have shown that, at some time near the transition between prehistory, flood waters from the Persian Gulf may have covered the southern sections of the Mesopotamian Valley."[707] The stories of the great flood suggest a worldwide catastrophe brought about by an earth-shattering eruption or by an astronomical collision with earth that changed both our planet's surface and human history. Current archaeological evidence shows that the sea level was much lower 7000 years ago and the great deluge and violent catastrophes might have been the cause of the sinking of large land masses, resulting in the legends of the lost continents of Atlantis and Mu (Lemuria). The feast and dance of the dead has been important in many cultures. It is observed by the Indians of South America and the southwest inhabitants of Asia, Africa, Australia, and by Christians all over the world.[708] Although the stories in *Genesis* trace the gradual expansion of human culture, they also document the fall of man. This same theme can be found in an "ancient cosmological myth of origin in Sumeria… called *The Poem (or Epic) of Creation*."[709]

Ceremony of the dead South America, de Bry, 1624

Feast of the Dead, Isleta Pueblo, by Charles Lummis, 1900

Themes of sacrifice, resurrection and the renewal of life occur in the stories of all the ancient civilizations, including those of the early Indians. An enormous number of these myths and legends have been recorded. We have included several condensed versions to enlighten the reader with the universal connection in all the folk myths passed down from generation to generation.[710]

The Abenaki emergence myth of Kloskurbeh is identified with the Glooskap of Algonquin legends. The Abenaki, or Wabanaki, are an Algonquin people of Maine and New Brunswick. First Manitou, the Great Spirit, made Kloskurbeh, the great teacher. One day, when the sun was directly overhead, a young boy appeared to Kloskurbeh. He explained that he had been born when the sea had churned up a great foam, which was then heated by the sun, congealed, and came alive as a human boy. The next day, again at noon, the teacher and the boy greeted a girl. She explained that she had come from the earth, which had produced a green plant which bore her as fruit. And so Kloskurbeh, the wise teacher, knew that human beings came forth from the union of sea and land. The teacher gave thanks to Manitou and instructed the boy and girl in everything they needed to know. Then Kloskurbeh went north into the forest to meditate. The man and the woman had many, many children. Unfortunately, they had so many children that they were unable to feed them all by hunting and picking wild foods. The mother was filled with grief to see her children hungry, and the father despaired. One day the mother went down to a stream, entering it sadly. As she reached the middle of the stream, her mood changed completely and she was filled with joy. A long green shoot had come out of her body, between her legs. As the mother left the stream, she once again looked unhappy. Later, the father asked her what had happened during the day while he was out trying to gather food. The mother told the whole story. She then instructed the father to kill her and plant her bones in two piles. The father, understandably, was upset by this command and questioned the mother many times about it. Naturally, it was shocking and disturbing to think that he had to kill his wife in order to save his children—but she was insistent. The father immediately went to Kloskurbeh for advice. Kloskurbeh thought the story very strange, but then he prayed to Manitou for guidance. Kloskurbeh then told the father that the mother was right; this was the will of Manitou. So the father killed his wife and buried her bones in two piles as he was commanded to do. For seven moons, the father stood over the piles of bones and wept. Then one morning he noticed that from one pile had sprouted tobacco and, from the other, maize. Kloskurbeh explained to the man that his wife had really never died, but that she would live forever in these two crops. To this day, a mother would rather die than see her children starve, and all children are still fed today by that original mother. Men like to plant in the cornfields extra fish they catch as a gift of thanks to the first mother and a remembrance that we are all children of the union of sea and land.[711]

Ojibway (Chippewa) Algonquin creation myths can be found throughout the Algonquin linguistic area, which extends from the Atlantic coast to the Mississippi River, and from North Carolina in the south to the Subarctic. The great Earth Mother had two sons, Glooskap and Malsum. Glooskap was good, wise and creative; Malsum was evil, selfish and destructive. When their mother died, Glooskap went to work creating plants, animals and humans from her body. Malsum, in contrast, made poisonous plants and snakes. As Glooskap continued to create wonderful things, Malsum grew tired of his good brother and plotted to kill him. In jest, Malsum bragged that he was invincible, although there was one thing that could kill him: the roots of the fern plant. He badgered Glooskap for days to find the good brother's vulnerability. Finally, as Glooskap could tell no lies, he confided that he could be killed only by an owl feather. Knowing this, Malsum made a dart from an owl feather and killed Glooskap. The power of good is so strong, however, that Glooskap rose from the dead, ready to avenge himself. Alive again, Glooskap also knew that Malsum would continue to plot against him. Glooskap realized that he had no choice but to destroy Malsum in order that good would survive and his creatures would continue to live. So he went to a

Alaska Totem, 1920s

stream and attracted his brother by saying that a certain flowering reed could also kill him. Glooskap then pulled a fern plant out by the roots and flung it at Malsum, who fell to the ground dead. Malsum's spirit went underground and became a wicked wolf-spirit that still occasionally torments humans and animals, but fears the light of day.[712]

Arikara creation myth tells of the Great Sky spirit, Nesaru, sometimes called the Great Mystery, who was the master of all creation. Below the sky was an endless body of water where two ducks eternally swam. Nesaru made two brothers, Wolf-man and Lucky-man, who commanded the ducks to swim to the bottom of the great water and bring up some earth. With this earth, Wolf-man made the Great Plains and Lucky-Man made the hills and mountains. The two brothers went down beneath the earth and found two spiders. They explained to the spiders how to reproduce. The two spiders produced many kinds of animals and plants, including human beings. However, they also produced a race of evil giants. These giants were so evil that Nesaru eventually had to destroy them with a great flood. However, Nesaru loved human beings and saved them from destruction.[713]

Aztec myths claims there were five creations. We are presently in the period of the fifth sun. The first was the Sun of the Ocelot. During this stage, the world was shrouded in darkness and humans lived by animal instinct alone, without the benefit of reason. Lacking thought, they were eventually all eaten by ocelots. The second sun was the Sun of Air, a world of spirits and transparent beings that may return some day. But the humans of this time did not understand the proper principles to be redeemed from their sins and the gods changed them all into monkeys. The third was the Sun of Fire. During this period, people were ignorant of the gods. All the rivers dried up and all creatures were killed by roaring flames with the exception of the birds, who flew to safety. The fourth sun was the Sun of Water, when Tlaloc, the rain god, destroyed all the people in a flood. The fifth is our own period. This is the sun where the other four principles, animal energy, air, fire and water are combined and in balance. We cannot take it for granted that this sun will last forever. Our existence is dependent upon following the "ladder of redemption" that is contained in the Aztec calendar and by observing all the rituals. If the gods are again ignored, then this sun will die with all of us.[714]

Blackfeet oral history records the crossing of a frozen body of water which broke open, dividing the people into two large groups, permanently. The ice break is said to have been caused by an old woman, following her grandchild's request to pull up a buffalo horn into the trail. Some believed this was in the middle of a river, breaking up two Indian tribes, while others believe this refers to the frozen Bering Strait, and recalls when Algonquin ancestors supposedly came to North America from Asia. The Gros Ventres, Cheyennes and the

Blackfeet ("Niitsitapi," the Real People) Indian Nation

Arapahos all share with the Blackfeet the Algonquin family of languages. In Blackfeet mythology the important person is called Napi, or Old Man. Napi is represented as the creator here on earth. Some say he is the creator's servant; others tell how Napi and the brother were children of the creators of the first two people, a man and a woman, who had trouble involving an evil magical snake. Napi had magical powers with which he sometimes helped his people and at other times tricked them. Legends claim that the people were first called Blackfeet because of the dark soil they walked through in their northern forest land before moving out into the plains.

Chinook oral creation myth relates that the first men of the tribe came from the sky because they were the offspring of Thunderbird. The Chinook creation story centers in Oregon, on Saddle Mountain. That's where Thunderbird laid its eggs. Thunderbird was part man, part spirit being. An ogress rolled five of Thunderbird's eggs down Saddle Mountain and five men, each of a different color, were born. They found their women growing in various states of development in the valley below. The chief man plucked his wife from a rock. Her arms went through the rock, as if she was hugging it. There is a rock with this feature in the Pacific Northwest. This group formed the first tribe and split up as they kept moving further and further along the Columbia River.

Choctaw leader Peter Pinchlin told George Catlin of their tribal flood myth. Our people have always had a tradition of the deluge, which happened in this way: There was total darkness for a great time over the whole of the earth; the Choctaw doctors or mystery-men looked out for daylight for a long time, until at last they despaired of ever seeing it, and the whole nation was very unhappy. At last a light was discovered in the north and there was great rejoicing—until it was found to be great mountains of water rolling on, which destroyed them all, except a few families who had expected it and built a great raft, on which they were saved.[715]

Cherokee (Tsalagi) prophecy myth was revealed after generations of secrecy. The Tsalagi Cherokees decided, in 1969, to share their teachings and prophecies. Some Cherokees still live according to their old traditions. They became the Kituwa society and are the eastern Cherokee nation of the Etowah presently living in the Carolinas, Tennessee and in parts of Oklahoma. The Cherokee oral traditions relating to their concept of reality have been passed down via the spoken word, through chants, drums and in the Cherokee dances for hundreds and thousands of years. Their world view of life and death was based on the fundamental principles of intention, compassion and doing good, and the inhabitants of the earth were considered as part of one sacred circle. The Indians' sacred teachings were passed down to enable them to become the best human beings they could possibly be. The sacred Cherokee teachings cover a 100,000-year time span. During this time they were told there had been four great upheavals to the earth. The first changed the Earth's rotation and polarity. The second was caused by intense

Cherokee
Courtesy Museum of the
Cherokee Indian

winds and confused thought and action, and it distorted the Earth's mantle. This second change brought about the separation of the male and female from one being into two. The third upheaval, due to volcanic activity, destroyed the Earth's sister planet located between Mars and Jupiter. The fourth change came about when rising water covered Atlantis. Those who listened to the prophecy would survive on high ground. The Cherokee timekeeping claims we are now in the Fifth World and in the ninth and last stage of purification, and we will be entering into the Sixth World, in which all people of the world will be united.[716]

Cherokee ritual dance

Cree flood myth tells of Wisagatcak the Trickster building a dam across a stream in an attempt to capture the Great Beaver as it left its lodge. He waited all day until finally, at dusk, the huge creature swam toward him. The Great Beaver possessed powerful magic and, as Wisagatcak prepared to spear the beaver, it created a spell that caused a muskrat to bite Wisagatcak in the behind, making him miss the target. Though spared, the Great Beaver was angry and wanted revenge. The next morning Wisagatcak was dumfounded. After being bitten he had dismantled his dam, but the water level had not gone down even though the stream was now flowing freely through the spot where the dam had been. Even more strange—the water level continued to rise higher and higher. The Great Beaver had worked powerful magic indeed; the entire world was flooding. For two weeks the Great Beaver and the little beavers kept busy making all the waters of earth rise until not one spot of dry land could be found. In great haste, Wisagatcak built a raft of logs and took many animals aboard with him. The water continued to rise for yet another two weeks. At the end of the two weeks, the muskrat left the raft to search for land, but even the muskrat, who is accustomed to living between earth and water, drowned. Then a raven left the raft. He flew around the entire world, but found no land, only water. Then Wisagatcak made his own magic with the help of a

161

wolf on his raft. During the next two weeks on the raft moss grew all over its surface. The wolf ran around and around on the raft, causing the moss to become magic, expanding earth—until the raft was a vast land mass. However, to this very day, water springs up through holes in the ground through the cracks of the original raft.[717]

Crow Indians share the Pipe, by Howard Terpning
courtesy Morales Art Gallery

A Crow myth passed down to their children predicted the coming of the white man. It relates the story of two brothers that split up in two different directions. Hidatsa, meaning "Nuxbaaga" or "Original People," split from the Mountain Crows and found tobacco. They now trace their origins to Devils Lake in North Dakota. The legend forecasts that the white man would come like an avalanche, and would smother the land and its people. The Crows great chief, Plenty Coups, received a similar vision in 1857.[718]

Iroquois creation myth relates of the first humans that lived up beyond the sky as there was no earth beneath. One day, a great chief's daughter became ill and no cure could be found. A wise old man recommended that they dig up the roots of a certain tree in order to cure her. The people all worked together and dug a great hole around the base of the tree. In time, however, both the chief's daughter and the tree fell through the hole into the world below. Below, there was only a vast sea where two swans continuously swam. When the tree and the girl fell into the water, there was a clap of thunder. The swans heard this and came to see what had happened. They saw that the girl had fallen from the sky and went to save her. As this was very strange to the swans, they went to the Great Turtle, wisest of all creatures, for advice. The Great Turtle told them that the tree and the girl were a good omen. He then commanded all the creatures to find the tree and bring up the magic soil that was attached to its roots. The swans were to take this magic earth and build an island for the girl to live on. All the animals were involved in the search for the tree, but only an old toad was successful in bringing up any of the soil. She swam to the bottom, returned to spit out

Working the fields of the League of the
Haudenosaunee (Iroquois), engraving by de Bry, 1734

a mouthful of the dirt, and then died. The mouthful of earth then turned into a vast land mass. The earth was still dark at this time. The girl told the Great Turtle that there was light in the world above. The Great Turtle showed the burrowing animals how to bore holes in the sky for light to shine through. The girl is the mother of all living things. There are a number of ways she conceived the first humans on earth. One is that she was impregnated when she fell into the sea. Another is that the action of the magic earth with the sea caused her to conceive. In any case, the human race is the result of the union of the land and sea, as well as having origins in the sky above.

Deganawidah was the prophet of the Iroquois (League of the Haudenosaunee), which consisted of five original tribes that formed their United Nations of the Iroquois. Deganawidah was reported to have been born in the mid-1400s in a Huron settlement, on the north shore of Lake Ontario near modern-day Kingston, Ontario, in Canada. The original five Indian tribes that made up the League consisted of Mohawks, Oneidas, Onondagas, Senecas and Cayugas. Ten years after the formation of the union, the Tuscaroras from the Carolinas joined, giving the Six Nations over 50 sachems (chiefs.) Their confederacy was considered sacred and was administered by their chiefs, who were spiritual priests. The purpose of their confederacy was

Iroquois false face mask

peace. In the Iroquois language peace was the same as "noble" or "Lord," or their symbol for Great Spirit (God).

The Iroquois league of tribes originated with a pact from five hostile tribes to achieve peace for all. Disease, intrigue and new weapons brought by the European settlers eventually caused their downfall. Deganawidah prophesied what their future would entail. Three main pairs of principles formed the rules of action of the confederacy . They were: health of body and mind; peace between individuals and tribes; and proper conduct and thought, with justice and respect for human rights. Preparedness for the defense of this league, and the maintenance and strengthening of their spiritual power, was important to the longevity of the confederacy. After finally bringing peace to the tribes, Deganawidah planted a large pine tree with four large, white roots to commemorate the alliance of friendship, prophesying that the roots of the tree would each grow in a different direction, eventually reaching to the far parts of the world to bring together all people and create one United Nation. Hiawatha became Deganawidah's chief disciple in spreading this new religion. It lasted over 300 years, until the white man came

Beaded Iroquois bag

and destroyed the confederacy. Many of the principles in Deganawidah's prophecies were incorporated into the American constitution. Deganawidah prophesied that after his death he would return from the east when he was needed. He vowed that when he reappeared he would not only unite the Six Nations of the Iroquois, but all the peoples of the Earth.[719]

Haida creation myth tells of a raven on the beach who noticed an enormous clam shell. Upon approaching, he saw that it was partially open and that people were peering from within. Raven hopped up and with his slick tongue, coaxed the people to come out and join him in his world. Hesitantly, the people crawled out and became the Haida, the first men on earth. The sun, moon and stars were then created by the raven and the eagle. Both the raven and eagle are the the two main clan crests of the Haida people of the Queen Charlotte Islands. Raven is said to have stolen a ball of light from the chief who kept it hidden. The trickster flew away with his prize, but was

Haida village of Yan, photo by E. Dossetter, 1881

chased by the eagle who caused him to drop it. This ball of light fell and shattered—the larger pieces becoming the sun and moon, and the smaller fragments the stars.

Hopi prophesy from the Great Spirit (Massaw), told the Hopi tribe they were to follow a giant star and build their villages high on cliffs. Massaw gave the Hopi his rules for living a good life, as well as a stone tablet to the Old Spider Woman who, they believed, accompanied the people on their journeys from the third world below. The Old Spider Woman broke the tablet in two and gave one half to the elder white brother who had emerged with them from the earth. The white brother went to the east. The Hopi prophesied he would one day return to unite with them as one. Before that day, white men would come and try to take their land and villages and attempt to lead them away from their spiritual ways into bad ways. They were told to hold on to their ancient spiritual beliefs. The Hopi leaders were told that a light would come from the east as a true white brother. He would wear a red cloak or a red hat and would bring with him the sacred stone tablets now held by the Hopi. They would bring powerful helpers (peoples of the world) with

Hopi Road of Life

them and would shake the earth to purify the world. With that the earth will become new and beautiful again with an abundance of food and animal life. All races will intermarry and all will speak one language. A new religion will come to help all people lead a spiritual life and transform the world.

The Hopi relate the story of a pair of stone tablets in their possession which are at least 10,000—and possibly 50,000—years old. These tablets were part of a series of four pairs passed on to four different races that were each given two of the stone tablets. The Hopi stone tablets are kept on their reservation in Arizona, at the four corners area on the third mesa. The stone tablets held by the black race are located at the foot of Mt. Kenya in Africa, and belong to the Kukuyu tribe. The Tibetans in Tibet keep the stone tablets of the yellow race. If you draw a line straight through the Hopi reservation to the other side of the world, it would be in the same latitude as in Tibet. The Tibetan word for sun is opposite the Hopi word for moon, and the Hopi word for sun is the Tibetan word for moon. In Europe the white race that guards the stone tablets are the Swiss. They celebrate a holiday at certain times of the year when each family brings out a mask with various colors that show a similarity to the Hopi kachinas and African masks.[720]

The Alaskan Inuit are known to have a similar spiritual language to the Hopi, as well as sacred stones similar to the ones held by the Hopi tribe. One of the Hopi prophecies is that there will be a third shaking of the earth. We have already had World Wars I and II. Before this third shaking it was prophesied that the Hopis and all other native people would be invited to enter the World Circle of all races. The Hopi stone tablets recorded the name of this circle: "The People of Pahana." In Hopi, "Ni" means "people of." The Hopi prophesied the return of the people of Pahana, a light-skinned people from the east, or rising sun. They would appear when needed as long lost brothers, and would use their awesome power to rebalance the world. Inuit elders passed down a forecast of the coming of a new prophet whom they would recognize by

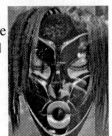

Northwest Indian face mask

his truthful teachings. Their prophet was to appear from the east in 1912 as a white man with a flowing white beard and long flowing hair. On his head he would wear a special kind of hat with a cloth wrapped around (turban). This prophet would not be the original prophet, but his messenger.[721]

Maya creation myth from the *Popol Vuh* tells of the four lords in heaven observing the world below. The yellow lord suggested that they make a man to enjoy the earth and offer praise to the gods. The other three agreed. So the yellow god took a lump of yellow clay and made a man from it. But his creation was weak; it dissolved in water and could not stand upright. The red god then suggested that they make a man out of wood, and the others agreed. So the red god took a branch from a tree and carved it into a human shape. When they tested it in water it floated; it stood upright without any problem whatsoever. However, when they tested it with fire, it burned. The four gods decided to try again. This time the black god suggested making a man out of gold. The gold man was beautiful and shone like the sun. He survived the tests of fire and water, looking better after each test. However, the gold man was cold to the touch; he was unable to speak, feel, move, or worship the gods. But they left him on earth anyway. The fourth god, the colorless lord, decided to make humans out of his own flesh. He cut the fingers off his left hand and they jumped and fell to earth. The four gods could hardly see what the men of flesh looked like, as they were so far away. From the seat of the four lords, they looked like busy little ants. The men of flesh worshipped the gods and made offerings to them. They filled the hearts of the four lords with joy. One day the

Mayan wall mural
Bonampak, Chiapas, Mexico

men of flesh found the man of gold. When they touched him, he was as cold as a stone. When they spoke to him, he was silent. But the kindness of the men of flesh warmed the heart of the man of gold and he came to life, offering praise to the gods for the kindness of the men of flesh. The word of praise from the previously silent creature woke the four gods from their sleep and they looked down on earth in delight. They called the man of gold "rich" and the men of flesh "poor", ordaining that the rich should look after the poor. The rich man will be judged at his death on the basis of how he cared for the poor. From that day onward, no rich man can enter heaven unless he is brought there by a poor man.

Mayan prophecy of the coming of the white men in the book *Chilam Balam*, forecasts the return of their great prophet from the east. In time the Mayans, with their vast knowledge, would again return. Although the Spaniards burned many of the Mayan books in 1562, some were saved, hidden and later transcribed into Spanish by Mayan scribes educated by the Spanish. The book by a Mayan prophet called *Chilam Balam* was written in Mayan hieroglyphics and was one of the survivors of the burning. The book has been called the "Book of the Prophet Jaguar" because *Chilam* means "prophet," and *Balam* means "jaguar."[722]

The Navajo have stories of creation and five worlds similar to the Aztec creation, and relate that the present world is the fifth world. In the first world, there were three beings living in the darkness: First Man, First Woman, and Coyote. The first world was too small and dark for them to live happily, so they climbed into the second world, which contained the sun and the moon. In the east there was blackness; in the west, yellowness; in the south, blueness; and in the north, whiteness. Sometimes the blackness would roll from the east and overshadow the entire world. When the three beings arrived in the second world, the sun tried to make love to First Woman. When she refused, there was discord. Coyote, who understood such things, called the other people of the four directions together. He advised them to climb up into the third world, a wide and peaceful land. Upon their ascent, they found that Coyote had been right; the new land was beautiful.

"Touch the Clouds"
Cheyenne chief, by Rinhardt

They were greeted there by the mountain people, who warned that they would all live in peace as long as they did not disturb the water serpent, Tieholtsodi. Telling Coyote not to do something was a guarantee that he would do it. Coyote's natural curiosity got the better of him and he wandered down to the sea. There he saw the water serpent and Tieholtsodi's children playing. He found them so attractive that he ran off with them under his arms. Tieholtsodi became very angry and searched the world for his children, but to no avail. Then he decided to flood the world and flush out the thief.

The fourth world was even larger than the third. However, it was dim and misty. There was a great river flowing through the fourth world. Human beings lived north of the river and human souls in animal form lived to its south. About this time, humans grew quarrelsome. The men constantly argued with the women about stupid things. Finally, the women decided to overlook what they considered the men's "faults" and the men "forgave" the women for theirs. When they finally did get back together it was a period of peace and happiness—and many, many children were born in that first year together. Their peace was short-lived, however, for Coyote still had the children of Tieholtsodi with him. Tieholtsodi's flooding of the third world had been so complete that the waters rose up into the fourth, making the ground soft. They were given permission for the people of the fourth world to enter the fifth. Having endured two floods because of Coyote's theft of Tieholtsodi's children, the people wanted to avoid the same problem in the fifth world. So they ordered Coyote to give the children back. He did so and Tieholtsodi was pacified.

Upon their entry into the fifth world, the people found themselves on an island in the middle of this vast lake. They prayed to the Darkness Spirit, who cut a ditch to drain away much of the water; this ditch is today the Colorado River. Then they prayed to the four winds to blow, day and night, to dry up the soil on their island until more land was available. The sun and the moon were thrown up into the sky, and for four days the people watched the sun ascend up to its proper place in the sky. However, when the sun reached that spot, it stopped, ceasing to move at all. Everything was in danger of being burned up. A great chief's wife came forward and told the people that she had recently dreamt that the sun would not move unless a human being died. She offered herself. The people wondered sadly where her spirit had gone until, one day, a man looked down a hole and saw the woman inside it, contentedly combing her hair. Since that time, one human being has had to die each day in order to make the sun move.[723]

The Nez Percé call themselves "Nimiipuu" (Nee-Me'-Poo), meaning "the Real People". According to one variation of their tribal legend, the Nez Percé were created from the "Heart of the Monster", whose entire body completely filled the valley of the upper Clearwater River in what is now north central Idaho. When Monster had devoured nearly all the animals in the land, Coyote slew Monster by jumping down its throat and cutting out its heart. Coyote then dismembered the body and flung the pieces to distant parts of the land, where different peoples sprang up. Last of all, Coyote took out the monster's heart and squeezed the blood out of it. These drops of blood from the monster's brave heart mingled with the earth and created the Nimiipuu people (Nez Percé).

Heart of the Monster, Idaho

Pawnee creation myth tells of Tirawa Atius (atius means "lord"), the great eternal god who created all things and supplies the needs of all creatures. He created the Path of the Departing Spirits, known to the white man as the Milky Way. East of the Path is the Male Principle—the Morning Star, and to the west is the Female Principle—the Evening Star. All that has happened and will happen has been ordained by Tirawa, and the stars are his servants. From the east, Morning Star began to pursue Evening Star in order to make love to her, but she continued to elude him. She put hindrances in his path, but continued to beckon him all the while. Why? Because it was not yet time to make living things on the earth, and females always tease and flirt with males, as well as demand tests to prove men's character. The number ten has always had significance for human beings, and this is because Evening Star placed ten obstacles in the way of her suitor. One of the hindrances was in the chaos beneath them. There was an endless sheet of water presided over by the Great Serpent. The Morning Star threw a ball of fire at the serpent, which caused the serpent to flee beneath the waves. As the fire hit the water, enough of the water dried up to reveal earth and rocks. From these materials, Morning Star threw a pebble into the sea of chaos and it became the Earth. When the Earth was in its proper place, Tirawa appointed four lesser gods to administer it. They were East, West, North, and South. They joined hands at the edge of the great sea on earth and a land mass emerged. Eventually, Morning Star caught up with Evening Star and made love with her. Soon Evening Star conceived a little daughter. When she gave birth to the little girl, she placed the child on a cloud and sent her to Earth. High above the Earth, Evening Star asked Morning Star to water her celestial garden and, as a love gift, he made the first rain. In the celestial gardens of Evening Star there grew a great many plants, including Mother Maize, the greatest of food plants. Evening Star gave maize to her daughter as a gift to plant on the newly emerged earth. Soon the Sun and the Moon produced a son, who married the daughter of Evening Star and Morning Star. Daughter-of-Evening-and-Morning-Star and Son-of-Sun-and-Moon are the parents of all living human beings, as well as the first beings to cultivate maize.

The Pawnee forecast the destruction of our world. Tirawa Atius is the lord of all things and it is he alone who determines fate. At the beginning of the world, he set a large bull buffalo in the sky to the far northwest. With the passage of each year, the bull loses one hair; when all these hairs are gone, the world will end. As that hair falls, there will be widespread meteor showers and the sun and moon will become dim. In the beginning, Tirawa Atius appointed the North Star and the South Star to control fate. The North Star once spoke directly to the Pawnee and told them that the South Star moved just a little bit to the north with each passing year. When the South Star catches up with the North Star, then the world will end. The command for the final destruction of the world is in the hands of the four gods of the directions. The West will issue the command that the

Buffalo Bill (but an Indian), Pawnee
by George Catlin, 1830s

world be destroyed and the East will obey. Then the stars in heaven will fall to the new earth and become people. The people left in this world at the time of destruction will fly high into the sky and become stars themselves.[724]

The Shuswap Indian Nation of the Kamloops region of Canada, now called Secwepemc, believe that in the beginning, the world was created by a powerful being known as the "Old One". He traveled the land creating the mountains, lakes, streams, everything. He left, but the task of creating the world was not complete. The Old One sent his helper, in the form of a coyote, to make the world right. Coyote and his powerful animal friends traveled the land and had many adventures. After each encounter the world changed. The Old One and Coyote created a balanced world for the Shuswap people to inhabit. They, in turn, were made responsible for the earth's care and were instructed to respect living things.

The Sioux creation myth relates that they originated beneath the Black Hills and before the creation of man. The Great Spirit's tracks appear on the stones at the Red Pipe in the form of a large bird. The bird used to slay buffaloes and eat them on the ledge of the Red Rocks, on top of the Coteau des Prairies, and their blood running on to the rocks turned them red. One day, when a large snake had crawled into the nest of the bird to eat his eggs, one of the eggs hatched out in a clap of thunder, and the Great Spirit, catching hold of a piece of the pipestone to throw at the snake, molded it into a man. This man's feet grew fast in the

Return of the White Buffalo, born 1994

ground where he stood for many ages, like a great tree, and therefore he grew very old; he was older than a hundred men at the present day. At last when another tree grew up by the side of him, a large snake ate them both off at the roots and they wandered off together—from these have sprung all the people that now inhabit the earth.

A Sioux healing prophesy was fulfilled in 1994 with the birth in Janesville, Wisconsin of Miracle, a white buffalo. "The birth of this white buffalo symbolized the beginning of a time of unity for all people, the joining of all races and colors of the world...." On May 9, 1996 *another* white buffalo, Medicine Wheel, was born on the Pine Ridge reservation in South Dakota. All the nations of the earth were asked to declare June 21, 1996, as the "Day of World Peace and Prayer". These amazing births gave meaning to an ancient Indian prophecy by bringing back recollections of a time when the White Buffalo Woman brought the sacred pipe to the Lakota, Dakota and Nakota nations in the sacred Black Hills. The legend of the white buffalo states, "One summer a long time ago, the seven sacred council fires of the Lakota Sioux came together and camped. The sun was strong and the people were starving for there was no game. Two young men went out to hunt. Along the way, the two men met a beautiful young woman dressed in white who floated as she walked. One man had bad desires for the woman and tried to touch her, but was consumed by a cloud and turned into a pile of bones. The woman spoke to the second young man and said, 'Return to your people and tell them I am coming.' This holy woman brought a wrapped bundle to the people. She unwrapped the bundle, giving to the people a sacred pipe and teaching them how to use it to pray. 'With this holy pipe, you will walk like a living prayer,' she said. The holy woman told the Sioux about the value of the buffalo, the women and the children. 'You are from Mother Earth,' she told the women.

"What you are doing is as great as the warriors do." Before she left, she told the people she would return. As she walked away, she rolled over four times, turning into a white female buffalo calf. It is said that after that day the Lakota honored their pipe, and buffalo were plentiful." Many considered the white buffalo births to be a symbol of hope, rebirth and unity for numerous Great Plains tribes. Unfortunately in March, 2000, Medicine Wheel was ordered to

Secwepemc National Heritage Park Museum

be killed by a police officer after the buffalo strayed from its pasture. He was later found with his throat slit and its hide scarred from being dragged down a gravel road. In September, 2004, Miracle, the remaining white buffalo, died of natural causes.[725]

Sioux prophesy of Black Elk's vision, the last of the Sioux holy men from the Oglala, Sioux tribe. In 1872, when he was nine years old, Black Elk had a great vision. It was not until after his death in 1950 that Black Elk's vision and prophecies were understood. His autobiography, *Black Elk Speaks*, has been translated into a number of languages and is well known throughout the world. Black Elk saw a vision of his people falling onto troubled times, losing spiritual contact with their culture. He foretold that his people would go through a great storm and time of peril, but would regain their strength and culture when they would have a spiritual awakening. His dream symbolized this spiritual awakening with the entrance of a bright red-colored man and a sacred herb. Black Elk foresaw that a star would rise out of the east. "It shall be a relative to them, and who shall see it shall see much more, for from there comes wisdom, and those who do

Esh-Ta-Hum-Leah
A Sioux Chief
McKenney & Hall, 1830s

not see it shall be dark." Black Elk's vision had foretold the coming of a prophet from the east who would bring wisdom and better times to all those who would listen.

In another part of his dream Black Elk looked down from the sky and saw his people blessed with a friendly rain. He then saw a flaming rainbow in the east that signified that we are all part of one rainbow and will eventually unite all the colors of the races, just like the colors of the rainbow, into one planet and one people. Black Elk also dreamed that he was on top of a high mountain, and below him he saw the hoop of the whole world with all the animals and people unified.[726]

Little Bear, Arapaho
by Rinhardt, 1890s

Toltec Indians of southern Mexico, in their prophecy of Quetzalcoatl, foretold that the white man would come to America from the eastern sea "in great canoes with white wings," in the form of a bird, with one foot being of a dove and the other of an eagle. The dove, symbolizing peace and the soul, foretold the coming of Christianity. A South American version represented the foot of the eagle for the way the white men treated the Indians by clawing them, killing them, enslaving and exploiting them. It also foretold that a few hundred years later, after the first coming of the white man, other white men would come with both feet of the dove and would lead the Indians out of the earth of despair and defeat, and into the sky of hope, freedom and triumph. As true brothers, both the Indian and white man would build a better world in which justice, peace and love between men would rule.[727]

Yuma creation legend recalls that in the very beginning there was nothing but water and darkness. The water sloshed around, splashing foam and spray. Some of the spray congealed and formed the sky. Kokomaht, the creator, lived underneath the water and was two beings in one. He rose up out of the water and said his own name, Kokomaht, the Father and creator of all. But out of himself came another being called Bakotahl. When the other being called to Kokomaht out of the water, he asked, "Did you rise up from the water with your eyes open or shut?" Kokomaht knew that this other being was evil, and decided to deceive Bakotahl, answering that his eyes had been open. So Bakotahl emerged from the water with his eyes open and became blind. Evil ones to this very day are still blind: "Bakotahl" means "the blind one." All things made by Kokomaht were good, while all things that Bakotahl produced were evil. The two stood on the waters, as there was no firm land created yet. Kokomaht asked his blind brother, "Where is the north?" But, being blind, Bakotahl pointed toward the south. Then Kokomaht responded, "That is not the north," and then he created the four directions. He faced west and said, "This shall be the west." Then he faced east and said, "This shall be the east," and so on. He took four steps to the south and the south came into being; he took four steps north to create the north.

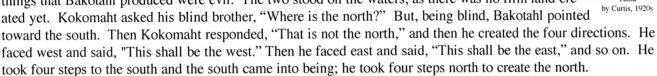

Yuma
by Curtis, 1920s

Then Kokomaht told his blind brother, "I will scatter the waters and make earth." So Kokomaht turned to face the north, creating a whirlwind that blew away enough water to create dry land. And Kokomaht then seated himself on the land. Bakotahl came to join him. Wishing to outdo his good brother, Bakotahl then said that he would make human beings. Feeling around in the wet clay, Bakotahl took clay and water and began to make human beings, but they did not have fingers and toes. When the creatures were finished Bakotahl showed them to Kokomaht, who knew that they were not right. So Kokomaht decided to make humans. Taking clay, he formed a male with complete hands and feet. Kokomaht took the male and swung it four times to the north and then four times to the south, and it came to life. Then he made a female and did the same thing. In the time that Kokomaht was busy making humans, Bakotahl had created seven beings. Kokomaht asked his brother what he was doing. Bakotahl responded that he was making humans, too. Kokomaht told his evil brother to examine the proper humans, perfectly made. Unlike the creatures made by Bakotahl, Kokomaht's humans had fingers that enabled them to make things and create works of art. Bakotahl was jealous and didn't like these perfect humans at all. Kokomaht stamped his feet and Bakotahl's creatures fell into the water and became ducks and geese. This angered Bakotahl, who made a whirlwind that created all the enemies of humankind: disease, bad intentions and plagues. Kokomaht was now alone on the land with only a man and a woman. So Kokomaht went to work creating more people—a male and a female of each race—the Cocopahs, the Mojaves, and the ancestral parents of all other peoples on earth. The last group he created were the white people. Kokomaht taught all these couples how to have intercourse and propagate the race. As the people scattered to their own places on the earth, Kokomaht saw that his work of creation was done. But among the people was the Frog (Hanyi), who rebelled against Kokomaht and

Ne-Sou- A-Quoit
A Fox chief
McKenney & Hall, 1830s

wished to destroy him through her powerful magic. Hanyi burrowed into the ground underneath the feet of Kokomaht and pulled out his breath until his throat became dry and he began to die. As he died, he taught the people the road of death. Kokomaht had made himself a son, Komashtam'ho, who took up the post of the creator. It was Komashtam'ho who made the sun that shines during the day by spitting into his hand, making a ball, and casting it into the sky. He threw it into the east, where the sun still rises. He spat into his hand and cast it into the heavens, where it became the stars. The death of Kokomaht caused the people to despair. Komashtam'ho decided to burn the body of his father, the creator, teaching the people of funeral rites. But there were no trees to burn in the fire. So, with a word, Komashtam'ho called trees out of the north and built a funeral pyre.

Tens- Kawau-Ta- Waw
Shawnee prophet
McKenney & Hall, 1930s

Before his death, Kokomaht had told the Coyote, "Take my heart; be good to all my creatures." But Coyote misunderstood the command. What Kokomaht had meant was, "Be as I was." Coyote thought that this command was to steal and eat the heart of Kokomaht. So the Coyote prowled around the funeral pyre waiting for just the right moment to climb up and eat the creator's heart. Komashtam'ho knew of Coyote's intentions and he dispatched the Coyote to travel to the east as the sun was rising, to fetch fire. Komashtam'ho knew very well that the humans would need fire in order to survive. When Coyote returned with the fire, he again plotted how to steal the heart of Kokomaht. However, the badger jumped up on the funeral pyre and succeeded in stealing the heart. All of the other animals tried to catch the badger, but none succeeded. Komashtam'ho told the Coyote, "You will always be a thief, living by stealing. Men will despise you and kill you to defend their flocks." And all the people heard this. Then Komashtam'ho spoke to all the people as the flames consumed the body

Wovoka and the Ghost Dance

of Kokomaht. He told them, "You will never again see Kokomaht in the flesh; he is dead. All of you will die someday as well. If Kokomaht had been allowed to live, then all of you would be immortal and the world would be overpopulated. But Kokomaht's spirit lives on and so will your spirits." Although the body dies, the spirit lasts forever. Each man's spirit, at death, leaves the body and goes off to live with the spirits of those whom it loved in life. The spirit of Kokomaht lives on to protect all that is good. Bakotahl lives under the earth and turns around, causing earth-quakes. Bakotahl still causes suffering and evil among men. But the good spirit of Kokomaht can overcome any evil.[728]

Wovoka, prophet of the Paiute tribe in Nevada, was born about 1856 and died in 1932. Wovoka brought the Ghost Dance to the Indians in the 1890s. In 1889, as he lay near death, the voice and vision from the Great Spirit told him to "go back to your people, and tell your people the things that you shall hear. You must teach that Jesus is upon the earth; that he moves as in a cloud; that the dead are all alive again; that when their (the Indians') friends die, they must not cry; that they must not hurt anybody, or do harm to anyone; they must not fight; they must do right always; they must not refuse to work for the whites, and to make trouble anymore with them. You must take the dance we will show you back to the earth. It is the dance of goodness. It comes from heaven; it has a purpose; it will make your people free, and it will make them glad." Wovoka's message to his fellow Indians was essentially that they should purify their hearts and do good deeds that would effect changes in their way of life. The Ghost Dance was to be a rallying point for teaching harmony between all men. White men were invited to join in, as some did, but it had a terrifying effect on the white population. It was entirely misunderstood and was finally banished by the whites with the use of force, resulting in loss of lives.[729]

Zuni Pueblo dance, 1880s

Zuni creation legends relate that in the beginning there was only moisture, which became clouds. The Great Father Sun, the creator Awonawilona, thickened the clouds into water that then formed a great sea. With his own flesh, Awonawilona fertilized the sea, and green algae grew over it. The green algae produced the earth and sky. The marriage of earth and sky and the action of the sun on the green algae produced all living things. From the lowest of the four caves of the earth, the seeds of men and animals were incubated as eggs. The creator provided enough warmth that the eggs were hatched and all living creatures were produced.[730]

CHAPTER 14 INDIAN MOVEMENTS TOWARDS SELF-DETERMINATION

"View of The Great Treaty Held At Prairie Du Chien."
September, 1825, with Sioux and other tribes, by James Otto

The nineteenth-century wars, the reservation system and contact with modern society left Indian society in disarray, and its response to poverty and despair has taken its own place in the sad history of the American Indian. Indians are, however, beginning to come to terms with their role in today's society. The problems of their past were put into proper perspective by Vine Deloria, Jr. in his 1970 book, *We Talk You Listen*. "From the late 1880s until 1934, self-government of Indian tribes had ceased, as the federal government exercised complete control over the lives and property of Indian people. Outbreaks in the 1890s, resulting from the Indians' helplessness and effort to retain their own culture and traditions inspired by Indian religious prophets resulted in the Ghost Dance and Wounded Knee massacre. Every effort was made to destroy Indian culture in order to break the hold of the tribe over individual Indians.... Indian children were kidnapped and taken thousands of miles away to government boarding schools. Once there, they were whipped if they used their native languages or made any reference to their former mode of life. All religious ceremonies were banned on Indian reservations. Priceless objects of art were destroyed on the advice of missionaries and bureaucrats because they were thought to be manifestations of the old pagan way of life. It was a time of forced obliteration of native culture and belief. People thought by banning everything Indian they could bring the individual Indians from Stone Age to Electric Age in one generation."[731]

By 1871, the ratification of over 372 treaties between the federal government and the Indians created immense problems. In addition to these agreements between the Indians and the government, there were also about 5000 laws governing Indians rights and religious freedom. The early treaties with the Indians gave them nation status and financial assistance, but not citizenship. These so-called "Treaty Indians" were considered independent landowners who had the right to negotiate the sale or exchange of their land. In fact, the U.S. government promised to protect their lands from white settlers. Soon after the federal government succeeded in removing most of the Indian tribal nations west of the Mississippi, it began to have misgivings about their reservation policy. The aim of the U.S. government began to shift in 1851 when the Commissioner of Indian Affairs declared, in a report to Congress, that the government was planning to integrate the Indians into the mainstream European population. "The great question", said the Commissioner, was "how shall the Indians be civilized?"[732]

In 1854 the new Commissioner of Indian Affairs, George W. Manypenny, negotiated treaties with the tribes in Kansas and Nebraska in order to have land to allocate to white settlers moving there. The treaty between the Oto and Missouri tribes set the stage for future appropriations of Indian land in the west, and led to Indian wars against these regulations. The 1854 treaty gave authority to the United States President and Congress to "...break up and fence one hundred acres of land at their new home; they shall receive from the United States the further sum of twenty thousand dollars.... The President may, from time to time, at his discretion, cause the whole of the land herein reserved or appropriated west of the Big Blue River, to be surveyed into lots, and assign to such Indians or Indians of said Confederate tribes as are willing to avail of the privilege, and will locate on the same as a permanent home.... And the residue of the land hereby received, after all the Indian persons or families of such Confederate tribes shall have had assigned permanent homes, may be sold for their benefit, under such laws, or regulations as may hereafter be prescribed by the Congress or President of the United States.... The

Peace Commission under General Sherman, 1868
Left to right: Red Dog, Little Wound, Red Cloud, American Horse, Red Shirt.
Standing J. Bridgeman

said Confederate tribes agree, that all the necessary roads and highways, and railways, which may be constructed as the country improves... shall have the right of way through their land west of the Big Blue River, shall have a right of way through the reservation, a just compensation being made thereof in money...."[733]

As the white settlers poured into the wide-open territory of Kansas and Nebraska, additional treaties were made with the other tribes. The U.S. government gradually extracted more and more concessions, one of which was the Treaty with Wyandot Indians in 1855, which attempted to give them citizenship and terminate their relationship with the United States government. The responsibility for Indian welfare was to be shifted to the individual states. The Wyandot treaty read, "The Wyandot Indians, having become sufficiently advanced in civilization, and desirous of becoming citizens... are hereby declared to be citizens of the United States... subject to the laws of the United States and the Territory of Kansas in the same manner as other citizens of said Territory."[734] This was followed in 1862 with similar provisions in the treaty with the Ottawa Indians.

Sioux treaty in tent, under General Sherman, 1868

Commissioner Manypenny, while congratulating himself on his work on these treaties, forecast the rapid United States expansion, and predicted the demise of the Indians unless the Indians were protected from further encroachments on their land. In his 1856 annual report to Congress on November 22, he said, "Since the 4th of March, 1853, fifty-two treaties with various Indian tribes have been entered into. These treaties may with few exceptions of a specific character, be separated into three classes: first, treaties of peace and friendship; second, treaties of acquisition, with a view of colonizing the Indians on reservations; and third, treaties of acquisition, and providing for the permanent settlement of the individuals of the tribes, at once or in the future.... The quantity of land acquired by these treaties, either by the extinguishments of the original Indian title, or by the re-acquisition of lands granted to Indian tribes by former treaties, is about one hundred seventy four millions of acres.... The existing laws for the protection of the persons and property of Indians wards of the government are sadly defective. New and stringent statutes are required.... The rage for speculation and the wonderful desire to obtain choice lands, which seems to possess so many... causes them to lose sight and entirely overlook the rights of the aboriginal inhabitants... trespasses and depredations of every conceivable kind have been committed on the Indians. They have been personally maltreated, their property stolen, their timber destroyed, their possessions enrouched upon... The rights and interests of the red man have been completely disregarded, the good conduct and patient submission of the latter contrasts favorably with the disorderly and lawless conduct of many of the white brethren.... That the red man can be transformed in his habits, domesticated, and civilized, and made a useful element in society, there is abundant evidence. With reference to his true character, erroneous opinions very generally prevail. He is, indeed the victim of prejudice.... The wonderful emigration to our newly acquired States and Territories, and its effect upon the wild tribes inhabiting them and the plains and prairies, is well calculated.... Not only are our settlements rapidly advancing westward from the Mississippi River towards the Pacific Ocean, and from the shores of the Pacific eastward towards the Mississippi river, but large

OUR INDIAN WARDS.

"Is not the government srong enough to keep its agreement with us?"— Chief Ouray, Report, George Mannypenny, 1880

settlements have been made in Utah and New Mexico between the two. Already the settlements of Texas are extending to El Paso and spreading Gadsden Purchase... to Puget Sound. Railroads built, and building from the Atlantic and Gulf cities... are extending west across to Louisiana, Arkansas, Missouri and Iowa.... It is impossible to avoid the conclusion that in a few years, in a very few, the railroads of the east... will extend westward up towards the Rocky Mountains, at least as far as good lands can be found, and that roads from the Pacific coast will be built as far east as good lands extend; and that in both cases an active population will keep up with the advance of the railroads—a population that will open farms, erect workshops, and build villages and cities. When that time arrives... where will be the habitation and what [will be] the condition of the rapidly wasting Indian tribes of the plains, the prairies, and of new States and Territories? As sure as these great physical changes are in pending, so sure will these poor denizens of the forest be blotted out

Ouray and chiefs from Utah, 1890s

of existence, and their dust be trampled under the foot of rapidly advancing civilization, unless our great nation shall generously determine that the necessary provision shall at once be made, and appropriate steps be taken to designate suitable tracts or reservations of land...." One year after this report by Manypenny, in 1858, Chief Plenty Coups of the Crow had a vision that forecast the end of the Indian's way of life. He foresaw many of the things that Manypenny mentioned in his report to Congress.[735]

Congress continued with the western displacement of the Indian in favor of the white settlers. Forty-two thousand Indians in the states of Oregon and Washington were moved to reservations. In 1858, Charles E. Mix, a new Commissioner on Indian Affairs, realized the extent of the Indians' predicament resulting from the loss of hunting lands and suggested educating the Indians in the white man's ways so as to support themselves, and limit reservations until these steps were taken. He advocated the use of military force to protect the Indians from the white settlers due to Congress, "extinguishing their [the Indians'] title to large tracts of country, which were needed for the extension of our settlements..."[736] With the discovery of gold in Colorado, the Pikes Peak gold rush brought an endless stream of emigrants following the Oregon trail out west, right through Indian lands. In 1858, large groups of miners and new villages in the area forced Congress to declare it a new territory under the surveillance of a Governor. Congress enacted a Homestead Law in 1862 for the white settlers, allotting them Indian land, and began debating to extend the notion of creating homesteads to the Indians in order to break up the reservations.

In his policy toward the Indians in 1862, the Commissioner on Indian Affairs, William P. Doyle, encouraged President Abraham Lincoln to keep the Indians on their reservations while they became accustomed to the idea of owning property and adapting to the white man's ways. It was expected that when this was achieved the Indians would then be allotted plots of land and would assume full United States citizenship. During and immediately after the Civil War, relations between many of the western tribes and the United States government became hostile. The Santee Sioux rebelled in 1862. They had been tricked in 1851 into signing away all their lands in Minnesota, Iowa and the Dakota area, while being allowed to keep a small twenty-mile wide reservation on the upper Minnesota River. As they watched more than 150,000 settlers move across their land to the west, the Senate passed laws that allowed these settlers to take another half of the Indian land. Under their Chief, Little Crow, they fought back and lost. Little Crow escaped into Canada, only to return later to Minnesota where he was killed by bounty hunters who were paid money for his scalp, initially in the amount "...of twenty-five dollars then, but when the authorities found whose scalp they had, the two hunters received an added five-hundred dollars."[737]

Little Crow

The Apache Wars began in 1862 under General Carleton, and lasted until 1871. On November 29, 1864, at Sand Creek, Colorado, 70 peaceful Arapaho and Cheyenne Indians were massacred while standing under the protection of the American Flag. This happened under Colonel Chivington, a former preacher, with more than 700 Colorado volunteers and 125 regular army troops. A joint committee of Congress started hearings in 1865, and on January 27, 1867, issued a stinging report of the massacre, calling for punishment of those involved. Congress explained the problem, stating that, "With an eager search for gold on fertile tracts of land, the boundaries of Indian reservations are wholly disregarded; conflicts ensue; exterminating wars follow, in which the Indian is, of course, at the last overwhelmed if not destroyed."[738]

As a result of the joint report by Congress and pressure from the public, a bill was passed on July 20, 1867, that provided for a commission of military and civilians as representatives to make peace treaties with the Plains tribal Indians. A report from the Peace Commission on January 7, 1868, reviewed the Indian problem, and condemned the white's treatment of them. They passed resolutions to govern the supply of food and clothing to the Plains Indians, but the commission also recommended that the Indian tribes should be placed on reservations and be prepared to be absorbed into the white civilization. It recommended that the United States government should stop negotiating new treaties with the Indians as independent nations, but should treat Indians as individuals subject to U.S. laws. It was recommended that the Indian Bureau should now be under War Department control. Parts of the report stated, "Now by educating the children of these tribes in the English language, these differences would have disappeared, and civilization would have followed at once. By civilizing one tribe, others would have followed. Indians of different tribes associate with each other on terms of equality; they have not the Bible, but their religion, which we call superstition, [which] teaches them that the Great Spirit made us all. In the difference of language today lies two-thirds of our trouble."[739]

Following the Peace Report, General Grant was elected as president and was persuaded by the Quakers, missionaries and other unpaid philanthropists to begin a "peace policy" with the Indians. In 1869 Grant appointed his former aide, Brigadier General Ely S. Parker, a Seneca, to become the first Indian to head the Indian Bureau under the War Department. Unfortunately, Grant's "peace policy" consisted of dividing up the Indian reservations among various religious denominations, with the missionaries appointed as agents for the Indians under their control. Putting the missionaries in control of their ceremonies and religion, as well as of the education of the Indian children, effectively completed the devastation of the Indian way of life. Parker himself did not trust the missionary's control and believed that he would be able to eliminate the corruption in the Indian Bureau. Unfortunately, he was caught up in the politics of Washington and instead, "...was blamed to the extent of being tried by the House in 1871. He was acquitted of any wrongdoing, but resigned six months later."[740] The problems related to the treaties negotiated between the United States government and the Indians ultimately resulted in a cover-up and a charade of inequality, with the United States enforcing unequal treaties with the Indians for many years. The

Modoc War Peace Commission, 1870s
Treaty with Modoc's never ratified by Congress

United States government promised the Indian Nations their independence; instead, the government treated the Indians as subservient tribes by attempting to change their culture and taking possession of their land. In his last annual report as Commissioner of Indian Affairs, dated December 23, 1869, Ely Parker, who was well aware of this problem, stated, "The Indian tribes of the United States are not sovereign nations capable of making treaties, as none of them have an organized government of such inherent strength as would secure a faithful obedience of its people in the observance of compacts of this character. They are held to be wards of the government, and the only title the law concedes to them to the lands they occupy or claim is a mere possessory one. But, because treaties have been made with them, generally for the extinguishments of their supposed absolute title to land inhabited by them, or over which they roam, they have been falsely impressed with the notion of national independence. It is time that this idea should be dispelled, and the government ceases the cruel farce of thus dealing with its helpless and ignorant wards. Many good men, looking at this matter only from a Christian point of view, will perhaps say that the poor Indian has been greatly wronged and ill treated; that this whole country was once his, of which he has been despoiled, and that he has been driven from place to place until he has hardly left to him a spot where to lay his head...."[741]

Eli S. Parker

General Grant and Brigader General Eli Parker, Civil War

The Congressional Act of March 3, 1871, ended all future treaty making with the Indians. A rider to an appropriation bill covering expenses to the Yankton Sioux tribe read, "No Indian nation or tribe within the territory of the United States shall be acknowledged or recognized as an independent nation, tribe, or power with whom the United States may contract by treaty; but no obligation of any treaty made and ratified with any such Indian nation or tribe prior to March third, eighteen hundred and seventy one, shall be hereby invalidated or impaired."[742]

In 1875 it was recommended that "legislation be sought in Congress looking towards the divorcement of the United States and Indians as citizens of a domestic sovereignty within our borders, and the transfer of the Indians and their property to the states where they reside, as rapidly as the states and the Indians are prepared therefore."[743] The states of New York, North Carolina, Michigan, Wisconsin and Minnesota followed suit and proposed similar legislation. There was a drive in Congress to pass an allotment bill from 1879 on, and there was also pressure from humanitarians to defeat the bill. Organizations sprang up with the aim of defending the Indians. Among them were the Indian Rights Association, the Indian Citizenship Committee, and Friends of the Indians. Among those standing for Indian rights was Helen Hunt Jackson, a woman who understood what the Indians faced on their removal from their ancestral lands, and consistently voiced her opinion against the allotment bill. In 1881 she was the author of *A Century of Dishonor*, a stinging indictment of the United States' Indian policy and the atrocities, broken treaties and the government's scandalous behavior to the Indians.[744]

Helen Hunt Jackson

The "Dawes Act" or "Allotment Act" was finally pushed through Congress on December 16, 1886, and Grover Cleveland signed the bill into law on February 8, 1887. The purpose of this act was to push the Indians into accepting United States citizenship at the expense of their land and tribal culture. The head of each family was allotted 160 acres. All other individual Indians over the age of 18 were to receive 80 acres of land. United States citizenship was contingent on their accepting this offer. The President of the United States was authorized to divide the Indian reservation into individual pieces and assign a parcel to each man woman and child, at his discretion. The remaining "surplus" lands would then be offered to the homesteaders for $2.50 per acre. A key provision requesting tribal consent was dropped from the bill. Tribes exempt from this act were the Five Civilized Tribes along with the Osages, Miamis, Peorias, Sauks and Foxes, the Seneca Indians in New York and Indians residing on a strip of Sioux land in Nebraska. An amendment to the Act, added on February 28, 1891, was in later years to prove even more disastrous to the Indians. It stated that, "Lands not needed for farming or agricultural purposes, and are not desired for individual allotments, the same may be leased by authority of the Council speaking for such Indians, for a period not to exceed five years for grazing purposes, or ten years for mining purposes...." This devastating act removed about "...ninety million acres, or almost two-thirds of their land base between the years 1887 and 1890. Without cost to itself, the federal government thus trans-

Senator Henry Dawes

Indian land for sale, 1900s

ferred land to white ownership, even requiring the tribes to pay the costs of surveying and allotting. In every case where allotment was carried out, the Indian tribe objected; and in most cases the lands were covered by treaties in which the United States government obligated itself to protect the tribe in its right of possession...."[745] The Dawes Act unleashed another series of acts to deprive the Indian tribes of their language, marriage rights and cultural heritage. An act passed on August 9, 1888, regulated the marriages between white men and Indian women and their rights to land. White men were prohibited from marrying Indian women. If a white man did marry an Indian woman, he would not be entitled to any of her property. The Indian woman marrying a white man had to accept the land allotment, which automatically made her into a United States citizen. The Five Civilized Indian Tribes were exempt from this act. The act of June 28, 1898, effectively destroyed and did away with all tribal governments in Indian Territory and declared Indian laws unenforceable in federal courts. This completed what the Dawes Commission could not arrange through negotiation. In addition to legalizing the leasing of the "excess" land of the Indian, the act allowed companies to access their mineral rights. On March 3, 1901, the Five Civilized Tribes and other small Indian tribes were granted United States Citizenship.[746]

Dawes agreement with five tribes (Cherokee, Chickasaw, Choctaw, Creek and Seminole)

Laws were enacted in 1875, telling the Indians that education "must be regarded as a fundamental and indispensable factor... in justice for the rich lands taken from the Indians... and it was the true policy in dealing with the Indian race, as with every other... [that] elevating them to the social and moral conditions of civilization, consists not so much in feeding or governing the adults as in educating the children." "The Friends of the Indians" was a society formed in 1883 by the Protestant and Catholic churches. Its mission was to fund boarding schools to reeducate Indian children. In 1885 the Federal Superintendent of Indian Schools announced that for an Indian to be considered "a member of a new social order", he must be re-educated. "To do this," he asserted, "we must re-create him, make him a new personality."[747] The best known of these schools was the Carlisle, Pennsylvania, Indian Industrial School, founded in 1879 by Captain and later General Richard H. Pratt. "Pratt hoped to destroy the 'Indian' in the 'race' in favor of the 'man', as he was so fond of saying."[748] Pratt's thinking was that the "Indians remain Indians because they are walled in on reservations and compelled by every force we can apply, even to the hedging about with guns, pistols and swords to remain Indians." Other Western countries followed the United States' example of forcibly removing children from their parents for reeducation. In Australia it was known as the "Stolen Generations."[749]

Captain Pratt with new Carlisle students, 1880s

On September 27, 1887, the Commissioner of Indian Affairs required all instructions in missionary or Indian schools to be only in English. Day schools for Indian children were found to be ineffective. A substitute boarding school was devised to remove the children far from their homes and reservations. Following the Carlisle school model, at least twenty-four day schools and more than eighty boarding schools were opened for Indian children. Once in these schools, the Indian children were subjected to many indignities, all intended to remove every trace of Indian culture. The children were deloused with DDT and had their names changed to American-sounding names upon arrival. They were forbidden to speak their native languages under threat of having their mouths washed with lye soap. They were subjected to religious indoctrination and all kinds of other abuse. Many of the children were taken from their families at the age of six and remained in the schools until age seventeen. The Carlisle School remained in operation until the end of the 1917-18 school year.

"Educating the Indians", 1884 Returning to Pine Ridge reservation from Carlisle

Thomas J. Morgan, Indian Bureau Commissioner from 1889 to 1893, made attendance in these schools compulsory for all Indian children aged five to eighteen. Rations and annuities, or even prison, would be used to coerce the Indian parents if they did not give up their children to the schools. Many parents secretly hid their children. The United Nations in their "Convention on Punishment and Prevention of the Crime of Genocide" in 1948 stipulated that forcibly removing children from their families was a crime against humanity. The Sioux filed a class action lawsuit in April, 2003, in the U.S. Court of Federal Claims for $25 billion on behalf of thousands of students abused at Indian boarding schools around the country. They accused the federal government of failing to live up to treaties dating to the 1800s that said the government would protect them from "bad men among the whites."[750]

Carlos Montezuma, 1890

Carlos Montezuma, physician and reformer from Yavapai parents, served as a medical officer at the Carlisle School in the 1890s. He realized that the incompetence of the staff and the prevailing paternalistic attitude towards the Indians were doing more harm than good. He called for the abolition of the Bureau of Indian Affairs, arguing that the Indians should have the right to determine their own talents, abilities, and be free to develop independently.

Left, Apaches arriving at Carlisle school. Right, five years later.

Montezuma founded the Society of American Indian Friends to help the Indian achieve self-determination. In 1914 he wrote an article entitled *What Indians Must Do*, in which he said, "We must free ourselves. Our peoples' heritage is freedom. Freedom reigned in their whole makeup. They harmonized with nature and lived accordingly. Preaching freedom to our people on reservations does not make them free any more than you can, by preaching, free those prisoners who are in the penitentiary. Reservations are prisons where our people are kept to live and die, where equal possibilities, equal education and equal responsibilities are unknown.... We must do away with the Indian Bureau.... On the reservation our people did not act without the consent of the Superintendents, and *they did not dare to think*, for that would be rival to the Superintendent."[751]

Arthur C. Parker

Arthur C. Parker, a member of the Seneca Tribe and editor of the *Society of American Indians' Quarterly Journal*, disagreed with Montezuma's stand that the Bureau of Indian Affairs should be abolished, but nevertheless, in 1915, he published an extensive article that criticized the failed government's policies. Parker wrote that his people have been robbed of intellectual life, social freedom, economic independence, moral standards, their good name, and a definite civic status. The government gave the Indians reserved tracts of his land, superintendents as guardians, schools with mechanical equipment, and access to clerks who handled their money, food and clothing, a new civilization and a great religion. Parker did not hesitate to emphasize that the cost was high: "As a price (the government) has denied the Indians a voice in their own affairs, any responsibility, the right to compete, [has] defined his own status in his country, his right to submit claims against the United States without special permission, a true and adequate education and the 'right to be a man', as other men in America. This has usurped his responsibility, demeaned his manhood, destroyed his ideals, broken his faith, humiliated his spirit, and created a nation without a country, and we have refused to listen to his petitions." Parker proposed an American Indian Day. The Congress of the American Indian Association issued a proclamation on Sept. 28, 1915, which declared the second Saturday of each May as an American Indian Day and contained the first formal appeal for recognition of Indians as citizens.[752]

The Dawes Act of 1887 resulted in putting the Indians' surplus land on to the open market to be snapped up by land-hungry whites as well as missionaries for their churches and cemeteries. The acreage given to the Indians in numerous cases—due to its poor use for farming—was sold or leased to whites for industry at a small price. This left the tribes psychologically and spiritually drained. Unemployment and poverty soared. Most important to the Indians was their loss of religious freedom.

Indian Land for Sale poster, 1900s

On October 15, 1917, the new Indian Commissioner, Cato Sells, in his annual report, declared another new Indian policy to free the Indians from government guardianship and force them into white society. This policy, also called the "Forced Patent", lasted until 1921 and was based on discontinuing any special privileges to competent Indians and supposedly to give closer attention to the less competent Indians. Cato Sells allowed for easier sale of Indian land, gave the competent Indians partial control of their own monies, and eliminated ineligible pupils from government schools, etc. The purpose of the act was explained. "It means, in short, the beginning of the end of the Indian problem..."[753] The commissioners of Indian Affairs, from 1917 up to the early 1940s, followed this path in attempting to transfer the responsibility to the states. Hearings were also held in Congress to transfer the appropriations to the individual states.[754]

The "Meriam Report" (Meriam Survey), taken in 1928 by Lewis Meriam for the Institute of Government Research, severely criticized the government's handling of the Indians and the allotment policy. A monumental work titled *The Problem of Indian Administration* became the basis for dealing with the Indians for the next twenty years. It reported that there were 340,541 Indians in the United States. They were scattered among 193 tribes in 200 Indian communities and reservations. The government operated 217 different schools, 132 of which were day schools. The survey found that services to Indians were inadequate, and that conditions and

Committee of 100 on Indian Affairs presents proposal for Indian citizenship to President Grover Cleveland, December 13, 1923

174

equipment were below standards, with employees being subjected to low pay and poor living conditions. The fundamental change in the way this report dealt with the Indian problem was in its assertion that a policy of self-determination would be established in the future. The report stated, "These Indians are as much entitled to direct their lives according to their desires as are the conservative Indians. It would be as unjust and as unwise to attempt to force them back to the old, or to withhold guidance in the achievement of the new ends they seek, as it would be to attempt to force the ones who love the old into the new. The position taken, therefore, is that the work with and for the Indians must give consideration to the desires of the individual Indians."[755]

During the 1920s, John Collier, executive secretary and spokesman for the American Indian Defense Association, emerged as a forceful spokesman for Indian rights and self-determination. Collier was impressed with the Pueblo community's spirituality and harmony with their environment. He felt that the non-Indian world could learn much from the Indians way of life. Collier was shocked to see the actions of the Indian Bureau against the Pueblo Indians. They first defamed their religious ceremonies as pornographic and then, as Collier wrote, "Commissioner Charles H. Burke visited Taos Pueblo and notified the old men in council that because they were non-Christians with their own religious rituals, they were half animals." The Bureau forbade the withdrawal of Pueblo boys from school for their initiation ceremonies. The Pueblo announced that they were ready for jail or any other penalty, saying that the initiation ceremonies would go forward. Then the whole governing body of Taos Pueblo was thrown into jail for violating the Bureau's religious crimes code."[756] Next, followed New Mexico's Senator Holm O. Bursum's bill of June 7, 1922, which declared a dominant advantage to the whites in title land disputes over the Pueblo Indians from grants going back to Spanish and Mexican occupation.

John Collier and Hopi friends

A new era for the Indians began when President Franklin D. Roosevelt announced the New Deal. In March, 1933, Roosevelt chose Harold L. Ickes as the new Secretary of the Interior and appointed John Collier as Commissioner of Indian Affairs.[757] To put into motion changes in our past dealings with the Indians, and to give them renewed status, responsibility and power, Congress passed the Wheeler-Howard Indian Reorganization Act in 1934. This Act, although way too late, reversed the policy of allotment, encouraged tribal organizations and allowed religious freedom. No longer would Indians be placed in prisons for practicing their ancient religious ceremonies. This act began a revival in Indian ceremonies that continues today. During the early 1940s, numerous commission hearings were held to end the Indians' protection under the Federal government and make them self-sufficient so as to assimilate into the United States social and economic life.[758]

By 1943 the political attitude of Congress changed once again, and they challenged Collier's method of dealing with the Indians, saying, "Instead of the original aim of the federal government to make the Indian into a citizen... the aim appears to keep the Indian an Indian... [to] attempt to help him recapture his ancient worn out cultures... which are but a vague memory... and [are] unable to function in his present world." In 1944 and 1945 Congress reduced the Bureau Of Indian Affairs (BIA) to a skeleton size.[759]

President Franklin Roosevelt with Indians

In 1950 Congress decided to terminate the special status of the Indians. This was followed by enactments in Congress from 1954 to 1959, ending federal government obligations to a number of Indian tribes. The Federal government passed along that responsibility to the states in which the Indian tribes lived, but a large number of tribes opposed termination and refused to enter into any programs that would make them self-sufficient. This forced the federal government to rethink their policy of termination. Secretary of the Interior Morris Udall advanced his plan for economic development and involvement during the 1960s by urging the federal government to help the Indians.[760] Presidents Nixon, Kennedy and Johnson all reaffirmed the reversal of the termination policy, recommending the reversal of state attitudes, and for the United States government to be directly involved with the Indian tribes.

In 1961 the Kennedy administration encouraged Indians to organize a united Indian voice in order to press their grievances. Four hundred Indians from sixty-seven tribes convened at the American Indian Chicago Conference held at the University of Chicago in mid June, 1961. They came up with a "Declaration of Indian Purpose." They stated that their common Indian beliefs to retain their spiritual and cultural values recognized today's complex society, and "a cultural climate will be created in which the Indian people will grow and develop as members of a free society." They stressed "Resource and Development", and programs on the reservations to provide employment and economic benefits to the Indians. Monies would be available from lands or assets held in trust by the federal government. Employment with "preference to Indians in BIA employment", given to Indian graduates of business schools, resulting in jobs on the reservations. Regarding treaty rights, they desired that all the "trust protected lands remain intact and beyond the reach of predatory men." The Indian was not looking for special treatment. Their only wish was for the United States government to honor it's past treaty obligations. "A treaty in the minds of our people is an eternal word." They concluded their Declaration by remembering that, "In the beginning the people of the New World, called Indians by accident of geography, were possessed of a continent and a way of life.... In region after region, Indian groups found their means of existence either totally destroyed or materially modified. Newly introduced diseases swept away or reduced regional populations. These changes were followed by major shifts in the internal life of tribe and family. The time came when the Indian people were no longer the masters of their situation. Their life ways survived subject to the will of a dominant sovereign power." The conference recognized that money alone would not solve their problems. They concluded that the land was taken from them with "...the loss of some millions of acres in real estate. They [meaning the Indians] have in mind that the land supported a universe of things they knew, valued and loved... what we ask of America are not charity, not paternalism, even when benevolent. We ask only that the nature of our situation be recognized and made the basis of policy and action. In short, the Indians asked for assistance, technical and financial, for the time needed, however long that may be, to regain in the America of the Space Age some measure of the adjustment they enjoyed as the original possessors of their native land."[761] In 1968, during his campaign speeches and in his message to Congress, President Nixon said that he disavowed the policy of termination, advocating instead "self-determination without termination." He also stated that, "We must recognize that American society can allow many different cultures to flourish in harmony and we must provide an opportunity for those Indians wishing to do so to lead a useful and prosperous life in an Indian environment."[762]

National Indian Congress dinner,
Davenport Hotel
Spokane, Washington, 1926

In 1969 the Senate Committee On Labor and Public Welfare formed a special subcommittee to investigate Indian education. It was initially headed by Senator Robert F. Kennedy, and later, after his death, by Senator Edward Kennedy. The subcommittee declared that the American policies on Indian education had been a failure. The committee traveled all over the United States visiting all types of Indian schools and homes and published a report listing sixty recommendations for improvement. In one section of the report, the committee declared, "We are shocked at what we discovered.... We have developed page after page of statistics. These cold figures mark a stain on our national conscience, a stain which has spread slowly for hundreds of years;... children who want to learn but are not taught; of adults who try to read but have no one to teach them; of families who want to stay together but are forced apart; or of nine year-old children who want neighborhood schools but are sent thousands of miles away to remote and alien boarding schools. . . . We have concluded that our national policies for educating Indians are a failure of major proportions. They have not offered Indian children—either in years past or today—an educational opportunity anywhere near equal to that offered to the great bulk of American citizens... what concerned us most deeply, as we carried out our mandate, was the low quality of virtually every aspect of the schooling available to Indian children. The school buildings themselves; the cost of materials and books; the attitude of teachers and administrative personnel; the accessibility of school buildings—all these are of shocking quality."[763]

AIM occupies Office of Economic
Development in Denver,
December, 1971.

The efforts of the United States government to make changes were doomed to failure by its historical lack of respect for the Indians. The Indians had been forced to give up their culture and their land, and began to form political organizations in an effort to strive for self-determination. A split developed between the older leaders and the younger, better-educated Indians as to ideology and the likelihood of making progress with an apathetic United States government. These more sophisticated, militant Indians opted for rapid changes, while the more traditional Indians preferred a more gradual approach. The National Congress of American Indians (NCAI) organization, founded in 1944, began to assert more power and in 1966 they rose up against another federal government plan of termination, drawing up their own plan of self-determination.[764] In 1960, college-educated students organized the National Indian Youth Council (NIYC). The youth were alienated from American society and alienated themselves from their own leaders on the reservations, whom they called "Uncle Tomahawks." They defied the organizations and tribal leaders set up under the Indian Reorganization Act (IRA), including the moderate National Congress of American Indians (NCAI). They were also against the federal government's Bureau of Indian Affairs (BIA) offices, which were located on the reservations, and which they called

Garry & Kathy Rowland
AIM Members - 2004
From Wounded Knee, S. D.

"Colonial Offices." The new movements issued a rallying cry of "Red Power", echoing that of the Black Panther movement in an attempt to change and redefine the priorities of their tribal chiefs. The NCAI 43rd Convention in October, 1986, took up the issue of blood quotas. The NCAI claimed the prerogative of determining that question lay with the Indian reservations, not the federal government. The National Congress of American Indians, aware of outrages against the Indians of South America, raised their voices of concern.

Militant Indian organizations formed during the 1960s—the most well known of which was the American Indian Movement (AIM). To bring attention to the United States government and their own tribal leaders, the Indian activist groups staged coastal "sit-ins" in the Pacific Northwest, an occupation of Alcatraz Island, along with the takeover of the BIA building in Washington, D.C. The leading militant American Indian Movement (AIM) fought pitched battles against the federal government on the Pine Ridge Lakota Indian reservation. From 1973 to 1976 approximately 60 AIM members, including twenty-one women and two children, were killed during battles at the Pine Ridge reservation in South Dakota. Many others were sent to federal prison. One of the lead-ers of AIM, Leonard Peltier, was still incarcerated as of this writing (in 2005) for allegedly killing an FBI agent. The American Indian Movement named this battle against the United States govern-ment as the "second battle of Wounded Knee."[765]

AIM occupies Alcatraz, 1969

With the end of armed violence on the reservations, the individual tribal chiefs were given the chance to assert their power, adapt and make changes. They banded together with other tribal chiefs at intertribal gatherings to gain additional bargaining power with the United States govern-ment and to combat the Inter-tribal rivalries that emerged in the overall Indian leadership.

In 1975 the U.S. federal government again recognized and began acting upon past abuses toward the Indians. The federal government passed a number of acts, all for the benefit of improving the conditions of the Indian and encouraging them to manage their own affairs and to determine their own destiny. This was a step in the right direction. However, the Indians were still under the control of either the Bureau of Indian Affairs or some other government-established trust that set the guidelines and controlled the monies awarded as a result of negotiations. A long-term dispute by the 14 tribes and bands that now make up the Confederated Tribes in the entire upper Columbia Basin in the Pacific Northwest sued the United States government for mining rights that went back to the first gold strikes in the 1850s, when their land was confiscated. The United States Supreme Court in 1975 affirmed their hunting and fishing rights. The Forest Service was supposed to protect the tribe's rights, but tribal attorney Steve Suagee, attorney for the Confederated Tribes, claimed the Forest Service managers have "acted more like a trustee for the mining company rather than the tribes. That needs to be reversed."[766]

On January 4, 1975, Congress passed the "Indian Self-Determination and Education Assistance Act." It allowed Indian participation in the education of their children and established a program to provide for the tribes to control their own educational programs in the schools. In addition to the "American Indian Religious Freedom Act" by Congress on October 2, 1978, the Bureau of Indian Affairs issued procedures for their new program of "Federal Acknowledgement of Indian Tribes." This recognized previously unac-knowledged groups of tribal members, as well as the already-recognized federal tribes. This allowed these groups to petition the federal government to be eligible for services and bene-fits. The Bureau acknowledged that "the tribe is entitled to the immunities and privileges available to other federally acknowledged Indian tribes...."[767]

Tesqueta Pueblo government house, 1920s

October 17, 1978, Congress passed an act that would assist tribally controlled community col-leges. On November 1, 1978, an "Education Amendments Act" was approved by Congress to set standards for the basic education of Indian children in Bureau of Indian Affairs schools. It provided for maintenance and repairs of the schools, qualified Indian teachers, etc.[768] In the same year, on November 8, 1978, Congress passed the Indian Child Welfare Act, accepting responsibility for the breakup of Indian families and acknowledging the importance of placing Indian children in an Indian environment.[769] On October 31, 1979, the Archaeological Resources Protection Act was passed. It stated that consent from Indian tribes and permits for any archaeological digs were required, in order to ensure the protection of their cultural heritage on Indian lands.[770]

In 1984, under the Reagan administration, the Bureau of Indian Affairs issued a "Statement of Policy." It stated: "The principal objectives of the Bureau of Indian Affairs are to actively encourage Indian and Alaska Native people to manage their own affairs through the contracting of programs and other means under a trust relationship with the federal government.... In discharging its duties, the

1925 Indian School, now a Secwepemc (Shuswap) tribal school Kamloops, Canada

Bureau does not attempt to manage the affairs of the four-hundred-eighty-eight federally recognized tribes served by the organization. The era of paternalism is dead. Instead, a viable policy of Indian self-determination, emphasized by President Reagan's January 24, 1983 Indian Policy statement, keys the direction of the Bureau.... While the Bureau of Indian Affairs supports tribal efforts to reach self-determination and control of their own affairs, it also has a solemn obligation to meet the dictates of the trust responsibility. And when self-determination and the trust face off in a head-to-head confrontation, as they sometimes do, the trust obligation under law takes precedence...." A follow-up to the Indian Self Determination and Education Assistance Act of 1975 resulted in the April 28, 1988 Tribally Controlled Schools Act. This provided for outright grants to the tribes for their schools for maintenance expenditures, school operations, guidance, counseling, etc. These grants were to be deposited into the funds of tribally-controlled schools. Congress recognized the unique educational needs of the Indians. Important in their Declaration of Policy was that it repudiated termination. "The Congress hereby repudiates and rejects House Concurrent Resolution 108 of the 83rd Congress and any policy of unilateral termination of federal relations with any Indian Nation." Although at present the United States government, Canada and most governments of Central and South America have recognized the Indians' right to self determination and their inherent right to coexist with other minorities, greed for gold and other material needs have not stopped the taking of Indians land.[771]

Indian Congress parade, 1920s

In Brazil, for some time a genocidal war had been waged against the Indians to take over their lands. Following the holocaust of the second World War, the United Nations set up a genocide convention. On December 11, 1946, a resolution was adopted defining genocide as "a denial of the right of existence of entire groups of human beings, as homicide is the denial of the right to live of individual human beings." The United Nations recognized the growing Indian population with a 1993 declaration as the "International Year of Indigenous People." Steve Newcomb of the Indigenous Law Institute assists Indian and other indigenous communities, while contending that "Indian nations and peoples have an inherent right to live free of all forms of empire and domination." A 1998 paper prepared by Newcomb for the United Nations Human Rights Commission Inter-Sessional Working Group, stated, in part, that, "The current draft of the Declaration was developed in a cooperative dialogue between states and indigenous peoples over thirteen years in the United Nations. It is the result of testimony and interventions by indigenous representatives from around the world regarding the oppression and hardships that their nations and peoples are subjected to by states and by corporations...."[772]

There are numerous lawsuits, launched on behalf of the Indian tribes, that are pending against the federal government and the states, as well as against timber, mining and land companies. Much of the approximately ten million acres of individually-owned land currently held in trust by the United States government was either leased or taken from the Indians as a result of treaties or agreements. A large portion of this land was leased to non-Indians and the Indian complaint is that the average purchase price of about half the land was less than a dollar an acre. A further third of a billion acres, mainly in the west, was confiscated without compensation. Indian tribes, due to the United States government extinguishing their titles to this land, claimed another two-thirds of a billion acres. Thirty five percent of the land in the United States is owned by the individual Indian nations. This land is leased to lumber, uranium and other mining interests. There are a large number of lawsuits against the United States government involving water, land and mineral rights that the American Indians have been deprived of. Payments for this land use to the Indian tribes have been negligible.[773]

Salmon factory, 1920s

The Indians lost much of their access to water and, along with this, their fishing rights, when dams were built and water was diverted to irrigate land owned by white farmers, and to supply houses owned by non-Indians. The United States government granted perpetual fishing rights in the 1850s to Indians in the Pacific Northwest and other areas. After fifteen years of abuse and harassment, followed by "fish-ins" and lawsuits, the Indians' case finally reached the United States Supreme Court in 1969. On July 8, 1969, the Boldt decision marked a sweeping tribal rights victory when the district court filed its opinion and decree defining the treaty rights of the Confederated Tribes and Bands of the Yakama Indian Nation, and the Confederated Tribes and Bands of the Umatilla Reservation (the Walla Walla, Cayuse, Umatilla and the Nez Percé Bands or Tribes and the Warm Springs Tribe). It interpreted the treaty right of "taking fish at all usual and accustomed places" on the Columbia River and its tributaries, and declared the manner and extent to which the state of Oregon could regulate Indian fishing. There are other lawsuits in the courts regarding water and mining rights on land leased by the corporations. Monies that were to be given to the Indian tribes were not accounted for and in many cases the paperwork that would account for these monies has vanished, making the finalizing of these settlements extremely difficult.[774] On October 10, 1980, the Maine Indian Claims Settlement Act was approved. In order to avoid a long lawsuit involving the removal of whites occupying the land, the state of Maine reached an agreement with the Passamaquoddy tribe, Penobscot nation, and the Houlton band of Maliseet Indians. In this act of Congress, in return for the relinquishment of all claims, the federal government recognized the tribes, allowed them to receive financial aid and set up a claims fund of $27,000,000. There are a number of other land claims throughout the United States involving small and large land tracts that remain in dispute. The Kerr-McGee Corporation, a company mining uranium, flooded Navajo lands in the 1950s. Birth defects, lung cancer and other problems continued into the 1980s, producing additional lawsuits.[775]

Black Hills Indian camp, 1900s

Red Cloud

General Custer enters the Black Hills

The Black Hills hold strong religious significance to the Sioux tribes. The 1868 Treaty of Fort Laramie promised the Sioux a large reservation and affirmed that no more land could be taken without the approval of three-fourths of the male adults. The Sioux never formally sold the Black Hills to the federal government. In 1871 gold was discovered within the Sioux reservations and in 1877 the government ordered the Sioux to move. The Sioux resisted and the battle with the U.S. Army ensued, resulting in the defeat of Custer at Little Big Horn. Although they won the battle, the Sioux were still forced to flee and the Homestead Mining Company removed much of the gold. A lawsuit eventually reached the United States Supreme Court in 1980. The Supreme Court decreed that, "A more ripe and rank case of dishonorable dealing will never, in all probability, be found in our (American) history." Following the United States Supreme Court's decision, the Indian Claims Commission awarded the Sioux $100 million. The offer was rejected, with the Oglala Sioux tribe filing a suit in U.S. District Court for title to the Black Hills, and for $11 billion in damages for the "denial of the absolute and undisturbed use and occupation of the Black Hills for 103 years." The Sioux refused to sell the Black Hills under any circumstances and the lawsuit remains in the courts. Attorneys representing more than 300,000 Indians are in the federal courts in a class-action lawsuit. They claim monies the Interior Department should have paid to the Indian Trust Fund (established since 1887), remains unaccounted for. On June 25, 1916, Chief Two Moons stated, "Forty years ago I fought Custer... until all were dead.... I was then the enemy of the white man. Now I am the friend and brother, living under the flag of our country." In 1991 Congress enacted Public Law 102-201 to establish an Indian memorial at the Custer site to "honor and recognize the Indians who fought to preserve their land and culture."[776]

Indian version, Battle of Little Big Horn

Two Moons, Cheyenne

Crazy Horse in battle

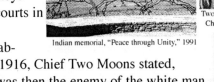

Indian memorial, "Peace through Unity," 1991

Crazy Horse at Black Hills, 2003

In 1996 gamblers wagered almost five billion dollars in Indian casinos. In 2003, 15 billion dollars was spent, more than the amount wagered in the Atlantic City and Las Vegas casinos combined. This revenue brought enormous profits. Some of this money has been distributed to tribal members or used to improve health care, infrastructure, and education on reservations—or to repurchase lost ancestral lands. According to the National Indian Gaming Commission, 182 tribes were operating 274 gaming facilities in 1996. Gambling on reservations has become a significant part of the nation's gambling picture as well as playing an important role in the Indians' quest for self-determination. Recognizing that few other sources of revenue offered hope, in the short term of providing economic independence, the Indian's interest in gambling as a producer of revenue began during the 1970s. Some tribes, such as the Navajo, forbid all gambling activities. Since the 1950s, both Congress and the federal courts arrived at a compromise concerning Indian sovereignty and state claims of jurisdiction over tribes. Legally, where state laws prohibit gambling, it applies equally to tribal lands. The federal government supports the Indians' right in gambling operations as long as they are not forbidden under state law.[777] On October 17, 1988, Congress confirmed the Indians' rights to gambling with the "Indian Gaming Regulatory Act" (IGRA), stating: "...Indian tribes have the exclusive rights to regulate gaming activity on Indian lands if the gaming activity is not specifically prohibited by federal law and is conducted within a state which does not, as a matter of criminal law and public policy, prohibit such gaming activity... gaming on Indian lands is within the exclusive jurisdiction of the Indian tribes. The act established within the Department of Interior a commission known as the "National Indian Gaming Commission "(IGRA).[778] There were attempts to stop Indian gambling. The State of Rhode Island forbid an Indian casino that would compete with its own future and the state of New Mexico, in their own plans for gambling, tried to shut down Indian casinos while it was starting its own lottery. These attempts have been defeated in the courts. The positive side of the Indians' gambling is that, in many cases, they have provided new schools and homes, have revived their language and culture, and are helping to defeat the grinding poverty facing many Indians.[779]

Yakama Indian Nation casino, Toppenish, WA

According to a United Nations report in 2003, indigenous people around the world and in the Americas are in great danger of losing their culture and are caught up in conflict as well as environmental degradation. As a result of acceleration of global warming, deforestation and technology, wild places are now easily accessible. Consequently, even people in the most remote regions now have environmental and social pressures. Western society must learn from and preserve all indigenous cultures in order for all of us to survive on this planet. Therefore, it is urgent now to find political and economic solutions to massive historical injustice; i.e. self-government, land claims and economic development. The plight of most indigenious people and the Indian in the Americas is one of cultural geonocide and degradation. The atrocities suffered by Indians, often sanctioned by governments throughout the Americas, left an indelible mark on the psyche of generations of Indians past and present. The amendments, treaties and other legal edicts of the United States Constitution have often worked to the detriment of the Indians. Malfeasance and chicanery on many occasions has resulted in broken treaties and forgotten promises. This conduct eventually has led to alcohol addiction, pillage, murder, bondage, usurping of ancestral homes, fragmentation of tribal structure, religion and philosophy, as well as the disintegration of the Indian culture. These horrendous injustices perpetrated on the Indians not only represent a dark chapter in United States history but also exposes this country's greatest contradictions.

Racial and religious prejudice is commonplace both in the United States as well as in other areas of the Americas. To change this attitude, our government and all of the Americas must be legally and morally committed to support all Indians in their quest for human rights. The United States is a proud nation with a rich heritage. Americans believe so strongly in human rights that we advocate it for the rest of the world. However, this has not been the fate of Indians in the United States. Our problems lie not with the Indians but with those who apparently have no regard for the most quoted sentence in the July 4, 1776 Declaration of Independence, "We hold these truths to be self-evident, that all men are created equal, that they are endowed with certain unalienable rights, that among these are life, liberty and the pursuit of happiness."

Jessica Jules (Little Green Hummingbird Woman) 2003, Secwepemc, with photo, Chief Petit Louis 1855-1915

Lisa Little Dog 1/2 Blackfeet, German & Irish, 2003

The Indian populations still face and must be able to surmount a large number of problems. Past excesses by governments and corporations that have taken the Indians' land and minerals have yet to be settled. Most other minorities have managed to integrate into society while retaining the ceremonies, food and music of their own cultures. The problem remains that of all the minorities, a large number of Indians are penned in on a reservation, dependent on the government's limited handouts of food and health care, available only to those who stay on the reservation. Our modern society has brought alcohol and drug addiction, along with the TV set. A shortage of jobs (many reservations have over 50% unemployment) has forced about 85 percent of the Indians to leave their land and culture and integrate into white society, or settle in large cities in Indian communities.

Today myths and stereotypes persist with new distorted untrue impressions: that all Indians are rich due to gambling, that the tribes have unlimited hunting and fishing rights and that the tribes are able to survive on government handouts. The Indians in the Americas and indigenous peoples throughout the rest of the world can only succeed by being treated as equals and allowed to hold on to their noble ceremonial traditions and languages that tie the family and community together. In the final analysis, America's success as a nation is dependent on the well-being of all its citizens—including the Indians here and in all the Americas. One conclusion from the many years of research and writing, is that in the past as well as in the present there has been a spread of genetic traits, practices, or other features from one culture to another. The reality is that we must all live in harmony with "Mother Earth" and all living things. We are all part of one human family, Mitakuye Oyasin—meaning, "We are All Related".[780]

September 21, 2004, marked a new era for the Indians in the Americas and the indigenous peoples throughout the world. In the largest gathering in Indian history, over 25,000 individuals representing tribal nations and indigenous communities, marched proudly in unison near the United States Capital in Washington, D. C. This was a celebration for the grand opening of the Smithsonian National Museum of the American Indian (NMAI).

September 21, 2004 Grand Opening Celebration - National Museum of the American Indian (NMAI)

Senator Ben Nighthorse Campbell - Northern Cheyenne

Senator Daniel Inouye - Hawaii

NMAI Director W. Richard West Southern Cheyenne

All Photos by Bill Marder

NOTES TO THE TEXT

[1] Jack Forbes, Professor of Native American Studies and Anthropology at University of California remarks that Columbus "wrote his letters in Latin, in which language he refers to the Americans as 'Indus', which is the Latin form for 'Indios.' Spanish typically adds an "I" in many Latin words...."

[2] Felix S. Cohen, *Handbook of Federal Indian Law*, Washington, D. C., 1942, p. 19. Revised 1982. The constitution of the United States specifically refers to Indian tribes where it says that "Congress shall have the power to regulate Commerce with foreign nations, among the several states, and with the Indian tribes." Cohen well versed in Indian laws in his legal definition of Indian wrote, "The term "Indian" may be used in an ethological or in a legal sense. If a person is three-fourths Caucasian and one-fourth Indian, that person would ordinarily not be considered an Indian for ethnological purposes. Yet legally such a person may be an Indian. Racial composition is not always dispositive in determining who are Indians for the purpose of Indian law. In dealing with Indians, the federal government is dealing with members or descendents of political entities, that is, Indian tribes, not with person of a particular race. Tribal membership as determined by the Indian tribe or community itself is often an essential element. In fact, a person of complete Indian ancestry who has never had relations with any Indian tribe may be considered a non-Indian for some legal purpose." At present there is no general agreement among Indians as to which term is preferred. The native peoples of Canada often use the terms *First Nations, Aboriginals, First peoples*, and *Indigenous peoples*. Most people of the Arctic prefer to be called *Inuit, Yuit,* or *Aleuts,* rather than the word *Eskimos* which they feel is derogatory. Many Indians prefer to identify themselves by tribal affiliation or clan. Many tribes acquired the names haphazardly from other groups. For example, the Navajo received their name from the Spaniards, who called them the *Apaches de Navajo* to distinguish them from the Apache. *Navajo* was a Pueblo Indian word for an area of the Southwest. The Navajo now refer to themselves as *Diné*, which means "the people." Other tribes also refer to themselves as, "We the People, The Humans, The Real People and the Earth People."

[3] Frances Gardiner Davenport, editor, *European Treaties bearing on the History of the United States and its Dependencies to 1648,* Carnegie Institution of Washington, 1917, Washington, D.C., pp. 75-78. The original text in Latin is in the same volume, at pp. 72-75. Columbus' discovery in 1492 of supposedly Asiatic lands threatened the unstable relations between the kingdoms of Portugal and Castile. Pope Alexander VI, a native of Valencia and a friend of the Castilian King, responded with the third bull May 4,1493, to appease the Portuguese. This Papal Bull has never been abrogated or annulled and remains in effect. The next year 1494 in the Treaty of Tordesillas, Pope Alexander VI with the emissaries of the Portuguese and Spanish crowns changed the wording to "divide" the non-Christian world between the two countries. Under that edict, Spain controls all of the Americas and Portugal receives Africa and Asia.

[4] Lewis Hanke, *The Spanish Struggle for Justice in the Conquest of America*. Philadelphia: University of Pennsylvania Press, 1949, p.34.

[5] Fernández de Gonzalo Oviedo, *Historia General y Natural de las Indias,* Primera, Parte, Lib.29, cap. 7. In 1514 Oviedo was appointed a notary and later supervisor of gold smelting at San Domingo. On his return to Spain in 1523 was appointed historiographer of the Indies. He paid five more visits to the Americas before his death, which took place at Valladolid in 1557. Oviedo wrote two extensive works of permanent value: *La General y Natural Historia de las Indias and Las Quinquagenas de la nobleza de Espana* and his shorter work above. Las Casas describes it as "containing almost as many lies as pages."

[6] Hanke, p. 34.

[7] Bartolomé De Las Casas, *History of the Indies*, New York: Harper Torchbooks, 1971, edited and translated and by Andree Collard, Book Three, section 57, p. 192-94. Las Casas began the *History of the Indies* in 1527 and finished about 1565. See Also Bartolomé de Las Casas, *Historia de las Indias,* edited by Augustin Millares Carlo and Louis Hanke, Mexico: Fondo de Cultura Economica, 1951. Lewis Hanke, *The Spanish Struggle for Justice in the Conquest of America*, Philadelphia:University of Pennsylvania Press, 1949, pp. 31-36. Robert S. Chamberlain, *Conquista y Civilizacion de Yucatan*, Mexico:

D. F. Porria, 1982, pp. 25-27. Wilcomb E. Washburn, ed., *The Indian and the White Man,* New York: Anchor Books, 1964, pp. 306-309. The decree of Pope Alexander VI, in 1493 preceded this later injunction. It gave the right "by the authority of almighty God", to give, grant and assign the New World to Isabella and Ferdinand. At the same time it gave them the power to convert the inhabitants of these "pagan lands." Queen Isabella was more sympathetic to the plight of the Indians and cautioned her representatives to treat the Indians justly. After the death of Queen Isabella in 1504, King Ferdinand and his daughter Juana resumed power. According to Las Casas Jurist Dr. Palacios Rubios who was sympathetic to the Indians plight prepared the original proclamation (requirement). Appointed by King Ferdinand as the new Governor Pedrarias Davila, a nobleman arrived in Darien in 1514. Chamberlain, pp. 25-27. Proclamation to the Incas. Washburn, pp. 306-309, another different worded proclamation, "And that we have said this to you, and made this Requisition, we request the notary here present to give us testimony in writing, and we ask the rest who are present that they are witnesses of this Requisition."

[8] Bartolomé de Las Casas, translated by John Phillips, *The Tears of The Indians: Being an Historical and True Account of the Cruel Massacres and Slaughters of above Twenty Millions People Committed by the Spaniards in the Islands of Hispaniola, Cuba, Jamaica & c. as also in the Continent of Mexico, Peru, & other Places of the West Indies, to the Total Destruction of those Countries,* Printed by J. C. for Nath, Brook, at the Angel in Cornhil: London, 1656.

[9] Ivan Van Sertima, *They Came Before Columbus*, NY, Random House, 1976, pp. 1-18. "The Secret Route From Guinea." The spear tips were found to contain an alloy with same proportions of gold and silver as similar spears in general use in West Africa. This was an arms technology equivalent today to the tipping of bullets and shells with uranium in order to make them more able to penetrate steel. See also John Boyd Thacher, *Christopher Columbus. His Life, His, Work, His Remains,* With an Essay on Pedro Martir of Angleria and Bartolomé de las Casas, the first Historians of America. New York: G. P. Putman's Sons, 1903- 1904, 1963, Vol. 2. p. 380. See also J. M. Cohen, editor, *The Four Voyages of Christopher Columbus,* London: Penguin Books, 1969. Leo Weiner, *Africa and the Discovery of America*, Chicago: Innes & Sons, 1933, Vol. I. Ivan Van Sertima, *They Came Before Columbus*, NY, Random House, 1976, pp. 1-18. Robert H. Fuson, translator, *The Log of Christopher Columbus,* Camden, Maine, International Marine Publishing Co., 1987. First Voyage of Columbus, Aug. 1492 to March 1493. Left Spain Aug., 1492. His flagship, the Santa Maria, had 52 men aboard while his other two ships, the Nina and Pinta, each held 18 men. Columbus arrived in the Bahamian Islands in the West Indies October 12, 1492. Second Voyage, Columbus left Spain, September 1493, with 17 ships and 1,200 men, all eager to find wealth and immense riches. Left the Canary Islands on October, 1493. After a 21-day voyage they sighted the West Indies. Columbus made landfall in Hispaniola November 22, 1493. Arriving November 28, 1493 Columbus found the La Navidad settlement of the first voyage burned and all his men dead. Of the twelve hundred crew, staff and passengers on this second voyage, three hundred died of disease in the new settlement of La Isabella, in Haiti that Columbus established. Columbus arrived back in Spain in June, 1496. Third Voyage, May 1498-October 1500. Columbus sailed on his third voyage, at the close of May 1498, with six ships. August 1, 1498 Columbus spotted the land of South America near the mouth of the Orinoco River. Columbus coasted for a while near the shores of South America, and then, broken in health by his labors, anxieties and failure to find gold he sailed on to his colony on Hispaniola. Shortly after Sebastian Cabot, an English navigator discovered North America. Fourth Voyage, May 1502-November 1504. Columbus sailed with four caravels and one hundred and fifty men, early in May 1502, supposedly to find a passage through "the sea" (now known as the Gulf of Mexico), into the Indian Ocean. After much suffering, Columbus returned to Cadiz in November 1504, sick and dejected. Nineteen days after his arrival, Queen Isabella died. Columbus died two years later at Valladolid on May 20, 1506. His last words were "Lord, into thy hands I commit my spirit."

[10] J. Lee Goff, *Medieval Civilization, 400-1500 AD*, 1900. See also J. H. Mundy, *Europe in the High Middle Ages, 1150-1300*, Under this feudal society the landowners, priests and leaders would pass down

the religious messages in simple pictorial images to the illiterate masses. Peter Garnsey, and Richard Saller, *The Roman Empire: Economy, Society Culture*, 1987. The Roman Empire reached its cultural peak in 31 BC. The empire evolved through its military genius. It had an aristocratic government that dominated its subjects based on Roman civil laws. It was not until the invasion of Southern Europe by the Muslims in 800 AD that Europe began to incorporate the Muslim's philosophy, science, literature, and architecture into their society.

[11]Russell Thornton, *American Indian Holocaust and Survival, A Population History Since 1492*, Norman: University of Oklahoma Press, 1987, pp. 15-41. See Also Alvin M. Josephy, Jr. *America in 1492*, New York: Random House, 1991, p. 6. Estimated the population of American Indians living in North and South America in 1492 at 75 million. Henry F. Dobyns, *Their Number became Thinned, American Indian Population Dynamics in Eastern North America*, Knoxville, University of Tennessee Press, 1983, pp. 25-33. Henry F. Dobyns, "Estimating Aboriginal American Population, an Appraisal of Techniques with a New Hemispheric Estimate", *Current Anthropology*, (Oct., 1966), vol. 7, No. 4, pp. 395-416. Dobyns estimated a low of 90 to a high of 112 million in North and South America. His breakdown of the American Indian population before the Europeans came to the New World was, North America with a low of 9,800,000 to a high of 12,250,000..." Dobyn's estimated before Columbus arrived, the following breakdown. Mexican civilization was as low as 25 million to a high of 37,500,000; Central America with a low of 10,800,000 to a high of 13,500,000; Caribbean Islands with a low of 443,000 to a high of 553,750; the Andean civilization a low of 30,000,000 to a high of 37,500,000; marginal sections of South America had a low of 9 million to a high of 11,250,000. Catlin, *Letters and Notes on the Manners, Customs, and Conditions of the North American Indians*, New York: Dover Publications, 1973, Vol. I, p. 6. Reprint of (1844) edition. Catlin writes in 1844 that in North America there, "were sixteen millions in numbers (American Indians)... over the bones and ashes of twelve millions of red men; six millions of whom have fallen victims to the small-pox, and the remainder to the sword, the bayonet, and whiskey; all of which means of their death and destruction have been introduced and visited upon them by acquisitive white men; ...Of the two millions remaining alive at this time..." Census figures for The United States Indian population in 1970 was 792,000, 50 percent more than the under estimated 1960 census. The 1980 census found 1,423,043 American Indians living in the United States and Alaska. The United States Department of Commerce, Bureau of Census, *We the First Americans*, Washington, DC, 1993, p. 2, reported the population in 1990 as 1,959,000 of American Indians living in the United States, and Alaska (Inuits and Aleuts). Each census shows a larger percentage increase of the American Indian population. Wilcomb E. Washington, *Red Man's Land, White Man's Law*, Norman: University of Oklahoma Press, 1971, 247. "Included in that total are individuals who report their race as Indian but include non Indian ancestry in their ethnic background, a category known as 'American Indians of Multiple Ancestry.' Over 5.5 million Americans identify themselves as non-Indian but claim Indian ancestry—they are known as 'Americans of Indian Descent' but are not included in the official Indian count. Sherburne F. Cook and Woodrow Borah, *The Aboriginal Population of Central Mexico on the Eve of the Spanish Conquest*, Berkley: University of California Press, 1963. The population of Central Mexico, the Aztec empire and its surrounding states was estimated in 1492 at about 25 million. *Handbook of Middle American Indians* by the University of Texas Press, 1982, and Barbara Grimes, "Ethnologue", estimates today's present population of Indians in South America, including Central America and Mexico, at about 50 million Indians of all tribes. This would help confirm Dobyn's, Cook and Borah's estimated past population figures. *Microsoft® Encarta® Online Encyclopedia 2004*, "Native Americans of Middle and South America", cites the populations in 2004 of indigenous peoples in South America and Middle America, from 40 to 49 million. "Indigenous peoples in Middle and South America today make up a large majority of all Native Americans throughout the world. At least 400 different groups count themselves as culturally distinct peoples." James Mooney, *The Aboriginal Population of America North of Mexico*. Washington, D.C., Smithsonian Publication No. 2955, 1928. Mooney's gave a deceiving low estimate of 1,153,000 for the Native populations in the

United States, Canada, Alaska and Greenland before Columbus. Older estimates by historians and anthropologists similar to Mooney have had ranges so different so as to indicate their methods of acquiring data as faulty and misleading. Europe's population in 1492 averaged 5 million people in England to about 8 million in Spain. The United States government signed treaties recognizing at least 550 American Indian Nations. Jack Forbes, *The Indian in America's Past*, Prentiss-Hall, 1964, pp. 2-3. "Over 6 million Mexican Americans and Spanish Americans contain a portion of Indian blood and are not counted as Indians.... Many states legally classify Mexican-Americans as 'White,' and the federal census does not enumerate them as Indians. In some instances there is more Native American blood among the Mexican-Americans than among the Indians on the reservations."

[12]John Bigelow, ed., *The Complete Works of Benjamin Franklin*, Chapter II. pp. 210, 365, 366. See also Leonard W. Labaree, ed., *The Papers of Benjamin Franklin*, New Haven: Yale University Press, 1967, Vol. 2. In the writings of Benjamin Franklin, Henry Morgan, Cadwallader Colden and others, they noted that the Indian Six Nations confederacy as a model to establish a confederacy of independent states and the foundation later of the United States form of government. The English knew them as the Five Indian Nations: the Mohawk, Oneida, Onondaga, Cayuga and Seneca. In 1722, when the Tuscaroras joined their league, the confederacy became known as the Six Indian Nations or Six Nations Confederacy. The people of the Six Nations designate themselves Haudenosaunee, which translates loosely as "people of the longhouse." In later years tribes and Nations throughout the United States, followed the example of the Six Nations to form the Confederacies of the Abenaki, Blackfoot, Creek, Powhatan, Confederated tribes of Umatilla, etc.

[13]Matthew W. Stirling, *Indians of the Americas*, National Geographic, Washington, D.C: (1955), pp. 183-216. See also Virgil J. Vogel, *American Indian Medicine*. Norman: University of Oklahoma Press, 1970. Munro S. Edmonson, *The Book of the Year: Middle American Calendrical Systems*, Salt Lake City: University of Utah Press, 1988. The calendar of the Maya is accurate to the day for up to 374,400 years. The Mayans were able to predict the eclipses and the rising and various positions of the stars. The Maya understood 17 different calendars based on the Cosmos. Some of these calendars go back as far as ten million years and are so difficult that you would need an astronomer, astrologer, geologist, and a mathematician just to work out the calculations. They also made tables predicting eclipses and the orbit of the planet Venus. Calendars that are most important to humans on earth are the Haab, the Tun-Uc and the Tzolkin Ritual calendar. The Tzolkin is the most important and the one with the most influence. The Tzolkin is a cycle of 260 days and the Haab is a cycle of 365 days. The tzolkin cycle and the haab cycle were combined to produce a cycle of 18,980 days, known as the calendar round. 18,980 days is a little less than 52 solar years. The Aztecs had similar calendars as the Mayans. The Aztec 52 year cycle (1507 to 1559) "Calendar Round" (Sun Stone), signaled the coming of Cortes and the catastrophic ending of the Aztec Empire ending the 52 year cycle.

[14]N. Watchel, *The Vision of the Vanquished: the Spanish Conquest of Peru through Indian Eyes*, Harvester Press, 1977. The Inca Empire was the largest and most advanced Empire on the American continent before its discovery by Europeans. At its height, the empire extended from northern Ecuador to central Chile and from the Andes to the coast. The Incas were originally a Peruvian highland tribe who spoke Quechua language. According to a mythological account, they came from the south and settled in the Cuzco basin, to which they were at first confined. The Incas expanded their rule on neighboring tribes about 1100 A.D., when governed by the first non-legendary ruler. The empire reached its peak in the fifteenth century. The Inca Empire developed an economy based on an intensive terracing of mountain slopes and irrigation. This civilization, which developed urban centers, a road network, and a well-organized and efficient administration, achieved remarkable skills in metal refining and metalworking, architecture, weaving, pottery, and other arts. The Inca suspension bridge across the Apurimac was 220 feet long and 118 feet above the river. It was immortalized in Thornton Wilder's *The Bridge of San Luis Rey*. By 1532, the Spanish conquest brought an end to the Inca Empire.

[15]Harold E., Driver, *Indians of North America*, Chicago: University of Chicago Press, 1969, pp. 70-77.

[16]Cadwallader Colden, *History of the Five Indian Nations*, New York:

New Amsterdam Book Co., 1902, 2 vols. Vol. I, pg. 182. "Their great Men, both Sachems and Captains are generally poorer than the common People for they affect to give away and distribute all the Presents or Plunder they get in their Treaties or in War, so as to leave nothing for themselves. There is not a Man in the Ministry of the five Nations, who has gained his Office, otherwise than by Merit; there is not the least Salary, or any Sort of Profit..." See also John McMaster, editor, *Merriwether Lewis, History of the Expedition Under the Command of Captains Lewis and Clark*, New York: Allerton Book, 1922, 2 vols. vol 2, p. 118. "Each individual is his own master, and the only control to which his conduct is subjected, is the advice of a chief supported by his influence over the rest of the tribe. The chief himself is in fact no more than the most confidential person among the warriors, a rank neither distinguished by external honor, nor invested by any ceremony, but gradually acquired from the good wishes of his companions and by superior merit."

[17]George Catlin, *Letters and Notes on the Manners, Customs, and Conditions of the North American Indians*, London: Piccadilly, 1841 Reprint, New York: Dover Publications, 2 Vols., 1973.

[18]Robert H. Ruby, and John A. Brown. *The Chinook Indians:Traders of the Lower Columbia River*. Norman: University of Oklahoma Press, 1976. There were numerous trails throughout the Americas utilized as trade routes before the arrival of the Europeans. Hopewell craftsmen had fashioned copper effigies of fish, birds, serpent heads, copper breastplates, copper axes, figures carved from mica, obsidian and stone, tortoise shell, and pearl ornaments. The variety of materials in all areas of the Americas shows the tribes carried on an extensive trade in all areas to get their raw materials and exchange goods.

[19] Bartolomé de las Casas, *De las Antigua's Gentes del Peru*, 3 Vols. Mexico,1851, Madrid, 1892. Writings to the Catholic Church and Spanish King in the 1500's in his fight against the abuse and civil rights of the American Indians.

[20]*Heritage Illustrated Dictionary*, Boston: Houghton Mifflin Co., 1979, vol. 2, p. 794. On "19th century 'Manifest Destiny' doctrine that the United States had the right and duty to expand throughout the North American Continent." A powerful editor, John L. Sullivan, wrote in 1845 that it is "the right of our manifest destiny to possess the whole of the continent which providence has given us...."

[21]*Journals of the Continental Congress*, 1774-1789. Washington, D. C., 34 vols., vol. XXVIII, pp. 118-120, 148-151, 475-479. The Hopewell treaties were negotiated during 1785-1786 with the Cherokees, Choctaws, and Chickasaws. It evolved into a United States policy of recognizing the Indian tribes as separate Nations. The Tribes acknowledged themselves to be under the protection of the United States only and no other power. This treaty recognized the Cherokees, Choctaws, and Chickasaws as sovereign Nations and allowed them to manage their own affairs. It supposedly fixed boundaries for Indian territory. It gave the Indian Nations protection from the settlers encroaching on their lands and promised that, "the hatchet shall be buried forever." This was the United States end wording in many of the treaties to the American Indian. The Treaty of Hopewell could not be enforced due to North Carolina having sole jurisdiction over the lands when the treaty was signed. North Carolina did not become a member of the Union until after the treaty. North Carolina ratified the constitution on Nov. 21, 1789. It ceded her lands to the United States on Dec. 12, 1789. By then it was too late to remove the entrenched settlers. Thomas Jefferson and Henry Knox Secretary of War were responsible for initiating the reservation policy in dealing with the Indians by giving them the right to own land. Their first recommendation to President George Washington was, "that they are not to be divested thereof, but in consequence of fair and bona fide purchases, made under the authority, or with the express approbation, of the United States." Knox reported to Congress July, 1788, that the settlers in North Carolina were breaking the Treaty of Hopewell against the Cherokees by their, "avaricious desire of obtaining the fertile lands possessed by said Indians of which and particularly their ancient town of Chota they are exceedingly tenacious... That he conceives it of the highest importance to the peace of the frontiers that all the Indian tribes should rely with security on the treaties they have made or shall make with the United States."

[22]*American State Papers*, Indian Affairs, Washington, D. C., 1882, 2 vols., 1832-1834, vol. 2, pp. 181-185. Research in Wilcomb E. Washington, *Red Man's Land White Man's Law*, Norman: University of Oklahoma Press, 1971, pp. 54-58. The communique by Calhoun stated, "The time seems to have arrived when our policy towards them should undergo an important change. They neither are, in fact, nor ought to be, considered as independent nations. Our views of their interest, and not their own, ought to govern them. By a proper combination of force and persuasion, of punishments and rewards, they ought to be brought within the pales of law and civilization.... Our laws and manners ought to supersede their present savage manners and customs.... The land ought to be divided among families: and the idea of individual property in the soil carefully inculcated."

[23]Frances G. Lombardi & Gerald Scott, *Circle without End*, Happy Camp, Naturegraph Publishers, Inc., p. 28.

[24] John Collier, *Indians of the Americas*, New York : W. W. Norton, p. 7, 1947.

[25]Robert H. Fuson, translator, *The Log of Christopher Columbus*, Camden, Maine: International Marine Publishing Co., 1987, p. 107. on the discovery of Cuba.

[26]Alvin M. Josephy, Jr. *The Indian Heritage of America*, New York: Alfred A. Knopf, 1970, p. 12.

[27]Harold Driver, *Indians of North America*, Chicago: University of Chicago Press, 1969, p. 457. This reduction of the Indian population through war and diseases was based on a conservative estimate of 75 million Indians when Columbus arrived in America.

[28]Luther Standing Bear, *Land of the Spotted Eagle*, Boston: Houghton Mifflin Co., 1933, p. 248. Luther Standing Bear was born in 1868 in a log cabin near the Pine Ridge & Rosebud reservation in South Dakota. At age 11 he was the first to enter the Carlisle Indian school in Pennsylvania.

[29]Commager & Giordanetti, *Was America a Mistake?* New York: Harper & Row, 1967.

[30]*The London Saturday Journal*, London, England: William Smith, May 2, 1840, No. 70, pp. 280-282. Titled, "The North American Indians: Are the Indians Capable of Civilization?"

[31]*The London Saturday Journal*, Feb. 15, 1840. No. 59, pp. 97-99, titled "Catlin's Indian Gallery". Catlin claimed he visited over 48 tribes. Catlin described a Mandan religious ceremonial buffalo dance. "To the strict observance of the Bull Dance they attribute the coming of the buffalo to supply them with food during the season...."

[32] Tom Jones, *The Last of the Buffalo*, Cincinnati: Tom Jones, 1909. "Comprising a history of the buffalo herd at the Flathead reservation and an account of the last buffalo roundup."

[33]John G. Neihardt, *Black Elk Speaks* (also called: *Being the Life Story of a Holy Man of the Oglala Sioux*), Lincoln: University of Nebraska Press, 1961. pp. 198-200. As told to Neihardt by Black Elk.

[34]James P. Grimes, *Ancient America*, July/Aug., 1995, Colfax, Wisconsin: Issue #12, pp. 35-36. *On Pre-Columbian Written Records of America*, chronology compiled from old manuscripts, maps, myths, histories, manuscripts and epics. See also Gunnar Thompson, *American Discovery*, Seattle, Washington: Argonauts, Misty Isle Press, 1994. Additional references are cited in the writings in the Shan Hai Jing, *Classic of Mountains and Seas* (2250 B. C.); in the Egyptian *Keftiu* (1600 B.C.); Homer's *Elysium* (800 B.C.); Plato (300 B.C.); Herodotus, *The Histories* (500 B.C.); Theophrastus (300 B.C.); Aristotle (350 B.C.); Liang Shu, *History of the Liang Dynasty,* (502 to 556 A. D.); Diodorus Siculus, Italian historian, *Bibliotheca Historica,*(56 B.C.); Proculus, (400 A.D.); Josephus, *Antiquities of the Jews, Land Beyond the Ocean* (80 A.D.), John W. Baldwin, *Ancient America*, Harper Brothers, NY, 1878. Arlington Mallory, *The Rediscovery of Lost America*, New York: E. P. Dutton, 1979. David A. Deal, *The Discovery of Ancient America*, Irvine, CA: Kherem La Yah Press, 1984.

[35]According to John Verano, a professor of anthropology at Tulane University trepanation is the process of cutting a hole in the skull. Trepanation is the oldest surgical practice and is still performed ceremonially by some African tribes. A trepanned skull found in France was dated at about 2200 B.C. About 1,000 trepanned skulls from Peru and Bolivia date from 500 B.C.E. to the 16th century.

[36]Leo Duel, *Conquistadors without Swords*, New York: Schocken Books, pp. 534-539, 1974. See also Junius B. Bird, *Travels and Archaeology in South Chile*, Iowa City, University of Iowa Press, 1988. Fell's Cave measures 36 feet wide, by 28 feet deep, and 11 feet tall from the original floor (the floor forming the earliest occupation). The deepest layer, Layer 5, represented the first occupation of the cave. It was very thin, only 3-9 inches thick, and contained lithic artifacts and faunal remains. Four hearths were identified, each about 5 inches deep and about 2 feet across. The hearths contained fine black ash, burned bones of horse, sloth, and guanaco and stone flakes.

37James Adair, *History of the American Indians*, London: 1775. Reprint 1930, p. 50, (footnote # 23). See also Pickett, *History of Alabama*, p. 106 says, "Many of the old Indian countrymen with whom we have conferred believe in their Jewish origin, while others are of a different opinion...." *Mysteries of the Ancient Americas*, Reader's Digest Books, Pleasantville, NY: 1986, pp. 34-41. Harry Errald Stafford, *The Early Inhabitants of the Americas*, New York : Vantage Press, 1959. Claims the Eskimos were the only ones of Mongol blood that crossed the Bearing Strait. The other tribes were descendants of the lost tribes coming from the Mideast and journeying to America in different migrations across the South Pacific and the Atlantic Ocean. Edward P. Kellog Jr., editor, *The True Origin of the Indians of the Americas or The Roots of the American Indian*, Walnut Creek, CA., Edward Kellog, 1980, translated from the Spanish, *El Verdadero Origen De Los Amerindios*, by Benjamin M. Rea, discusses various origin theories of the American Indian.

38John Noble Wilford, "Findings Plunge Archaeology of the Americas into Turmoil", *New York Times*, May 30, 1989, p. 65, See also Eliot Marshall, "Clovis Counterrevolution", *Science*, 1990, 249:738. Clovis or Folsom named after area where first found in New Mexico. The Clovis fluted stone points are in fact scattered throughout North and South America in soil layers up to 11,500 years in age. A smooth channel extending lengthwise along both faces distinguishes Folsom Points. Clovis points have striking stone projectile point. Its distinctive characteristics include a central groove, or flute, along both of its faces and finely worked edges. Clovis tools were usually made from high quality stone, such as chert and obsidian. In 1934, evidence of an older inhabitant, Sandia Man, dating roughly 20,000 years, was found in Sandia Cave near Albuquerque, New Mexico.

39Roger Lewin, *In the Age of Mankind*, Washington, D.C: Smithsonian Books, 1988.

40J. Madelene Nash, *Time Magazine*, New York: Dec. 4, 1995, pp. 64-74. See also Scotese and Glonka, *Paleomap, Timeline on the Geological Evolution of the Earth*, Arlington: University of Texas, 1992. Nick Lane, *Oxygen: The Molecule that Made the World*, New York: Oxford University Press, 2003.

41K. C. Condie, "Plate Tectonics and Crustal Evolution" Butterworth/Heinemann, pp. 282, 1997.

42 Stephen L. Harris, *Agents of Chaos*, Missoula, Montana: Mountain Press Publishing Company, 1990. Harris claims Indian legends "preserve an amazing number of geologic facts." In Chapter 26 he described the "world's largest flood", that came about by the breaking up of a glacial dam at Lake Missoula about 12,000 years ago. The flood waters carved out an area in east-central Washington of almost 2000 square miles in a matter of days. The flood waters reached heights of up to 1200 feet at the Wallula gateway. Harris notes that there are Indian legends of a great flood in this area.

43Tabitha M. Powledge and Mark Rose, "The Great DNA Hunt, Part II, Colonizing the Americas", *Archaeology Magazine*, Nov./ Dec., 1996, p. 62. See also Richard E. Leakey and Roger Lewin *Origins*, New York: E. P. Dutton, 1977. W. W. Bishop, & J. A. Miller, *Calibration of Huminoid Evolution*, 1972. G. L. Isaac, *Archaeology of Human Origins*, 1989. DNA analysis traced human ancestry back to an African "Eve", setting off debate about how modern humans evolved. While there was general agreement that *Homo erectus* traveled from Africa and dispersed across Asia between 1 and 2 million years ago, what happened next remained a question. The "Out-of-Africa" hypothesis contended that modern humans developed in Africa and migrated from there recently, driving *Homo erectus* into extinction. Proponents of a "multiregional" hypothesis held that *Homo erectus* populations evolved into modern humans in many regions, and that these groups later bred with each other and with groups that emigrated from Africa. The Eve study examined mitochondrial DNA (mtDNA), which is passed only by mothers to their offspring. The researchers, Rebecca Cann, Mark Stoneking, and the late Allan Wilson, estimated that the ancestor of all surviving mtDNA types lived between 140,000 and 290,000 years ago. When did the migrations from Africa take place? They dated the oldest cluster of mtDNA types with no modern African representation to between 90,000 and 180,000 years ago. These populations might have left Africa at about that time, but the mtDNA data could not determine exactly when. The most recent research on modern human origins, by John Armor, examined nuclear DNA of populations from around the world. Armor and his colleagues concluded that the evidence fits with the development of modern humans in Africa, a small number of whom emigrated and became the basis for non-African populations. These observations, they say, are more difficult to reconcile with a multiregional model for the origin of modern humans. Early ancestors of our modern man were the *Australopithecus man* (found in South Africa), *Java man, Peking man, Heidelberg man, Cro-Magnon, Neanderthal man*, etc. Kenneth Kidd and Sarah Tishkoff of Yale University & Trefor Jenkins of Wintersrand University in South Africa, *Science Magazine*, 1996. Part of a research team in a cooperative international study, they examined the DNA of people from all over the world in a DNA segment of 1600 people from 42 populations. The oldest DNA variant came from sub-Saharan Africans, suggesting they evolved in Africa first. Africans had 21of 24 discovered DNA variations. People from the Middle East and Europe had the second oldest DNA variant, suggesting they moved out of Africa into Europe at least 100,000 years ago. There was a decrease in variations on the borders of Africa. The youngest DNA was found in Asians and North and South Americans.

44*USA Today*, "Fossil Discovery Shakes Human Family Tree", July 11, 2002, p. 5D. Ian Tattersal, curator of anthropology at the American Museum of Natural History in New York City, traveled around the world and personally examined every hominid fossil that has been found. After careful observation of the many fossils that were presumed to be related, Tattersal concluded that the fossils were in fact from different groups. "And there is a lot more species out there than we have had the courage to recognize." Tattersal claimed, "There are lots of different ways to be a hominid and ours is only one of them.... The new skull will have to be added to the hominid tree, but there is no way you can shoehorn this discovery into any scenario that exists today." See also Paul S. Martin, *Natural History Magazine*, "Pleistocene Overkill", Dec., 1966. Edward P. Lanning and Thomas C. Patterson, "Early Man in South America", *Scientific American*, Nov., 1967. NBC Television programs aired in Feb., 1996, and Oct. 11, 1997 on the "The Mysterious Origins of Man", featured questionable Jurassic art that has created a controversy in the scientific community as to whether this is true or a hoax. Two collections were discovered. Called the Ica carved stones, they were found in 1967 in a cave near the mysterious Nazca Lines of Ancient Peru and secondly, 3000 miles away in Mexico, Acambaro figurines were found that depict realistic carvings of dinosaurs such as Stegosaurus, Tyrannosaurs Rex, and Pterodactyls. This so-called Jurassic art depicts ancient pilots herding dinosaurs, men attacking dinosaurs with hand axes, and advanced surgical procedures. The figurine carvings show mythological figures (which suggests that ancient Egyptians traveled to Mexico), and reptilian creatures resembling extinct dinosaurs. This, along with discoveries of human footprints found side by side with dinosaur tracks, suggested man lived in America at the time of the dinosaurs 200 million years ago.

45*Science News*, May 31, 1997, vol. 151, p. 333, Oct. 18, 1997, vol. 152, pg. 134. Reports of new fossil findings of a 1.5 million-year old human ancestor possessing more biological variations than have often been assumed. Another fossil analysis found that an upright stance had developed in 9 to 7 million year-old apes, upsetting notions that only members of the human evolutionary chain possessed this feature. See also *Time Magazine*, "Early Man", July 22, 2002, Vol. 160, No. 4. Marsha Walton, *CNN, Sci-Tech*, July 11, 2002, "A team of researchers in Central Africa say they've uncovered what appears to be the earliest evidence of the human family ever found — a skull, jawbone and teeth between 6 million and 7 million years old. Scientists say the discovery, unearthed in the Djurab desert of northern Chad, is of considerable importance." Ian Tattersal, a paleoanthropologist and curator at The American Museum of Natural History, claimed it is the first hominid fossil found in Central Africa. John Noble Wilford, *New York Times*, June 12, 2003. Also in *Nature*, which claimed, "The discovery of the oldest near modern human remains... probably about 150,000 years ago, as genetic studies have suggested in Africa."

46Milford Wolpoff and Rachel Caspari, *Race and Human Evolution: A Fatal Attraction*, New York: Simon and Schuster, 1997.

47 M. J. Morwood, P. B. O'Sullivan, and D. M. Raup, "Fission Track Ages of Stone Tools and Fossils on the East Indonesian Island of Flores." *Nature*, 1998, 392: pp. 173-176. See also *Antiquity*, #73 (1999): pp. 273-86. Stated "More recent work has shown that stone artifacts definitely occur *in situ* at Mata Menge (Morwood *et al.*, 1997), while fission track dates of 880,000-800,000 and 900,000

years for Mata Menge and Tangi Talo, respectively, show that both sites are of Early Pleistocene age (Morwood *et al.* 1998). These findings have significance for assessing the capabilities of early hominids, for their dispersal and for insular evolutionary processes." Paul, Recer, AP Science editor, *Ocala Star Banner Newspaper,* Ocala, Florida, Dec. 12, 1996. Henry Gee, *Macmillan Magazines Ltd. Nature News Service,* "The Sign of the Ancient Mariner" 1998. Stating "Fossil humans belonging to the species *Homo erectus* could have made boats and gone island-hopping across deep-water straits in what is now Indonesia almost a million years ago."

[48]O. L. Bandy, editor, *Radiometric Dating and Paleontology Zonation,* 1970. See also L. A. Currie, editor, *Nuclear and Chemical Dating Techniques,* 1982. R. E. Taylor, Radiocarbon Dating, 1987. G. Lissac, "Archaeology of Human Origins", *Journal of Human Evolution,* 1989. William Kimball, Donald Johnson, and Robert Walter, along with 14 co-authors, "Report by the Institute of Human Origins", Dec., 1996. Recorded the findings of William Kimball who directed the discovery and analysis of a human fossil, upper jawbone found in Ethiopia along with a scattering of crude stone tools. The fossil's age of 2.33 million years was determined by an accurate radiometric method that measured minute quantities of the elements of potassium and argon in the rocks around the fossil. Willard Libby, an American chemist, introduced radiocarbon dating in 1949.

[49]Leakey and Lewin, *Origins,* New York: E. P. Dutton, 1977. See also Leakey and Lewin, *People of the Lake,* New York: Anchor Press/Doubleday, 1978., W.W. Bishop &, J.A. Miller, *Calibration of Hominoid Evolution,* 1972.

[50]R.V. Fodor, *Frozen Earth: Explaining the Ice Ages,* Hillside, NJ: Enslow Publishers, 1981. See also A. Post and E.R. La Chapelle, *Glacier Ice.* Seattle, WA: University of Washington Press, 1971. Shows aerial photographs of glaciers in western North America extending from the Cascade Range, Pacific Coast of North America and the interior ranges of Alaska.

[51]Scott Elias, *The Ice Age History of Alaskan National Parks,* Washington, D. C.: Smithsonian Institution Press, 1995

[52]Tabitha M. Powledge and Mark Rose, *Archaeology Magazine,* "The Great DNA Hunt, Part II Colonizing The Americas" Nov./Dec., 1996, p. 60. See also David M. Oestreicher, "Unraveling the Walam Olum." *Natural History Magazine,* Oct., 1996, Volume 105, No. 10, pp. 14-21, Rafinesque's unpublished drawings and notes can be located in the archives of the *American Philosophical Society* in Philadelphia. Rafinesque in 1836 announced that he had deciphered an ancient hieroglyphic document, painted and engraved on wooden tablets. Rafinesque's hoax was confirmed by Lucie Parks Blalock of Quapaw, Oklahoma. Born June 14, 1906, she is one of a handful left who can speak the Unami (a Lenape dialect) of the Delaware language. Oestreicher's article had pointed out that Rafinesque's "...text was full of fractured constructions, including Lenape versions of English idioms." Rafinesque made up hieroglyphs in the Walam Olum that Oestreicher wrote were, "...hybrids concocted from ancient Egyptian writing, ancient Chinese Kuwen script, Ojibway Midewiwin pictographs, and even some Maya symbols." Rafinesque was a native of Constantinople, raised in France and Italy. He migrated to the United States in 1815. He was a well known eccentric Naturalist who made many wild claims, among which was a cure for tuberculosis, an investment program where one was never liable for losses, and a plan for sink-proof boats.

[53]Oestreicher, p. 16.

[54]Oestreicher, p. 19.

[55]Oestreicher, p. 16.

[56]James W. Loewen, *Lies My Teacher Told Me,* New York: The New Press, 1995, pp. 92, 93. See also John Fiske, *The Beginnings of New England,* Boston: Houghton Mifflin Co., 1889, p. 184. Fiske wrongly claimed that the New England Indians were paid for all their land and said of the Pequots, "it is wrong to suppose that savages, whose business is to torture and slay, can always be dealt with according to the methods in use between civilized peoples." John Bach McMaster, *History of the People of the United States from the Revolution to the Civil War,* New York, Farrar Straus & Co., 1964. p. 15 stated, "The Indian was, moreover, only an idle shiftless savage." George Bancroft, *History of the United States of America,* New York, D. Appleton & Co., 1964. pp. 128-129, 165, Chapter 1, discusses the Indians as having wrought their own destruction due to their " hasty cruelty... inconsiderate revenge..." and that the Indians disappeared "...leaving no enduring memorials, but the names of rivers and moun-

tains." Richard N. Current, Harry T. Williams and Alan Brinkley, *American History: A Survey.* The 1987 edition states, "The story of this new world... is a story of creation of a civilization where none existed." R. Carlyle Buley, *The Old Northwest,* Bloomington: University of Indiana Press, 1964, 2 vols., Vol. 2, 127. Buley won a Pulitzer prize for his history. In one demeaning part Buley stated, "The Potawatomi and the Menaminee were... a fairly dirty, lazy, and harmless lot."

[57]Oestreicher, p. 19. See also Vine Deloria, Jr., *God is Red,* Golden Colorado: Fulcrum Publishing, 1994, pp. 41-42. Hill went on to produce a film, *Mystic Warrior,* from accounts in her book.

[58]Maximum V. V. Pitulko, P. A. Nikolsky, E. Yu Girya, A. E. Basilyan, V. E. Tumskoy, S. A. Koulakov, S. N. Astakhov, E. Yu Pavlova, and M. A. Anisimov, "The Yana RHS Site: Humans in the Arctic Before the Last Glacial", *Science,* Jan. 2, 2004. 303: 52-56. *Science,* Jan. 2, 2004, 303: 52-56. Quote on Siberian discovery by Daniel Mann of the University of Alaska, Fairbanks and on Thomas Lee in Michael Cremo & Richard Thompson, *Forbidden Archaeology,* Los Angeles: Bhaktivedanta Book Publishing, 1993. See also P. J. Julig,editor, *Mercury Series Paper,* "The Sheguindah Site: Archaeological, Geological and Paleobotanical Studies at a Paleoindian Site on Manitoulin Island, Ontario", in Canadian Museum of Civilization, Archaeologiocal Survey of Canada, 2002, No. 161. Carl M. Wright, "Avocational Archaeology: Paleo-Geography and Migrations of the First Americans", *Central States Archaeological Journal,* July, 2001, Vol. 48, No. 3, pp. 116-117.

[59]Tom Dillehay, "A Late Ice-Age Settlement in Southern Chile", *Scientific American* (1984), #251, pp. 106-117. See also Tom Dillehay, *Nature,* and Michael B. Collins, "Early Cultural Evidence from MonteVerde, Chile" (1988), 332:150. Tom Dillehay, "Monte Verde, A Late Pleistocene Settlement in Chile", *Smithsonian Institution Press,* 1989, Washington, D.C. Tom Dillehay a University of Kentucky archaeologist has been working at the Monte Verde site for 20 years. Dillehay published a 1300 page second volume report on his findings in the spring of 1996. Found as evidence at the Monte Verde site was "six artifacts that are unequivocally artifacts", says archaeologist and geologist C. Vance Haynes, Jr., at the University of Arizona in Tucson. "These are projectile points, a slate rod, and a grooved stone. Layers of peat shut off oxygen, protecting mastodon meat, wooden lances, planks and stakes, knotted reeds, animal hide, and chewed plant leaves.... The wooden planks and stakes formed the frame of a large tent, once draped with mastodon hides and divided internally by more flaps of hide." These ancient people lived 30 miles from the Pacific. Near a firepit a person, probably a child, had stepped into soft clay, leaving a tiny footprint. See also *New York Times,* Science Section, Tuesday, Aug. 25, 1998. Dr. Pino and Dr. Tom D. Dillehay of the University of Kentucky in Lexington, the archaeologist who has directed the Monte Verde explorations, are planning more extensive excavations of the knoll site in Jan., 2001. They plan to strip away six feet of topsoil with a bulldozer, then begin fine-tooth digging in the lower layers where evidence of human activity has emerged. "There's no doubt about the age—it's 33,000 years old", Dr. Pino said of the sediment layers bearing the apparent artifacts under the knoll. The date, which would put the occupation during a warm interlude in the ice ages, is based on radiocarbon examination of burned wood that scientists suspect came from hearths at the hunting camp. Archaeologists found the charcoal in three shallow depressions lined with scorched clay. Other hints of human occupation include 24 fractured pebbles, several of which were probably flaked by people using them to cut and scrape meat, hides and plants. When independent archaeologists visited Monte Verde last year and authenticated the younger campsite, Dr. Pino said that they also examined the material from the deeper, 33,000 year-old layer. "They said there is no doubt these are real human artifacts", he said. "We were surprised. We expected another fight."

[60]*Baltimore Sun,* "Strand of Hair May be Proof", May 6, 1991, p. 3a. See also Robert S. Peabody Foundation, "Preliminary report on Archaeological investigations at Tornillo Shelter, Southern Organ Mountains, New Mexico." David L. Chandler, "Dig Finds Signs of Humans in N.M. 35,000 Years Ago." *Archaeology Res. Paper No. 1.* D. Chrisman, *Society for American Archaeology,* "Human Modification of Animal Bones in Pre-Clovis Zones of Pendejo Cave Orogrande, NM", March 26, 1998. Seattle, WA: At the 63rd annual meeting D. Chrisman stated: "...we selected 6 specimens showing evidence of human modification of animal bones. These indicate

manufacture of bone tools and ornaments and marrowing. They come from well-defined and dated layers, ranging from ca. 13,000 to 50,000 YBP. Included are a pendant, an awl-knife and a serrated knife, all showing incised or ground grooves. Of three broken bones, one was probably caused by a worked stone wedge; another by impact of a tool or spear point whose broken tip remains stuck; and a bison humerus which was broken, marrowed, then retouched. Techniques used include stereolithography and 3-D groove reconstruction."

Robert MacNeish, after a distinguished career as an archaeologist, died on Jan. 16, 2001. In his memorial biography, Kent V. Flannery and Joyce Marcus related that "In 1989 south of Alamogordo, New Mexico, MacNeish researched two caves. One of them, Pendejo Cave, was in a limestone cliff overlooking the dry beds of glacial lakes. Accompanied by project administrator Jane G. Libby and a team from the Andover Foundation, MacNeish dug at Pendejo Cave from 1990 to 1992. It had 22 "extremely well defined" strata and produced 72 radiocarbon dates, 60 of which were pre-Clovis. Levels G and H were at least 25,000-31,000 years old; there were no dates available for Level O (the oldest), but Level N had a date in excess of 36,240 B.C. The older hair sample, dating to 19,180 B.C., was initially identified as Mongoloid rather than Indian, suggesting a very early stage in the peopling of the New World. What appear to be human finger and palm prints were found on clay in Level I and could be older than 30,000 B.C. The two lowest levels had extinct Pleistocene animals. Controversy was stirred up by Pendejo Cave. He knew that at least one group of Paleoindian specialists, widely known as the "Clovis Police", would be skeptical of any attempt to push human occupation of the New World back to 30,000 B.C. They would question whether the "artifacts" found with extinct fauna were really of human manufacture. A few would suggest that the alleged hearths from which some radiocarbon dates had come were simply burned pack-rat middens."

[61]William R. Corliss, *Science Frontiers*, Jul.-Aug. 1991, #76.
[62]Niede Guidon, "Cliff Notes", *Natural History,* vol. 96, no. 8, 1987. See also Guidon and G, Delibrias, *Nature*, 1986, vol. 321, pp. 769-771. *Discover Magazine, The World of Science.* Special Science issue, Jan., 1998 pgs. 100-101. Guidon and Delibrias wrote, "Carbon 14 dates point to Man in the Americas 32,000 years ago." Guidon stated archaeologists are now realizing that "People were in North America long before 12,500 years ago." They arrived long before the ice sheets blocked off the Bering Strait and Canada 20,000 years ago. D.J. Meltzer, *Antiquity* "On a Pleistocene Human Occupation at Pedra Furada, Brazil", 1994, pp. 68, 695. Meltzer and several more conservative archaeologists visited the Brazilian site and criticized Guidon's discovery, contending that the 500 or more supposedly human-made stone "artifacts" collected by Guidon's team were actually "geofacts", chipped and flaked naturally as rocks fell one upon the other from nearby cliffs. N. Guidon, Pessis, A.M. Parenti, Fabio; Fontugue, Michel, and Claude Guerin. Reply to Meltzer, Adovasio, and Dillehay on the "Nature and Age of the Deposits in Pedra Furada, Brazil." *Antiquity* (1996) 70: 408-421. Guidon responded by saying, "The article by Meltzer in 1994 is based on partial data and false information. Its battery of questions takes us by surprise; none of the three colleagues came up with these questions during the 1993 meeting. It was mounted precisely to generate direct dialogue on the peopling of the America. We disagree with their statement, 'the comments on Pedra Furada are not offered lightly' (p. 696). The commentaries are worthless because they are based on partial and incorrect knowledge...."
[63]Peter Muello, "Find Puts Man in America at Least 300,000 Years Ago." *Dallas Times Herald,* 16 June, 1987, A-1. See also Stuart J. Fiedel, "Older than we Thought: Implications of Corrected Dates for Paleoindians", *American Antiquity*, 1999, 64(1):95-115.
[64]Sharon Begley, "The First Americans", *Newsweek*, Oct., 1992. See also David Hatcher Childress, *Lost Cities & Ancient Mysteries of South America*, Stelle, Ill: Adventures Unlimited Press, 1986, p. 10. Robert E. Gentet, "Geological Evidence of Early Man", *Creation Research Society Quarterly,* 1991, 27:122. Gold miners gravel in California during the 1850s and 1890s turned up human skulls, mortars/pestles, stone sinkers, double-headed stones, and other artifacts at depths to 130 feet, underneath thick lava beds in sediments estimated to be 1.6 million year old.
[65]Ruth D. Simpson, "Updating the Early Man Calico Site, California", *Anthropological Journal of Canada*, 1982, 20:8, no. 2.

Article states, "Continuation of the Calico investigation, both in the field and laboratory, has conclusively established the presence of Early Man, through the demonstration of numerous tools in several categories, as proven by a number of significant traits or attributes familiar to archaeologists. Microscopic examination reveals use-wear patterns. Uranium-thorium tests yield a date of 200,000 ± 20,000 years for the artifacts." See also George F. Carter, *Earlier than You Think, A Personal View of Man in America*, College Station, Texas: A&M University Press, 1980, pp. 239, 302, 311. Carter compared European and African pebble tools with tools found at sites in California and found all the ancient pebble tools were virtually identical and differed from pebbles found near the man-made tools and from those occurring as a result of avalanches and earthquakes. James G. Duvall III and George F. Carter, "Calico Revisited", *Science News*, 1987, 131:227, and "Calico Defended", *Science News*, 1987, 131:339. William R. Corliss, *Ancient Man: A Handbook of Puzzling Artifacts,* Glen Arm, Maryland: The Sourcebook Project, 1980. Michael Cremo, & Richard Thompson, *Forbidden Archeology*, Los Angeles: Bhaktivedanta Book Publishing, 1993, pp. 203-206, on the Calico Site.
[66]Dr. Virginia Steen McIntyre, *Ancient American*, 1997, vol. 3, issue 19-20, pp. 72-78. This site was originally discovered by an amateur archaeologist, Juan Armenta Camacho, a local paleontologist from the city of Puebla, who stumbled across mammoth bones in June, 1933. In 1962 the American Philosophical Society of Harvard University and the National Science Foundation funded this project. Cynthia Irwin-Williams, a young archaeologist worked with Juan. During 1962 they both discovered four sites around the perimeter of an ancient basin turned into a reservoir where fossil bones and stone artifacts were found together. These sites were named El Horno, El Mirador, Tecacaxo, and Hueyatlaco. Additional excavations uncovered many stone tools at the higher Hueyatlaco site in 1964 and 1966. Hueyatlaco yielded what is arguably the oldest piece of art in the New World, possibly the world: a mineralized mastodon pelvis with engraved images of extinct elephants, a speared feline, and other etchings. Juan Armenta Camacho found it in 1959, fifty meters from the later Hueyatlaco excavations. By 1960 it was on display at the Smithsonian, and *Life Magazine* featured the find. All fossil bones and artifacts from the"Valsequillo Project" were removed to Mexico City and taken over by the Mexican government. Butchered bones from the newer (Hueyatlaco) site and the older site (El Horno), was sent away to Barney Szabo, a geochemist at the U.S. Geological Survey to test with the newest uranium-series dating method. The tests revealed dates of 80,000 years for the Hueyatlaco site and approximately 280,000 years for a tooth from a butchered mastodon from the El Horno site. See also Michael Cremo & Richard Thompson, *Forbidden Archaeology*, Los Angeles: Bhaktivedanta Book Publishing, 1993, p. 376. Book states: "In 1975, Virginia Steen-McIntyre learned of the existence of another site with an impossibly early date for stone tools in North America—Sandia Cave, New Mexico, U.S.A., where the implements of advanced type (Folsom points) were discovered beneath a layer of stalagmite considered to be 250,000 years old."
[67]Virginia Steen-McIntyre, Ronald Fryxell and Harold E. Malde, "Geologic Evidence for Age of Deposits at Hueyatlaco Archaeological Site, Valsequillo, Mexico", *Quaternary Research*, 1981, 16:1-17. See also Barney J Szabo, Harold E. Malde, and Cynthia Irwin-Williams, "Dilemma Posed by Uranium-Series Dates on Archaeologically Significant Bones from Valsequillo, Puebla, Mexico", *Earth and Planetary Science Letters*, 1969, 6:237-244. Virginia Steen-McIntyre wrote to Estella Leopold, associate editor of *Quaternary Research*, that she had a difficult time getting her dating study on Hueyatlaco published. "The problem as I see it is much bigger than Hueyatlaco. It concerns the manipulation of scientific thought through the suppression of 'Enigmatic Data', data that challenges the prevailing mode of thinking. Hueyatlaco certainly does that! Not being an anthropologist, I didn't realize the full significance of our dates back in 1973, nor how deeply woven into our thought the current theory of human evolution has become. Our work at Hueyatlaco has been rejected by most archaeologists because it contradicts that theory, period."
[68]Readers Digest Books, *The World's Last Mysteries*, Pleasantville, New York: 1978, pp. 99-100.
[69]Geoffrey Ashe, Thor Heyerdahl, Helge Ingstad, J.V. Luce, Betty J. Meggers, Birgitta L. Wallace. *The Quest for America*. New York/

Washington: Praeger, 1971. pp. 201-204.

[70]*The Quest for America*, p. 204. See also D. Wilson, *Prehistoric Man: Researches into the Origins of Civilization in the Old and New Worlds*, London: 1862, Vols. I and II. Vol. II, pp. 228. Wilson noted the various textures of hair among the Peruvian mummies and further concluded, "to disprove the assumed unity of physical type throughout the western hemisphere. No feature of the Modern Indian is more universal, or yields more slowly even to the effacing influence of hybridity than the long, coarse, black hair..."

[71]"Egyptians find 5,000 Year-Old Mummy", *Science and Technology*, April 4, 2003. See also Stuart Fleming, Bernard Fishman, David O'Connor and David Silverman, *The Egyptian Mummy: Secrets and Science*. Philadelphia: The University of Pennsylvania, 1980. G. E. Smith and W. R. Dawson, *Egyptian Mummies*, 1924, repr. 1988. E. W. Barber, "The Mummies of Ürümchi", *The Columbia Encyclopedia*, Sixth edition, 1999, New York: Columbia University Press, 2003, www.bartleby.com/65/. The Chinchoros culture of the northern Chilean coast practiced artificial mummification around 5000–3000 B.C. and around 4000 B.C. corpses were deliberately salted at La Paloma, in central Peru. Pre-Columbian burials on the arid coast of Peru and Chile tended to become naturally mummified. In the late 1990s a cache of late prehistoric mummies of the Chachapoyas culture was found in a rock shelter in humid Northeastern Peru. In 1974 in the Changsha area of China, an embalmed woman, later identified as a matron of the Han dynasty, was disinterred, along with many artifacts, from an air and watertight tomb in a remarkably well-preserved state. In Ürümqi (Urumchi), the capital of Xinjiang, China (Turkistan), other exceptionally well-preserved mummies, dating back as far as 4000 years and having European features, have posed a mystery to anthropologists. Some believe they may be Tokharians, members of a so-called lost tribe of Indo-Europeans, known from later inscriptions.

[72]*The Quest for America*, pp. 202-208. See also M. Trotter, "Hair from Paracas Indian Mummies", *American Journal of Physical Anthropology*, 1943, Vol. 1. *Ancient American*, Vol. 8, No. 58, pp. 35-38.

[73]Gunnar Thompson, *American Discovery*, Seattle: Washington, 1984, pp. 13-15. On Native Diversity.

[74]James Bailey, *The God Kings and the Titans*, New York: St. Martin's Press, 1973, p. 33. See also Ivan Van Sertima, *They Came Before Columbus*, NY: Random House, 1976, p. 258. Christopher Columbus reported in his diaries sightings of black Africans in America. Richard Deacon Madock, *The Discovery of America*, New York: George Braziller, 1966, p. 110. Joseph Gardner, editor, *Mysteries of the Ancient Americas: The New World Before Columbus*, New York: Readers Digest, 1986, pp. 19, 34.

[75]Pedro Martir de Angleria, Editorial Bajel, Buenos Aires, Argentina: *Decadas del Nuevo Mundo*, First Argentine edition, (First Latin Edition, 1530), p. 200. See also Pedro Martir de Angleria, Francis MacNutt, trans. *De Orbe Novo, The Eight Decads of Pedro Martir de Angleria*. New York: G. P. Putnam's Sons, 1912 (original, 1530). Richard Poe, *Black Spark, White Fire*, Rocklin, CA: Prima Publishing, 1997, p. 259. Pedro Martir received the earliest reports on New World civilizations in Mexico, Central, and South America. Martir was an Italian humanist from Florence who served during the 1490s as tutor in the court of Ferdinand and Isabella, and was later appointed the Spanish Royal Chronicler by Charles V of Spain. In these posts, Martir got many of his accounts from the discoverers themselves. Besides personally interviewing these explorers, he also saw the materials (gold and trade goods) they brought back to Spain. He himself had a great understanding of geographical problems. Martir realized the significance of the Gulf Stream and, in 1494, was the first to know that Columbus did not reach Asia.

[76]Willard P. Leutze, *Ancient American*, Colfax, Wisconsin, issue #13, pp. 10-12. See also *Présence Africaine Magazine*, No. XVIII-XIX, Feb.-May. 1958, p. 180. Cheikh Anta Diop, *Pre Colonial Black Africa*, Brooklyn, NY: Lawrence Hill Books, 1987, pp. 208-211. Arab documents relate that the Emperor of Mali, Kankan Mussa's predecessor, made two attempts to explore the Atlantic. On the first attempt, 200 ships were equipped and spent two years at sea. On returning, the captain gave a glowing report of his voyage. A second expedition was taken by the King who turned his throne over to Sultan Mussa. He reportedly left with two thousand ships in 1310 and never returned. The African ships were equipped with outriggers, which prevented capsizing and rendered them capable of venturing out into the high seas.

[77]Leo Deuel, *Conquistadors Without Swords*, New York: Schocken Books, 1974, pp. 219-223, 226-228. See also James Bailey, *The God Kings and the Titians*, New York: St. Martin's Press, 1973, p. 9. Regarding the giant basalt balls in Ivan Van Sertima's *They Came Before Columbus*, New York: Random House, 1976.

[78]Dr. Andrzej Wiercinski, "Inter-and-Intrapopulational racial differentiation of Tlatilco, Cerro de Las Mesas, Teothuacan, Monte Alban and Yucatan Maya", *XXXIX Congreso International de Americanistas*, Lima, (1970) Vol. 1, pp. 231-252. See also Clyde A. Winters, "The Decipherment of Olmec Writing", April, 1997, paper presented at the 74th meeting of the Central States Anthropological Society, Milwaukee, WI. Clyde Winters, "Blacks in Ancient America", *Colorlines*, 3(2), 27-28. Clyde Winters, "Mexico's Black Heritage", *The Black Collegian*, (1979) 76-82. Clyde Winters, "Manding Writing in the New World, Part 1", Journal of African Civilization, (1979) 1 (1), 81-97. Clyde Winters, "The Migration Routes of the Proto-Mande", *The Mankind Quarterly*, (1986) 27 (1), 77-96.

[79]Michael Coe, *Mexico*, New York: Praeger Publishers, 1962, p. 88.

[80]J. Eric Thompson, *Maya History and Religion*, Oklahoma, University of Oklahoma Press, 1970, pp. 45, 137, 306, 307. Thompson considered the black figure as a traveling trader (or merchant). The merchants were painted black to indicate power and fear. See also Maria Longhena, *Mayan Script*, New York: Abbeville Press, p. 89. The Mayan god of merchants is called "Ek Chauah". Also called the Mayan god of the cocoa plant (chocolate). The cocoa bean was the universal currency for the Maya and associated with traveling merchants. It is still conjecture as to whether this black painted figure is an African.

[81]Diego de Landa, translated by William Gates, *Yucatan Before and After the Conquest*, Dover Publications, 1978. p. 46. See also Leo Deuel, *Conquistadors without Swords*, New York: Schocken Books, 1974, p. 215.

[82]Alexander von Wuthenau, *Unexpected Faces in Ancient America*, New York: Crown Publishers, 1975, Figure 97, p.136, black with kinky hair.

[83]Ivan Van Sertima, *They Came Before Columbus*, New York: Random House, 1976, pp. 32-33.

[84]Gregorio Garcia, *El origen de los Indios de el Nuevo Mundo e Indias occidentals*, 1607, p. 6. Garcia, a monk from the Dominican Order, devoted himself to the studies of the antiquities of the country and the manners and customs of the native Indians. He was a writer of high authority and his work is of great value and importance. The fifth book contains the various native accounts of the origin of the Indians and a discussion of the Indians in the Americas.

[85]Wuthenau, p. 170.

[86]Pedro de Angleria Martir, Editorial Bajel, Buenos Aires: Argentina, *Decadas del Nuevo Mundo*, First Argentine edition (First Latin Edition, 1530), p. 200. See also Karl E. Meyer, *Pleasures of Archaeology*, New York, Antheneum Press, 1970, p. 224. Alvise da Cadamosto, "Description of Capo Bianco and the Islands Nearest to It", in J. H. Parry, *European Reconnaissance: Selected Documents* New York: Walker, 1968, pp. 59-61. Among the findings were the caduceus, an upright design of entwined serpents. This was a religious symbol in ancient Kush adopted by the Egyptians. Physicians in America associate this symbol with their profession.

[87] Dr. Andrzej Wiercinski, on "An Anthropological Study on the Origin of Olmecs", *Swiatowit*, 1972, 33, 143-174. See also Willard P. Leutze, *Ancient American*, Colfax, Wisconsin, issue #13, pp. 10-12. Dr. Andrzej Wiercinski, "Inter-and-Intrapopulational Racial Differentiation of Tlatilco, Cerro de Las Mesas, Teothuacan, Monte Alban and Yucatan Maya", *XXXIX Congreso International de Americanistas*, Lima (1970), Vol. 1, pp. 231-252. A. Wiercinski, & R. A. Jairazbhoy, *The New Diffusionist*, (1975) 5 (18). Wiercinski discovered that 13.5% of the skeletons from Tlatilco and 4.5% from Cerreo de las Mesas were Negroid. This was determined by craniometric and cranioscopic methods compared to other racial populations.

[88]FranciscoTomas Hermenegildo Garces (1738-1781), *Diario, de las ultimas peregrinaciones del Padre Fr. Francisco Garces, hasta la provincia del Moqui, y noticias de varias nuevas naciones exparcidas hasta el Rio Colorado en Califonia*, 1777. Padre Francisco Garces's diary chronicles his travels in 1777 through Arizona and California

with the Second Anza Expedition.

[89]Armond de Quatrefages, *The Human Species*, London: Kegan Paul & Co., 1879, 2nd Edition. See also General Thomas Woodard of Louisiana in his 1859 book *Reminiscences of the Creek, or Muscogee Indians, Contained in Letters to Friends in Georgia and Alabama.* General Thomas Woodard quotes a letter by Stephen Richards of West Florida describing the Yamassees, "...as having dark skins, coarse hair, thick lips and flat feet...." At the time of its discovery Uruguay was inhabited by about 4000 Indians, incluing the Charruas, who dwelt on the north shore of the Río de la Plata as far as the Río San Salvador. The Charruas were very dark in colour, thick-lipped, small-eyed, and very warlike, but were not cannibals as some called them. They made constant war on the other Indians and were a source of terror to the Spaniards, whom they prevented for over a century from establishing colonies. In the seventeenth century the Jesuits began to convert and civilize the Indians. After their expulsion in 1767 the white Europeans began to occupy their lands. Violence evolved over the years until the dwindling minority of the Charruas were slaughtered by the first President of Uruguay when he assumed power in 1832.

[90]Frank Russell, *Twenty-Sixth Annual Report of the Bureau of Ethnology*, Washington, DC, 1908. Frank Russell, an ethnologist, lived among the Pima Indians from 1901-1902 and made a crude translation into Roman letters of their creation chant. It was later recognized and translated into an ancient poetic Semitic hymn. Part of the translation read, "In the beginning the World-Magician created the Earth. As time went by he set the plants upon his handiwork.... Then the Word-Magician created rains by magic, to water his handiwork, so the crops would ripen." Barry Fell realized that the Pima and traditional religious chants were not a mysterious secret religious language of their shamans but a corrupt "creolinized" Arabic, derived apparently from North African Berber sources, somehow being superimposed upon the native tongue in much the same way as religious vocabulary of Latin or French origin was superimposed upon Anglo-Saxon after the Norman Conquest of England. According to Fell, the story-content and the actual vocabulary of these North African tales may have reached the Pima from visiting Arab-Berber traders in pre-Columbian times or even later. There are petroglyphs in the deserts of Nevada, California, and Idaho (Wees Bar) that are similar to those of North Africa.

[91]Barry Fell, *America B.C.*, New York: Simon & Schuster, 1976, 1989, pp. 177-191. Dr. Fell concluded that the Zuni language appears to be largely derived from North African dialects, the linkage being very marked with Coptic, Middle Egyptian, and Nubian of the Nile Valley. While there is evidence of much loan vocabulary, too, from adjacent tribes (from the Algonquian dialects to the north and the Mexican tongues to the south), the main vocabulary is North African. See also Frederick E. Hoxie, *Encyclopedia of North American Indians*, Boston, Houghton Mifflin, 1996, p. 710. Originally called the Ashiwi people by the Spanish, the Zuni tribe, a matriarchal society, has a language, religion, and blood type startlingly different from all other tribes.

[92] Lyle Campbell, *American Indian Languages: The Historical Linguistics of Native America*, Oxford University Press, 1997. See also Marianne Mithun, *The Languages of Native North America*, Cambridge Language Surveys, Cambridge University Press, UK, 2001. *Britannica Concise Encyclopedia, Encyclopedia Britannica Premium Service*, "American Indian Languages" (18 April, 2003). Languages spoken by the original inhabitants of the Americas and the West Indies and by their modern descendants show an extraordinary structural range. Before Columbus, more than 300 distinct languages were spoken in North America north of Mexico by an estimated population of 2–7 million. Today many are becoming extinct. Fewer than 170 languages exist today, of which the great majority are spoken fluently only by older adults. A few widespread language families are: Algonquian (Algic), Iroquoian, Siouan-Catawaba, Muskogean, Athabaskan, Uto-Aztecan, Salishan, Caddoan, Eskimo-Aleut, Wakashan, Timucuan, Arawakan, etc. account for many of the languages of eastern and interior North America, though in the far west, and especially in California, there was an abundance of linguistic extremes. In Mexico and northern Central America (Mesoamerica), an estimated 15–20 million people spoke more than 300 languages before Columbus. The large Otomanguean group of languages, for example, uses tone to change the word meaning, similar to the Chinese. Otomanguean and the Mayan families, along with a single language, Nahuatl, spread throughout Mesoamerica. More than 10 of these languages and language complexes still have over 100,000 speakers. Mayans originally had about 31 languages. Chol was used during their classical period from 200 to 900 A. D. South America and the West Indies had an estimated pre-Columbian population of 10–20 million, speaking more than 500 languages. Important language families include Chibchan in Colombia and southern Central America, Quechuan and Aymaran in the Andean region, Arawakan in the Caribbean, and Tupian in northern and central lowland South America. Aside from Quechuan and Aymaran, with about 10 million speakers, and the Tupian language, Guaraní, most remaining South American Indian languages have very few speakers, and some are faced with extinction before linguists can adequately record them.

[93]Joseph H. Greenberg, Christy Turner II, and Stephen Zegura, "Settlement of the Americas", *Current Anthropology*, (1986) 27:477-497. See also Joseph H. Greenberg, *Language in the Americas*, Stanford: Stanford University Press, 1987.

[94]Joseph H. Greenberg, comments by Wallace Chafe, Regna Darnell, Ives Goddard, Dell Hymes, Richard Rogers and David Sapir. "Review of Language in the Americas", *Current Anthropology*, (1987) 28(5). See also Ruth Gruhn, "Linguistic Evidence in Support of the Coastal Route of Earliest Entry into the New World." *Man (N.S.)*, (1988), vol. 23, pp. 77-100. Tabitha M. Powledge and Mark Rose, "The Great DNA Hunt, Part II: Colonizing the Americas", *Archaeology Magazine*, Nov./Dec., 1996, pp. 59-68. Goddard, Ives and Lyle Campbell, 1994, "The History and Classification of American Indian Languages: What are the Implications for the Peopling of the Americas?" In Robert Bonnichsen and D. G. Steele, eds., *Methods and Theory for Investigating the Peopling of the Americas*, pp. 189-207. Corvallis: Oregon State University, 1994. Lyle Campbell, *American Indian Languages: The Historical Linguistics of Native America*, Oxford University Press, 1997.

[95]S. L. Bonatto and F. M. Salzano, "A Single and Early Origin for the Peopling of the Americas Supported by Mitochondrial DNA Sequence Data." *Proceedings of the National Academy of Sciences, USA*, 94 (1997): pp. 1866-1871. See also Ann Gibbons, "Geneticists Trace the DNA Trail of the First Americans", *Science*, Jan. 15, 1993, vol. 259, no. 5093, pp. 312-313. Studies of mummified remains from Chile 3000 to 5000 years ago found two of the four DNA lineages. Testing 40 living Mayans found all four of the DNA lineages. Hohokam mummies at the collection of the University of Arizona found similar results. DNA is the chemical blueprint of the human being abbreviated from the word deoxyribonucleic acid.

[96] M. D. Brown, " Haplogroup X: An Ancient Link Between Europe/ Western Asia and North America?" *American Journal of Human Genetics*, (1998), 63:1852-1861. See also Carl Ortwin Sauer, editor John Leighly, *Land and Life*, Berkley, University of California Press, 1969, pp. 239. William W. Fitzhugh and Aron Crowell, editors, *Crossroads of the Continent: Cultures of Siberia and Alaska*, Washington, D. C., Smithsonian Institution, 1968.

[97]Jerry E. Bishop, "A Geneticist's Work On DNA Bears Fruit for Anthropologists, Variations in Fragments Hint some American Natives may Hail from Polynesia: The Controversy Over Eve", *Wall Street Journal*, Sept. 10, 1993, p. 1, col. 1. Bishop writes, "Douglas C. Wallace can see the future in a tiny strand of DNA... but he also can peer deep into the past. He has looked back more than 100,000 years to the first humans in Africa. And recently, at a gathering here of science reporters, he painted a picture of prehistoric migrations emerging from DNA that is exciting anthropologists. The scene depicts groups of prehistoric, intrepid mariners moving not out of Siberia, as anthropologists have long assumed, but out of Southeast Asia, across the Pacific, and into the Americas 6000 to 12,000 years ago. If this picture is accurate, it makes many Indians distant cousins of the Polynesians."

[98]D. C. Wallace, K. Garrison, and W. C. Knowles, "Dramatic Founder Effects in Amerindian Mitochondrial DNA Species", *American Journal of Physical Anthropology*, (1985) 68:149-156 .

[99]Christy G. Turner II, "Teeth and Prehistory in Asia." *Scientific American*, Feb. 1989, pp. 88+. See also M. H. Crawford, *The Origins of Native Americans: Evidence from Anthropological Genetics*. Cambridge University Press, 1998. Christie G. Turner II., pp. 113-115. In "Ancient People of the North Pacific Rim", Turner claimed that the Arctic inhabitants of North America shared a common trait

with their Siberian ancestors: incisors which were scooped out at the back. J. H. Greenberg, C. G. Turner II, and S. L. Zegura. "The Settlement of the Americas: A Comparison of Linguistic, Dental and Genetic Evidence", *Current Anthropology*, (Dec. 1986): 27, 477-497. W. C. Boyd, *Genetics and the Races of Man: An Introduction to Modern Physical Anthropology*, Boston, Little Brown, 1950, p. 227. See also Ann Gibbons, "Geneticists Trace the DNA Trail of the First Americans", *Science*, vol. 259, no. 5093. R. S. Malhi and D. G. Smith, *American Journal of Physical Anthropology*, Jan. 15, 1993, pp. 312-313, Sept., 2002, 119(1): 84-6. Article states: "Haplogroup X represents approximately 3% of all modern Native North American mitochondrial lineages. The presence of haplogroup X in prehistoric North America, along with recent findings of haplogroup X in southern Siberians, confirms the hypothesis that haplogroup X is a founding lineage.... In studies of Native American mtDNA diversity, the co-occurrence of the same haplogroup at significant frequencies in both the modern Native American and European populations is unique. Recent European genetic admixture cannot explain the presence of haplogroup X in the Amerindians. First, if the occurrence of haplogroup X were the result of female gene flow from Europeans, then other more common European mtDNA haplogroups should also be present in the northern Native Americans, and they are not. Second, the Native American and European mtDNAs are very different and are connected only through an ancient common ancestor. Hence, Native American and European haplogroup X mtDNAs diverged long ago. Finally, Native American haplogroup X mtDNAs encompass substantial continent-specific diversity, implying an ancient arrival in America. Thus, haplogroup X represents a fifth founding mtDNA haplogroup for the Native Americans, supporting the conclusions of Bailliet et al. (1994), Forster et al. (1996), and Scozzari et al. (1997) "... An ancient arrival of haplogroup X in the Americas could be corroborated by the presence of haplogroup X in pre-Columbian human remains. A coalescence time of 23,000 to 36,000 years ago would suggest that haplogroup X arrived in the Americas during the initial major Amerindian migration 20,000 to 30,000 years ago."

[100]Tabitha M. Powledge and Mark Rose, "The Great DNA Hunt, Part II, Colonizing The Americas", *Archaeology Magazine*, Nov./Dec., 1996, p. 62. Merriwether analyzed both contemporary Indian humans and ancient remains (mummies) from all over America and Asia. The nine types of mtDNAS variants are A1, A2, B, C1, C2, D1, D2, X6 and X7. *National Academy of Sciences* (1997), studied American Indians from the Navajo, Chamorro and Flathead tribes. They determined that all three groups possess a unique type of retrovirus gene, JCV, found only in China and Japan, suggesting travel by boat.

[101]Dr. Andrew Merriwether, Francisco Rothhammer and Robert E. Ferrell, "Distribution of the Four Founding Lineage Haplotypes in Native Americans Suggests a Single Wave of Migration for the New World", *American Journal of Physical Anthropology*, (1995) vol. 98, pp. 411-30. Merriwether did not believe the Indians and the Siberian people were descended from a common ancestor. He believed the Indians to be related to the Tibetans who, he claimed, were displaced Mongolians. The Tibetans were found to have eight of the nine mtDNA variants that are also found in the Indians. Merriwether was unable to prove a date for this one big migration. This date coincides with the earliest archaeological findings in America. The following individuals played a major role in the research on mtDNA during the mid to late 1990s. Michael Crawford, an anthropologist, looked to DNA for the origins of Indians. He found 4 distinct groups of mutation in the mtDNA and dated them to around 30,000-9000 B.C. He has written various article which are compiled in his book, *The Origins of Native Americans*. Michael D. Brown looked at a new region (not A, B, C, or D haplogroups) and called it haplogroup X. This haplogroup is in the minority of Indians and is not found in any Asia populations, yet is found in some European populations. It is distinctly related to the European haplogroup X. He also mentions that haplogroup X is found in pre-Columbian burials. Douglas Wallace worked on the haplogroups A, B, C and D and with the populations in which these occurred. He estimated that the first wave of migration was around 25,000 B.C., the second around 13,000 B.C., and the third around 8,000 B.C. Andrew Merriwether looked at a different region he called haplogroup X-6, and X-7.

[102]Lyle Campbell, *American Indian Languages: The Historical Linguistics of Native America*, Oxford University Press, 1997. Evaluates proposals of distant linguistic relationships, with a full bibliography. See also John M. Cooper, *Bibliography of the Tribes of Tierra del Fuego and Adjacent Territory, Bureau of American Ethnology*, Bulletin 63, Washington, D.C: 1917. *Magellan's Voyage: Narrative Account of the First Circumnavigation*, 2 vols., translated and edited by R. A. Skelton, 1969. Carleton Beals, *Nomads and Empire Builders*, New York: Citadel Press, 1965, pp. 14-16. Describes these people as having a giant stature.

[103]A. Hyatt Verrill, *The American Indian*, New York: The New Home Library, 1947, p. 414.

[104]Verrill, pp. 414-415.

[105]Associated Press Report, *The Washington Post*, Feb. 29, 1975, p. A17. *Ancient American*, Colfax, Wisconsin, Vol. 3, #22, Jan./Feb. 1998, p. 25. See also Richard Poe, *Black Spark, White Fire*, Rocklin, CA: Prima Publishing, 1997, p. 260.

[106]George A. Barton, *Archaeology and the Bible*, 3rd Ed., Philadelphia: American Sunday-School Union, 1920, pp. 342-343.

[107]Lloyd de Mause, editor, *The History of Childhood*, The Psycho History Press, 1974, p. 27, "Global Child Sacrifice." See also J. Quaegebeur, ed., *Ritual and Sacrifice in the Ancient Near East*, Leuven: Peeters, 1993. Gary A. Anderson, *Sacrifices and Offerings in Ancient Israel: Studies in their Social and Political Importance*, HSM, Atlanta: Scholars Press, 1987. A. M. Eckstein, "Human Scrifice and Fear of Military Disaster in Republican Rome." *American Journal of Ancient History* (1982), 7 69-95. Michael H. Jameson, ed. M. Grant & R. Kitzinger. "Sacrifice and Ritual: Greece", in *Civilizations of the Ancient Mediterranean: Greece and Rome*. New York: Scribner's, 1988. 2:959-79. W. W. Hallo, "The Origins of the Sacrificial Cult: New Evidence from Mesopotamia and Israel." In P. D. Miller, Jr., *Ancient Israelite Religion*, Philadelphia: Fortress, 1987. pp. 3-14. In the Old Testament, Abraham was prepared to sacrifice his son as an offering to God. At the last moment Abraham substituted a ram.

[108]Gerhard Herm, *The Phoenicians*, New York: William Morrow and Co., 1975, pp. 118-120. To offer a living human as a sacrifice in primitive times was the best way to appease the gods. See also Gunnar Heinsohn, "The Rise of Blood Sacrifice and Priest-Kingship in Mesopotamia: A "Cosmic Decree"? *Religion*, 22 (1992): 109-134.

[109]Diego de Landa, *Relacion de Las Cosas de Yucatan*, Alfred M. Tozzer, ed. Cambridge, Mass: 1941. See also "Papers of the Peabody Museum of American Archaeology and Ethnology", vol. XVIII. Zecharia Sitchin, a scholar with a knowledge of ancient Hebrew and Sumerian languages and author of the *Earth Chronicles* series, claims mythology is based on the repository of ancient memories. Sitchin believes that ancient Hebraic instructions for building altars and using precious and semiprecious stones are identical to those used by Native Americans.

[110]Sylvanus Griswald Morley, *The Ancient Maya*, Standard, CA: Standard University Press, 1946, p. 236.

[111]Bernardino de Sahagun, *Florentine Codex: General History of the Things of New Spain*. Santa Fe, New Mexico: The School of American Research, 1959.

[112]G. C. Vaillant, *The Aztecs of Mexico*, Baltimore, MD, Penguin Books, 1961, pp. 98-100, 111-112, 120, 124, 126. See also Bernardino de Sahagun, *Historia General de las Cosas de Nueva España*, translated by Fanny Bandelier, Nashville, TN, 1938, Books 1-4. On "Dual gods", Miguel Leon Portilla, *Aztec Thought and Culture*, Norman: University of Oklahoma Press, 1963, pp. 81-82. Aztec dualism is also represented by Quetzacoatl, who stood for harmony, and his brother Tezcatlipoca, who stood for conflict. The twin of Quetzalcoatl was Xolotl, a double monster god. In Babylonia, dualist myths involve Ishtar, the mother goddess of insatiable love, and Ereshkigal, the evil god from the infernal regions. In Egypt, dualism developed between Osiris (good) and his brother Set (evil). Persephone and Hades represented dualism in Greek mythology, and Persephone was only partially successful in overcoming the evil Hades.

[113]Hernando Cortés, *Letters from Mexico*, trans. & ed., A. R. Pagden, New York: Grossman Publishers, 1971, pp. 35-37. See also Hernándo Cortés, *The Despatches of Hernando Cortes, the Conqueror of Mexico, Addressed to the Emperor Charles V, Written during the Conquest, and containing a Narrative of Its Events*. Edited and trans. by George Folsom, New York: Wiley and Putnam, 1843. At the heart of Aztec religion lay the belief that in the past the world had been created and demolished by the gods four times. At the end of each era the sun was destroyed and the earth depopulated. The Aztecs believed

that their own world, the Fifth Sun, was created at the ancient site of Teotihuacan through the sacrifice of a god who flung himself into a fire in order to reappear in the sky as the sun. This sun, however, was unable to move across the heavens until other gods also sacrificed themselves by providing their own blood as sustenance for the movement of the sun. The human sacrifices, which were the focal point of many religious rituals, symbolized the continual effort of the Aztec people to repay this blood debt to the gods, to provide energy for the movement of the sun across the sky and to prevent their own world of the Fifth Sun from coming to an end.

[114]Austen Henry Layard, *Nineveh and Its Remains, Volume I,* and *Discoveries in the Ruins of Nineveh and Babylon,* Volume II, New York, NY: George P. Putnam, 1953. p. 456. In April, 1840, Layard and his team entered the region of Mesopotamia at Mosul, where he first sighted the ancient Mesopotamia monuments. After remaining a night in Mosul to explore the mounds of Nineveh, Layard left for Baghdad and stayed at Hammam Ali, where he first sighted Nimrud. In late 1845 he began his excavation at Nimrud.

[115]Samuel Morrison, *The European Discovery of America: The Southern Voyages, A.D. 1492-1616,* New York. Oxford University Press, 1974. pp. 284-286. Vespucci wrote this letter to his former employee after he returned from his voyage to Brazil. The Guarani tribe, who were related linguistically to the Tupi tribe, were spread out into the Amazon and Bolivian jungles. Their captives were well cared for, but were eventually eaten. See also Ian Heath, *Armies of the Sixteenth Century: The Armies of the Aztec and Inca Empires, other Native Peoples of the Americas, and the Conquistadores, 1450-1608.* Great Britain : Foundry Books, 1999. Heath writes, "The large cannibalistic Tupi tribe was one of the first that the Portuguese and Spaniards came into contact with when they landed on the coast of Brazil. The term "Tupi" actually embraced numerous related tribes.... By the time the Spaniards and Portuguese had first contact with this tribe, they had overrun most of the Brazilian coastline.... Each tribe consisted of many palisaded villages that were made up of between four to eight communal houses. Each of these communal houses could accommodate up to 30 families.... They were able to field armies somewhere in the range of 20,000 men. There was constant inter-tribal warfare. This conflict provided victims for their sacrificial rituals and cannibalism." At present, modern civilization has wreaked havoc with these isolated indigenous tribes. In Brazil the search for gold, along with diseases, have almost made these long-isolated tribes extinct.

[116] Yuan Ke, *The Classic of Mountains and Seas with Annotations,* Shanghai: Shanghai Guji, 1980, reprint, Harmondsworth: Penguin, 1999. In 2250 B.C. a Chinese geographer, *Shan Hai Ching, (Classic of Mountains and Seas),* describes a land across the oceans called Fusang and refers to a Grand Canyon there as the "Great Luminous Canyon." See also A. V. Schaerffenberg, *The Chinese Connection,* Stelle, IL, Adventures Unlimited Press, 1994. *Ancient American,* Colfax, Wisconsin, Vol. 1, #4, Jan./Feb., 1994, p. 28. Chinese accounts of overseas expeditions date from 3000 B.C. R. A. Jairazbhoy, *Ancient Egyptians and Chinese in America,* NJ, Rowman & Littlefield, 1974, p. 17. Diodorus of Sicily, in his book *Library of History,* writes in ca. 21 B.C. of a country that took a voyage of many days through the Atlantic. This land had navigable rivers, big houses, forests and fruits. He wrote that the Phoenicians discovered this country a long time ago and had kept its location a secret. Additional writings of possible landings in America were by Herodotus in ca. 480 B.C. He wrote of Phoenicians trading beyond the Pillars of Hercules; Avienus in ca. 450 B.C. of the journey of Himilco and Hanno; Plato ca. 400 B.C. in his *Dialogues* writes of Atlantis and other continents beyond; Aristotle ca. 360 B.C. writes "of a country outside the pillars of Hercules as being fertile, well wooded, fruitful with navigable rivers." Theopompus, a 4th cent. BC Greek historian, wrote in ca. 378 B.C. of an island of immense size out in the ocean, with strange people quite different from the Greeks; Strabo, Roman geographer, about ca. 100 B.C. wrote of Phoenician traffic outside the Straits of Gibraltar; Roman playwright Lucius Annaeus Seneca, ca. 30 A.D., theorized that there may be land on the opposite side of the Atlantic; Pomponius Mela, a Spaniard and contemporary source for Pliny wrote his *Description of the World,* ca. 44 A.D. He wrote of Indians adrift in the Atlantic until they were blown by high winds to the shores of Germany; Plutarch, ca. 70 A.D., states, "Far West in the ocean in the latitude of Britain, lie islands beyond which stretches a great continent. Greek language is spoken there." Pausanias,

ca. 150 A.D. writes, "West of the Atlantic are a group of islands whose inhabitants are red-skinned and whose hair is like a horse's." Aelianus, ca. 200 A.D., reported that it was common knowledge among the Phoenicians of Cadiz that a huge island existed out in the Atlantic; Proclus, ca. 440 A.D., insisted that the new land had stones and pillars erected by Egyptians and the inscriptions found on the pillars told the history of the people.

[117]*The Quest for America,* New York/Washington: Praeger, 1971. "Contacts From Asia". See also Jessie D. Jennings, editor, *Ancient Native Americans,* San Francisco: Freeman, 1978 on "Pre-Columbian Transoceanic Contacts". Graham Hancock, *Fingerprints of the Gods,* NY: Three Rivers Press, 1995, pp. 1-32. Discusses Piri Reis map of 1513 and other maps possibly made before 4000 B.C. Areas of the yet undiscovered Antarctica are shown without ice as well as areas of South America and the Andes undiscovered at this time.

[118]R.C. Murphy, "The Seaworthiness of Balsa-wood Sailing Rafts in Early South America." *Hispanic American History Review* (1941), Durham, NC, Vol. XXI, p. 204. See also Bjorn Landstrom, *The Ship,* Garden City, NY, Doubleday & Co., 1961, pp. 10-11, on "primitive boats". K.R. Fladmark, "Routes: Alternate Migration Corridors for Early Man in North America", *American Antiquity* (1979), vol. 44, No. 1. Malcolm Ritter, " Study: Human Ancestors made Watercraft much Earlier than Thought", *Associated Press,* 1998. Brian M. Fagan, *The Great Journey, the Peopling of Ancient America,* New York: Thames & Hudson, 1987. J. de Saamanos, *Relacion de los Primeros Descubrimientos de Francisco Pizarro y Diego Almagro,* Madrid: vol. V, 1844. Collection of documents edited on the history of Spain, originally recorded by Saamanos in 1526. Writes "ship" is derived from the Greek word "skaphe", meaning "to hollow out".

[119]Rex Gilroy, "Mysterious Australia: The Lost Civilization of Australia", *The Australasian Ufologist Magazine,* 1995, extracts from Vol. 4 No. 1, pp. 27-33.

[120]M. J. Morwood, F. Aziz, P. B. O'Sullivan, Nasruddin, D. R. Hobbs & A. Raza, "Archaeological and Palaeontological Research in Central Flores, East Indonesia: Results of Fieldwork, 1997-98". *Antiquity* (1999) 73: 273-286. M. J. Morwood, P. B. O'Sullivan, F. Aziz, & A. Raza, "Fission-track Ages of Stone Tools and Fossils on the East Indonesian Island of Flores", *Nature* (1998), 392: 173-176. See also Paul Recer, AP Science Editor, *Ocala Star Banner Newspaper,* Ocala, Florida: Dec. 12, 1996. See also Henry Gee, "The Sign of the Ancient Mariner", *Macmillan Magazines, Ltd., Nature News Service* (1998). "Such navigational ability has always been assumed to have been the prerogative of our own species, *Homo sapiens.*" M. J. Morwood of the University of New England, New South Wales, and colleagues, discuss stone tools and bones of fossil elephants and other animals buried between 800,000 and 900,000 years ago on Flores, in the Lesser Sunda island chain, east of Java. "When the sea-level was at its lowest during the last ice age, much of what is now Indonesia was a single landmass which included Borneo, Java and Sumatra. Even then, Flores was separated by three deep-water channels, the narrowest being 19 km wide. To reach Flores, animals would have had to fly or swim, or be carried on boats or rafts. Suggestions that stone tools on Flores and elsewhere in offshore Indonesia could represent a very early phase of human navigational ability has been discounted because it is difficult to establish that the stone tools were deposited at the same time as the animal bones, and not made later and mixed in by processes of erosion and re-disposition. Morwood and colleagues have laid that criticism to rest, with firm dates showing that the tools at a site called Mata Menge, on Flores, really are around 800,000 years old. But a site called Tangi Talo, around 100,000 years older, has a different set of animals and no stone tools, suggesting (but not proving) that humans were not in the area at that time. This age suggests that the makers of the tools were *Homo erectus* because, as far as we know, there were no members of *Homo sapiens* in Asia at the time. Not only that, these creatures would have to have crossed the open sea not once, but three times. Current fossil evidence suggests that *Homo erectus* appeared in Africa around 2 million years ago. They travelled far and fast: 1.8-million-year old specimens have been recovered from Java (access to Java, which was joined to Asia for significant periods during the Ice Age, would have been easy). Sapiens, although a close relative of *Homo erectus,* appeared much later, also in Africa. *Homo sapiens* may have reached Flores by 900,000 years ago, though it is unlikely: *Homo erectus* seems to have been the toolmaker and, perhaps, the boatmaker. The finding has several implications. Although *Homo*

erectus is thought to have been able to have made fire, its cultural abilities have traditionally been thought rather inferior to that of *Homo sapiens*. For example, *Homo erectus* made hand-axes in more or less the same way for a million years, and examples have been found throughout the Old World." "Ancient Mariners?" *Nature*, Australia, Thursday, 6 Sept., 2001, states "Stone artifacts on the Indonesian island of Flores indicate the presence of humans over 840,000 years ago and therefore the likelihood of remarkably early sea crossings. These discoveries help fill a gap in the fossil record of South-East Asia. Although skeletons thought to be *Homo erectus* have been found in Java and dated to over a million years old, there were no other secure indicators of human presence in the region until after 40,000 years ago. The virtual absence of confirmed stone tools prior to this time presented a bit of a problem. Were the early hominids in this part of the world a spanner short of a tool box, or did they simply use archaeologically invisible technologies (like bamboo)? The findings on Flores offer new insights. This work appears to confirm an older idea, first floated in the 1960s, that stone artifacts from Mata Menge (central Flores) were found in association with an extinct fauna (fossil elephants and others) thought to be about 750,000 years old. The idea was rejected at the time because few archaeologists accepted that the stones were definitely of human origin, or were the same age as the fauna. However, Mike Morwood (University of New England) and colleagues revisited the area and have now published details of at least 20 stone artifacts found in situ (14 from Mata Menge, six from nearby Boa Lesa). The researchers are convinced that these are in fact stone tools. And age estimates, based on fission track dating of sediments below and above the artifacts, demonstrate they must be between about 880,000 and 800,000 years at Mata Menge and older than 840,000 at Boa Lesa. Even with the lowest sea levels imaginable, Bali appears never to have been connected to Lombok, nor was Sumbawa connected to Flores. Therefore the new findings from Flores, although still not accepted unequivocally, suggest that whoever made the artifacts (probably *Homo erectus*) would have had to have made two sea crossings: 25 kilometres from Bali to Lombok (which was probably joined with Sumbawa at low sea levels), and 19 kilometres from Sumbawa to Flores."

[121]John Noble Wilford, "New Answers to an Old Question: Who Got Here First?" *New York Times*, Nov. 9, 1999, sec. F: 1, 4. See also "First Americans may have Arrived 33,000 Years Ago", *CNN Interactive* (1998). "First Americans Were Australian", *Time Warner*, *Online, BBC News*, Aug. 26, 1999. Lucia may not have been the first, judging from artifacts found at early sites in America. If human ancestors sailed across 12 or more miles of water nearly 1 million years ago, to the Indonesian island of Flores, then couldn't the early humans navigate the Pacific? This find suggests that the first Americans might have been Negroid in origin but that Mongoloid races later eliminated these first settlers. However, there is evidence that Mongoloid and black races lived side by side in Mexico. At the La Venta site in Mexico, the ancient Olmecs, with black features and Mayan artifacts, date to about 1000 BC. There is evidence that both modern Australians and Blacks (along with Melanesians, Papuans, Veddoids and some others) come from the same original immigrant stock along similar routes, and are thus related.

[122]"Early Americans were Caucasian?" *Ancient American*, Colfax, Wisconsin: Vol. 8, #9, 2003, pp. 7, 11.

[123]Theodore Schurr, "Mitochondrial DNA and the Peopling of the New World", *American Scientist*, May-June 2000, Vol. 88, No. 3. See also Guy Gugliotta, "Earliest Americans seen as More Diverse." *The Washington Post*, Tuesday, July 31, 2001, page A01. According to Schurr the genetic evidence is, instead, more consistent with a complex migration pattern involving at least two ancient expansions of ancestral populations who may have come from widely separated parts of the Asian continent. The body of Hour Glass Cave man, found in 1988 in the Colorado Rockies, was estimated to be 7500 years old and was reburied by the Southern Ute tribe; Wizards Beach man, 9200 years old, now in at the Nevada State museum; Arlington Springs woman, Channel Island, California, estimated to be 10,000 to 12,000 years old; Wilson-Leonard, Texas, skeleton, 9000 to 12,000 years old, to be DNA tested at the Texas Archaeological Research laboratory, University of Texas in Austin. J. A. de Villiers, *The East and West Indian Mirror*, London, 1906. This gives a good bibliographical account of Schouten and le Maire's round-the-world voyage via the le Maire Straits and Cape Horn, and includes a visit to

giant burial grounds.

[124]Jack D. Forbes, *Native Americans of California and Nevada: A Handbook*, Healdsburg, CA: Naturegraph Publishers 1969.

[125]Thor Heyerdahl, *Early Man and the Ocean*, NY: Vintage Books, Random House, 1980, pp. 39-47.

[126]Carrol L. Riley, Charles Kelley, Cambell W. Pennington & Robert L. Rands, editors, *Man Across the Sea: Problems of Pre-Columbian Contacts*, Austin, University of Texas Press, 1971. See also Eugene R. Fingerhut, *Who First Discovered America? A Critique on Pre-Columbian Voyages*, Claremont, California, Regina Press, 1984. J. J. Graydon, "Blood Groups and the Polynesians", *Mankind*, (1952) vol. IV, #8, Sydney, pp. 329-339. A. E. Mourant, "The Distribution of Human Blood Groupings", *Scientific Publications* (1954), Oxford: Blackwell.

[127]Ruth Gruhn, "Linguistic Evidence in Support of the Coastal Route of Earliest Entry into the New World", *Man (N. S.)* (1988), vol. 23, pp. 77-100. George F. Carter, "Plant Evidence for Early Contacts with America, *Southwestern Journal of Anthropology*, Summer, 1950, 86, pp. 444-456. See also Carl O. Sauer, "Agricultural Origins and Dispersals", *American Geographic Society*, *Bowman Memorial Lectures* (1952), Series 2, New York.

[128]*Early Man and the Ocean*, pp. 52-55.

[129]R. C. Murphy, "The Earliest Spanish Advances Southward from Panama along the West Coast of South America", *Hispanic American History Review* (1941), Durham, NC, Vol. XXI.

[130]J. de Saamanos, *Relacion de los Primeros Descubrimientos de Francisco Pizarro y Diego Almagro*, Madrid, vol. V, 1844. In the collection of documents edited for the history of Spain, originally recorded by Saamanos in 1526.

[131]*Early Man and the Ocean*, pp. 216 -228.

[132]Joseph de Acosta, *Historia natural y moral de las Indias (Natural and Moral History of the Indies)*, Mexico: FCE, 1590, reprint 1940. Acosta was from a family of converted Jews. A Jesuit from the age of 26, he taught in Jesuit colleges in Spain. At his own request, he went to the Americas in 1572. He was in Peru for fourteen years where he fulfilled various duties for the order.

[133] Leo Deuel, *Conquistadors without Swords*, New York: Schocken Books, 1974, pp. 125-127.

[134] Deuel, p. 126.

[135] Deuel, p. 127.

[136] Deuel, p. 127.

[137]*Early Man and the Ocean*, p. 193. See also Thor Heyerdahl, *American Indians in the Pacific: The Theory behind the Kon-Tiki Expedition*, London: Allen & Unwin, 1952, pp. 561, 558-59. Reference to the horse in Pedro de Gamboa Sarmiento, *History of the Incas*, Cambridge: Hakluyt Society, 1907. Originally published 1572, p. 135. Father Joseph de Acosta, *The Natural and Moral History of the Indies*, reprinted from the English Translated Edition of Edward Grimston, 1604. Edited, with Notes and an Introduction, by Clements R. Markham, Volume I: The Natural History (Books I, II, III, and IV), 1880 (1879), pages XIV, 295.

[138] Deuel, p. 127.

[139] Deuel, p. 127.

[140]Gerhard Herm, *The Phoenicians*, New York: William Morrow and Co., 1975, pp. 83-93, 98. King Solomon's copper mines produced a vast quantity of goods to trade for gold, silver, ivory, panther skins, spices, etc. These were transported in Phoenician ships to the marketplaces of Ophir via routes through the India Ocean, or around Africa.

[141]Herm, *The Phoenicians*, pp. 99, 150. The keels for the Phoenicians ships were cut from logs over 60 feet long. At around 500 BC the Phoenicians were at the height of their power, controlling the Mediterranean Sea routes from their coastal sea cities, pp. 201-202, 206, 207. Chapter on "The Punic Empire of the Phoenicians". In 500 BC the Carthaginians formed an alliance with the Phoenicians. Their main city was Carthage on the Mediterranean. "Sailors must have been more popular than soldiers in Carthage. The navy was more useful than the army; it had to be kept up, was continually modernized and was used for commercial as well as military purposes." By 500 B.C. Phoenicians were building much larger ships which had a deck running the full length, with a pointed ram at the bow. There were two banks of oars instead of one on two decks. Their speed was about 5 or 6 knots without a wind. By the 3rd century ships were built with 30 oarsmen to an oar. The Carthaginian merchant ships were much larger than boats such as the Mayflower, which went to America in

the 17th century, with a displacement of 180 tons, most probably similar to the Roman corn freighters that had a displacement of 1000 tons. See also Fell, *Saga America*, NY: Times Book, 1980, pp. 62-65, 79-83. Fell describes Phoenician and Carthaginian coins, stone artifacts and inscriptions found in America. Coins date from 325 B. C.

[142]Barry Fell, *America B.C.*, New York: Simon & Schuster, 1976, 1989, pp. 138-145. A subterranean stone chamber dedicated to the sun god Bel was found in South Royalton, VT. It was originally thought to be a colonial root cellar. The mother goddess was called Tanit. Over the chamber's entrance was a stone lintel that had, in Ogam Celtic letters, a Phonecian monogram. It was a deeply engraved dedication to the sun god Bel. Inside the chamber was another inscription, "Pay heed to Bel, his eye is the sun."

[143]Gunnar Thompson, *American Discovery*, Seattle, WA, 1984, pp. XIII, XIV, 56-58, 103, 131, 163-165, 173, 288-289. See also James P. Grimes, "Larger than the Santa Maria", *Ancient American* (1995), Colfax, Wisconsin: Vol. 2, #10, pp. 35-39. Excellent article illustrating ancient ships.

[144]Robert and Jennifer Marx, *In Quest of the Great White Gods: Contact Between the Old and the New World from the Dawn of History*, NY: Crown, 1992. See also R. F. Marx, *Oceans* (1984), 17.4:18-21 and A. Santarelli, *Mondo Sommerso* (1983), 270: 252-3. Both *Oceans* and *Mondo Sommerso* write of an alleged Roman wreck in Guanabara Bay on the Brazilian coast, less than ten miles from Rio de Janeiro. In 1976 a diver discovered two unbroken amphoras at the bottom of the bay. Amphoras were commonly made and used by the Romans. In 1982 an archaeologist discovered thousands of fragments from more Roman amphoras in the same area. Among the fragments were 200 amphora necks. Several hundred ancient Roman silver and bronze coins were unearthed near Recife, Brazil, that might have been from the Roman ship. In addition to this evidence there are numerous examples of Roman amphora and coins found in New England, indicating that Roman vessels were aware of a Northern route to reach North America via Iceland, Greenland, Nova Scotia and Newfoundland. Elizabeth Lyding Will, "The Roman Amphora— Learning from Storage Jars", *Archaeology Odyssey Archives*, Jan./Feb. 2000. She writes, "From about the third century B.C. to the fifth century A.D., energetic Roman traders sailed huge cargo ships to the ends of the known earth, as we can tell from shipwrecks and excavations. They ventured out into the Atlantic, at least to the west coast of Scotland and to the Canary Islands; they traveled by river deep into western and eastern Europe; and they sailed to India and, probably, beyond.... The capacious holds of Roman cargo ships were filled in a herringbone pattern with hundreds, sometimes thousands, of heavy, thick-walled, six-gallon clay containers roughly 3 feet in height, called amphoras.... Just how far did the Romans go? Is there a Roman ship off the Azores, as some say?... The highly publicized amphoras Robert Marx found in the ship are in fact similar in shape to jars produced in kilns at Kouass, on the west coast of Morocco. The Rio jars look to be late versions of those jars, perhaps datable to the third century A.D. I have a large piece of one of the Rio jars, but no labs I have consulted have any clay similar in composition...." Robert Heine-Geldern, "A Roman Find from Pre-Columbian Mexico", *Anthropological Journal of Canada* (1967), Vol. 5, No. 4, pp. 21-22. Refers to a late Roman torso of Venus from Veracruz and a hoard of Roman coins washed up on a beach in Venezuela. A small hoard of Roman coins, dating to several decades after the Severian period, was found in 1963 during construction work on a bridge over the Ohio River opposite Louisville, KY. Heine-Geldbern also writes on the Roman terracotta head shown at bottom of page 40. The Calixtlahuaca head was rediscovered in 1992 by Romeo H. Hristov, an archaeologist, in the back storage rooms of the National Museum of Anthropology in Mexico City. The Roman looking terra-cotta head was originally found in Tecaxic-Calixtlahuaca, Mexico, in 1933, when a Mexican archaeologist named Jose García Payón unearthed an oddity while digging in the burial mounds of the Toluca Valley of central Mexico. In 1961 the Austrian anthropologist, Robert Heine-Geldern, examined the head and declared that it derived "unquestionably" from the Hellenistic-Roman school of art. Questions to the authenticity have surfaced due to the fact that when found, it was not documented using standard archaeological procedures.

[145]Steven Darian, "Other Faces of the Makara", *Artiobus Asia* (1976), vol. 38, no. 1, p. 30.

[146]Robert von Heine-Geldern, "Trans-Pacific Diffusion", *Handbook of Middle American Indians* (1966), Vol. IV, Austin: University of

Texas Press, p. 293.

[147]Geldern, pp. 130-131.

[148] Bill S. Balinger, *Lost City of Stone*, New York: Simon & Shuster, 1978, p. 109.

[149]Gunnar Thompson, *American Discovery*, Seattle, WA: 1984, pp. 106-114. "Chinese Merchants" refers to travels to America (3000 BC-1850 AD). See also G. R. G. Worcestor, *Junks and Sampans of the Yangtze*, Anapolis: Naval Institute Press, 1971, p. 11, on "Chinese bone inscriptions of plank boats." Robert von Heine-Geldern, *Handbook of Middle American Indians*, Austin: University of Texas Press, 1966, vol. IV, pg. 292, on "Trans- Pacific Diffusion."

[150]"A New Discovery, China Presses Claim that it Found America." *Los Angeles Times Service*, *Milwaukee Journal*, Sept. 15, 1980. Also Marx, *In Quest of the Great White Gods*, NY: Crown Pub., 1992, pp. 32, 33, 35, on Chinese compass and stone anchors. Stephen C. Jett, "Diffussion versus Independent Development: The Basis of Controversy", in Riley, pp. 5-53. In about 200 B. C. China had, in addition to large wooden ships, a dagger-board sailing type raft of flexible construction that was more likely to survive a long sea voyage.

[151]Robert Ellis Cahill, *New England's Viking and Indian Wars*, #12. See also Gwyn Jones, *The Norse Atlantic Saga*, London, Oxford University Press, 1964. Radiocarbon C-14 data from charcoal found at the archaeological site in Newfoundland was dated to 1000 A.D. Paul Chapman, *The Norse Discovery of America*, One Candle Press, 1981. Robert A. Hall Jr., *The Kensington Stone is Genuine: Linguistic, Practical and Methodological Considerations*: Columbia, SC: Hornbeam, 1982. Yarmouth inscribed rock with runic inscriptions, found in Nova Scotia as early as the 1850s.

[152]R.A. Skelton, Thomas E. Marston and George D. Painter, *The Vinland Map and the Tartar Relation*, New Haven: Yale University Press, 1965, p. 140, is a translation of the Vinland Map. See also "Vineland Map is 20th Century Forgery", *Ancient American*, Colfax, Wisconsin, Vol. 7, #10, Sept/Oct., 2002. Leonard Bloomfield, Harry Hoijer, ed., "Algonquian in Linguistic Structures of Native America", *Smithsonian Institution*, NY, 1971: Johnson reprint, July 29, 2002. The Algonquin Indians are the most populous and widespread North American Native group, with tribes originally numbering in the hundreds and speaking several related linguistic dialects. They inhabited most of the Canadian region south of Hudson Bay between the Rockies and the Atlantic Ocean, bypassing certain territories held by the Sioux and Iroquois, who had driven them out of their territory along the St. Lawrence and Ottawa rivers in the 17th and 18th centuries. The word Algonquin means "at the place of spearing fishes and eels." See also Evan T. Pritchard, *No Word for Time: The Way of the Algonquin People*, San Francisco, CA: Council Oak Books, 2002.

[153]Samuel Morrison, *The Great Explorers: The European Discovery of America*, New York: Oxford University Press, 1978. Verrazano sent detailed letters back to King Francis I to provide valuable first-hand information about the eastern North American coastline and potential resources, as well as the first accounts of several Indian cultures. Giovanni Verrazano was the first European to sail up the mid-Atlantic coast, passing through and, at some points, describing the region of future early English colonies. See also Ingeborg Marshall, *A History and Ethnography of the Beothuk*, Montreal and Kingston: McGill-Queen's University Press, 1996.

[154]Roy W. Drier and Octave J. Du Temple, *Prehistoric Copper Mining in the Lake Superior Region*, published privately by the authors, Calumet, MI: 1961. Dr. Roy W. Drier (died 1974), was Professor of Metallurgy at Michigan Technological University. He was an acknowledged local authority on the prehistoric copper culture in the Keweenaw. See also Susan R. Martin, *Wonderful Power: The Story of Ancient Copper Workings in the Lake Superior Basin*, Detroit: Wayne State University Press, 1999. Martin's recent scholarly study of the prehistoric mining of copper along the Keweenaw Peninsula and Isle Royale is the definitive work on ancient copper in the Lake Region. A respected prehistoric archaeologist, she discusses how native copper was worked and traded throughout the North American continent. *Michigan History Magazine*, John R. Halsey, "Red Metal: The Roles Played by Michigan's Copper in Prehistoric North America", Eagle Harbor: Keweenaw County Historical Society, 1992. From an article published in Sept./Oct., 1983. Felix M. Kessing, *The Menominee Indians of Wisconsin*, Philadelphia: American Philosophical Society, 1939.

[155]Emil Veakis, *Archaeometric Study of Native Copper in Prehistoric*

North America, Ph.D. Dissertation (Anthropology), State University of New York at Stony Brook, 1979. See also Aboriginal Research Club (various authors), *The Ancient Copper Mines of Northern Michigan*, Aboriginal Research Club: Detroit, MI 1940. Collection of 21 papers, mostly reprints of earlier publications, 112 pages, few footnoted sources, 2-page bibliography. Tyler Johnson Bastian, *Prehistoric Copper Mining in Isle Royale National Park, Michigan*. M.A. Thesis (Anthropology), University of Utah, 1963. Jesse D. Jennings, *Prehistory of North America*, Second Edition, McGraw-Hill Book Company, 1974. *Annual Report, Bureau of American Ethnology*, Cyrus Thomas, "Report on the Mound Explorations of the Bureau of Ethnology", (1894), Washington, D.C: Smithsonian Institution, Volume 12, pp. 292-311. H. Trawick, *Time before History: The Archaeology of North Carolina*, ed. R. P. Ward and Stephen Davis Jr., University of North Carolina Press, 1999. On Pee Dee Culture.

[156]Partick Huyghe, *Columbus Was Last*, New York: *Hyperion*, 1992, pp. 57-64. "A Copper Trade". Huyghe described Fell's qualifications as, "Barry Fell was born in New Zealand, has studied Greek, Latin, German, French, and Danish. He also learned Gaelic and acquired a working knowledge of Sanskrit, Egyptian hieroglyphics, Kufic Arabic, and other African and Asian languages. Language has always been his passion."

[157]Arlington Mallery and Mary Roberts Harrison, *The Rediscovery of Lost America*, New York: E. P. Dutton, 1951, 1979. Chapter on "The Clash of Theories", pp. 37-49, 223-224. See also E. G. Squier, and E. H. Davis, "Ancient Monuments of the Mississippi Valley", *Smithsonian Contributions of Knowledge*, (1848), No. 1. E. G. Squier, "Aboriginal Monuments of the State of New York", *Smithsonian Contributions of Knowledge*, (1850) No. 2, Gunnar Thompson, *America Discovery*, Seattle, Washington: 1984, p. 103, on African Lost Wax process. Egypt search for copper deposits in America, on p. 77. Also metal-casting and forging technology. Irish and Welch refugees introduced North European culture to Native tribes living in the Eastern Woodlands of North America, circa 12th century, on p. 207. The French decimated the Natchez Indians with disease and war. Elaborate funeral ceremonies for the Natchez elite were conducted on the mound plazas in the Grand Village of the Natchez. The rituals included the sacrifice of relatives and servants of the deceased. At times a sacred perpetual fire was kept burning day and night.

[158]Susan R. Martin, *Wonderful Power: The Story of Ancient Copper Workings in the Lake Superior Basin*, Detroit: Wayne State University Press, 1999. See also John R. Halsey, *Miskwabik—Red Metal: The Roles Played by Michigan's Copper in Prehistoric North America*, Eagle Harbor: Keweenaw County Historical Society, 1992. Roy W. Drier and Octave J. Du Temple, *Prehistoric Copper Mining in the Lake Superior Region*, published privately by the authors: Calumet, MI, 1961.

[159]Salvatore Michael Trento, *The Search For Lost America: The Mysteries of the Stone Ruins*, Chicago: Contemporary Books, Inc., 1978, pp. 86-87, the "Knapp Stone".

[160]Roger Lewin, *In the Age of Mankind*, Washington, D.C: Smithsonian Books, 1988, pp. 208-214.

[161]Sir John Marshall, *Mohenjo-Daro and the Indus Civilization*, 1931, 3 vol. See also S. Piggott, *Prehistoric India* (1950); Sir Mortimer Wheeler, *The Indus Civilization* (3rd ed., 1968); James A. Mellart, *Earliest Civilizations of the Near East*, New York: McGraw Hill, 1965. Dora Jane Hambin, *The First Cities*, New York: Time Life Books, 1973, pp. 123, 150, 151, on "Ancient toilets and sewer network."

[162]"Uncovering a Ritual Center in Veracruz", *National Geographic*, Aug., 1996, Vol. 190 #2. Unearthed in the state of Veracruz, Mexico by archaeologists Jaime Cortes Hernandez and George Stuart from *National Geographic*. They found over 50 buildings covered by vegetation. Dora Jane Hambin, *The First Cities*, New York: Time Life Books, 1973, pp. 108-109. On the many-terraced Ziggurat of Ur. "Builders of the Ancient World", *National Geographic*, Washington, DC: "The Pyramid of the Niches", *National Geographic*, (1986), pp. 90-91. A site in Tajin, a part of Veracruz, Mexico contains ruins built about 300 A.D. of a step pyramid called "the Pyramid of the Niches." Center stairway and flat top constructed initially of mud earth brick with stone slabs added later. The pyramid strongly resembles the step pyramids of Southeast Asia. The Sumerians lived in the southern portion of Mesopotamia. The Sumerian people lived in twelve city states, famous among which are Sumer and Ur. They shared a common language, Sumerian. The Sumerians were an agricultural people. Sumerian seems to have disappeared as a spoken language, but lived on as a written language. The most lasting impact on the modern world was the innovation of the Sumerian system of writing. The Sumerian writing system is called cuneiform, or "wedge-shaped" writing. As their vocabulary expanded, pictograms of cows and sheep were replaced by the wedge-shaped writing of cuneiform.

[163]Victor W. Von Hagen, *The Ancient Kingdoms of the Americas*, Cleveland and New York: The World Publishing Company, 1961, p. 450. See also Charles Singer, E. J. Holonyard and A. R. Hall, editors, *The History of Technology*, New York: 1954, 1957, volumes 1, 3. Dora Jane Hambin, *The First Cities*, New York: Time Life Books, 1973, pp. 48-51, "An Urban Sprawl of Hillside Houses."

[164]Hugh Fox, *Gods of the Cataclysm*, Dorset Press, N. Y: 1981, pp. 96-100, on "Easter Island and Indus Valley Scipt", "The Viracocha People in the Pacific." See also *Oxford Studies in Anthropological Linguistics, 14*, Steven Roger Fischer and Hackett Fischer, "Rongorongo: The Easter Island Script: History, Traditions, Texts", Clarendon Press, March, 1998. "Rapanui's rongorongo script comprises one of the world's most fascinating writing systems. This is principally because *rongorongo* is Oceania's only indigenous script that predates the twentieth century and because it represents one of the world's most eloquent graphic expressions. Like the Indus Valley script of Mohenjo Daro and Harappa of approximately 2000 BC, or the Etruscan writing of central and northern Italy of the first millennium BC, *rongorongo* has also been, until very recently, one of the world's very few undeciphered writing systems. Most of Rapanui's *rongorongo* inscriptions consist of parallel lines of signs or glyphs that represent human figures, birds, fishes, plants, geometrics, and other things...." Sir John Marshall, director of the archaeological research at Mohenjo-Daro, discovered similarities in the Sumerian, Indus Valley and other cultures. These were first discovered in 1923 (Asia, March 1932). A New York Times dispatch of Sept. 17, 1932, revealed that hieroglyphic script discovered at Mohenjo-Daro "corresponds exactly to inscriptions on tablets found on Easter Island off the Chilean coast."

[165]Sir Mortimer Wheeler, *The Indus Civilization*, Cambridge: Cambridge Press, 1968. Sir Daniel Wilson, *The Lost Atlantis and other Ethnographic Studies*, Edinburgh: David Douglas, 1892.

[166]Hugh Fox, *Gods of the Cataclysm*, Dorset Press, N. Y: 1981, pp. 75- 77, 102. Pages relating to "A Mochica Quetzalcoatl".

[167]Andrew Robinson, *Lost Languages: The Enigma of the World's Undeciphered Scripts*, London: BCA, 2002. Florian Coulmas, *The Blackwell Encyclopedia of Writing Systems*, Oxford: Blackwell Publishers, 1996. Peter T. Daniels, William Bright, Eds. *The World's Writing Systems*, NY: Oxford University Press, 1996. Fox, pp. 98-100.

[168]Fox, pp. 44, 45, 18-20. See also Julio Tello on "Discovery of the Chavin Culture in Peru", *American Antiquity*, (1943-45), Menashia, Wisconsin: vol. IX, pp. 135-160. Kwang—Chih Chang, *Shang Civilization*, New Haven and London: Yale University Press, 1980.

[169]Nigel Davies, *The Ancient Kingdoms of Peru*, Penguin Books, 1997. See also Dr. Susan Imhoff, Dr. Ailbhe MacShamhrain and Richard Killeen. *Timelines of World History*, Quadrillion Publishing Ltd., 1998. Michael E. Moseley and Carol Mackey, "Chan Chan, Peru's Ancient City of Kings", *National Geographic*, (March 1973): 318-345. Michael E. Moseley and Kent C. Day, editors, *Chan Chan: Andean Desert City*, University of New Mexico Press, 1982.

[170]Joe W. Saunders, "A Mound Complex in Louisiana at 5400-5000 Years Before the Present", *Science*, (1997) 277: 1796-1799. See also Peter N. Spotts, "Dirt Mounds Yield Clues to Antiquity", *The Christian Science Monitor*, Friday Sept. 19, 1997 edition. "Man Made Mounds said Oldest in North America", *The Japan Times*, Sept. 20, 1997.

[171]R. Silverberg, *Mound Builders of Ancient America: The Archaeology of a Myth*, New York Graphic Society Ltd., 1968. See also H.C. Shetrone, *The Mound Builders*, New York, London: D. Appleton and Company, 1930. Alan D. Harn, "The Prehistory of Dickson Mounds: The Dickson Excavation", *Illinois State Museum Reports of Investigations*, (1980), No. 35.

[172]R. S. Thorpe and O. Williams-Thorpe, "The Myth of Long Distance Megalith Transport", *Antiquity*, (1991), New York: G. P. Putnam's Sons, 65: 64-73. See also Dr. Joe W. Saunders, regional archaeologist for the State of Louisiana, "Earliest Mound Site",

Archaeology News Briefs, (Jan/Feb. 1998, Vol. 51, No. 1. Mound sites were located throughout much of the Eastern United States from the Ohio Valley all the way down into Florida. Mound sites have been found spread throughout Southeastern Alabama, Georgia, Northern Florida, South Carolina, and Central and Western North Carolina and Tennessee. Many of these cultures that constructed the temple mounds or burial mounds utilized corn agriculture. A form of chiefdom government operated within this entire area, and these chiefdoms controlled specific territories. The mounds were built by a people who found food in nearby rivers and forests, and occupied the site over hundreds of years. Bones and shells reveal that the mound builders ate lots of fish, mussels and aquatic snails. Turtles and small animals were unearthed in the mounds, as were large deposits of fire-cracked gravel, suggesting that the people used red-hot rocks to bake or steam their food. The leftovers also indicate that the people came in the spring and left in the fall. Scores of flint drills were found, each about half a centimeter long, which were used to make beads. The Mississippi's waters were used as a network for travelers from near and far to exchange the sought-after pearls, copper, jasper, and mica.
[173]Barry Fell, *America B.C.*, New York: Simon & Schuster, 1976,1989, pp. 256-275, on "The Egyptian Presence." See also J. D. Fage, editor, *The Cambridge History of Africa*: Vol. 2: from 500 BC to AD 1050, Cambridge University Press, England, 1978. "Megalithism is one of the most ancient forms of sacred architecture." Jean-Pierre Mohen, *Standing Stones, Stonehenge, Carnac and the World of Megaliths*, Thames and Hudson: London, 1999. John North, *Stonehenge: Neolithic Man and the Cosmos*, London: Harper Collins Publishers, 1996. Contains excellent glossary on terms for man-made ancient constructions.
[174]Joseph J. Thorndike Jr., ed., *Discovery of Lost Worlds*, New York: American Heritage Publishing Co., 1979. pp. 8-31, on "The Earliest Cities." See also Henri-Paul Eydoux, *In Search of Lost Worlds*, London: Hamlyn Publishing Group, 1972. Peter Tompkins, *Mysteries of the Mexican Pyramids*, New York: Harper & Row, 1976. Ciff Tarpy, "Maya Royal Grave, Place of the Standing Stones", *National Geographic*, May, 2004, pp. 66-78. Paul Recer, AP ScienceWriter, *Mobile Register*, Washington, D.C: page 2a, April 27, 2001. John F. Ross, "The Lost Pyramids of Caral, " *Smithsonian*, Washington, D.C. (Aug., 2002), Smithsonian Institution. On BBC, http://www.bbc.co.uk/science/horizon/2001/caraltrans.shtml, Jan. 31, 2002 it was reported, "The magnificent ancient city of pyramids at Caral in Peru hit the headlines in 2001. The site is a thousand years older than the earliest known civilization in the Americas and, at 2627 BC, is as old as the pyramids of Egypt. Many now believe it is the fabled missing link of archaeology—a 'mother city'.... The mother of all cities. For over a century, archaeologists have been searching for what they call a mother city. Civilization began in only six areas of the world: Egypt, Mesopotamia, India, China, Peru and Central America."
[175]Neil Steede, "The Bricks of Comalcalco", *Ancient American*, 1:8, Sept./Oct. 1994. See also Barry Fell, "The Comalcalco Bricks: Part 1, the Roman Phase", *Occasional Papers, Epigraphic Society*, (1990), 19:299. Peter Tompkins, *Mysteries of the Mexican Pyramids*, Toronto, Canada: Fitzhenry & Whiteside, Ltd., 1976, pp. 304-325.
[176]John F. Ross, Abstract of an article "First City in the New World?" *Smithsonian* (Aug., 2002), Vol. 23, #5, pp. 57-64. Arturo Posnansky, *Tiahuanacu, The Cradle of American Man*, 4 vols., translated by James F. Shearer, Locust Valley, NY, 1945. The orientation of the Kalasasaya at Tiahuanaco caught the attention of Prof. Arturo Posnansky, a German engineer who was studying the ruins. Our earth is now tilted at an angle of 23 degrees and 17 minutes. In the past it was tilted differently. The Earth's axis moves back and forth between 22 degrees and 1 minute to an extreme of 24 degrees and 5 minutes. One complete oscillation takes roughly 41,000 years to complete. The astronomers, by measuring the tilt of the earth on its axis in respect to the plane of the solar system, were able to determine a date of the site at approximately 12,500 BC. The transport of extremely large stones over immense distances might have been accomplished by an unknown civilization with advanced technologies. It's out of the question that a worldwide cataclysm could create mountains almost overnight is certain places, raising a seaport high above its original level. Graham Hancock in *Fingerprints of the Gods*, surmises the Pleistocene extinction sank Atlantis and ended the Ice Age around 12,000 years ago. Scholars including Posnansky, Becker, Kohlschutter and Muller have concluded from astronomical investigations of the ecliptic "that the site may well have been constructed as far back as 12,000 BC (before the Great Flood), making Tiahuanaco one of the oldest cities on the planet, if not the oldest!"
[177]Arnold Jacoby, *Senior Kon-Tiki, The Life and Adventures of Thor Heyerdahl*, Rand McNally, 1967, pp. 90-1, 212-13, 345, 349. See also Thor Heyerdahl, *Early Man and the Ocean*, New York, Vintage Books, Random House, 1980, p. 118. Astri A. Stromstead, *Ancient Pioneers: Early Connections between Scandinavia and the New World*, Erick Fris, New York: 1971. *The Quest for America*, p. 208.
[178]*The Quest For America*, pp. 218-22. See also Deuel, pp. 175-185, 318. *Theosophy Magazine* of the Theosophical Society, vol. 16, No. 2, pp. 70-76. No. 23 of a 59-part series, Dec., 1927, on the legend as chronicled by the Theosophists in the 1920s. Covers the Toltec ancient wisdom and history; also on Quetzalcoatl, who played a prominent role in virtually all the other Mesoamerican deities. "The origin of the Toltecs is variously given. Some identify them with the populations in Guatemala and also in Yucatan... from which it has been inferred that the Mayas and the Toltecs were one people. Ixtlilchochitl, a native chronicler, represents them as coasting down Lower California and Mexico, arriving at a place called Tlapallan in 378 A.D. Turning inland they finally settled on the site of modern Tula and built Tollan, the city from which they took their name. Here they erected temples and palaces, the walls of which were incrusted with rare red and black stones. Some think this is reminiscent of Atlantean architecture in which white, red and black stones were decoratively combined, and that Tlapallan—the traditional home of Quetzalcoatl, the "land of black and red stones", generally translated as "the land of writing" because the Mayas used both red and black inks—was in Atlantis."
[179]Juan de Torquemada, *Los veinte y un libros rituales y Monarchia Indiana*, Seville: Matthias Clauijo, 1615. See Also Juan de Torquemada, *Monarquía Indiana*, Porrúa: México, 1723, 1969, recording the ancient oral records told to Torquemada in Mexico. In a chapter called *De la Poblacion de Tulla y su Senorio*, Torquemada wrote that Quetzalcoatl, on landing in Central America, contacted the Toltecs who described Quetzalcoatl and his men as "...great in stature, excellent gold-and-silver smiths. When they landed at Panuco, Quetzalcoatl was at their head and they marched inland, under his direction. They built the splendid city of Tulla, with fine and beautiful houses, temples and palaces, all of greatest magnificence." The Toltecs intermarried with the natives of the country and by command of Quetzalcoatl, colonized other parts of Central America. Fernando de Alva Ixtlilxochitl, Alfredo Chavero, ed., *Obras Históricas*, Mexico: Editora Nacional, 2 vols., originally published about 1600, republished 1892. Ixtlilxochit's first volume was *Relaciones: The Historia de la Nación Chichemeca*, and was his last work. It was left unfinished, recording only the period up to the siege of Mexico. His work contains very important data on the history of Mexico. Illustrations are of ancient Indian hieroglyphic paintings, and the traditions and songs of the Indians. David Hatcher Childress, *Lost Cities & Ancient Mysteries of South America*, and *Lost Cities of North and Central America*, Adventures Unlimited Press, Stelle, Ill., 1986. See also Gunnar Thompson, *American Discovery*, Seattle, Washington: 1984, pp. 86, 87. Mexican historian Mariano Cuevas concurs on these similarities. Harold T. Wilkins, *Mysteries of Ancient South America*, Secaucus, New Jersey: Citadel Press, 1956, pp. 98-99, refers to Quetzalcoatl.
[180]Dane Coolidge and Mary Roberts, *Last of the Seris*, New York: Dutton, 1939. Friar Juan Torquemada, *Monarquia, Indiana*: 1723 Edition. Harold T. Wilkins, *Mysteries of Ancient South America*, Secaucus, New Jersey: Citadel Press, 1956, pp. 98-99 Refers to Quetzalcoatl. Francisco Saverio Clavigero, *The History of Mexico Collected from Spanish and Mexican Historians from Manuscripts and Ancient Paintings of the Indians*, 2 vols., 1st English Edition, London: G. G. Robinson, 1787. As a result of the Spanish Kings' suppression of the Society of Jesus, the author (1731-1787) had to leave South America in 1767. His history of Mexico is based also on sources such as Torquemada. It was first published in Italian.
[181]*The Quest for America*, pp. 236, 237.
[182]Wilkins, pp. 98-99, on Viracocha.
[183]Dora Jane Hambin, *The First Cities*, New York: Time Life Books, 1973, pp. 42, 65, 67. Wall Paintings similar to Indian pictographs on stone, pp. 108-109, showing pyramid type temples.
[184]Aidan and Eve Cockburn, editors, *Mummies, Disease and Ancient Cultures*, Cambridge, MA :Cambridge University Press, 1980, pp. 1-17, 13:5-143.

[185]Leonard Cotter, *Lost Cities*, New York: Grosset & Dunlap, 1963, p. 188.

[186]Gunnar Thompson, *American Discovery*, Seattle, Washington: Argonauts, Misty Isle Press, 1994, pp. 84-89. Refers to many Egyptian artifacts discovered in America. See also *Ancient American*, vol. 2 no. 8, 1995, p. 33. Gunnar Thompson writes on Egyptian amulets.

[187]Gunnar Thompson, "Egyptian Statuettes in Mexico", *Ancient American*, (1995), vol. 2 no. 8, pp. 32-33. Entire issue by different authors titled "Ancient Egyptians Sail to America." Mariano Cuevas, *Historia de la Nacion Mexicana*, Mexico: Talleres Tipograficos Modelo, 1940, pp. 14, 16. Writes and shows illustrations on Egyptian Statutes. About 1971 Gareth W. Lowe, Director of the BYU-New World Archaeological Foundation, photographed the two figurines located in a display case in the National Museum of Archaeology (Museo Nacional de Antropologia David J Guzman), founded in 1883 in San Salvador, El Salvador in April, 1997.

[188]David Hatcher Childress, "Archaeological Coverups?" *World Explorers Club*, http://www.keelynet.com/unclass/canyon.txt., 1993.

[189]Paul White, "The Oz-Egyptian Enigma", *Exposure Magazine* (1996), vol. 2 No. 6. White writes of Egyptian relics in Australia. "After 5000 years Australia's amazing hieroglyphs still struggle for recognition! Because this site is non-Aboriginal, the Aussie government still fails to protect it." Leading Australian researcher Paul White brings us this astounding story and translations of the Egyptian hieroglyphs found in New South Wales. He states, "It is located approx 2 hrs. drive north of Sydney, a rocky outcrop that contains about 250 Egyptian hieroglyphics, etched into 2 opposing wall surfaces.... Visual observation of the site makes it obvious that the very worn carvings exposed to the coastal weather would have to be several centuries to a thousand years old at least.... When first found the site was completely overgrown with thick vegetation and filled in with smashed rock and a much higher soil line." Numerous additional findings in Australia point to Egyptian and Phoenician exploration in Australia thousands of years ago. British museum scientists discovered that from 1000 BC onwards eucalyptus resin was employed in the embalming of the dead in Egypt. Eucalyptus was only found in Australia and New Guinea at that time. The tomb of a woman was uncovered in Feb., 1964 in the Jordan Valley using Eucalyptus Resin. Boomerangs have been found in the tombs of Egyptian kings and queens. They were introduced around 100 BC.

[190]Hugh Thomson, *The White Rock: An Exploration of the Inca Heartland*, London: Weidenfeld & Nicolson, 2001. See also Kenneth Wright, *Machu Picchu A Civil Engineering Marvel*, Virginia: ASCE press, 2000. John H. Rowe, "An Introduction to the Archaeology of Cusco", *Papers of the Peabody Museum*, (1994), Vol. 27, No. 2, Boston: Harvard Press. Clarke & Engelbach, *Ancient Egyptian Construction and Architecture*, London: Oxford University Press, 1930, New York: Dover Publications, 1990.

[191]Barry Fell, *America B. C.*, New York: Demeter Press, 1976, pp. 174-191, on the Libyans of Zuni. See also Nigel Davies, *Voyagers to the New World*, Albuquerque, University of New Mexico, 1979, pp. 89-91. Hugh Fox, *Gods of the Cataclysm*, Dorset Press, NY: 1981, p. 155, on Ashanti-Nicaragua throne-stool. Charles Darwin, *The Descent of Man*, New York: Appleton, 1879, p. 168. Charles Darwin revealed that when he was in Egypt he had recognized the features of a statue of the Pharaoh Amunoph III as remarkably Negroid. In a footnote he wrote that what he had seen with his own eyes and what he wrote has been since firmly established in Egypt. See also Cheikh Anta Diop, *Civilization or Barbarism: An Authentic Anthropology*, New York: Laurence Hill, 1981, p. 70. Black Pharaohs were Taharka of the 25th dynasty and Rahotep. Nubian kings reigned from 800 BC to 625 BC. Riane Eisler, *The Chalice and the Blade*, New York, San Francisco: Harper and Row, 1987, p. 40, writes on Darwin and black pharaohs. R. A. Jairazbhoy, *Ancient Egyptians and Chinese in America*, New Jersey: Rowman & Littlefield, 1974, p. 17.

[192]*Quest for America*, pp. 236-237. See also Ferdinand Columbus, *The Life of Admiral Christopher Columbus*, Rutgers University Press, 1959, p. 232. Thacher, p. 380. Ivan Van Sertima, *They Came Before Columbus*, p. 268. *Popol Vuh: The Sacred Book of the Ancient Quiche Maya*, translated from the Spanish (of Adrian Recinos) by Delia Goetz and Sylvanus G. Morley, Norman: University of Oklahoma, 1950. 1st edition refers to "black people, pale-skinned people", as illustrated in the Mayan murals.

[193]A. D. Godley, translator, *Herodotus, History*, Vol. 4, Cambridge, MA: Harvard University Press, 1963. See also W. S. Hett, editor, *Minor Works*, Cambridge, MA: Harvard University Press: 1955. *Strabo, The Geography of Strabo*, Cambridge, MA: Harvard University Press, 1961, Book 1, Section 1. G. Bury, translator, Cambridge, MA: Harvard University Press, Cambridge, MA: 1961. R. G. Bury, translator, *Plato's Dialogues*, Harvard University Press, 1961. C. H. Oldfather, *Diodorus of Sicily*, Library of History, Vol. 3, Cambridge, Ma., Harvard University Press, 1952. Editor, *St. Jerome's Chronology*, stated that by 49 B.C. Siculus was an established historian, to have "exercised considerable historical acumen and a measure of originality in the composition of *Bibliotheke*." The *Chronology* also credits *Bibliotheke* (56 BC) to be a "...universal history, in forty books. Siculus covered the story of creation until the Roman Republic."

[194]*Ancient American*, Colfax, Wisconsin: Vol. 17, #10, 1997, pp. 20-22. Findings discovered by Dr. Mark McMenamim, professor of geology and paleontology at Mount Holyoke College, South Hadley, Massachusetts. McMenamim was the author of *Hypersea: Life on Land*, that argued that evolutionary life started in the sea, not on land.

[195]Robert F. Marx & Jennifer G. Marx, *In Quest of the Great White Gods: Contact Between the Old and New World from the Dawn of History*, New York: Crown Publishing Co., 1992.

[196]Gerhard Herm, *The Phoenicians*, New York: William Morrow and Co., 1975, pp. 83-93. Peruvian textiles with the red dye have been radio-carbon dated to 200 A.D. See also Gunnar Thompson, *American Discovery*, Seattle, Washington, 1984, pp. 83-85, regarding serpent connections, pp. 149-151; see also pp. 151-153 for Phoenician artifacts in America.

[197]Hugh Fox, *Gods of the Cataclysm*, Dorset Press, NY, 1981, pp. 114-158. Covers "Phoenicians in the New World."

[198]Fox, pp. 75-77. See also Maria Longhena, *Mayan Script*, New York: Abbeville Press, 2000, p. 60. J. Asar Jubal, *The Black Truth*, Black Truth Enterprises, Long Beach: CA., 1991, pp. 24-29. "Dwarfs" (pygmies) were called by the ancient Ethopians Tangu (Tengu), possibly related to ancient Lucy (ca. 3 million years old) that stood about three feet in height. In Egypt the word "gnome" was called "tang", referring to a dwarf (pygmy). "Gnome" was derived from a Greek word referring to a wise person held in high esteem in Egyptian society. The term "Gnosis" (or Gnostic) refers to one with "superior wisdom, knowledge of the mysteries or spiritual truth."

[199]Salvatore Michael Trento, *The Search For Lost America: The Mysteries of the Stone Ruins*, Contemporary Books, Inc., Chicago, 1978. See also Cyrus H. Gordon, *Before Columbus: Links between the Old World and Ancient America*, New York: Crown, 1971.

[200]Michael Lawrence Morton, "The Miami Stone Circle", *Miami Herald*, Jan. 31, 1999. The circle was part of the town of Tekesta that preceeded Miami.

[201]Ray A. Williamson, *Living the Sky: The Cosmos of the American Indian*, Boston: Houghton Mifflin Co., 1984, p. 138. Williamson writes on the Acoma Pueblo myth, relating to the kivas. Under the foundations in the north they placed yellow turquoise, under the west foundation blue turquoise. In the south was red turquoise and in the east white turquoise. See also Maria Longhena, *Mayan Script*, New York: Abbeville Press, pp. 66-71. In the Mayan culture East is red, west is black, south is yellow and north is white. Center is blue and green.

[202]Ray A. Williamson. *Living the Sky: The Cosmos of the American Indian*, Boston: Houghton Mifflin Co., 1984. See also S. H. Lekson, T. C. Windes, J. R. Stein, and W. J. Judge, Jr., "The Chaco Canyon Community", *Scientific American* (July, 1988), pp. 100-109. Anna Sofaer, edited by Baker Morrow and V. B. Price, "The Primary Architecture of the Chacoan Culture: A Cosmological Expression." *Anasazi Architecture and American Design*, (1997) Albuquerque, NM: University of New Mexico Press. M. Zeilik, "A Reassessment of the Fajada Butte Solar Marker", *Archeaoastronomy* (1985) (JHA), no. 9, S69-S85.

[203]Ray A. Williamson *Living The Sky*, 1984, pp. 199-217, on "Medicine Wheels and the Plains Indians."

[204]M. Oldfield Howey, *The Encircled Serpent*, New York: Authur Richmond Co., 1955. The Carnac serpent, constructed from about 10,000 upright stones, some as high as 15 feet, wound for eight miles. See also Ken Johnson, *The Ancient Magic of the Pyramids*, New York: Simon & Schuster, Dec., 1977. pp. 124-136, on the serpent, mounds and stones, and the serpent's egg. L. G. Brisbin, "The Stone Serpent Mound in Kentucky and Other Monuments", *West Virginia*

Archaeologist, (1976), 25: 26-36.

[205]B. Mundkur, "The Cult of the Serpent in Mesoamerica: Its Asian Background", *Current Anthropology,* (1976) 17: 429-455. See also Iron Thunderhorse, "Secrets of the Snake Dance, *Ancient American,* Colfax, Wisconsin, Feb., 2000, Vol. 5, #31, pp. 26, 27. Earle D. Forest, *The Snake Dance of the Hopi Indians,* New York: 1911. Dr. Jesse Walter Fewkes, "Ceremonials at Walpi", *Journal of American Ethnology and Archaeology,* (1895) Vol. 4, Cambridge, MA, Snake Tower Books. The Hopi Snake Dance requires two weeks of ritual preparation during which the snakes are gathered. Children watch over them until it is time for the dance. Most of the snakes are rattlesnakes, but all are handled freely. The dancers then take an emetic and dance with the snakes in their mouths, with an Antelope Priest in attendance. He strokes the snakes with a feather and sometimes helps support the weight of the larger snakes. After the dance the snakes are released to carry prayers.

[206]Anthony F. Aveni, "The Nazca Lines: Pattern in the Desert." *Archaeology,* (July, 1986), 39(4): 32-39. See also Gerald Hawkins, *Beyond Stonehenge,* New York: Harper and Row, 1969.

[207]M. Reiche, *Mystery on the Desert,* Stuttgart: Heinrich Fink Gmb., 1968. M. Reiche, *Peruvian Ground Drawings,* Munich: Kunstraum Munchen, E.V., 1974.

[208]Charles Hillinger, "Mazes Remain Enigmas of Ancient Indian Art", *Los Angeles Times* (June 11, 1991), p. A3. See also Frank Joseph, "California's Mysterious Maze Stone", *Ancient American,* Colfax, Wisconsin, 1997, vol. 3, issue 24, pp. 38-39. Joseph speculated these maze stones were related to the Hopi flood legends. The Hopis climbed mountains to escape drowning. These maize stones might have been utilized as ceremonial markers to imitate migration from this enormous catastrophe. The Hopis celebrate this flood in their ceremonial "Crown Dance."

[209]Roger Joussaume, *Dolmens for the Dead: Megalithic Building throughout the World,* Ithaca: Cornell University Press, 1985, 1988. See also Evan Hadingham, *Circles and Standing Stones: An Illustrated Exploration of Megalith Mysteries of Early Britain,* Garden City, NJ: Anchor Press/Doubleday, 1976. David Hatcher Childress, *Lost Cities of North & Central America,* Stelle, IL: Adventures Unlimited Press, 1992. John L. Sorenson and Martin H. Raish, *Pre-Columbian Contact with the Americas across the Oceans,* Provo, UT: Research Press, 1996.

[210]John Gallagher, "Dighton Rock", *Ancient American,* Colfax, Wisconsin: (March/April/2003), Vol. 8, #50, pp. 17-19.

[211]Barry Fell, *America B. C., Ancient Settlers in the New World,* New York: Demeter Press, Book Quadrangle—The New York Times Book Company, 1976. Robert Silverberg, *Mound Builders of Ancient America: The Archaeology of a Myth,* Greenwich, Connecticut: New York Graphic Society, 1968.

[212]Barry Fell, "The Etymology of some Ancient American Inscriptions", *Epigraphic Society Occasional Publications* (Sept., 1976), Vol. 3, No. 76, Part 2. See also Barry Fell, *America B.C.,* New York, Demeter Press, 1976, p. 111. Fell, p. 21, on the Grave Creek Stone Tablet. See also *Western Reserve and Northern Ohio Historical Society Tract* (April, 1879), No. 44, pp. 65-68.

[213]Gordon, *Before Columbus,* pp. 120-127.

[214]Donald Y. Gilmore and Linda S. McElroy, editors, "The Bat Creek Stone." A Reply to Critics in *Across Before Columbus? Evidence for Transoceanic Contact with the Americas Prior to 1492,* Edgecomb, ME: NEARA Publications, 1998, pp. 203-215. See also Cyrus Thomas, *Twelfth Annual Report of the U. S. Bureau of Ethnology,* Washington, D.C., Smithsonian Institution Press, 1894. Report on Mound Explorations of the Bureau of Ethnology. J. Huston McCulloch, "The Bat Creek Inscription: Did Judean Refugees Escape to Tennessee?" *Biblical Archaeology Review,* (July/Aug. 1993), pp. 46-53. Cyrus H. Gordon, *Before Columbus: Links between the Old World and Ancient America,* Crown Pub., New York, 1971, p. 187, notes "The significance of the excavations of Bat Creek is that they attest inscriptionally and archaeologically to a migration in early Christiian times from Judea to our Southwest."

[215]George E. Moorehouse, "The Los Lunas Inscriptions: A Geological Study", *Epigraphic Society Occasional Publications,* 13 (1985), pp. 44-50. Michael Skupin, "The Los Lunas Errata", *Epigraphic Society Occasional Publications,* 18 (1989), pp. 249-52. Barry Fell, "Ancient Punctuation and the Los Lunas Text", *Epigraphic Society Occasional Publicatons* 13 (1985), 32-43, cover

photo. Cyrus Gordon "Diffusion of Near East Culture in Antiquity and in Byzantine Times", *Orient,* 30-31 (1995), 69-81. Jay Stonebreaker, "A Decipherment of the Los Lunas Decalogue Inscription", *Epigraphic Society Occasional Publications* 10 (1982, Part 1), 74-81. James D. Tabor, "An Ancient Hebrew Inscription in New Mexico: Fact or Fraud?" *United Israel Bulletin,* Vol. 52, Summer 1997, pp. 1-3. Lyle L. Underwood, "The Los Lunas Inscription", *Occasional Publications* 10 (1982, Part 1), 57-67. J. D. Purvis, "The Samaritan Pentateuch and the Origin of the Samaritan Sect", *Harvard Semitic Monographs* (1968), vol. 2, Harvard University Press. Associated with the inscription is the mountain itself, which shows evidence of fortification and ancient habitation. The Decalogue inscription is located at the north side of the mountain at the foot, close to the only accessible pathway up. The top is a flat plateau with many ruins. The whole area is covered with drawings on rocks called petroglyphs. One of the most interesting of these petroglyphs is what appears to be a sky-map, laid out on a flat rock, recording the positions of the planets and constellations during a solar eclipse. Researcher David Deal, who did a drawing of the site, has identified the eclipse astronomically as occurring on Sept. 15, 107 B.C. Samaria was an Israeli city, circa 500 BC.

[216]Robert Alrutz, "The Newark Holy Stones: The History of an Archaeological Tragedy", *Journal of the Scientific Laboratories,* Denison University, 1980, 57: 1-57. David Allen Deal, *Discovery of Ancient America, 1st ed.,* Irvine CA, Kherem La Yah Press, 1984. Cyrus H. Gordon, "Diffusion of Near East Culture in Antiquity and in Byzantine Times, "*Orient* (1995), vol. 30-31: 69-81. J. Huston McCulloch, "The Newark Hebrew Stones: Wyrick's Letter to Joseph Henry", *Midwest Epigraphic Journal,* Vol. 6 (1989), pp. 5-10. "The The Newark, Ohio Inscribed Head: A New Translation", *Epigraphic Society Occasional Papers* (1990), vol. 19 : 75-80. Joseph Schenck, *Mysteries of the Holy Stones,* Pheasant Run Publications, St. Louis, 1982. Charles Whittlesey, "Archaeological Frauds: Inscriptions Attributed to the Mound Builders, Three Remarkable Forgeries", *Western Reserve Historical Society Historical & Archaeological,* 1872, Tract #9.

[217]Wuthenau, pp. 168-169.

[218]Gordon, pp. 175-89. See also Jeremiah F. Epstein, "Pre-Columbian Old World Coins in America", *Current Anthropology,* (Feb., 1980) Vol. 21 No. 1, pp. 1-20. Article on Hebrew Bar Kokhba coins.

[219]S. F. Balabanova, Parsche and W. Pirsig, "First Identification of Drugs in Egyptian Mummies." *Naturwissenschaften* (1992), 79, 358, Springer-Verlag. Dr. Balabanova ran samples from the mummies through a system which uses antibodies to detect the presence of drugs. The results confirmed the presence of drugs. Before Columbus, these plants had not been found anywhere in the world outside of the Americas. One of the UK's foremost authorities on mummies is Rosalie David, Keeper of Egyptology, Manchester Museum. When she was informed that cocaine had been found in Egyptian mummies she was highly skeptical of Balabanova's results and decided to get some samples from her own mummies and have them tested. It turned out that the results from the Munich mummies were not the only evidence from the dead. Balabanova, while conducting her normal research into the metabolism of drugs, had requested samples of other ancient human remains from universities. She received more results from Egypt. She tested tissue from 134 naturally preserved bodies from an excavated cemetery in the Sudan, once part of the Egyptian empire. About a third of them tested positive for nicotine and cocaine. A percentage of bodies from all these other regions also contained nicotine. The walls of the grand temple of Karnak are covered in depictions of the lotus flower, including the tops of the vast columns to the pictograms on the walls. The lotus was a very powerful narcotic which was used in ancient Egypt and presumably, was widespread in use. The pharaohs clearly indulged in drugs. Hashish—which Balabanova also found in the mummies—is an Egyptian tradition which has survived for thousands of years. For thousands of years people in the Andes have been chewing cocoa leaves to get out the cocaine with its stimulant, anaesthetic and euphoric properties. There are actually species of the cocoa family which grow in Africa, but only the South American species has ever been shown to contain the drug. Since cocaine is not in any African or Asian plants, Balabanova was completely mystified, but she thought she might have just one possible idea. Indians in America have also indulged in the pleasures of smoking tobacco and chewing cocoa leaves for thousands of years. Perhaps there was trans-oceanic

trade relationships long before Columbus, and cocoa plants had been imported into Egypt even then. Balabanova questioned if an ancient Egyptian drug trade stretched all the way across the Atlantic Ocean. Balabanova surmised that the idea was so far-fetched, it could only be considered when all the others had been eliminated.

220Barry Fell, *America B.C.*, New York: Demeter Press, 1976, pp. 125-155, "The Celts in America." A stamp from Portugal on page 32 illustrates stone dolmens like those found in North America. The Ogam Celtic scripts had been found inscribed on stones in England, France, Spain, Portugal and in the United States. These dolmens, as they are called, were made of large boulders and carefully trimmed stone roof-slabs and lintels, each weighing several tons. See also T. G. E. Powell, *The Celts*, London: Thames & Hudson, 1958. L. Winkler and R. E. Stone, "Construction and Use of America's Stonehenge", *New England Antiquities Research Association Journal* (1999), V. 33, No. 2.

221Letter by John Sevier, Knoxville: Oct. 9, 1810. Tennessee's first governor (1745-1815) responded to a request in 1810 by a researcher into the history of Louisiana. Seiver replied, "Your letter of Aug. 30 is before me. With respect to the information you have requested, I shall with pleasure give you so far as my own memory will now serve me; and also aided by a memorandum taken on the subject, of a nation of people called the Welsh Indians.... I took an opportunity of enquiring of a venerable old chief called Oconostota (died 1783), who then and had been for nearly sixty years the ruling chief of the Cherokee Nation, if he could inform me what people it had been which had left such signs of fortifications in their country and in pre-Columbian explorer sites in the Southeast, particular the one on the bank of Highwassee River...." Seiver in his reply reports Oconostota told of fighting between the white (Welsh) and Indians that was settled when, " the whites proposed to the Indians that they would exchange prisoners and cease hostilities, they would leave the Country and never more return, which was acceded to; and after the exchange parted friendly.... They (Welsh) descended the Tennessee down to the Ohio, thence down to the big river (the Mississippi), then they ascended it up to the Muddy River (the Missouri) and thence up that river for a great distance..." Oconostota had stated, "they are no more a white people; they are now all become Indians, and look like the other red people of the Country...." Seiver claimed he knew, "a French-man, who had lived with the Cherokees and said he had formerly been high up the Missouri. He informed me he had traded with the Welsh tribe; that they certainly spoke much of the Welsh dialect, and tho' their customs was savage and wild, yet many of them, particularly the females, were very fair and white, and frequently told him that they had sprung from a white nation of people."

222Paul Shao, *Asiatic Influences in Pre-Columbian American Art*, Ames: Iowa State, 1976. See also J. Soustelle, H.R. Lane, trans. *The Olmecs: The Oldest Civilization in Mexico*, Norman, Oklahoma: University of Oklahoma Press, 1985. M. D. Coe, *The Maya*, Sixth Edition, Singapore: Thames & Hudson. M. D. Coe, *Mexico: From the Olmec to the Aztecs*, 2001. Poem by Lao Tzu (600-300 B.C.), Chinese Taoist philosopher in *Tao-Te Ching*, that speaks of Quipu's. "A small country has fewer people.... The people take death seriously and do not travel far... though they have armor and weapons, no one displays them.... Men return to the knotting of rope in place of writing...."

223B. Mundkur, "The Cult of the Serpent in Mesoamerica: Its Asian Background", *Current Anthropology* (1976), 17: 429-455.

224V. Mansfield, West/Wadsworth, Belmont, California, "Mandalas and Mesoamerican Pecked Circles", *Current Anthropology* (1981), 22: 269-284. "The Alleged Diffusion of Hindu Divine Symbols into Pre-Columbian Mesoamerica: a Critique." *Current Anthropology* (1978), 19: 541-583.

225Paul Tolstoy, "Paper Route", *Natural History* (June, 1991), 100:6 . Shun-Sheng Ling, *Barkcloth, Impressed Pottery, and the Inventions of Paper and Printing*, Nanking (Taipei) Institute of Ethnology Academia Sinica, 1963, p. 42. Sir Harry Johnson, *The Uganda Protectorate*, London, 1902, p. 104. Victor W. Von Hagen, *The Aztec and Maya Papermakers*, Hacker Art Books, 1977. Fox, Hugh; *Gods of the Cataclysm*, New York: Dorset Press, 1981, pp. 19-27, "Chavin, The Prehistoric Transpacific." Samuel Dunn, *North America as Divided amongst the European Powers*, London: Prt., for Rob Sayer, No. 53 Fleet St., June 10, 1774.

226Hewitt R. Jackson, "Are We Living in the Land of Fou Seng?" *48° North* (July, 2001).

227Donald L. Cyr, ed., Donald Gilmore and Linda McElroy, *Across before Columbus?: Evidence for Transoceanic Contact with the Americas Prior to 1492*, Edgecomb, ME, New England Antiquities Research Association, 1998, pp. 280-83. A.V. Schaerffenberg, "Ancient Chinese Maps of the World", *The Chinese Connection*, Stelle, Ill.: Adventures Unlimited Press, 1994. See also *Ancient American*, Colfax, Wisconsin: Vol. 1, #4, Jan./Feb., 1994, pg. 28. Chinese accounts of overseas expeditions date from 2500 B.C. Buddhist historian Kuan-Mei identified America as "Fusang" and as the "Isle of the Blest", common Chinese names for America. Kuan-Mei also identified the Grand Canyon of Fusang as the site of astronomical observations during the reign of Emperor Shi Hwang-ti, about 246 B.C. Kuan-Mei noted, "It was in Fusang that Hwang-ti's astronomers resided, who were charged with observing the rising sun." Indians have long observed that natural rock formations in the Grand Canyon corresponded to the rising of the sun at solstices. The presence of Chinese astronomers in the area is confirmed by ancient Taoist Yin-Yang motifs on petroglyphs found in the area. Gavin Menzies, *1421: The Year China Discovered the World*, London: Transworld, 2002. "Oldest Map in China Found—2200 Years Old." *Pravada News*, May, 2002.

228Yuan Ke, *The Classic of Mountains and Seas*, with annotations, Shanghai: Shanghai guji, 1980, pp. 195, 199, 211, 214. Reprint, Harmondsworth: Penguin, 1999. Chinese Emperor Shi Huang-Ti, about 259-209 B.C., was the first ruler to unify all of China. In 221 B.C. his armies annexed the six states, and he assumed the title of First Emperor (Shi Huang-ti) of a new dynasty. He ordered his chancellor to burn all the literary classics of the past and began that immense work, the Great Wall of China. See also Hendon Harris, *The Asiatic Fathers of America*, Taiwan: Wen Ho Printing Co., 1975, pp. 302-303.

229Hendon Harris, *The Asiatic Fathers of America*, Taiwan: Wen Ho Publishing Co., 1975, pp. 302-303.

230*The Classic of Mountains and Seas*, Anne Birrell, trans. Harmondsworth: Penguin, 1999. See also Joseph Deguignes, *Recherches sur les Navigations des Chinois du Cotede L' Amerique*. in *Memoires de L'Academie des Inscriptios et Belles Lettres*, Vol. xxxviii, 1761. Charles G. Leland, *Fusang; or The Discovery of America by Chinese Buddhist Priests in the Fifth Century*, New York: Barnes & Noble, 1973. Henriette Mertz, *Pale Ink: Two Ancient Records of Chinese Exploration in America*, Chicago: Swallow Press, 1972, 1-2, 98-157. Donald Cyr, editor, Santa Barbara, CA., *Dragon Treasures*, Stonehenge Viewpoint, 1989, pg. 29, listing of Chinese world maps. George F. Carter, "Chinese Contacts with America: Fu-Sang Again." *Anthropological Journal of Canada* (1976), Vol. 14, No. 1. For detailed information on *History of the Liang Dynasty*, compiled in 628-35 A.D., see Wilkinson, *Chinese History: A Manual*, 1999, W-777.

231Donald Cyr, ed., *Dragon Treasures*, Stonehenge Viewpoint. See also *48° North*, Nov. '91 (on the Japanese currents). Partick Huyghe, *Columbus Was Last*, New York, Hyperion, 1992, on the Land of Fu-Sang, pgs. 113-128. Joseph Campbell, *The Mythic Image*, Princeton, NJ: Princeton University Press, 1974, pp. 122-129, pp. 130, 133. Pictured on pages 128-129 are a Ya Vessel from the Shang Dynasty, 1523-1027 B.C., and a Moche jar, 500 A.D. Both items are remarkable for their beauty and in their similarity. Joseph Deguignes, *Histoire Generale des Huns*, (1756-8); Joseph Deuignes, *Ch'ienlung, Emperor of China, 1711-1799*, Paris: N. M. Tilliard, 1770. Robert E. McKechnie, *Strong Medicine*, Vancouver, B.C., J. J. Douglas, Ltd., 1972, p. 7. Reports evidence of a visit by Chinese Buddhist monks or merchants in the area of British Columbia, Canada. The account of the travels of Hsu Fu is incorporated in the official yearbook of the Chinese empire during that year. It is also recorded that Hui-Shen (Buddhist priest) introduced Buddhism to Fusang. Hui-Shen was reported to have come from Cophene (Kophene), in Afghanistan. *Milwaukee Journal*, Sept. 15, 1980, On Fusang, "A New Discoverer, China Presses claim that it Found America." *San Francisco Chronicle*, Nov. 25, 1979, writes of archaeologist James R. Moriarty of the University of San Diego, California, unearthing Chinese stone anchors near Palos Verdes Peninsula and off Point Mendocino. In the latter case, the anchors were encrusted with manganese, which showed that it had been lying on the seabed possibly as long as 2000 or 3000 years.

232Joseph Campbell, *The Mythic Image*, Princeton, NJ: Princeton University Press, 1974, pp. 146-147. "It now appears that the Mayan table registered in the *Dresden Codex* matches to a fault the Han Chinese. According to the so-called phase coincidence cycle of the Han astronomers, the Mayan figures simply triple the Chinese; the proportions are the same." The Han Chinese dynasty existed from 206 B.C. to 220 A.D. and was noted for a revival of its culture and the introduction of Buddhism.

[233]Dr. Youliang, trans., *Neolithic Site at Bampo Near Xian*, printed and published in China, 1982. Pottery designs unearthed and pictured are remarkable in their resemblance to the ancient Anasazi (ancient ones) pottery finds that predate the Pueblo culture that began to develop about 700 A.D.

[234]Hartwig Hausdorf, *Die Weisse Pyramide*, Munich: Knaur Publishers, 1994. Published in German with photographs of the Chinese pyramids. It was reported that the large pyramid was originally painted black on the North side, blue-gray or faded green on the East, red on the South and white on the West. From approximately the same time period that the large pyramids were built in Egypt. See also *National Geographic*, Oct., 1996, p. 74, which shows a diagram of the Qin Shi Huang burial mound in Xian.

[235]*Ocala Star Banner*, Ocala, Florida, Tuesday, Feb. 25, 1997. Reported from Barnaul, Russia, by Interfax.

[236]Betty J. Meggers, Clifford Evans and Emilio Estrada, *Early Formative Period of Coastal Ecuador: The Valdivia and Machilillia Phases*, Washington, D. C., Smithsonian Institution Press, 1965. Joman pottery shards can be seen at the Bank Museum of Ecuador. See also Tadayoshi Kawamura, *Mayan God and Joman God*, self-published, 2002.

[237]Gunnar Thompson, *American Discovery*, Seattle, Washington: 1984, pp. 32-33. Shows "Japanese voyagers." These symbolic motifs were common both in Japan's Ainu folk culture and are also found in the Northwest Indian tribes.

[238]R. A. Jairazbhoy, *Ancient Egyptians and Chinese in America*, Totowa, NJ: Rowman and Littlefield, 1974.

[239]David H. Kelley, *Deciphering The Mayan Script*, Austin: University of Texas, 1976. The Zero date is astonishingly precise. The date on the Mayan calendar, when converted into the date on the Julian calendar, becomes Aug. 12, 3113 B.C. Their calendar is only one day short in every 5000 years while our modern calendar is one and a half days too long in 5000 years.

[240]Helmut de Terra, translated from German by Alan Houghton Broderick, *Man and Mammoth in Mexico*, London: Hutchinson & Co., 1957, pp. 160-171. W. D. Strong, "Indian Oral Traditions Suggest a Knowledge of the Mammoth", *American Anthropologist*, (1934) Vol. 36: 81-88.

[241]Leo Deuel, *Conquistadors Without Swords*, New York: Schocken Books, 1974, p. 522. See also Gunnar Thompson, *American Discovery*, Seattle, Washington: 1984, pp. 218-219.

[242] Thompson, pp. 218-219.

[243]Edward P. Lamming, *Peru Before the Incas*, Englewood N.J., Prentice Hall, Inc., 1967, pp. 164-165.

[244]Carl L. Johannessen, D. Y. Gilmore and L. S. McElroy, eds., "Maize Diffused to India before Columbus came to America", *Across Before Columbus?: Evidence for Transoceanic Contact with the Americas Prior to 1492*, New England Antiquities Research Association, Edgecomb, Maine: 1998, pp. 109-24. Article on Maize in America and sculptured statues in India.

[245]Shakti M. Gupta, *Plants in Indian Temple Art*, Delhi: B. R. Publishing Corp., 1996, pp. 17-20, 30. *Midwest Epigraphic Journal*, vol. 12/13, 1998-99, pp. 43-44. Book review writes, "Gupta's book contains a wealth of evidence for pre-Columbian contacts between the New World and the Old despite the fact that she is not particularly interested in, or even aware of, the possibility. Gupta does not stop with maize, but goes on to identify sunflower, pineapple, cashew, and custard apple as all new world species in pre-Columbian temple art. Monstera, a split-leaf philodendron large evergreen climber, native to Central America, appears in Hindu and Jain temples in Gujarat and Rajastan from the 11th to 13th centuries. Sunflower, a native of Central and South America, is found in the Rani Gumpha cave, Udaigiri, from the 2nd century B.C. Guptya also finds pineapple as a plant indigenous to Brazil, 'clearly depicted' in the Udayagiri cave temple, Madhya Pradesh, circa 5th century A.D."

[246]Jaweed Ashraf, "Maize in India: Introduction or Indigenous", *Annuals, NAGI*, (Dec. 1994) Vol. XIV, #2, pp. 6-26. See also Johannessen, "Indian Maize in the Twelfth Century A.D", *Nature*, 1988. See also Johannessen & Parker "Maize Ears Sculptured",

Economic Botany (1989), Veena and Sigamani, "Do Objects in South India Represent Maize Ears?" *Current Science*, Vol. 61, pp. 395-396.

[247]A. Hyatt Verrill, *Old Civilizations of the New World*, Indianapolis: Bobbs Merrill Co., 1929, p. 116. A reproduction of this bas relief shows two deities with a corn plant. See also Edward P. Kellog Jr., ed., *The True Origin of the Indians of the Americas or The Roots of the American Indian*, Walnut Creek, CA., 1980. Translated by Benjamin M. Rea from the Spanish, *El Verdadero Origen De Los Amerindios*, pgs. 91-94, 178. "Definitive illustration of sculptured maize." *Scottish Banner* (May, 1996), Lewiston, NY, vol. 19, #11.

[248]Sertima, p. 258, note 28, on "How Ancient is West African Maize?" See also Gunnar Thompson, p. 105, on maize in Africa.

[249]Johannessen & Parker, "Maize Ears Sculptured..."*Economic Botany*, (1989). Objects in the hands of the male and female deities sculptured on the exterior of the Kesav temple at Somnathpur near the city of Mysore, India, represent maize. See also Veena & Sigamani, "Do Objects in South India Represent Maize Ears?" *Current Science*, Vol. 61, pp. 395-396. M. M. Payak, & J. K. S. Sachan, "Maize Ears not Sculpted in 13th Century Somnathpur Temple in India", *Economic Botany*, April 1, 1993, vol. 47, No. 2, p. 202. Claims maize now grown near the temple originates from the 1960s and the sculpture would not show maize but instead an "imaginary fruit bearing pearls known in Sanskrit as Muktaphala."

[250]Campbell, *The Mythic Image*, Princeton, NJ, Princeton University Press, 1974, pp. 151-154, 330-335.

[251]Alvin M. Josephy, Jr., *America in 1492*, New York: Random House, 1991, pp. 378-379.

[252]Fewkes, "Snake Ceremonials at Walpi", *Journal of American Ethnology and Archaeology*, Vol. 4, Cambridge, MA, 1895.

[253]Alan Landsburg, *In Search of Lost Civilizations*, New York, Bantam Books, 1976, pp. 153-155. "The Indus basin is an oblong valley eight hundred miles long, one or two hundred miles across, and an especially uninviting part of what is now India." It covered an area of land more extensive than Egypt.

[254]Geoffrey Parrinder, ed., *World Religions, From Ancient History to the Present*, New York, Facts on File, 1971, pp. 212-219. "Philosophically, the great Goddess is the shakti or power of Shiva, who represents the opposite pole of maleness, consciousness and rest;..."

[255]Dr. Allen C. Ross, *Mitakuye Oyasin: We are All Related*, Denver, Colorado, Wiconi Waste Pub. Co, 1989, pp. 76-90. See also J. R. Conrad, *The Horn and the Sword – The History of the Bull as Symbol of Power and Fertility*, New York: Dutton, 1957, pp. 20-21.

[256]Professor W. Masaaki Kimura,' "Ryukyu in the Late Quaternary", in *Journal of Geography* (in Japanese), (1996) 105 (3), pp. 261-268. Article on the Continent of Mu as part of the Ryukyu Islands dating back over 10,000 years. "Archaeological similarities have been found between immigrant and indigenous groups scattered throughout the ten thousand nautical miles of the Pacific in what has come to be called the "Lapita" 3 culture." See also Col. James Churchward, *The Books of the Golden Age*, Albuquerque, N.M.: Brotherhood of Life Publishing, 1997. Reprint of four books pertaining to the investigation of Mu. Mu is specifically discussed in one of the four books: *The Sacred and Inspired Writings of Mu*. Churchward, by studying various ancient texts, had discovered the existence of what he believed was a long lost continent with an advanced civilization that 60,000 years ago had sunk below the Pacific Ocean after a cataclysmic earthquake. Churchward claimed 64 million people died in the sinking, that dated back over 50,000 years. The Hawaiian Islands and the Pacific Islands are the remaining mountain peaks of the lost continent.

[257]Professor Nobuhiro Yoshida, "Stone Tablets of Mu, The Motherland of Mankind", *Ancient American*, Colfax, WI, Nov./Dec., 1997, vol. 3, #21, pp. 18-22. Professor Nobuhiro Yoshida is Japan's leading authority on ancient petroglyphs. Trushar Barot, "Divers find World's Oldest Building", *The Sunday Times*, London, April 26, 1998, p. 4. Frank Joseph, "Underwater City found near Japan" *Ancient America*, (March/April 1997), vol. 3, #17, pp. 2-6. Robert M. Schoch, with Robert Aquinas McNally, *Voices of the Rocks: A Scientist Looks at Catastrophes and Ancient Civilizations*, New York: Harmony, Crown Publishing, Random House, 1999.

[258]Yoshida, p. 21. Sa refers to Sacred. Ra is the same sun god as that worshipped by the Egyptians. Mu refers to the Earth Goddess. The name SA-Ra-Mu appears in old Japanese writing. On p. 19: Petroglyphs of similar ships have been found engraved on stone in an

Inca ruin in Peru, and in Borobudur, Java, dated to the 8th century B.C. See also Henriette Mertz, *Atlantis: Dwelling Place of the Gods*, Chicago: Private Printing, 1976; Col. James Churchward, *The Lost Continent of Mu*, New York: Ives Washburn, 1931.

[259]Garcilaso De La Vega, El Inca (The Inca), *First Part of the Royal Commentaries of the Incas*, Clement Markham, editor, Hakluyt Society, 1869, 1871.

[260]John Hemming, *Discovery of Lost Worlds*, edited by Joseph J. Thorndike Jr., New York: Simon & Schuster, 1979. See also Alden J. Mason, *The Ancient Civilizations of Peru*, Middlesex: Penguin Books, 1968; John Mitchell, *The New View over Atlantis*, Great Britain: Sago Press, 1969; Philip Van Ness Myers, *Ancient History*, New York: Ginn & Co., 1904.

[261]Churchward, pp. 130-132. On the buried civilizations of Mexico City and Tiahuanaco as a colony of Mu. See also Wendell C. Bennett, "Excavations at Tiahuanaco", *Anthropological Papers of the American Museum of Natural History*, (1934) Vol. xxxiv, Part III; Gordon R. Willey, *An Introduction to American Archaeology, Volume Two: South America*, Prentice-Hall, Englewood Cliffs, 1971; Pedro Cieza de Leon, *Chronicle of Peru*, London: Hakluyt Society, 1864 and 1883, Part I, Chapter 87, as reproduced in Graham Hancock, *Fingerprints of the Gods*, New York: Crown, 1995, p.73. See also Garcilaso de la Vega, El Inca, *Royal Commentaries of the Inca & General History of Peru (Part One)*, Harold Livermore, trans. from 1616 original, Austin: University of Texas Press, 1987. Garcilaso de la Vega made the following notes about Tiahuanaco soon after the Spanish conquest: "We must now say something about the large and most incredible buildings of Tiahuanaco. There is an artificial hill, of great height, built on stone foundations so that the earth will not slide. There are gigantic figures carved in stone... these are much worn which shows their great antiquity. There are walls, the stones of which are so enormous it is difficult to imagine what human force could have put them in place. And there are the remains of strange buildings, the most remarkable being stone portals, hewn out of solid rock; these stand on bases anything up to 30 feet long, 15 feet wide and six feet thick, base and portal being all of one piece.... How, and with the use of what tools or implements, massive works of such size could be achieved are questions which we are unable to answer... nor can it be imagined how such enormous stones could have been brought here." The two stone carvings in the "Gate of the Sun" (Tiwahaku) show animals which were extinct more than 10,000 years ago—the elephant and the toxodon. Professor Denis Saurat of France identifies the carvings as the head of a toxodon, a prehistoric animal now extinct. The elephant disappeared from the Americas over 10,000 years ago and the toxodon was believed to have disappeared from the South American landmass around 1.6 million years ago. The toxodon and the family toxodontidae were South American notoungulates of the Pliocene and Pleistocene eras. The toxodon itself is described as rhinoceros-like, about 10 feet long. See also Marcel F. Homet, *Sons of the Sun*, England: Neville Spearman, 1963. Suggests the possibility that a Sumerian colony established itself around Titicaca, in what is now known as Bolivia. According to legend the first Inca, Manko-Kapak, appeared in Lake Titicaca and tradition held that the Incas were red or brown-haired—a characteristic alien to American Indians, but many mummies discovered there confirm this fact. Huge blocks of stone found at Tiahuanaco were once held together by copper and even gold rivets. This was a method of building construction almost identical to that used in Assyria and Eritrea thousands of years ago. The colony even used solid stone wheels, just like the ones in use by the Sumerians themselves, and were thought to have transported the huge stone blocks in this manner. The tribe living around Lake Titicaca is called the Uru and elders retain memories of people of their tribe being sacrificed under the foundations when Tiahuanaco was built. The name Uru suggests Ut, which again is linked to the Sumerian civilization. The Incas carried out mummification and, like the Sumerians, placed a metal disc in the mouth of a corpse. They also built pyramids and obelisks, while using cups, plates, spoons and goblets much like those in the Old World. Both the Sumerians and the Incas held the rainbow as sacred and each carried their notables around in litters. A temple in Chavin, Peru, contains an ingenious system of air conduits that still carries fresh air to every room in the building and is very similar to one discovered in the Cretan palace at Knosses. Posnansky had several astronomers from highly respected institutions check the alignment of the site and the tilt of the Kalasasaya temple to compare the tilt to a distant era of time. Kalasasaya Court marked the rising of the sun at the solstice, as would have been observed around 12,000 B.C. The rectangular enclosure, marked out by roughly hewn megaliths interspersed by dry-stone walling, was a solstice marker. It was oriented east towards the rising sun at the equinoxes, and had four megaliths positioned at the eastern wall. The megaliths in the north-east and south-east corners were, respectively, 23.5 degrees north and south of east, suggesting they were solstice markers, since this was within the parameter of rising and setting in previous ages. The exact angle of the solstice risings, north and south of east, varies in accordance with a 41,000 year wobble of the earth known as the "Obliquity of the Ecliptic."

[262]I. K. Fedorova, *Versions of Myths and Legends in Manuscripts from Easter Island*, 1965. In T. Heyerdahl et al., *Miscellaneous Papers: Reports of the Norwegian Archaeological Expedition to Easter Island and East Pacific*. Vol. 2. Stockholm: *Forum*, pp. 395-401. See also J. A. Van Tilburg, *Easter Island: Archaeology, Ecology and Culture*: Smithsonian Institution Press, Washington: D. C., 1994. Also, *The Quest for America*, pp. 208-211.

[263]Arturo Posnansky, *Tiahuanacu: The Cradle of American Man*, 4 Vols., translated by James F. Shearer, Locust Valley: NY, 1945. The orientation of the Kalasasaya at Tiahuanacu caught the attention of Prof. Arturo Posnansky, a German engineer who was studying the ruins. Our earth is now tilted at an angle of 23 degrees and 17 minutes. The Earth's axis moves back and forth between 22 degrees and 1 minute to an extreme of 24 degrees and 5 minutes. One complete oscillation takes roughly 41,000 years to complete. By measuring the tilt of the earth on its axis in respect to the plane of the solar system, astronomers were able to determine a date of the site at about 10,000 B.C. See also J. M. Bird, *Plate Tectonics*: Washington: D.C., American Geophysical Union, 1980, p. 986. R. S. Dietz, "Continent and Ocean Basin Evolution by Spreading of the Sea Floor", *Nature* (1961), vol. 190, pp. 30-41. X. Le Pichon, "Sea-floor Spreading and Continental Drift", *Journal of Geophysical Research* (1968), v. 73, pp. 3661-3697. D. P. McKenzie and R. L. Parker, "The North Pacific: An Example of Tectonics of a Sphere", *Nature*, 1967, vol. 216, pp. 1276-1280; A. Wegener, *The Origin of Continents and Oceans*, New York: Dover, 1966; T. Wilson, "A New Class of Faults and their Bearing on Continental Drift", *Nature* (1965), v. 207, pp. 343-347. Plate tectonics, the branch of science that deals with the process by which rigid plates are moved across hot molten material, has helped to explain, in global-scale geology, the formation of mountains and the distribution of earthquakes and volcanoes. Almost every society in the world has their own flood legends.

[264]Michael Bradley, *The Black Discovery of America*, Toronto: Personal Library, 1981, pp. 4, 9. See also Sertima, p. 45.

[265]Dbyani Ywahoo, *Voices of our Ancestors*, Boston and London: Shambhala Publications, Inc., 1987, pp. 15-16.

[266]Barry Fell, *America B.C.*, New York: Demeter Press, 1976, pp. 253-285.

[267]Maria Longhena, *Mayan Script*, New York: Abbeville Press, p. 172, covers a system of "Bean Writing", by the Moche. Victor W. Von Hagen, *The Ancient Kingdoms of the Americas*, Cleveland and New York: The World Publishing Company, 1961, pp. 186-188. William Burns worked as a professor of textile engineering besides teaching some Quechua classes on the side. He studied Guamán Poma's book, *The First New Chronicle and Good Government*, 800 pages, and the 400 pages of pen and ink drawings. In 1978, in the pictures, Burns noticed some symbols on the robes of Guamán Poma's two leaders. The names of the leaders were above the pictures in Spanish. Reading from the Spanish and comparing the names of the two leaders, Burns was able to decode some of the symbols as letters. Examinations of more and more drawings and textiles from the Incan empire allowed him to interpret more and more of the cryptic symbols. According to Burns, the ancient writing system consists of twelve letters and ten numbers, with numbers doubling as letters. As in Hebrew, the vowels are left out. Burns' findings have been disputed based on his non-scientific background.

[268]Julian H. Steward, ed., *Handbook of South American Indians*, Washington, D.C., 1946-1950, 6 vols., Vol. 2. Refers to the Andean Civilizations.

[269]Priscilla S. Meyer, "Rewriting America's History: Genetics and the South Pacific", *Ancient American*, (1996) Colfax, Wisconsin: Vol.2, issue #9, pp. 12-15.

[270]Douglas C. Wallace, "Dramatic Founder Effects in Amerind

Mitochondrial DNAs", *American Journal of Physical Anthropology*, (1985) vol. 68, pp. 149-155. T. G. Schurr, "Amerind Mitochondrial DNAs have Rare Asian Mutations", *American Journal of Human Genetics* (1990), vol. 46 #3, pp. 613-623.

271Carol Riley, J. Kelley, C. Pennigian & R. Rands, editors, *Man Across Sea*, Austin: University of Texas Press, 1971, p. 413. Gunnar Thompson, *America Discovery*, Seattle, Washington: 1984, p. 105.

272Carleton Beals, *Nomads and Empire Builders*, New York: Citadel Press, 1965, pp. 98-99. Describes pre-Inca, Chavin culture building techniques of enormous blocks fitted together. See also Robert F. Spencer, Jesse D. Jennings, *The American Indians*, New York: Harper and Row, 1965, pp. 404-405. Also J. B. Griffin, *Archaeology of Eastern United States*, Chicago University Press, 1952, pp. 221-238. Covers prehistoric cultures of the Central Mississippi Valley. Irvin M. Peithmann, *Echoes of the Red Man*, New York: Exposition Press, 1955, pp. 43-61. "The Hopwellians were busy trading up and down the river, farming and becoming more settled in their habits centuries before the Roman Empire fell in A.D. 476." See also Time-Life Books, *The Age of God-Kings, Time Frame: 1500 to 3000 B.C.*, covers Mesopotamia and Egypt. One of the great two centers of Harrapan culture, the city of Mohenjo-Daro, was divided by a corridor 200 yards wide along the Indus river, separating the city into two sections.

273Friedrich Katz, *The Ancient American Civilizations*, New York: Praeger, 1969, 1972.

274John R. Swanton, "Indian Tribes of the Lower Mississippi Valley and Adjacent Coast of the Gulf of Mexico", *Bureau of American Ethnology* (1911), Bulletin 43, Smithsonian. See also Jim Barnett, *The Natchez Indians*, Mississippi Department of Archives and History Popular Report, Natchez, 1998. Wendall H. Oswalt and Sharlotte Neely, "The Natchez: Sophisticated Farmers of the Deep South", in *This Land was Theirs*, 5th edition, Mayfield Publishing Co., Mountain View, CA., 1996, pp. 467-491. In 1901 in Ross County in Southern Ohio, mounds were discovered on a country estate named Adena. These mounds extended into five states. There are records of Thomas Jefferson exploring mounds as early as 1780. It was not believed at that time that they were the work of the Indians. In 1842 the *American Ethnological Society* was founded by Albert Gallatin and Henry Schoolcraft to support research in American prehistory. In 1892 more than 30 mounds were discovered in southern Ohio on a farm belonging to Captain M. C. Hopewell. The largest mound was 23 feet high on 110 acres. The mounds extended north and south along the Mississippi river.

275Robert Silverberg, *The Mound Builders*, Athens, Ohio: Ohio University Press, 1986. Martha A. Potter, *Ohio's Prehistoric Peoples*, Ohio Historical Society, Columbus, OH, 1968. Also David G. Anderson, *The Role of Cahokia in the Evolution of Southeastern Mississippian Society in Cahokia: Domination and Ideology in the Mississippian World*, edited by Timothy R. Pauketat and Thomas E. Emerson, Lincoln: University of Nebraska Press, 1997, pp. 248-268. Monks mound in Cahokia was built with a larger base than the Khufu pyramid.

276Marija Gimbutas, *The Language of the Goddess*, San Francisco: Harper & Row, 1989, p. 53, fig. 89. See also Barry Fell, *Saga America*, New York, NY, Times Books, 1980, p. 66; Jamake Highwater, *Native Land*, New York: Barnes & Noble, Inc., 1995, p. 180.

277*The Log of Christopher Columbus: First Voyage to America in the Year 1492*, noted in preface, "as copied out in brief by Bartholomew Las Casas, one of his companions." London: W. H. Allen & Co., Ltd., Illustrations by J. O'H Cosggrave. " Preamble to the book beginning with "In the Name of Our Lord Jesus Christ."

278Francis de Beer, ed. "We Saw Brother Francis", Chicago: *Franciscan Herald Press*, 1983. See also John L. Kessell, *Friars, Soldiers, and Reformers: Hispanic Arizona and the Sonora Mission Frontier, 1767-1856*, Tucson: University of Arizona Press, 1976. The Franciscans were an important presence in the New World from the early 1500's to 1763. There were Franciscan missionaries as far south as Colombia and Venezuela, and as far north as Canada. See also Lewis Hanke, *The Spanish Struggle for Justice in the Conquest of America*, Philadelphia: University of Pennsylvania Press, 1949, pp. 83-86, 89.

279William H. Prescott, *History of the Conquest of Mexico*, New York: Harper and Brothers, 1843. William H. Prescott, *History of the Conquest of Peru*, New York: Harper and Brothers, 1847, republished by Reprint Heritage Press, 1957. Pedro de Gamboa Sarmiento, *History of the Incas*, trans. Sir Clements Markham, Cambridge, England, 1907. The Aztec Codex books that survived were printed on deerskin or bark paper, in exquisite colored pictorial hieroglyphics depicting mythological and historic writings related to their calendar and religious ceremonies.

280Diego de Landa, *Relacion de Las Cosas de Yucatan*, Alfred M. Tozzer, ed., Cambridge, Mass., 1941. See also "Papers of the Peabody Museum of American Archaeology and Ethnology", vol. XVIII. Landa's book was found in 1864 by Charles Etienne Brasseur. Three important books written by the Maya before the conquest were also found. They were the books of *Chilam-Balam* that contained an abridged history of the Maya, and the *Popol-Vuh*, that translates as a "Collection of Writings." The third famous book was the *Dresden Codex*, now at the Royal Library in Dresden. It contains 39 leaves of bark paper, totaling 78 pages, painted on both sides with vibrant colors of dark red, light red, black, blue, yellow, brown, green, and a rich shiny black. The books were printed from the bark of the ficus tree. The bark was pulled from the tree, soaked in water and then beaten until it was about .079 inch thick. Finally it was covered with white sizing, upon which the hieroglyphics were painted in different colors.

281Frances Gardiner Davenport, editor, *European Treaties Bearing on the History of the United States and its Dependencies*, Washington, D.C., Carnegie Institution of Washington Publications, 1914, 254, I, info on The Bull Romanus Pontifex, p. 23. See also Luis Weckman, *Las Bulas Alejandrinas de 1493 y la Teoria Politica del Papado Medieval*, Mexico, 1949.

282France V. Scholes and Ralph L. Roys, "Friar Diego de Landa and the Problem of Idolatry in Yucatán", *Co-operation in Research*, Washington, D.C. (1938), pp. 585-620. See also Inga Clendinnen, *Ambivalent Conquests: Maya and Spaniard in Yucatán, 1517-1570*, Cambridge, MA, Cambridge University Press, 1987, pp. 72-111. Contains detailed accounts of Landa and the inquisition. Landa was the provincial head of Merida, under the provincial administrator of the Yucatan.

283Inga Clendinnen, *Ambivalent Conquests*, Cambridge, MA, Cambridge: University Press, 1987, pp. 75-76, 100-102. See also Frances V. Scholes and Eleanor B. Adams, eds., *Don Diego Quijada, Alcalde Mayor de Yucatan, 1561-1565*, Mexico, Editorial Porrua, 2 volumes, 1938, vol. 2, pp. 209-221.

284Clendinnen, p. 108. The regulation granting leniency to the Indians was invoked as a result of the excessive sufferings inflicted previously on the Indians by Bishop Landa and the other missionaries in Mexico. Las Casas appealed in 1551 in his book, *In Defense of the Indians*, and a subsequent debate resulted in an edict attempting to restrict the inhuman treatment against the Indians.

285Clendinnen, p. 102. See also Antonio de Remesal, *Historia de la Provincia de S. Vicente de Chyapa y Guatemala*, Madrid: Francisco de Angulo, 1619.

286Garcilaso de la Vega, *Primera Parte de Los Commentarios Reales, Lisboa, 1609*. Reprint, *Royal Commentaries of the Incas and General History of Peru*, Austin: University of Texas Press, 1966. In a conversation with the Inca King, Vega wrote down the chronology of succession.

287John L. Kessell, *Friars, Soldiers, and Reformers: Hispanic Arizona and the Sonora Mission Frontier, 1767-1856*, Tucson: University of Arizona Press, 1976, pp. 69-71. On treatment by missionaries in Arizona. See also Henry Warner Bowden, *American Indians and Missions: Studies in Cultural Conflict*, Chicago: University of Chicago Press, 1981, pp. 52-57, 127-128. Ramon A. Gutierrez, *When Jesus Came, the Corn Mothers Went Away: Marriage, Sexuality, and Power in New Mexico, 1500-1846*, Stanford, CA: Stanford University Press, 1991, pp. 73-80. Gutierrez casts this as a replay of the legend of Francis, renouncing his natural father to completely serve God. Friars joining the order had to turn their backs on their families in a similar fashion, and now they forced Indians to make the same choice, rejecting their fathers, their traditions, and their way of life. Some of the strictest punishments were specifically designed to humiliate the older generation, stripping them of power and respect. Using drama as a teaching tool to bridge the language gap, the friars cast children as angels or Christians, and their parents as devils, infidels or enemies. See also pp. 127-128 on Father Salvador de Guerra's whipping a Hopi.

288Frances Gardiner Davenport, ed., *European Treaties Bearing on the History of the United States and its Dependencies*, Washington,

D.C., Carnegie Institution of Washington Publications, 1914, 254, I, The Bull Romanus Pontifex, p. 23. See also Luis Weckman, *Las Bulas Alejandrinas de 1493 y la Teoria Politica del Papado Medieval*, Mexico, 1949. The Treaty of Tordesillas pushed the line of demarcation 1175 miles west, giving Portugal the rights to colonize Brazil. P. Maxwell-Stuart, *Chronicles of the Popes*, Thames & Hudson, 1997. J. Brusher, *Popes through the Ages,* New Advent, 1996. E. Chamberlain, *The Bad Popes*, Barnes & Noble, 1993. Alexander VI, known as Borgia, had at least 10 illegitimate children including Cesare and Lucrezia, by Vanozza. When he was 58 he was infatuated with a 15-year old beauty, Giulia Farnese, who had been recently married. The Pope openly acknowledged his children by her—Laura, Juan and Rodrigo. He made Guilia's brother cardinal and the future Paul III. His son Cesare became Archbishop of Valencia and a Cardinal a year later. Pope Paul III (Alessandro Farnese, 1468-1549) fathered four children by a Roman mistress and reigned as head of the papacy from 1534 to 1549. He convened the Council of Trent to clarify the Catholic doctrine on the reformation and initiated reforms within the church.

[289]Lewis Hanke, "Pope Paul III and the American Indians", *Harvard Theological Review* (April, 1937), Vol. 30, #2, p. 77.

[290]Bartolomé de Las Casas, *Historia de las Indias,* Mexico: Fondo de Cultura Economica, 1951, 3 volumes, translated by Andre Collard. An important history of the Spanish conquest and subjugation of the Indians in the new world. See also *Natural History*, Oct., 1996, Vol. 105, No. 10, p. 29.

[291]*Royal Decrees, Leyes y Ordenancas*, Printed at Alcala, Spain, 1543. This book is the earliest of printed ordinances for America. A later edition was printed in Madrid, Spain, in 1585. A copy is in the Harvard College Library, Boston, Massachusetts, USA. Another edition was printed in Valladolid, Spain, in 1603.

[292]Justin Winsor, ed., *Narrative and Critical History of America* (8 vol., 1884–89), New York: Houghton Mifflin Co., 1886, Vol. II. On Spanish explorations in America from the fifteenth to the seventeenth century, Vol. 2 pp. 320-323. Lists La Casas' 30 propositions. *Royal Decrees Leyes y Ordenancas,* printed at Alcala, Spain, 1543.

[293]Robert Himmerich y Valencia, *The Encomenderos of New Spain, 1521-1555*, University of Texas Press, Dec., 1991. See also Robert Stoner Chamberlain, *Pre-Conquest Labor Practices in Indian Labor in the Spanish Indies*, Boston: D.C. Heath and Co., 1966. Crown of Spain, "The Laws of Burgos" in *Indian Labor in the Spanish Indies*, D. C. Heath and Co., Boston, 1966. Lewis Hanke, *The Spanish Struggle for Justice in the Conquest of America*, Philadelphia, University of Pennsylvania Press, 1949, pp. 83-86, "The Encomienda System." Robert Valencia Himmerichy, *The Encomenderos of New Spain*, Austin: University of Texas Press, 1991. Lesley Byrd Simpson, *On the New Laws in Indian Labor in the Spanish Indies,* Boston: D. C. Heath and Co., 1966. D. O. Flynn, A. Giráldez (1997), *Mines of Silver and Gold in the Americas*, edited by Peter Bakewell, in *An Expanding World: The European Impact on World History*, pp. 1450-1800, vol. 19, series edited by A. J. R. Russell-Wood. Fr. Joel S. Panzer, *The Popes and Slavery*, Staten Island, NY, Alba House, 1996, pp. 8, 75-7.

[294]Alvin M. Josephy Jr. (ed.), William Brandon (Narrative), *American Heritage Book of Indians*, New York, Random House, 1961, p. 139. In 1551 "Indian slaves in Mexico mines—160,000 of them—were to some degree actually, not only technically, freed from forced labor..." In 1552 a special court was set up for the protection of Indian rights in Mexico. In 1573 Spain passed additional "New Laws", again subjecting the Indians to slavery. See also John Collier, *Indians of the Americas*, New York, W. W. Norton, 1947, pp. 80-98. Gold was the important factor against any changes. In the late 1500s Spain, facing bankruptcy due to new ships, threats from the Moors, and its invasion of Portugal, abrogated all of its promises. Indians were forced into more brutal labor in the gold and silver mines, which reduced their numbers from 1,490,000 in 1563 to 612,000 in 1754. Unrest by the majority of peasant Indians against Spain and the succeeding power structures in Central and South America continued off and on until modern times.

[295]Justin Winsor, ed., *Narrative and Critical History of America* (8 vol., 1884–89), New York: Houghton Mifflin Co., 1886, 2: 217-230. On Spanish explorations in America from the fifteenth to the seventeenth century. Lists La Casas' 30 propositions. See also *Royal Decrees Leyes y Ordenancas*, printed at Alcala, Spain, 1543, pp. 320-323.

[296]Winsor, p. 333. See also Bartolomé De Las Casas, trans., and C. M. Stafford Poole, ed., *In Defense of the Indians*, De Kalb, Illinois: Northern Illinois University Press, 1992, p. 46. Don Antonio Sepulveda, a wealthy Spanish merchant, spent his lifetime and died in his search for Eldorado (the land of gold). Sepulveda was a member of the business community in Columbia. All that concerned him was his greed for gold. With the permission of the Spanish nobility in 1580 Sepulveda dredged a lake in Columbia to look for a fortune in lost gold. An army of Indians was forced to drain the lake and found an egg-sized emerald and a few gold objects. Sepulveda died before he could arrange for another expedition.

[297]Winsor, p. 320.

[298]Bartolomé de Las Casas, trans., and ed. C.M. Stafford Poole, *In Defense of the Indians*, De Kalb, Illinois: Northern Illinois University Press, 1992, p. 11. Translation of a 1552 Latin manuscript by Bartolomé De Las Casas in the Paris National Library.

[299]Casas, p. 12.

[300]Casas, p. 14.

[301]Casas, p. 15.

[302]Casas, p. 15.

[303]Casas, p. 28.

[304]Casas, p. 39.

[305]Casas, pp. 42-43.

[306]Casas, pp. 45, 43-44, 47. Paola Giovio, *History of His Times*, 1500s. Giovio left an early testimony of the Spanish conquest. Speaking on human sacrifice, Bishop Giovio stated, "The rulers of the Mexicans have a right to sacrifice men to their Gods, provided they have been condemned for a crime."

[307]Casas, pp. 54, 287, 360, 362.

[308]Casas, p. 9.

[309]Daniel J. Boorstin, *The Discoverer's*, New York: Random House, 1983, p. 634.

[310]Friar Bernardino de Sahagun, translated by Fanny R. Bandelier from the Spanish version of Carlos Maria de Bustamante, *History of Ancient Mexico*, Nashville: TN., Fisk University Press, 1932.

[311]Jack Weatherford, *Native Roots,* New York: Faucet Columbine, 1991, p. 112.

[312]Malcolm Margolin, *The Ohlone Way*, Berkeley, CA, Heyday Books, 1978, p. 37.

[313]Margolin, 29, 37, 89, 94, 150, 154.

[314]Friar Francisco Palou, *Life and Apostolic Labors of the Venerable Father Junipero Serra*, Pasadena, CA: G. W. James, 1913.

[315]Margolin, p. 161.

[316]Weatherford, p. 111.

[317]Jean Francois de Galoup de LaPerouse, *A Voyage Round the World in the Years 1785-88*, J. Johnson, 1794.

[318]Weatherford, pp. 134-135.

[319]Jack Forbes, *Native Americans of California and Nevada*, Healdsburg, California: Naturegraph, 1968, pp. 39, 40.

[320]Margolin, p. 166.

[321]Frederick E. Hoxie, ed., *Encyclopedia of North America*, New York: Houghton Mifflin, 1996, pp. 381-382.

[322]Albert Henry Smyth, ed., *The Writings of Benjamin Franklin, 1706-1790*, New York: NY, Macmillan, 1906, vol. 10, pp. 97-105. Benjamin Franklin in France published in 1783 his ironic, "Remarks Concerning Savages of North America, 1784."

[323]Nancy Black and Bette S. Weidman, eds, *White on Red*, Port Washington, NY: Kennikat Press, 1976, p. 104.

[324]Samuel G. Drake, *Biography and History of the Indians of North America*, Boston: 1851, pp. 594. Red Jacket's 1805 speech in reply to Reverend Cram. Cram was sent to Buffalo, NY by the Evangelical Missionary Society of Massachusetts to tell the Six Nations that the only true religion was Christianity. The speech was considered genuine by Drake, as Red Jacket would not speak English although he understood it. The speech was translated into English. After Red Jacket finished the speech he and others went to the missionary (Cram) to take him by the hand. Instead, Cram hastily arose from his seat and stated that "...there is no fellowship between the religion of God and the works of the devil, therefore, I could not join hands with them." The Indians then all left smiling politely. Seneca Chief & Orator Red Jacket lived from 1751 until 1830. Opposed to the Christian missionaries, he tried to preserve the Six Nations and their culture. He succumbed to alcohol addiction in later years.

[325]Lydia Maria Child, *An Appeal for the Indians*, New York, William P. Tomlinson, 1868. Reprint, *Hobomok and other Writings on*

Indians, Rutgers State University Press, 1968.

[326]Eldridge S. Brooks, *The Story of the American Indian*, Boston: D. Lothrop Company, 1887, p. 148.

[327]Nicholas P. Canny, *The Ideology of English Colonization: From Ireland to America*, William & Mary Quarterly, 3rd Series, XXX, 1973, 575-598. Francis Jennings, *The Invasion of America*, New York: W. W. Norton, reprinted 1976, p. 46. In 1395 Richard II of Christian England called the Irish, who were seeking independence of his rule, wild heathen savages. Ireland, Scotland and Wales were inhabited by independent Celtic tribes and clans who lived in rural parts of England. They were called barbarians, pagans, and a "savage nation" that lived "like beasts."

[328]John Lankford, editor, *Captain John Smith's America*, New York: NY, Harper and Row, 1967, p. 19, titled "Virginia: The Land and It's Native Inhabitants."

[329]Lydia Maria Child, *Hobomok and other Writings on Indians*, Rutgers University Press, 1986. Writes on "An Appeal for the Indians", p. 225.

[330]James A. Wilson, ed., *The Cabot Voyages and Bristol Discovery under Henry VII*, Cambridge: Hakluyt Society Publications, 2nd Ser. CXX, 1962, pp. 49-53, 204-205. This law gave Henry VII his Christian right to act on his own without the approval of the Pope.

[331]Paul Schilpp, ed., *The Philosophy of Bertrand Russell*, 1963. The word "pagan", translated from the Latin in Webster's dictionary, is associated with a peasant or countryman. It is also used as a synonym for one who has no religion. "Heathen" was often used in the same vein. The dictionary translates this as one who is a wasteland dweller or one who lives in a wild, rustic or rural area. A logical explanation for the degradation of the Indian was given by author, philosopher, and Nobel Prize-winner, Bertrand Russell. In his essay on "*The Superior Virtue of the Oppressed*", Russell wrote that the conquering nations and ruling classes built up comforting myths about the subjects of their oppression in order to deflect their own guilt.

[332]Roger Williams, *Christenings Make not Christians, or a Briefe Discourse Concerning that Name Heathen, Commonly Given to Indians, as also Concerning that Great Point of Their Conversion*, 1645. Also found in "Rhode Island Historical Tracts", Providence, RI, XIV, pp. 1-21, 1881. Roger Williams, an English clergyman, was expelled from Massachusetts for his beliefs. With Quakers and other refugees he founded Rhode Island and took shelter among his Indian friends, the Narragansetts, who at that time inhabited over 30 villages. Roger Williams lived in peace among the Narragansetts.

[333]John W. Bohnstedt, "The Infidel Scourge of God: The Turkish Menace as seen by German Pamphleteers of the Reformation Era", *American Philosophical Transactions* (1968), LVIII, part IX, pp. 18-19.

[334]Lydia Maria Child, *An Appeal for the Indians*, New York: William P. Tomlinson, 1868. Reprint, *Hobomok and other Writings on Indians*, Rutgers State University Press, 1968.

[335]Henry T. Malone, *Cherokees of the Old South*, Athens: The University of Georgia Press, 1956. The upper towns (Georgia, North Carolina and Eastern Tennessee) were under the leadership of James Vann, a half breed. By 1800 Vann became the richest man in the Cherokee nation. Vann and his followers accepted the missionaries. Opposed to Christianity and the missions in the lower towns along the Tennessee River were other Cherokees called Chickamaugans, under the main leadership of Chief Little Turkey and the principal speaker Doublehead. Vann, Ridge and many others embraced missionaries not because of a belief in the Christian religion. It was mainly due to the bad blood or greed between the Cherokee's two divisions, Aniyunwiya and the Chickamaguans. The two divisions of the Cherokee were originally called the Aniyuniwa and the Aniyuntikwalaski. The Cherokees believed they were immune to the U.S. policy of using one nation to wipe out another, then coming in themselves and wiping out any survivors. Dragging Canoe warned them this would happen, but his words fell on deaf ears. They soon learned he was correct—in their forced removal in 1838 to Oklahoma called the "Trail of Tears." In 1809 Doublehead (of the opposing faction of the Cherokees) was killed at the hands of Ridge, James Vann and Alexander Saunders.

[336]Walter Brownlow Posey, *The Baptist Church in the Lower Mississippi Valley, 1776-1845*, Lexington: University of Kentucky Press, 1957.

[337]U.S. Department of Interior, "Statistics Concerning Indian Education", *Branch of Education, Bureau of Indian Affairs* (1956), Washington, D.C.

[338]Samsom Occom, *A Short Narrative of My Life*, typescript, Dartmouth College Archives, in Bernd Peyer, *The Elders Wrote* (Berlin, Dietrich Reimer Verlag, 1982), pp. 12-18.

[339]Francis Paul Prucha, *American Indian Policy in the Formative Years*, Lincoln: University of Nebraska Press, 1970, p. 220.

[340]Henry T. Malone, *Cherokees of the Old South*, Athens: The University of Georgia Press, 1956.

[341]Robert F. Berkhofer, Jr., *Salvation and the Savage: An Analysis of Protestant Missions and American Indian Response, 1787-1862*, Lexington: University of Kentucky Press, 1965, pp. 1-15, 152-160. In Francis Paul Prucha, ed., *The Indian in American History*, New York: Holt Rinehart and Winston, 1971, pp. 76.

[342] Berkhofer, p. 78.

[343] Berkhofer, p. 78.

[344]Cephas Washburn, Hugh Park, editor, *Reminiscences of the Indians 1862*, Press-Argus, 1955. In the Turkey Town Treaty of 1817 the Cherokees agreed to exchange 1/3 of the lands in the East for equal acreage located between the White River on the Northeast boundary and the Arkansas River on the Southwest boundary in the then Arkansas Territory.

[345]*American Baptist Missionary Union Annual Report*, 1841, p. 51. Concerns the "Report of Evan Jones." Evan Jones reports that one hundred and seventy people were converted during the revivals in the concentration camps and one hundred and thirty were baptized into the church upon their arrival in Indian Territory.

[346]"Annual Report of the Commissioner of Indian Affairs, Sept. 21, 1887." Quoted in Francis Paul Prucha, ed., *Documents of the United States Indian Policy*, 2nd ed., expanded, Lincoln: University of Nebraska Press, 1990, pp. 174-175.

[347]Reuben Gold Thwaites, *Original Journals of the Lewis and Clark Expedition, 1804-1806*, 8 vols., New York: Arno Press, 1969. The Nez Percé were a tremendous help to the explorers, saving them from starvation after they crossed the Bitterroot mountains and on their return from the west. Meriwether Lewis wrote in the journals that the Nez Percé were the most honest, hospitable and sincere people on earth. They each promised eternal friendship and the Nez Percé promised they will always remain at peace with the United States. Frederick Turner, *The Portable North American Indian Reader*, NY, Viking Press, 1973, pp. 231-232. On the oral tales of the Nez Percé in "The Advent of the Missionaries." See also Melville Jacobs, *Northhwest Sahaptin Texts*, New York: Columbia University Press, Contributions in Anthropology, Vol. 19, Part 1, 1934. L. V. McWhorter, *Hear Me, My Chiefs! Nez Percé History and Legend*, Caldwell: Idaho, Caxton Printers, 1952. Nez Percé received their wrong name from an intepreter with the 1805 Lewis and Clark expedition. The name, meaning pierced nose, is not common to the tribe. Henry Harmon Spaulding established a Nez Percé Indian mission at Lapwai. The first school in Idaho for Indian children opened at Lapwai. The first white child born in Idaho was Eliza Spaulding, born at Lapwai. In 1839 Henry Spaulding started publishing the Bible in Lapwai on the earliest printing press used in the Pacific Northwest. Chief Timothy, the first native Christian leader, was baptized on Nov. 17, 1839. Young Chief Joseph was only 38 years old and had been chief since the death of his father in 1871. On Jan. 14, 1879, Chief Joseph, head of the Wallowa band of Nez Percé, spoke to a gathering of Congressmen and other leaders in Washington, D.C. in which he presented a brief history of his people's dealings with the white man, and mentioned Henry Spaulding. In his speech, Chief Joseph pointed with pride to a long history of friendship with the white man. When his father was young, a white man named Rev. Henry H. Spaulding came to the Nez Percé and "talked of spirit law". The people listened because he spoke good things to them. Old Joseph became a Christian and received a Bible as a gift from Rev. Spaulding. Then other white men started trickling in, building houses and making farms. "At first," says Joseph, "our people made no complaint. They thought there was room enough for all to live in peace, and they were learning many things from the white men that seemed to be very good. But we soon found that the white men were growing rich very fast, and were greedy to possess everything the Indian had. My father was the first to see through the schemes of the white men, and he warned his tribe to be careful about trading with them. He had suspicion of men who seemed anxious to make money. Then, in 1855, Governor Isaac Stevens of the Washington Territory invited the Nez Percé to a meet-

ing. He said there were a great many white people in our country, and many more would come; that he wanted the land marked out so that the Indians and the white men could be separated. It was then that the Rev. Spaulding showed his true colors and urged Old Joseph to sign the treaty. Old Joseph was incensed that his friend in spirit matters should be urging him to sign away his country. Some of the other chiefs signed the treaty for their bands and so received blankets and annuities. Old Joseph cautioned his people against taking anything from the white man because it will be claimed that he has purchased your land with his gifts. The time would soon come when Old Joseph would even tear up the Bible that Rev. Spaulding had given him. You can sense his frustration at being invaded, pushed and shoved from every direction."

348Clark Wissler, *Indians of the United States*, Garden City, NY, Doubleday, 1949.

349Herbert S. Klein, *African Slavery in Latin America and the Caribbean*, New York: Oxford University Press, 1986.

350Fr. Joel S. Panzer, *The Popes and Slavery*, Staten Island, NY, Alba House, 1996, pp. 8, 75-78. Reference to Canary Islands.

351José Ignacio Lasaga, *Vidas Cubanas, Volume I*, Editorial Revista Ideal, II volumes, Miami: 1984. Edición bilingüe, p. 4. Queen Isabella's Codicil or Appendix on her last will and testament.

352Eric Williams, *From Columbus to Castro: The History of the Caribbean*, New York: Random House, Inc., 1970, p. 41. See also Charles Gibson, *Spain In America*, New York: Harper and Row Publishers, 1966, pp. 51-52.

353Carl Otwin Sauer, *The Early Spanish Main*, Berkeley: University of California Press, 1966, p. 196. "Negroes had proved hardy in the gold fields. They were next thought of to replace the Indians who had been relieved of forced labor. Las Casas, who had been in Spain during the regency of Cisneros, recalled that the vecinos of the island had asked him in 1517 to give his support to the introduction of negro slaves, to which he agreed as protection for the Indians, the Casa de Contratacion approving the importation of four thousand." See also Gustavo Gutierrez, *Las Casas: In Search of the Poor Jesus Christ*, trans. Robert R. Barr, Maryknoll, New York: Orbis Books, 1993, p. 27.

354James Muldoon, *The Americas in the Spanish World Order: The Justification for Conquest in the Seventeenth Century*, Philadelphia: University of Pennsylvania Press, 1994, p. 57.

355Longtrail Snowbird, "Essays on Native American Life and Relations with Non-Natives, 1600-1850", Native Tech Home Page, by Tara Prindle, 1996.

356William K. Boyd, editor, *Histories of the Dividing Line between Virginia and North Carolina*, New York, 1967, pp. 3, 4.

357Albert Ellery Bergh, *The Writings of Thomas Jefferson*, Washington, D. C., 1907, vol. 16, p. 452.

358*The Heritage Illustrated Dictionary of the English Language*, Boston: Houghton Mifflin Company, 1979, Vol. I, p. 594. Definition of "Half-blood, half-breed." See also Jack Weatherford, *Native Roots*, New York: Faucet Columbine, 1991, p. 275. "While the Métis (Indian-French) controlled the buffalo hunt, the "half-breeds" (Indian-English) worked as laborers for the Hudson Bay Company and as small farmers along the Red River."

359Jack D. Forbes, *Africans and Native Americans*, Chicago: University of Illinois Press, 1993, pp. 40, 106, 119, 154-189, 221-250.

360Bartolomé de Las Casas, *Historia de las Indias*, edited by Augustin Millares Carlo and Louis Hanke, Mexico: Fondo de Cultura Economica, 1951, 3 volumes. Reprint, New York, 1971, trans. Andre Collard, vol. I, pp. 366, 397-98, 405, 408-10, 421-423, 439, 465, 467; vol. 2, pp. 74, 87, 93.

361Daniel J. Boorstin, *The Discoverer's*, New York: Random House, 1983, p. 631. Pulitzer-prize winning author.

362Boorstin, p. 631.

363Lewis Hanke, *The Spanish Struggle for Justice in the Conquest of America*, Philadelphia, University of Pennsylvania Press, 1949, pp. 83-86. On the Encomienda system, a trusteeship system, by which conquistadors were granted the towns of the indigenous people they conquered. See also *The Heritage Illustrated Dictionary of the English Language*, Boston, Houghton Mifflin Company, 1979, Vol. I, p. 668. The definition of indenture is "a deed or contract executed between two or more parties... binding one party into the service of another for a specified term." The system of indenture used by the English and the Spanish encomienda system, were both basically a forced work agreement.

364Jack D. Forbes, *Africans and Native Americans*, Chicago: University of Illinois Press, 1993, pp. 55-58.

365Forbes, p. 55.

366Frederick E. Hoxie, ed., *Encyclopedia of North America*, New York: Houghton Mifflin, 1996, pp. 475-477. The Pequot population was approximately 4000 in the 1500s. They were almost annihilated by war, disease, and slavery. Although low in numbers, they survive to this day. Federally recognized as the Mashantucket Pequots and another non-Federally recognized tribe, the Paucatuck Pequots.

367Hoxie, p. 140. Metacom, son of Massasoit, befriended and fed the Pilgrims when they first arrived in New England in 1620.

368William Loren Katz, *Black Indians*, New York: Aladdin Paperbacks, 1997, p. 102.

369Katz, 104.

370Katz, 110.

371Katz, 105.

372Katz, 110.

373George Milligen, *A Short Description of the Province of South Carolina, with an Account of the Air, Weather, and Diseases at Charles-Town*, London: 1770, p. 26. See also James H. Cassedy, Demography in Early America, Beginnings of the Statistical Mind, 1600-1800, Cambridge, Mass: 1969, p. 86.

374R. Price, editor, *Maroon Societies: Rebel Slave Communities in the Americas*, 3rd ed. Baltimore: Johns Hopkins Press, 1997. Describes maroon societies formed by escaped slaves in the United States, Latin America and the Caribbean in the 17th, 18th and 19th centuries. European and American slave owners attempted to destroy the settlements. Frequent wars were fought between maroons and the slave owners. See also Fernandez Gonzalo de Oviedo, *Historia General y Natural de las Indias*, Madrid, Biblioteca de Autores Espanoles, book 16, p. 107; book 24, p. 418, 1959.

375Katz, p. 63-69. Seminole wars extended over forty years, finally ending in 1858. During this time many of the Seminoles and maroons were forcibly removed to various western areas of the United States for resettlement. In 1911 Executive Order number 1379 granted the remaining Seminoles in Florida three areas for reservations.

376Katz, pp. 35-36.

377 Katz, p. 47.

378Forbes, p. 37.

379 Forbes, p. 247.

380Weatherford, p. 380.

381*The Heritage Illustrated Dictionary of the English Language*, Boston, Houghton Mifflin Company, 1979, Vol. II, p. 824.

382Marvin Harris, *Patterns of Race in the Americas*, N. Y.: Walker and Company, 1964. See also Magnus Morner, *Race Mixture in the History of Latin America*, Boston: Little Brown, 1967.

383Harris, pp. 127, 139.

384*The Heritage Illustrated Dictionary of the English Language*, Boston: Houghton Mifflin Company, 1979, Vol. II, p. 824.

385William Bridgewater, ed., *The Columbia Viking Desk Encyclopedia*, New York: Viking Press, 1953, p. 627.

386Jack D. Forbes, *Africans and Native Americans*, Chicago: University of Illinois Press, 1993, p. 183. See also Frederick P. Bowser, *The African Slave in Colonial Peru, 1524-1650*, Stanford: Stanford University Press, 1974, p. 254; Jack Forbes, ed., *The Indian in America's Past*, Prentis-Hall, 1964, pp. 2-3. "Over 6 million Mexican-Americans and Spanish-Americans have Indian blood yet are not counted as Indians. Many states legally classify Mexican-Americans as 'White', and the federal census does not enumerate them as Indians."

387Inga Clendinnen, *Ambivalent Conquests*, Cambridge: Cambridge University Press, 1987, pp. 38, 42, 59-60, 65, 102. Concerning brutalities committed, pp. 38, 55-56.

388Jack D. Forbes, *Apache, Navajo and Spaniard*, Norman: University of Oklahoma Press, 1960, p. 91.

389Verner W. Crane, *Southern Frontier, 1670-1732*, Durham, N.C., Duke University Press, 1928.

390Crane, p. 92. See also William Smith, on "The Slave Trade", "The North American Indians." *The London Saturday Journal*, March 14, 1840, London, England: p. 195; also May 2, 1840, p. 282.

391Robert F. Heizer and Alan J. Almquist, *The Oher Californians: Predjudice and Discrimination under Spain, Mexico and the United States to 1920*, Berkeley: University of California Press, 1971, pp.

60, 95-104, 115-117. See also Wilcomb E. Washburn, *Red Man's Land/White Man's Law: A Study of the Past and Present Status of the American Indian*, New York: Charles Scribner's, 1971, p. 165.

392Washburn, *Red Man's Land/White Man's Law*, p. 164. Felix S. Cohen, *Handbook of Federal Indian Law*, Washington, D.C., 1940, pp. 527-529. U.S. Department of Interior, Federal Indian Law, Washington, D.C., 1958. In Dec. of 1923 a committee of 100 Indians visited Washington, D.C. Ruth Muskrat, a Cherokee Indian, presented Calvin Coolidge with a copy of *The Red Man in the United States*, on a survey of the Indian in America.

393Jack D. Forbes, *Africans and Native Americans*, Chicago: University of Illinois Press, 1993, pp. 192-195.

394John Codman Hurd, *The Law of Freedom and Bondage in the United States*, New York: Negro Universities Press, 1968, vol II, p. 128.

395Robert F, Heizer and Allan J. Almquist, eds., *The Other Californians*, Berkeley: University of California Press, 1971, p. 236.

396Adam Hodgson, *Remarks During a Journey through North America in the Years 1819, 1820 and 1821*, New York: 1823, pp. 218-20. Letter quoting Dr. Elias Boudinot.

397Helen T. Cattteral, *Judicial Cases Concerning American Slavery and the Negro*, Washington, D. C., Carnegie, 1929, vol. 2, p. 401. See also Jack D. Forbes, *Africans and Native Americans*, Chicago, University of Illinois Press, 1993, pp. 196-197.

398 Cattteral, pp. 415- 416.

399 Forbes, pp. 202-203.

400Jack Weatherford, *Native Roots*, New York, Faucet Columbine, 1991, p. 275.

401Maria Cambell, *Halfbreed*, Lincoln: University of Nebraska Press, 1973, pp, 9-12. A. S. Lussier, ed., *Louis Riel and the Metis*, Winnipeg, Canada: Pemmican Publications, 1988. Olive Patricia Dickinson, *Canada's First Nations*, Toronto: McCelland & Stewart Inc., 1994. pp. 263-272, 292-293, 307-315.

402Olive Patricia Dickinson, *Canada's First Nations*, Toronto: McClelland & Stewart Inc., 1994. pp. 406-409.

403Frederick E. Hoxie, ed., *Encyclopedia of North America*, New York: Houghton Mifflin, 1996, p. 555.

404M. Annette James, ed., *The State of Native America Genocide, Colonization and Resistance*, Boston: South End Press, 1992, pp. 23-53.

405Robert E. Bieder, "Scientific Attitudes Towards Mixed-bloods in Early Nineteenth-century America."*Journal of Ethnic Studies* (1980), no. 8, pp. 17-30.

406D. S. Otis, *The Dawes Act and Allotment of Indian Lands*, Norman, and Oklahoma: University of Oklahoma Press, 1973.

407Russell Thornton, *American Indian Holocaust and Survival, A Population History since 1492*, Norman, University of Oklahoma Press, 1987, pp. 15-41.

408Thornton, p. 203.

409Charles E. Dawes, *The Uset Calumet*, Nashville, TN: Feb., March, 1988, pp. 7-8. "Tribal Leaders see Danger in Use of Blood Quantum as Eligibility Standard."

410Alexander Ross and Kenneth A. Spaulding, ed. *The Fur Hunters of the Far West*, Norman: Oklahoma Press, 1956, pp. 196-198.

411Alexander Ross, *The Red River Settlement: Its Rise, Progress, and Present State, with some Account of the Native Races and its General History to the Present Day*, London: Smith, Elder, 1856, reprint Minneapolis: Ross & Haines, Inc., 1957, pp. 193, 242.

412Francis Parkman, *The Oregon Trail*, 1849, reprint, Norwalk Ct: Heritage Press, 1943, 1971, p. 315.

413Hazel W. Hertzberg, *The Search for an American Indian Identity*, Syracuse: Syracuse University Press, 1971, p. 122.

414Fernández de Gonzalo Oviedo, *Historia Generaly Natural de las Indias*, Asuncion, Editorial Guarania, 1944, 14 volumes. See also Oliver C. Dunn and James E. Kelley Jr., *The Diary of Christopher Columbus' First Voyage to America: 1492-1493*, Norman: University of Oklahoma Press, 1987. Bartolomé de Las Casas, *Historia de las Indias*, edited by Augustin Millares Carlo and Louis Hanke, Mexico: Fondo de Cultura Economica, 1951, 3 vols., Bartolomé de Las Casas, *Apologética Historia Sumaria*, Mexico, Universidad Nacional Autonoma de Mexico, 1967. Hernándo Cortés, trans. by J. Bayard Morris, *Five Letters, 1519-1526*, New York: 1929. Diego de Landa, *Relacion de Las Cosas de Yucatan*, ed. Alfred M. Tozzer, Cambridge, MA, 1941, sourced from "Papers of the Peabody Museum of American Archaeology and Ethnology", vol. XVIII. Bernardino de Sahagún, trans. by Fanny R. Bandelier, *Historia General de las Cosas de Nueva España (A History of Ancient Mexico)*, Nashville, TN, 1932. William H. Prescott, *History and Conquest of Mexico*, New York: 1843. William H. Prescott, *History and Conquest of Peru*, New York: 1847. Early reports on the first colonists to the New World.

415William Smith, "The North American Indians: Are the Indians Capable of Civilization?", *The London Saturday Journal*, London, England, May 2, 1840, No.70, pp. 280-282.

416Robert H. Fuson, translator, *The Log of Christopher Columbus*, Camden, Maine, International Marine Publishing Co., 1992, covers his "Discovery of Espanola", p. 105.

417Fuson, p. 144.

418 Fuson, p. 147.

419Fuson, p. 149.

420"The Columbus Letter of March 14, 1493, Chicago: The Newberry Library, pp. 6-10.

421Fuson, p. 77.

422Fuson, p. 79.

423 Fuson, pp.79, 80.

424 Samuel Morrison, Samuel Eliot Morrison, *Christopher Columbus: The Voyage of Discovery, 1492*, CT: Dorset Press, 1991.

425Fuson, p. 77.

426Fuson, p. 129.

427Fuson, p. 174. Navidad translates as Nativity.

428Fernando Columbus, *The Life of the Admiral Christopher Columbus*, translated by Benjamin Keen, Rutgers, 1959, reprint 1978, pp. 147-148.

429Bartolomé de Las Casas, *The Tears of the Indians*, translated by John Phillips, printed by J. C. for Nath, Brook, at the Angel in Cornhil: London, 1656, p. 5.

430Casas, p. 6.

431Bartolomé de Las Casas, *Historia de las Indias*, edited by Augustin Millares Carlo and Louis Hanke, translated by Andre Collard, Mexico: Fondo de Cultura Economica, 1951, 3 volumes.

432Casas, *Historia de las Indias*, Vol. III, Section 57, p. 193. King Ferdinand (1452 to 1516) ruled over the following areas: Aragon, Castile, Sicily and Naples. Along with Queen Isabella I, he established the Spanish Inquisition and financed the explorers to America in return for gold.

433Fernando Columbus, *The Life of the Admiral Christopher Columbus*, translated by Benjamin Keen, Rutgers, 1959, reprint 1978, pp. 147-148.

434Richard Eden, editor, *The Decades of the Newe Worlde or West India* (The First Three Books on America), Birmingham, England: Turnbull & Spears, 1885. Taken from the first *History of the New World*, by Pedro Martir de Angleria, an Italian in the Spanish court. The first thin volume was for the first ten years. It was written in Latin and first published in Seville, Spain in 1511. Pedro Martir followed up in Latin with additional decades of this important first history, totaling eight decades in all. The Eden edition covers the first three decades.

435Samuel Morrison, *Journals and other Documents on the Life and Voyages of Christopher Columbus*, translated and edited by Morrison, New York, 1963, pp. 121, 136. Andrés Bernáldez, author of *Historia de Los Reyes Católicos*, wrote down the information given to him by Christopher Columbus. Columbus stayed with him after his voyage.

436Robert H. Fuson, translator, *The Log of Christopher Columbus*, Camden, Maine: International Marine Publishing Co., 1987, p. 146. The Indian name Cacique referred to the leader or head of a tribe, and was translated to the word "chief." Some tribes had a number of chiefs that controlled the town or the entire countryside. Guacanagaric had five tribal chiefs (caciques) under his authority. Guacanagaric, also pronounced Guatiguaná, befriended Columbus on his first voyage to Haiti on Dec. 22, 1492. Columbus, in his meetings with Guacanagaric, constantly talked of finding "as much gold as we desire." Columbus left Haiti to sail back to Spain. His journal on Jan. 2, 1492, noted, "I left on this Isle of Espanola 39 men in the fortress, under the command of three officers, all of whom were friendly with King Guacanagaric...." Columbus also noted that when he returned, he expected that "I might find a lot of gold waiting, and a place to establish a settlement for this harbor is not to my liking." The rumored gold was thought to come from the east. Columbus wanted their new settlement closer to the gold and Spain, which was also towards the east.

[437]John Boyd Thatcher, *Christopher Columbus: His Life, His Work, His Remains*, New York: G. P. Putnam's Sons, 1903-1904, 3 vols., p. 348, vol. 2. Guacanagaric came to the aid of Columbus when the Santa Maria ran aground on a reef. His people unloaded all the supplies before the ship sank. Guacanagaric fought back against the Spanish brutalities, but was defeated. Thatcher wrote that Guacanagaric was "a wanderer in the mountains, ruined and deprived of his state." There were five major chiefs when Columbus landed. Chief Guacanagaric was from the Northeast coast and the interior of the Dominican Republic by the Bay of Samana. Columbus lured Chief Caonabo from Maguana into a trap and then forced him to wear iron chains. He was shipped to Spain as a slave. Chief Guarionex, from the province of Magua (Huhabo), was imprisoned in 1494 and forced to watch the Spanish rape his wife before her, and then he was executed. The Spanish killed Chief Behechio of the province of Xaragua. Behechio's sister and widow of Caonabo, Anacaona, succeeded her husband. Ovando, Columbus' successor, went to her village under false pretenses, tricked Anacaona, slaughtered and burned her village and then hanged Anacaona in Santo Domingo. Chief Cotubanama (Cayacoa) was from the province of Higuey (Caizcimu). The Spanish attacked and the chief was hanged in Santo Domingo. It was in his province that rumors spread of there being gold. In 1503 Ponce De Leon led an army that massacred as many as 7000 Tainos.

[438]Samuel Morrison, *The European Discovery of America: The Southern Voyages, A.D. 1492-1616*, New York: Oxford University Press, 1974, pp. 135-136. See also Bartolomé de las Casas, *Breuissima Relacion de la Destruycion de las Indias*, Seville, Spain, 1552-1553. Las Casas printed a series of nine tracts detailing his allegations against the Spanish oppressors. He describes the atrocities and tortures the Spanish Conquistadors inflicted upon the Indians.

[439]Christopher Columbus, *The Diario of Christopher Columbus's First Voyage to America, 1492-1493*, abstracted by Fray Bartolome de las Casas. Ed. by Oliver Dunn and James E. Kelley, Jr., trs. Norman: University of Oklahoma Press, 1989.

[440]Kirkpatrick Sale, *The Conquest of Paridise*, New York: Alfred A. Knopf, 1990, p. 161. See also William Deneven, editor, *The Native Population in the Americas in 1492*, Wisconsin, 1976.

[441]Bartolomé de Las Casas, *Historia de las Indias,* edited by Augustin Millares Carlo and Louis Hanke, Mexico: Fondo de Cultura Economica, 3 volumes, 1951.

[442]Kirkpatrick Sale, *The Conquest of Paradise*, New York: Alfred A. Knopf, 1990, pp. 160-161. See also Fernandez Gonzalo de Oviedo, *Historia General y Natural de las Indias*, Madrid, Biblioteca de Autores Espanoles, 1959. According to the Spanish census, taken in 1508 through 1518, the population started out at "under 100,000 and declined precipitously."

[443]Samuel Morrison, *Journals and other Documents on the Life and Voyages of Christopher Columbus*, translated and edited by Morrison, New York: 1963. Christopher Columbus, *The Diaro of Christopher Columbus' 1st Voyage to America*, edited by Oliver Dunn & J. E. Kelley Jr., 1989. Fernando Columbus, *The Life of the Admiral Christopher Columbus*, translated by Benjamin Keen, Rutgers, 1959, reprint 1978. Fernando Columbus was the son of Columbus.

[444]Kirkpatrick Sale, *The Conquest of Paridise*, New York: Alfred A. Knopf, 1990, p. 158

[445]Friedell, pp. 217-223.

[446]G.C. Vaillant, *The Aztecs of Mexico*, Baltimore, MD: Penguin Books, 1961, pp. 230-233. An ancient legend prophesied that Quetzalcóatl, the bearded, fair-skinned Toltec ruler-god, would return from the east in the year Ce Acatl to reclaim his kingdom. Evil omens that had confounded the Aztec priests and sorcerers over the previous decade only heightened Montezuma's anxiety. First, despite fair weather, the waters of Lake Texcoco had suddenly boiled up, flooding the island of their capital city. Then an inexplicable conflagration had consumed the temple of their chief god, Huitzilopochtli. The voice of a woman wailing in the night had repeatedly disturbed the city's slumber. Immense comets with fiery tails had been seen shooting through day-time skies and a great column of fire had appeared in the east every night for an entire year. All were taken to be signs of Quetzalcóatl's imminent return.

[447]Egon Friedell, trans. by Charles Francis Atkinson, *A Cultural History of the Modern Age*, London: Alfed A. Knopf, 3 vols., 1930,

vol. 1, pp. 217-223.

[448]Bernal Diaz del Castillo, *The Discovery and Conquest of Mexico, 1517-1521*. New York: Grove Press, 1956. See also William H. Prescott, *The Conquest of Mexico*, ed. Beatrice Berler, San Antonio, Texas: Corona Publishing Company, 1988 p. 13. Hernán Cortés, ed. and trans. by George Folsom. *The Despatches of Hernando Cortes, the Conqueror of Mexico, Addressed to the Emperor Charles V, Written during the Conquest and Containing a Narrative of Its Events*, New York: Wiley and Putnam, 1843. Ten years after allying with Cortés in the siege of Tenochtitlán, the people of Huejotzingo asked him for help in a legal battle against the extremely burdensome tributes exacted by Spanish administrators sent to rule New Spain.

[449]Sylvanus Griswald Morley, *The Ancient Maya*, Standard University, CA: Standard University Press, 1946, pp. 85.

[450]Inga Clendinnen, *Ambivalent Conquests*, Cambridge, MA, Cambridge University Press, 1987, p. 36.

[451]Clendinnen, pp. 51-52.

[452]G. C. Vaillant, *The Aztecs of Mexico*, Baltimore, MD: Penguin Books, 1961, p. 67. See also J. Eric Thompson, *The History of the Maya*, N. Y., Charles Scribner's & Sons, 1931, p. 81.

[453]Herbert Edward Thompson, *People of the Serpent*, London: G. P. Putnam & Sons, 1913. Niebuhur was referring to Bishop Diego Landa.

[454]John Hemming, *The Conquest of the Incas*, Hamondsworth, England: Penguin, 1983, p. 25.

[455]Robert S. Chamberlain, *Conquista y Civilizacion de Yucatan*, Mexico: D. F. Porria, 1982, pp. 25-27.

[456]Ronald Wright, *Stolen Continents*, New York: Penguin Books, 1993, p. 82.

[457]Ann Kendall, *Everyday Life of the Incas*, New York: Dorset Press, 1973, pp. 167-172, on metallurguy and mining. See also *The Gilded Image*: "Pre Columbian Gold from South and Central America", *Minerva* (2003), 7. 3, 1016, http://www.pamp.ch/Gold /pp/precolom. html. Anne Millard, *The Inca*, New York: Warwick Press, 1980. The gold was hammered into a thin foil and placed in the hands and mouth of a youth upon burial. This gold foil is the first evidence for the working of metals in South America. Placer gold was plentiful in the rivers coming down from the high Andes to the coastal plains of Peru, but much of it had a relatively high silver or copper content (the mixture still mined in Peru and Chile today). The goldsmiths had to learn to work with this combination of metals. Gold was often 40-60%, silver 25-40% and copper 15-20%.

[458]Boleslao Lewin, *La Rebelion de Tupac Amaru*, Buenos Aires: Libreria Hachette, 1957, pp. 497-498. Tupa Amaru II was the great-great-great grandson of Tupa Amaru. Educated and fluent in Spanish, he started the rebellion with Quechua words, translated as: "From this day forth, no longer shall the Spaniard feast on your property."

[459]Egon Friedell, trans. by Charles Francis Atkinson, *A Cultural History of the Modern Age*, London: Alfed A. Knopf, 3 vols., 1930, vol.1, pp. 217-223.

[460]Ronald Wright, *Stolen Continents*, New York: Penguin Books, 1993, p. 192. See also Rolena Adorno, *Guamán Poma and His Illustrated Chronicle from Colonial Peru: From a Century of Scholarship to a New Era of Reading/Guamán Poma y su crónica ilustrada del Perú colonial: un siglo de investigaciones hacia una nueva era de lectura*. Copenhagen, Denmark: Museum Tusculanum Press, University of Copenhagen, and The Royal Library, 2001. 88 pages + maps, illustrations, and 15 color plates. Felipe Guamán Poma may have begun writing this book as early as 1587 when about age 50. The book was completed in 1615 when he was in his 70s. Guamán Poma's 800 pages of text and 400 full-page drawings gives an account of Andean history through the conquest to the early 1600s. Felipe Guamán Poma, a convert to Christianity, was half Indian and half Spanish. His mother was a great grandchild of the tenth Inca, Tupac Inca Yupanqui. His father, Martin de Ayala, was Spanish. When he attended a Spanish school he was mistreated due to his half Indian ancestry. He spoke to as many native people as possible to insure he could put down all they knew about the way of the Incas. His book is a thorough, truthful report of Inca society, culture, daily life and also their religious ways. Guamán Poma defended and helped the Inca people and had read the work of Las Casas. Poma tried to send his book to Spain. His book found its way to northern Europe and was forgotton until it was found in 1908 in the Royal Copenhagen Library where it resides today, some 300 years after its

completion. The celebrated English historian of Peru, Sir Clements Markham, said of Guamán Poma and his work: "How the book, with all those damning illustrations, escaped destruction and how it was ever allowed to be sent home, is a mystery. One would give much to know the fate of the author, so full of compassion for his ill-fated countrymen, diligent as a collector of information of all kinds, proud of his ancestry, a gifted artist, full of sympathy, fearless in the exposure of injustice and cruelty. Guamán Poma was a hero of whom any country might be proud. At length this most important work is in good and sympathetic hands, and will be given to the world. It is, without exception, the most remarkable as well as the most interesting production of native genius that has come down to our time."

461Charles Wilson Hackett, *Revolt of the Pueblo Indians of New Mexico and Otermin's Attempted Reconquest, 1680–1682*, Albuquerque: University of New Mexico, 1942, Volume 2: 245–49.

462Joe S. Sando, *The Pueblo Indians*, San Francisco: The Indian Historian Press, 1976, pp. 53-62.

463Garcilaso de la Vega, *Primera Parte de Los Commentarios Reales*, Lisboa, 1609, reprint, Royal Commentaries of the Incas and General History of Peru, Austin: University of Texas Press, 1966.

464Lyon G. Tyler, ed., *Narratives of Early Virginia, 1606-1625*, New York: Scribner, 1907. See also Robert Beverley, *The History and Present State of Virginia, ca. 1673-ca. 1722*, printed London: for B. and S. Took, 1722, "in four parts", reprint, Chapel Hill, 1947. In Lankford, pp. 37-41, 360, 364, excellent detailed history of the customs and religion of the Virginia Indians.

465Alden T. Vaughn, *New England Frontier*, Boston: Little Brown & Co., 1965, p. 20. Quote from Cotton Mather in *Magnalia Christi Americana*. Canonicus, head of the Narragansets, regarded the coming of the white man with a jealous fear. Roger Williams, exiled from Massachusetts, found a friend in Canonicus who gave Williams all the land around Providence, R. I.

466William Bradford, editor: William T. Davis, *History of Plantation*, New York: Charles Scribner's, 1908, pp. 339-350. Section covering "The Destruction of the Pequots", 1836.

467Bradford, pp. 339-350, on the "Destruction of the Pequots." See also William Bradford, edited by Harvey Wish, *Of Plymouth Plantation*, Capricorn Books, New York: 1962, pp. 40, 41, 60, 62-63, 72-73, 76. Covers the Pilgrims at Plymouth, 1620. The Puritans were first met by Samoset of the Abnaki Indian tribe, who introduced them to Squanto, more fluent in English. George W. Manypenny, *Our Indian Wards*, New York, Dacapo Press, 1972, Introduction pp. XX-XXI, on the Pequoit War. Thanksgiving Day was declared an official holiday by George Washington to replace the many holiday days held to celebrate their victories over the Indians. During the Civil War in the 1860s, Abraham Lincoln declared Thanksgiving Day a legal National holiday. That same day Lincoln ordered his troops to march against the Sioux in Minnesota.

468George W. Manypenny, *Our Indian Wards*, New York: Dacapo Press, 1972, pp. 11-15.

469Manypenny, pp. 19-20. See also Historical Society of Pennslvania, *Memoirs of the Historical Society of Pennsylvania*, Vol. VI, Philadelphia: 1858. "Penn Wampum Belts" were given to William Penn about 1684 at the treaty of Kensington. This was the first of many given by Indian tribes to the Europeans to seal their friendships and as a sign of peace.

470Henry Steele Commager and Elmo Giordanetti, *Was America a Mistake?*, New York: Harper Torchbooks, 1967, p. 137. Raynal's anti-clerical sentiments provoked the wrath of the government of France. In 1779 his book *Histoire des Deux Indes* was prohibited from entering France in foreign country editions. In 1781 it was officially banned by the French parliament of Paris.

471Manypenny, p. 18.

472Robert M. Utley and Wilcomb E. Washington, *Indian Wars*, Boston: Houghton Mifflin Co., 1977, p. 100. General Amherst "had been determined to eradicate the Indian vermin—if necessary by the further use of smallpox-infected blankets...." See also Olive Patricia Dickinson, *Canada's First Nations*, Toronto, Ontario, Canada, McClelland & Stewart, Inc., 1992, p. 183. John W. Harpster, ed., *Pen Pictures of Early Western Pennsylvania*, University of Pittsburgh Press, 1938. William Trent was commander of the local militia of Pittsburgh during Pontiac's seige of the fort. Trent's entry for May 24, 1763, stated "...we gave them two blankets and a handkerchief out of the Smallpox Hospital. I hope it will have the desired effect." General Amherst in 1763, in his war against the Pontiacs, urged every method

be used against them including that notorious directive about distributing smallpox-infected blankets in their encampments. Amherst also advocated the use of drugs. T. E. Rose M. D., *From Shaman to Medicine Man*, Vancouver, Canada, Mitchell Press, 1972, p. 129. Canada had its own deliberate policy of genocide against their Indian populations. "The first epidemic of smallpox occurred in 1862, when the Indians suffered principally from its ravages. In those days they died like rats and their bodies could be seen lying around Ogden point by the fifties." Joanne Drake-Terry, *The Same as Yesterday*, Lillooet, Canada, Lillooet Tribal Council, 1989, p. 107. "When the white people came in the spring, they had sealed Hudson's Bay blankets with them. When they opened them, they handled them with gloves, from here, the smallpox epidemic started. The white people's intention was to kill us all, but we were saved by the great Indian doctors."

473Wilcomb E. Washburn, *Red Man's Land, White Man's Law: A Study of the Past and Present Status of the American Indian*, New York: 1971. See also Monroe E. Price, *Law and the American Indian: Readings, Notes and Cases*, Indianapolis, IN, 1973.

474Charles J. Kappler, ed., *Indian Affairs, Laws and Treaties*, Washington: Govt. Printing Office, 5 vols., 1903-1941. See also Wilcomb E. Washburn, ed., *The American Indian and the United States: A Documentary History, Volumes I-IV*, New York: Greenwood Press, 1973.

475Jared Sparks, *The Writings of George Washington; Being His Correspondence, Addresses, Messages and other Papers, Official and Private*, New York, Boston: Charles Tappan, 1846, Harper & Brothers, 1847, vol. 6, pp. 264-66. The position of the Iroquois Confederacy during the Revolutionary War was to remain neutral, although both the British and the Americans asked them to join sides. Lee Miller, editor, *From the Heart*, New York: Vintage Books, 1996, p. 102. Little Abraham of the Mohawks stated, "The Resolution of the Six Nations are not to be broken or altered.... This then is the determination of the Six Nations, not to take any part, but as it is a family affair, to sit still and see you fight it out."

476Sparks, pp. 263-266.

477Angie Debo, *The Road to Disappearance: A History of the Creek Indians*, Norman: University of Oklahoma Press, 1941. These vigilante groups intensified after 1808 when a federal law prohibited further importation of slaves into America. Florida during this period was under Spanish rule.

478John K. Mahon, *History of the Second Seminole War, 1835-1842*, Gainesville: University of Florida Press, 1992. See also Grant Foreman, *The Five Civilized Tribes*, Norman: University of Oklahoma Press, 1934. Zachary Taylor was elected President of the United States in 1848.

479*The London Saturday Journal*, London, England: William Smith, May, 1840. pp. 280-281.

480George Catlin, *Letters and Notes on the Manners, Customs and Conditions of the North American Indians*, New York: Dover Publications, 1973, Vol. 1, p. 6.

481Walter Hart Blumenthal, *American Indians Dispossessed*, Philadelphia:, George S. MacManus Co., 1955, pp. 46-65, Chapter 2 titled, "Exploitation, Speculation and the Land Companies." Covers George Washington and others in the early stages of taking Indian lands. Wilcomb E. Washburn, ed., *The American Indian and the United States: A Documentary History, Volume I-IV*. New York: Greenwood Press, 4 vols. 1973, reprint, 1979. Albert Ellery Bergh, ed., *The Writings of Thomas Jefferson*, Washington, D.C., 1907, 20 volumes. Jefferson on June 20, 1803, followed up his confidential letter: "To Meriwether Lewis, esquire, captain of the first regiment of infantry of the United States of America: Your situation as secretary of the president of the United States has made you acquainted with the objects of my confidential message of Jan. 18, 1803, to the legislature; you have seen the act they passed, which, though expressed in general terms, was meant to sanction those objects, and you are appointed to carry them to execution...." Robert J. Muckle, *The First Nations of British Columbia*, Vancouver, B.C., UBC Press, 2002, p. 140. In Canada there were 68 major treaties and a number of smaller treaties starting with the first on Dec. 15, 1727 and ending in 1930. These treaties covered most of Ontario, the Prairie Provinces, and parts of Vancouver Island, the Northwest Territories, and Atlantic Canada. It was ironic that King George III's proclamation in 1763 was to have set the example in the colonies and was to be the foundation of all North American treaties. It was based on the belief that the Indian Nations had rights and ownership of the lands. It established a system of extinguishing those rights only through treaty negotiations.

482Felix S. Cohen, *Handbook of Federal Indian Law, with Reference Tables and Index*, Washington, D.C., 1942, revised 1958. See also Wilcomb E. Washburn, ed., *The American Indian and the United States: A Documentary History*, New York: 1973, 4 vols. See also *Sixty Years of Indian Affairs: Political, Economic, and Diplomatic, 1789-1850*, Chapel Hill, N.C., 1941. Initially the early Cherokee leaders resisted assimilation under Dragging Canoe (Tsi'yu-gunsini), the son of Attakullakulla and cousin of Nancy Ward.

483Henry A. Washington, ed., *The Writings of Thomas Jefferson*, 9 vols., Washington, D.C., Taylor & Maury, 1853-54. Jefferson had slaves of his own and in the Constitution of the United States African Americans at one time were considered as three-fifths of a person.

484Robert M. Utley and Wilcomb E. Washington, *Indian Wars*, Boston, Houghton Mifflin Co., 1977, p. 139. See also Grant Foreman, *The Five Civilized Tribes*, Norman: University of Oklahoma Press, 1934. The Cherokee nation ruled over 135,000 square miles from the Ohio River in the north and southward into Georgia and Alabama, covering what are now eight states.

485Wayne Moquin and Charles Van Doren, Eds., *Great Documents in American Indian History*, New York: De Capo Press, 1995, p. 109.

486James D. Richardson, compiler, *A Compilation of the Messages and Papers of the Presidents*, Washington, D.C., 1896-1899, 10 Vols.

487Virgil J. Vogel, *This Country was Ours*, New York: Harper and Row, 1972, p. 107.

488Grant Foreman, *Indian Removal*, Norman, University of Oklahoma Press, 1932, pp. 129-190. Covers Creek removal by force. The Creek tribes were members of the Muskhogean family of tribes that were known as one of the "Five Civilized Tribes."

489Vogel, p. 106. See also Grant Foreman, *The Five Civilized Tribes*, Norman: University of Oklahoma Press, 1934. pp. 229-312. Covers Cherokee removal.

490Foreman, pp. 229-231. See also Angie Debo, *The Road to Disappearance*, Norman: University of Oklahoma Press, 1941.

491Francis Paul Prucha, *American Indian Policy in the Formative Years*, Lincoln: University of Nebraska Press, 1970. pp. 250-273. Covers the laws of 1834.

492James Richardson, ed., *Messages and Papers of the Presidents*, New York: Dec. 6, 1830, Andrew Jackson's Second Annual Message, Vol. III, 1082-85.

493Samuel G. Drake, *Biography and History of the Indians of North America*, Boston: 1841, p. 450.

494Foreman, p. 235.

495Foreman, pp. 267, 268.

496Foreman, pp. 294-312, covers the "Trail of Tears." See also Wilcomb E. Washburn, editor, *The American Indian and the United States: A Documentary History*, New York: 1973, 4 vols. Peter Nabokov, editor, *American Indian Testimony*, New York: Viking Penguin, 1991, pp. 147-149. Angie Debo, *The Road to Disappearance*, Norman: University of Oklahoma Press, 1941.

497Foreman, pp. 315-386, on Seminole removal. See also John K. Mahon, *History of the Second Seminole War, 1835-1842*, Gainesville: University of Florida Press, 1992.

498Chief Seattle, *The Washington Historical Quarterly*, Seattle, WA: Washington University State Historical Society, Oct., 1931, issue 22, no. 4. See also *Seattle Sunday Star*, Oct. 29, 1887. In a column by Dr. Henry A. Smith, he makes it clear that his version is not an exact copy, but rather the best he could put together from notes taken at the time. Seattle's speech, spoken from the heart, was delivered through an interpeter with Dr. Smith carefully writing it down. Chief Seattle (also called Seath, See-Yat), chief of the Suquamish and Duwamish tribes, spoke on surrendering his land to Governor Issac Stevens.

499Charles J. Kappler, ed., *Indian Affairs, Laws and Treaties*, Washington, D.C., Govt. Printing Office, 5 vols. 1903-1941. Covers the 1868 Shoshone Treaty. In 1878 U.S. President Grant had given Chief Washakie a very expensive saddle to honor his loyalty. Chief Washakie was their chief for about 60 years.

500Lyon G. Tyler, ed., *Narratives of Early Virginia, 1606-1625*, New York: Scribner, 1907, pp. 37-41, 360-364, reprint, 1959.

501Reginald Horseman Jr., "American Indian Policy and the Origins of Manifest Destiny", *University of Birmingham Historical Journal* (1968), XI, pp. 128-140. In Francis Paul Prucha, ed., *The Indian in American History*, New York, Holt, Rinehart and Winston, 1971, pp. 22.

502Horseman, pp. 22, 23.

503Gaillard Hunt, editor, *The Writings of James Madison*, New York, G. P. Putman & Sons, 1908, vol. 8, p. 404. Letter to President James Monroe discussing land rights.

504Reginald Horseman Jr., "American Indian Policy and the Origins of Manifest Destiny", *University of Birmingham Historical Journal* (1968), XI, pp. 128-140. In Francis Paul Prucha, ed., *The Indian in American History*, New York: Holt Rinehart and Winston, 1971, p. 27.

505C. F. Campbell, *The Plains Indian in Literature and in Life*, Boulder, CO, 1930. Covers "The Trans-Mississippi West", pp. 175-194.

506Roy Harvey Pearce, *The Savages of America: A Study of the Indian and the Idea of Civilization*, Baltimore: The John Hopkins Press, 1967. Also in Francis Paul Prucha, ed., *The Indian In American History*, New York, Holt, Rinehart and Winston, 1971, p. 17.

507Alvin M. Josephy, Jr., *The Indian Heritage of America*, New York: Alfred A. Knopf, 1970, pp. 329-330. Young Chief Joseph continued in his speech, saying, "Let me be a free man—free to travel, free to stop, free to work, free to trade where I choose, free to choose my own teachers, free to follow the religion of my fathers, free to think and talk and act for myself—and I will obey law, or submit to the penalty." Chief Joseph, exiled from his homeland in the Wallowa valley of Oregon, was never allowed to return. Considered a military genius, he steadfastly refused to ever sell any of his land to the United States government. Joseph died at age 64 on Sept. 21, 1904. His attending physician said it was from a broken heart.

508Seth K. Humphrey, *The Indian Dispossessed*, Boston: Little Brown & Co., 1905, covers the removal of the Poncas, pp. 143-201.

509Helen Hunt Jackson, *A Century of Dishonor*, Boston: Roberts Brothers, 1885, reprint, Harper Torchbooks, 1966, pp. 186-217, 359-374, covers the Poncas and Standing Bear's trial. See also U.S. Department of Interior, *Federal Indian Law*, Washington, U.S. Government Printing Office, 1958. John G. Neihardt, *Black Elk Speaks, Being the Life Story of a Holy Man of the Oglala Sioux*, Lincon: University of Nebraska Press: 1961, pp. 257-268. Covers the account of the Wounded Knee Massacre. In 1863 the Santee Sioux were banished to a reservation in what is now Minnesota; in 1864 the Navajos began their long walk to Fort Sumner in Eastern New Mexico and reservation life. In 1871 the United States government forced the removal of the Flathead tribe in the Bitter Root Valley of Western Montana to a reservation. In 1872 the war against the Modocs in Southern Oregon caused their defeat and final exile to Oklahoma. From 1862 to 1886 a long war persisted against the Apache tribes in an attempt to place them on reservations. In 1878 a war with the Paiutes sent the remnants of the tribe to their final banishment on the Yakama reservation in the State of Washington. In an attempt to end Indian power through the revival of the Indian Ghost Dance religion, Sitting Bull was murdered. On Dec. 29, 1890 near Wounded Knee Creek, South Dakota, about 300 Lakota Sioux men, women and children were killed in what was called the Wounded Knee Massacre.

51011th Annual *U.S. Bureau of Census*, Washington, D.C., U.S. Government Printing Office, 1894, pp. 637-638.

511Alexis de Tocqueville, *Democracy In America, 1835-1840*, NY, Ramdom House, 1945. Although Alexis de Tocqueville praised America's ideals as a young country with the words, "the most democratic, most egalitarian, most religious, most prosperous, most charitable nation on earth...", at the same time, however, he feared that the virtues he valued—freedom, civic participation and creativity— would be imperiled by "the tyranny of the majority", individualism, and other democratic despotisms. This was starting to take place in the treatment of the Indians, African Americans, and other minorities. Tocqueville believed that America's spirit and democratic institutions "awaken and foster a passion for equality which they can never entirely satisfy." Alexis de Tocqueville was fearful that the American system would take root in Europe and change their old aristocratic institutions to a system based on the U.S.—as a land of opportunity.

512Washington Irving, *Sketch Book of Geoffrey Crayon Gent*, Philadelphia: J. B. Lippincott, 1875. Short story collection by Washington Irving. First published in 1819-20 in seven separate parts. Six chapters deal with American subjects.

513Ernest Thompson Seton and Julia M. Seton, compilers, *The Gospel of the Redman*, Santa Fe: Seton Village, 1963, p. 40. Ernest

Thompson Seaton was once head of the Boy Scouts of America.
[514]Rupert Costo, ed., *Textbooks and the American Indians*, San Francisco: American Indian Society, 1970, pp. 2-3.
[515]A. D. Godley, trans., *Herodotus, History*, Vol. 4, Cambridge, MA: Harvard University Press, 1963.
[516]William Meyer, *Native Americans: The New Indian Resistance*, New York: International Publishers, 1971, p. 17.
[517]Irvin M. Peithmann, *Echoes of the Red Man*, New York: Exposition Press, 1955, p. 125.
[518]Virgil J. Vogel, *This Country was Ours*, New York: Harper and Row, 1972, pp. 51-52. "Cash Reward Offered for Indian Scalps." Poster stated, "By His Excellency William Shirley, Esq. Captain-General and Governor in Chief, in and over His Majesty's Province of Massachusetts-Bay, in New-England, and Vice-Admiral of the same, and Major-General in His Majesty's Army. A Proclamation, Whereas the Indians of Norridgewock, Arresaguntacook, Weweenock and St. John's Tribes, and the Indians of the other Tribes inhabiting in the Eastern and Northern Parts of His Majesty's Territories of New-England, the Penobscot Tribe only excepted, have, contrary to their solemn Submission unto His Majesty long since made and frequently renewed, been guilty of the most perfidious, barbarous and inhuman Murders of divers of his Majesty's English subjects;... I have therefore thought fit to issue this Proclamation, and to Declare the Indians of the Norridgewock Arresaguntacook, Weweenock and St. John's Tribes, and the Indians of the other Tribes now of late inhabiting in the Eastern and Northern Parts of His Majesty's Territories of New-England, and in Alliance and Confederacy with the above-recited Tribes, the Penobscots only excepted, to be Enemies, Rebels and Traitors to His Most Sacred Majesty.... I have sought fit to punish the same; and I do hereby promise, that there shall be paid out of the Province-Treasury to all and any of the said forces, over and above their Bounty upon Enlistment, their Wages and Subsistence, the Premiums or Bounties following, For Every Male Indian Prisoner above the Age of Twelve Years, that shall be taken and brought to Boston, Fifty Pounds. For every Male Indian Scalp, brought in as Evidence of their being killed, Forty Pounds. For every Female Indian Prisoner, taken and brought in as aforesaid, and for every Male Indian Prisoner under the Age of Twelve Years, taken and brought in as aforesaid, Twenty-five Pounds. For every Scalp of such Female Indian or Male Indian under Twelve Years of Age, brought in as Evidence of their being killed,, as aforesaid, Twenty Pounds..."
[519]Peithmann, p. 125.
[520]William Bartram, *Travels through North and South Carolina, Georgia, East and West Florida*, London, 1792. See also *White on Red*, eds. Nancy Black and Bette S. Weidman, Port Washington, NY: Kennikat Press, 1976, p. 116.
[521]Glenn Tucker, *Tecumseh: Vision of Glory*, Indianapolis, & New York: Bobbs-Merrill Co., Inc., 1957.
[522]Edward Eggleston, *A First Book in American History*, New York: D, Appleton & Co., 1889, p. 151. See also Cadwallader Colden, *History of the Five Indian Nations*, New York: New Amsterdam Book Co., 1902, 2 vols., Vol. 1, pg. 182.
[523]Michael E, Melody, *The Apache*, New York: Chelsea House Publishers, 1989. pp. 63-64. See also Winfred Buskirk, *The Western Apache*, Norman: University of Oklahoma Press, 1986.
[524]John Bigelow, ed., *The Complete Works of Benjamin Franklin*, New York, G. P. Putman's Sons, 1887. See also Leonard W. Labaree, ed., *The Papers of Benjamin Franklin*, New Haven: Yale University Press, 1967, Vol. 2.
[525]A. Hyatt Verrill, *The American Indian*, New York: The New Home Library, 1947, p. 478.
[526]Frederick E. Hoxie, ed., *Encyclopedia of North America*, New York: Houghton Mifflin, 1996, pp. 570-572. See also James Axtell and William C. Sturtevant, "The Unkindest Cut, or Who Invented Scalping?" William and Mary Quarterly, 37 (1980): 451-472. "Although the American Indian took scalps long before 1492, the Europeans promoted the spread and frequency of scalping by trading the natives guns (leading to more deaths) and knives (making scalp removal easier) and, from 1637 on, by offering bounties for Indian scalps and, after 1688, European scalps." Robert M. Utley & Wilcomb E. Washington, *Indian Wars*, Boston: Houghton Mifflin Co., 1987, pg. 100. Describes an incident in 1743, "of 57 (white) vigilantes who surrounded the village and scalped, hacked, stabbed, and mangled the three men, two women, and one young boy who were present..." Benjamin Franklin was so outraged by this incident that he wrote, "But the wickedness cannot be covered, the guilt will lie on the whole land till justice is done on the murderers. The blood of the innocent will cry to heaven for vengeance." J. P. Dunn, Jr., *Massacres of the Mountains: A History of the Indian Wars of the Far West, 1815-1875*, New York, Capricorn Books, 1886, covers Christian atrocities toward Apaches. U. S. Congress Report, "Massacre of the Cheyenne Indians", The Joint Committee on the Conduct of the War, 2nd session, 38th Congress, vol. III, Washington, D.C., Govt. Printing Office, 1865. J. C. B., *Travels in New France by J. C. B.*, ed. Sylvester K. Stevens, Harrisburg: The Pennsylvania Historical Commission, 1941. While Europeans did not originate scalping, they did encourage its spread through the establishment of bounties. J. C. B. writes that "the French and English were accustomed to pay for the scalps, to the amount of thirty francs worth of trade goods. Their purpose was then to encourage the savages to take as many scalps as they could, and to know the number of the foe who had fallen." Edmund Atkins, English Superintendent of Indian Affairs for the Southern Colonies, wrote a letter to Maryland Governor Horatio Sharpe on June 30, 1757 stating that: "large publick Rewards for Scalps given by Provincial Laws to Indians are attended with very pernicious Consequences to his Majesty's Service.... The Cherokees in particular have got the Art of making 4 Scalps out of one man killed. Here are now 20 Scalps hanging out to publick View, which are well known to have been made out of 5 Frenchmen killed."
[527]Henry F. Dobyns, *Their Number became Thinned, American Indian Population Dynamics in Eastern North America*, Knoxville: University of Tennessee Press, 1983, pp. 25-33. See also Henry F. Dobyns, *Current Anthropology*, Oct., 1966, Vol. VII No. 4, United States census figures for 1970 indicated approximately 792,000—50 percent more than the under-estimated 1960 census. The 1980 census showed that there were 1,423,043 Indians living in the United States and Alaska. The United States Department of Commerce, Bureau of Census, *We the First Americans*, Washington, D.C., 1993, p. 2, reported the population in 1990 of Indians in the United States and Alaska (Inuits and Aleuts) as being 1,959,000. Each census shows a larger increase in the Indian population. Over 5.5 million Americans identify themselves as non-Indian but claim they are of Indian ancestry. In Central and South America the majority of the population is of mixed ancestry from the intermarriages with their Portuguese Spanish conquerors. Many who are of a lighter skin color pass for Caucasian (White or Hispanic), yet are Spanish speaking people in that culture, refusing to acknowledge their Indian ancestry.
[528]J. M. Cooper, *The Northern Algonquian Supreme Being*, Washington, D.C., covers primitive man, No. 6, 1933, pp. 3-4, 41-111.
[529]M. E. Sharpe. *Shamanism: Soviet Studies of Tradition Religion in Siberian and Central Asia*, Armonk, NY: 1990, See also William S. Lyon, *Encyclopedia of Native American Shamanism: Sacred Ceremonies of North America*, Santa Barbara, CA: Abc-Clio, 1998. William S. Lyon, *Encyclopedia of Native American Healing*, New York: W. W. Norton & Company, 1998. Michael J. Winkelman, *Shamans, Priests and Witches: A Cross-Cultural Study of Magico-Religious Practitioners*, Arizona State University Anthropological Research Papers, Jan., 1992.
[530]Robert H. Ruby and John A. Brown, *Dreamer-Prophets of the Columbia Plateau: Smohalla and Skolaskin*, Norman, Oklahoma: University of Oklahoma Press, 1989. See also Major J. W. McMurray, *Transactions of the Albany Institute*, Albany, NY, 1887, vol. XI, pp. 240-248. Read before the Albany Institute, Jan. 19, 1886. George Simpson and J. Milton Yinger, editors, *American Indians and American Life*, Boston: Russell & Russell: pp. 127-136, section on "Religion Among American Indians", by Ruth Underhill.
[531]Charles Alexander Eastman, *The Soul of the Indian*, Boston: Houghton Mifflin, 1911, pp. 3-5, section on "The Great Mystery."
[532]Harold E. Driver, ed., *The Americas on the Eve of Discovery*, Englewood Cliffs, New Jersey: Prentice-Hall, Inc., 1964, pp. 87-91. Ruth L. Bunzel, "The Self-Effacing Zuni of New Mexico", *Bureau of American Ethnology Annual Report* (1932), Washington D. C., #47, pp. 474-87, titled "Introduction to Zuni Ceremonialism."
[533]Black Elk (Hehaka Sapa), *Les Rites Secrets des Indiens Sioux*, recorded and edited by Joseph Epes Brown, Paris, Payot, 1979, p. 26.
[534]Georges E. Sioui, *For an Amerindian Autohistory*, Montreal & Kingston: McGill-Queen's University Press, 1992, pp. 10-11.

535Christopher Vecsey and Robert V.W. Venables, eds., *American Indian Environments: Ecological Issues in Native American History*, Syracuse: 1980, from the Introduction.
536Ake Hultkrantz, trans. Monica Setterwall, *The Religions of the American Indians*, Los Angeles: University of California Press, 1979. See also Natalie Curtis, recorder and ed., *The Indians Book: Songs and Legends of the American Indians*, New York, Dover Press, 1950. Alice Marriott and Carol K. Rachlin, eds., *Plains Indian Mythology*, New York: New American Library, 1975. "Race of the American Indians", *The United States Democratic Review* (May, 1851), Vol. 28, Issue 155.
537Edward Goodbird, *Goodbird the Indian*, New York: Fleming H. Revell Co., 1914, pp. 37-38. Goodbird was a member of the Sioux family of Indian tribes. Hidatsa is located in the Upper Missouri in North Dakota.
538J. R. Walker, "The Sun Dance and Other Ceremonies of the Oglala Division of the Teton Dakota", *Anthropological Papers of the American Museum of Natural History* (1921), Vol. 16. The introduction is devoted to the attitudes of the Oglalas toward their ceremonies. The rest describes the Sun Dance, Hunka and Buffalo ceremonies in great detail, and the role of the Shaman and each participant in the ceremony.
539George Bird Grinnell, *Pawnee Hero Stories and Folk Tales; with Notes on the Origin, Customs, and Character of the Pawnee People*, Lincoln, Neb: Univ. of Nebraska Press, 1963. The Pawnees were about the only Indians who did not go to war with the U.S. They worked as scouts against other Indians. Eventually they were forced to move from their native land in Nebraska and forced to settle in Oklahoma. Diseases reduced their number from about 10,000 to 1000.
540Alice C. Fletcher, "The Hako, A Pawnee Ceremony", *Bureau of American Ethnology*, Washington, Government Printing Office, 22nd Annual Report, part 2, 1900-1906.
541Thomas Gann & J. Eric Thompson, *The History of the Maya*, New York: Charles Scribner's Sons, 1931, pp. 118-120, 248-249.
542Alfred Metraux, *The Incas*, Studio Vista, 1965. Quote found by Father Christobal de Molina in 1957. Pachacuti was born in 1440. First of the recognized historical Inca rulers, Pachacuti was responsible for the Inca expansion into an empire. His son, Tupac Inca, became the new Inca king after Pachacuti's death in 1470. Pedro Sarmiento De Gamboa, translated by Clements Markham, *History of the Incas*, Cambridge: The Hakluyt Society, 1907, pp. 138-139. Recording the death of Pachacuti, De Gamboa wrote of his last words, "I was born as a flower of the field. As a flower I was cherished in my youth, I came to my full age, I grew old, now I am withered and die."
543Charles Alexander Eastman, *The Soul of the Indian*, Boston: Houghton Mifflin, 1911.
544Helen Hunt Jackson, *A Century of Dishonor*, 1909, p.7.
545Henry Benjamin Whipple, *Lights and Shadows of a Long Episcopate*, New York: 1899, pp. 50-53.
546Ernest Thompson Seton & Julia Seton, *The Gospel of the Redman*, Santa Fe: Seton Village, 1966, pp. 2-3.
547Joseph Francois Lafitau, eds. William N. Fenton & Elizabeth L. Moore, *Customs of the American Indians Compared with the Customs of Primitive Times*, Toronto: The Champlain Society, 2 vols., 1974, vol. 2, pp. 151-152. Translated from Lafitau's 2 volumes, *Moeurs des Sauvages Ameriqains, Compares aux Moeurs des Premiers Temps.*
548Washington Irving, *The Adventures of Captain Bonneville*, New York: R. Worthington, 1884, p. 171.
549John James, *My Experience with Indians*, Austin, TX: Gammel's Book Store, 1925, p. 67.
550Lafitau, Fenton and Moore, pp. 151-152.
551Philip Drucker, *Indians of the Northwest Coast*, Garden City, N. Y., The Natural History Press, 1963, pp. 154-157.
552Richard Erdoes, *The Rain Dance People*, New York: Alfred A. Knopf, Inc., 1976, pp. 175-203, Covers "Birth, Life and Death." *Theosophy*, Vol. 16, No. 2, pp. 70-76. No. 23 of a 59-part series, Dec., 1927. Section called "Ancient Landmarks XXIII, The Feathered Serpent."
553George W. Manypenny, *Our Indian Wards*, New York: Dacapo Press, 1972, pp. 28, 29.
554Kintana Garibay and Angel Maria, *Historia de la Literatura Nahuatl*, Mexico: 1953. This book is the translation from the original texts made in 1558, and transcribed in the Nahuatl language. It was translated into Spanish by the two writers who were fluent in both languages.
555William W. Warren, *History of the Ojibways, Based upon Traditions and Oral Statements*, First Published, 1885, Reprint, *History of the Obijway Nation*, Ross & Haines, 1957, pp. 72-73.
556Dbyani Ywahoo, *Voices of Our Ancestors*, Boston and London: Shambhala Publications, Inc., 1987, p. 187.
557Grace Steele Woodward, *The Cherokees*, Norman: Univ. of Oklahoma Press, 1963, pp. 23-24. "Lady of Cofitachequi" is mistakenly referred to as the niece of the chieftainess, but was the actual chief.
558Dr. H. C. Yarrow, *North American Indian Burial Customs*, Ogden, Utah: Eagle View Publishing Co., 1988, pp. 12-13, 32. See also Harold E. Driver, *Indians of North America*, Chicago: University of Chicago Press, 1969, pp. 374-375. C. L. Sonnichsen, *The Mescalero Apaches*, Norman: University of Oklahoma Press, 1958.
559G. E. Lankford, ed., *Native American Legends: Southeastern Legends: Tales from the Natchez, Caddo, Biloxi, Chickasaw, and other Nations*, Little Rock, AR: August House Publishers, 1987, pp. 116, 117.
560W. David Baird, *The Choctaw People*, Phoenix, Indian Tribal Series, 1973, pp. 2, 8.
561Baird, p. 7. See also Frankie Sue Gilliam, ed., *Twin Territories Newspaper*, Oklahoma, 1995, pp. 6-10, "The Choctaws, an Enduring Race." In 2003 there were 96,350 Choctaws worldwide.
562Dr. H. C. Yarrow, *North American Indian Burial Customs*, pp. 40, 53. See also E. Adamson Hoebel, *The Cheyenne, Indians of the Great Plains*, New York, Holt, Rinehart, and Winston, Inc., 1960, pp. 86-88. G. B. Grinnell, *The Cheyenne Indians, Their History and Ways of Life*, New Haven: Yale University Press, 2 vols., 1923.
563The Museum of Civilization, *Secrets of Amazonia*, Quebec, Canada, National Library of Canada, 1996, p. 39. See also Alanson Skinner, "Social Life and Ceremonial; Bundles of the Menomini Indians", *American Museum of Natural History, Anthropological Papers of the American Museum of Natural History,* New York: 1913.vol. XIII, part I, p. 85. The Menominee tribe of California believed that humans possessed two souls. One resided in the head and was the intelligent soul that wandered about in the graveyard after death. Offerings of food were made to satisfy this soul. The other soul resided in the heart and it was this soul that traveled to the next world.
564The Museum of Civilization, *Secrets of Amazonia*, p. 45.
565Reg Ashwell, *Coast Salish, Surrey, B.C.*, Hancock House Publishers, 1989, p. 69. See also James A. Teit, ed. by Franz Boas, *The Salish Tribes of the Western Plateaus*, 45th Annual Report of American Ethnology, Washington, D.C., Smithsonian, 1930.
566Philip Drucker, *Indians of the Northwest Coast*, Garden City: The Natural History Press, 1963, pp. 175-176
567Lewis Henry Morgan, *The Indian Journals 1859-62*, Ann Arbor: The University of Michigan Press, 1959, pp. 144-145, covers the Shawnee tradition of heaven.
568George Irving Quimby, *Indian Life in the Upper Great Lakes*, Chicago: The University of Chicago Press, 1960, pp. 120-121.
569Quimby, 120-121.
570John de Verrazano, *The Voyage of Verrazano along the Coast of North America*, Joseph G. Cogswell, trans. New York Historical Society Collections, 1841, 2nd series, I, pp. 37-67.
571Adriaen van der Donck, *Description of the New Netherlands*, New York Historical Society Collections, 1841, 2nd series, I, p. 190.
572Grove A. Day, *Coronado's Quest: The Discovery of the Southwestern States*, Berkley: University of California Press, 1964.
573John Josselyn, *An Account of Two Voyages to New England*, London: 1674, Reprint Boston Ma: Veazie, 1865, p. 124.
574John Lankford, editor, *Captain John Smith's America*, New York: NY: Harper and Row, 1967, pp.118-119.
575 Lankford, pp. 118-119.
576Carleton Beals, *Nomads and Empire Builders*, New York: Citadel Press, 1965, p. 12.
577Chief Red Fox with Cash Asher, *The Memoirs of Chief Red Fox*, New York: Ballantine Books, 1981, p. 19.
578Carleton Beals, *Nomads and Empire Builders*, Philadelphia and New York: Chilton Co., 1961, pp. 16-20. They lived in the area of Peru and wore floor-length wool dresses. Women of rank ate from gold or silver vessels while the ordinary women ate from wooden or

clay vessels. "They dwelt in seventy villages connected by fine roads.... Their capital had fine buildings and temples dedicated to the Sun, with many gold vessels for the services, brightly painted walls and ceilings, and these were lined with gold and silver female idols. The women were unmarried and no man was permitted to remain in their dominion after sundown. They did bear children. When the desire came to them, they assembled a hoard of warriors and made war on a great overlord, in colder country... captives were brought back to their own land—white men of great stature—and the women kept them as long as their caprice lasted or until pregnant; then they sent them back to their country. If the women gave birth to a male child, they killed them and sent the body to the father; if a female child, they raised her with great solemnity and instructed her in the arts of war." See also Orlando Villa Boas, with Claudio Villas Boas, edited by Kenneth S. Brecher; illustrations by Wacupia. *Xingu; The Indians, Their Myths,* New York: New York: Farrar, Straus and Giroux, 1973. p. 125. G. C. Rothery, *The Amazons in Antiquity and Modern Times,* F. Griffiths, London: 1910, pp. 118-119. Hugh Fox, *Gods of the Cataclysm,* Dorset Press, N. Y., 1981, pp. 195-203, Writes on the Xingu legend and others, titled "God the Mother." *The Hakluyt Society Series* number 24, *Expeditions into the Valley of the Amazons,* trans. and ed. by C. Markham, London: 1959, p. 36.

579Alfonso Ortiz and Richard Erdoes, *American Indian Myths and Legends,* NY: Pantheon, 1984. White Buffalo Calf Woman Brings the First Pipe, as told by John Fire Lame Deer, in 1967. "The Sioux are a warrior tribe, and one of their proverbs says, 'Woman shall not walk before man.' Yet White Buffalo Woman is the dominant figure of their most important legend."
580M. Annette Jamimes with Theresa Halsey, *State of Native America, American Indian Women,* Boston: South End Press, 1992, p. 319. See also Paula Gunn Allen, *The Sacred Hoop,* Boston, Beacon Press, 1986, p. 45.
581Lewis Henry Morgan, *League of the Ho-de-no-sau–nee, Iroquois,* Massachusetts: JG Press, 1995. p. 199.
582Thomas E. Sanders and Walter W. Peek, eds. *Literature of the American Indian,* New York: Glencoe, 1973, pp. 41-43, refers to "The Woman Who Fell from the Sky: A Seneca account." One of many similar versions by the Indian tribes.
583Natalie Curtis, recorder and editor, *The Indians Book: Songs and Legends of the American Indians,* New York: Dover Press, 1950.
584Clyde Kluckhohn and Dorothea Leighton, *The Navajo,* Garden City, N. Y., Anchor Books, 1962, p. 180.
585Clyde Kluckhohn and Dorothea Leighton, pp. 181-182.
586 Marija Gimbutas, *The Civilization of the Goddess: The World of Old Europe.* Harper, San Francisco: 1991. See also Marija Gimbutas, *The Language of the Goddess,* Harper Collins, New York, 1989. George Thomson, *The Prehistoric Aegean,* Lawrence and Wishart, London, 1954, p. 152. Refers to "Khasis of India." Bruhns, Karen Olsen, and Karen E. Stothert, *Women in Ancient America,* Norman: University of Oklahoma, 1999. Douglas L. Oliver, *Native Cultures of the Pacific Islands,* Honolulu: University of Hawaii Press, 1989. Joseph Campbell, *The Masks of God: Primitive Mythology,* Viking, 1959. Joseph Campbell, *The Mythic Image,* Princeton University Press, 1974. The Mother goddess was continuously worshipped for thousands of years from about 3500 to 500 B.C. during the ascendance and decline of civilizations that flourished and were conquered. Her names were many: Ishtar, Astarte, Anahita, Ma Asherah, but she was first known as Inanna, the beloved and revered deity of Sumer. Inanna played a greater role in Sumerian myth than any other deity. Her story has been restored from fragmented cuneiform tablets comprising the cycle of Inanna. The Hymn to Inanna was sung at the sacred marriage rites between the goddess and the Sumerian King to ensure the fertility of the land and to legitimize the king's rule. The cosmic powers of the Goddess had to be transferred to the king to ensure his powers of leadership and fertility. These peaceful, agricultural societies existed for thousands of years until, in 2500 B.C., waves of Indo-European sky-worshipping pastoral tribes invaded from the East. Archaeological evidence indicates that the two cultures were completely different. The invaders brought their love of conquest and weapons with religions that had their male gods at the head, and put an end to the matriarchal societies. Two matriarchal societies based on a similar structure as the Indians in the Americas were the Nagovisi of Bougainvillea in the South Pacific and the Khasi of Meghalaya, India. The Khasi of India were forbidden to marry within their clan, and all the land was passed on through the woman. "Not only is the mother the head and source and only bond of the family; she is the only real owner of the property.... The father has no kinship with his children, who belong to his mothers clan...."
587Ake Hultkrantz, trans. Monica Setterwall, *The Religions of the American Indians,* Los Angeles: Univer. of Calif. Press, 1979. p. 53.
588W. Jones, ed. by M. W. Fisher, "Ethnography of the Fox Indians", Washington, D.C., *Smithsonian Bulletin of the Bureau of American Ethnology,* 1939, p. 125.
589Ake Hultkrantz, trans. Monica Setterwall, *The Religions of the American Indians,* Los Angeles: Univ. of California Press, 1979, p. 54.
590Paula Gunn Allen, *The Sacred Hoop,* Boston: Beacon Press, 1986, p. 254.
591Harold E. Driver, *Girls' Puberty Rites in Western North America,* University of Calif., Anthropological Records, 1941, VI, pp. 21-90.
592Nathan Rutstein and Michael Morgan, eds., *Healing Racism: Education's Role,* Springfield, MA, Whitcomb Publishing, 1996, pp. 44-45. The child is called "wakan yeja" in Lakota. The English translation is "sacred being."
593Howard S. Russell, *Indian New England before the Mayflower,* Hanover, NH: University Press of New England, 1980, p. 36.
594Melvin R. Gilmore, *Uses of Plants by the Indians of the Missouri River Regions,* U. S. Bureau of American Ethnology, Annual Report, Washington, D. C., 1911-12, vol. 33, p. 64.
595Robert F. Spencer and Jesse D. Jennings, *The American Indians,* New York: Harper and Row, 1965, pp. 146, 364.
596Richard Erdoes, *The Rain Dance People,* Mew York: Alfred A. Knopf, Inc., 1976, p. 181.
597Norman A. Chance, *The Eskimo of North Alaska,* New York: Holt Rinehart and Winston, 1966, pp. 20-21, section on "Birth to Infancy."
598Thomas Gann, & J. Eric Thompson, *The History of the Maya,* New York: Charles Scribner's Sons, 1931, p. 166.
599George A. Petititt, "Primitive Education in North America", University of California Publications in *American Archaeology and Ethnology* (1946), Vol. XLIII, pp. 9-11.
600Mari Sandoz, *These Were the Sioux,* New York: Hastings House Publishers, 1961, p. 243.
601Chief Red Fox, *The Memoirs of Chief Red Fox,* New York: Fawcet, 1981, p. 18.
602Wilcomb E. Washburn, *The Indian in America,* New York: Harper and Row, 1975, p. 15.
603Thomas Alford, *Civilization,* Norman: University of Oklahoma Press, 1936, pp. 19-21.
604Charles Alexander Eastman, *The Soul of the Indian,* Boston: Houghton Mifflin, 1911, pp. 32-35.
605Leo W. Simmons, ed. *Sun Chief: The Autobiography of a Hopi Indian,* New Haven: Yale University Press, 1942, pp. 51-52. Chief Don Talayesva, Hopi of Oraibi Arizona, was born in 1890. He was caught between two cultures: his own and that of white society.
606Harold E. Driver, *Indians of North America,* Chicago: University of Chicago Press, 1969, pp. 370-371. C. L. Sonnichsen, *The Mescalero Apaches,* Norman: University of Oklahoma Press, 1958. The entrance of the woman into motherhood was attached to important ceremonial practice by most of the Indian Tribes.
607Jane B. Katz, *I am the Fire of Time,* New York: E. P. Dutton, 1977, p. xvii. Quote from E. Adamson Hoebel, *The Cheyennes,* New York: Holt, Rinehart & Winston, 1960, p. 26.
608Adriaen van der Donck, "Description of the New Netherlands" *New York: Historical Society Collections* (1841), 2nd series, I, p. 190.
609John Witthoft, *The American Indian as Hunter,* Harrisburg, PA: Pennsylvania Historical and Museum Commission, 1967, p. 5.
610 Frederick E. Hoxie, *Encyclopedia of North American Indians,* New York: Houghton Mifflin Co., 1996, p. 195.
611Paula Gunn Allen, *The Sacred Hoop,* p. 26. See also Robert Grumet, "Sunksquaws, Shamans, and Tradeswomen: Middle Atlantic Coastal Algonkian Women during the 17th and 18th Centuries", in Women and Colonization: *Anthropological Perspectives,* ed. Mona Etienne and Eleanor Leacock, New York: Praeger, 1980.
612M. Annette Jaimes, editor, *The State of Native America,* South End Press, Boston, MA, 1982. Annette Jaimes and Theresa Halsey, "American Indian Women", p. 317. See also Robert Grumet, "Sunksquaws, Shamans, and Tradeswomen: Middle Atlantic Coastal Algonkian Women during the 17th and 18th Centuries." Writes, "The women were known as Sunksquaws or in English as Queens. Article 45 of the Iroquois Constitution called the women that presided at

their councils, Royaneh."

613Sir Iain Moncreiffe, *The Highland Clans*, 1967. See also R. Fox, *Kinship and Marriage* (1984); E. Gellner, *The Concept of Kinship*, 1987. Lorna Blackie, *Clans and Tartans: The Fabric of Scotland*, London: Quintet Publishing, Ltd., 1987. Some tribes that were based on the matrilineal clan system were the Cherokee, Crow, Delaware, Oto, Hidatsa, Mandan, Pawnee, Shawnee, and the Six-Nation Confederacy of Iroquois, Mohawk, Cayuga, Seneca, Tuscarora and Oneida. The clan system later disappeared in some tribes, as with the Dakotas. Patrilineal tribes included the Omaha, Ponca, Iowa, Kansa and Osage, Ojibway, Menominee, Potawatomi, Ho-chunk etc.

614Edward W. Gifford, *Clans and Moieties in Southern California*, Coyote Press, 1918.

615Frederick E. Hoxie, *Encyclopedia of North American Indians*, New York: Houghton Mifflin Co., 1996, p. 195.

616Lewis Henry Morgan, *League of the Iroquois*, Secaucus, New Jersey: The Citadel Press, 1972, pp. 78-92. See also Paul Bohannan, and John Middleton, eds., *Kinship and Social Organization*, Garden City, NY, Natural History Press, 1968. CM Barbeau, "Iroquoian Clans and Phratries, *American Anthropologist*", March-June, 1917, 19(3):392-402. Barbeau labels the many different clans in the Iroquois nation and examines the relationship between the clans and the phratries. They appear to have been a political unit, not common to all tribes of the Iroquois. The Iroquois covered an area from the Carolina states to the Great Lakes. Total population was between eighty and one hundred thousand, with their people making up various tribes. These tribes were the Cherokee, the Tuscarora, the Five Nations, or Iroquois proper, the Huron-Wyandot, the Neutral, and the Erie. Each one of these peoples was further divided into smaller nations. He identifies all of their different clans. All of the clans personify animals with the name of their clan, the most popular ones being wolf, deer, bear, turtle, etc. It seems that the wolf clan was the most important among the Iroquois, as well as the Algonkian, Siouan, and other eastern, southern and central nations. Bear and Deer clans also are very important, while the turtle clans were limited to mostly eastern clans. The clans were federated into larger, exogamous bodies, now called phratries. They served as political units and also as a way to distribute power evenly among the tribes and clans. Of the eight Iroquois nations, however, only four were part of a phratry. Most believe that these phratries were based on the kinship of the clans but this has been widely argued. There is a lack of uniformity in the arrangement of clans in the phratries that hint at a sense of arbitrariness in their purpose. The totemic qualities of the clans were absent in the phratries. A minority of the Iroquois were in a phratry, while it was essential to be in a clan. The continued inactivity of the phratries proved to be a cause of their eventual extinction. In general, the phratries did not have the influence or personality that they were intended for.

617Thomas Sanders and William Peek, eds., *Literature of the American Indian*, New York: Glencoe Press, 1973, pp. 208-239. Covers "The Law of the Great Peace." *The Syracuse Newspapers, Herald American*, "The Six Nations of the Iroquois" (July 22, 1990). Published by *The Herald Company*. The other clans like Mohawk, Wyandot, Oneida, Onondaga, Cayuga and Seneca arranged their tribes in yet a different order and sometimes even further subdivided them. Some using phratries, or moites or other classifications.

618Sam D. Gill and Irene F. Sullivan, *Dictionary of American Indian Mythology*, Oxford University Press 1994, pp. 49, 126. See also John L. Stoutenburg Jr., *Dictionary of the American Indian*, NY: Philosophical Library, 1956, p. 72.

619Robin Fox, *Kinship and Marriage*, NY: Penguin Books, 1967.

620Lewis Henry Morgan, *The Indian Journals, 1859-62*, Ann Harbor: University of Michigan Press, 1959, p. 170.

621William Bartram, *Travels through North and South Carolina, Georgia, East and West Florida*, London: 1792. See also *White on Red*, ed. by Nancy Black and Bette S. Weidman, Port Washington, NY: Kennikat Press, 1976, p. 116.

622Lewis Henry Morgan, *The Indian Journals, 1859-62*, Ann Harbor: University of Michigan Press, 1959. Discusses clan relationship and the status of women among the various tribes.

623Richard S. Brandt, *Hopi Ethics*, Chicago: University of Chicago Press, 1954, p. 260. See also Laura Thompson and Alice Joseph, *The Hopi Way*, Chicago: University of Chicago Press, 1944.

624Robert Steven Grumet, "Sunksquaws, Shamans, and Tradeswomen: Middle Atlantic Coastal Algonkin (Algonquin) Women During the 17th and 18th Centuries." The women were known as Sunksquaws or in English, as Queens. Article 45 of the Iroquois Constitution called the women that presided at their councils Royaneh. See also Mona Etienne and Eleanor Leacock, editors, *Women and Colonization: Anthropological Perspectives*, New York: Praegar, 1980.

625William Penn, *A Letter from William Penn, Proprietary and Governor of Pennsylvania in America to the Committee of the Free Society of Traders*, London: 1683. Reprint London: J. Coleman, 1881. In reference to "A Description of Pennsylvania in 1683."

626Cybercasting Services Division of the *National Public Telecomuting Network (NPTN)*, ed. by Gerald Murphy, "The Constitution of the Iroquois Nation, 1836."

627Joseph Francois Lafitau, ed. by William N. Fenton & Elizabeth L. Moore, *Customs of the American Indians Compared with the Customs of Primitive Times*, Reprint 1974, p. 69.

628Pierre de Charlevoix, *Journal of a Voyage to North America*, London, 1761.

629Bernal Del Castillo Diaz, A. P. Maudslay, translator, *The Discovery and Conquest of Mexico, 1517-1521*, New York: 1956.

630J. G. Frazer, *Totemism and Exogamy: A Treatise on Certain Early Forms of Superstition and Society*, London: Macmillan, 1910, 4 vol., repr. 1968. See also Emile Durkheim, *The Elementary Forms of the Religious Life*, Karen E. Fields (translator), New York, NY, Free Press, 1995. C. Lévi-Strauss, *Totemism*, Beacon Press, 1963. C. M. Barbeau, "Parallel Between the Northwest Coast and Iroquoian Clans and Phratries", *American Anthropologist*, 1917, vol. 19: 403-405. Ronald Preston Rohner, *The Kwakiutl: Indians of British Columbia*, New York: Holt, Rinehart and Winston, 1970. Franz Boas, *The Social Organization and the Secret Societies of the Kwakiutl Indians*, 1897. In a report of the U.S. National Museum for 1895: 311-738, Government Printing Office.

631Philip Drucker, *Indians of the Northwest Coast*, Garden City: The Natural History Press, 1963, pp. 131-143. The Potlach evolved into our modern day "potluck suppers." A potlatch was a festive ceremony with singing, dancing and the giving of gifts. It was generally used to show a change of status in the community, enabling the youth and distant relatives to socialize and be together. A potlatch might be held on the occasion of a wedding, the birth of a child, or the attainment of new position in the tribe.

632Drucker, p. 131. See also H. G. Barnett, *American Anthropologist*, July to Sept., 1938. Helen Codere, "Fighting with Property: A Study of Kwakiutl Potlatching and Warfare 1792-1930." *Monographs of the American Ethnological Society* 18, University of Washington Press, WA, 1950.

633Jerald T. Milanich and Susan Milbrath, eds., *First Encounters*, Gainesville: University of Florida Press, 1989, p. 203.

634Jerald T. Milanich and Susan Milbrath, pp. 206-208.

635John P. Brown, *Old Frontiers*, Kingsport, Tenn: Southern Publishers, 1938, p. 79.

636Grace Steele Woodward, *The Cherokees*, Norman: University of Oklahoma Press, 1963, p. 43. See also *Tennessee Historical Quarterly*, Vol. 21, 1962, p. 354. Quote on Nancy Ward who died in 1822 at age eighty-four.

637Carolyn Thomas Foreman, *Indian Women Chiefs*, Washington, D.C., Zenger Publishing, 1976. See also Paula Gunn Allen, *The Sacred Hoop*, Boston: Beacon Press, 1986, p. 38.

638Doreen Jensen and Cheryl Brooks, eds., *In Celebration of Our Survival*, Vancouver, BC: University of British Columbia, 1991, pp. 65-79. See also Shirley Joseph (1991), "Assimilation Tools, Then and Now", *In Celebration of Our Survival*. Also, Pamela Paul, The Trojan Horse: *An Analysis of the Social, Economic and Political Reaction of First Nations People as a Result of Bill C-31*. M.A. thesis for degree of Master of Arts, Department of Anthropology, University of New Brunswick, Canada.

639Wilcomb E. Washburn, ed., *The American Indian and the United States: A Documentary History*, New York: 1973, 4 vols. On treaties and acts of Congress, debates with court decisions and the reports of the Commissioner of Indian Affairs, showing the United States government relationship with the Indians. The United States "Freedom of Indian Religion Act" was passed in Nov. 1978, and signed by President Carter. Before this act, an Indian could be punished by 10 years in jail or a $10,000 dollar fine for singing native songs or performing their ceremonial dances.

640John Bigelow, ed., *The Complete Works of Benjamin Franklin*, pp. 210, 365-366. See also Cadwallader Colden, *History of the Five Indian Nations*, New York: New Amsterdam Book Co., 1902, 2 vols. Paul Wallace, *White Roots of Peace*, Santa Fe: Clear Light Publishers, 1994. Thomas Henry, *Wilderness Messiah*, Wm. Sloan Assoc., 1955; Morgan, MA: JG Press, 1995. Reprint of 1851 edition on the origins, structure and customs of the Confederacy.

641William Bridgwater, editor, *The Columbia Viking Desk Encyclopedia*, New York: Viking Press, 1953, pp. 602, 617. The Thanksgiving that we celebrate today was taken and copied from the ceremonial feast the Plymouth colonists were invited to by the Indians, even to the foods eaten, on their first Thanksgiving in 1621 after landing in New England (p. 602). Mardi Gras was an occasion for merrymaking during the middle ages (p. 617).

642George William Douglas, *The American Book of Days*, New York: The H. W. Wilson Co., 1948, p. 252. See also Barbara G. Walker, *The Women's Encyclopedia of Myths and Secrets*, San Francisco, CA: Harper & Row, 1983, p. 625. According to Walker, the Maypole was not originally European, but finds its origins in the phallic festivals of India and Egypt, celebrating the fertility of the spring.

643Marija Gimbutas, *The Language of the Goddess*, San Francisco: Harper & Row, 1989, p. 141.

644Gimbutas, Introduction. See also Ake Hultkrantz, trans. by Monica Setterwall, *The Religions of the American Indians*, Los Angeles, University of California Press, 1979, pp. 168-169. Frederick E. Hoxie, *Encyclopedia of North American Indians*, p. 386.

645Ake Hultkrantz, trans. by Monica Setterwall, *The Religions of the American Indians*, Los Angeles: Univ. of California Press, 1979, p. 168.

646Francis Densmore, *The American Indians and Their Music*, New York: The Woman's Press, 1926. See also Francis Densmore, "The Songs of the American Indian", *American Mercury*, VIII, Jan., 1926, pp. 65-68. John C. Fillmore, *The Harmonic Structure of Indian Music*, New York: G. P. Putman's Sons, 1899.

647Ruth M. Underhill, *Red Man's America*, Chicago: University of Chicago Press, 1971, pp. 274, 275.

648Charles S. Myers, *Reports of the Cambridge Anthropological Expedition to the Torres Straits*, Cambridge: 1912, Vol. 4, Chapter 12.

649Erich M. Von Hornbostel, "The Music of the Fuegians, *Ethnos* (July, 1948), Vol. 13, nos. 3-4.

650Charlette Heth, editor, *Native American Dance: Ceremonies and Social Traditions*, Washington, D.C., National Museum of the American Indian, Smithsonian Institution, Golden Colorado: Fulcrum Publishing, 1992.

651William Bartram, *Travels through North and South Carolona, Georgia, East and West Florida*, Mark Van Doren, editor, New York: Dover Publications, 1959, p. 396.

652Paul Recer, AP Science writer, *Mobile Register*, page 2A, Washington, D.C., April 27, 2001.

653Inez Hilger, *Henun Namku, An Araucanian Indian of the Andes Remembers the Past*, Norman: Univ. of Oklahoma Press, 1966, pp. 74-79.

654Ake Hultkrantz, trans. by Monica Setterwall, *The Religions of the American Indians*, Los Angeles: University of California Press, 1979, pp. 56-58. On p. 57: " It is therefore interesting to observe that in the cult she is represented by a corncob among the Indians in Central America, Mexico, the southwestern United States, and on the Plains." See also Richard Erdoes, *The Rain Dance People*, New York. Alfred A. Knopf, Inc., 1976, pp. 227-231. An old proverb, "Corn is the Hopi's heart.... Corn is our mother, the giver of life to our people...."

655Lewis Henry Morgan, *The Indian Journals, 1859-62*, University of Michigan Press, 1959, p. 77. Among the Shawnee, dances performed in the 1860s were the Bread Dance (used in the spring and fall), New Corn Dance (For the Green Corn Festival), two War Dances (before leaving and returning), False Face Dance (to ask the spirits to drive away an illness), Pumpkin Dance (similar to Bread Dance), Wolf Dance (giving dance to be shared later by tribe), Bird Dance (performed by women to honor the first bird appearing in Winter and Spring), Fish Dance (social dance for men and women), Horse Dance (women stand by singers and the men trot into the dance), Dance for the Dead (adoption of one in place of the deceased), Swan Dance (men and women), Bear Dance, Bean Dance, Rocking Dance, Cherokee Dance, Scraping Dance, Squat Dance, Turkey Dance, etc.

656Edward Morris Opler and Mircea Eliade, ed., "Apache Religion", in *The Encyclopedia of Religion*, New York: Macmillan Publishing Company, 1987, pp. 331-333.

657 William K. Powers, Mircea Eliade, ed., "Lakota Religion", in *The Encyclopedia of Religion*, New York: Macmillan Publishing Company, 1987, pp. 434-436.

658Louis Lamphere, Mircea Eliade, ed., "Navajo Religion", in *The Encyclopedia of Religion*, New York: Macmillan Publishing Company. 1987, pp. 337-340.

659Albert B. Reagan, "A Navajo Fire Dance", *American Anthropologist* (1957), 36(3): pp. 434- 437.

660Joe S. Sando, *The Pueblo Indians*, San Francisco: Indian Historian Press, 1976. See also J. S. Sando, *Pueblo Nations: Eight Centuries of Pueblo Indian History*, Santa Fe, NM: Clear Light, 1992. E. P. Dozier, *The Pueblo Indians of North America*, Prospect Heights, IL: Waveland Press, 1983. E. W. C. Parsons, *The Pueblo of Jemez*, New Haven: Yale University Press, 1925.

661Frank Waters, *The Book of the Hopi*, NY: Penguin, 1963, p. 258.

662Richard Erdoes, *The Rain Dance People*, pp. 230.

663Frederick J. Dockstader, *The Kachina and the White Man*, Albuquerque: University of New Mexico Press, 1985. See also Neil David, *Kachinas, Spirit Beings of the Hopi*, Albuquerque: Avanyu Publishing, Inc., 1993. Frank Waters, *The Book of the Hopi*, New York: Penguin, 1963.

664 Elsie Clews Parsons and Ralph L. Beals, "The Sacred Clowns of the Pueblo and Mayo-Yaqui Indians", *American Anthropologist* (1934), vol. 36, pp. 491-514. See also David Maybury-Lewis, *Millenium: Tribal Wisdom and the Modern World*, NY: Viking Press, 1992, pp. 210-213.

665Dr. Jessie Fewkes, "Snake Ceremonials at Walpi", *Journal of American Ethnology and Archaeology*, Vol. IV, Cambridge, 1894. See also Fewkes, Tusayan Snake Ceremonies: Sixteenth Annual Report of Bureau of Ethnology, Washington, D.C., 1896. Tusayan Snake and Flute Ceremonies: Nineteenth Annual Report of Bureau of Ethnology, Washington, D.C., 1897.

666Edward S. Curtis, *The North American Indians*, Vol. 12, 1907-1930. Curtis visited the Hopi reservation every year after 1900. A total of 14 photographs of the snake ceremony, priest and snake catchers are shown in Vol. 12.

667Ruth M. Underhill, *Red Man's Religion*, Chicago: University of Chicago Press, 1965.

668M. Inez Hilger, *Henun Namku, An Araucanian Indian of the Andes Remembers the Past*, Norman: University of Oklahoma Press, 1966, pp. 44-46.

669Willard Z. Park, "Paviotso Shamanism", *American Anthropologist*, 36 (1): pp. 99-113, Jan.-March 1934. Park's report on Paviotso shamanism begins with a history of these people before they were placed on reservations in the western part of Nevada. He also briefly describes the local environment and some of the Paviotso food gathering ways. This is an account of their history, environment and environmental interaction.

670John G. Neihardt, *Black Elk Speaks: Being the Life Story of a Holy Man of the Oglala Sioux*, Univ. of Nebraska Press: Lincon, 1961.

671S. R. F. Price, *Rituals and Power: The Roman Imperial Cult in Asia Minor*, Cambridge: Cambridge University Press, 1984. See also "Mysteries of the Ancient World", Washington, D.C., *National Geographic*, 1979, p. 94. Adela Yarbro Collins, "The Origin of Christian Baptism", *Studia Liturgica* 19 (1989), pp. 28-46. On the "Manual of Discipline", 2-3. The Dead Sea Scrolls provide us evidence that immersion was used as an initiatory rite by Jewish sects prior to the time of John. The Dead Sea Scrolls proved to be the ancient writings of a Jewish community that lived in Qumran from about 125 B.C. to A.D. 68. According to the Manual of Discipline, initiates to the Qumran community were required to immerse themselves before being accepted into the community.

672John G. Neihardt, *Black Elk Speaks: Being the Life Story of a Holy Man of the Oglala Sioux*, Univ. of Nebraska Press: Lincon, 1961.

673Wayne Moquin and Charles Van Doren, Eds., *Great Documents in American Indian History*, New York: De Capo Press, 1995, p. 361.

674William Sturtevant, editor, *Handbook of North American Indians*, Washington: Smithsonian Institution, 1984. David Damas, editor, *Artic*, vol. 5.

675Reginald Laubin with Gladys Laubin, *North America; Civilization of the American Indian; Indian Dances of North America; Their Importance to Indian Life*. Norman: University of Oklahoma Press 1977.

676J.R. Walker, "The Sun Dance and Other Ceremonies of the Oglala Division of the Teton Dakota", *Anthropological Papers of the American Museum of Natural History*, Vol. 16, 1921. See also Frances Densmore, *The American Indians and their Music*, New York, Womans Press, 1926, pp. 30-41, covers "Ceremonies and Dances." Elsie Clews Parsons, Pueblo Indian Religion, Lincoln, University of Nebraska Press, 1996, vol. I, pp. 170-266, covers "The Spirits", pp. 267-492 on "Ritual."

677Thomas E. Mails, *Fools Crow*, Lincoln: University of Nebraska Press, 1979, pp. 80, 81.

678Ruth M. Underhill, *Red Man's Religion*, Chicago, University of Chicago Press, 1965, pp. 106-115, on "Indian Ceremonialism." See also A. Hyatt Verrill, *The American Indian*, NY, The New Home Library, 1947, pp. 135-155. Covers "Dances And Ceremonials."

679Powwow was an Algonquin term, "pau-wau" or "pauau", which referred to a gathering of medicine men and spiritual leaders. "Pau-wauing" referred to a religious ceremony, usually one of curing. In the 1800's the European explorers observing these religious gatherings and dances mispronounced the word as powwow. Jennings, *The Invasion of America*, p. 241. In 1646 the Massachusetts General Court decreed that "no Indian shall at any time pawwaw, or perform outward worship to their false gods, or to the devil...."

680Joseph H. Cash and Gerald W. Wolf, *The Three Affillated Tribes, Mandan, Arikara, and Hiidatsa*, Phoenix: Indian Tribal Series, 1974, pp. 6-10.

681Lewis Henry Morgan, *The Indian Journals, 1859-62*, University of Michigan Press, 1959, pp. 183-189.

682J. G. Jorgensen, *The Sun Dance Religion*. Chicago: University of Chicago Press, 1974. See also L. Spier, "The Sun Dance of the Plains Indians: Its Development and Diffusion", *Anthropological Papers of the American Museum of Natural History*, 1921, 16, 7.

683Dale McGinnis and Floyd Sharrok, *The Crow People*, Phoenix: Indian Tribal Series, 1972. pp. 30, 31.

684Murry L. Wax, *Unity and Diversity*, Engelwood Cliffs, New Jersey: Prentice Hall, 1971, pp. 138, 139.

685James Mooney, *The Ghost Dance Religion and the Sioux Outbreak of 1890*, Lincoln: University of Nebraska Press, 1991.

686Alexander Lesser, "Cultural Significance of the Ghost Dance", *American Anthropologist* (1933), Vol. 35:18, pp. 108-115.

687Stanley Vestal, *New Sources of Indian History, 1850-91*, Norman: University of Oklahoma Press, 1934, pp. 309-311.

688Christopher Vecsey, editor, *Handbook of the American Indian Religious Freedom*, New York: Crossroad Publishing Co., 1991.

689Emory Dean Keoke and Kay Marie Porterfield, *Encyclopedia of American Indian Contributions to the World*, Facts on File, Inc., 2001.

690John R. Swanton, *Indians of the Southeastern United States*, Bulletin No. 137, BAE, Washington, D.C., 1946, p. 285. See also Bernard Romans, *A Concise History of East and West Florida, Vol. 1*, New York: Romans, 1775.

691James Adair, *History of the American Indians*, New York, New York: Promontory Press, 1930, pp. 435-439.

692Munro S. Edmonson, *The Book of the Year: Middle American Calendrical Systems*, Salt Lake City,:University of Utah Press, 1988.

693J. Eric Thompson, *Maya History and Religion*, Oklahoma: University of Oklahoma Press, 1970. See also Maria Longhena, *Maya Script*, New York: Abbeville Press, 2000, p. 89.

694John Lawson, Hugh Taldmedge Lefler, editor, A New Voyage to Carolina, Chapel Hill: Univ. of North Carolina Press, 1967, p. 184.

695Ann Kendall, *Everyday Life of the Incas*, NY: Dorset Press, 1973.

696Garcilaso de la Vega, El Inca, trans. by Harold V. Livermore, *Royal Commentaries of the Incas and General History of Peru*, Austin: University of Texas Press, 2 vols., 1,530 pgs., 1966.

697James Adair, *History of the American Indians*, New York, New York: Promontory Press, 1930, p. 433.

698Adair, pp. 432-434.

699Victor Wolfgang von Hagen, *The Aztec: Man and Tribe*, New York: The New American Library, Inc., 1958, 1961.

700George Catlin, *Letters and Notes on the Manners, Customs, and Conditions of the North American Indians*, New York: Dover Publications, 1973, p. 142.

701*Quest for America*, pp. 218-223.

702Stuart Culin, "American Indian Games", Presidential Address to American Folk-Lore Society, Baltimore, MD, Dec., 1897, published in *The Journal of American Folk-Lore*, (Oct.-Dec., 1898), Volume XI, No. XLIII, pp. 245-252. Culin researched the following American Indian tribal games and found them related among the following tribal groups: "Algonquian: Arapaho, Cheyenne, Chippeway, Illinois, Massachusetts, Menominee Micmac, Narranganset, Nipissing, Ojibway, Passamaquoddy, Penobscot, Siksika; Athapascan: Apache, Navajo; Caddoan; Arikara, Pawnee; Eskimauan: Eskimo (Inuit); Iroquoian: Delaware, Huron, Iroquois, Mohawk, Onondaga, Seneca, Tuscarora; Keresan: Keres (Acoma, Cochite Laguna, San Felipe, Sia); Kiowan: Kiowa; Koluschan: Tlingit; Lutuainian: Klamath; Mariposan: Yokut; Natchezan: Natchez; Piman: Papago, Pima, Tarahumara, Tepeguana; Punjunan: Nishinam; Salishan: Clallam, Cowlitz, Lkungen, Lummi, Nisqalli, Nslakyapamuk, Queniut, Skagit, Snohomish, Soke, Sushwap, Twana; Shahaptian: Klikitat; Shoshonean: Comanche, Paiute, Shoshoni, Unikaret; Siouan: Assinaboin, Dakota (Sisseton, Teton [Brule] Yankton), Iowa, Mandan, Minnetaree, Omaha; Tanonan: Tewa (Isleta, Santa Clara, San Ildefonso, Taos, Tesuque); Waukeshan: Kwakiutl, Macah; Yuman: Cocopa, Havasupai, Mohave and Zuni."

703Ann Kendall, *Everyday Life of the Incas*, New York: Dorset Press, 1973, pp. 167-172. On "Metallurguy and Mining." See also "The Gilded Image: Pre-Columbian Gold from South and Central America", *Minerva* 7.3, 1016.

704W. P. Clark, *Indian Sign Language*, Philadelphia, 1885. See also Emory Dean Keoke and Kay Marie Porterfield, *Encyclopedia of American Indian Contributions to the World*, Facts on File, Inc., 2001. The American Indians left a permanent linguistic legacy of names for half of the U.S. states, as well as many of the towns, rivers, mountains, and other geographical features. The names were given by both Indians and non Indians. The names were taken from chiefs, Indian expressions, events etc. Some names were fictional, and many names contained mispronounciations by their conquerors.

705Charles J. Opitz, *Wampum*, Ocala, FL, First Impressions Printing Co., 1995.

706Yuri E. Berezkin, "The Fourth Source." April 4, 1996 paper based on author's catalogue of Central and South American mythology with parallels from the Mediterranean to Central Asia and Australia. E. R. Emerson, *Indian Myths, or Legends, Traditions and Symbols of the Aborigines of America*, Minneapolis, MN: Ross & Haines, Inc., 1965. See also S. H. Hooke, Middle Eastern Mythology, New York: Penguin Books, 1963. Robert Boissiere, *The Return of Pahana*, Santa Fe, New Mexico: Bear & Company Publishing, 1990, pp. 60-65. Boissiere found many similarities between Indian prophesies, mythologies and ancient Mid-Eastern legends.

707W. Gunther Plaut, *The Torah: A Modern Commentary*, New York: Union of American Hebrew Congregation, 1981. Gerhard von Rad, translator. Also, J. H. Marks, *Genesis: A Commentary*, revised edition, 1972. See also E. A. Speiser, ed., *Genesis*, 1964. Ronald Youngblood, *The Genesis Debate*, 1986. Mesopotamia is located in the extreme southeastern part of present day Iraq. Human occupants settled in this area, covered with swamps at the head of the Persian Gulf, at least 7000 years ago and gradually spread northward up the lower Tigris-Euphrates Valley.

708Vincent H. Gaddis, *American Indian Myths & Mysteries*, Radnor, Pa: Chilton Book Company, 1977, p. 9.

709Boissiere, pp. 60-65. Helen Bauer, *California Indian Days*, N Y, Doubleday & Co., 1963, pp. 80, 81. Towards the end of summer a dance for the dead was performed by California tribes. Wood and food was burned in the village along with people wailing for those who died that year. As they danced, one gift after the other was thrown into the flames. After all was consumed the names of the dead were never mentioned again.

710Richard Erdoes and Alfonso Ortiz, *American Indian Myths and Legends*, New York: Pantheon Books, 1984. See also Joseph Campbell, *The Masks of God: Primitive Mythology*, New York: Penguin Books, 1976. Also Ake Hultkrantz, translated by Monica Setterwall, *The Religions of the American Indians*, Los Angeles: University of California Press, 1979.

711Stories from Canada's First Peoples: The Inuvialuit, the Algonquin, the Métis and Cree, the Nisgaa, the Abenaki and the Mikmaq. *Tales of the North American Indians* – http://www.sacred-texts.com/nam/tnai/.

712Mamit Innuat: *Innu Mythology Overview* from the website of the Innu Nation http://www.innu.ca/myth.html (formerly known as Montagnais or Naskapi) of Nitassinan (eastern (Quebec and Labrador).

713http://www.earthbow.com/native/contents.htm, *Native American Indian Folklore*. Folklore, stories, myths, and legends from various Native American tribes.

714Karl Taube, *Aztec and Maya Myths: The Legendary Past*, Austin: University Of Texas, 1993.

715George Catlin, *Letters and Notes on the Manners, Customs, and Conditions of North American Indians*, New York: Dover, 1973.

716Dbyani Ywahoo, *Voices of our Ancestors*, Boston and London, Shambhala Publications, Inc., 1987, pp. 21, 88.

717Richard Erdoes and Alfonso Ortiz, *American Indian Myths and Legends*, New York: Pantheon Books, 1984.

718Frank B. Linderman, *Plenty Coups, Chief of the Crows*, Lincoln: University of Nebraska Press, 1930, 1957.

719Paul Wallace, *White Roots of Peace*, Santa Fe, Clear Light Publishers, 1994. Thomas Henry, *Wilderness Messiah*, Wm. Sloan Associates, 1955, pp. 25, 32-33, 37, 38.

720George Yamada, ed., *The Great Resistance: A Hopi Anthology*, self-published March, 1957. From "He Will Use any Means to get What He Wants", by Dan Katchongva, a Hopi spiritual leader from Hotevilla, Arizona. In 1955 when 80 years old, he told this prophesy that had been passed down orally for generations to a congressional hearing in Washington, D.C. Also, *Independent Hopi Nation, The Hopi Message*, published by the Hopi Nation, 2nd edition in mimeographed form, Sept. 13, 1961. See also Richard Erdoes and Alfonso Ortiz, *American Indian Myths and Legends*, New York: Pantheon Books, 1984.

721William Willoya and Vinson Brown, *Warriors of the Rainbow*, Happy Camp: Naturegraph Publishers, 1962, pp. 68-70. See also Ella Clark, *Indian Legends of the Pacific Northwest*, Berkeley: University of California Press, 1953. Also, *Mamit Innuat: Innu Mythology*, http://www.innu.ca/myth.html. Overview from the website of the Innu Nation (formerly known as Montagnais or Naskapi) of Nitassinan (eastern Quebec and Labrador).

722Ralph Roys, *The Book of Chilam Balam of Chumayel*, Washington D.C., Carnegie Institute of Washington, 1933. See also New Edition, Univ. of Oklahoma Press, 1976. Eric J. Thompson, *The Rise and Fall of Maya Civilization*, Norman: University of Oklahoma Press, 1954.

723Hasteen Klah, *Navajo Creation Myth, The Story of the Emergence*, Museum of Navajo Ceremonial Art, AMS Press,1942.

724Richard Erdoes and Alfonso Ortiz, *American Indian Myths and Legends*, New York: Pantheon Books, 1984.

725*The Houston Chronicle*, "American Legend is made Flesh", (Sept. 24, 1994). No longer mythical White Buffalo a beacon to Plains tribes. See also *The New Phoenix* (the national newspaper of the free Cherokees), Winter, 1996. "White Buffalo Calf Woman Brings the First Pipe", http://www.kstrom.net/isk/arvol/buffpipe.html. A Lakota myth, as told by Joseph Chasing Horse.

726John G. Neihardt, *Black Elk Speaks*, Lincoln: University of Nebraska Press, 1961. Also called "Being the Life Story of a Holy Man of the Oglala Sioux", told to Neihart by Black Elk.

727John H. Cornyn, trans., *The Song of Quetzalcoatl*, Antioch Press, 1931, pp. 44-48. See also William Willoya and Vinson Brown, *Warriors of the Rainbow*, Happy Camp: Naturegraph Publishers, 1962, pp. 21-22.

728http://www.earthbow.com/native/contents.htm, *Native American Indian Folklore*. Folklore, stories, myths, and legends from various Native American tribes.

729Paul Bailey, *Wovoka, the Indian Messiah*, Westernlore Press, 1957.

730Barton Wright, *The Mythic World of the Zuni*, as written by Frank Hamilton Cushing, Univ. of New Mexico Press, 1992. See also Hamilton A. Tyler, *Pueblo Animals and Myths*, Univ. of Oklahoma Press, 1975.

731Vine Deloria, Jr., *We Talk You Listen*, New York: The Macmillan Company, 1970, p. 109.

732 *House Executive Document, Annual Report of the Commissioner of Indian Affairs*, no. 2, 32nd Congress, 1st session, serial 636, pp. 273-74, Nov. 27, 1851. See also Francis Paul Prucha, *Documents of United States Policy*, Lincoln: University of Nebraska Press, 1990. Excellent reference to U.S. Congressional Acts and documents between the U.S. and Indians from Sept. 7, 1783 to Oct. 17, 1988.

733Charles J. Kappler, ed., *Indian Affairs, Laws and Treaties*, Washington: Govt. Printing Office, 5 vols., 1903-1941. 2: 608-10.

734Article One of *Treaty of Wyandotte*, Jan. 31, 1855, 10, 12, Stat. 1159.

735*Senate Executive Document, Annual Report of the Commissioner of Indian Affairs*, no. 5, 34th Congress, 3rd session, serial 875, pp. 571-575, Nov. 22, 1856.

736*House Executive Document, Annual Report of the Commissioner of Indian Affairs*, no. 2, 32nd Congress, 1st session., serial 636, pp. 273-74, Nov. 27, 1851.

737*Chronicles of American Indian Protest*, Greenwhich, Conn: Fawcett Publications, 1971, pp. 190-191.

738*Joint Special Committee of Congress Report, Condition of the Indian Tribes*, Senate Report, no. 156, 39th Congress, 2d sess., serial 1279, pp. 3-10, Jan. 26, 1867. See also Stan Hoig, *The Sand Creek Massacre*, Norman: University of Oklahoma Press, 1961.

739*House Executive Document, Report of the Indian Peace Commission*, no. 97, 40th Congress, 2d sess., serial 1337, pp. 15-17, 20-22, Jan. 7, 1868.

740Virgil J. Vogel, *This Country was Ours*, New York, Harper and Row, 1972, pp. 165-66. Covers "On the Indian Problem, 1872."

741"Annual Report, Commissioners of Indian Affairs, House Executive Document, Report of the Indian Peace Commission", no. 97, 41st Congress, 2d sess., serial 1414, pp. 448, Dec. 23, 1869. Indian Commissioner Parker on the treaty system. Parker wrote the surrender terms that were given to General Robert E. Lee at Appomattox, Virginia.

742Charles J. Kappler, ed., *Indian Affairs, Laws and Treaties*, Washington: Govt. Printing Office, 5 vols., 1903-1941, Sec. 2079.

743"Annual Report, Commissioner of Indian Affairs", Edward P. Smith, 1875, p. 17.

744Francis Paul Prucha, *American Indian Policy in Crisis: Christian Reformers and the Indian, 1865-1900*, Norman: University of Oklahoma Press, 1976, pp. 242-255. See also Helen Hunt Jackson, *A Century of Dishonor*, New York: Indian Head Books, 1994. Four days before her death on Aug. 12, 1885, Helen Jackson sent the following letter to President Grover Cleveland: "Dear Sir: From my death-bed I send you a message of heartfelt thanks for what you have already done for the Indians. I ask you to read my *Century of Dishonor*. I am dying happier for the belief I have that it is your hand that is destined to strike the first steady blow toward lifting this burden of infamy from our country, and righting the wrongs of the Indian race. With respect and gratitude, Helen Jackson." Instead of honoring her request, the Dawes Act of forced land allotment aimed at the obliteration of tribal life was signed into law on Feb. 8, 1887 by President Grover Cleveland.

745D'Arcy McNickle, "Indian and European White Relations from Discovery to 1887", in George Simpson and J. Milton Vinger, ed., *American Indians and American Life*, New York: Russell & Russell, vol. 311, May, 1957, pp. 10-11. First Published in *The Annuals of The Academy of Political and Social Science*. McNickle is a member of the Flathead tribe of Montana and spent 16 years as a staff member of the Bureau of Indian affairs. See also Charles J. Kappler, ed., *Indian Affairs, Laws and Treaties*, Washington: Government Printing Office, 5 vols., 1903-1941, 33-36, 56-58. On the Dawes Act and Amendment.

746Curtis Act, June 28, 1898, *United States Statute at Large Indian Affairs: Laws and Treaties*, 30:497, 98, 502, 504-05. *Annual Report, Commissioner of Indian Affairs*, Cato Sells, 1917, pp. 3-5.

747Commissioner of Indian Affairs, Edward P. Smith, "Annual Report", 1875, pp. 8-9. Angie Debo, *A History of the Indians of the United States*, Norman, University of Oklahoma Press, 1970, p. 287. Wilcomb E. Washburn, ed., *The American Indian and the United States: A Documentary History*, New York: 1973, 4 vols. On treaties and acts of Congress, debates with court decisions and the reports of the Commissioner of Indian Affairs, showing the United States government relationship with the Indians.

748Robert F. Berkhofer, Jr., *The White Man's Indian*, New York: Vintage Books, 1978, p. 171. Pratt was the former commander of the infamous Fort Marion Prison near St. Augustine where Osceola of the Seminoles had been assasinated in 1836. Carlisle school remained open until the end of the 1917-18 school year.

749Richard Henry Pratt, *How to Deal with the Indians: The Potency of Envioronment*, Pennsylvania: Carlisle, 1903, p. 3.

750Ian Brownlie, ed., *Basic Documents on Human Rights*, London, New York: Oxford Press, 1971.

751Carlos Montezuma, "What Indians Must Do", Society of American Indians, *Quarterly Journal*, 2, 1914, pp. 294-99. Carlos Montezuma (Wassaja), (1866?-1923) considered himself an Apache Indian, fortunate enough to be sold to Carlos Gentile, a photographer. Gentile placed him under the care of a Baptist minister. He was educated, excelled in school and received a medical degree from Chicago Medical College.

752Hazel Whitman Hertzberg, "National Anthropology and Pan-Indianism in the Life of Arthur C. Parker (Seneca)", *Proceedings of the American Philosophical Society*, (1979), 123, no. 1, pp. 42-72. Parker was related to Ely Parker, Presidents Grant's aide and head of the Indian Bureau. Arthur Parker worked as an anthropologist, ethnologist and archaeologist. He was involved with the Seneca and Handsome Lake supporters. As a Christian he realized the injustices to the Indians and fought to change it.

753"Annual Report, Commissioner of Indian Affairs", Cato Sells, 1917, pp. 3-5.

754"Annual Reports, Commissioners of Indian Affairs, 1917-1923." Hearings before the Subcommittee of the Committee on Indian Affairs, Washington, D.C., 69th Congress, U. S. Senate, Feb., 10, 1927.

755Lewis Meriam, *The Problem of Indian Administration*, Baltimore: John Hopkins Press, 1929, pp. 89. See also Mrs. Lawrence Riggs Howard, *A Century of Indian Progress*, New York: American Missionary Association, 1928, p. 44.

756John Collier, *The Indians of the Americas*, New York: W. W. Norton & Company, 1947, p. 256.

757John Collier, *The Indians of the Americas*, W. W. Norton & Co., 1947, covers "The Indian New Deal", pp. 261-287. John Collier was a great friend of the Indians, as well as being Indian Commissioner. He was the originator of the 1934 Wheeler-Howard Indian Reorganization Act.

758Hoover Commission, 1948 *Survey of Conditions of the Indians in the United States*, (1928-1943): Report, No. 310, Washington, D.C., 78th Congress, 1st Session, U. S. Senate, June 11, 1943, pp. 1-22, and supplement report, May, 2, 1944.

759Report, No. 310, Washington, D. C., 78th Congress, 1st session, U.S. Senate, June, 11, 1943.

760Theodore W. Taylor, "The States and their Indian Citizens", *U.S. Department of the Interior, Bureau of Indian Affairs*, Washington, D.C., 1972, pp. 64-70.

761American Indian Chicago Conference, "Declaration of Indian Purpose", June 13-20, 1961.

762Nixon's pre-election speech, Sept. 27, 1968.

763Vine Delloria, Jr., *Behind the Trail of Broken Treaties: An American Indian Declaration of Independence*, Austin, Texas: University of Texas Press, 1985, pp. 29-32.

764"Report of the Special Subcommittee on Indian Education: A National Tragedy—A National Challenge", Senate Report no.501, 91st Congress, 1st session, serial 12836-1, pp.xi-xiv. Washington, D.C., U. S. Govt. Printing Office, 1969.

765M. Annette Jaimes, ed., *The State of Native America*, Boston, MA: South End Press, 1982, pp. 291-308, 327, 328. See also Vine Delloria, Jr., *Behind the Trail of Broken Treaties: An American Indian Declaration of Independence*, Austin, Texas: University of Texas Press, 1985.

766Chris Carrel, "Tribes Strike Back at Mining", *High Country News*, Paonia, Colorado, Aug. 31, 1998. Confederated tribes and bands of the Yakama Indian Nation signed the Treaty of 1855 near Walla Walla, Washington. The 14 tribes and bands consisted of Klickatat, the Klinquit, the Kow-was-say-ee, the Kah-milt-pah, the Li-ay-was, the Oche-chotes, the Palouse, the Pisquouse, the Skin-pah, the Se-ap-cat, the Shyiks, the Wenatchapam, the Wish-ham, and the Yakama.

767Code of Federal Regulations, *Federal Register*, 43:39362-64, Sept. 5, 1978, 54.

768*United States Statute at Large Indian Affairs: Laws and Treaties*, 92:2316-22, 2327.

769*United States Statute*, 92:3069, 3071-73, 3075-76.

770*United States Statute*, 93:721-23.

771*United States Statute*, 102: 385-87.

772Steve Newcomb (Shawnee/Delaware) of the Indigenous Law Institute, "Position Paper on the 1998 United Nations Human Rights Commission Inter-Sessional Working Group on the United Nations. Draft Declaration on the Rights of Indigenous Peoples." In *Akwesasne Notes* (Autumn 1981), Vol. 13, No. 4, p. 21.

773Russel Barash, "Indian Land Claims Policy in the United States." *North Dakota Law Review*, (1982) No. 58, pp. 1-82.

774Sohappy v. Smith (D. Ore. 1969), 302 F. Supp. 899.

775*United States Statute at Large Indian Affairs: Laws and Treaties*, 94:1785-89, 1793-95. Oct. 10, 1980 "Maine Indian Claims Settlement Act."

776Blumenthal, pp. 174-176. The Indian Claims Commission Act of Aug. 13, 1946, empowered the Indian tribes to seek redress to numerous claims for violation of treaties or alleged fraud that have been pending for years. These violations date back to the Hopewell treaty of 1786 to the present day. In 1928 Senator Linn Frazier stated: "At the rate the Court of Claims had functioned it would take 172 years to settle or dismiss the eighty-six then pending claim cases...." Most of the Indian claims appear to drag out forever. Also, *U.S. Reports*, 374, 423-24, "United States v. Sioux Nation of Indians", June 30, 1980. On Dec. 2, 2002, the Bush administration asked the Supreme Court to limit lawsuits filed by American Indian tribes contending the Interior Department failed to protect tribal resources. Otherwise, the government, which manages 56 million acres of land for the benefit of tribes, could be the subject of a mountain of lawsuits.

777U.S. Reports, "California v. Cabazon Band of Mission Indians" (1987), 202, 480. Also Levin, "Betting on the Land", pp. 126-27.

778*United States Statute*, "Indian Gaming Regulatory Act" (Oct. 17, 1988), 102: 2467-69, 2472, 2476.

779John R. Emshwiller & Christina Binkley, "Indian Gambling", *The Wall Street Journal* (Aug. 23, 2004), pp. A1, A8. See also William Eadington, "Economic Development and the Introduction of Casinos: Myths and Realities", *Economic Development Review* (Fall, 1995), 13/4, pp. 52-53.

780George Simpson and Milton Yinger, eds., *American Indians and American Life*, New York: Russell & Russell, 1975.

BIBLIOGRAPHY
BOOKS AND PERIODICALS

Acosta, Joseph de. *Historia natural y moral de las Indias* or *Natural and Moral History of the Indies.* Mexico: FCE, 1590, Reprint 1940.

Adair, James. *History of the American Indians.* London, 1775. Reprint 1930.

Adamson, Hoebel, E. *The Cheyenne.* Indians of the Great Plains, New York: Holt, Rinehart, and Winston Inc., 1960.

Allen, Paula Gunn. *The Sacred Hoop.* Boston: Beacon Press, 1986.

Anderson, David G. ed. by Timothy R. Pauketat and Thomas E. Emerson. *The Role of Cahokia in the Evolution of Southeastern Mississippian Society In Cahokia: Domination and Ideology in the Mississippian World.* Lincoln: University of Nebraska Press: 1997.

Angleria, Pedro Martir de. *Decadas del Nuevo Mundo.* Buenos Aires, Argentina: Editorial Bajel, First Argentine edition, First Latin Edition, 1530.

Ashe,Geoffrey, and Thor Heyerdahl, and Helge Ingstad and J.V., Luce and Betty J. Meggers, and Birgitta L. Wallace. *The Quest for America.* New York/Washington: (Praeger), 1971.

Ashwell, Reg. *Coast Salish.* Surrey, B.C.: Hancock House Publishers, 1989.

Bancroft, George. *History of the United States of America.* New York, D. Appleton & Co., 1964.

Bailey, James. *The God Kings and the Titans.* New York: St. Martin's Press, 1973.

Bailey, Paul. *Wovoka, The Indian Messiah,* Westernlore Press, 1957.

Baird, W. David. *The Choctaw People.* Phoenix, Indian Tribal Series, 1973.

Bakewell, Peter. ed. *Mines of Silver and Gold in the Americas. An Expanding World: The European Impact on World History, 1450-1800.* vol. 19. Series ed. by A. J. R. Russell-Wood. Brookfield, Vt.: Ashgate/Variorum, 1997.

Baldwin, John W. *Ancient America.* New York: Harper Bros, 1878

Balinger, Bill S. *Lost City of Stone.* New York: Simon & Shuster, 1978.

Bandy, O.L, ed. *Radiometric Dating and Paleontology Zonation.* 1970.

Barton,George A. *Archaeology and the Bible.* Philadelphia: American Sunday-School Union, 1920.

Bartram,William, *Travels through North and South Carolina, Georgia, East and West Florida.* Philadelphia: James & Johnson, 1792. Reprint, Macy-Masius, 1928.

Bauer, Helen, *California Indian Days.* Garden City, New York: Doubleday & Co., 1963.

Beals, Carleton. *Nomads and Empire Builders.* New York: Citadel Press, 1965.

Bear, Luther Standing. *Land of the Spotted Eagle.* Boston: Houghton Mifflin Co., 1933.

Bergh, Albert Ellery. *The Writings of Thomas Jefferson.* Washington, D. C., 20 vols.1907.

Berkhofer, Robert F Jr. *Salvation and the Savage: An Analysis of Protestant Missions and American Indian Response, 1787-1862.* Lexington: University of Kentucky Press, 1965.

Berkhofer, Robert F. Jr. *The White Man's Indian.* New York: Vintage Books, 1978.

Beverley, Robert. *The History and Present State of Virginia,1673-ca.1722.* In Four parts., London: B. and S Took, 1722. Pub. University of North Carolina (Aug. 1, 1960).

Bigelow, John ed., *The Complete Works of Benjamin Franklin.* New York, G. P. Putman's Sons, 1887.

Bird, J.M. *Plate Tectonics.* Washington, DC: American Geophysical Union, 1980.

Black, Nancy and Bette S Weidman,.eds. *White on Red.* Port Washington, New York: Kennikat Press, 1976.

Blumenthal, Walter Hart. *American Indians Dispossessed.* Philadelphia: George S. MacManus Co., 1955.

Boissiere, Robert. *The Return Of Pahana.* Santa Fe, New Mexico: Bear & Company Publishing, 1990.

Boorstin, Daniel J. *The Discoverer's.* New York: Random House, 1983.

Bowden, Henry Warner. *American Indians and Missions: Studies in Cultural Conflict.* Chicago: University of Chicago Press, 1981.

Boyd, William K. ed. *Histories of the Dividing Line Between Virginia and North Carolina.* New York: 1967.

Bradford, William ed. William T. Davis. *History of Plantation.* New York: Charles Scribner's, 1908.

Brandt, Richard S. *Hopi Ethics.* Chicago: University of Chicago Press, 1954.

Brown, D. A., *Bury My Heart at Wounded Knee: An Indian History of the American West .* New York: Henry Holt & Company, 1970.

Buley, R. Carlyle. *The Old Northwest.* Bloomington: University of Indiana Press, 1964.

Bury, R. G. translator, *Plato's Dialogues.* Harvard University Press. 1961.

Buskirk, Winfred. *The Western Apache.* Norman:University of Oklahoma Press, 1986.

Cambell, Maria. *Halfbreed.* Lincoln: University of Nebraska Press, 1973.

Campbell, Joseph. *The Mythic Image.* Princeton, NJ: Princeton University Press, 1974.

Campbell, Lyle. *American Indian Languages: The Historical Linguistics of Native America.* Oxford University Press, 1997.

Carter, George F. *Earlier than You Think, A Personal View of Man in America.* College Station, Texas: A& M University Press, 1980.

Casas, Bartolomé De Las, trans. and ed. C.M. Stafford Poole. *In Defense of the Indians.* De Kalb, Illinois: Northern Illinois University Press, 1992.

Casas, Bartolomé de las. *Breuissima Relacion de la Destruycion de las Indias.* Seville: Spain, 1552-1553.

Casas, Bartolomé de las. *De las Antigua's Gentes del Peru.* 3 Vols. Mexico: 1851, Madrid: 1892.

Casas, Bartolomé de Las. *Historia de las Indias,* edited by Augustin Millares Carlo and Louis Hanke, Mexico: Fondo de Cultura Economica, 1951, 3 volumes.

Casas, Bartolomé De Las. ed. and trans. by Andree Collard. *History of the Indies.* New York: Harper Torchbooks, 1971.

Casas, Bartolomé de Las. *The Tears Of The Indians.* trans. John Phillips, Printed by J. C. for Nath, Brook, at the Angel in Cornhil: London, 1656.

Cash, Joseph H. and Gerald W. Wolf. *The Three Affiliated Tribes, Mandan, Arikara, and Hidatsa.* Phoenix: Indian Tribal Series, 1974.

Castillo, Bernal Diaz del. *The Discovery and Conquest of Mexico.* 1517-1521. New York: Grove Press 1956.

Catlin, George. *Letters And Notes on the Manners, Customs, and Conditions of the North American Indians.* London: Piccadilly, 1841 Reprint, New York: Dover Publications, 2 Vols. 1973.

Cattteral, Helen T. *Judicial Cases Concerning American Slavery and the Negro.* Washington, D. C.: Carnegie, 1929.

Chamberlain, E. *The Bad Popes.* Barnes & Noble, 1993.

Chamberlain, Robert S. *Conquista y Civilization de Yucatan.* Mexico: D. F. Porria, 1982.

Chamberlain, Robert S. *Pre-Conquest Labor Practices in Indian Labor in the Spanish Indies.* Boston: D.C. Heath and Co. 1966.

Chance, Norman A. *The Eskimo of North Alaska.* New York: Holt Rinehart and Winston, 1966.

Chang, Kwang-Chih. *Shang Civilization.* New Haven and London: Yale University Press, 1980.

Chapman, Paul. *The Norse Discovery of America.* One Candle Press, 1981.

Charlevoix Pierre de. *Journal of a Voyage to North America.* London: 1761.

Childress, David Hatcher. *Lost Cities & Ancient Mysteries of South America.* Stelle, Ill.: Adventures Unlimited Press, 1986.

Chronicles of American Indian Protest, Greenwhich, Conn: Fawcett Publications, 1971.

Churchill, W. *Indians Are Us? Culture and Genocide in Native North America.* Monroe, ME: Common Courage Press, 1994.

Churchill, W. *A Little Matter of Genocide: Holocaust and Denial in the Americas, 1492 to the Present.* San Francisco, CA: City Lights Books, 1998.

Churchward, Col. James. *The Lost Continent Of Mu.* New York: Ives Washburn, 1931.

Clarke & Engelbach. *Ancient Egyptian Construction and Architecture,* New York: Dover publications, 1990.

Clark, Ella. *Indian Legends of the Pacific Northwest.* Berkeley: University of California Press, 1953.

Clark, W. P. *Indian Sign Language.* Philadelphia, 1885.

Clavigero, Francisco Saverio. trans, Italian by Charles Cullen. *The History of Mexico Collected from Spanish and Mexican Historians from Manuscripts and Ancient Paintings of the Indians.* 2 vols, 1st English Edition, London: G. G. Robinson, 1787.

Clendinnen, Inga. *Ambivalent Conquests.* Cambridge, Ma.: Cambridge University Press, 1987.

Cockburn, Aidan and Eve editors, *Mummies, Disease and Ancient Cultures.* Cambridge, MA :Cambridge University Press, 1980.

Coe Michael. *The Maya.* Sixth Edition. Singapore: Thames & Hudson. 2001.

Coe, Michael. *Mexico*/ New York: Praeger Publishers, 1962.

Cohen, Felix S. *Handbook of Federal Indian Law.* Washington, D.C., U. S. Government Printing Office, 1942, revised 1958, 1982.

Colden, Cadwallader. *History of the Five Indian Nations.* New York: New Amsterdam Book Co., 2 vols., 1902.

Collier, John. *Indians of the Americas.* New York: W. W. Norton, 1947.

Columbus,Christopher. *The Diario of Christopher Columbus's First Voyage to America, 1492-1493.* Abstracted by Fray Bartolome de las Casas, ed. by Oliver Dunn and James E. Kelley, Jr., trs. Norman: University of Oklahoma Press, 1989.

Columbus, Fernando. *The Life of the Admiral Christopher Columbus.* trans. by Benjamin Keen, Rutgers, 1959.

Commager, Henry Steele and Elmo Giordanetti. *Was America a Mistake?* New York: Harper & Row, 1967.

Cook-Lynn, E. *Anti-Indianism in Modern America: A Voice from Tatekeya's Earth.* Urbana, IL: University of Illinois Press, 2001.

Cook, Sherburne F, and Woodrow Borah. *The Aboriginal Population of Central Mexico on the Eve of the Spanish Conquest.* Berkley: University of California Press, 1963.

Cooper, J. M. *The Northern Algonquian Supreme Being.* Washington, DC: Primitive Man, No.6, 1933.

Corliss, William R. *Ancient Man: A Handbook of Puzzling Artifacts.* Glen Arm, Maryland: The Sourcebook Project, 1980.

Cortés, Hernándo. *Letters From Mexico.* trans.& ed. A. R. Pagden , New York: Grossman Publishers, 1971.

Cortés, Hernándo. *The Despatches of Hernando Cortes, the Conqueror of Mexico, Addressed to the Emperor Charles V, Written during the Conquest, and Containing a Narrative of Its Events.* ed. trans. by George Folsom. New York: Wiley and Putnam, 1843.

Costo, Rupert ed. *Textbooks and the American Indians.* San Francisco: American Indian Society, 1970.

Cotter, Leonard. *Lost Cities.* New York: Grosset & Dunlap, 1963.

Council on Interracial Books for Children. *Chronicles of American Indian Protest,* Greenwich, CT, Fawcett Publications, 1971.

Crawford, M.H, *The Origins of Native Americans: Evidence From Anthropological Genetics.* Cambridge University Press, 1998.

Cremo, Michael & Richard Thompson. *Forbidden Archeology.* Los Angeles: Bhaktivedanta, Book Publishing, 1993.

Culin, Stuart. *American Indian Games.* Presidential Address, American Folk-Lore Society, Baltimore, Maryland, Dec., 1897, published in *The Journal of American Folk-Lore,* Volume XI, Oct.-Dec., 1898, No. XLIII.

Currie, L. A., ed. *Nuclear and Chemical Dating Techniques.* 1982.

Curtis, Edward S. *The North American Indians. The Complete Portfolios.* 1907-1930. Taschen, 2003.

Curtis, Natalie. Recorder and ed. *The Indians Book: Songs and Legends of the American Indians,* New York, Dover Press, 1950.

Cyr, Donald L. ed., and Gilmore, and Donald Linda, McElroy. *Across before Columbus?:Evidence for Transoceanic contact with the Americas prior to 1492.* Edgecomb, Me.: New England Antiquities Research Association, 1998.

Cyr, Donald, ed. Santa Barbara, CA, *Dragon Treasures.* Stonehenge Viewpoint, 1989.

Darwin, Charles. *The Descent of Man.* New York: Appleton, 1879.

Davenport, Frances Gardiner. ed. *European Treaties bearing on the History of the United States and its Dependencies to 1648.* Carnegie Institution of Washington, 1917, Washington, D.C.

David, Neil, *Kachinas, Spirit Beings of the Hopi.* Albuquerque: Avanyu Publishing, Inc. 1993.

Davies, Nigel. *The Ancient Kingdoms of Peru,* Penguin Books, 1997.

Day, Grove A. *Coronado's Quest,:The Discovery of the Southwestern States.* Berkley: University of California Press, 1964.

Deal, David Allen, *Discovery of Ancient America.* 1st ed., Irvine CA,: Kherem La Yah Press, 1984.

Debo, Angie. *The Road to Disappearance: A History of the Creek Indians.* Norman: University of Oklahoma Press, 1941.

Delloria, Vine Jr. *Behind the Trail of Broken Treaties: "An American Indian Declaration of Independence."*Austin,Texas: University of Texas Press, 1985.

Deloria , Vine Jr. *We Talk You Listen.* New York: The Macmillan Company, 1970.

Deloria, Vine Jr. *God is Red.* Golden Colorado: Fulcrum Publishing, 1994.

Densmore, Francis. "The Songs of the American Indian", *American Mercury,* VIII, Jan., 1926.

Densmore, Francis. *The American Indians and their Music.* New York: The Woman's Press, 1926.

Deuel, Leo. *Conquistadors Without Swords.* New York: Schocken Books, 1974.

Diaz, Bernal Del Castillo, A. P. Maudslay, transl. *The Discovery and Conquest of Mexico 1517-1521.* New York: 1956.

Dickason, Olive Patricia. *Canada's First Nations.*Toronto: McCelland & Stewart Inc., 1994.

Dillehay, Tom D. *Monte Verde. A Late Pleistocene Settlement in Chile.* Washington, D.C: Smithsonian Institution Press: 1989.

Diop, Cheikh Anta. *Civilization or Barbarism: An Authentic Anthropology.* New York: Laurence Hill, 1981.

Dobyns, Henry F. *Their Number Became Thinned, American Indian Population Dynamics in Eastern North America.* Knoxville: University of Tennessee Press, 1983.

Dockstader, Frederick J. *The Kachina and the White Man.* Albuquerque: University of New Mexico Press, 1985.

Donck, Adriaen van der. *Description of the New Netherlands.* New York Historical Society Collections, 1841.

Dozier, E. P. *The Pueblo Indians of North America.* Prospect Heights, IL: Waveland Press, 1983.

Drake, Samuel G. *Biography and History of the Indians of North America.* Boston: 1851.

Drier, Roy W. and Octave J. Du Temple, *Prehistoric Copper Mining in the Lake Superior Region,* Published privately by the Authors: Calumet, MI: 1961.

Driver, Harold E. *Girls' Puberty Rites In Western North America.* University of Calif., Anthropological Records, 1941.

Driver, Harold E. *Indians of North America.* Chicago: University of Chicago Press, 1969.

Drucker, Philip. *Indians of the Northwest Coast.* Garden City, N. Y: The Natural History Press, 1963.

Dunn, Oliver C. and James E Kelley. Jr. *The Diary of Christopher Columbus' First Voyage to America:1492-1493.* Norman: University of Oklahoma Press, 1987.

Dunn, J. P. Jr. *Massacres of the Mountains: A History of the Indian Wars of the Far West, 1815-1875.* New York, Capricorn Books, 1886.

Eastman, Charles Alexander. *The Soul of the Indian.* Boston: Houghton Mifflin, 1911.

Eden, Richard ed., *The Decades of the Newe Worlde or West India (The First Three Books on America,)* Birmingham, England: Turnbill & Spears, 1885.

Edmonson, Munro S. *The Book of the Year: Middle American Calendrical Systems.* Salt Lake City: University of Utah Press, 1988.

Eggleston, Edward. *A First Book in American History.* New York: D, Appleton & Co., 1889.

Elias, Scott. *The Ice Age History of Alaskan National Parks.* Washington, D. C.: Smithsonian Institution Press, 1995.

Emerson, E. R. *Indian Myths, or Legends. Traditions and Symbols of the Aborigines of America.* Minneapolis, MN: Ross & Haines, Inc., 1965.

Erdoes, Richard. *The Rain Dance People.* New York: Alfred A. Knopf, Inc., 1976.

Etienne, Mona and Eleanor Leacock, eds. *Women and Colonization: Anthropological Perspectives.* New York: Praegar, 1980.

Fagan, Brian M., *The Great Journey,* The Peopling of Ancient America, New York: Thames & Hudson, 1987.

Fell, Barry. *America B.C.* New York: Simon & Schuster, 1976, 1989.

Fell, Barry. *Saga America.* New York, N Y: Times Books, 1980.

Fillmore, John C. *The Harmonic Structure of Indian Music.* New York: G. P. Putman's sons, 1899.

Fischer, Steven Roger, and Hackett Fischer. *Rongorongo: The Easter Island Script: History, Traditions, Texts.* Oxford Studies in

Anthropological Linguistics, 14" Clarendon Press, March 1998.

Fitzhugh, William W. and Aron, Crowell, ed. *Crossroads of the Continent: Cultures of Siberia and Alaska*. Washington, D. C., Smithsonian Institution, 1968.

Fleming, Stuart, Bernard Fishman, David O'Connor, and David Silverman. *The Egyptian Mummy: Secrets and Science*. Philadelphia: The University of Pennsylvania, 1980.

Fodor, R.V. *Frozen Earth: Explaining the Ice Ages*. Hillside, NJ: Enslow Publishers, 1981.

Forbes, Jack D. *Africans and Native Americans*. Chicago: University of Illinois Press, 1993.

Forbes, Jack D. *Native Americans of California and Nevada: A Handbook*. Healdsburg, CA: Naturegraph Publishers 1969.

Forbes, Jack. *The Indian in America's Past*. Prentiss-Hall, 1964.

Foreman, Carolyn Thomas. *Indian Women Chiefs*. Washington, D.C: Zenger Publishing, 1976.

Foreman, Grant. *The Five Civilized Tribes*. Norman:University of Oklahoma Press, 1934.

Fox, Hugh. *Gods of the Cataclysm*. N. Y: Dorset Press, 1981.

Fox, Robin. *Kinship and Marriage*. New York: Penguin Books, 1967.

Frazer, J. G. *Totemism and Exogamy A Treatise on Certain Early Forms of Superstition and Society*. London: Macmillan, 1910.

Fuson, Robert H. trans. *The Log of Christopher Columbus*. Camden, Maine: International Marine Publishing Co., 1987.

Gaddis, Vincent H. *American Indian Myths & Mysteries*. Radnor, Pa: Chilton Book Company, 1977.

Garcia, Gregorio. *El origen de los Indios de el Nuevo Mundo e Indias occidentals*, 1607.

Geldern, Robert von Heine. *Handbook of Middle American Indians*. Vol. IV, Austin: University of Texas Press, 1966.

Gifford, Edward W. *Clans and Moieties in Southern California*. Coyote Press, 1918.

Gill Sam D. and Irene F. Sullivan. *Dictionary of American Indian Mythology*. Oxford University Press, 1994.

Gilmore, Melvin R. *Uses of Plants by the Indians of the Missouri River Regions*. U. S. Bureau of American Ethnology, Annual Report, Washington, D. C., 1911-12, vol. 33.

Gimbutas, Marija. *The Language of the Goddess*. San Francisco: Harper & Row, 1989.

Godley, A. D. trans. *Herodotus, History*. Vol. 4, Cambridge, MA: Harvard University Press, 1963.

Goetz, Delia and Sylvanus G. Morley, *Popol Vuh*. The Sacred Book of the Ancient Quiche Maya. trans. from the Spanish (of Adrian Recinos) Norman: University of Oklahoma, 1950.

Goodbird Edward. *Goodbird the Indian*. New York: Fleming H. Revell Co., 1914.

Gordon, Cyrus H. *Diffusion of Near East Culture in Antiquity and in Byzantine Times*. Orient 30-31, 1995.

Gordon, Cyrus H. *Before Columbus, Links between the Old World and Ancient America*. New York: Crown. 1971.

Greenberg, Joseph H. *Language in the Americas*. Stanford: Stanford University Press, 1987.

Griffin, J. B. *Archaeology of Eastern United States*. Chicago: Chicago University Press, 1952.

Grinde, D. A., Jr., & Johansen, B. E. *Ecocide of Native America: Environmental Destruction of Indian Lands and Peoples*. Sante Fe, NM: Clear Light Publishers, 1995.

Grinnell, G. B. *The Cheyenne Indians: Their History and Ways of Life,* New Haven: Yale University Press, 2 vols., 1923.

Grinnell, George Bird, *Pawnee Hero Stories and Folk Tales; with notes on The Origin, Customs, and Character of the Pawnee People*. Lincoln, Neb: University of Nebraska Press 1963.

Grumet, Robert Steven. Mona Etienne and Eleanor Leacock, eds. *Women and Colonization: Anthropological Perspectives.*New York: Praegar, 1980.

Gupta, Shakti M. *Plants in Indian Temple Art*. Delhi: B.R. Publishing Corp, 1996.

Gutierrez, Gustavo. *Las Casas: In Search of the Poor Jesus Christ*. trans. Robert R. Barr, Maryknoll, New York: Orbis Books, 1993.

Gutierrez, Ramon A. *When Jesus Came, the Corn Mothers Went Away: Marriage, Sexuality, and Power in New Mexico, 1500-1846*. Stanford, CA: Stanford University Press, 1991.

Hackett, Charles Wilson. *Revolt of the Pueblo Indians of New Mexico and Otermin's Attempted Reconquest, 1680–1682*. Albuquerque: University of New Mexico, 1942, Volume 2: 245–49.

Hadingham, Evan. *Circles and Standing Stones: An Illustrated Exploration of Megalith Mysteries of Early Britain*. Garden City, NJ: Anchor Press/Doubleday, 1976.

Hagen, Victor Wolfgang. Von. *The Ancient Kingdoms of the Americas.*
Cleveland and New York: The World Publishing Company, 1961

Hagen, Victor W. Von. *The Aztec and Maya Papermakers*. Hacker Art Books, 1977.

Hagen, Victor Von. *The Aztec: Man and Tribe*: New York: The New American Library Inc, 1958, 1961.

Hall, Robert A. Jr. *The Kensington Stone is Genuine: Linguistic, Practical and Methodological Considerations:* Columbia, S. C: Hornbeam, 1982.

Halsey, John R. *Miskwabik - Red Metal: The roles played by Michigan's Copper in Prehistoric North America*. Eagle Harbor: Keweenaw County Historical Society, 1992.

Hancock, Graham. *Fingerprints of the Gods*. New York: Three Rivers Press, 1995.

Hambin, Dora Jane. *The First Cities*. New York: Time Life Books, 1973.

Hanke, Lewis. *The Spanish Struggle for Justice in the Conquest of America*. Philadelphia: University of Pennsylvania Press, 1949.

Harris, Marvin. *Patterns of Race in the Americas*. New York: Walker and Company, 1964.

Harris, Stephen L. *Agents of Chaos*. Missoula, Montana: Mountain Press Publishing Company, 1990.

Hawkins, Gerald. *Beyond Stonehenge*. New York: Harper and Row, 1969.

Heath, Ian. *Armies of the Sixteenth Century: The Armies of the Aztec and Inca Empires, other Native peoples of the Americas, and the Conquistadors 1450-1608*. Great Britain : Foundry Book, 1999.

Heizer, Robert F. and Allan J. Almquist, ed. *The Other Californians*. Berkeley: University of California Press, 1971.

Hemming, John. *Discovery of Lost Worlds*. Ed. by Joseph J. Thorndike Jr., New York: Simon & Schuster, 1979.

Hendon, Harris. *The Asiatic Fathers of America*. Taiwan: Wen Ho Printing Co., 1975.

Herm, Gerhard. *The Phoenicians*. New York: William Morrow and Co., 1975.

Hertzberg, Hazel W. *The Search For An American Indian Identity*. Syracuse: Syracuse University Press, 1971.

Heth, Charlette ed., *Native American Dance: Ceremonies and Social Traditions*. Washington, D.C., National Museum Of the American Indian, Smithsonian Institution, Golden Colorado: Fulcrum Publishing, 1992.

Heyerdahl, Thor. *Early Man and the Ocean*. NY: Vintage Books, Random House, 1980.

Hilger, Inez Henun. *Namku, An Araucanian Indian of the Andes Remembers the Past*. Norman: University of Oklahoma Press, 1966.

Hoig, Stan. *The Sand Creek Massacre*. Norman: University of Oklahoma Press, 1961.

Howard, Lawrence Riggs. *A Century of Indian Progress*. New York: American Missionary Association, 1928.

Howey, M. Oldfield. *The Encircled Serpent*. New York: Authur Richmond Co., 1955.

Hoxie, Frederick E. *Encyclopedia of North American Indians*. Boston: Houghton Mifflin, 1996.

Hultkrantz, Ake trans. Monica Setterwall, *The Religions of the American Indians*. Los Angeles: University of California Press, 1979.

Humphrey, Seth K. *The Indian Dispossessed*. Boston: Little Brown & Co., 1905.

Hunt,Gaillard ed, *The Writings of James Madison*. New York, G. P. Putman's Sons, 1908.

Hurd, John Codman. *The Law of Freedom and Bondage in the United States*. New York: Negro Universities Press, 1968.

Huyghe, Partick. *Columbus Was Last*. New York: Hyperion, 1992.

Indian Tribal Series, circa 1970s, 40 vols., each pertaining to a different tribe. Each vol. is numbered (from an edition of 15,000) and signed by the tribal chief at time of publication, Phoenix Press.

Irving, Washington. *Sketch Book of Geoffrey Crayon Gent*. Philadelphia: J. B. Lippincott, 1875.

Isaac, G.L. *Archaeology of Human Origins*. 1989.

Jackson, Helen Hunt. *A Century of Dishonor*. Boston: Roberts Brothers, 1885, 1901, 1966.

Jacoby, Arnold. *Senior Kon-Tiki, The Life and Adventure of Thor Heyerdahl*. Rand McNally, 1967.

Jairazbhoy, R. A. *Ancient Egyptians and Chinese in America*. N.J., Rowman & Littlefield, 1974.

James, M. Annette, ed. *The State of Native America Genocide, Colonization, and Resistance*. Boston: South End Press, 1992.

Jameson, Michael H. Ed., and M. Grant and R. Kitzinger, *Civilizations of the Ancient Mediterranean: Greece and Rome*. New York: Scribner's, 1988.

Jamimes, M. Annette with Theresa Halsey. *State of Native America, American Indian Women*. Boston: South End Press, 1992.

Jennings, Jesse D. *Prehistory of North America*. McGraw-Hill Book Company, 1974.

Jennings, Francis. *The Invasion of America: Indians, Colonialism, and the Cant of Conquest*. New York: W. W. Norton, reprinted, 1976.

Jensen, Doreen and Cheryl Brooks, eds. *In Celebration of Our Survival*. Vancouver, BC: University of British Columbia, 1991.

Johansen, B. E. *Forgotten Founders: How the American Indian Helped Shape Democracy*. Boston, MA: Harvard Common Press, 1987.

Johannessen, Carl L. "Maize Diffused to India before Columbus Came to America", D.Y. Gilmore, and L.S. McElroyeds. *Across Before Columbus?: Evidence for Transoceanic Contact with the Americas prior to 1492*. New England Antiquities Research Association, Edgecomb, Maine: 1998.

Johnson, Ken. *The Ancient Magic of the Pyramids*. New York: Simon & Schuster, Dec., 1977.

Jones, Tom. *The Last of the Buffalo*. Cincinnati: Tom Jones, 1909.

Jones, W. ed. by M. W. Fisher. *Ethnography of the Fox Indians*. Washington, D. C.: Smithsonian Bulletin of the Bureau of American Ethnology, 1939.

Jorgensen, J. G. *The Sun Dance Religion*. Chicago: University of Chicago Press, 1974.

Josephy, Alvin M. Jr. *The Indian Heritage of America*. New York: Alfred A. Knopf, 1970.

Josephy, Alvin M. Jr. *America In 1492*. New York: Random House, 1991.

Joussaume, Roger. *Dolmens for the Dead: Megalithic Building throughout the World*. Ithaca: Cornell University Press, 1988.

Kappler,Charles J. ed. *Indian Affairs, Laws and Treaties*. Washington: Government Printing Office, 5 vols., 1903-1941.

Katz, Friedrich. *The Ancient American Civilizations*. NY Washington, D. C. Praeger, 1974.

Katz, Jane B. *I am the Fire of Time*. NY: E. P. Dutton, 1977.

Katz, William Loren. *Black Indians*. NY: Aladdin Paperbacks, 1997.

Kawashima, Yasuhide. *Igniting King Philip's War*. Lawrence, Kansas: University of Kansas Press, 2001.

Ke,Yuan. *The Classic of Mountains and Seas with Annotations*. Shanghai: Shanghai guji, 1980, Reprint, Harmondsworth: Penguin, 1999.

Kellaway, William. *The New England Company, 1649-1776: Missionary Society to the American Indians*. London: Longmans, 1961.

Kelley, David H. *Deciphering The Mayan Script*. Austin: University of Texas, 1976.

Kellog Jr. Edward P. ed. *The True Origin of the Indians of the Americas or The Roots of the American Indian*. Walnut Creek, CA, Edward Kellog, 1980.

Kendall, Ann. *Everyday Life of the Incas*. NY: Dorset Press, 1973.

Keoke, Emory Dean and Kay Marie Porterfield. *Encyclopedia of American Indian Contributions to the World*. Facts on File, Inc., 2001.

Kessell, John L. *Friars. Soldiers, and Reformers: Hispanic Arizona and the Sonora Mission Frontier*. 1767-1856.

Kessing, Felix M. *The Menominee Indians of Wisconsin*, Philadelphia: American Philosophical Society, 1939.

Klein, Herbert S. *African Slavery in Latin America and the Caribbean*. New York: Oxford University Press, 1986.

Kluckhohn, Clyde and Dorothea Leighton. *The Navajo*. Garden City: New York: Anchor Books, 1962.

Labaree, Leonard W. ed.*The Papers of Benjamin Franklin*. New Haven: Yale University Press, 1967.

Lafitau, Joseph Francois, eds. William N. Fenton & Elizabeth L. Moore, *Customs of the American Indians Compared With The Customs of Primitive Times*, Toronto: The Champlain Society, 2 vols., 1974.

Lamming, Edward P. *Peru Before the Incas*. Englewood N.J.: Prentice Hall Inc.,1967.

Landa, Diego de. *Relacion de Las Cosas de Yucatan*. Alfred M.Tozzer, ed. Cambridge. Mass: 1941.

Landa, Diego de. trans. by William Gates. *Yucatan Before and After the Conquest*. New York: Dover Publications, 1978.

Landsburg, Alan. *In Search of Lost Civilizations*. New York,: Bantam Books, 1976.

Lane, Nick. *Oxygen: The Molecule that Made the World*. New York: Oxford University Press, 2003.

Lankford, G. E., ed. *Native American Legends: Southeastern Legends: Tales from the Natchez, Caddo, Biloxi, Chickasaw, and other Nations*. Little Rock, Arkansas: August House Publishers, 1987.

Lankford, John, editor. *Captain John Smith's America*. New York: NY: Harper and Row, 1967.

Laubin, Reginald With Gladys Laubin. *North America; Civilization of the American Indian; Indian Dances of North America; Their Importance to Indian Life*. Norman: University of Oklahoma Press 1977.

Layard, Austen Henry. *Nineveh and It's Remains, Volume I* and *Discoveries In the Ruins of Neneveh and Babylon, Volume II*, New York: George P. Putnam, 1953.

Leakey, Richard E. and Roger, Lewin. *Origins*. New York: E. P. Dutton, 1977.

Leland, Charles. G. *Fusang; or, The Discovery of America by Chinese Buddhist Priests in the Fifth Century*. New York: Barnes & Noble, 1973.

Leon, Pedro Cieza de. *Chronicle of Peru*. London: Hakluyt Society 1864.

Lewin, Boleslao. *La Rebelion de Tupac Amaru*. Buenos Aires: Libreria Hachette, 1957.

Lewin, Roger. *In the Age of Mankind*. Washington, D. C: Smithsonian Books, 1988.

Ling, Shun-Sheng. *Barkcloth, Iimpressed Pottery, and the Inventions of Paper and Printing*. Nanking (Taipei) Institute of Ethnology Academia Sinica, 1963.

Loewen, James W. *Lies My Teacher Told Me*. New York: The New Press, 1995.

Longhena, Maria. *Mayan Script*. New York: Abbeville Press, 1999.

Lussier, A. S. ed. *Louis Riel and the Metis*. Winnipeg, Canada: Pemmican Publications, 1988.

Lyon, William S. *Encyclopedia of Native American Shamanism: Sacred Ceremonies of North America*. Santa Barbara, CA: Abc-Clio, 1998.

Madock, Richard Deacon. *The Discovery of America*. New York: George Braziller, 1966.

Mahon, John K. *History of the Second Seminole War 1835-1842*. Gainesville: University of Florida Press, 1992.

Mails, Thomas E. *Fools Crow*. Lincoln: University of Nebraska Press, 1979.

Mallory, Arlington and Mary Roberts Harrison. *The Rediscovery of Lost America*. New York: E. P. Dutton, 1979.

Mancall, Peter C. *Deadly Medicine: Indians and Alcohol in Early America*. Ithaca, New York: Cornell University Press, 1955.

Manypenny, George W. *Our Indian Wards*. New York, Dacapo Press, 1972.

Marriott, Alice and Carol K. Rachlin. eds. *Plains Indian Mythology*, New York: New American Library, 1975.

Marshall, Ingeborg. *A History and Ethnography of the Beothuk*. Montreal and Kingston: McGill-Queen's University Press, 1996.

Martin, Susan R. *Wonderful Power: The Story of Ancient Copper Workings in the Lake Superior Basin*. Detroit: Wayne State University Press, 1999.

Marx, Robert F. and Jennifer Marx. *In Quest of the Great White Gods: Contact Between the Old and the New World from the Dawn of History*. New York: Crown, 1992.

Mason, Alden J. *The Ancient Civilizations of Peru*. Middlesex: England, Penguin Books, 1968.

Mitchell, Johnm. *The New View Over Atlantis*. England: Sago Press, 1969.

Mause, Lloyd De ed. *The History of Childhood*. The Psycho History Press, 1974.

Maxwell, Stuart, P. *Chronicles of the Popes*. England: Thames & Hudson: 1997.

McGinnis, Dale and Floyd Sharrok. *The Crow People*. Phoenix: Indian Tribal Series, 1972.

McKechnie, Robert E. *Strong Medicine*. Vancouver, B.C: J. J. Douglas, Ltd., 1972.

McMaster, John Bach. *History of the People of the United States from the Revolution to the Civil War*. New York: Farrar Straus & Co., 1964.

McMaster, John ed. *Merriwether Lewis, History of the Expedition Under the Command of Captains Lewis and Clark*. New York: Allerton Book, 1922.

McWhorter, L. V., *Hear Me, My Chiefs! Nez Percé History And Legend*. Caldwell: Idaho, Caxton Printers, 1952.

Meggers, Betty J. and Clifford Evans, and Emilio Estrada. *Early Formative Period of Coastal Ecuador: The Valdivia and Machilillia Phases*, Washington, D. C.: Smithsonian Institution Press, 1965.

Mellart, James A. *Earliest Civilizations of the Near East*. New York: McGraw Hill, 1965.

Melody, Michael E. *The Apache*. New York: Chelsea House Publishers, 1989.

Meriam, Lewis. *The Problem of Indian Administration*. Baltimore: John Hopkins Press, 1929.

Mertz, Henriette. *Atlantis: Dwelling Place of The Gods*. Chicago: Private Prt., 1976.

Metraux, Alfred. *The Incas*. Studio Vista, 1965.

Meyer, Karl E. *Pleasures of Archaeology*. New York, Antheneum Press, 1970.

Meyer, William, *Native Americans: The New Indian Resistance*, New York: International Publishers, 1971.

Milanich, Jerald T. and Susan Milbrath, eds. *First Encounters*. Gainesville: University of Florida Press, 1989.

Millard, Anne.*The Inca*. New York: Warwick Press, 1980.

Milligen, George A. *Short Description of the Province or South Carolina, with an Account of the Air, Weather, and Diseases at Charles-Town*. London: 1770.

Mooney, James. *The Aboriginal Population of America North of Mexico*. Washington, DC: Smithsonian Publication, No. 2955, 1928.

Mooney, James. *The Ghost Dance Religion and the Sioux Outbreak of 1890*. Lincoln: University Of Nebraska Press, 1991.

Mooney, James. *Myths of the Cherokee and Sacred Formulas of the Cherokees*. Nashville, TN: Charles & Randy Elder, 1982.

Moquin Wayne and Charles Van Doren. ed., *Great Documents In American Indian History*. New York: De Capo Press, 1995.

Morgan, Lewis Henry, *The Indian Journals 1859-62*. Ann Arbor: The University of Michigan Press, 1959.

Morgan, Lewis Henry. *League of the Ho-de-no-sau–nee (League of the Iroquois)*. Massachusetts: JG Press, 1995.

Morley, Sylvanus Griswald. *The Ancient Maya*. Standard CA: Standard University Press, 1946.

Morrison, Samuel. *Christopher Columbus: The Voyage of Discovery 1492*. CT: Dorset Press, 1991.

Morrison, Samuel. *The European Discovery of America, The Southern Voyages, A.D .1492-1616*. New York. Oxford University Press, 1974.

Moseley, Michael E and Kent C., Day, eds. *Chan Chan: Andean Desert City*. University of New Mexico Press, 1982.

Muldoon, James. *The Americas in the Spanish World Order: The Justification for Conquest in the Seventeenth Century*. Philadelphia: University of Pennsylvania Press, 1994.

Neihardt, John G. *Black Elk Speaks*. Lincoln: University of Nebraska Press, 1961.

Occom, Samsom. *A Short Narrative of My Life*. typescript, Dartmouth College Archives, in Bernd Peyer, The Elders Wrote, Berlin: Dietrich Reimer Verlag, 1982.

Oldfather, C. H. *Diodorus of Sicily*. Library of History, Vol. 3, Cambridge, Ma: Harvard University Press, 1952.

Oliver, Douglas L. *Native Cultures of the Pacific Islands*. Honolulu: University of Hawaii Press. 1989.

Olsen, Karen and Karen E. Stothert. *Women in Ancient America*. Norman: University of Oklahoma, 1999.

Opitz, Charles J. *Wampum*. Ocala, Fl. First Impressions Prt. Co., 1995.

Otis, D. S. *The Dawes Act and Allotment of Indian Lands*. Norman: University of Oklahoma Press, 1973.

Oviedo, Fernandez Gonzalo de. *Historia General y Natural de las Indias*. Madrid, Biblioteca de Autores Espanoles, 1959.

Palou, Friar Francisco. *Life and Apostolic Labors of the Venerable Father Junipero Serra*. Pasadena: G. W. James, 1913.

Panzer, Fr. Joel S. *The Popes and Slavery*. Staten Island, NY, Alba House, 1996.

Parrinder, Geoffrey ed. *World Religions, From Ancient History to the Present*. New York: Facts on File, 1971.

Parsons, E. W. C. *The Pueblo of Jemez*. New Haven: Yale University Press, 1925.

Parsons, Elsie Clews. *Pueblo Indian Religion*. Lincoln, University of Nebraska Press, 1996.

Pearce, R. H. *Savagism and Civilization: A Study of the Indian and the American Mind*. Berkeley, CA: University of California Press, 1998.

Peithmann, Irvin M. *Echoes of the Red Man*. New York: Exposition Press, 1955.

Penn, William. *A Letter from William Penn, Proprietary and Governor of Pennsylvania in America to the Committee of the Free society of Traders*, London: 1683.Reprint London: J. Coleman, 1881.

Poe, Richard. *Black Spark White Fire*. Rocklin, CA: Prima Publishing, 1997.

Poma, Felipe Guamán. Ed. by John Murra, and Rolen Adorno and Jorge Urioste, *Felipe Guamán Poma de Ayala, New Chronicle and Good Government (Nueva Coronica y Buen Gobierno)*, Siglo Veintiuno Editores, Mexico City, Mexico, 1980.

Portilla, Miguel Leon. *Aztec Thought and Culture*. Norman: University of Oklahoma Press, 1963.

Posnansky, Arturo. *Tiahuanacu, The Cradle of American Man*. 4 Vols, (trans. by James F. Shearer), Locust Valley, NY, 1945.

Post, A. and E.R La Chapelle. *Glacier Ice*. Seattle, WA: University of Washington Press, 1971.

Potter, A. *Ohio's Prehistoric Peoples*. Columbus: Ohio Historical Society, 1968.

Pratt, Richard Henry. *How to Deal with the Indians: The Potency of Envioronment*. Pennsylvania: Carlisle, 1903.

Prescott, William H. *History of the Conquest of Peru*. New York: Harper and Brothers, 1847.

Prescott,William H. *History of the Conquest of Mexico*, New York: Harper and Brothers,1843.

Price, Monroe E. *Law and the American Indian: Readings, Notes and Cases*. Indianapolis, 1973.

Price, R., editor. *Maroon Societies: Rebel Slave Communities in the Americas*. 3rd ed. Baltimore: Johns Hopkins Press, 1997.

Prucha, Francis Paul. *American Indian Policy in the Formative Years*. Lincoln: University of Nebraska Press, 1970.

Prucha, Francis Paul, ed., *The Indian in American History*, New York: Holt Rinehart and Winston, 1971.

Prucha, Francis Paul. *American Indian Policy in Crisis Christian Reformers and the Indian*. 1865-1900, Norman: University of Oklahoma Press, 1976.

Prucha, Francis Paul. *Documents of United States Policy*. Lincoln: University of Nebraska Press, 1990.

Quaegebeur, J., ed. *Ritual and Sacrifice in the Ancient Near East*. Leuven: Peeters, 1993.

Quatrefages, Armond de. *The Human Species*. London: Kegan Paul & Co., 1879, 2nd Edition.

Quimby, George Irving, *Indian Life in the Upper Great Lake*. Chicago: The University of Chicago Press, 1960.

Reader's Digest Books. *Mysteries of the Ancient Americas*. Pleasantville, New York: 1986.

Richardson, James D. compiler. *A Compilation of the Messages and Papers of the Presidents*. Washington, D. C.: 1896- 1899, 10 Vols.

Riley, Carrol L and Charles Kelley, and Cambell W Pennington and Robert L. Rands. Eds. *Man Across the Sea: Problems of Pre-Columbian Contacts*. Austin: University of Texas Press.,1971.

Rohner, Ronald Preston. *The Kwakiutl: Indians of British Columbia*. New York: Holt, Rinehart and Winston, 1970. Franz. Boas, 1897.

Rollins, P. C., & O'Connor, J. E. Eds. *Hollywood's Indian: The Portrayal of the Native American in Film*. Lexington, KY: Press of University Kentucky, 1998.

Rose, T. E. MD. *From Shaman to Medicine Man*. Vancouver, Canada: Mitchell Press, 1972.

Ross, Alexander, and Kenneth A Spaulding. eds. *The Fur Hunters of* the *Far West*. Norman: Oklahoma Press, 1956.

Ross, Alexander. *The Red River Settlement, its Rise, Progress, and Present State. With some Account of the Native Races and its General History to the Present Day*. London: Smith, Elder 1856.

Rowe, John H. *An Introduction to the Archaeology of Cusco*. Papers of the Peabody Museum Vol. 27, No. 2, Boston: Harvard Press, 1994.

Roys, Ralph, *The Book of Chilam Balam of Chumayel*. Washington, DC, Carnegie Institute of Washington, 1933.

Ruby, Robert H. and John A. Brown. *Dreamer-Prophets of the Columbia Plateau: Smohalla and Skolaskin*, Norman, Oklahoma: University of Oklahoma Press, 1989.

Ruby, Robert H. and John A., Brown. *The Chinook Indians:Traders of the Lower Columbia River*. Norman: University of Oklahoma Press, 1976.

Russell, Frank. *Twenty-Sixth Annual Report of the Bureau of Ethnology*. Washington, DC: 1908.

Rutstein, Nathan and Michael Morgan. eds. *Healing Racism Education's Role*. Springfield. Ma., Whitcomb Publishing, 1996.

Saamanos, J. de. *Relacion de los Primeros Descubrimientos de Francisco Pizarro y Diego Almagro*. Madrid: vol. V, 1844.

Sahagun, Friar Bernardino de. translated by Fanny r. Bandelier from the Spanish Version of Carlos Maria de Bustamante, *History of Ancient Mexico*. Nashville: TN., Fisk University Press, 1932.

Sale, Kirkpatrick. *The Conquest of Paradise*. New York: Alfred A. Knopf, 1990.

Sanders, Thomas E. and Walter W. Peek, eds. *Literature of the American Indian*. New York: Glencoe, 1973.

Sando, J. S. *Pueblo Nations: Eight Centuries of Pueblo Indian History*. Santa Fe, New Mexico: Clear Light, 1992.

Sando, Joe S. *The Pueblo Indians*, San Francisco: The Indian Historian Press, 1976.

Sandoz, Mari. *These Were the Sioux*. New York: Hastings House Publishers, 1961.

Sarmiento, Pedro de Gamboa. *History of the Incas*. Cambridge: Hakluyt Society, 1907.

Sauer, Carl Otwin. *The Early Spanish Main*. Berkeley: University of California Press, 1966.

Schaerffenberg, A. V. *The Chinese Connection*. Stelle, Ill., Adventures Unlimited Press, 1994.

Schoch, Robert M. with Robert Aquinas McNally. *Voices of the Rocks: A Scientist Looks at Catastrophes and Ancient Civilizations*. New York: Harmony, Crown Publishing, Random House, 1999.

Sertima, Ivan Van. *They Came Before Columbus*. New York: Random House, 1976.

Seton, Ernest Thompson and Julia M. Seton. *The Gospel of the Redman*. Santa Fe: Seton Village, 1963.

Setterwall, Monica. *The Religions of the American Indians*. Los Angeles: University of California Press, 1979.

Shao, Paul. *Asiatic Influences in Pre-Columbian American Art*. Ames: Iowa State, 1976.

Sharpe, M.E. *Shamanism: Soviet Studies of Tradition Religion in Siberian and Central Asia*, Armonk, New York: 1990.

Silverberg, R. *Mound Builders of Ancient America*. Greenwich, Connecticut: New York: Graphic Society, 1968.

Simmons, Leo W. ed. *Sun Chief: The Autobiography of a Hopi Indian*.
New Haven: Yale University Press, 1942.

Simpson, George and Yinger, Milton, eds., *American Indians and American Life*. New York: Russell & Russell, 1975.

Skelton, R. A. and Thomas E. Marston, and George D. Painter. *The Vinland Map and the Tartar Relation*. New Haven: Yale University Press.

Smyth, Albert Henry ed. *The Writings of Benjamin Franklin, 1706-1790*. New York: 1906.

Sorenson, John L. and Martin H. Raish. *Pre-Columbian Contact with the Americas across the Oceans*. Provo, UT: Research Press, 1996.

Soustelle, J. and H.R. Lane, trans. *The Olmecs: The Oldest Civilization in Mexico*. Norman, Oklahoma: University of Oklahoma Press, 1985.

Sparks, Jared. *The Writings of George Washington; Being His corre spondence, addresses, messages and other papers, official and private*. New York: Harper & Brothers, 1847.

Spencer, Robert F. and Jesse D. Jennings. The American Indians. New York: Harper and Row, 1965.

Spier, L. "The Sun dance of the Plains Indians: Its development and diffusion." *Anthropological Papers of the American Museum of Natural History*, 1921.

Stafford, Harry Errald. *The Early Inhabitants of The Americas*. New York: Vantage Press, 1959.

Stedman, R. W. *Shadows of the Indian: Stereotypes in American Culture*. Norman, OK: University of Oklahoma Press, 1982.

Stern, K. S. Loud Hawk: *The United States Versus the American Indian Movement*. Norman, OK: University of Oklahoma Press, 1994.

Steward, Julian H, ed. *Handbook of South American Indians*. Washington: Smithsonian, 1946-1950, 6 vols plus vol. 7, index.

Stirling, Matthew W. *Indians of the Americas*. Washington, D. C: National Geographic, 1955.

Stoutenburg , John L. Jr., *Dictionary of the American Indian*, New York: Philosophical Library, 1956.

Strauss, C. Lévi, *Totemism*. Beacon Press 1963.

Stromstead, Astri A. *Ancient Pioneers: Early Connections Between Scandinavia and The New World*. Erick Fris, New York: 1971.

Sturtevant, William ed. *Handbook of North American Indians*. Washington: Smithsonian Institution, 1984.

Swanton, John R. *Indians of the Southeastern United States*. Bulletin No.137, BAE, Washington, D. C: 1946.

Taube, Karl. *Aztec and Maya Myths:The Legendary Past*. Austin: University of Texas, 1993.

Taylor, Theodore W. *The States and Their Indian Citizens*. Washington, D. C., U.S. Department of the Interior, Bureau of Indian Affairs, 1972.

Teit, James A., ed. by Franz Boas. *The Salish Tribes of the Western Plateaus*. Washington, D. C., Smithsonian, 1930.

Terra, Helmut de, tran. from German by Alan Houghton Broderick. *Man and Mammoth in Mexico*. London: Hutchinson & Co., 1957.

Terry, Joanne Drake. *The Same as Yesterday*, Lillooet, Canada, Lillooet Tribal Council, 1989.

Thacher, John Boyd. *Christopher Columbus. His Life, His Work, His Remains*. With an Essay on Pedro Martir of Angleria and Bartolomé de las Casas, the first Historians of America. New York: G. P. Putman's Sons, 1903- 1904, 1963.

Thompson, Gunnar. *American Discovery*. Seattle, Washington: Argonauts, Misty Isle Press, 1994.

Thompson, Herbert Edward. *People of the Serpent*. London: G. P. Putnam's Son's, 1913.

Thompson, J. Eric. *Maya History and Religion*. Oklahoma: University of Oklahoma Press, 1970.

Thomson, Hugh. *The White Rock: An Exploration of the Inca Heartland*. London: Weidenfeld & Nicolson, 2001.

Thornton, Russell. *American Indian Holocaust and Survival, A Population History Since 1492*. Norman: University of Oklahoma Press, 1987.

Thwaites, Reuben Gold.*Original Journals of the Lewis and Clark Expedition, 1804-1806*. 8 vols., New York: Arno Press, 1969.

Tilburg, J. A. Van. *Easter Island, Archaeology, Ecology and Culture*. Washington :1994.

Tocqueville, Alexis de. *Democracy In America*, 1835-1840.

Tompkins, Peter. *Mysteries of the Mexican Pyramids*. Toronto, Canada: Fitzhenry & Whiteside, Limited, 1976.

Torquemada, Friar Juan. *Monarquía Indiana*. Porrúa: México, 1723, 1969.

Trawick, H. *Time before History: The Archaeology of North Carolina*. by R. P Ward and Stephen Davis Jr., University of North Carolina Press, 1999.

Trento, Salvatore Michael. *The Search for Lost America: The Mysteries of the Stone Ruins*. Chicago: Contemporary Books, Inc. 1978.

Tucker, Glenn. *Tecumseh: Vision of Glory*. Indianapolis, & New York: Bobbs-Merrill Co. Inc., 1957.

Turner, Frederick. *The Portable North American Indian Reader*. New York: Viking Press, 1973.

Tyler, Lyon G. ed. *Narratives of Early Virginia, 1606-1625*. New York: Scribner, 1907.

Underhill, Ruth M. *Red Man's America*. Chicago: University of Chicago Press, 1971.

Underhill, Ruth M. *Red Man's Religion*. Chicago: University of Chicago Press, 1965.

Utley, Robert M. and Wilcomb E. Washington. *Indian Wars*. Boston:

Houghton Mifflin Co., 1977.

Vaillant, G.C. *The Aztecs of Mexico*. Baltimore, Md: Penguin Books, 1961.

Valencia, Robert Himmerich y. *The Encomenderos of New Spain, 1521-1555*. University of Texas Press, Dec. 1991.

Veakis, Emil. *Archaeometric Study of Native Copper in Prehistoric North America*. Ph.D. Dissertation (Anthropology), State University of New York at Stony Brook, 1979.

Vecsey, Christopher ed. *Handbook of The American Indian Religious Freedom*. New York: Crossroad Publishing Co. 1991.

Vega, Garcilaso de la, *Primera Parte de Los Commentarios Reales, Lisboa,1609. Reprint, Royal Commentaries of the Incas and General History of Peru*, Austin: University of Texas Press, 1966.

Verrazano, John de. *The Voyage of Verrazano along the Coast of North America*. Joseph G. Cogswell, trans. New York Historical Society Collections, 1841.

Verrill, A. Hyatt. *Old Civilizations of the New World*. Indianapolis: Bobbs Merrill Co., 1929.

Verrill, A. Hyatt. *The American Indian*. New York: The New Home Library, 1947.

Vestal, Stanley. *New Sources of Indian History*. 1850-91, Norman: University of Oklahoma Press, 1934.

Vogel, Virgil J. *This Country was Ours*. NY: Harper and Row, 1972.

Vogel, Virgil J. *American Indian Medicine*. Norman: University of Oklahoma Press, 1970.

Walker, Barbara G. *The Women's Encyclopedia of Myths and Secrets*. 1983.

Walker, J. R. "The Sun Dance and Other Ceremonies of the Oglala Division of the Teton Dakota." *Anthropological Papers of the American Museum of Natural History*, Vol. 16, 1921.

Wallace, Paul. *White Roots Of Peace*. Santa Fe: Clear Light Publishers, 1994.

Warren, William W. *History of the Ojibways, based upon Traditions and Oral Statements*. First Published, 1885.

Washburn, Cephas, and Hugh Park ed., *Reminiscences of the Indians 1862*. Press-Argus, 1955.

Washburn, Wilcomb E., ed., *The American Indian and the United States: A Documentary History Volume I-IV*. New York: Greenwood Press, 1973.

Washburn, Wilcomb E., ed., *The Indian and the White Man*. New York: Anchor Books, 1964.

Washington, Henry A. ed. *The Writings of Thomas Jefferson*. 9 vols., Washington, D.C. Taylor & Maury, 1853-54.

Washington,Wilcomb E. *Red Man's Land White Man's Law*. Norman: University of Oklahoma Press, 1971.

Watchel, N. *The Vision of the Vanquished: the Spanish Conquest of Peru through Indian Eyes*. Harvester Press, 1977.

Waters, Frank. *The Book of the Hopi*. New York: Penguin, 1963.

Wax, Murry L. *Unity and Diversity*. Engelwood Cliffs, New Jersey: Prentice Hall, 1971.

Weatherford, Jack. *Native Roots*. New York: Faucet, Columbine, 1991.

Weckman, Luis. *Las Bulas Alejandrinas de 1493 y la Teoria Politica del Papado Medieval*, Mexico: 1949.

Wegener, A. *The Origin of Continents and Oceans*. New York: Dover, 1966.

Weiner, Leo. *Africa and the Discovery of America*. Chicago: Innes & Sons, 1933, Vol. 1.

Wheeler, Sir Mortimer. *The Indus Civilization*. Cambridge: Cambridge University Press, 1968.

Whipple, Henry Benjamin. *Lights and Shadows of a Long Episcopate*. New York: 1899.

Willey, Gordon R. *An Introduction to American Archaeology*. Volume Two: South America, Prentice-Hall, Englewood Cliffs: 1971

Williams, Eric. *From Columbus to Castro: The History of the Caribbean*. New York: Random House Inc., 1970.

Williamson, Ray A. *Living The Sky: The Cosmos of the American Indian*. Boston: Houghton Mifflin Co., 1984.

Willoya,William and Vinson Brown. *Warriors Of The Rainbow*. Happy Camp: Naturegraph Publishers, 1962.

Wilson, Sir Daniel, L.L.D., F.R.S.E. *The Lost Atlantis and other Ethnographical Studies*. Edinburgh: David Douglas, 1892.

Wilson, Sir Daniel. *Prehistoric Man: Researches into the Origins of Civilization in the Old and New Worlds*. London: Vols. 1, 11. 1862.

Winkelman , Michael J. *Shamans, Priests and Witches: A Cross-*

Cultural Study of Magico-Religious Practitioners, Arizona State University Anthropological Research Papers, Jan. 1992.

Winsor, Justin ed. *Narrative and Critical History of America*. (8 vol., 1884–89), New York: Houghton Mifflin Co., 1886.

Wissler, Clark. *Indians of the United States*. Garden, City New York: Doubleday, 1949.

Witthoft, John. *The American Indian as Hunter*. Harrisburg, Pennsylvania: Pennsylvania Historical and Museum Commission, 1967.

Wolpoff, Milford and Rachel Caspari. *Race and Human Evolution: A Fatal Attraction*. New York: Simon and Schuster, 1997.

Woodward, Grace Steele. *The Cherokees*. Norman: University of Oklahoma Press, 1963.

Wright, Barton. *The Mythic World of the Zuni*. as Written by Frank Hamilton Cushing, University of New Mexico Press, 1992.

Wright, Ronald. *Stolen Continents*. New York: Penguin Books, 1993.

Wuthenau, Alexander von, *Unexpected Faces in Ancient America*. New York: Crown, 1975.

Yamada, George ed. *The Great Resistance: A Hopi Anthology*. Self-published, March, 1957.

Yarrow, Dr. H. C. *North American Indian Burial Customs*. Ogden, Utah: Eagle View Publishing Co., 1988.

Youliang, Dr. trans., *Neolithic Site At Bampo Near Xian*. Printed and published in China, 1982.

Ywahoo, Dbyani. *Voices of our Ancestors*. Boston and London: Shambhala Publications Inc., 1987.

PERIODICALS

Annual Report of the Commissioner of Indian Affairs, Sept. 21, 1887. Quoted in Francis Paul Prucha, ed., *Documents of the United States Indian Policy*, 2nd ed., expanded, Lincoln: University of Nebraska Press, 1990, pp. 174-175.

Adovasio, J. M. and Pedler, D. R. 1997. "Monte Verde and the antiquity of humankind in the Americas." *Antiquity 71*:573-580.

Ancient American. Colfax, Wisconsin, bi-monthly, 1994-2003.

Ancient American, Colfax, Wisconsin, Vol.7, #10, "Vineland Map is 20th Century Forgery." (Sept./Oct., 2002).

Ashraf, Jaweed. "Maize in India: Introduction or Indigenous." *Annuals, NAGI*, Vol. XIV, #2, pp. 6-26, (Dec., 1994).

Balabanova, S.F. and Pirsig, Parscheand W. "First Identification of Drugs in Egyptian Mummies." *Naturwissenschaften*, Springer-Verlag, 79, 358 (1992).

Barbeau, CM. "Iroquoian Clans and Phratries, *American Anthropologist*", March-June, 1917.

Bennett,Wendell, C. "Excavations at Tiahuanaco", *Anthropological Papers of the American Museum of Natural History*, Vol. xxxiv, Part III (1934).

Bieder, Robert E. "Scientific Attitudes Towards Mixed- bloods in Early Nineteenth Century America."*Journal of Ethnic Studies*, no. 8, pp. 17-30 (1980).

Bishop Jerry E. "A Geneticist's Work On DNA Bears Fruit For Anthropologists, Variations in Fragments Hint Some American Natives May Hail From Polynesia, The Controversy Over Eve." *Wall Street Journal*, Sept. 10, 1993, p. 1, col. 1.

Bonatto, S.L., F.M Salzano, "A Single and Early Origin for the Peopling of the Americas Supported by Mitochondrial DNA Sequence Data." *Proceedings of the National Academy of Sciences USA*. 94 (1997): pp.1866-1871.

Brooke, J. "Indian lawsuits on school abuse may bankrupt Canada churches." *New York Times*, Nov. 2, 2000, pp. A1, A8.

Brown, M.D. "Haplogroup X: An Ancient Link Between Europe/Western Asia and North America?" *American. Journal of Human Genetics*, 63 (1998).

Canny, Nicholas P. The Ideology of English Colonization: From Ireland to America, *William & Mary Quarterly*, 3rd Series, XXX (1973).

Carter, George F. "Calico Defended", *Science News*, 131:339, (1987).

Carter, George F. "Plant evidence for early contacts with America", Southwestern *Journal of Anthropology*, 86, Summer, (1950).

Chandler, David L. "Dig Finds Signs of Humans in N.M. 35,000 Years Ago." *Society for American Archaeology*, Seattle WA: (March 26, 1998).

Codere Helen, "Fighting with Property: A Study of Kwakiutl Potlatching and Warfare 1792-1930." *Monographs of the American Ethnological Society* 18, 1950. University of Washington Press, Wa.

Commissioners of Indian Affairs", Annual Reports " (1917-1923).

CNN Interactive. "First Americans May have Arrived 33,000 Years Ago", 1998; *Time Warner*, Online. *BBC News*, "First Americans were Australian", Aug. 26, 1999.

Corliss, William R., "Declaration of Indian Purpose."*Science Frontiers* #76, Jul.-Aug. 1991. American Indian Chicago Conference, June 13-20, 1961.

Dietz, R.S. "Continent and ocean basin evolution by spreading of the sea floor:" *Nature*, vol. 190, pp. 30-41 (1961).

Dillehay , Tom D., and Collins, Michael B. "Early Cultural Evidence from Monte Verde, Chile." *Nature*, 332:150, (1988).

Dillehay, Tom D., "A Late Ice-Age Settlement in Southern Chile." *Scientific American*, 251, pp. 106-117 (1984).

Dobyns, Henry F. "Estimating Aboriginal American Population, an Appraisal of Techniques with a New Hemispheric Estimate." *Current Anthropology*, vol.7, No. 4. (Oct., 1966).

Duvall James G. III, "Calico Revisited", *Science News*, 131:227, 1987.

Eadington, William. "Economic Development and the Introduction of Casinos: Myths and Realities", *Economic Development Review*, 13/4. (Fall, 1995).

Egan, T. "New prosperity brings new conflict to Indian country." *New York Times*, March 8, 1998, pp. 1, 24.

Egan, T. "Backlash growing as Indians make a stand for sovereignty." *New York Times*, March 9, 1998, pp. A1, A16.

Epstein , Jeremiah F., "Pre-Columbian Old World Coins in America" *Current Anthropology*, Vol. 21 No. 1, pp. 1-20. (Feb. 1980).

Federal Register, 43:39362-64 (Sept. 5, 1978).

Fell, Barry "The Etymology of some Ancient American Inscriptions", *Epigraphic Society Occasional Publications*, Vol. 3, No. 76 part 2, (Sept. 1976).

Fell, Barry. "The Comalcalco Bricks: Part 1, the Roman Phase", Occasional Papers, *Epigraphic Society*, 19:299, (1990).

Fewkes, Dr. Jesse Walter, "Ceremonials at Walpi." *Journal of American Ethnology and Archaeology*, Vol. 4, Cambridge, Ma.: Snake Tower Books. (1895).

Fletcher, Alice C. "The Hako, A Pawnee Ceremony." *Bureau of American Ethnology*, Washington: Government Printing Office, 22nd Annual Report, part 2 (1900-1906).

Franciscan Herald Press. Francis de Beer, ed. "We Saw Brother Francis." Chicago: 1983.

Gee, Henry, "The sign of the Ancient Mariner." *Macmillan Magazines Ltd, Nature News Service*, 1998.

Geldern, Robert Heine. Vol. 5, No. 4, pp. 21-22, "A Roman Find from Pre-Columbian Mexico. " *Anthropological Journal of Canada,*1967

Gibbons, Ann, "Geneticists Trace the DNA Trail of the First Americans", *Science,*vol. 259, no. 5093 (Jan. 15, 1993).

Greenberg, Joseph H, and ChristyTurner II, and Stephen Zegura, "Settlement of the Americas" *Current Anthropology*, 27:477-497 (1986).

Grimes, James P. "Pre Columbian Written Records of America", *Ancient America*. Colfax, Wisconsin: Issue #12, (July/Aug., 1995).

Gruhn, Ruth, "Linguistic Evidence in Support of the Coastal Route of Earliest Entry into the New World." *Man (N.S.)*, vol. 23 (1988).

Grumet, Robert. "Sunksquaws, Shamans, and Tradeswomen: Middle Atlantic Coastal Algonkian Women during the 17th and 18th Centuries", in Women and Colonization: *Anthropological Perspectives*, ed. Mona Etienne and Eleanor Leacock, New York: Praeger, 1980.

Guidon Niede and Delibrias, G., *Nature*, vol. 321, pp. 769-771 (1986).

Guidon, Niede, Cliff Notes, *Natural History*, vol. 96, no.8 (1987).

Gilliam, Frankie Sue, ed. "The Choctaws, an Enduring Race." *Twin Territories Newspaper*. Oklahoma, 1995, p.6-10.

Hanke, Lewis, "Pope Paul III and the American Indians", *Harvard Theological Review*, Vol. 30, #2, p. 77 (April, 1937).

Harn, Alan D. "The Prehistory of Dickson Mounds: The Dickson Excavation", *Illinois State Museum Reports of Investigations*, No. 35 (1980).

Hertzberg, Hazel Whitman."National Anthropology And Pan-Indianism in the life of Arthur C. Parker (Seneca)", Proceedings of the *American Philosophical Society,* (1979).

High Country News, Paonia, Colorado, Chris Carrel, "Tribes strike back at Mining." Aug. 31, 1998.

Hillinger, Charles, "Mazes Remain Enigmas of Ancient Indian Art."

Los Angeles Times, June 11, 1991, p. A3.

Hoover Commission, 1948, "Survey of Conditions of the Indians in the United States*"* Report, No.310, Washington, D. C. (1928-1943), 78th Congress, 1st Session, U. S. Senate (June 11, 1943).

Horseman, Reginald Jr. "American Indian Policy and the Origins of Manifest Destiny", University of Birmingham Historical Journal XI, (1968).

House Executive Document, Annual Report of the Commissioner of Indian Affairs, no.2, 32nd Congress, 1st sess, serial 636, pp.273-74 (Nov. 27, 1851).

Johannessen, "Indian Maize in the Twelfth Century A.D.", *Nature*, (1988).

Johannessen & Parker, "Maize Ears Sculptured." *Economic Botany*, (1989).

Joint Special Committee of Congress Report, "Condition of the Indian Tribes", Senate Report, no.156, 39th Cong., 2d sess.serial 1279, pp. 3-10, (Jan. 26, 1867).

Journals of the Continental Congress, Washington, D. C., 34 vols. (1774-1789).

Kessing, Felix M., *Michigan History Magazine*. "The Menominee Indians of Wisconsin", Philadelphia: American Philosophical Society, (1939).

Lanning , Edward P. and Patterson, Thomas C. "Early Man in South America", *Scientific American*, (Nov., 1967).

Lekson, S. H. T. C. Windes, J. R. Stein, and W. J. Judge, Jr. "The Chaco Canyon Community", *Scientific American*, July 1988, pp. 100-109, 1988.

Lesser, Alexander. "Cultural Significance of the Ghost Dance." *American Anthropologist*, Vol. 35:18, (1933).

Lissac, G. *Archaeology of Human Origins*, 1989. Journal of Human Evolution, (Dec., 1996).

London Saturday Journal."The North American Indians, Are The Indians Capable Of Civilization."London, England: William Smith, May 2, 1840. No.70, pp. 280-282.

Los Angeles Times Service, Milwaukee Journal, Sept. 15, 1980. "A New Discovery, China Presses Claim that it found America."

Malhi, R.S. and D.G. Smith. "Haplogroup X", *American Journal Physical Anthropology*, 119 (1):84-6 (Sept., 2002).

Mansfield, V. and Wadsworth, Belmont California: "Mandalas and Mesoamerican Pecked Circles." *Current Anthropology*, 22: 269-284 (1981), and "The Alleged Diffusion of Hindu Divine Symbols into Pre-Columbian Mesoamerica: a Critique." *Current Anthropology*, 19: 541-583 (1978).

Martin, Paul S, "Pleistocene Overkill." *Natural History Magazine*, (Dec., 1966).

McIntyre, Dr. Virginia Steen, *The Ancient American*, vol. 3 issue 19-20 (1997).

McIntyre, Virginia Steen and Ronald Fryxell, and Harold E. Malde, "Geologic Evidence for Age of Deposits at Hueyatlaco Archaeological Site, Valsequillo, Mexico", *Quaternary Research* 16:1-17 (1981).

Merriwether, Dr.Andrew Francisco Rothhammer and Robert E. Ferrell. "Distribution of the Four Founding Lineage Haplotypes in Native Americans Suggests a Single Wave of Migration for the New World", *American Journal of Physical Anthropology*, vol. 98, 411-30 (1995).

Meyer, Priscilla S. "Rewriting America's History: Genetics and the South Pacific."*The Ancient American*, Colfax, Wisconsin: Vol.2, issue #9, pp. 12-15 (1996).

Miami Herald, "The Miami Stone Circle", Jan. 31, 1999.

Microsoft® Encarta® Online Encyclopedia 2004. "Native Americans of Middle and South America."

Montezuma, Carlos. "What Indians Must Do", *Society of American Indians, Quarterly Journal*, 2 (1914).

Moorehouse, George E. "The Los Lunas Inscriptions: A Geological Study", *Epigraphic Society Publications*,13 44-50 (1985).

Morwood, M. J. and P. B.O'Sullivan and D. M. Raup. *Nature*, (1998).

Muello, Peter. "Find Puts Man in America at Least 300,000 Years Ago." *Dallas Times Herald*, June 16, 1987.

Mundkur, B. "The Cult of the Serpent in Mesoamerica: Its Asian Background." *Current Anthropology*, 17: pp. 429-455 (1976).

Murphy, R. C. "The Seaworthiness of Balsa-wood Sailing Rafts in Early South America", Durham, North Carolina: *Hispanic American History Review*, Vol.XXI. p. 204 (1941).

Museum of Civilization, *Secrets of Amazonia*. Quebec, Canada:

225

National Library of Canada, 1996.

National Geographic, "Uncovering a Ritual Center in Veracruz", Vol. 190 #2 (Aug., 1996).

Petititt, George A. "Primitive Education in North America." *University of California Publications in American Archaeology and Ethnology*, 1946, Vol. XLIII. pp. 9-11.

Pichon, X. Le, 1968, "Sea-floor spreading and continental drift:" *Journal of Geophysical Research*, v. 73, p. 3661-3697.

Powledge, Tabitha M. and Mark Rose, "The Great DNA Hunt, Part II, ColonizingThe Americas."*Archaeology Magazine*, (Nov., Dec., 1996).

Reagan, Albert B. "A Navajo Fire Dance." *American Anthropologist*, 36(3): pp. 434- 437.

Recer, Paul, AP Science Writer, "The Lost Pyramids of Caral." *Mobile Register*, Page 2A, Washington, D.C: April 27, 2001.

Report of the Special and Subcommittee on Indian Education, "Indian Education: A National Tragedy - A National Challenge", Washington, DC: U. S. Government Printing Office, (1969).

Ross, John F. "First City in the New World?" *Smithsonian*, Aug., 2002, Vol. 23, #5, pp. 57-64.

Sauer, Carl O., "Agricultural Origins and Dispersals", *American Geographic Society*, Bowman Memorial Lectures, New York:

Saunders, Joe W. "A Mound Complex in Louisiana at 5400-5000 Years Before the Present." *Science*, Vol. 277 (Sept. 19, 1997), 5333 Abstract of the full report of 1996.

Scholes, France V. and Ralph L. Roys. "Friar Diego de Landa and the Problem of Idolatry in Yucatán", in *Co-operation in Research* Washington, D.C., 1938, pp. 585-620.

Schurr, T. G. "Amerind Mitochondrial DNAs have rare Asian Mutations." *American Journal of Human Genetics*, vol. 46 #3, pp. 613-623 (1990).

Schurr, Theodore, "Mitochondrial DNA and the Peopling of the New World."*American Scientist*, Vol. 88 No. 3 (May-June 2000).

Scottish Banner, "Definitive illustration of sculptured maize." Lewiston, New York, vol. 19, #11 (May, 1996).

Seattle Chief. *The Washington Historical Quarterly*, Seattle, Washington: Washington University State Historical Society, issue 22, no.4. (Oct., 1931).

Senate Executive Document, "Annual Report of the Commissioner of Indian Affairs", no.5, 34th Cong. Sess, serial 875, pp. 371-375 (Nov. 22, 1856).

Simpson, Ruth D."Updating the Early Man Calico Site, California", *Anthropological Journal of Canada*, (1982) 20:8, no. 2.

Skinner, Alanson. "Social Life and Ceremonial; Bundles of the Menomini Indians", *American Museum of Natural History, Anthropological Papers of the American Museum of Natural History*, New York: 1913.vol. XIII, part I, p. 85.

Snowbird, Longtrail "Essays on Native American Life and Relations with Non-Natives 1600-1850", Native Tech Home Page, by Tara Prindle, (1996).

Sofaer, Anna "The Primary Architecture of the Chacoan Culture: A Cosmological Expression." *Anasazi Architecture and American Design*, edited by Baker Morrow and V.B. Price, Albuquerque, NM: University of New Mexico Press, 1997.

Squier, E. G. "Aboriginal Monuments of the State of New York", *Smithsonian Contributions of Knowledge*, No. 2, (1850).

Squier, E. G. and Davis, E. H., "Ancient Monuments of the Mississippi Valley", *Smithsonian Contributions of Knowledge*, No. 1, (1848).

Steede, Neil, "The Bricks of Comalcalco", *Ancient American*, 1:8, (Sept./Oct. 1994).

Stonebreaker, Jay , "A Decipherment of the Los Lunas Decalogue Inscription", *Epigraphic Society Occasional Publications*, 10 part 1, pp. 74-81 (1982).

Strong, W.D. "Indian oral Traditions Suggest a Knowledge of The Mammoth" *American Anthropologist*, Vol. 36: 81-88 (1934).

Superintendent of Indian Education Annual Report (1887).

Swanton, John Rindian, "Tribes of the Lower Mississippi Valley and Adjacent Coast of the Gulf of Mexico", *Bureau of American Ethnology*, Smithsonian, Bulletin 43 (1911).

Theosophy, "Ancient Landmarks XX111, The Feathered Serpent." Vol. 16, No. 2, pp, 70-76. No. 23 of a 59-part series, (Dec., 1927).

Tarpy, Ciff. "Maya Royal Grave, Place of the Standing Stones", *National Geographic*, May, 2004, pp. 66-78.

Tello Julio. "Discovery of the Chavin Culture in Peru." *American*

Antiquity, Menashia, Wisconsin: 1943-45, vol. ix. pp. 135-160.

Thomas, Cyrus, "Report on the Mound Explorations of the Bureau of Ethnology", *Annual Report, Bureau of American Ethnology*, Washington, D.C: Smithsonian Institution, Volume 12, pp. 292-311 (1894).

Thompson, Gunnar Ph.D. "Egyptian Statuettes in Mexico", *Ancient American*, vol.2 no. 8, p. 32-33. 1995.

Thorpe, R. S., and Thorpe, O. Williams, New York: J. P. Putnam's Sons, "The myth of long distance megalith transport." *Antiquity*, 65, pp. 64-73 (1991).

Tolstoy, Paul, "Paper Route." Shun-Sheng Ling, "Barkcloth, Impressed Pottery, and the Inventions of Paper and Printing", (1963): Nanking (Taipei Institute of Ethnology Academia Sinica, *Natural History*, p. 42. 100:6 (June, 1991).

Trotter, M. "Hair from Paracas Indian Mummies", *American Journal of Physical Anthropology*, Vol.1, 1943.

Turner, Christy G. II. "Teeth and Prehistory in Asia."*Scientific American*, 88+ (Feb. 1989).

U.S. Reports, 374, 423- 24. "United States v. Sioux Nation of Indians", (June 30, 1980).

U.S. Bureau of Census, Washington, D.C: U. S. Government Printing Office, 11th Annual, (1894).

United States Statute at Large Indian Affairs: Laws and Treaties, Curtis Act, 30:497,98, 502, 504-05. 614 H (June, 28, 1898).

Veena and Sigamani, "Do objects in South India represent Maize ears?" *Current Science*, Vol. 61, pp. 395-396.

Wallace, Douglas C. "Dramatic Founder Effects in Amerind Mitochondrial DNAs." *American Journal of Physical Anthropology*, vol.68. pp.149-155 (1985).

Whittlesey, Charles "The Grave Creek Inscribed Stone", *Western Reserve and Northern Ohio Historical Society*, Tract, No. 44, pp. 65-68 (April, 1879).

Whittlesey, Charles, "Archaeological Frauds: Inscriptions Attributed to the Mound Builders. Three Remarkable Forgeries", *Western Reserve Historical Society Historical & Archaeological* Tract #9, (1872).

Wiercinski, Dr.Andrzej. "Inter-and-Intrapopulational racial differen tiation of Tlatilco, Cerro de Las Mesas, Teothuacan, Monte Alban and Yucatan Maya", *XXXIX Congreso International de Americanistas*, Lima, Vol. 1, pp. 231-252, 1970.

Wiercinski,Dr.Andrzej. "An Anthropological Study on the Origin of Olmecs", *Swiatowit*, 33, 143-174, 1972.

Wilford, John Noble "New Answers to an Old Question: Who Got Here First?" *New York Times*, Nov. 9, 1999.

Will, Elizabeth Lyding, "The Roman Amphora Learning from Storage Jars." *Archaeology Odyssey Archives*, (Jan./Feb., 2000).

Wilson, T. "A New Class of Faults and Their Bearing on Continental Drift:" *Nature*, vol. 207, p. 343-347 (1965).

Winkler, L., and R. E. Stone. "Construction and Use of America's Stonehenge", *New England Antiquities Research Association Journal*, V. 33, No. 2. (1999).

Winters, Clyde A. "The Decipherment of Olmec Writing." Paper presented at the 74th meeting of the Central States Anthropological Society, Milwaukee, WI (April, 1997).

Winters, Clyde A. "The Migration routes of the Proto-Mande, *"The Mankind Quarterly,* 27 (1), 77-96, (1986).

Wright, Carl M. "Avocational Archaeology: Paleo-Geography and Migrations of the First Americans", *Central States Archaeological Journal*, Vol. 48, No. 3. p. 116-117, July, 2001.

Yoshida, Professor Nobuhiro, "StoneTablets of Mu, The Motherland of Mankind." *Ancient American*, Colfax, Wisc: vol. 3, #21, pp. 18-22. (Nov., Dec., 1997).

INDEX

227

228

230

234

Tumacacori, Arizona, 60
Tupa (Tupac), Inca Kings, see individual names
Turkana, 15
Turkey, (Turkish), 31, 69
Turner, Christy G. 11, (Physical Anthropoligist), 15
Turner, Philip, 74
Turtle Dance Ceremony, (Pueblo), 138
Tuscarora tribe, 128, 158
Twisted Hair, Chief of Nez Percé, 70
Two Moons, Chief of Cheyenne, 179
Tyrrhenians, 41
Tzolkin Calendar, 3, 151 (notes, 13) (photo, 151)
Uaxactum, Guatemala, 35
Udall, Morris, (Secretary of the Interior), 175
Uhle, Max, 50
Umatilla tribe, 105, 178
Underhill, Captain John, 92
Underhill, Ruth, 134
United Foreign Missionary Society, 70
United Nations, 158, 166, 173, 178, 180
United States Census, 76, 80, 81, 105 (notes, 11, 386, 527)
United States government, 70, 77, 78, 81, 82, 94-97, 99, 101, 103-105, 107, 147, 148, 169, 171, 173, 175-178
Universities of, Chicago, 175; Emory, 15, 57; Kentucky, 11; Michigan, 9, 16; Montreal, 50; New Mexico, 48; Pennsylvania, 21, 82; Salamanca, 76; San Diego, CA, 24; Washington, 32; Wayne State, 11; Yale, 25, 46, 88
Unyoro tribe, Uganda, 50
Uruk, 30, 31 (photo, 7)
Utah, 134, 170
Ute tribe, 78, 146
Uweepe Ceremony, 145
Uxmal, 39
Uzbek pyramids, 37
Valdivia, Ecuador, 52
Valsequillo, site, Puebla, Mexico, 12
Vancouver, British Columbia, 50
Vargas, General Don Diego de, 89
Vasquez, Sebastian, 60
Vega, Garcilasso de la (the Inca), 23, 55, 89, 90, 153
Velasquez, Diego, (Governor of Cuba), 86
Velloso, Reverend Senior, 39
Ventura, Charles Savona, 54
Veracruz, Mexico 13, 30, 48, 86
Vermont, (sun god Bel), 24
Verrazano, Giovanni de, 26, 121 (notes, 153)
Verrill, Hyatt, 16
Vespucci, Amerigo, 18
Viking, 25, 26
Vinland, (Wineland), 25
Viracocha, 31, 37, 38, 56, 113, 114
Virgin Islands, U. S., 17
Vision Quest, 44, 134, 136, 142, 143
Wales, 7, 49
Walker, J. R., (physician), 112
Wallace, Douglas C., 15, 16, 57 (notes, 97)
Wallam Olum, *(Red Score)*, 10
Wampanoag Confederacy, 127
Wampanoag tribe, 92
Wampum, 31, 93, 116, 158
Wanapan tribe, 109
Ward, Nancy, 131, 132 (photo, 132)
Warren, William H., 118
Washakie, Chief of Shoshones, 102
Washani, Dancers creed, 109
Washburn, Cephas, 70
Washington, D. C., 6, 17, 47, 103, 106, 155, 156, 172, 177
Washington, George, 94, 96, 102, 158 (photo, 96)
Washington, Ohio, 26
Washington, State, 170
Watson Brake, 32
Wayne, General Anthony, 96
Wayonaoake, Queen, 126
Waywaka, Andes, Peru, 88
Weeden Island culture, Florida, 32

Weetamoo, Queen and chief of Pocasset, 126, 127
Welsh, 7, 49
Wessex, Earl of, 107
West Indies, 16, 59, 76, 78, 83, 92, 127
West Virginia, 14, 45, 47,49, 58
Wheeler-Howard Indian Reorganization Act, 175
Wheelock, Reverend Eleazer, 69
Whipple, Henry Benjamin (1822-1901), 67, 115
White Buffalo Woman, 54, 122, 166, (notes, 579, 725) (photo, 166)
White Buffalo, 54, 166 (photo, 166)
White Wolf, 5
Whitman, Walt, 82
Wiercinski, Dr. Andrzej, 13 (notes, 87)
Willet, Edward, 82
Williams, Dr. Cynthia Irwin, 12
Williams, Eric, 72
Williams, Roger, 68
Wilson, Sir Daniel, LLD., F.R.S.E., 25
Wilson, Dr. Peter, 157
Wilson, John (Big Moon), 149
Winnebago tribe, 109, 115
Winter dance ceremony, (Salish), 143, 144
Wintun tribe of California, 112
Wisconsin Historical Society, 29
Wisconsin, 10, 15, 26, 28, 29, 32, 80, 96, 135, 166, 172
Wissler, Clark, 71
Woden - lithi, (King from Ringerike, Norway), 27
Wolpoff, Milford, 8, 9
Women, (Indian), 16-18, 24, 26, 30, 38, 47, 50, 51, 66, 71-74, 77, 78, 80-86, 88, 90-92, 94, 95, 101, 107-109, 114,117, 118, 120-133, 135-137, 139, 141, 142, 147, 148, 150, 153, 154, 157, 158, 164, 166, 173, 177
World Explorers Club, 39
Wounded Knee, South Dakota, 105, 148, 169, 177 notes (509) (photos, 105)
Wovoka, (Jack Wilson), Paiute, 147, 168 (photos, 148, 168)
Writing systems, forms of hieroglyphic, pictographic, 8, 13, 30, 31, 36, 40, 42, 44, 46, 47, 49, 50, 51, 57, 60, 86 (notes, 78, 162, 164, 267) (photos, 31)
Wuthenau, Alexander von, 48
Wyandot tribe, (Huron), 93
Wyoming, 39, 44, 102, 134, 155, 157
Wyrick, David, 48 (notes, 216)
Xavier, Francisco, 89
Xian, China, 37, 51 (notes, 233)
Xingu tribe, 121
Xochicalco, 35
Yakama (Yakima), tribe, 16, 52, 143, 168, 178 (notes, 509)
Yamassee tribe (Jamassi), 14
Yankton Sioux, 172
Yaquis tribe, 89
Yellowstone, 10
Yokut tribe, 45
Yonaguni Island, (Japan), 54
Yopis, Mexico, 42,
Yu, Emperor of China, 15
Yucatan, Mexico, 13, 32, 38, 39, 48, 50, 52, 59, 60, 87, 157
Yuchi tribe, 118
Yugoslavia, 122,
Yuma, 39,78, 89, 134, 167
Yupanqui, Tupac (King of Inca, 1471- 1493), 113
Yuwipi, Sioux ceremony, 137
Zenu tribe, Colombia, 156
Zero, 3, 31, 86 (notes, 239)
Zia Pueblo, 45 (photo, 134)
Ziggurats, 31-34, 54 (notes, 164) (photos, 7, 30, 31, 34
Zuazo, Licenciado, 71
Zumarraga, Friar Juan de, (missionary), 59
Zuni, 14, 15, 30, 43, 45, 110, 123, 125, 134, 138, 155, 168 (notes, 91)
Zunta, Alonso de, 59

Printed in the United States
141148LV00001B/127/A